HOUSE OF WITS

An Intimate Portrait
of the

JAMES
FAMILY

PAUL FISHER

HENRY HOLT AND COMPANY • NEW YORK

D0003742

Henry Holt and Company, LLC
Publishers since 1866
175 Fifth Avenue
New York, New York 10010
www.henryholt.com

Henry Holt® and 🏛® are registered trademarks
of Henry Holt and Company, LLC.

Distributed in Canada by H. B. Fenn and Company Ltd.

Owing to limitations of space, permissions to use previously published
and unpublished material appears on page 669.

Library of Congress Cataloging-in-Publication Data
Fisher, Paul, 1960–
    House of wits: an intimate portrait of the James family / Paul Fisher.–1st ed.
        p.   cm.
    Includes bibliographical references and index.
    ISBN-13: 978-0-8050-7490-1
    ISBN-10: 0-8050-7490-2
    1. James family.   2. Upper-class families—New York (State)—
New York—Biography.   3. Manhattan (New York, N.Y.)—Biography.
4. Europe—Biography.   I. Title.
    CT274.J35F57 2008
    974.7'10430922—dc22   2007043214

Henry Holt books are available for special promotions
and premiums. For details contact: Director, Special Markets.

First Edition 2008

Designed by Victoria Hartman

Printed in the United States of America

1   3   5   7   9   10   8   6   4   2

For Charlotte

Contents

INTRODUCTION:
A CONTEMPORARY PORTRAIT
OF THE JAMESES

Success has always been the biggest liar . . . "great men," as they are venerated, are bad little fictions invented afterwards.

Friedrich Nietzsche, *Beyond Good and Evil*

In everything they undertake they do well and often excellently; they are admired and envied; they are successful whenever they take care to be—but all to no avail. Behind all this lurks depression, the feeling of emptiness and self-alienation, and a sense that their life has no meaning.

Alice Miller, *The Drama of the Gifted Child*

When you travel, your first discovery is that you do not exist.

Elizabeth Hardwick, *Sleepless Nights*

L ate in his life, the American expatriate novelist Henry James longed to memorialize his entire remarkable family, all of whom remained poignantly alive in his imagination. "We were, to my sense, the blest group of us," he wrote in his autobiography in 1913, "such a company of characters and such a picture of differences . . . so fused and united and interlocked, that each of us . . . pleads for preservation." But although there have been admirable James biographies, it has been difficult to break through the decorum of the family and even their finest chroniclers to truly capture this iconoclastic group, whose oversized collective achievements—as great as those of any other family in American history—grew out of a very troubled, impassioned, and often dysfunctional home life.

Some of the Jameses—a close-knit New York dynasty—ended their lives as depressed and disappointed bankrupts; others became eminent writers whose wit and invention helped lay the foundations for what we now think of as modern America. The family is best known for its two eldest sons, Henry James Jr. and William James, the philosopher and psychologist. The former's sumptuous fictions about Americans in Europe—*The American* (1877), *The Portrait of a Lady* (1881), and *The Wings of the Dove* (1902), among many others—captured the glittering international world of the so-called Belle Epoque, the "beautiful epoch" between the Civil War and World War I. Henry James epitomized high literary achievement, and his works, known for their psychological depth, have been seen as groundbreaking "modern" classics. Only a shade less well known than his brother, William James established a considerable reputation as a pioneer of modern psychology and as a proponent of "pragmatism"—a characteristically American philosophy that empowered each individual to determine his or her own truths.

History has immortalized these brothers in isolation and has only secondarily considered them in the light of their less prominent relatives and the struggles those relatives embodied. Critics have sometimes regarded William and Henry as grand self-generated "geniuses" in their respective realms, as figures who stood above their family circumstances. But Nietzsche's warning about success obscuring the real complexity of famous lives applies well to these two American icons. Suffering and deep human complexity fueled their work, and for six decades the two men remained remarkably close, engaged, and competitive blood brothers. They were locked in a lifelong relationship that weirdly echoed their parents' marriage and whose turbulent and complex dynamics crucially shaped their most famous books.

Besides Henry and William, the James clan contained other figures who have also fascinated many: Henry James Sr., their father, was a rebellious prophet of American social reform; their sister, Alice James, was a career invalid and clandestine diarist who documented her own struggles in an extremely male-oriented family and society. But these two additional Jameses, reclaimed and recovered only in the last few decades, are just the beginning of the family story. I believe that all seven of the Jameses—the parents and their five extraordinary children—were in fact so "fused and united and interlocked" that it is impossible fully to understand any one of them without the rest, without investigating the moving drama of their complex family life that unfolded in some of the most interesting cities of the era—New York, Newport, Boston, London, Paris, and Rome—between the social upheavals of the 1840s and the outbreak of the First World War in 1914.

For years, the Jameses lavished on one another a rich moveable feast of family life. Their father's intellectual ambitions and shifting moods swept them capriciously from city to city, continent to continent. When the five children were still young, before constant mobility had become the American norm, the family moved through Europe and America like vagabonds, surviving years of shifting houses, hotels, and boarding schools knitted together by long rail journeys and Atlantic steamship crossings. Traveling continually, with only the family for stability and continuity, they alternately adored, defended, and excoriated one another with an intensity that only people who passionately love each other can generate. They became the only real "country," as William James later put it, to which any of them ever belonged.

Driven to leave his mark on the world as well as to travel, Henry Senior passed on many of his obsessions to his children; with high expectations and elusive approval, he helped spur them all toward the anxieties of overachievement. Henry Junior and William James were especially caught up, but their less famous siblings were not immune to it. Their superhuman efforts to be seen, acknowledged, and understood dominated their private and professional lives, spawning grandiose plans, remarkable accomplishments, and deep, long-lasting depressions.

Somewhere between the Alcotts and the Royal Tenenbaums, the Jameses come into the American story and add much to our perception of it. In their ambitions, ambiguities, and affectations, the Jameses can strike us as curiously contemporary—the forerunners of today's Prozac-loving, depressed or bipolar, self-conscious, narcissistic, fame-seeking, self-dramatized, hard-to-mate-or-to-marry Americans. This side of the Jameses has often been downplayed, and much of the story has remained untold, buried under generations of propriety, convention, and veneration. But the Jameses' dysfunction sheds crucial light on the origins and full range of their influential achievements. Henry Senior's bold social experiments, Henry Junior's exquisite fiction, Alice's exploration of women's hidden lives, and William's seminal contributions to American psychology—all grow directly from this sometimes unseemly experience. Accordingly, this book is an effort to interpret these people by way of their interior family and household experience, as Henry James himself longed to do, and to understand their hidden passions and vulnerabilities both as deeply moving and highly relevant to our own present-day lives.

IN NEW YORK'S Washington Square, you can still see scraps of the Jameses' family world: cast-iron railings, steep steps, porticoes, and fanlights. Back when I was an undergraduate, I roamed expectantly with an old address, hoping to look them up, hoping to establish a personal link. For years, I've "collected" James houses: on Beacon Hill, on the rue St.-Honoré, in St. John's Wood, at Newport, at Chocorua, in New Hampshire. With Henry Senior's determination to give his family a "sensuous education," each house represented a slice of his experiment in unconventional living, each a new phase of the family's remarkable development. Most of the numerous James residences are ghostly now, thanks to the American mania for tearing down and rebuilding that Henry James so deplored in *The American Scene*. (I was almost as shocked as he was to discover that both his mother's house in Washington Square and his birth house in nearby Washington Place no longer exist.) Of some of these houses, not even a photograph remains; they were ordinary domestic properties, part of the family life of the nineteenth century that almost nobody bothered to document.

The half-effaced domestic story of the James family has fascinated me for many years, and I found one unexpected living link in Edinburgh in 1988, when I met H. S. ("Jim") Ede (1895–1990), a distinguished art critic, then in his nineties, who as a young art student in London had met the elderly Henry James at the house of the actress Ellen Terry and had walked with the grandfatherly novelist through the streets of Kensington. Here was someone who had shaken Henry James's hand and who remembered the man as having a "melodious voice" and once remarking, when a child walked into the room, "Oh, you angel from an antique age."

Did I like Henry James? Did people still read him? Jim Ede asked me; he was passionately interested in the novelist's legacy, as well as, more generally, in the living relevance of art. Vital links to the past come in many forms, and many generations of readers have felt, as I did when I first read these books, an almost disquieting connection with the authors of *The Turn of the Screw* (Henry Junior's gripping ghost story) or *The Varieties of Religious Experience* (William's heartfelt exploration of human spirituality), and have wondered what might be behind the unexpected immediacy of these works. I have spent many tantalizing days at Harvard's Houghton Library, that great storehouse of Jamesian artifacts, looking for those surprising details that bring people of the past alive for us and make them relevant. There and elsewhere, I have found, among more "distinguished" papers, scrawled love letters and confessions, cartoons and shopping lists, and blurred photographs of loved ones that the Jameses carried with them on their travels.

Though superlative biographical work has been done on almost all the Jameses—and collectively on the family by F. O. Matthiessen in 1947 and R. W. B. Lewis in 1991—a more complete and modern portrait of this family has simply not been possible until recently. The Jameses' papers were thoroughly combed through by an earlier generation of scholars, but few have looked at these documents with an up-to-date critical perspective. Whole new theoretical structures about gender and sexuality have emerged since most of the James biographies were written, and incisive research has bared the contradictions of their personal lives and their historical era.

Before the last decade or two, few people talked or wrote about the most intimate issues in the Jameses' lives: mental illness, alcoholism, love, sex, homosexuality, money, the roles of women and men, and the pressures of professional and artistic success on personal lives. Even meticulous, monumental biographies of the past—exemplary ones, like Leon Edel's careful and comprehensive multivolume account of Henry James Jr., completed in 1985—do not adequately address many issues of the James family's confidential lives. We can talk about the Jameses now without holding back or turning our heads, and we are significantly more able to interpret what lies behind their hard-to-read expressions.

The Jameses methodically kept from the public eye the substantial history of mental and physical illnesses that ran in the family. Along with a history of psychological problems, Henry Senior lived for nearly three decades as an alcoholic, a factor in his and his children's lives that has largely gone unmentioned in the James biographies. Henry Senior's desperation to avoid the depression of everyday life made him imagine better places on far horizons. At least one of his sons had a severe drinking problem, and all of his offspring developed coping mechanisms and character traits common to children of alcoholics. For all of the Jameses, dysfunction and illness operated as a safety valve: breakdowns gave the unknown Alice a mode of self-assertion, and deep depressions dogged William and Henry, the most conspicuously "gifted" of the children.

Sex counted as a prime James family secret, one that stirred and stimulated them behind the moral propriety they had inherited from both of their parents. In fact, the common Victorian conflation of romance and family love caused a special confusion in a family whose closeness bordered, psychologically at least, on the incestuous. Until recently, there has been little frank discussion about the Jameses in love, about the affairs and half affairs and private obsessions that they carried on, in private and in public, throughout most of their adult lives, and the instability of the younger generation's relationships in comparison to their parents'. These rich stories are not a matter of labels; to more deeply understand Alice James's ambiguous "Boston marriage" with Katharine Peabody Loring, for example, it helps to adopt a contemporary understanding of the complexities of women's sexual desires. Henry James Jr.'s London bachelorhood provides a similar puzzle, one whose implications were largely taken at face value until recent studies called his motivations into question and started a lively debate about the novelist's sexuality.

Henry, the great letter burner of the family, imposed his own uneasiness about eroticism (and especially homoeroticism) during a time when middle-class Victorian silence was yielding to greater sexual openness— his own father's agitations on behalf of "free love" in the early 1850s, for example, or William's musings on his own sexual fitness for marriage in the 1870s. Henry's genteel obfuscations about sex create a frustrating though not an impenetrable smoke screen. But even William James's apparently more conventional marriage turns out not to look so simple and in fact helps to build a rich picture of love and its complications for the James family and their era.

The role of women in the James household is essential to their story. The rediscovery and republication of Alice James's diary in 1964, Jean Strouse's brilliant *Alice James: A Biography* (1980), and Alfred Habegger's *Henry James and the "Woman Business"* (1989) have admirably redressed this imbalance. Even so, the James women have been methodically sidelined. At the center of the family drama, I have tried to place Mary Walsh James, the only member of the immediate family about whom a biography has not been written but whose shrewd maneuvers kept her family together and halfway functional. I would also like to shed light on Kate Walsh, the travel-hungry maiden aunt, who often lived with the family and chaperoned Alice without much understanding her; Alice Gibbens James, William's wife, who objected to Alice James's intense friendship with the Bostonian feminist Katharine Loring but otherwise coped with her husband's contradictions; and the Jameses' first cousins, Kitty and Minny Temple, headstrong and wayward orphans whom the Jameses adored and idolized and who prefigured the greater liberties of the twentieth century.

Just as important, confusions and conflicts over the roles of women and men played a huge part in the Jameses' lives, especially as nineteenth-century feminism challenged traditional understandings. The elder Jameses counted as a somewhat unconventional couple—Mary James the more forceful and practical character, Henry Senior more emotive and sensitive—who still embodied quite a bit of Victorian propriety. To their children, they offered both rigidity and veiled permission to be different. Raised with their father's obsession with "manliness" and his disdain for women as anything but homemakers, the young Jameses had to work hard to carve out identities for themselves, and their rich solutions to these questions reflect many of our contemporary concerns.

Finally, it is revelatory to look at the Jameses as a Victorian (and not-so-Victorian) household—the family's fascinating interrelations with their era and its emerging middle-class culture. As well-to-do middle-class forerunners, the Jameses belonged to a group trapped in between worlds. Like Isabel Archer in Henry James's *Portrait of a Lady*, they inherited enough money to pursue the personal and professional lives they wanted, though not really enough to qualify them for the mansions, cotillions, and commercial empires of the Gilded Age. Yet, more than such luxuries, the Jameses craved intellectual independence, and with that freedom came many difficulties: they were all too free to consider their own happiness and satisfaction. (At least some of them were; the parents largely indulged their two oldest sons while putting the younger two out to earn their livings, effectively creating two classes of Jameses, the "successes" and "the failures.") Just rich enough to worry about whether or not they were fulfilled, all the Jameses tended to fall victim to introspection and self-scrutiny. Their richly textured private lives forecast the increasing leisure and prosperity (but also the competition and dysfunction) of coming generations. The Jameses were crucial pioneers of middle-class aspiration, anxiety, and self-realization.

For this reason, in hunting for a more compelling image of the Jameses, it is essential to look at their houses, their servants, their luggage, their ships, their friends, their connections to the institutions and manias of their day—and to consider these contexts as mysterious and complicated, not as given facts of life. Seeing more of the Jameses' historical world can give us more access to their inner lives. Such a thickly populated Victorian topography of temperance meetings, department stores, financial panics, and nerve asylums helps take the Jameses out of the elite shell in which they have often been trapped. Far from being a mythical or exalted dynasty, living in artistic isolation, the Jameses interacted with a burgeoning America and its developing institutions: they witnessed the creation of the Erie Canal, the transcontinental railroad, the New York Public Library, the modern form of Harvard University, and the Brooklyn Bridge.

To be sure, the iconoclastic and misfit Jameses didn't epitomize their era in an obvious way. They lived to trounce customs and violate norms, beginning with Henry Senior and Mary's unconventional civil marriage in 1840. But the Jameses stood at a remarkable intersection of worlds. In their long collective lifetimes, they penetrated some of the most glittering intellectual, literary, artistic, financial, and even political enclaves of their times. They met everybody. They knew everybody. And any understanding of the Jameses remains incomplete without a portrait of the ever-changing nineteenth- and twentieth-century Atlantic world— its terrain of attic nurseries, drawing-room séances, thronged lecture halls, and blood-spattered Civil War field hospitals—through which the Jameses adventurously roved.

In Washington Square more than twenty years ago, I looked for a vanished mansion. But what I've discovered since, and especially in the many years of writing this book, is something almost as ghostly but much more personal: the moving, hidden story of this family whose vulnerabilities tell us something crucial about their remarkable works. Ultimately, I think, the Jameses reveal something profound not only about "genius" but also about the misfortunes and triumphs of ordinary families. And even more surprisingly, they tell us something striking and unexpected about how a modern family can survive and thrive in love and in trouble, despite the tangles of the past.

· 1 ·

THE VOYAGE
OF THE *ATLANTIC*

T hough small, spare, and unbalanced in his gait, Henry James
Sr. loved to pit himself against the uncomprehending world.
Sometimes he walked with canes, to cope with a childhood injury, but more often this self-appointed prophet of social reform cast
away all artificial forms of support and navigated on his own. Such was
the case on this steamy and momentous June day in 1855, when the
forty-four-year-old patriarch lowered himself down the steps of his
Fourteenth Street brownstone, ready to take on just about everyone.

The James family party was leaving New York: one lame man, Henry
himself; three bonneted women; five young children; and a Himalaya of
luggage. On this "thoroughly hot" summer morning, as the *New York Tribune* described it, they were striking out toward a Europe that, thanks to
the lithographs and novels that had stoked their imaginations, felt more
real to them, in a sense, than the scorching streets of Manhattan. It was as
if they were going home, though the places they envisioned were as yet
unknown. Defiantly, Henry was preparing to snatch his young family—
Alice, his smallest child, was only six—away from the city that had
counted as the only genuine home they'd ever known. The Jameses were
moving to the lake country of Switzerland, where, Henry insisted, his
children would blossom in the experimental hothouses of Swiss schools.
He was, after all, a social engineer of sorts. His children, he believed,
should be the beneficiaries of the world's most enlightened thinking.

The "acquisition of the languages" by young patricians was all the vogue—an educational "New York fetish" of the 1850s, as Henry's novelist son would later claim. But Henry wasn't only following a trend; he was intoxicated by the idea that these groundbreaking schools could help his children fulfill the ambitious destinies he had marked out for them. Liberated from the bad moral influences of rough-and-tumble New York, their father felt, his sons would soon acquire exquisite manners and impeccable French. To anyone who questioned his decision to transplant them across the ocean, the cane-wielding Henry—often armed, literally and figuratively, with a stick—bristled with justifications.

For years, Henry had waged a single-minded campaign to rid himself and his family of their solid Manhattan address. He'd leveled various crafty arguments at his wary, stiff-collared listeners. He'd persuaded his friend Horace Greeley, the slender and bespectacled editor of the *New York Tribune*, with his visions of instructive European cities. He'd even defied his idol, the New England philosopher Ralph Waldo Emerson, who had testily declared European travel to be a "fool's paradise" in his influential 1841 essay "Self-Reliance."

Of course, Henry loved to argue as much as he loved to travel. And partly, his insubordination was Emerson's own fault, as the protégé had adopted his mentor's own radical American individualism with gusto. "Society everywhere is a conspiracy against the manhood of every one of its members," Emerson had written a decade before in "Self-Reliance"; "Whoso would be a man must be a nonconformist." But Emerson hadn't intended for Henry to be as maddeningly, perversely singular as he was currently showing himself. Sitting serene among his flush green New England orchards, remote from the family upheaval now unfolding at Henry's front door, Emerson may have wondered if he'd created a monster. Others, posed the question, would certainly have responded in the affirmative.

To be sure, Henry's diatribes explaining the upending of his family rang with the same high principles he had shown in public debates over slavery, utopian socialism, women's role in society, and "free love." He had spoken out on almost every controversial issue of his time, with a sometimes bewildering mix of radicalism and conservatism. On free love he had been at least a theoretical extremist; on women's rights, he was a notorious reactionary—and these strong and often contradictory opinions would impact the development of his children. But Henry's many enthusiasms also concealed a deeper truth behind his present urgency. Henry James Sr. was "different," a jumble of discordant notes. At times he seemed unbalanced.

He had previously suffered from restlessness, nervousness, and melancholia. For years "blue devils" and "black devils" had plagued the man with a phantasmagoria of symptoms as well as depression and anxiety. Such burdens made it difficult for him to concentrate or sustain interest in much of anything. On top of everything else, Henry suffered from visual hallucinations: a decade before, he'd blundered onto a devil crouching on a hearthstone—a dramatic mental thunderclap that had brought on a severe nervous breakdown in 1844.

Henry also had a decades-long history as an alcoholic—a usually unspoken-of feature of his life and his children's. He had been drinking hard liquor since the age of eight or nine and had been addicted to alcohol since his troubled adolescence. His adult life, too, had been dominated by his addiction. But six years before, he had consulted a doctor friend in England; and four years prior, in 1851, he had made a public declaration, in the *New York Tribune*, that he had given up drinking. He had done it, he claimed, by sheer force of will.

The nineteenth century, to be sure, scarcely understood and rarely discussed such demons. Both alcoholism and mental illness still invited derision and superstition. But sanatoriums for drinking problems had begun to appear, and reformist crusaders such as the Quaker-inspired Dorothea Dix had started to lobby northeastern states to create bona fide mental hospitals in order to ease psychological afflictions. Dix herself—dark-chignoned and straight-backed—was a victim of recurrent depression. She longed to provide refuge for those whom she saw as suffering from a vast, crippling, and invisible epidemic. For generations, the inmates of "charitable" institutions had been poked with sticks, made to froth, rant, and tear at one another for mob amusement.

More fortunate, with his independent income, Henry was in no danger of incarceration. He didn't even appear "mad." On the contrary, he was capable of charming and disarming many of the New Yorkers he met. Vastly intelligent and tenderhearted, he was the sort of man that women warmed to and even fell in love with; several receptive New York ladies had succumbed, among them Mary Walsh, whom he had married fifteen years before. His children, too, felt his magnetism, and all of them would be shaped by his alcoholism and mental illness, as well as by his charm, his nonconformity, and his radiant intelligence.

AS THEY SPILLED down the steps of their former home, the five James children—William, Henry, Wilkie, Bob, and Alice—must have looked fresh and willing enough, caught up in their father's enthusiasm and the excitement of the day. By moving to Europe, Henry hoped to provide his offspring with what he called a "sensuous education"— sensuous in this case implying a broad and lively development of faculties, under the tutelage of nature, and not frivolous sensuality. Henry's interest in his children's education was an extension of his social theories about the moral improvement of the human race. For this reason, the progressive Henry was also morally and certainly sexually as strict as many a nineteenth-century patriarch. Instead of budding libertines, the young Jameses would become guinea pigs of Henry's theories about "social consciousness"—Henry's version of the human progress that the nineteenth century often believed in. Lovingly, Henry treasured his children as "chickens" who sheltered under his paternal wings every night. Yet when he gazed at them—at thirteen-year-old William and twelve-year-old Henry Junior especially—he saw not only overdressed Victorian children kitted out for a sea voyage but also the forerunners of a new and improved "race."

Whatever his eventual plans for his brood, Henry's first goal was to get the family to their steamship—a journey of several stages, the first a drive from their Fourteenth Street residence to the Hudson River ferry. The family kept no carriage, so they hired conveyances arrived from Mr. Hathorn's livery stable in nearby University Place. With Henry's thin sons helping Hathorn's hired hands—doing their utmost to budge some of the cumbersome baggage—the hacks were soon loaded. Iron-rimmed steamer trunks, leather portmanteaus, cylindrical hatboxes, and patterned carpetbags would litter the next six decades of the family's life, but the disarray of this departure, though outwardly gay and optimistic, also hinted at Henry's personal desperation as well as the tension underlying this family scene.

Henry held his head high as he struggled to find his seat in the carriage—not a good sign for his steadiness on an ocean passage. For all his protestations about his offspring's education, Henry had also launched his plan for his own narcissistic reasons: he knew he had to make something of himself, and he hoped Europe could help. He'd kicked off this family hegira not only to soothe his anxiety but also to nudge his own stalled literary career back to life, in order to write philosophical letters for the *New York Tribune*. Henry was in his midforties, and he wanted to make more of his life. He wanted to produce a series of articles about his family's precarious life in transit, about their future careers as "hotel children."

ꙮ

THE BIG CARRIAGES, "lolling and bumping," started off for the Jersey ferry. Regal, dark-haired Mary Walsh James, Henry's wife, cut a commanding figure. Forty-five and a year older than Henry, she had organized the move with a cool head and the tactical eye of a general. Yet she too must have been excited. Secretly, she loved to travel; the notion of being a woman who actually visited foreign countries had counted as one of the attractions of her marriage. But more than her husband, Mary had been able to foresee how hellish it would be to cross the ocean with five extremely curious children—not to mention one somewhat childlike husband.

Mary had firsthand knowledge of these challenges: the Jameses had sailed for Europe before, a decade earlier, when William and Henry Junior were mere babies. But this time around, they were going not for a tour, not for the yearlong hobnob in which wealthy Americans sometimes indulged, but for good—for years, anyway. Tiresome arrangements had been necessary to rent the house, charge letters of credit to European banks, and move a sprawling family out of the home in which they'd resided for seven years. Henry had schemed. Mary had budgeted, sorted, and packed for months. Travel in the mid-nineteenth century involved a welter of setbacks and dangers, even before stepping into a hired carriage.

Mary well understood that her husband, a moral philosopher turned vagabond, fretted less about his family's travel arrangements than about his own particular luggage, a "vast, even though incomplete, array of Swedenborg's works," as his son Henry would remember it. All over Europe, these tomes by an arcane eighteenth-century Swedish mystic, carefully arranged in an enormous trunk, would startle many a porter and weigh down many a conveyance. The prolific Emanuel Swedenborg had managed to scribble more than ninety books before giving up the ghost, and a significant number of these effusions constituted the traveling library of his zealous American follower.

For a whole decade of Henry's marriage, the frayed red Swedenborgs had put a "strain"—though an "accepted" one—on Mary James's patience. When trying to explain their inexplicable father to her children, Mary would refer to their "Father's Ideas"—the capital *I*, as her son Henry remembered it, implied in her voice.

Against Henry's ideas, Mary marshaled her own allies. Two other women accompanied the family in their carriage, to help Mary look after the children: one aunt and one nanny. Mary's younger unmarried sister, Catharine, as usual, had her hands full with the excitement of her niece and nephews, who jostled and elbowed one another to claim better views of the streets. The children had read in Charles Dickens about London, their first stop; twelve-year-old Henry Junior especially had soaked in the luxurious lithographs of Joseph Nash's *Mansions of England in the Olden Time* on the drawing room carpet, swinging his heels in the air. And now that the Jameses had actually started, Mademoiselle Cusin, their French governess, could hardly govern them.

Deliberately sweet and detached, Mary liked to stay above such a fray, with her children as well as her husband. But she probably didn't savor the prospect of a voyage on the *Atlantic*, the steamship that awaited them on the other side of the Hudson. Henry had been so eager to get to Liverpool that he'd even booked his family on one of the most notorious and luckless steamers ever to cross the Atlantic Ocean.

Like the later *Titanic*, the leviathan *Atlantic* had at least a sporting chance of sinking, no matter how unsinkable it billed itself. The 1850s had already seen some of the worst maritime disasters in American history. So much sidewheeler luxury tonnage had split on icebergs or foundered in wind-lashed seas that some of the James family's friends had felt that it was an exception when crossing the Atlantic "not to be drowned." Henry and Mary's "laughing assurances to the contrary [were] received with uplifted eyes and hands and . . . incredulous 'Ohs!' " The Jameses' friends read the newspapers; they knew what happened to unlucky steamers. Wreck after wreck had unfolded in lithographic splendor.

⤋

IN COMPARISON TO the high-latitude, iceberg-strewn shipping lanes, New York must have seemed safe and predictable. The place, after all, had counted as home for a family who would afterward spend their lives perpetually in search of an equivalent emotional anchorage. In Manhattan, over the past decade, the younger Jameses had enjoyed what they would remember as idyllic childhoods. They'd wolfed iced custards. They'd bounded alongside side-whiskered uncles and ringletted aunts. They'd frequented matinees, dame schools, and music shops with gas lamps shaped like harps. They'd haunted bookshops stuffed with gorgeous English bindings, where bells tinkled cheerfully over the doors. But the New York of 1855 had already begun to gather its modern momentum. The city, pushing toward a million inhabitants, was the world's most thriving port as well as its second largest city, after London. Mary James's ancestral home was a burgeoning metropolis surrounded by river traffic, a populous island overflowing with polyglot crowds. Walt Whitman, a young and as yet unknown Brooklyn poet, celebrated New York in 1854 as a magnificent hive of New World democracy.

As the Jameses headed out down Broadway—at the time slicing five miles across Manhattan from the Battery to the mushrooming fifties, where the vast urban pleasure ground of Central Park would soon be staked out—they threaded a canyon of commerce. New York no longer amounted to a provincial town of narrow Federal townhouses and quaint Dutch gables, as Henry and Mary could easily remember. Downtown, the city was now sprouting six-story commercial buildings in brown sandstone, native brick, sooty granite, and pillared marble.

Among the most monstrous of the new Manhattan hotels was the St. Nicholas, between Broome and Spring streets. The largest such establishment in the world, it boasted more than six hundred rooms. In its gilded and mirrored dining room, exotic dishes were kept warm over spirit lamps, prepared by French chefs according to the latest New York craze. Blue flames cast a glow at every table, while a fleet of liveried waiters whisked in plates of the era's ubiquitous oysters.

Elsewhere along the Jameses' route from Fourteenth Street to lower Manhattan, other monuments to New York's muscular adolescence would have been visible. On Lafayette Place, the recently completed Astor Library imitated Venice with its ruddy round-topped "Byzantine" arches. (This precursor of the New York Public Library, with its two hundred thousand volumes, had been built by John Jacob Astor, the fur and real estate tycoon—and incidentally America's first millionaire—who, with his temper and whims almost matched Henry James Sr. in oddness.)

Alexander T. Stewart's dry-goods shop, on Broadway, at Chambers Street, overflowed from a six-story marble cube. This forerunner of New York's soon-to-be-legendary department stores employed a platoon of four hundred people and even featured a "telegraph line on the premises" for lightning-quick orders. Stewart's damasks and brocades, lace collars and Valenciennes flounces commanded mind-boggling prices, but it was the imported luxury fabrics that mesmerized wealthy New York women, among them Mary James. The children had "wearily trailed through it," hanging to their entranced mother's or their aunt Kate's skirts.

Also on Broadway, P. T. Barnum's theater, his Great American Museum, was "covered with gaudy paintings" and flew eye-catching flags. During the month of the Jameses' departure, Barnum had hosted a "National Baby Show" in which he had paraded "one hundred of the finest babies in America." (In antebellum America, this show rigorously excluded black infants.) Barnum's spectacle of a museum more usually housed "bottled mermaids, 'bearded ladies,' and chill dioramas," as the younger Henry recalled, which had both fascinated and repelled the James children. Thanks partly to their father's big plans, some of the children would feel, in the future, like Barnum monstrosities or carnival freaks—as the perspicacious Alice James would later put it—who'd "missed fire."

Just as the family was poised to encounter Europe, New York was ready to compete head-to-head with London. In 1851, London had astounded the world with its Great Exhibition in Hyde Park. (A schoolmate of the younger Henry James had shown him an "iridescent and gilded card" advertising this dazzling fair enclosed in a gigantic vaulted greenhouse.) New York countered in 1853 with its own Crystal Palace, a vast domed Taj Mahal of cast iron and glass. Like its imperial British competitor, this first U.S. world's fair showcased what the well-known Manhattan diarist George Templeton Strong called "covetable things." It plugged American-made jewelry and furniture as well as displaying "appetizing nuggets and bars and chunks" of freshly mined California gold.

A shrine to American style and ingenuity, the Crystal Palace also stood beside the terminal reservoir of the Croton aqueduct, a fortresslike structure that towered between Fortieth and Forty-second streets, near where the New York Public Library would go up fifty years later. In one of the engineering miracles of an optimistic century, these new public waterworks had recently begun to pump public water into the astonished bathrooms of up-and-coming New Yorkers like the Jameses. Such modern conveniences hadn't graced the lives of previous generations, but the Jameses and their peers would pioneer all manner of modern improvements, and plumbing was only the beginning.

∽

ACROSS THE HUDSON, the massive steamship *Atlantic* awaited them—huge and blunt, with its beetle-black hull, dark rigging, and massive sidewheels. Already this ship had loomed large in popular legend. As the James boys were well aware, it had figured in one of the most disturbing maritime cliffhangers of the day. A few winters before, the ship had gone missing. Some speculated that it was locked in pack ice. Others thought it had gone down with all hands. Anxiety about the vessel's fate ran high during the freezing January and drizzling February of 1851.

On February 4, the *New York Tribune* announced a series of public lectures by "Mr. James," the first on the "Legitimacy and Significance of the Institution of Property." But while Henry was spinning his social philosophy, the city was gripped with the potential loss of both property and life, as steamer after steamer coasted into port with "no news," "no tidings," and "no trace" of the *Atlantic*. "I am surprised a vessel or vessels has not been sent to the neighborhood of Cape Race to look for the Atlantic," one New Yorker fretted to Horace Greeley's paper. "Surely the lives of the persons on board are worth the effort."

After many a false alarm, news finally came. The missing leviathan reemerged in a belling headline: THE ATLANTIC SAFE AT CORK! The Cunard liner *Africa* brought the revelation that the American ship had broken its mainshaft in mid-Atlantic and, thus crippled, had inched its way back to Ireland on canvas.

The news spread through the city like wildfire. Breathless, a grease-painted New York actor appeared in the smoking footlights of his downtown theater. The crowd, in a hush, awaited his announcement. "Ladies and gentlemen, I rejoice to be able to tell you that the good ship Atlantic is safe!" At this, the house, including nine-year-old William and seven-year-old Henry James, let loose with roars of joy and applause.

In past decades, travelers like the Jameses who were bound for Europe had crowded to Packet Row, the fringe of docks on the lower tip of Manhattan. There "packets"—fast wooden sailing ships outfitted to carry mail and grandees—had departed on the first of every month. With the advent of steamers, and of goliath steamships like the *Atlantic*, the bustle of the Manhattan docks had outgrown these quaint facilities and had transplanted itself across the river.

At the departure of a big steamship, bedlam reigned at the Collins Line depot in Jersey City. Young Henry later described the waterside "*abords* [outskirts] of the hot town"—as the James children knew them from other summertime sailings. He remembered the "rank and rubbishy" quarters of the city on both sides of the Hudson,

> where big loose cobbles, for the least of all base items, lay wrenched from their sockets of pungent black mud and where the dependent streets managed by a law of their own to be all corners and the corners to be all grocers; groceries indeed largely of the "green" order, so far as greenness could persist in the torrid air, and that bristled, in

glorious defiance of traffic, with the overflow of their wares and im-
plements. Carts and barrows and boxes and baskets, sprawling or
stacked, familiarly elbowed in its course the bumping hack (the
comprehensive "carriage" of other days, the only vehicle of hire
then known to us).

Pandemonium reigned as Henry Senior shouted to porters, and Mary
and her sister shepherded the children. One or two of them were likely
to bolt off; the others remained quietly observant.

The gangways of the *Atlantic*, meanwhile, thronged with well-to-do
travelers and their dependents. As they boarded, the James children were
confronted by the big, gaudily painted figurehead on the steamship's
prow, "supported right and left by a gilded mermaid." Was this muscled
male torso supposed to be the sea god Neptune? Or was it William
Wordsworth's famous Triton, sounding his vine-and-leaf-twined horn?
Witty English travelers joked that the figure represented Edward Knight
Collins, the bullish American shipping magnate and owner of the *Atlantic*,
blowing his own bugle.

Like Barnum, Collins operated with the hyperbolic instincts of a
Yankee showman. And his ambitions far outstripped the mere building
and running of Atlantic steamships. With his three-hundred-foot liner—
heavily subsidized by Congress—Collins had aspired to trounce the
speed records set by the ever-fleeter British passenger ships. And Collins
likewise hoped to outstrip the opulent furnishings of the more established
Cunard Line.

As for the *Atlantic*, American newspapers cried it up as a "floating
palace." They touted it as "the most beautiful specimen of marine architecture afloat." Passage on the ship cost a staggering $130 for a first-
class cabin, $325 for "exclusive use of extra-size state-rooms." An
"experienced surgeon" also patrolled the ship, a precaution against the
seasickness and influenza that dogged Victorian steamers.

The *Atlantic*'s huge boilers heated ample water for bathrooms, an
unheard-of convenience at sea. It packed forty tons of ice, cut on New
England ponds in the winter, to keep its luxurious provisions chilly and
to provide iced drinks for the passengers: "lemonade (frozen)," as the
ship's menu advertised.

When the James children scurried down belowdecks, they discovered a whole enticing fantasyland. Grandiose carved escutcheons of the states erupted on the panels between their staterooms. In the main salon—almost seventy feet long and crafted out of brocatelle marble, stained glass, and rare woods like "white holly, satin-wood, and rose-wood," as other observers noted—the children threaded through a profusion of columns and mirrors and overstuffed plum-colored sofas, "their numbers quadrupled by the reflection." At the ship's stern, the young Jameses could marvel over stained-glass windows radiating the hastily concocted arms of the cities of Baltimore, Philadelphia, Boston, and New York. They could glimpse stirring spread eagles, five-pointed stars, and an operatic oil painting of Liberty crushing a feudal prince underfoot.

Were they, the James children, the embodiment of liberty—embarking on an unorthodox "sensuous education"? Or were they, with their French governess and attendant aunt, with their cushion of family money, young nobility themselves? The *Atlantic*'s contradictions of democracy and elitism matched the Jameses' own contradictions. And by coming aboard, they'd launched their own perilous equivalent of its career; they too had fired a shot across the bow of Europe.

AT THE RAIL, as the *Atlantic* steamed out to sea, its coal-fired boilers smudging a long strip of evening sky, the James family watched their familiar New York dwindle. But as the *Atlantic* punched through waves in the open ocean out past Fire Island, seasickness seized them. One after another, they succumbed to what the family unanimously called the "Demon of the Sea." As the voyage continued, they would plunge into "very nasty weather nearly the whole of the passage," as Henry would note in one of his first letters to the *Tribune*. What's more, the staterooms or sleeping cabins of the *Atlantic* were tiny, each with two bunks and only one small porthole. For the convenience of large Victorian families, these miniature rooms offered communicating doors. But these hardly spread cheer when the vomiting began and circulated from one child to the next.

Mary and her sister, Kate, who rightly claimed the constitutions of horses, carefully shepherded their sickness-prone charges, including the hypochondriacal Henry. But as the *Atlantic* surged into deeper, rougher water, even these hardy women crumpled, groaning, into the fold-down bunks. The *Atlantic* rolled and plunged, and only the narrow precautionary bedrails kept the sisters from sprawling out onto the floor.

Though elegantly paneled and floored with "rich carpeting," the *Atlantic*'s staterooms quickly grew as airless as cupboards. The grand steamer provided tight quarters even on a good day of its ten- or twelve-day voyage. No wonder that the children hurried up on deck to escape these claustral cubicles whenever their equilibrium permitted.

Mary, always so well dressed, would, in other circumstances, have relished announcing herself in the dining salon in her best crinolines, with her five handsome children in tow. But only two members of the family felt well enough regularly to appear at dinner: Henry Senior and his youngest son, Bob, who later would become an accomplished sailor and who now managed to sidestep the green-gilled misery of his all-too-sensitive siblings.

Henry and Bob made an odd-looking twosome. Henry, wobbly but cheerful, navigated the rolling decks with his canes as eight-year-old Bob darted about, bright-eyed and birdlike, basking in the rare windfall of his father's complete attention. The abundant wine and spirits no doubt tempted Henry, but he could glory in his abstinence and in his sense that, after so many delays, he was making something of himself. His appearance marked him as a New York gentleman of means, with confidence, wit, and condescension; but he added more novel distinctions: the cachet of being a writer and a newspaperman, a contributor of high-profile travel letters to the *Tribune*.

Henry, often desperately insecure and self-conscious, felt equal to the company he met every evening at the captain's table. He conversed fearlessly with James Renwick, an eminent professor of physics and geology at Columbia, and with the illustrious Sir Allan MacNab, premier of Upper and Lower Canada, as he perused the baroque menu that included a first course of green turtle soup, made with captured sea turtles. Diners could then move on to turkeys in oyster sauce or "*epigram*" of lamb with truffles. For dessert, there were apple fritters, almond-cup custards, cranberry tarts, or "Coventry puffs." (Bob's fingers got sticky.)

And the famous frozen lemonade—especially good for a recovering alcoholic—was available morning, noon, and night.

From these suppers, Henry no doubt brought to his incapacitated family entertaining or indignant anecdotes. The children lived on stories, and they appreciated their father's. As he vowed to confide to *Tribune* readers, Henry objected to a young woman at the table who'd struck him as belonging "to 'the lower classes' in manners and deportment." But mostly he returned with updates from Captain West on the *Atlantic*'s course and position. The ship was plying north as well as east. It was thrusting deep into stormy northern latitudes—to avoid icebergs, the captain counterintuitively insisted.

Henry admired Captain West as "manly and good-hearted . . . full of kindness." In his company, Henry felt "the menace plucked out of every storm." But although the *Atlantic*'s experienced skipper spoke calmingly of his sharp-eyed lookouts, of his iceberg-free course, both Mary and Henry no doubt worried as the *Atlantic* crossed the Grand Banks and headed toward even more polar waters. Another Collins monster ship, the *Arctic*, had met a terrible fate off Newfoundland only the year before, in 1854, in one of the greatest maritime disasters of the decade.

The *Arctic*, an even speedier and more luxurious seagoing palace than its sister ship, had embodied high-stakes ambition. In a dense fog it had collided with another ship and quickly sunk; three hundred people died, including Edward Knight Collins's own wife, daughter, and son. Its loss in the Grand Banks had dealt the United States a tragic loss that seemed like a punishment for hubris. The Jameses could not know, in 1855, that the Collins Line was doomed, that American ships would never overtake the European passenger companies in the coming heyday of transatlantic liners. But they keenly understood during this tense northern voyage the vulnerability of their own hopes.

EVEN WHEN LAID low by seasickness, Mary worked her magic to stitch her high-strung family together. She alleviated the ravages of Henry's demons, calming him with her sweet, steady gaze. *She* wouldn't have moved the family to Switzerland, if it had been up to her. True, she'd learned to share Henry's enthusiasm for those top-notch Swiss schools. But *she* wouldn't have chosen to stow her children on an ill-fated ship, to toss and turn with nightmares of ice grinding into the prow. And yet she'd chosen Henry. And to choose Henry, she might well recall, was to choose a universe of icebergs.

Mary Walsh James was nothing, though, if not resilient—yet, lacking her husband's wit, she hadn't been missed at the captain's table. Like her younger sister, Kate, like her small daughter, Alice, Mary was at times easy to overlook. She was a distinct personality, with a roster of definite likes and dislikes, but she also cultivated the invisibility of Victorian wives, mothers, and daughters. And yet it is not possible to understand the Jameses or their America without her. Her favorite son, at least, roundly defended her importance. Henry Junior would ask, "What account of us all can pretend to have gone the least bit deep without coming to our mother at every penetration?" Mary James, with her Victorian solidity and prudery—and with her un-Victorian assertiveness—would shape her children's careers, their anxieties and ambitions, quite as much as their volatile father. She was the world as it should be, in the eyes of nineteenth-century mothers: a place where her children didn't always fit comfortably.

As the first week passed and the *Atlantic* steamed past Ireland, Mary revived and was soon figuring accounts and rooting in trunks for some of the elaborate pleated frocks she'd laid in to wear on the voyage. By the time the *Atlantic* sailed into the waters of Liverpool Bay, Mary was magnificently dressed and at the rail with her children, ready to return to terra firma when the gangplanks went down.

It was July 8, 1855—four days after an Independence Day spent tossing at sea—when the James children disembarked at the Liverpool docks and, at a stroke, became expatriates and foreigners. When she looked at her children, wide-eyed at the spectacle of the strangely dressed and strangely accented international throngs around them, Mary could hardly have foreseen how this dislocation would transform her children. Years before, she had told a friend that sometimes her "mother's heart paints a future for [her] boys, & the thought . . . adds a brighter tint of happiness to the picture." Her boys as well as her little girl lit up, eager to engage with the unknown train stations and hotels that now spread in front of them. She watched as all five of her children drank in the smoke-smudged horizons of Europe's busiest port and the world's most extended empire.

The Jameses had avoided the fate of the *Arctic*, but they hadn't dodged the consequences of becoming a family in transit, a group of close-knit exiles adrift among the palaces and ruins of Europe. Though plenty of well-to-do nineteenth-century American families routinely lived and traveled in Europe—the Continent of 1855 teemed with Yankee top hats and steamer trunks—the Jameses were already no ordinary tourists, and their coming travels would rarify them further. The young Jameses would grow up believing the answer to their problems could be found in the next city, the next country. At the same time, they would be thrown onto one another for company and comfort, sometimes in terrible isolation; they would be outsiders everywhere. Psychological survival, from this point on, would prove challenging enough for these émigrés, and their careers in dislocation had only just begun.

· 2 ·

PANIC

O ne might argue that the seed of the Jameses' 1855 decampment
to Europe was planted a long time before, in the summer of
1824, in a peaceful park in front of the Albany Academy in upstate New York. It all began, in a manner of speaking, with a miniature
hot-air balloon rising into the optimistic blue sky—and with a doomed
experiment which would critically shape the child who would become
the crippled, anguished father of later times.

The year 1824 ought to have been just another pleasurable interlude
in Henry Senior's carefree youth. As he joined his tutor and classmates
on the academy lawn, thirteen-year-old Henry James—innocent of the
"Senior" he'd adopt later in life—personified the lively chaos of a new
adolescent: he was ready to try almost anything. With the other academy boys milling around him in the park, Henry looked more like an
excited child than a young man. A portrait from several years later
shows him in a frock coat, wide-eyed and baby-faced, with narrow
shoulders and wispy hair brushed forward at the temples; he resembled
a Napoleonic corporal or a Romantic poet.

On this summer afternoon in 1824, Joseph Henry, a brilliant young
tutor and rising scientific star at the Albany Academy, gathered the students in front of the main hall of the school, a graceful Federal-style hall
built in 1815. He would become the Albert Einstein of his era, with his
later discoveries in electromagnetism, aeronautics, and acoustics, but on

this day he was entertaining the boys with an educational demonstration of "balloon-flying." Hot-air balloons, besides transfixing idle teenagers, had attracted curious adults ever since the Montgolfier brothers, Joseph and Etienne, launched a sheep, a duck, and a rooster in a silken balloon near Paris in 1783.

Earlier in 1824, coincidentally, the first rubber balloons had been contrived at the Royal Institution in London, by a visionary who'd later fascinate the adult Henry, one Professor Michael Faraday. Grander balloons were sometimes made from silk, but simple inflatables for boys might be made from animal intestines. In any case, the boys' sausage-casing balloons remained small—experiments and not conveyances. Their "motive power" came from "heated air supplied from a tow ball saturated with spirits of turpentine," as one of the boys later remembered. The tow, the fibers of hemp or flax, burned hot like a wick, so that these small airships caught fire easily.

Sometimes these soaring balloons proved even more combustible than the excited boys who launched them. After the midair demise of one of the airborne fire hazards on that fateful day, its tow ball plummeted meteorlike to earth among the academy students on the lawn. The boys, unable to resist, booted this "roll of fire" here and there, improvising a frenzied game from the fallen coals.

When one of the boys kicked the blazing tow ball extra high, it sailed right into the open window of a nearby stable. Completing its fateful arc, the ball alighted in the worst possible spot: in the vast dry tinderbox of the hayloft. In a flash, a horrifying panorama opened up to the astonished observers—the houses and warehouses of Albany going up in flame. Fires in stables could spread, and this one might well have sparked the Albany equivalent of the great fires that had historically razed swaths of American cities: New York City in 1776 (and again in 1846), New Orleans in 1788 and 1794, and Boston repeatedly throughout its clapboard-and-thatch colonial history.

Such a disaster apparently flashed into the mind of the young Henry. In a burst of heroism or daring, "thinking only of the conflagration," he rushed into the hayloft. To keep the fire from spreading, he stamped at the flame, smothering it before long—and so saving the stable, if not Albany itself. But in the process, his own trousers, sprinkled with turpentine from the earlier balloon experiment, burst into flame. And the fire seared into his leg before he or anyone else could put out the blaze.

∾

EVEN BEFORE HIS accident, the barely pubescent Henry James knew how to play with fire. At an even more tender age, he'd roamed and hunted in the wooded hills of the Hudson Valley, packing a temperamental flintlock, a combustible supply of powder, and a "glowing fire of animal spirits." As he later poetically recalled, he'd chased "under the magical light of the morning the sports of the river, the wood, or the field." But the truth was that, with such high spirits, Henry basically amounted to an accident waiting to happen.

While still very young, Henry had rebelliously joined a boys' gang, which had coalesced around a pair of cheerful shoemakers addicted to gambling, drinking, and dares. These two cobblers were brothers who played Fagin to the younger urchins they adopted, though also with a strong element of working-class rebellion. Yet Henry and the felonious waifs—like something out of Charles Dickens's *Oliver Twist* (1837)— didn't hail from the squalor of the river docks or from the hardscrabble farms up-country. They sprang instead from the quality class of Albany, from the grand gabled mansions of the city.

William James, Henry's father, had been born poor in Ireland and still spoke with a strong Scots-Irish accent. He had emigrated from Ulster sometime between 1789 and 1794 and hammered his way out of poverty. Through force of will, flinty Presbyterian zeal, entrepreneurial grit, and lucky timing, he had amassed a colossal fortune based on shrewd merchandizing and opportunistic land speculation in Albany as well as on his stake in the Erie Canal, which opened in 1825 when his son Henry was fourteen. At his death, William James of Albany would be worth $1.2 million, a figure that made him one of the richest men in New York State, a robber baron in the style of his richer contemporary and rival, the fur tycoon John Jacob Astor. With profits from waterside warehouses, liquor trade, moneylending, and other rackets, this entrepreneurial father had opened up broad horizons for his numerous family.

The Jameses' rambling mansion on North Pearl Street, on the city's then-posh east side, overflowed with servants, siblings, and hangers-on. Even before his death, Henry's father—later known grandly as William James of Albany—was already dreaming up a princely future for his son. But, a little like Shakespeare's famous prodigal, Prince Hal, Henry tended to prefer the rebellious Falstaffian fringes of low life to the up-holstered parlors of new wealth.

Henry's father was a friend of De Witt Clinton, the 1812 presiden-tial candidate who'd lost to James Madison, later becoming the larger-than-life governor of New York who'd masterminded the Erie Canal. Two of the young hoodlums in the shoemakers' gang were Clinton's sons, and that much is telling about their relation to their prominent and overwhelming father. In Henry's case, his father was evidently not a tyrannical man, and Henry later claimed that William James hardly ever made an "exhibition of authority towards us." The problem, as Henry's biographer Alfred Habegger has suggested, may well have been just the opposite: that this flinty, self-made tycoon mostly kept his emotional distance. With such a busy man, in a family of eleven children, it was hard to get any attention; and Henry wanted his father's engagement even if the boy didn't have the inclination, as some of his older brothers did, to follow in the family business.

Harmlessly enough, the boys' antics had begun with the swiping of fruit, cakes, and eggs from their parents' well-stocked larders. (This al-lowed Henry, in some way, to thwart a tightfisted father, renowned for his genius at scrimping and saving.) But before much time had passed, Henry and the Clinton boys—these out-of-control heirs—branched into gin, rum, and Madeira wine.

Word of their exploits spread through Henry's hometown of Albany—a sleepy, prosperous, hill-hemmed place, which had previously resembled the quaint Dutch-gabled villages glimpsed in Washington Irving's tales. Yet, thanks to the Erie Canal, the place had ballooned into a boomtown by the mid-1820s. Rough, turbulent vices took hold, and soon the city was "awash in spirits," as Habegger has described it. This metamorphosis, in fact, took place partly because of Henry's fa-ther, William James, and his business ventures, namely the importation of liquor from Europe and the Caribbean. Because of entrepreneurs like

James, alcohol was cheap and available. A gallon of corn whiskey cost only about twenty-five cents.

Young Henry took full advantage, developing a knack for swigging from all the wrong bottles. As he later recalled, he plunged into "the habit of taking a drink of raw gin or brandy on my way to school morning and afternoon." Significantly, Henry later described even his early drinking as a "habit." Even at the age of ten, three years before his accident at the fire, the boy was veering, rather scarily, toward chronic alcoholism. In his walks to school, he weaved down the bypaths of Albany—just as later, for decades, he'd lurch and zigzag his way through life.

That Henry's parents evidently didn't notice or intervene shows something about their distance or distraction. A problem like Henry's, though, may not have attracted much attention during an era when, as one historian has observed, even babies and toddlers were fed strong spirits. Drinking small amounts early on, the theory went, would "protect them from becoming drunkards." Such preventatives, however, weren't working. The 1820s saw the highest per capita consumption of alcohol in American history. Estimates range from between four and seven gallons of pure alcohol, per person, per year. In any case, it was more than twice the amount now consumed in the United States. In an era when water was often polluted and coffee and tea cost dearly, stiff drinking had become a daily ritual for most Americans. Beer and hard cider were staples of households, drunk at every meal including breakfast. Especially among men, whiskey, brandy, rum, and gin flowed freely both in homes and taverns. Liquor dominated most public social occasions, including weddings, funerals, militia musters, barbecues, balls, horse races, barn raisings, and even elections.

But Henry's childhood drinking evidently went way beyond even the lax norms of this alcohol-drenched period before the rise of temperance movements in the 1830s and 1840s. It is difficult to explain why an alcoholic gets hooked, but Henry's case certainly seems to have been exacerbated by family troubles. Though documentation from this period of the young man's life is scarce and sometimes "strangely self-contradictory," as Henry's biographer has put it, the root of much of the boy's turmoil isn't difficult to discover. A single figure throws an enormous shadow over Henry's early life.

William James of Albany had turned forty in 1811, the year Henry came into the world. Henry was the fifth of what would become eleven children, the son of William's third and final wife, Catherine Barber James. In contrast to the "anxiety" and painstaking care of his mother, Henry later described his father, perhaps euphemistically, as "certainly a very easy parent." "Easy" could well have meant absent, and with his many businesses to manage, Henry's father probably didn't monitor his young son's rovings or confront Henry about his slumping marks in school. Though he evidently had strong opinions, the elder James held back from expressing them directly to his children—a lifelong habit that would later be crowned by the harsh, angry injustice of his will, a piece of would-be discipline on his recalcitrant children, inflicted after his death. Henry felt his father's absence, and more: he even went so far as to hint that he disapproved of his father's own hard drinking, his stormy temperament, and his run of three wives.

Such unarticulated tensions were probably one reason that Henry was "never so happy at home as away from it"—a remark with great portent for his itinerant future. Some of his happiest memories were "horse talk" with the coachman, visiting rabbits with the outdoor servant, and arguing with the cook and waiter about "rheumatism, [M]ethodism, and miracle." It says a lot about Henry's loneliness and his alienation from his family that he clung to the servants, drank heavily, and took an interest in the agitations about religion and miracle-working that were beginning to erupt around him in New York State.

MUCH WAS IN the wind in 1824. The Erie Canal—called "Clinton's ditch" after the governor who'd promoted it—was forty feet wide and four hundred miles long, comparable to later ambitious American megaprojects like the Panama Canal (1904–14) and the Hoover Dam (1931–35). Thanks to the canal, New York City would be connected to the Great Lakes, and important towns would spring up, Utica and Syracuse and Rochester and Buffalo, now able to ship their goods on the canal barges. Such development would contribute to the Jameses' later income: for example, William James took over a salt manufactory in Syracuse, and his shrewd investments there would fuel the family's future intellectual endeavors. Their money, much as they hated to admit it, came from William James's ventures in the part of the state the canal had opened up.

The canal swept new immigrants to the rich lake-streaked farmlands of western New York State. Many came from the rocky, failing farms of New England, and certain counties of New York acquired the flavor of craggy Vermont or marshy Connecticut. But the influx was also sprinkled with other elements, Germanic or else Anglo-Celtic like the Jameses—including an influx of Catholic migrants, mostly Irish, as early as the 1820s, when the fire of a Protestant revival also spread across the region, the famous "burned-over district" of western New York, where the woods echoed with the shouts and hymns of camp meetings. The swelling towns sprouted new plank or brick churches whose steeples vied for the attention of the newly pious adherents of the so-called Second Great Awakening.

Between 1825 and 1835, more than thirteen hundred revivals erupted across the state. Western New York swarmed with chiliasts, millenarians, visionaries, crackpots, utopians, communitarians, and wild-eyed enthusiasts of every stripe. Old and new sects proliferated. In Palmyra in the 1820s, a young man only a few years older than Henry—one Joseph Smith Jr., the future founder of Mormonism—claimed to have witnessed a radiant angel carrying mysterious golden plates, ancient records of New World Hebrews.

Henry's passionate extremes and grandiosity weren't out of place in this region whose peculiar energy would fuel him and his children for decades. The pent-up fire of Protestant revivalism, raging during Henry's youth, would later propel him into theology, though the secular effects of his enthusiasm would arguably prove even more important and more lasting. In manifold ways, the values and attitudes of the burned-over district would help inspire Henry's later brand of maverick utopianism. Its attitudes would also feed the séance spiritualism that would emerge with the so-called Rochester rappings of 1848.

In the New York State of Henry's youth, millenarian sects often based their end-of-the-world predictions not only on ingenious readings of scripture but also on astronomical displays: eclipses, auroras, and meteor showers. Millenarian preachers gained adherents in the wake of natural catastrophes like floods, crop failures, and fires. Their movements promised to superimpose a divine plan on human uncertainty, to substitute a sense of cosmic order for the impulse of panic. Both the fears and hopes of utopian revivalism would influence Henry's future meditations on society, and his future conception of the education of his children. But the severe burn Henry got in the stable fire in 1824 would scar his future children as well as himself.

∞

NO RECORD REMAINS of the scene at the school or the panic at the James home on Pearl Street when thirteen-year-old Henry arrived home with his burned and blistered leg. Henry's mother, Catharine Barber James, had given birth to seven of her eight children by 1824 and had dealt with manifold accidents and illnesses. As a retiring, quiet woman, who had had to play a muted part as the third wife of a moody, preoccupied man, Catharine had been forced to practice patience. But she was in for gory scenes and long-lasting turmoil with her son's injury. Henry's leg was so badly charred that soon it "had to be amputated," one family friend remembered, just below the knee. In spite of William James's position, the job turned out to be "ill-done." Such surgery, performed without anesthetic, put Henry through unimaginable horrors, and Henry would spend most of the next two years, from the ages of thirteen to fifteen, confined to his bed. To help him cope with the pain, his father and his doctors plied him with whiskey and other strong spirits—exacerbating his drinking problem. Then, at the age of sixteen, Henry suffered another setback. Alarming black specks of disease broke out on his damaged leg, where the skin had never completely healed or even grown over the exposed bone. The leg had to be amputated again, this time above the knee—a grisly operation that took place, in May 1828, with only more liquor standing between Henry and the pain.

In a fictionalized account of his ordeal written later in life, Henry substituted a "gun-shot wound" in his arm for his burned leg. Why did he imagine this version of his formative adolescent trauma? Did a shooting accident better suit his sense of manhood, brave as he'd actually been to save the stable? Instinctively, Henry transferred the injury to his arm instead of his leg, as if he wanted to remove the injury from his legs and lower body, where it potentially interfered with his powers of locomotion and mobility (so necessary to a "man") and where an injury might be thought to impair masculine sexual potency—figuratively if not literally. Many of Henry's future issues with "manhood," anyway, were tied up with this critical injury in a significant place.

Henry would spend two years under virtual house arrest; in his fictionalized version, he portrayed his father as showing an exquisite tenderness, betraying "an exalted sense of his affection."

> My wound had been very severe, being followed by a morbid process in the bone which ever and anon called for some sharp surgery; and on these occasions I remember . . . his sympathy with my sufferings was so excessive that my mother had the greatest possible difficulty in imposing due prudence upon his expression of it.

No doubt William James of Albany was indeed moved by his young son's horrific mutilation. This rather hard-bitten anti-English merchant must have melted at times, as this passage suggests. Still, Henry must have at least partly fantasized his father's tenderness, just as he'd imagined a gunshot wound, just as he'd spared his leg by sacrificing his arm. In his lived experience, Henry's hurt probably amounted, at best, to a touching, uneasy truce with his father. Later, as he entered his young manhood, Henry would once again pit himself against his father in a long decade of what seems to have been intense although mostly indirect father-son conflict: disputes over his education, his career, and his increasingly unorthodox Presbyterian beliefs.

Thanks to his injury, Henry entered adult life as an alcoholic, one-legged young man when he went off to Union College in Schenectady in September 1828, at the age of seventeen. He was grateful to leave home behind, but he had hardly escaped the complications of his upbringing. In coming years, after a maladjusted and unsuccessful start, he would abandon his studies and sidestep becoming a lawyer—he eyed such a career, which his no-nonsense father favored, with "revulsion." He would then hide out in the isolated town of Canandaigua, at the western end of the Finger Lakes region—with one of Governor Clinton's ex-criminal sons. This period of Henry's young life is particularly murky, but it's likely that he drank and gambled his days away. At any rate, Henry's amputation, with its visible and invisible layers of damage, would inflict a brittle intensity and an incurable sense of mutilation that would determine not only his own subsequent development but also that of his children.

His future son Henry Junior would describe his injury as "an excellent whip" to his father's strong nature, an encouragement for him to persevere in the face of his disadvantages. His injury would certainly spur his desire for fame, recognition, and success, as the psychologist Alice Miller has famously described in the case of abused and gifted children. Along with his alcoholism, his injury would sometimes generate narcissistic grandiosity. But Henry's attendant depression and self-flagellation would also prove much, much darker, and this whip would savage others besides himself.

Fortunately for Henry's future children, however, they could claim another legacy, too—and one much more serene than Henry's chaotic adolescence. The James family could also trace its history back to the tranquil marble porticoes of Washington Square, where a sensible young woman was learning to cope with the difficulty of women's lives.

৵৶

BEFORE THE PANIC, the view from the big front windows of her drawing room had provided young Mary Walsh with welcome distraction. With her needlework on her lap, she could sit for hours and watch Manhattan's well-tailored society pass by. Mary's home, fittingly situated on the north side of Washington Square Park, stood near the base of Fifth Avenue, where she could enjoy the greenery of the square and keep track of passing carriages, laundry carts, and neighbors out for a stroll. Beyond the trees, she could see redbrick mansions with identical fanlights, and farther south, the shingled rooftops of less fashionable townhouses.

But by the spring of 1837, the big jewel box of Washington Square, which had thoroughly encased Miss Walsh in the velvet of middle-class security, had come a little unhinged. This showpiece of New York City had fallen deadly quiet, though knots of rough, hatless men occasionally passed through the square and hackneys raked along the cobbles at breakneck speed. Mostly, though, the sidewalks remained deserted, with no young couples out roving to admire the clusters of the acacia trees or take in the peppery smell of the blooming ailanthus. Mary and her mother and sister hardly dared to leave the house. Throughout the spring, the city had plunged ever deeper into a new and frightening financial crisis, the worst the United States had yet encountered. During this, the so-called Panic of 1837, New York banks and trading companies toppled like dominoes. Investments plummeted, flattening the city's newfound wealth and raising the fear of mobs.

To cope with the crisis, the twenty-seven-year-old Mary Walsh resorted to time-honored expedients for women in distress. When things were trying, she matched colored yarns or perhaps read leftover tea leaves, trying to foretell her own fate and Catharine's. But she couldn't deny to herself or to her sister what she believed to be true. Though almost no records from this time have survived, it seems clear that Mary was not a silly or scheming young woman, exclusively concerned with her marriage prospects; nor was she easily prone to anxiety. Yet one of the goals of her life had been to marry and have a family, and that simple dream was looking more and more unlikely, as she grew older and as suitable gentlemen lost their fortunes.

These days, a fresh tap at the silver knocker on the front door might announce an abashed servant in a frock coat delivering a note, flush with more bad news from a friend or a relative. Railroad stocks had crashed; canal shares were worthless. Two hundred and sixty trading houses had failed. "The militia are under arms, as riots are expected," one foreign observer noted. Mary, with her good head for finance, understood these matters well enough.

Mary knew her own legacy wouldn't by itself furnish a mansion like her family's. The Walshes' holdings, it's true, had fared better than most. Elizabeth Walsh, Mary's widowed mother, had proved a canny and prudent investor in an age when women were believed to have no head for money. Thanks to Mrs. Walsh, the three women hadn't joined the thousands who'd lost everything in land speculation. Nor had they found themselves, in the absence of any reliable U.S. currency, exchanging IOUs for gloves or plates of oysters, though Mary's mother probably wrung her hands about how to pay the servants, with New York banknotes worthless, coinage unavailable, and domestic help already impossible to find and keep.

Even before this disaster, Mary and Catharine (or Kate, as she was called) had attracted precious few suitors, despite their wealth and social standing. Both of the Walsh sisters were tall, florid, serious women, rather plain except for their elegant wardrobes, and without the obvious "accomplishments"—harp playing or pencil drawing—by which young women were meant to ensnare husbands. The two young ladies were fairly typical members of the conservative and inexpressive Presbyterian elite: dressy but pious, elegant but sober. In 1837, Mary turned twenty-seven and Kate twenty-five. By the standards of their time, they'd already ossified into "spinsters." (Even years later, Mary, self-conscious about her age, would sometimes lie about it.) Yet Mary's position wasn't as rare as she probably thought, and she could hardly have guessed that late marriage, that feared fate, actually held the keys to women's future in the United States—in autonomy and education—as well as her own future.

Mary, if the truth were known, didn't trouble much about women's issues—even though, within a decade, many of her peers would be focused on the "Woman Question." Rising consciousness of injustice to women would result in the Seneca Falls Declaration of 1848, which claimed, among other things, American females' rights to education, professional careers, and suffrage. During New York's troubled days, Mary Walsh probably grasped at a more tangible consolation than equality: her family's splendid new house. Washington Square, grandly built up over the past decade, felt as solid as the bedrock of Manhattan itself, and it was this very quality that endorsed Mary's own prospects: the townhouse remained redolent of wealth and embodied the kind of life young women of Mary's caste felt they deserved from marriage.

The impressive width of the house (a recognized mark of a merchant's prosperity since colonial times) and its costly slabs of marble broadcast the status of her family, just as the dimensions of Henry's father's mansion grandly announced his wealth to the citizens of Albany. Even when land values shriveled along with stock in railroads and canals, Elizabeth Walsh still had an estate valued at $25,000; her three-story brick Washington Square residence alone added an additional $18,000, a staggering sum at the time.

Inside this newly built mansion, with its gilt-framed mirrors and marble-topped tables, Mary had the run of two large drawing rooms or parlors whose retractable panel doors could convert them into one huge ballroom or dining room—not that the family had found the occasion, or the social daring, for a gala. Years later, Mary would look back fondly on Washington Square and would pass on to her children a flawless vision of "quiet and genteel retirement." That much stood in stark contrast to Henry's turbulent childhood in Albany.

By European standards, however, the Walshes' house counted as "vulgar" in its newness. It wasn't the venerable, almost aristocratic enclave that it would later seem, especially to her son Henry Junior. Even the magnificent square—in a previous century an Indian village called Sapokanikan and for many years a place of public execution—looked startlingly fresh and contrived in 1837. It flaunted new wealth, and insofar as the Walshes qualified as nouveau riche—like the Jameses of Albany, self-made immigrants only a generation before—such a display showed both their pride and their insecurity.

Like other members of their circle, the Walshes adhered to Calvinistic Presbyterianism, a conservative tradition in contrast to the enthusiasm of upstate revivalism. Mary's religion, with its manifold constraints on the activities of a "virtuous" unmarried woman, had set limits on relationships with the opposite sex, among other restraints. Though her natural bent was hardly scriptural, the bracing piety of her home helped Mary cope with the crisis as the financial panic worsened—even if such devout living often counted as a hardship itself.

Mary and her family had faced hardship before. Her father, James Walsh, had died mysteriously on a business trip in Richmond, Virginia, in 1820, when Mary was ten, Kate eight. His death stranded their mother with six children (four boys, two girls) to bring up alone. James Walsh's death came as a "great shock" to his wife, as William Walsh, a cousin, remembered. Elizabeth Walsh was "overwhelmed . . . with grief," so that "she secluded herself from all society, except a chosen circle of family relatives, and a few other families with whom she had always had intimacy." Fortunately, though, Mary's mother had also inherited a good deal of grit from her own father, an energetic Scottish merchant named Alexander Robertson, who'd boldly immigrated to New York just before the Revolution.

Elizabeth Walsh, in fact, had become heir to both her Scottish father's business sense and his stern Presbyterian sentiments. She was economical to a fault, according to one of her Walsh relatives; when visiting in the country upstate, she wore her second-best dresses, even if her daughters were "allowed to display their finery." (The Walsh women sorted their clothes into categories of "best, second best, and calico.") With careful management, this tycoon's daughter had maintained a mansion and sent her sons off to prime American institutions like Columbia College in New York. In spite of her thriftiness, Elizabeth Walsh was "warm-hearted, kind, [and] hospitable," the family remembered. She and her daughters pioneered their own entrepreneurial innovation: a loyal and close-knit female household in which, by 1837, only the occasional grown-up brother lingered.

Mary loved her brothers, but she also probably enjoyed the influence she had as the eldest daughter in a household with no man around to lay down the law. She'd always played the obedient daughter, but Mary must have savored her importance to her mother and such worldly wisdom as she'd laid away over her twenty-seven years. The genes of Alexander Robertson had bestowed on her (her middle name was Robertson) two monumental qualities: financial acumen and administrative genius. Both would prove crucial for the future of her children—not one of whom, incidentally, would inherit Mary's bracing executive efficiency.

As of yet, however, Mary's practicality had found few outlets beyond helping her mother keep the household accounts. Young women weren't supposed to exhibit pluck, decisiveness, or a head for finances, though Mary had all of these qualities in spades. She appeared calm and self-possessed, but she would soon prove herself capable of some surprisingly headstrong acts.

If in her childhood she'd confided such aspirations to her sister, Kate would have proven the most reliable of confidantes. Many years later, Kate would burn Mary's early letters and papers in order to keep Mary's secrets and her own. Thus Mary's childhood remains largely in darkness: her worries about her plainness; her dolls with rich costumes and porcelain faces; her sorrows over her father's death—all such details of her early life, if they existed, would be crumpled into the flames, for the sake of silence, discretion, and good form.

By 1837, Mary's enigmatic character had already rooted itself in her essential privacy, in her guarded preservation of her Presbyterian version of a respectable Victorian front. Like the fictional daughter in her son's future novel *Washington Square* (1880), Mary qualified as "strong" and "properly made," as fresh and robust in appearance as a milkmaid. Surviving photographs from later in her life confirm Mary's resemblance to Catherine Sloper, the modest but vigorous young protagonist of Henry's novel. If Mary later saw herself in Catherine, she never acknowledged the likeness. But she appreciated the novel, as if assenting to its portraiture of her young womanhood. And it could well have been his youthful mother that Henry Junior later conjured up.

> Her appearance of health constituted her principal claim to beauty; and her clear, fresh complexion, in which white and red were very equally distributed, was, indeed, an excellent thing to see. Her eyes were small and quiet, her features were rather thick, her tresses brown and smooth. A dull, plain girl she was called by rigorous critics—a quiet, lady-like girl, by those of the more imaginative sort.

Kate, being two years younger, tended to curl her hair more inventively than her sibling. She may well have qualified as the livelier, the more sportive, the more outwardly adventurous sister—the more marriageable, too, given her youth and ringlets. Mary might have assumed that any passing man would be attracted to her sister rather than to her. In this, though, she underestimated her own appeal, as she held a trump card: Mary had a more impressive character than her sister, and many early Victorian men based their matrimonial searches on "character" (even if Mary's morality hadn't brought many young men to the house).

Elizabeth Walsh preferred "character" herself, and she was a shrewd monitor of its presence or absence. With new-moneyed Scots pride, she seems to have expected considerable financial, familial, and religious credentials from young men who called on her daughters. Such exacting qualifications, in the nineteenth century, often led families to choose candidates who were close family friends or even relatives. In the calculations of Jacksonian mothers, first cousins often figured as the ideal spouses: intermarriage kept capital (as well as dangerous rogue genes) in the family. But, for whatever reason, Mary and Kate didn't fall for any of their Robertson and Walsh cousins, though several hovered around the right connubial age.

In future years, Mary's children would tease her about her lack of experience with romance, with anything like a "love-story," as her son Henry would note. The Walshes didn't hold with frivolous entertainments like novel reading and card playing. In New York, anyway, card parties chiefly attracted rakish men who reeked of chewing tobacco or cigars. And Elizabeth, as the Walsh cousin noted, also barred her daughters from other "worldly" entertainments: operas, theaters, or even more devout "oratorio concerts."

Most often confined behind the green shutters of Washington Square, Mary actually shared more with Henry, who had been housebound during his convalescence, than would first appear. She followed a rigid and predictable daily schedule that, dutiful as Mary tried to be, couldn't help but tax her patience. From other accounts of the time, we can glimpse the kind of daily ritual that Mary probably performed, along with other young ladies of means: early rising and meticulous dressing, family prayers, coffee and tea at set hours, and breakfasts of fried ham and salt fish and gummy half-baked rolls, served to the family by surly Irish or free black servants.

Quiet, order, and elegance dominated the Walshes' staid routine. After breakfast and for most of the day, Mary and her sister must have set to work, sometimes baking or cooking, for which they would have donned snowy aprons over their cotton housedresses. Fine watered silks were for company, for callers (if any). Servants executed most of the housework, but Elizabeth Walsh trusted in the virtue-instilling effect of her daughters' domestic tasks. Thus Mary and Kate plied at their needlework, embroidering fancy cushion covers or knitting small plain items for charity. So stood the starched decorum of Elizabeth Walsh's elegant but devout household, with its well-mannered rustlings of figured satin.

❧

BY LATE 1837, the threat of riots had subsided, even though the dark worries of economic depression would linger on until the mid-1840s. Mary, meanwhile—to judge from her later love of excursions—jumped at any opportunity to get out of the house. Eagerly she would tie on one of her bonnets. (Women wore neat white caps while at home.) She'd set out in the carriage, with her mother and sister. They would shop, go to church, or visit her favorite cousin, Helen Wyckoff. As one of her few entertainments, Mary could mingle with other rich and pious women, in elegant drawing rooms very much like the ones she'd left behind in Washington Square. Like other moneyed Presbyterian ladies, Mary no doubt also ran charitable errands, carrying her work basket and "a large roll of all those indescribable matters which ladies take as offerings to Dorcas societies"—articles she'd sewn for the poor.

Poverty might have distressed Mary and her family, who were piously philanthropic: Elizabeth Walsh had a reputation in her family as a "prudent dispenser of charities." The Walshes kept their distance from the grit of New York, from the muddy streets, beggars, dandies, and mobs. When temporarily freed, Mary couldn't help but glimpse what her son would later call the "long, shrill city," with its horizons of church steeples (New York had more than a hundred churches in the 1830s), with its surrounding thicket of ships' masts, the carriers of the city's commerce. In the rutted streets, the Walshes' carriage jostled with hard-shoving handcarts, swerved against gaudily painted omnibuses drawn by four horses and crammed with miscellaneous New Yorkers. Behind the carriages—as Dickens noticed in 1842—pigs often trotted. They complicated traffic and roved in jubilant American independence (Dickens thought), a strange signature feature of the biggest city of the Americas, which was as yet devoid of garbage collection.

But the city's rising wealth also glittered around the Walshes on their excursions. Broadway in the early 1830s gaped eighty feet wide and already stretched almost three miles long. Although patchily built up in places, it sported attractive shops that vied in splendor with those of London and Paris. On Broadway, fripperies that Mary admired promenaded boldly in broad daylight. Her tastes in fashion, like those of many New Yorkers, would have tended to French rather than English styles. Only a stray pair of cotton stockings might betray a hidden (and shameful) allegiance to English ways.

Fashion plates having existed for a couple of centuries, Mary would have known about the latest tastes of the French capital though she had never been there, and she would have seen with rapture the Broadway promenade that observers of her time described as "a moving bed of tulips": the ladies had a "flaunting air" with "their streaming feathers and flowers, silks and satins of all colours . . . like so many nymphs of the *pavé* [pavement]." But if the Walsh sisters wished to show off their own flourishes of dress in public, their mother limited their exhibitions of finery chiefly to home and church.

As something of a clotheshorse and a "high flyer at Fashion," in Dickens's later famous phrase, Mary loved especially to patronize milliners' shops. As a plain woman, she didn't stoke her vanity. In this way too she resembled the future heroine of *Washington Square*, who, "in spite of her taste in fine clothes," had "not a grain of coquetry, and her anxiety when she put them on was as to whether they, and not she, would look well."

To this end, Mary and her sister favored the stores where the old-fashioned many-paned sash windows had recently been replaced with glossy sheets of plate glass. There they could examine all the latest and finest fabrics: watered silk, satin, velvet, nankeen, muslin—the Walshes insisted on the best. As the granddaughter of a linen tycoon, Mary understood the value of that useful flaxen material; she, like many nineteenth-century ladies, had a penchant for its finer grades, called cambric and lawn, for her petticoats. (Poorer women wore coarser stuff, like the material now found in Scottish dishtowels.) Mary would have cultivated an exhaustive knowledge of muslins as well. These refined cotton fabrics, in close derivatives of white, provided the chief dress material for the Walsh sisters and their circle: muslin was chaste, delicate, the very flag of feminine virtue. Mary also fingered satins and silks—frock materials for visiting, for evening, or just for feeling elegant.

More often than to the shops, however, Mary traveled to the Murray Street Church, their mother's Presbyterian congregation. Here was at least one place where she could show off the latest confections of her dressmaker. As Mary and her sister slid into the family pew, they could feel the evaluating or envious eyes of their friends upon them; if the Walsh sisters weren't daintily pretty, at least they were immaculately dressed.

The Murray Street Church typified the contradictions of Mary's upbringing and indeed of an 1830s America that frequently combined austere Calvinism with rank materialism. Visiting this congregation in their new quarters decades later, during the Civil War, Mary's son Henry would marvel at the severity of the "old Scotch Presbyterian divine" under whom his mother had sat in her youth. "Darkly must her prospect of heaven have been obscured!" he wrote.

The church was awash with Scots, formerly hard-bitten and austere, who'd made fortunes in America and now, like the Walshes, lived lavishly. Dr. Mason, the formidable "divine," had earlier vigorously managed up-and-coming Columbia College; the congregation, pious but socially ambitious, expected no less distinction from its spiritual leader. Dr. Mason tended to "fulminate" (according to Mary's son) and to preside over services that ran hypnotically long. But Mary was patient. Elizabeth Walsh schooled both of her daughters in that premier female virtue. Both of the Miss Walshes were good listeners, or at least good at appearing to listen—a skill, useful in the marriage market, that would figure strongly in both their futures.

Although she'd voluntarily joined the church at an early age, Mary didn't necessarily hold deep convictions about her mother's brand of Old School Presbyterianism. But church ranked as a relief and a pleasure for her. Pious young ladies depended almost wholly on "public worship, and private tea-drinkings" for their society. In church, Mary had a chance of glimpsing and perhaps even meeting moneyed men.

There in church, when Mary was turning thirteen in 1823—the year before Henry's accident upstate—she'd listened for six months to a temporary minister, the Reverend William James, then twenty-six years old, the second-eldest son of William James of Albany, by a previous marriage. Reverend James had recently returned from a "retreat" in the wilds of Scotland. A dark-haired, intense young man, he married one Marcia Ames in 1824, shortly after his preaching engagement at the Murray Street Church.

If Mary had taken note of this young minister, he must have faded to a dim memory by 1837. And her church didn't often showcase such young preachers; it hadn't provided many potential matches. Still, it was through the family's association with the Presbyterian Church—through her younger brother Hugh, who was studying to be a minister—that an intriguing marital prospect finally arrived in Mary's life.

∽

JUST WHEN MARY'S prospects looked bleakest, Hugh Walsh brought his roommate from Princeton Theological Seminary, Henry James, to Washington Square. The exact month of his introduction is uncertain. If his first appearance took place in February 1837, Henry made his way into the Walshes' drawing room on one leg, propping himself up with two canes; this was how he managed to navigate the world. He traveled with a free black manservant, the charismatic Billy Taylor, who would soon accompany Henry to Europe. (Billy was not employed for long after this trip, but he remained a family legend.) If Henry's first visit fell in October 1837, he came fresh off the Atlantic packet—just excitedly back from London. He walked in on the "good Cork leg" he'd had specially constructed and fitted to him in the English metropolis.

Henry had grown into a mild-looking man of twenty-six, with a somewhat moon-shaped face, large eyes, and thinning hair. Though he was still an active alcoholic and carried other scars from his difficult youth, he looked like a gentleman in company and was carefully tailored enough to appeal to Mary Walsh—to judge from the miniature of him painted in the late 1820s. Yet his gentle looks deceived; his eyes grew intense when he spoke. Since his adolescent injury, Henry had had a fairly disastrous career. He'd failed in his studies at Union College in Schenectady; he'd run away to Boston, where he'd supported himself by proofreading; and he'd hidden out in frontier New York doing little, it is very possible, besides drinking.

In 1835, though, Henry had at least tried to deal with his alcohol addiction, as part of a personal religious renewal; he had felt his own emptiness and tried to fill it with God. His hope to find healing as well as his fascination with theology had sent him to the Princeton Theological Seminary and helped him find his feet there. But even this early in his life, Henry wasn't one to toe an orthodox line, and in Princeton he was getting himself involved in heated religious controversies. And controversy, as the Walsh sisters soon found out, allowed Henry to manifest his deep passion for life. Once he began, it was a journey—mad, enticing, unfamiliar, and perhaps occasionally incomprehensible.

The tumultuous current of Henry's colorful and unorthodox conversation soon wrinkled the calm surface of Washington Square. He told exciting stories—how on his trip to England he'd been so impatient to see the country that he'd disembarked prematurely at Plymouth, the first port of call; how he'd been "so intoxicated with the roads and lanes and hedges and fields and cottages and castles and inns that [he] thought [he] should fairly expire with delight." Henry had visited his relatives in Bailieborough, County Cavan, Ireland, in 1837, and Billy Taylor, his lively and intelligent black servant, had been a hit as well as a novelty. Henry's wealth gave him "the power to dazzle," as his novelist son would later put it. But Henry had this power largely, too, from the sheer charismatic force of his personality.

To the Walsh sisters, Henry also talked doctrine—having had, even in his misspent youth, a "morbid doctrinal conscience," which he'd recently thrown off for a more exotic theology. Henry rendered the otherwise stupefying subject of reformed Presbyterianism intriguing to the young women. Where had Henry gotten this gift—the knack of injecting his arcane ideas with such urgency, as well as with such "colour and savour"? The Walsh sisters had been schooled in ministers; they had served their own successive clergymen coffee year after year in the very parlor where Henry discoursed. But not until Henry's appearance had they heard such vivid and adamant protestations. This visitor was full of charm, energy, and grandiose plans—features, to be sure, of the revivalism of the burned-over district—but also character traits typical of an alcoholic.

The girls' equally infatuated brother Hugh had primed them for Henry's compelling heresies. Yet they hadn't taken their brother too seriously, and Henry himself, in person, brought a note of prophetic and millenarian excitement—not to mention a reconstruction of the Walshes' entire theological universe—by means of his hero, an obscure Presbyterian dissenter named Robert Sandeman.

According to this visionary Scottish maverick, Henry told them, they didn't need to look to the clergy to understand God; they could search their own hearts. Though Mary didn't claim to be "clever" about doctrine, she inhaled this new oxygen deeply. Henry's "talk and temper," as his children would later appreciate, had a highly "original charm." It also had a highly charged spirit behind it, and Mary may also have had a more physical inducement, as Henry radiated a certain roguish, sexual edge left over from his rakish young manhood. Henry's "superior intellect, easy and affable manners, and his fine personality," as Mary's cousin William Walsh described it, introduced a "new element" for Mary; he brought fresh possibilities to their rigidly organized world.

Though Elizabeth Walsh evidently found Henry less beguiling than her children did, she tolerated his visits: she was well known for her warmheartedness and her "generous hospitality," and Henry carried the reassuring credential of his ministerial candidacy at Princeton. As a marriage prospect, he had the added allure of being the son—prodigal though he was—of the now-deceased William James of Albany, the owner of hotels, canals, and a good portion of the Albany waterfront. The Walshes' grandfather had expanded his fortune with linen, Henry's self-made father had inflated his fortune with salt—"solar evaporated salt" produced in Syracuse. With such ventures, there was enough money there, Elizabeth Walsh might have judged, to supply all fourteen of William James's children.

Much had happened in the James family since Henry's tortured adolescence. When William James of Albany died in 1832, his will had reduced his widow to a miserly pension. And in yet another traumatic episode for Henry, the old man had virtually cut off his rebellious son from his million-dollar estate, giving Henry the smallest share of any. Henry and many of his siblings (who had their own objections to their father's tangled stipulations) had challenged the will in court and, after an ordeal that was all too vivid in the disinherited son's mind, had restored some equity to William of Albany's estate. Even after his father's death, Henry's conflicts with this formidable man had continued to feed the intensity of his heretical religious views. He would have a lifelong dislike for arbitrary authority.

In Washington Square, Henry proved himself to be no typical seminarian. As he grew more intimate with the Walshes, he revealed himself as a verbally pungent visionary, an obscurantist, and a theological barnburner. His trenchant criticism of ministers struck the Walsh family as a contradiction, in that Henry was the half brother of the now-famous Reverend William James, whose ministerial debut Mary remembered. There was also the fact that Henry was training to be a minister himself.

Yet, as if the recent schism at Princeton between the Old School Presbyterians and the revivalist New School didn't provide his iconoclastic spirit enough traction, Henry had slashed his own theological path across both camps. Henry didn't just admire Robert Sandeman. He'd coined himself as an ardent disciple who dreamed, like his obscure eighteenth-century Scottish grassroots hero, of a primitive Calvinist church freed from the corrupt clergy and their tyranny. Henry, ever spoiling for an obscure argument, had already won Hugh Walsh over to his point of view. And now he wasted no time in starting on Hugh's two attentive sisters.

⁓

WHEN SHE FIRST met the singular visitor, Mary—for all her polite upbringing—couldn't have helped wondering about his missing leg. What Henry told her or when hasn't been recorded, but the amputated leg perhaps worked on her sympathy, if not her imagination—at the same time that Henry himself chipped away at her conventional religious ideas.

The Walsh sisters, their cousin William reported, felt a "strong attraction" for the newcomer. The word *attraction* in the nineteenth century didn't often mean sexual attraction, but it seems clear that their cousin remembered both young women as deeply impressed by their magnetic visitor. Henry continued to arrive, by carriage or by cab—he was often "reduced to driving," as he "could circulate to any convenience but on even surfaces." He continued to charm the young women, though down deep he didn't have a high opinion of female intelligence. He plowed down anyone, male or female, who argued with him, so the sisters vied with each other through their capacity for listening to his tirades and expressing pleasure and interest.

Though other nineteenth-century gentlemen wooed women by means of flattery or romantic delicacy, Henry was happiest when railing against the clergy or lionizing his obscure theological heroes—not only Robert Sandeman, but later the more erudite John Walker, whose vitriolic attacks on pastoral authority were very much to Henry's taste.

To show their admiration for Henry, both Mary and Kate "converted"—in a calm Walsh way, preserving their own inward equilibrium—to his insubordinate ideas. They took the momentous and daring step of leaving their mother's well-heeled church and joining Henry's radical Separatists.

Faced with such a visitor on a continuing basis, Elizabeth Walsh was beside herself. Her daughters' wild conversion to a fringe sect struck "grief" into the genteel mother, according to a Walsh cousin. But because Hugh took Henry's side—and no doubt because male authority still counted with her, independent as she was—Mary's mother didn't banish Henry from the house. Still, the disturbed Mrs. Walsh watched uneasily as, chaperoned by Hugh, her two daughters shouldered in among Henry's group of "Scotch Baptists" in New York. This congregation of radical and anticlerical Presbyterian Separatists had the merit, at least, of being gathered by the socially respectable British consul in New York, a Scotsman named James Buchanan—not to be confused with the later bachelor president of the United States from Pennsylvania.

Elizabeth Walsh must have fretted about a fringe splinter group that met on rough-and-tumble Canal Street, no matter how distinguished some of its members were. And she would have worried still more when Henry, in keeping with his anticlerical principles, gave up Princeton's seminary altogether. Henry still hung on to his income, but he lacked that other necessary prop of masculine respectability, a settled career.

Even though their mother didn't intervene, this three-way courtship of the Walsh sisters didn't proceed smoothly or quickly. For one thing, the restless Henry, often in emotional turmoil, seldom remained for long in New York. Instead, he was living at home with his mild and proper mother, Catharine Barber James, in Albany, quarreling at Princeton, or haring off on European tours. He saw other women, wielding his strange charisma in many settings, with maternal and safely married women especially. (Later evidence suggests that Henry was a flirt, but no proof of other sexual liaisons survives.)

In October 1838, Henry headed abroad again, plunging across the Atlantic to visit Michael Faraday, the electromagnetic physicist—the inventor of the rubber balloon in 1824—who also counted himself as a Sandemanian. It was April 1839 before he returned to Manhattan, loaded with a whole new battery of stories, theories, and tirades. He was enraged with Frenchmen urinating in public and fascinated by the first noisy but fleet transatlantic steamship, the *Ontario*, on which he'd voyaged. In spite of his flightiness and his absences—or because of them—he brought gusts of the wide world to the sedate precincts of Washington Square.

In New York, Henry also paid visits to his older sister Jannet's in-laws, the Barkers, an elegant and good-looking family of bankers with whom he'd bonded during his family lawsuits in the mid-1830s and who would figure prominently in his own family's future. Henry targeted one Barker for special attention. Anna Hazard Barker, a high-strung and intelligent beauty, had a fine-boned face and dark ringlets that later led Ralph Waldo Emerson to pronounce her the "loveliest of women." In Anna Barker, Mary Walsh had a true rival, known or unknown, in addition to her own charming younger sister, Kate. Both contenders had the advantage of being younger than Mary was (Mary had a year on Henry, in fact) and by the standards of the day prettier.

But Mary, in her stiff, rather architectural costumes, with her quiet but strong listening presence, carried her own appeal to the intense and unsettled Henry. Anna Barker magnified Henry's own nervousness. Like him, she was febrile and excitable; her company could be both a delight and torment. Eventually marrying into a Boston banking clan, the Wards, Anna would afterward represent for Henry—who avidly corresponded with her in the 1850s—a road not taken.

IN LANDING HENRY'S affection, Mary played to her strengths. Her soothing maternal quality put the overwrought Henry at his ease. She could flatter him with her silence if not with her agreement. She could "listen with the whole of her usefulness, which needed no other force, being as it was the whole of her tenderness," as her favorite son would later put it.

But Mary also had—though Henry seldom glimpsed it—a rather blunt and earthy wit. She would later roll her eyes at some of Henry's "Ideas." Her strict upbringing had given her patience—and an iron self-control. She offered Henry, in her son's words, "complete availability, and could do it with a smoothness of surrender." And that exactly fit Henry's bill—though his preference for Mary probably emerged only gradually. If she had any designs on Henry for herself, Kate eventually accepted his choice with a good grace, to judge from her continuing closeness to her sister. The Walsh family remained calm through the courtship, quietly looking after one another. Even Henry's religious heresy didn't shatter the close-knit tranquillity of the household.

The Walshes' strength, mildness, and serenity evidently appealed to Henry James, with his own agonized personal and family history. Steady, modest, supportive, and maternal, Mary was an icon of domesticity with a skeptical streak.

No record of Henry's proposal or the drama surrounding it survives. But Henry no doubt focused all his eloquence on this request. Later he'd tell his children that Mary had completely won his heart, and that he would have been lost without her.

Mary's support would prove vitally necessary to him. But was he just as necessary to Mary? He personified everything she couldn't have as a spinster in Washington Square: a bright, bold, talkative husband, worlds away from the staid merchants of the Murray Street Church. Though her mother wondered about Henry's direction, Mary envisioned him as a bold intellectual upstart who wanted to storm the world and who had chosen her as his personal comrade. She believed in him, "caught the reverberations of the inward mystic choir," as her son put it. Through the convention of marriage, Mary fastened onto Henry as her hope for a wider, richer, and freer life.

But Mary didn't have to wait for challenges to throng in. First, she had to face the challenge of securing her mother's consent. Elizabeth Walsh may not have proved a delicate obstacle. If Henry's children could later imagine their father's "romantic youth" as spent in "Bohemia," Elizabeth Walsh no doubt took a dimmer view of Henry's dissolute young manhood. But he, at least, wasn't hunting Mary's fortune; Elizabeth must have given him that much credit. Nevertheless, in 1839, Elizabeth Walsh amended her will to ensure that her two daughters' inheritance could not be subject to their future husbands' debts.

❧

BEFORE IT WAS done, Henry had to cajole, strategize, and maneuver in order to marry Mary Walsh. His eventual success invigorated him; it gave him a triumph that would become one of the most important of his life—and not only because his previous career had counted as lackluster, at best. He had faced his demons, previously, without such sympathy and tenderness as he had now found.

Henry's eloquence, maniacally persuasive to some, probably moved Elizabeth Walsh less than her daughter's quiet yet unyielding determination. Mary later admitted to her children that holding "a firm rein" amounted to "especially [her] forte." In this first test of her strength, indeed, she proved herself more than just a mindless follower of her future husband—though some biographers have too easily accepted this evaluation. Mary had made up her mind to cast her lot with Henry, and she carried through on her resolve. This decision matches the forceful handwriting and sure expressions of her later surviving letters. Though not particularly known for her cleverness, Mary was resourceful. And in the late 1830s, in this crucial conflict with her mother, Mary's rebellion paved the way for her to become a force in the James family.

Henceforth, Mary would take the reins and steer her own life, usually by manipulating her role as a "devoted" Victorian wife. Though her unconventionality would remain less visible, less spectacular than her husband's—less dramatic than her children's would eventually be—in the quiet precincts of Washington Square Mary declared her own independence and helped lay the foundation for her family's long struggle with norms and conventions.

Further conflicts over the wedding inevitably arose. When considering her daughters' marriages, Elizabeth Walsh may have envisioned august ceremonies inside the portals of the Murray Street Church. But Henry abhorred and emphatically rejected all bonds solemnized by ministers. Along with his guiding light, John Walker, Henry insisted that marriage had nothing to do with the corruption of organized churches. He regarded marriage as "essentially a *civil* contract." To Mary's mother, as to most Americans of the time, a civil wedding counted as a travesty—hardly a marriage at all—a convenience for couples who had "sinned" and couldn't persuade any minister or priest to join them.

Henry's own mother, Catharine Barber James, evidently shared this dark opinion of civil unions. And in her objection to Henry's and Mary's plans, she did Elizabeth Walsh one better. She refused to countenance any such breach of propriety and did not come down from Albany to attend her own son's wedding.

That Elizabeth Walsh did attend, that she went so far as to host this unorthodox union in her own house in Washington Square—throwing open the folding doors between the two big drawing rooms for the occasion—shows how thoroughly Mary had worked her will on her silenced, compliant mother.

As a concession to her mother's pride, Mary and Henry arranged for the mayor of New York, Isaac Leggett Varian, an eminent Democrat, to perform the ceremony; the event took place on July 28, 1840, by which time Washington Square, its pungent ailanthus trees heavy in the summer heat, had regained the sedate composure of the years before the bank panic.

If Kate felt a twinge of envy at all that was happening for her sister, she hid it well. Her attendance at the wedding suggested that she and Mary wouldn't be separated by Henry's decision, that they would remain close. Mary showed her own form of hopefulness: for the ceremony, she wore dazzlingly fine white Indian muslin and a "wondrous gold headband" appropriate to her social status and her high expectations.

In a strange coincidence, Henry and Mary married only a few months after Queen Victoria wed the younger son of the Duke of Saxe-Coburg-Gotha in February 1840. Victoria's finery may have surpassed Mary's. Yet the two women had more in common, sentimentally and dynastically, than Mary might have imagined. Victorian marriage would seem to have begun its august and sometimes tyrannical reign as a dominant social institution in the Anglo-American world. But already the Jameses' civil marriage had undercut the middle-class decencies of their century. And the young couple's unusual relationship, with Mary a firm and commanding partner, also signaled—as did Victoria's own union with the deferential and ancillary Prince Albert—unconventional reversals of the accepted roles of husbands and wives. In the future, the Jameses' lives would sometimes follow and sometimes run counter to the family norms that the queen of England had begun to lay down.

❧

AFTER HER WEDDING, Mary got her first real taste of the wider world at the establishment where she and Henry roomed as newlyweds, the legendary Astor House Hotel. Her novelist son would refer to it as the "ancient Astor House," but in the summer of 1840, this grand Broadway hotel counted as crisply new. The stone of its Greek revival pediment had been freshly cut, the Doric pillars, the volutes, and the central seashell over the monumental entrance newly erected.

John Jacob Astor, the crotchety fur magnate and the richest man in America, had built the hotel for $400,000. He grandly opened it in May 1836 as the showpiece of his financial empire—an empire not dissimilar to that of another immigrant, William James of Albany. Sheathed in marble, the Astor House claimed to be the grandest hotel not only in America but in the world. Bigger than any hotel in London or Paris, it boasted three hundred rooms and (a novelty in the 1830s) toilets and bathrooms on each of its five floors.

While in residence there, Mary James could glimpse in the rich vestibule the grandees whose arrivals and departures the New York newspapers also announced. When Mary stood on the steps, she not only commanded the luxurious shops in the ground floor of the hotel, with their bright striped awnings, but also the changing panorama of Broadway, where a person could view "better than anywhere else," as one traveler remarked, "the concourse of passengers and vehicles" that increasingly enlivened New York.

From this vantage point, the new life Mary had chosen looked glamorous and colossal. Ever grandiose, impulsive, and visionary, her husband had ambitions to match this brave new hotel—if not the inflated and imperial aspirations of the new Victorian era itself. Henry had decided to make a name for himself as a writer—though he wasn't sure, yet, what kind he wanted to be. Mary, schooling herself to be a good Victorian wife, pledged to support him. Though he had a little money, Henry was an unknown, an eccentric one-legged man in an era of masculine grit and action, just one of a robber baron's retinue of children. Henry felt he was something more than that, and he was hellbent to distinguish himself. Later on, the fame Henry craved would carry a high price for both him and his family. But in this early honeymoon phase of the Jameses' life, Mary no doubt hoped that her new husband's fiery wit and dogged will could lift him above his disappointments and old hurts and earn his family the kind of future he had promised her.

· 3 ·

SHADOW PASSIONS

S ometimes, during the first months of their marriage in the autumn of 1840, in the carriage they hired as newlyweds, Henry
and Mary rattled past the just-finished New York Society Library at the corner of Broadway and Leonard Street in lower Manhattan. The structure resembled a Greek temple in brownstone; and
although Henry couldn't have known it, a New England oracle would
soon appear behind its columned facade, one that would soon bestow on
him the essential sense of purpose and direction that his life had lacked
so far. Henry had perpetually longed for something that would motivate
him with an intellectual passion as great as his love for his wife.

The library itself gave little enough hint of such a potential; it appeared calm and stodgy, with little of the grandeur of Parnassus. The
institution's origins were actually humble: in 1754, six book-loving citizens banded together to create the first subscription library in New
York. Only a few decades later, during the Revolution, the British soldiers occupying Manhattan had looted the books or else slashed them
up for musket wadding. But now, in 1840, the library's brand-new home
towered in three grand stories over the wagon ruts of Broadway, with
Ionic columns of the city's signature brown sandstone. As a Greek Revival centerpiece—striking a Greco-Roman claim to authority and dignity in the rough, expansionist America of the 1840s—this ambitious
new institution betrayed an architectural kinship to the palatial Astor

House Hotel. But unlike the hotel, the library hinted at New York's Athenian, intellectual aspirations. It issued a challenge not only to scholarly Europe but also to Boston, New York's old bookish rival.

As yet Henry didn't subscribe to this particular institution, which was run collectively by New York's ivory-caned elite. In spite of its attractions (the penniless young Herman Melville would also haunt this building), the place also served as a gentlemen's club for an intermarried collection of Manhattan notables. Henry, despite his father's wealth, hardly belonged to this circle. As an outsider usually intent on maximizing his own difference, uninterested in their intrigues, he could only appreciate, from the street, the high-ceilinged reading room, which he and Mary saw "brilliantly lighted" at night. At any rate, Henry didn't often work in libraries. He wasn't a man to sit still for long or conform to regulations. He was at the mercy of the impatience that had already driven him from one belief system to another and which made much conventional endeavor impossible. As Mary would learn, he was a man who had to keep moving. He and his wife were out vigorously hunting for a house; they couldn't go on living at the sumptuous Astor House forever, running up bills.

Henry pursued a home with his unusual determination and vigor; it was the first quest of his married life. He and Mary scoured the fashionable areas that, at the time, included the neighborhood around St. John's Park, with its freshly planted shade trees, terraced houses, and Georgian-style Episcopal chapel. The Jameses would also have known Bond Street, where the Astors set a high moneyed tone, and Gramercy Park, with its newly minted porticoes and its railed-off garden in the center of the square. For up-and-coming Manhattanites, the right neighborhood was de rigueur.

None of these places or their social circles, however, quite suited Henry's notions or the couple's combined financial resources—rents from shops in Syracuse and some railroad investments—which yielded a comfortable but narrow middle-class income.

❧

IN 1840–41, THE first winter of their marriage, Henry and Mary sensibly rented a house at 5 Washington Place, just around the corner from Mary's old home in Washington Square. (They would soon arrange to buy the property at a discount from Henry's ne'er-do-well younger brother, John Barber James.) As Henry wrote to a friend, he enjoyed being "in my own house, at my own tea-table, with my own wife, and all of my things around me."

Henry genuinely loved his new domestic life—it was a soothing, unfamiliar comfort after the turmoil of his anxious youth. "I love the fireside rather than the forum," he later wrote, but his very domestic habits also reinforced his long-running problems with drink: he later observed how much easier it was for a "passive" man, devoted to a reflective inner life, to fall victim to drunkenness. Men of action, by contrast, had fewer temptations, and partly because they were "manly" in a less ambiguous way than Henry felt himself to be. And Henry wasn't alone in these sentiments; in a century increasingly influenced by temperance movements, a habit of drink was thought to strip men of their masculine virtues.

Henry's new tea-table existence may have been the least of the burdens of his jobless, stay-at-home life. Men of the time frequently drank rum, whiskey, or gin mixed with bitters even before breakfast; took a liquor break at midmorning, for "elevens"; then drank hard spirits at midday dinner and on into the afternoon and evening, with a fireside nightcap before turning in. Temperance movements would gradually persuade Americans to put aside some of these alcoholic rituals, but the norms of the 1840s favored hard drinking and no doubt camouflaged Henry's ongoing addiction. But if certain friends were to notice his problem later in the 1840s, Mary must have done so, too, and probably early in their marriage.

Partly because Henry spent many hours shut away in his study, the Jameses' improvised rental was probably the first place Mary acted with real independence. Although hierarchy dictated that Mary follow her husband's instructions on pretty much everything, he rarely laid down the law. Their situation was hardly unconventional, in any obvious way, but it could have exposed Henry, especially as an alcoholic, to accusations of unmanliness. In the temperance tracts of the time—the formulaic stories about drunkards and the saintly women who compensated for their vices—wives sometimes had to take on tasks usually reserved for men when their husbands drank. Mary rarely acknowledged such an imbalance; she was too loyal to refer to her husband's difficulty with spirits. Yet Henry's occasional incapacity, due to depression or alcohol, must have led to Mary's taking charge—though Henry mostly remained active, driven, and, to use one of his own favorite words, manly.

But, as Henry's friends recognized, he was "an unbusinesslike character," who knew little of the "value of money." His intimates trembled for him whenever he had to interact with "Wall Street people." Mary, fortunately, had a good head for figures: even when she couldn't make money for the family through its investments, she could save it by means of the thrifty household management lauded by the popular tracts and women's periodicals of the time. Mary sometimes read books that Henry recommended and caught onto his enthusiasms, but she instinctively belonged to what Americans had begun to call the Cult of True Womanhood—the nineteenth-century adulation for women's domesticity that was growing along with the number of prosperous middle-class households. Mary saw her home as her true sphere, and she wanted to make their new house a refuge for the man who had chosen her for his wife.

In Washington Place, Mary found herself settled reassuringly—or perhaps depressingly—close to her mother and her sister. But Kate's proximity proved especially useful when, in the spring of 1841, Mary figured out that she was pregnant. Despite this, she strove to preserve her independence, even though she was already establishing herself in the Victorian role that the British poet Coventry Patmore would famously describe as "the Angel in the House." But she was an assertive and businesslike angel, although she undoubtedly grew more subdued by early 1842 when she prepared for her first childbed.

A minor mystery surrounds this first family birth. Family tradition later located the event at the Astor House Hotel, where the Jameses may indeed have relocated due to an emergency. Grand hotels sometimes kept physicians on call or on the premises; a doctor might prove useful during the later stages of a woman's confinement. It's equally possible, though, that the baby was born at home in Washington Place—and that the legendary Astor House just fit better into subsequent family mythology. Both Henry and Mary, in fact, with the lavish invention of yarn tellers or novelists, subsequently altered or suppressed at least a few aspects of their early life together. In any case, there were ultimately no problems in Mary's first delivery.

Henry and Mary named their new son William, honoring Henry's late father. (Mary also had a William in her family tree, her great-grandfather.) But this christening wasn't a simple matter for Henry. Writing later in his life about his childhood, Henry referred to "a certain lack of oxygen which is indeed incidental to the family atmosphere"; given such memories, his motive for naming his son must have been more dynastic than sentimental. Henry continued to live with the scars he had received from his father, and his new parental role set off a blizzard of conflicting feelings.

With his persistent mental demons, Henry's serene, tea-tabled household—that sine qua non of nineteenth-century bourgeois life—both pleased and galled him. (He moved his family to a new redbrick townhouse, down the street at 21 Washington Place, early in 1842.) Despite his intellectual ambitions, he may have felt emasculated by the fact that he had no profession to take him out of the house—no career at all, except as a private scholar, a theological dilettante who had yet to prove himself. His hours at home, as much as he loved Mary, as much as he gloried in his new son, often sapped his spirits and made him feel useless. Fatherhood, that unfamiliar and surprisingly demanding burden, intensified Henry's desire to forge for himself a reputation as a writer and thinker. More impatient than ever for something that would help him justify his existence, he grew ripe for a fresh infatuation.

❧

ON THE EVENING of March 3, 1842, the Greek temple of the New York Society Library blazed with costly light. A tasteful placard advertised, as the *Evening Post* had also done a few days before, a lecture series grandly titled THE TIMES. Not every speaker tackled so unboundaried a subject, but not every lecturer was Ralph Waldo Emerson.

Even when not delivered by speakers like the author of *Nature* (1836) and "Self-Reliance" (1841), lectures spelled high entertainment in 1842. Lecture halls, or lyceums, as they were called, had sprouted up in cupolaed halls or borrowed churches in almost every self-respecting town in Yankee America. They attracted large audiences accustomed to fiery

stump speeches, improbable yarns, and vigorous sermons. Bent on education and self-improvement, Americans filled the chairs.

Lyceum programs featured mesmerists or foreign opera singers and
other popular acts who could profitably cram a hall. Early in the 1840s,
two colorful performers—who styled themselves as Signor Blitz and
Dr. Valentine—actually shared the lyceum circuit with the more staid
Emerson, performing "humorous scenes" (fast-paced dialogues that
portended vaudeville). In case their high energy show fell flat, these two
enterprising entertainers also contrived a stirring sideshow: a Barnum-
style "mermaid" pickled in a huge jar and—a priceless addition to any
stage production—an "exhibition of learned canary birds."

Emerson, though a more distinguished lecturer, had his own history
of spectacle and knew how to deliver a memorable performance. In
1838 he had shocked the latest crop of Harvard Divinity School graduates with his unorthodox humanistic view of Christianity, in which the
historical Jesus was only a teacher and every man had access to his own
spiritual light. Then, in 1841, he'd published his *Essays: First Series*—a
volume of ruminations, mild in appearance, which nevertheless inspired
his readers to espouse abolitionism, draw up blueprints of utopias, or
hole up in ramshackle cabins in the woods. To be sure, Emerson
brought a fare of a higher intellectual caliber than most who bowed to
the crowds from the lyceum stage. His seriousness and import would
appeal to a man like Henry James. Emerson wielded his own secret
power of mesmerism, to which Henry would prove highly susceptible,
but which matched the passionate, entrepreneurial optimism of the expansionist 1840s, the era of the Oregon Trail and the invention of the
telegraph. Emersonian individualism, rooted in the glories of nature but
passionately unconventional, would suit many a young man and woman
who, having rejected orthodox religion as Henry had done, was in need
of a compelling philosophy.

Tickets at the New York Society Library were available for one night
or for the whole series of six lectures. Unlike some of the extortionate
showmen of his time, Emerson preferred to charge "low prices"; the philosopher exacted his fee in other, more subtle ways. But either in spite of
Emerson's reputation or because of it, few New Yorkers descended the
back stairs of the library and claimed seats in the lecture room, with its

"commodious" seating rising in a circular arrangement meant to invoke a Greek amphitheater.

Ralph Waldo Emerson, undaunted by the size of the audience, entered, "punctual as a clock." As one observer recalled, Emerson often made his appearance without causing much of a stir, wearing his "time-worn black body-coat and trousers." Stooping a little, he plodded up the aisle, his top hat in one hand and the packet containing his speech clutched in the other. After climbing up to the platform, Emerson laid his manuscript on the reading desk, rummaging for somewhere to prop his hat. If the audience politely clapped, he would "scarcely acknowledge the applause, having as yet done nothing to merit it." Then he would lift his head and look, "not at us"—as one audience member remembered—"but at another audience above our heads, visible to him only."

On that March evening, the thirty-eight-year-old Emerson no doubt resembled a remarkable 1842 daguerreotype of him, which revealed a bony man of middle height, with a scrupulous cravat, a Roman nose, and lucid blue eyes. His voice carried a "grave music," one Concord friend noted.

> His gestures were few and restrained. I never saw him lift his arm as high as the shoulder-level: his favorite emphasis was to bring up his clenched right hand at right angles, and then to lower it powerfully, as his voice sounded forth with the resonance of high waves breaking in calm weather on the shore. On that sea we voyaged with him, he endowing us with his vision, so that, for an hour, we were all Emersons.

Emerson—enthralling and impressive—would eventually inspire hyperbole, with some adulatory observers making reference to "the Eagle of Olympian Jove." But on this evening relatively early in his lecture career, the sage began a shade "cold and embarrassed," the *Post*'s reviewer found. Yet he soon "warm[ed] into genuine eloquence," speaking feelingly, in a voice "deep and clear": "The Times are the masquerade of the Eternities," Emerson intoned; "trivial to the dull, tokens of noble and majestic agents to the wise; the receptacle in which the Past leaves its history; the quarry out of which the genius of to-day is building up the Future."

Emerson inspired both with a palpable conviction of his own genius—and, even more contagiously, with the hope that each of his listeners might also qualify as a "genius of to-day"—that each of them might go out and do something extraordinary. During his New York debut, in fact, Emerson cast this spell over a scruffy twenty-two-year-old journalist, the editor of the *New York Aurora*, who found Emerson's lectures "one of the richest and most beautiful compositions, both for its matter and style, we have heard anywhere, at any time." This commentator, slouching among the well-tailored New York Society Library crowd, was the budding poet Walt Whitman.

Whitman wouldn't count as Emerson's only Manhattan conquest. The evening left Henry James in a state of admiration bordering on delirium. To Henry, Emerson, a fellow ministerial dropout, seemed infused with the purpose and confidence that he had so long tried to discover in himself. Henry listened, rapt, to each illuminating word. Emerson must have seemed to be speaking straight to him, when he talked about the kind of depressive suffering common to cultivated men who were restlessly striving after novelty. "This *Ennui*, for which we Saxons had no name, this word of France, has got a terrific significance. It shortens life, and bereaves the day of its light. Old age begins in the nursery, and before the young American is put into jacket and trowsers, he says, 'I want something which I never saw before'; and 'I wish I was not I.'" Emerson wondered aloud about the cause of this dangerous cast of mind. "Is there less oxygen in the atmosphere? What has checked in this age the animal spirits which gave to our forefathers their bounding pulse?"

As soon as the lecture was over, Henry hurried with his canes back to Washington Place, seized a sheet of writing paper, and poured out his stirred-up feelings. As he'd listened to the address, Henry confessed, he had "glowed with many a true word" that had fallen from Emerson's lips. Finally, he felt, here was a man who lived "truth and goodness" and might comprehend how Henry himself, in his own small way, had always wanted to understand the "truth that surround[ed] and embrace[d]" him. Henry's letter alternated, excitedly, between the abstract language of his theological studies and the warmer tone of a person looking to be rescued by someone from what he called, tellingly, the "barrenness of our most unloving world."

Hungrily, Henry seized on Emerson's high moral ideas as a cure for the "barrenness" that had haunted his life almost without remission. The idea of moving beyond these troublesome emotions was challenging, even with Emerson's thoughts as guide and comfort. Emerson beckoned to Henry, as well as to other male disciples, with an almost physical promise of love, support, and purpose. Emerson's poetic language, infused with longing and aspiration, elicited similarly passionate responses from some of his listeners. Sudden assumptions of intimacy, like Henry's, were not uncommon.

In his first note, Henry confided to Emerson that he was "severed from friends and kindred." He felt alienation beneath his eccentric social facade—a feeling he had attempted to keep absolutely private. As his main standby, Mary offered him one vital kind of love, but he needed another kind of reassurance; he seems to have suspected that Emerson, as guide and friend, could help him discover the kind of higher purpose he craved.

Henry's note was strikingly charged with yearning and conveyed a level of deep emotion that Emerson could summon from many of his devotees. Emerson's wife, Lidian, wittily called missives like Henry's, which her husband inspired and received with startling frequency, "love letters."

❦

HENRY PUSHED AND cajoled to see Emerson at the Globe Hotel on the day following the lecture at the library. When he actually succeeded in gaining the philosopher's complete attention, he was even more inspired by his electric presence. Emerson was at least well enough pleased with his new admirer to entertain Henry for an extended talk. Both of these men evidently sensed that they needed each other, and they came together with intensity, Emerson playing gracious prima donna to Henry's infatuated admirer.

Oddly enough, for all his Bostonian refinement and aloofness, Emerson didn't object to Henry's "love letter" or his feverish intrusions. The philosopher—who made his home in the tranquil village of Concord, Massachusetts—craved society, but in Manhattan, the crowds always made him feel a little lost. True, he admired this "city of magnificence and steam" and forecast "an imperial prosperity" for the years to come. Yet he was intimidated by Manhattan's cosmopolitanism ("Me my cabin fits better") and by the hard-knuckled practical men whom he met there. Money-hungry and pragmatic, they seemed to foreshadow a country of singularly material concerns. But also he had his own reasons, in the spring of 1842, for needing to counteract an "unloving world."

For one thing, Emerson had grown tired of defending his less-than-popular transcendentalism—his signature philosophy that invited Americans to connect to higher spiritual meanings not through traditional religion but through the worship of nature. Many down-to-earth, practical types, even in Boston, had ridiculed such romantic and eccentric notions. In *Nature* (1836), Emerson had memorably illustrated this inspirational process through the metaphor of the "transparent eyeball": "I become a transparent eyeball—I am nothing; I see all; the currents of the Universal Being circulate through me; I am part or particle of God," Emerson had written.

But this unusual image had grown into a derided tag; in 1836, it had been caricatured by the poet Christopher Cranch, in a sketch of a long-legged eyeball wearing a hat and tails, striding out for an inspirational walk in the hills. Although Emerson had a circle of enthusiastic collaborators in Boston, where he'd helped establish the Transcendental Club in 1836, he considered himself "wholly guiltless" of founding this much-satirized movement and increasingly shied away from being identified as its prophet, insisting that there was no such thing as a "pure" transcendentalist—himself or anybody else. Emerson had signed up for his New York lectures not because he wanted to spread doctrine but because he had urgent debts to pay.

Also, Emerson, like Henry, pined for friendship; he conceived of it as something that occurred most satisfyingly between men and that offered a curious Platonic superiority to marriage. The year before he met Henry, Emerson had devoted one of his most passionate essays, "Friendship" (1841), to this lofty subject. Emerson's panegyric to male bonding reflected a whole body of "respectable" work on this topic including an essay by one of his important models, the sixteenth-century French essayist Michel de Montaigne. In fact, Emerson's idealism on the subject matched that of Shakespeare's sonnets addressed to the so-called fair youth. Emerson's evident enthusiasm was rooted in an infatuation he'd had at Harvard with his fellow student Martin Gay. This undergraduate with "cold blue eyes," as Emerson noted, formed just one part of Emerson's hard-to-pigeonhole erotic life. There were also Emerson's two wives: his present wife, Lidian; and his first wife, Ellen Louisa Tucker, who had died tragically young, from tuberculosis, in 1831. Such complexities definitely gave Emerson's high-minded friendship, for both men and women, some of its frisson.

During Emerson's stay in Manhattan, Henry pursued him eagerly, always ready for further discussion. Emerson judged the eager New Yorker to be "a very manlike thorough seeing person" and, as he told his friend Margaret Fuller, "an independent right minded man." Still, Henry's talk, at parties, could sometimes be rude or offensive—another characteristic quality traceable to his love of liquor and his strong opinions. Emerson may have blanched when his new friend delivered a strong diatribe against Rebecca Black, a self-educated spiritual thinker who made her living by sewing slopwork for tailors, whom Emerson also met in New York. Even though Henry later apologized for it, the bile was hard to sponge away.

But, all in all, Henry made a unique impression on the guest lecturer, the rest of whose series he ardently attended. Henry joined an inner circle of "ten or twelve" men in New York who, Emerson reported to his wife, "expressed a strong sympathy in opinion"—agreed with Emerson's views. And ultimately Emerson rated Henry highly—as a select friend, a "true comfort,—wise, gentle, polished, with heroic manners, and a serenity like the sun."

☙

VISITING THE JAMESES in Washington Place that March, Emerson got a peep at two-month-old William James. Later, members of the James family would mythologize the encounter in their characteristic style, as the philosophical titan of one generation visiting the cradle of his successor. But if Emerson was moved by his nursery visit, he was probably thinking of his own lost son. A little more than a month before, Emerson's five-year-old son, Waldo, had died suddenly and without warning of scarlet fever—another reason why the New England philosopher might have welcomed Henry's company.

In his letters home, Emerson didn't mention Mary James, whom so many important men would later overlook and underrate. The philosopher didn't usually view women as intellectually significant any more than Henry tended to do, although in Boston he often spent time with his insightful friend Elizabeth Hoar as well as his learned colleague Margaret Fuller, the editor of the *Dial*. On his visit to the James household, Emerson did, however, notice a copy of this financially strapped transcendentalist magazine on Henry's table. Previously, Henry had avoided subscribing to the *Dial*, but now he had an incentive.

The elegant brick facade of 21 Washington Place spread twenty feet wide and rose three stories. It seemed an appropriate setting for the revivification of Henry's intellectual aspirations. The house lay just east of the newly built "castellated and gabled" hall of New York University. This accidental proximity to academe "hallowed" it, in Henry's view, and his house also had ample room for the servants and plumbing fed by the brand-new Croton waterworks, rivaling the modern conveniences at the Astor House. The grandeur and spirit of Washington Place, the most expensive and fashionable property the Jameses would ever own, was further enhanced by the optimism that Emerson had inspired in his aficionado. The question that remained, however, was whether Henry could sustain his new enthusiasm in the outside world.

In late January 1843, ten months after his introduction to Emerson, Henry stood up to his own malevolent self-doubts, daringly climbing up to the podium of the Stuyvesant Institute to deliver a lecture. Housed in a new building on Broadway since 1837, the institute—lavishly supported by the wealthy Peter G. Stuyvesant and Samuel Ward—was a meeting place for the wealthy Bond Street coterie with whom Henry didn't always harmonize. Henry's appearance was a social as well as an intellectual coup even if it was partly engineered by Ward, an influential banker and old friend. The institute had hosted many distinguished political, religious, and scientific speakers, and it prided itself on its place on the cutting edge: in 1839, D. W. Seager had given the first public demonstration of photography in America, an exhibition of the French daguerreotype process, in its chandeliered hall.

Henry's debut as a lecturer was accompanied with high expectations that might have seemed unreasonable without his mentor's influence. Emerson's example had reinforced Henry's own love of grand, ambitious topics along with his intermittent conviction of an almost-messianic mission—a form of grandiosity perhaps spurred by Henry's drinking. "When I take a few glasses of wine," Henry later wrote, "I am ready to measure my strategy with Bonaparte, and . . . to encounter Anthony in rivalry for Cleopatra."

Henry found himself in an enviable venue, commanding another lecture room modeled on a Greek amphitheater, with a sheaf of papers he'd been working on at home through the autumn of 1842. Out of modesty or self-doubt, Henry offered his four lectures for free. (With his greater reputation, Emerson sometimes walked away with as much as forty dollars per lecture.) To advertise his appearance, Henry recruited his old Princeton Theological Seminary friend Parke Goodwin at the *New York Evening Post*, who billed him as "an accomplished scholar, a profound thinker, and one who has given much study to the subject of which he treats."

Unfortunately for those who wished him success, Henry took for his subject "Literal Christianity." He'd follow this soporific opening with three more lectures on the subject of the "Inward Reason of Christianity." Henry was attacking literal or orthodox Christianity, but his iconoclasm was cerebral and difficult for his listeners to follow. He hadn't adopted any of Emerson's theatrical devices—his energizing themes, dramatic cadence, or stirring poetry. In spite of his adulation, Henry seemed to have missed the essence of what made his hero compelling. Instead, Henry, who seemed oblivious to the presence of his listeners, concentrated on the arid theological subjects that had fascinated him since his discovery of the Presbyterian dissenters—the same obscure theological figures he'd once spoken of to Mary. His new audience found these meanderings less than edifying and grew glassy-eyed as Henry spun out his dizzying abstractions.

Only a week into his endeavor, in early February, it grew clear to Henry that this first step in his "outgoing to the world" had failed spectacularly. "I came to night from my lecture," he wrote a friend, "a little disposed to think from the smart reduction of my audience that I had about as well not prepared my lectures, especially that I get no tidings of having interested one of the sort (the religious) for whom they were wholly designed."

Sadly for Henry's sense of self-respect, Emerson had returned to New York, buoyed on a wave of enthusiasm from recent appearances in Philadelphia, to deliver a series of stimulating new lectures on "New England Genius." He garnered many fresh admirers, including the youthful New Yorker William Tappan, "the most tranquil and wise of all the Round Table" (a joking name for Emerson's fans) and the "young Washington phoenix," Giles Waldo—who'd later import Emerson's idealism to Hawaii. For Emerson, young admirers were eminently replaceable, and Henry may well have wondered if he'd been supplanted by more recent converts. But Emerson still saw Henry "a good deal"—even if he hadn't actually attended Henry's lectures. Henry, of course, could not avoid seeing Emerson's continued triumphs as a painful contrast to his own embarrassment.

❧

AS SPRING UNFOLDED, Henry and Mary celebrated the birth of their second son. Henry wrote to Emerson that he had "another fine little boy," and Emerson replied with characteristic grace: "Tell Mrs. James that I heartily greet her on the new friend . . . that has come to her hearth."

The new baby's arrival, however, did little to lift Henry's despondency after his debacle at Stuyvesant. His previous enthusiasm had now been replaced by a dark depression—both fueled, no doubt, by drinking. The Jameses' new son, born April 15, 1843, stood in line to be named after Henry, but following the fiasco of his lectures, the honor must have rung hollow to his father, whose fantasies of fame had abruptly evaporated. What did the world need with a second Henry James, when the first had so far made so small a mark? Henry was approaching the age of thirty-two, and his career was moribund.

Henry regretted how much his empty unhappiness distanced him from Mary and the special feelings of fatherhood. He told Emerson in a letter how hard it was for him to stick to his paternal duties: "But I must stop, ere

I be stopped. My wife is grateful for your remembrance, and thinks nothing would so help me as a little intercourse with Concord. Another fine little boy now lying in her lap preaches to me that I must be settled at home."

As a cure for his malaise, Henry had considered a visit to Emerson in Massachusetts—not an easy journey at a time when the rail link between New York and Boston still remained incomplete. He may even have contemplated settling his family in Concord. Emerson maddeningly half invited, half evaded such a development. A relocation wasn't out of the question; Emerson's personal magnetism frequently attracted his disciples to Concord, and in 1842 the transcendentalist Sophia Peabody would persuade her husband, the novelist Nathaniel Hawthorne, to move to Emerson's neighborhood. Hawthorne had just emerged from literary obscurity with his *Twice-Told Tales* (1837), and the young couple's residence in the barn-gabled clapboard Old Manse would allow him to write *Mosses from an Old Manse* (1846), even if he himself didn't care very much for Emerson.

If Emerson had also attracted Henry, and Henry had succumbed, the history of the James family and indeed of American letters might have been drastically altered. The first memories of the two James infants would have featured dry stone walls, the bare trees of the Concord Revolutionary battlefield, and Emerson holding court in this literary Camelot with his fine-boned wife and "queen," Lidian, beside him.

Yet Henry, agitated and far from hopeful, entertained increasing reservations about Emerson. Even before his lecturing disappointment, he'd yearned for an "Invisible Emerson"—his personal and private friend, not the famous and bewitching lecturer for whom the public clamored. He needed the encouragement of a man who shared his passion and didn't withhold his attention. Henry complained to his mentor that he constantly disheartened him: "Whenever I am with you I get no help from you," Henry grumbled. Emerson struck Henry as a "man without a handle." With Emerson and Concord no longer the panacea he needed, with his old demons lying as close to him as his liquor cabinet, Henry began to consider his next move.

❧

DURING THE EMOTIONAL turbulence of his years at Princeton Theological Seminary, Henry had twice chosen escape. Twice he had

resorted to European travel—those visits to London and Paris that had
interrupted his courtship of Mary—as a cure for his disagreements with
his father and as a focal point for his philosophical infatuations; he'd
gone to meet theologians and scientists in England but also to seek out
his relatives in Ireland. Now, even though he had a brand-new family
and a brand-new mansion, he began to think again of steamships, the
outlines of unknown hills, and the drawing rooms of eminent European
thinkers. When self-doubts attacked him, Henry counterattacked, characteristically, with dreams of a place where all would be different.

In 1840s America, European travel had an immediate and incon-
trovertible air of importance; no one had to defend or explain it. The
Jameses' neighbors and acquaintances were continually in the frenzy of
getting ready to sail, always disembarking from Atlantic packets bearing
marble busts, clever anecdotes, and leatherbound books acquired in
London or Rome. To a disaffected man with a little money, Europe
beckoned like an irresistible mirage. And soon Henry had made his
decision.

Emerson lost his habitual serenity when, in August 1843, he heard
about Henry's travel plans. He complained that "the best people flow
off continually in the direction of Europe." Only "rovers & bad husbands," he wrote a friend, ever hankered to leave their own house—in
this case America—and go roaming. (The array of Emerson's friends
who were leaving resembled "bad husbands" to him, however they actually treated their own families.) "Every week I hear of some conspicuous American who is embarking for France or Germany," Emerson
complained, "and every such departure is a virtual postponement of the
traveller's own work & endeavour." He concluded that he "must write
to Henry James and inquire why he should go to Europe when America
has such claims & invitations."

A heated quarrel erupted between the two men. Henry answered
Emerson's arguments (Emerson said) by claiming that going to Europe
would be "good for his health, as he ha[d] some uneasiness in his chest."
Travel was often considered curative—a change of "air" was thought
beneficial for the lung diseases of the era, and fashionable European
spas offered mineral waters for other ailments—and the hypochondriacal James family would bank on this particular belief.

In Henry's case, however, the need for Europe was more emotional than medical, as Emerson seemed to sense. But even if he didn't approve of his friend's cure for restlessness, Emerson prepared letters of introduction for his protégé to literary Europeans. He sent Henry his "love," however, only by proxy; his disapproval of his friend's travel plans lingered—and the two men were to hover on troubled terms until 1847.

Mary no doubt fought her own misgivings about Henry's plan; it seemed drastic to sell their comfortable house, as Henry put it, to "winter in some mild English climate, Devonshire perhaps." If Europe attracted her, she—ever more down to earth than her husband—also knew that transporting two infants across the Atlantic would not be easy and that, even with a nursemaid, many of the burdens would fall on her. She also worried about the family's limited income and how far it might stretch in a foreign country. By October 1843, William had not yet reached his second birthday, and Henry Junior—the family called him "Harry" to distinguish him from his father—was merely a six-month-old baby. In itself, an Atlantic voyage in the 1840s could last two weeks or more. Even with the vaunted comforts of the new steamships, the journey could prove an ordeal even for unencumbered adults—as it had for Charles Dickens, who had found his own stormy crossing "appalling and horrible to the last degree."

This prospect of travel with children no doubt spurred Mary to enlist Kate's help. Maiden sisters were assumed to be available to help with babies, and during her nearly three years of pregnancy and new motherhood, Mary had probably drafted her sister before, though little or no record remains of the unmarried woman's early self-sacrifice; even at this early stage, women's work in the James family was discounted. Henry in his self-absorption, in his obsession with his health and his career, almost never mentioned Mary or considered her predilections.

❧

ON OCTOBER 19, 1843, the almost certainly ill-advised adventure began with Mary, Henry, the two babies, Kate, and a nursemaid named Fanny setting out on the Atlantic Ocean. The voyage counted as Mary's first to Europe—her first trip, almost, outside of New York. In spite of the rough crossing he had earlier endured, Dickens had extolled the vibrant, chaotic docks of lower Manhattan, where the Jameses embarked: "Where the bowsprits of ships stretch across the footway, and almost thrust themselves into the windows, lie the noble American vessels which have made their Packet Service the finest in the world."

When the *Great Western* had departed New York, on the return leg of its maiden voyage in May 1838, it had steamed away with great fanfare, "escorted down the bay by seventeen steamboats." Excited crowds had gaped at it, packing the Battery wharves and scrambling up on woodpiles for clearer views. After all, the steamer—the brainchild of British engineer Isambard Kingdom Brunel—had smashed the Atlantic speed record: it had just dashed over from Bristol in only fourteen days, in a dramatic head-to-head race with a vessel called the *Sirius*, beating the rival ship, which had burned everything on board in an attempt to win. The *Great Western*, an iron-bound wooden vessel, paddled with a massive, brand-new steam engine that, because it used distilled water, didn't have to shut down for desalting, as other steamships did, every two or three days—though this gargantuan engine took up half of its hull and kept the passengers awake with its throbbing.

The *Great Western* also sported a grand saloon seventy-five feet long and twenty-five feet wide. Like a floating art gallery, the saloon was adorned with fifty huge panels oil-painted in the ornate and playful style of the eighteenth-century French painter Jean-Antoine Watteau. According to the newspaper accounts, the ship vied with "club-houses of London in luxury and magnificence." But what London club stocked armchairs that pitched as if on rockers? The Jameses, on their first family trip abroad, were definitely in for some turbulence.

The voyage started out with silken seas, but it wasn't long before the late-autumn roughness of the North Atlantic took hold. In spite of the *Great Western*'s splendors, the Jameses probably found it as uncomfortable as Dickens had judged his *Britannia* steam packet. The famous English novelist had recoiled from his tiny unheated cabin furnished only with "a horsehair slab" to sit on. He bedded down with only "a very flat quilt, covering a very thin mattress, spread like a surgical plaster on a most inaccessible shelf." Even in a magnificent dining room, Dickens noticed, tortuous racks gripped wineglasses and cruet stands—hinting dismally at chronically churning seas. On the stormy Atlantic, one's exquisite many-course dinner might easily hurtle off the table.

For its part, the *Great Western* enthusiastically advertised a newly invented system of bells that allowed every cabin to importune the ship's stewards. But even an attentive shipboard staff couldn't have hushed Mary's high-strung infants (William in particular; little Henry was calmer and gave less trouble), especially if they'd been introduced to the family "demon" of seasickness and had started to throw up. Mary herself no doubt suffered plenty of misery, moments when memories of her comfortable Washington Square home must have taunted her like happy dreams. But, hardy and capable, Scottish to the bone, Mary rose to the challenge of her first transatlantic ordeal with children.

∽

SHORTLY AFTER THE *Great Western* put in at Liverpool on November 1, the James party caught a train to London, that imperial and coal-reeking metropolis of the Victorian world. For Mary, this autumnal arrival in the winter dark, endlessly ramifying brick-and-stucco city of London provided her with her first foreign experience. Quaint differences in dressmaking, child rearing, and the behavior of servants no doubt struck her—to judge from future stays during which she would become a great critic of foreign methods of housekeeping. For Henry, the arrival had less novelty and more personal urgency. After his spat with Emerson, he yearned impatiently for a substitute—a father, a friend, a mentor. But life had its own pace in England, and two weeks went by before Henry could arrange his next step. Then, armed with a letter of introduction, he targeted Emerson's close friend, the eccentric British philosopher Thomas Carlyle.

Carlyle had climbed to a pinnacle of fame after publishing his lively and unconventional autobiography, *Sartor Resartus*, in 1832, and his *French Revolution*, a scandalous and stirring history of this world-shattering event, in 1837. More recently, he'd embarked on a stormy lecture series of his own about "Heroes and Hero Worship"—a stimulating subject for a man like Henry who craved a hero, even if Henry arrived on Carlyle's doorstep critical of the essayist's extravagant and Romantic style.

Carlyle lived in Chelsea, on the Thames west of Westminster, in a half-dilapidated Queen Anne house at 24 Cheyne Row. This narrow and tall row house of the previous century, with its streaky russet brick, must have looked a little seedy to the Jameses, as they came to call on the first available Sunday. In rapidly progressing New York, most eighteenth-century houses had either been torn down or turned into warehouses. And in 1843, the out-of-the-way riverside district of Chelsea was not yet fashionable; the astute Carlyles lived here because they had made a real-estate steal in 1834. But the residence of the "sage of Chelsea" and his entertaining wife, Jane Welsh Carlyle, had already helped lift and gentrify this cholera-prone neighborhood.

Servants guided Henry, Mary, and Kate through the pine-paneled entryway and into the Carlyles' snug parlor. Amateur artworks, graceful pen sketches and portraits of Carlyle and his wife, covered the walls. Carlyle's long clay pipe and his favorite flask lurked somewhere about. The Jameses had entered the abode, clearly, of artistic and intellectual people. Still, both Henry and Mary met these British celebrities with some trepidation. Carlyle, at forty-eight a handsome Scotsman with a well-trimmed graying beard, greeted his visitors heartily, although he reputedly abhorred Americans. But in this case, he attempted to be generous to the man who came ecstatically recommended by his valued friend Emerson.

Carlyle's wife hung back a little more, thorough in her courtesies but keenly watching. A sleek and popular dark-haired beauty in her youth, Jane Welsh Carlyle combined good taste with a satirical streak very much ready to vent itself on Americans. She slept upstairs in a crimson bed—and to some it may have seemed as if the bedspread had been bloodied by the victims of her verbal thrusts. Around the same time that the Jameses introduced themselves at Cheyne Row, Jane Carlyle complained to a relative that "really these Yankees form a considerable item in the ennuis of our mortal life. I counted lately *fourteen* of them in one fortnight!" She had wanted to "take the poker" to all of them except one, she had said. "If Mr Carlyle's '*increasing reputation*' bore no other fruits but *congratulatory* Yankees and the like I should vote for its proceeding to *diminish* with all possible dispatch!" She lampooned what she perceived as the "drawling and *Sir*-ring" of her transatlantic visitors.

With such a blustery temperament in their host, with such a masked hostility in their hostess, no wonder the Jameses trembled a little on their first and on subsequent visits to the Carlyles. Even under more welcoming circumstances, Henry was a nervous and hesitant man, or so Carlyle described him in a prompt letter to his friend Emerson.

> James is a very good fellow, better and better as we see him more— Something shy and skittish in the man; but a brave heart intrinsically, with sound earnest sense, with plenty of insight and even humour. He confirms an observation of mine . . . that a stammering man is never a worthless one. Physiology can tell you why. It is an excess of delicacy, excess of sensibility to the presence of his fellow creature, that makes him stammer.

Carlyle identified Henry's shyness as a form of sincerity. The sage of Chelsea viewed Henry's fragility sympathetically, at least in his report to Emerson. But Jane Carlyle, with cruel wit, latched onto a different aspect of Henry's physical makeup.

> "Not a *bad* man" (as C. would say) "nor altogether a fool,"—but he has only one leg—that is to say only one real available leg—the other, tho the fellow of it to appearance consisting entirely of cork—Now a man needs to take certain precautions . . . to use some sort of *stick* instead of trusting to Providence as this Mr James does. So that every time he moves in the room . . . one awaits with horror to see him rush down amongst the tea-cups, or walk out thro the window glass, or pitch himself foremost into the grate! from which . . . dangers he is only preserved by a continual miracle!

Of the "wife and wifes-sister," Jane Carlyle sketched an equally scathing picture: "Of his two women what could anybody say?—unless that they giggled incessantly, and wore *black* stockings with light-colour[e]d dresses." The Walsh sisters' otherwise uncharacteristic laughter probably came from their social discomfort—though perhaps they merely appreciated Carlyle's jokes.

As for Mary's fashion sense, which Jane Carlyle so fiercely lampooned, it probably resembled what her son would later describe in his novel *Washington Square:* like Catherine Sloper, Mary James tended to "make up for her diffidence of speech by a fine frankness of costume," as she knew she wasn't a "witty person." Mary wasn't talkative or literary, like Jane Carlyle; and she may have made the faux pas of wearing light-colored dresses at the wrong time of year or of combining light and dark colors. But it is also possible that Jane Carlyle derided her for clothes that were quite acceptable in New York. As a matter of principle, New York followed French rather than British fashions—and increasingly tailored its own versions of all these borrowed European styles.

For his part, Henry welcomed Carlyle's hospitality, "the many hours of unalloyed entertainment his ungrudging fireside afforded me." Henry was impressed enough with Carlyle's parlor—where he was to meet such notable figures as the poet Alfred Tennyson—that he kept a detailed notebook of the conversations that unfolded there.

But Henry hardly aspired to be a second James Boswell—recording the table talk of a great man—and he was less disposed than the eighteenth-century biographer to adore uncritically. Henry would ultimately grow as disparaging and pungent in his criticisms as Jane Carlyle had been, and his irritability probably owed partly to the uncomfortable meetings he had that winter in Chelsea—he, Mary, and Kate—with the babies safely left in the care of a nursemaid at home.

Carlyle, Henry soon found, was no Emerson. Though Henry and this Scotsman shared Presbyterian ancestry, Henry judged that the "old Covenanting stock" in Carlyle made him too pessimistic about human potential. Carlyle hated the kinds of "liberal reform" that Henry himself would increasingly espouse—nineteenth-century liberalism, that is, with its middle-class emphasis on individual and societal progress toward higher morality. The skeptical and bad-tempered Carlyle, Henry felt, "gnashed his teeth upon you if you should have claimed any scientific knowledge or philosophic insight into the social problem,—the problem of man's coming destiny on the earth." The insecure Henry felt this snub strongly.

Even so, Henry allowed that Carlyle was a "great critic." Henry de-scribed his friend as a "man of genius"; but the compliment was barbed, because in Henry's private vocabulary, a "genius" was a potentially im-moral or untrustworthy figure—a prejudice his talented sons would eventually inherit. But even more damningly, Henry didn't categorize

Carlyle as a "man of ideas"—the ultimate achievement, as far as Henry was concerned—and what he aspired to be himself. Henry issued these judgments decades later, after Carlyle's death, in one of his most successful public lectures. But he evidently knew early on—and devastatingly for his mood in the winter of 1843–44—that Carlyle, like Emerson, was "almost sure finally to disappoint one's admiration." For Henry, Carlyle also presented a dead end.

TO ENJOY THE British capital, the James family settled for the winter at the Piccadilly end of Mayfair—a more aristocratic area than the Carlyles'. Here Henry tried to work. But with his "bibliomanical propensity" and passion for the arcane, he easily strayed from his writing. He ventured into "musty shops in queer places," the splendid labyrinthine antiquarian bookshops in London. Aware of Henry's already-crammed steamer trunks, Mary registered "astonishment at [his] accumulations."

Henry, gravely disappointed by his own state of mind, found himself as malcontent and unsettled in England as he'd been in New York, subject to the same self-reproach and dark moods. The idea of further travel seemed therapeutic to him. In the spring of 1844, the Jameses uprooted themselves from their London digs and journeyed to Paris. Everyone got seasick on the Channel. Two-year-old William "screamed incessantly to have 'the hair taken out of his mouth'"—a sample of Mary's early trials as a traveling mother and of William's precocious hypersensitivities.

The infant Harry had barely passed his first birthday. But he afterward claimed to remember seeing the Place Vendôme with its monumental column: "as a baby in long clothes, seated opposite to [my parents] and in the lap of another person, I [was] impressed by the view, framed in the clear window of the vehicle as we passed, of a great stately square surrounded with high-roofed houses and having in its center a tall and glorious column." He also recalled being "conveyed along the Rue St.-Honoré, while [he] waggled [his] small feet," as he claimed distinctly to remember doing.

Harry's parents later humored him by marveling at this prodigy of his memory. Harry probably confabulated it. Yet perhaps, even more than most babies, he was all eyes.

⚜

BY MAY 1844, after a tour of English beauty spots in the green flush of spring, Henry and Mary settled down just west of London, at Windsor. Ever aristocratic in their tastes, the Jameses rented Frogmore Cottage from the Duchess of Kent. Surrounded by tempting "long walks and drives," their "cottage" in fact amounted to a good-sized stone house with towering chimneys. It lay in pastoral serenity, sandwiched between two great oak-studded royal parks, so that the Jameses could stroll in a garden bursting with flowers and blossoming fruit-trees. At last they commanded enough bedrooms and drawing rooms to accommodate their entire extended entourage. With Windsor Castle overtopping the trees, Henry imagined the young Queen Victoria "looking down from her castle windows upon our modest residence." The slim young queen had risen to the throne seven years before. She'd married Prince Albert in 1840, the same year the Jameses had married; and, like Mary, she now had a crop of small children.

Henry continued to hunt for his own sense of importance in these idyllic precincts, within hailing distance of royalty. His professional goal was to create an improved lecture series and a magnum opus out of his latest theological broodings. But he continued to suffer from racking self-doubt—the painful shyness that Carlyle had observed a few months before. Henry's insecurities were rendered all the more agonizing by contrast to the famous men, like Carlyle, at whose tables he'd drunk and with whom he often violently disagreed.

Also, Henry hadn't yet worked out his troubled relation to a family that deprived him of "oxygen," as he later put it. To Henry, the family would eventually figure as a "Divine seed" that carried the future progress of humanity in it. But the actual day-to-day muddle and expatriate isolation of his own family life often appalled him. In his European travels, out of touch with his intellectual friends, Henry felt more and more mired in his domestic life and in the public and private drinking that no doubt accompanied it. At Windsor, hemmed in by royal preserves, he felt more isolated than ever. He had recently taken a fresh interest in his little sons, but he also continued to feel the crushing associations of this family for whom he felt responsible. Would he ever learn to manage as other men did? He simply did not know and found himself reviewing all the old and hurtful conflicts with his father and his own forced isolation as an adolescent amputee in the 1820s.

⁂

TOWARD THE END of May, having eaten an ample English dinner ordered and supervised by Mary, Henry sat contemplating the "embers in the grate, thinking of nothing." That he had just consumed his big meal—a throwaway detail for past biographers—may also indicate that Henry had also drunk, and possibly heavily. In the nineteenth century, wines accompanied every course, and strong spirits (particularly for men) came ritually both before and after. But whether or not he was inebriated, Henry had evidently worked himself into a state. Suddenly, out of nowhere, "in a lightning flash" as he later remembered it, he suffered a bolt of fear and panic that shook him to his foundations. Henry faced an "insane" terror that he couldn't trace to any cause. It presented itself to him visually, viscerally, as "some damned shape squatting invisible to [him] within the precincts of the room."

Before this hallucinating horror had lasted even ten seconds, Henry found himself volcanically reduced from what he called "firm, vigorous, joyful manhood" to a state of helpless babyhood. He stifled his first impulse to call to Mary, to run pell-mell to the foot of the stairs and cry out for her to help. Instead, trying desperately to regain his "manhood," he exerted all of his will to govern these "frenzied impulses," refusing to budge from his chair until he'd recovered his self-control. For an agonizing hour, Henry held his ground. But an "ever-growing tempest of doubt, anxiety, and despair" lashed him. At last he shouted for his wife.

In fact, Henry had been living on a knife-edge at Frogmore Cottage. He'd embarked on what he later described as an "insane career" of guilt and self-recrimination. Whenever he sulked around his wife or snapped at his children or yelled at the cook—all features of psychological stress but also indicators of drinking—he ferociously blamed himself. Under the strains of family life, his self-hatred had been worsening toward what he described as an "infernal" pitch. The language of the time, decades before the emergence of scientific psychology, offered few enough terms to diagnose troubles of the mind and of the "nerves." Instead, Henry used theological words to describe his volatile state. But it must soon have grown clear to Mary that her husband's agitation had hit a dangerous pitch, something worse than his former sufferings. This time, Henry's disquiet wouldn't just go away.

For what we now call anxiety, the medical science of the time sometimes prescribed powerful doses of narcotics like laudanum. If he had followed this course, Henry might well have started on his way to becoming, like the English essayist Thomas de Quincey a generation earlier, an "opium eater," as he clearly had addictive tendencies. The "eminent physicians" whom Henry and Mary consulted in London, however, concluded that Henry had "overworked [his] brain." Evidently, they didn't consider alcoholism as one of Henry's problems; drinking was still largely considered a moral as opposed to a medical issue. In any case, alcoholism was only one of Henry's problems, and not the primary cause of his spectacular breakdown.

Henry's doctors prescribed "a life in the open air" and "cheerful company"; they had apparently spotted Henry's obsessiveness and his tendency toward what we would now call depression. They also recommended hydropathy, a form of water cure from the German spas that was newly in vogue in England. Some of the so-called water cures of the time involved drinking mineral waters or bathing in hot springs. But, as Henry found when Mary installed him at a local Georgian mansion called Sudbrooke Park in Petersham, this new hydropathy called for a different and more radical regimen. Henry could look forward to mummification in hot wet sheets followed by immersion in cold plunge baths.

Still feisty and independent in spite of his malaise, Henry hated this "interference with [his] personal liberty." He resented having to live "at this dismal water-cure and listening to its endless 'strife of tongues' about diet, and regimen, and disease." During the moments when his misery lightened, though, he appreciated the semirural setting of Richmond. He enjoyed its royal park, "the rich light and shade of English landscape, the gorgeous cloud-pictures."

For herself, the hardy Mary preferred long drives through the great city's bosky western suburbs in a pony chaise. The fresh air, though a variable benefit for Henry's health, suited her perfectly. In later years one of her favorite memories of London was that of a jaunt "one early spring morning through Hampstead." In nostalgic retrospect, the couple could mutually reminisce to their children about a "happy time spent in and about London with their two babies."

During the course of this cure, Henry and Mary visited a Concord-group connection in the area, one Sophia Chichester. Luckily, this widowed baronet's daughter proved more useful to Henry's recovery than plunge baths. Henry confided his problems to the well-read Mrs. Chichester, whom he found "a lady of rare qualities of heart and mind, and singular personal loveliness as well." (Sophia also "charmed" Mary.)

The Jameses' new friend diagnosed Henry's maladies according to the beliefs of Emanuel Swedenborg, the eighteenth-century Swedish theologian, with whom she was passingly familiar and whom Henry had previously encountered through his physician friend J. J. Garth Wilkinson. Though Swedenborg had started his career as a zoologist, mapping out anatomical studies of animals, he'd suffered his own crisis in 1744 and had begun hearing voices and dreaming of angels and demons; his visions had steered him away from science and into religious mysticism. "It is very much as I had ventured to suspect," Sophia Chichester told Henry, "you are undergoing what Swedenborg calls a *vastation*."

A "vastation," according to Swedenborg, constituted a vital stage in a spiritual journey. It marked "one of the stages of a regenerative process." Swedenborg argued that a person had to be emptied out before he or she could find meaning, the widow told Henry. This hopeful scientific-theological concept immediately made sense to Henry; this fresh perspective was just what he needed. Escaping his asylum, he hurried to his old favorite bookshops in London and "possessed himself of certain volumes of the writings of the eminent mystic."

Henry's physicians had forbidden him to read, so Henry started out by coyly glancing into the pages, then quickly shutting up his books. But his desire to read Swedenborg soon overcame him and grew "frantic." So, "instead of standing any longer shivering on the brink," he decided to "boldly plunge into the stream." Henry had discovered an even more bracing version, for him, of the water cure. And, unlike his previous torture with towels and dunkings, this new regimen seemed actually to do him good. Henry impatiently seized on Swedenborg's framework; he was especially eager to embrace a philosophy that could satisfyingly account for his own particular suffering.

At a crucial point, Swedenborg gave Henry the hope and courage to battle his inward demons, arriving in his life just in time to fill the place of idol and spiritual guide that he had longed to find in Emerson and Carlyle. Even though Henry came to consider himself what his son Harry would call an "independent and disturbingly irregular" follower of Swedenborg, he had at least found a friend he could live with, and without any of the turbulence his other mentors had brought to his mind. He could even share his new pursuit with the loyal Mary. But, at the same time, Swedenborg, dead and in book form, would also lack the warmth and the relevance of a live flesh-and-blood friend like Emerson.

And Henry's "cure" certainly wasn't instantaneous. Even after he took up Swedenborg, his "ghastly condition of mind" dogged him. But he would soon experience gradually lengthening intervals of relief. After four months of recovery, in October 1844, Mary braced herself for the next step: to take her husband back to New York.

THE NURSERY OF GENIUSES

A fter her adventures abroad, Catharine Walsh found herself back in Washington Square in the fall of 1844, once again inhaling the peppery smell of the ailanthus trees, devoting herself to a pair of toddlers who, in spite of her increasing responsibility for their welfare, didn't actually belong to her. Their belonging or not belonging to her would grow into one of the primary conflicts of her life.

To anyone who might have glanced at this decorous young lady in that park, Kate, now thirty-two years old, might have appeared an unlikely contributor to America's cultural future. It wasn't just that she was "only" a woman—that second-class, auxiliary being of the nineteenth-century United States—without a vote, without representation in the fields of medicine, law, or religion. Women were beginning to be conscious of such injustices. Margaret Fuller, the editor of the *Dial*, was organizing women's discussion groups in Boston, to articulate female views on literature, education, and what was now being called the "Woman Question"; she would argue for sexual equality in her brilliant book, *Woman in the Nineteenth Century* (1845). Also in Boston, Elizabeth Cady Stanton was immersing herself in the abolitionist movement; by 1848, in upstate New York, her anger at injustice against women would spur her, with Lucretia Mott and others, to organize the first women's rights convention and issue the famous Seneca Falls Declaration of Sentiments. Stanton believed in what she called "voluntary motherhood"—women having a say in reproduction and child care—though the strains of her overwhelming duties as a mother of six helped inspire her outrage.

Kate's "motherhood" was only partly voluntary; she had much of the same stress, with little of the praise heaped on Victorian mothers. She was unmarried; in the eyes of her world she amounted to a second-class woman, a "spinster" who had failed to snag a man or to reproduce. Strollers in Washington Square might well have ignored Kate, who did not seem a person of any special importance. Yet her role in the lives of the James family, though downplayed or misunderstood by some biographers, would in fact radiate fascinating and far-flung repercussions.

When the *Great Western* dropped the James family on the pavements of Manhattan, it was almost November. The sharp weather was already setting in, the leaves shriveling from the saplings in the square. In such autumnal gloom, the family's prospects must have felt shrunken, especially with Henry still weakened and convalescent. Their immediate need for housing was solved when Mary's elder brother, Alexander, an increasingly successful businessman, moved his expanding family out of the marble-fronted Washington Square townhouse where Mary and Kate had once resided to make room for the returning exiles. Not surprisingly, Alexander also consigned to his sisters the care of their ailing mother, Elizabeth. And the sixty-three-year-old wasn't the sisters' only charge; they also had Mary's two small children, both still under two, and her convalescent husband. It is unlikely that Henry himself, still shaky and hollow-eyed, could yet cope with the practical matters surrounding the resettlement of his family in New York.

This fresh centering of the Jameses' lives on Washington Square would have profound consequences for the children's sense of themselves as New Yorkers, as young Henry would remember almost four decades later.

> It was here, as you might have been informed on good authority, that you had come into the world . . . it was here that your grandmother lived in venerable solitude, and dispensed a hospitality which commended itself alike to the infant palate; it was here that you took your first walks abroad, following the nursery-maid with unequal step, and sniffing up the strange odor of the ailanthus-trees which at that time formed the chief umbrage of the Square.

Harry may well have embarked on his first steps with the nursemaid, Fanny or her Irish replacement. But with servants hard to find and keep in New York and his mother so often preoccupied with his grandmother's and his father's illnesses, he and William may well have been led by the hand or wheeled through New York by their intrepid aunt Kate.

Though she was still "without prospects," Kate was different from the young woman who had once lived with her sister in the staid precincts of the square. She had changed and grown more sophisticated. She bore the stamp of Europe and wore frocks she had picked up in London and Paris. Like her sister, Mary, she no doubt loved showing off her clothes—and by extension her new European experience. She was, after all, a woman who had met Carlyle and rattled in a phaeton through the Place Vendôme.

No photographs of Kate survive from this time, because of either her modesty or her resistance to daguerreotypes. An undated photo from Kate's middle age, however, reveals a stocky, solemn woman with a regal mien, a squarish jaw, and a downturned mouth. She seems to embody the celebrated figure of a dour Victorian aunt—the species of aunt gleefully stereotyped in both England and America and humorously lampooned in the 1890s by Oscar Wilde in the formidable, daunting, and Wagnerian Lady Bracknell.

In 1844, however, Kate probably wasn't sour or hard-faced. Even in her later photograph, the many pleats of Kate's dark dress and the starch-white curls on either side of her face hint at qualities that caused people to rank her as "buoyant" or "delightfully amiable & genial." Unlike Mary, Kate had really enjoyed herself in London and Paris. On her return to New York, she probably came off as livelier than her sister—more audacious, opinionated, and imaginative—even if she'd crossed the Atlantic as an au pair for her infant nephews, an adjunct to her older sister, an unpaid servant almost. Kate came back bitten by the splendors of the world she'd seen and readier than her sister to reminisce about them.

Did Kate return from England in triumph or in disappointment? Had she entertained hopes of meeting some unattached baronet? Historical evidence remains mute on this point. And Kate herself is part of the reason; she would later be the most fanatical letter burner in the family, a guardian of propriety, silence, and privacy.

Beginning in the Walsh's family mansion that winter, Kate no doubt plied her young nephews with stories—unwittingly preparing them for their cosmopolitan and transatlantic futures. The "treasure" of her memories would in fact imprint the fascination of Europe on at least one of her charges, the impressionable Harry. As he later remembered it, his aunt had "imbibed . . . in Europe the seeds of a long nostalgia"— a hankering for the Old World that she'd nurture most of her life. Kate's enthusiasm would eventually transform her into a more daring and able-bodied traveler than either Mary or her brother-in-law Henry; she was a Victorian voyager-aunt who would write letters and bring back exotic gifts from distant capitals.

Though she could hardly have guessed it herself, Kate foreshadowed whole generations of women who would travel excitedly to Europe in the late nineteenth century, among them her nephew's later protégées Constance Fenimore Woolson and Edith Wharton. She could hardly be described as a feminist, but Kate provided her nephew the future novelist with an early model for both his avant-garde women friends and for his poignantly aspiring novelistic heroines. Kate's relishing of Europe in 1843–44 dropped an early hint of the vigorous independence for which she instinctively longed. But women in the James family often found their work rendered unimportant and invisible; their labor, expression, and intelligence annexed on behalf of the men in the family. And so far, Kate's sacrifices for her sister's sons had given her no position at all, and none she could reasonably look forward to.

❧

DURING THE WINTER of 1844–45 in Washington Square, the thirty-four-year-old Mary had her own concerns. Henry's breakdown and convalescence had punched a hole in the customary Victorian procession of children. But now Mary was once again pregnant. A few months later, during the hot weather of July 1845, she gave birth to a third son. With their English residence still fresh in their minds, they named him after Henry's enthusiastic Swedenborgian friend and correspondent in London, Dr. J. J. Garth Wilkinson.

"Wilky" or "Wilkie," as the family afterward called Garth Wilkinson James, meant one more infant whose care Kate shared with the nursemaid. As a Victorian matriarch and moral guardian, Mary kept a distance between herself and her squalling infants. It couldn't hurt, she felt, to let a baby "bawl a good bit." A mother "ought to husband all her strength and vigor, to nourish her baby, and not exhaust herself by taking sole care of it." It is not clear whether Mary's philosophy extended to other caretakers or whether Kate resented her burdens as a live-in aunt. A long-suffering Victorian, Kate didn't permit herself to carp.

The weight of the James nursery, though, was soon lifted from Kate, at least temporarily. Henry and Mary decided, after struggling for a year in Manhattan, to move upstate to Henry's hometown of Albany—with Kate staying behind in New York to look after her failing mother, whose decline now struck Mary as "extreme."

Excitedly, the family traveled north by river. Their journey up the Hudson, in the days before the completion of the railroad in 1851, triggered an adventure on a "primitive steamboat"—a very poor, dirty, and backwoods cousin of the transatlantic liners. But it was on this very Hudson River route that, some forty years before, Robert Fulton had piloted the very first operational steamboat in 1807. Steam power as an essential American technology had improved, but the voyage, always an ordeal, both terrified and stimulated the small James children. As Harry later remembered it, they all suffered a "night of huge strange paddling and pattering and shrieking and creaking," ending in "the thrill of docking in dim early dawns" at Albany's bustling waterfront.

Once they arrived in the mansion district, however, the family's lives grew richer and calmer. The young Jameses settled in with their "softly-sighing widowed grandmother," Henry's sixty-two-year-old mother, Catharine Barber James. As Harry later remembered, his paternal grandmother lived in a "much-shaded savoury house," where the garden overflowed with tasty and aromatic peaches. Her family circle teemed with the "many-sized" paternal aunts, uncles, and cousins, waited on by "strange legendary domestics, inveterately but archaically Irish." Here the young Jameses got a taste of their father's childhood—without the disadvantages he had suffered.

For the two years of their Albany sojourn, Henry, Mary, and their three small sons lived in a family-owned property, a sturdy three-story brick house across the road from the grandmother's estate. Harry recalled this place as quintessentially Dutch and "pinkish red picked out with white." It was a cheerful dwelling, like something out of a Washington Irving sketch, contrasted with the "grayish-brown and very grave" mansion across the road, which intimidated sensitive children with its "oh so high white stone steps," possibly made of marble, and its dignified fanlight over the door. Here other aunts, not the familiar Kate, hovered over the James boys.

In spite of the famous line of elm trees on North Pearl Street, Albany may not have particularly pleased Mary, after her grander New York upbringing and after her taste of Europe. But she was better off than her sister; Kate was "confined to [her] mother's sickroom" for six months, or so Mary reported to her friend Emma Wilkinson. To help, Mary made occasional steamboat trips down from Albany, leaving her three little boys in Henry's care.

While she was away in the city, Henry proved a "faithful nurse," in Mary's exacting opinion. He showed surprising domestic competence during an era of fatherly indifference—when, as the popular *New York Ledger* columnist Fanny Fern joked in 1855, clueless husbands were as likely to hoist a baby by its heels as right-side up.

At least once, Kate got to dash up to Albany to see what her sister blithely described as her "little pets." But with Mary mostly at a distance upstate, Kate no doubt sought solace and companionship in her other "sister," her cousin and close friend Helen Wyckoff Perkins, who lived nearby in Manhattan. Harry later commemorated Helen as a "stout brave presence" who would continue to weather her own high waves in life. (These included a housebound cipher of a husband, a scoundrely wastrel of a brother, and a more pitiable brother—also, rather confusingly, named Henry—who suffered from an impaired mind and vocabulary. For Henry, Helen bravely took primary responsibility.)

Helen, though married, strongly resembled Kate as a principled and unselfish caregiver. The two women had been struck from the same mold—so much so that decades later Kate even took a turn at taking care of Cousin Henry. "Our admirable aunt, not less devoted and less disinterested than his former protectress, had yet much more imagination,"

Harry remembered. Kate had a spark; but what difference had it made so far in her life?

❧

BY THE SUMMER of 1847, Henry, Mary, and the children had shifted back to Manhattan once more—and they needed all the auntish help they could get. The family returned from Albany with *four* boys now, all under the age of six. The newest James had materialized during the summer of 1846. Henry thought his new son was better looking than any of his brothers had been at the same age, though in a rare burst of irony, Mary joked that this was "Henry's philoprogenitiveness" (his love of accumulating offspring) rather than "any increase of beauty in the family." In a piece of dynastic optimism, the couple had named the new baby after Mary's grandfather, the dry-goods tycoon Alexander Robertson.

Robertson, or "Bob," as the new infant was called, hurried in on the heels of his brother Wilkie, born the year before. Mary noted that Wilkie grew more assertive once Bob was born and he was "shoved off," as she put it to Emma Wilkinson, into the care of others. Wilkie began to walk when his brother was just two weeks old, to get attention (Mary thought), to take "into his own hand the redress of his grievances, which he seems to think are manifold." In a typical move among the James children to win parental attention, Wilkie became, in competition with his baby brother, "the ruling spirit of the nursery."

Bob's birth also highlighted other key aspects of the family's child-bearing. How could Mary have conceived a new baby in the first place if she were already nursing Wilkie? Such an unexpected conception may have come to Mary as a surprise, as lactation doesn't always prevent pregnancy, despite the fact that women of the time often trusted to nursing as a form of natural birth control.

Mary's dignity prevented her from discussing the bodily details of her child rearing, even with Emma Wilkinson. But middle-class Victorian women often employed hired lactation. During her mother's illness in 1846, Mary had occasionally left her children, including her baby Wilkie, for days at a time—a suggestion that the servant Mary called a "nurse" was that characteristic feature of Victorian class conflict, a wet

nurse. Such surrogates were often labeled as depraved or dangerous: after all, they often put the needs of their own children second to those of
their employers', out of economic hardship. Put more poignantly, as
one historian suggests, "wet nursing often involved trading the life of a
poor baby for that of a rich one." Nineteenth-century servants upped
the birthrate and survival rate of their middle-class masters, at their own
expense.

During the fall of 1847, the Jameses found temporary digs on Fifth
Avenue between Eighth and Ninth streets. Mary put up with crumbling
plaster in her tea room and divided the care of her children with Kate,
who was boarding with their mother in nearby Waverly Place. During
adversity, Victorian women knew how to team up. Soon Mary and Kate
also had to manage the round-the-clock care of Elizabeth Walsh, whose
condition had worsened and who saddened the holidays for them by
dying three days before Christmas in 1847.

Through these dark and transitional times, Kate proved herself devoted and indispensable. But after her mother's death she would be
drawn even deeper into a household that would finally grow more like a
settled family and less like a troupe of unfortunate houseguests.

∽✸✸

IN THE SPRING of 1848, a rosy and mostly recovered Henry brought
five-year-old Harry to see the new and as yet vacant house he'd bought
for the family on West Fourteenth Street. It would count as the first domestic real estate the family had actually owned since their days in
Washington Place, back at the beginning of the decade.

This new house—smaller, narrower, and farther uptown—lay just
east of Sixth Avenue. It lodged in a row of bay-windowed houses, some
of them (in the style increasingly archetypical of New York) built in
brownstone. The neighborhood lay, Harry would remember, in "a region where the extension of the city began to assume a theoretic air"—
where the area had been only patchily built up. Here the fresh, ongoing
construction left many vacant lots, some filled with "the poplars, the
pigs, the poultry, as well as the ramshackle 'Irish houses'" that would inspire shame in the James children about their own Irish heritage.

Rough-and-tumble, more workaday, West Fourteenth Street, with its "rural picturesqueness," marked a step down for the Jameses. As Harry remembered, it didn't aspire to a "world of quieter harmonies," like the marble porticoes owned by the merchant dynasties in and around Washington Square. But the new house offered compensations.

Inside, the young Harry saw workmen sporting hats folded out of newspapers. Perched on scaffolding, they cast plaster molds and pasted up long strips of yellowish wallpaper that was printed with "dragons and sphinxes and scrolls and other fine flourishes." This pattern suggested the traditional arrangements of a bona fide middle-class Victorian family; it fit a dwelling that would become an icon, for Harry at least, of a rooted home. The Fourteenth Street house was destined to figure as an "anchorage of the spirit" for the James children. Still, when the family moved in, Kate found herself squashed into a third-floor room, like a servant sequestered in the attic. What's more, the nursery often overflowed into her own bedroom, bringing waves of importunate James offspring into her own bed.

In August 1848, the house became more crowded. Only a few months after the Jameses' arrival on Fourteenth Street, Mary (who had been pregnant on yet another moving day) gave birth to a fifth child, and this time it was a girl.

Alice, the Jameses' first and only daughter, initially occupied her mother and the nursemaid. Two-year-old Bob was now correspondingly "shoved off" to Aunt Kate, and he later resented this transfer. As the snubbed youngest son, he came early on to abhor what he called his aunt's "mandatory ways." He long carried a grudge over a transfer he considered a kind of crime. But Alice too would suffer from the intense competition that would increasingly characterize the Jameses' nursery.

In a telling pecking order, Kate took responsibility for the younger children, especially Bob and Alice—and was consequently especially resented by them. Ironically, Kate's presence in the family only helped heighten all the children's clamor for parental care. Her role promoted a hierarchy whereby William and Harry, as the oldest sons, attracted most of their parents' attention. Wilkie and Bob, as a younger set of brothers, won less of Mary and Henry's interest and approval than their more dynastically privileged elder brothers.

Alice, the baby of the family and, moreover, a girl, ranked last. As such, she was almost entirely consigned to the care of Aunt Kate. "How feeble and diluted, of necessity, must the parental instinct be, trickling down," she would later observe, with respect to a Victorian family with twenty-five children. But she herself, with four older brothers, experienced a similar thinning of parental attention.

Along with the other James children, Alice felt the paradox of being heavily mothered and at the same time unmothered, distanced from their own mother's care. All of the children essentially had two mothers—not an entirely unprecedented situation in a time before the nuclear family had reduced family to a self-contained, Dick-and-Jane unit in a subdivision. The Jameses pioneered a modern family distinctiveness at the same time that, like most nineteenth-century families, their lives involved swarms of more distant relatives and the live-in presence of at least one.

For her part, Kate had chosen a career that had opened up the world to her but could also be monotonous and stultifying. Mary called Kate "Aunt Kate." But Kate had to address Mary as "Mother," as the children did—an indignity, in itself. In later letters the James children, especially William, called Kate "Aunt" or (in a more satirical vein) "the Aunt"— with wit, scorn, and fondness. In their minds selfless aunthood indeed summed up Kate's assigned and inescapable role.

Kate transported the children downtown on the horsecars, buslike wagons drawn on rails, to the "torture chamber" of the family dentist on Wall Street. This old man, with a purplish face, a polite manner, and a glossy wig reminiscent of a Mozart stage character, had previously figured as Kate's and Mary's "haunting fear," according to Harry, in their own childhoods.

Kate may not have chosen to have this "ruthless care" assigned to her. But she carried it through with the starch and discipline of a Victorian aunt. During the children's illnesses, however, Kate often summoned more patience, more indulgence than their own mother. Her health wasn't as ironclad as Mary's, and she often tended the illness-prone James children with something more like sympathy. In contrast, Mary hardly ever suffered a sick day. But Kate increasingly discovered ailments that by later in her life she absorbed, according to her niece, "lying with folded hands fostering her own aches & pains." With her feel for illness, Kate made a handy nurse. Nineteenth-century women, in fact, were expected to understand nursing intuitively, as if they had been born to do it.

All in all, the stubborn patience of Victorian matriarchy both had its own power and did its own damage. Kate, energetic and firm, with her "mandatory" ways, no doubt hovered over the young James children. Mary could also oppressively supervise her offspring. These doubled mothers did much to stifle Harry and even caused him to cherish a secret fantasy about turning into an orphan. With this much mothering, orphanage held a real allure.

⁂

ON FOURTEENTH STREET in the late 1840s, Mary and Henry nurtured the children in contrasting ways. Mary took them on trips to the massive and cavernous dry-goods store on Broadway, Stewart's. There they followed her, "hanging on [her] skirts," and got "the familiar Stewart headache from the prolonged strain of selection." For his part, Henry undertook the development of his children's minds. He took them to a bookshop on Broadway ("overwhelmingly and irresistibly English") and lavished on them the English books and periodicals they loved—notably a journal called the *Charm*, "a small periodical in quarto form, covered in yellow," that Harry thought smelled like England. Such treats as this had never materialized during Henry's own childhood.

Now that William and Harry had reached school age, Henry and Mary signed them up with schoolmarms, like the "broad-bosomed, broad based old lady" near Washington Square that Harry vividly remembered. This authoritative woman drank tea from a "blue cup, with a saucer that didn't match." She also carried a ferrule—that common prop of nineteenth-century education, a stinging stick of discipline. Mary and Kate didn't tote such a stick—but they looked, sometimes, as if they might.

Likewise, the James children were now getting old enough for theater excursions—outings that would strongly color their memories of Manhattan. They were, as Harry remembered, "'at home' among the theatres—thanks to [their] parents' fond interest in them." One evening, the James children attended a dramatized version of Harriet Beecher Stowe's *Uncle Tom's Cabin*. They adored it. Harry, at least, caught the bug of the melodrama that stirred so many Americans before the Civil War: he "lived and moved, at that time, with great intensity, in Mrs. Stowe's novel." Kate may have also loved this gripping best seller of 1852. The book after all embodied the very concepts of sentimental motherliness by which she lived. But no record survives of her presence beside them at the little "lecture-room" of a theater on the Lower East Side, where—in one of the many popular adaptations of Stowe's dramatic antislavery epic—the James children thrilled at the dramatic escape of the slave Eliza, her "flight across the ice-blocks of the Ohio."

Such high points illuminated the Jameses' early childhood memories. But home life wasn't completely harmonious for them, and not only because of the sibling rivalry that the two mother figures had already fostered in the crowded upper rooms of their brownstone. The favored children, William and Harry mostly, got more from Mary—and Harry, increasingly, the most. Henry had his own predilection for William, his eldest, though often he qualified in general as a warm stay-at-home father, fascinated by the budding intellectual abilities of his children. But he could also quixotically become disciplinary, especially with his headstrong oldest son. William, who turned eight in 1850, sometimes defied his father. And when their disputes heated up, his father, who was still prone to drink, sometimes curbed him with whippings.

❧

AS WILLIAM GREW, the father's tie with his eldest son intensified. In contrast to Harry, William had always qualified as a "motor," as he described himself—an assertive, bright, brazen boy who had early on taken his father and his father's dogmatic style as his model. While Harry worked hard to please his mother with quiet good behavior and politeness, with his careful dress and manners, William tried to catch and hold his father's wandering attention with stunts, antics, and displays of precocious genius. With his alcoholic habit, Henry's attention may sometimes have been hard to attract.

Henry could delight in all of his children but increasingly favored his eldest son. Remembering his own adolescent conflicts, he vowed to adopt a different form of parenthood, more lenient and understanding, than his own flinty father had provided. He tried to be easygoing, but he often lapsed back to the more confrontational model he'd inherited from his own father, especially with William. And all the while William admired and imitated his parent, craving even more of Henry's approval than Henry generally gave and resorting to extreme behavior when it was withheld.

The very intensity of this father-and-son dynamic had already ignited violent disturbances. When Henry back in New York had complained about the "shocking bad manners" his sons were picking up in the street, he no doubt worried about his tough and pugilistic eldest son more than his gentle and courteous second one. William was rebellious, prone to rudeness, and sometimes the conflict between Henry and his eldest son led to blows. William long remembered the pain of those occasions when "Father used to spank me with a paper cutter" in the Fourteenth Street house. Worsened by his own frustrations, Henry's complicated paternal love sometimes resulted in reddened welts. The young Jameses were children of an alcoholic, and time would unfold damage more complicated even than the violence that William so long remembered.

Though Harry lagged behind William by only one year, William always seemed, in his brother's eyes, to stride far ahead of him. More aggressive and more confident, William warned his brother, "*I* play with boys who curse and swear!" ("All boys," the milder Harry found, "were difficult to play with—unless it was that they rather found me.")

But, even more sharply, Harry felt his brother's intellectual advantage. Harry especially admired his brother's artistic gifts: the sketching and crayoning and painting that William had taken up in spite of his philosopher father. Henry didn't believe in art, but William loved to draw. In a little back room at Fourteenth Street, Harry remembered his brother "at seated play with his pencil under the lamp": "When I see him he is intently . . . rapidly drawing, his head critically balanced and his eyebrows working." And William had talent, at least in his brother's judgment: "No stroke of it that I have recovered but illustrates his aptitude for drawing," Harry would later observe.

Harry himself also "plied the pencil." But he didn't do it, he felt, as "critically, rapidly, or summarily" as William did. Yet Harry was already beginning to find something he *could* do, as, claiming some private place in the overcrowded house, he lost himself in penning and illustrating stories and plays. Still, William seemed always to outstrip him in wit and talent—staging performances for the father who, increasingly, found distractions away from home.

❧

MASTER OF HIS own house again in 1848, Henry Senior was back in the pink. At about this time Henry described himself, optimistically, as "standing five feet six or eight inches in [his] shoes, with fair hair and blue eyes, a competent knowledge of Greek, and an amiable disposition."

In Albany, Henry had begun lecturing again, to small but mostly appreciative audiences. His discovery of Swedenborg, still fresh, had given him both a philosophical framework and a club to belong to—the mystical yet scientific Swedenborgians. But Henry, ever idiosyncratic, hardly qualified as an orthodox follower of the Swedish mystic who was now in such vogue in America. Henry maintained a "frankly independent and disturbingly irregular . . . connection," as his son called it, to his intellectual mentor.

As a sign of his refreshed ambitions, Henry joined the New York Society Library, the scene of his meeting with Emerson. Henry also reconnected with his old mentor and established a friendship that was calmer, if also cooler, than before. Thus the growing James children knew the only guest room in their overcrowded townhouse as "Mr. Emerson's room."

When Emerson stayed with the Jameses in New York, he impressed the young Harry—who also with his father had met the now-legendary Washington Irving on a Hudson steamboat—with one of his first close-up views of a literary giant.

> I "visualise" . . . the winter firelight of our back-parlour at dusk and the great Emerson—I knew he was great, greater than any of our friends—sitting in it between my parents, before the lamps had been lighted, as a visitor consentingly housed only could have done, and affecting me the more as an apparition sinuously and, I held,

elegantly slim, benevolently aquiline, and commanding a tone alien, beautifully alien, to any we heard roundabout, that he bent this benignity upon me by an invitation to draw nearer to him, off the hearth-rug, and know myself as never yet, as I was not indeed to know myself again for years, in touch with the wonder of Boston.

This "wonder of Boston" hinted at the literary and intellectual superiority of the New England metropolis, which, in the late 1840s, towered over New York. To be sure, Walt Whitman was simmering in Brooklyn, and Herman Melville was frequenting the same book stacks at the New York Society Library as Henry. But Henry cultivated famous New England thinkers and welcomed them to his house, and that marked his continuing high ambitions.

Still, Henry no longer looked to Emerson for inspiration; instead, he'd discovered a new prophet to guide his thinking. During the slow years of Henry's recovery, in 1845–46, his well-heeled friend Edmund Tweedy had introduced him to the social theories of a French socialist named Charles Fourier. Fourier had proposed a new model for a utopian community, a village-sized unit of fifteen hundred people that he referred to as a phalanx. These enlightened few would live in egalitarian social harmony. Each would follow his passions, for work and love, while remaining committed to the collective good.

The well-traveled Henry had actually encountered Fourierists before—in Emerson's lecture rooms and also in England. In fact, he and Mary originally caught their enthusiasm for Fourier from a book translated by their old friend Sophia Chichester, the woman who had helped with Henry's cure in London. But especially after his breakdown and following his discovery of Swedenborg, Henry was primed to embrace an extravagant new utopian theory.

In his own tormented way, Henry had always been hunting for an ideal social arrangement. He had even tried to manifest this quest in his family life, as he engineered their many moves from one city to the next. Social progress and social experimentation fascinated Henry—a mania he shared with many reform-minded intellectuals of his time. In the 1840s, widespread seedlings of utopian communities had sprung up all over in America. Fourierist Associationists, for example, had nailed together a "phalanstery," or utopian village, at Red Bank, New Jersey.

But the most famous experimental community, and the best known to Henry, lay among rocky fields in West Roxbury, Massachusetts. At Brook Farm, a group of radical transcendentalists led by the ex–Unitarian minister George Ripley had been learning primitive agriculture, to go back to the earth and to get dirt on their hands as "yeomen scholars." (The community barely scraped by on its crops, although it eventually made money out of a school these uprooted intellectuals also seeded.) These utopians had founded their highly charged experimental community in 1841 and then converted to the still-higher voltage of Fourierism in 1844.

With his tendency to leap before he looked, Henry might well have transplanted his family to Brook Farm's dreamland of fence-building and late-night socialist rants. The Jameses too might have lived the life broodingly satirized by Nathaniel Hawthorne—a brief sojourner among these utopians—in *The Blithedale Romance* (1852). But Henry resisted moving his family to West Roxbury; maybe he valued his paternal authority, as well as his highly idiosyncratic personal freedom in New York City. Henry didn't always work well with groups.

Still, Henry wrote extensively for the *Harbinger*, the mouthpiece of the Brook Farm circle and the then most wild-eyed radical magazine in America. In comparison to this new organ, Emerson's old "transcendental" *Dial* looked tame. By 1848, in fact, when the magazine moved to New York, Henry's involvement with the publication was so deep that he worked at a desk in its office and helped with the editing—Henry's nearest approach to a formal job so far. That he had never had to earn money had enabled his alcoholism, as Henry himself recognized; but he was fortunate, with all his personal problems, that his family's welfare hadn't depended on his work in a demanding profession like the law. Would Henry have ever been able to keep such a job? Even now, with penniless visionaries like George Ripley as his colleagues, Henry most likely worked without pay and maybe even donated his own money to the cause. Still, this editorship constituted the high-water mark of Henry's reputation and prominence as an iconoclast, even if his dogmatic style and offbeat opinions continued to earn him as many detractors as admirers.

In the first years of his family's residence on Fourteenth Street,

Henry threw himself into work he'd ostentatiously titled "The Divine Life in Man." His new magnum opus, a soup of theology and social reform, inevitably bogged down. But that didn't keep Henry from rocking every possible boat by publishing bold articles and delivering resounding and polemical lectures in New York and Boston.

As a rule, Mary didn't care much for theories, even Henry's. But as befit the woman she imagined herself to be, she did her best to share her husband's new enthusiasm. During the family's residence in Manhattan, Mary wrote to her mother-in-law about Henry's latest manuscript, "You will like it better than anything he has ever written." Henry rationally addressed the difficulties of religious faith, Mary thought. "It fills too with new meaning and beauty, so many of the old Scriptures, which we have all been taught to revere, by giving them true spiritual significance that no one I think can read it attentively without going with new delight to their Bible." Such was Mary's rather vague and hopeful appreciation of her husband's thorny, argumentative, and arcane work.

Mostly, though, Mary fostered her husband's confidence by listening. In these years, as young Harry remembered, his mother often composed herself, in the parlor at the Fourteenth Street house, for the formidable task of listening to her husband. Henry read out to Mary "with an appreciation of that modest grasp of somebody's attention, the brief illusion of publicity . . . some series of pages from among his 'papers' that were to show her how he had this time at last done it." Henry read not just a paragraph or two but, instead, large swaths of his work.

Tactfully, Mary entertained herself with some piece of mending or sewing as she listened to "the full music of the 'papers.'" But she gave Henry all of her apparent attention. Evidently she didn't believe, as her son Harry came to, that Henry's "Ideas" were "somehow too philosophic for life, and at the same time too living . . . for thought." But even Harry, trained to respect his father, never committed the faux pas of thinking that his father "might be 'wrong.'"

Likewise William, Henry's eldest son—the child who would most follow Henry's philosophical example—resisted his parent's ideas. He later admitted his father's theories counted as "singularly unvaried and few." Not many writers, he thought, had spent so much time working their way through a single obsessive "bundle of truths."

But if even Mary could sometimes joke and even roll her eyes at her husband's oddities ("Your father's *ideas*, you know—!"), she remained proud of him. Her unwavering partisanship, in fact, rendered her more satirical children "delightedly derisive" about *her*. As a bonus, they could laugh at both of their parents at the same time.

Mary, though, took a genuine interest in Henry's pursuits. In the view of her son Harry, she remained profoundly in tune with her husband. His children took for granted the "vague grand things within" that Henry carried with him as he paced around the house. But Mary "sat on the steps" of Henry's temple and "caught reverberations of the inward mystic choir."

⤜⤛

TRAPPED IN THIS same house, Kate didn't at all worship in her sister's cult of Henry. Sometimes she might join Mary in a listening pose—as she'd done, more convincingly perhaps, during Henry's courtship. William sketched the typical family scene: "the lovely Mother and Aunt in armchairs, their hands crossed in front of them, listening to Father, who walks up and down talking."

Kate, though, had less incentive than Mary to indulge Henry's whims or put up with his bombast. For one thing, she was the sister that Henry hadn't chosen—for all that she was living in his house and filling a role that struck some of the Jameses' contemporaries as that of a second, if nonsexual, wife. If Kate had ever harbored any personal feelings about Henry—and no definitive evidence for or against this melodramatic possibility survives—her relations with Henry in the Fourteenth Street house in the late 1840s were marked with what William later described as a "sort of sub-antagonism." And their hidden conflict came to a boil in the late 1840s and early 1850s as Henry and Kate struggled to survive under the same roof.

With his abrasive style, Henry no doubt showed little respect for Kate's point of view. He had a low opinion of female intelligence, even though he corresponded with several brilliant and cultivated women. For her part, Kate held a number of strong opinions that may equally have irked Henry. Unlike the authoritative but milder Mary, Kate spoke with what Henry called "cheery strenuousness"—to the children, to the servants, and to Henry himself.

Kate's cheery strenuousness often found pet causes. In 1848, the year of dramatic revolutions in Europe, Kate declared herself a partisan, as Henry was not, of Lajos Kossuth, the dashingly bearded Hungarian nationalist and resistance fighter. Surprisingly, Kate often held political opinions that were more liberal than those of her sometimes fanatical, sometimes stodgy brother-in-law. In an era before women even had a vote, Kate wasn't called upon to express her ideas—and certainly not in Henry's household. But she expressed them all the same.

During this period, too, Kate had also apparently involved herself in some religious unconventionality. Though Kate herself expunged all records of this period, one of Henry's confidants preserved a scrap of some kind of unorthodox involvement in 1847. "So Miss Walsh is in hot water!" Dr. Wilkinson wrote Henry from England. "We do not wonder at it, and it seems to be a warning to us all, not at present to interlock ourselves very closely with any sect or party, & perhaps not to leave that in which we are born." Kate's "doctrinal" interests had evidently entangled her in some unfeminine and unconventional activities in New York City.

Even when not in "hot water," Kate didn't always observe the deferential silence prescribed for antebellum women. The James children stood in no doubt of Kate's crystal-clear opinions and predilections. They grew up hearing about Kate's strong value on sentiment—that unassailable stronghold of feminine prerogative. William later joked that to live "more in the intellect than the affections" qualified, for Kate, as a *low* form of life. In this protest, she more or less declared her disapproval of Henry's overzealous intellectualism.

≈

WHEN HENRY LECTURED in New York, he not surprisingly took Mary with him and not Kate. Kate most likely got to stay behind and tend the children. Harry remembered his parents' departure "at about the hour of our upward procession to bed." His father strode out the door—with the jerking gait that passed for his stride. Mary followed, bejeweled, well-dressed, in "earnest and confident though slightly fluttered attendance."

Mary added her own anxiety to the departure—"made more of a thrill" for the children—by worrying about Henry's absentmindedness. Were she and Henry leaving the house without "the *corpus delicti* or manuscript itself"? Henry had been known to forget his speech. He'd had to return home for it in a devil of a hurry. Harry remembered watching from the bay window of the parlor, as his father stood under a "gusty street-lamp" beside the door of the carriage, fishing his lecture from the pocket of his coattails, and shaking it, for Mary's "ideal comfort."

Henry didn't invite Kate to his lectures probably because he knew she was a critic. Even in this era of his relative success, he was plagued by his own inner self-doubts and self-loathing, without any contribution from Kate. In 1853, Henry delivered three catastrophic and abortive lectures (out of an advertised series of six) at the Masonic Temple in Boston. He came away horrified with their and his own "loud-mouthed imbecility." During such anxiety attacks, Mary could soothe Henry and reassure him.

But in her wifely appearances at Henry's lectures, Mary increasingly played another role—and one that must have particularly pained her. Mary had to reassure Henry's audience that he wasn't a libertine rabble-rouser but instead a respectable married man. For Henry, under the influence of his new hero Fourier, had begun to broadcast in his writings and from his podium not his usual dry theological harangues. Instead, to the horror of many of his friends, he had begun to air some potent and controversial assertions about marriage.

The Jameses had begun their wedded life as nonconformists, with their civil marriage. But in the late 1840s, Henry preached an even more radical departure from tradition. In 1848, when Europe was burning with revolutionary fires, Henry boldly published a translation of a pamphlet by Victor Hennequin, a French Fourierist, which promoted so-called free love.

Fourier qualified as an antinomian; he believed that a person with a high spiritual development could ignore or rewrite society's laws. In

Fourier's utopia, erotic passions could freely and naturally manifest themselves outside of marriage—between men and women only, of course.

With his signature enthusiasm and recklessness, Henry adopted what qualified as mind-boggling ideas at the time. What's more, he exerted himself to publicize them, surging to their defense in the pages of the *Harbinger* when, inevitably, they came under attack. Other American Fourierists shied away from this controversy, which tended to batter the Associationist cause—and in fact, through Henry, it caused 1840s American socialism no end of trouble.

Even Henry's friends saw "poltroonery" in his new ideas, though they recognized that Henry himself might actually observe "the old rules . . . to Mrs. James's very great consolation." Henry's prominent and vehement espousal of this radical point of view earned him high-profile notoriety. But it also tarred him with the brush of "free love" even years after he'd given up on the notion.

Curiously, Henry made himself a lightning rod for free love during an era when he was living, however chastely, with a second woman under his roof. The Fourierists, like the Mormons, in 1840s America sometimes flirted with the idea of polygamy. But the prevailing sentiment of the era militated against any such irregularities.

Kate, with her belief in an "affectional" side (and its consequent implication of women's sphere and women's experience), may well have looked askance at Henry's male-centered theories, especially because she couldn't help but wonder how Henry's "Ideas" might affect her sister, Mary. Others too wondered about Henry's conduct. And Kate, who'd observed Henry's pandemic flirtation firsthand, must have had her reasons for suspicion.

What's more, Henry's fulminations against marriage also coincided with the birth of the Jameses' last child, Alice, and with a subsequent miscarriage or abortive full-term birth that Mary suffered when, approaching forty, she became pregnant for a sixth time. Mary's "hemorrhage" apparently also endangered her life, much to Henry's alarm. This close call rendered future pregnancies perilous—a complication in Henry and Mary's sex life in an era when couples had few reliable forms of contraception besides abstinence. Here was another source of Henry's fulminations against marriage.

In this, Henry's most radical phase, he went so far as to champion divorce—a controversial and unthinkable idea in the early 1850s when he proposed it. His fascination, Henry claimed, was purely philosophical; he had no desire, in spite of some sexual tensions after Mary's miscarriage, to divorce *her*.

Peculiarly and contradictorily, Henry also defended marriage as necessary, especially for women. Henry declared in 1853, in a high-profile article called "Woman and the 'Woman's Movement'" in *Putnam's Monthly*, that women were strictly subsidiary to men and "inferior to man . . . in passion, his inferior in intellect, and his inferior in physical strength." Henry thus believed that "learning and wisdom do not become her." As far as he was concerned, a woman's role was to bear and raise men's children, "simply to love and bless man."

Henry's narrow ideas would ultimately affect Alice, the only daughter of the house, most powerfully. In the meantime, his views rendered him infamous among the newly energized feminists of the time. (One published a brisk rebuttal titled "The Proper Sphere of Men" in 1854, observing that "man has shown no reluctance to become the instructor and counselor of woman," and then repaying the favor by laying out men's duties toward women.) Henry didn't even flinch: his antiwoman stance stood as a further piece of notoriety that the argumentative and fame-hungry social theorist perversely savored.

Deeply domestic and staunchly loyal, Mary appeared to fit Henry's reactionary ideal. Her husband hailed her virtue but denigrated her intelligence. But far from being "dependent" on Henry, Mary quietly belied his theories by rendering him thoroughly dependent on her.

Henry was known to flirt and even steal a kiss when he could. But Mary had her own indispensable strengths. She supervised the household and the investments—seeing the comfort and coherence of their home as her main mission. But, as she'd proved in London, she could also manage Henry's health and emotional stability. Consequently, Henry's "free love" agitation never roved very far beyond the academic.

As for Henry, his own feelings through this stormy period remained conflicted and contradictory. "Who will then ever be caught in that foolish snare again?" Henry wrote one of his many female correspondents, referring to erotic passion. "I did nothing but tumble into it from my boyhood to my marriage; since which great disillusioning—yes!—I feel that the only lovable person is one who does not permit himself to be loved."

Whether or not Henry was "lovable," or permitted himself to be loved, Mary did love him. And if love sometimes failed a little in her marriage, Mary coped with him—sweetly, deftly, with an apparent innocence about what she was doing. Under Mary's influence, Henry tempered passionate unconventionality with Victorian restraint—a paradox he would bequeath to his children.

❧

SOMETIME AROUND 1850, Henry showed even more impressive restraint. As he asserted publicly in an editorial in the *New York Tribune* in August 1851, he stopped drinking cold, and by a sheer act of will. It was a courageous step in itself, and all the more so for being public, but Henry had a new impetus to grapple with his old habit. During the summer of 1849, Dr. Wilkinson, Henry's friend in England, had urged him to give up alcohol. Wilkinson combined the influence of a trusted companion with the authority of a medical doctor. His scientific opinion may well have carried weight with Henry, since the latter now believed alcoholism neither a sin nor a crime—as popular opinion defined it—but instead an illness. It was, he theorized in his *Tribune* piece, "quite as curable under proper care as any more material form of disease."

"How stupid to preach to the drunkard upon the evils of intemperance!" Henry asserted in his essay. An alcoholic had an "infinitely keener sense" of these evils than anybody who might criticize him. "The drunkard never lived who, in the very sabbath of his delirium, would not have given his right hand to be able to drink no more." Henry kept to such generalities about alcoholics without often speaking, explicitly, from his own experience; but his sufferings were present in every line of this bold, moving essay—one of Henry's most intriguing works, though it has attracted surprisingly little notice.

Through this essay, Henry reinforced his own determination to stay sober. Previously, he had sometimes had the motivation, but now he also had a method of doing so. Previously, "drunkards"—Henry's own negative term—had only been able to find help through jails, church ministries, and temperance missions. Well-to-do alcoholics were just beginning to be treated in sanatoriums, and Henry had heard of at least one such hospital on Long Island. Still, the understanding of alcoholism had a long way to go; Alcoholics Anonymous—whose creation was inspired, incidentally, by William James's *Varieties of Religious Experience* (1902)—would not be founded for another eighty-four years, in 1935.

In 1851, Henry's plan of action was characteristically idiosyncratic and based on his arcane philosophical principles. Alcoholism amounted to a habit, Henry theorized. "*Like all habits, its strength lies in a diseased will*"; Henry used italics in his intemperance article, showing the pitch of his determination to get the better of it. "Will," in Henry's mind, belonged to a person's moral character—especially to a man's. It was the manly assertion of will that could cure his disease. What concrete steps Henry took to quit drinking, if he confided them to anyone, have not survived the later letter burners in the James family. It is not certain if Henry gave up only hard spirits and kept imbibing beer and wine—which seems probable, from hints in family accounts—or if he actually gave up alcohol for good. But in 1851, at least, he portrayed himself as what is now known as a "recovered alcoholic," who had quit by virtuous self-assertion, as well as through the "sympathy and help" that he thought all people with drinking problems deserved.

Henry's self-transformation appears to be one of the most laudable acts of his life, and it coincided with a lift in his career as a lecturer. In 1850, he had published a volume called *Moralism and Christianity; or, Man's Experience and Destiny*. His next volume was *Lectures and Miscellanies* (1852), in which he courageously included his confessions about alcohol. It proved one of Henry's most popular publications, and it almost ran into a second edition. It contained lectures on democracy, art, and science, as well as on his perennial subjects of religion and morality. His article on "Intemperance" was tucked in the back of this collection, along with a piece on "Spiritual Rappings," even though it was arguably one of the most personal and resonant of all of these writings. Yet the story of the effects of his alcoholism on his children, unfortunately, had only just begun.

⁂

KATE, MEANWHILE, WAS about to make dramatic and life-changing decisions of her own. She was on the brink of taking a dramatic furlough from her role as maiden aunt and live-in nursery aid. By the autumn of 1851, a family illness divided Kate's loyalties. Alice, the baby of the family, had just turned three years old. But Kate gave up nurturing the little girl in order to nurse her grown-up brother John, who'd fallen seriously ill. She was not particularly close to John, but still it was her duty as a sister to take care of him.

Kate's removal to Eighth Street from Fourteenth Street didn't cut her off entirely from her surrogate children. (Even Henry, who for all his bluster had a warm heart, admitted that he was lonely without her.) But her brother's sickness distracted Kate and seems to have changed her frame of reference. John died in April 1852, one of a procession of uncles that to Harry seemed prone to dying—in an age when an abundance of uncles was counterbalanced by a high mortality rate.

But as soon as she returned again, Kate stumbled onto a serendipitous new purpose, a fresh interest that looked as if it would make up for her previous misfortunes. The coming months would curiously demonstrate how flares of idiosyncrasy, if not of passion, could erupt on the Walsh as well as the James side of the family.

East of Fifth Avenue on Fourteenth Street, in another newish row house, lived a sun-reddened, well-traveled acquaintance of the Jameses— and one, in a strange coincidence, who connected them back to Henry and Mary's earlier Atlantic rovings. Charles H. Marshall had retired ashore after a spirited career as a tough sea captain and a flinty shipping magnate. Though Marshall had started his maritime life as a cabin boy and worked away his youth in whaling, he'd more recently claimed fame by taking over the infamous Black Ball Line.

The Black Ball Line counted as a household name—when it didn't feature as a hiss and a byword. In another link between the James family and the fast ships of the era, the Black Ball, or "Old Line," had led the way as one of the first private sailing-packet companies in New York. It had grown famous, in its heyday earlier in the century, both for its speedy crossings of the Atlantic in the days before steam—"sixteen days and a pirouette" while transporting a Viennese dance company in one celebrated instance—as well as for its brutal discipline of sailors. One sea chantey that satirized the company, sung to the tune of "Blow the Man Down," enjoyed meteoric popularity in Jacksonian New York.

Marshall himself, having captained Atlantic packets, breathed the fresh air of discipline, as Henry illustrated in a playful sketch of his living habits. Captain Marshall "rises at five winter and summer," Henry wrote, "musters first-mate (or second-mate as the case may be) and crew, takes a look at the weather and a pull at the newspaper, opens all hatches, examines the condition of the hencoop, and finally brings himself to anchor at the breakfast table with every sail of his appetite and helm fast-down." And this wealthy old sea salt was soon to become Aunt Kate's suitor.

Captain Marshall's courtship of Kate progressed at least partly at the Fourteenth Street house, where Kate lived or visited frequently. Here the captain was aided too by accidental (or deliberately accidental) encounters that forwarded his suit. Marshall, a widower, may have admired Kate's forthright and practical shipshapeness, her command of the unruly James children—even though the captain's own children were older and had more or less sailed away.

But Kate's family duties also complicated his winning of her. Six-year-old Bob, the youngest James boy, who often slept in Kate's bed, claimed to remember the romance that his presence had perhaps impeded. Henry recalled the courtship differently: "Captain Marshall's assiduities this winter were boundless, and although Aunt Kate began by the old story of total and permanent insensibility, she finally 'give out,' as they say in Rutland and Danbury, about a fortnight since."

Kate apparently resisted the captain's advances. Did she balk because the captain had reached sixty, because he was twenty years older than she was? Or did she, at the sober age of forty, hesitate to commit herself? Whatever her reservations, Kate's upbringing had fitted her to wear a wedding ring. Kate had always taken advantage of her opportunities, few though they had been, and she knew the social value of this one, the greater respect paid to married women.

After a due interval, Kate accepted her suitor and indulged in wedding preparations. Her satirical brother-in-law observed a "steady stream of skirt and chemisette setting in towards the third story"; he felt the comic need to "speak to the Captain about the dimensions of Mrs. M.'s dressing room." Henry's joke confirms both Kate's love of millinery and Henry's scornful judgment on such "frivolous" female accoutrements.

Kate braved matrimony, however, with Walshlike earnestness. The whole of her sister's family attended her wedding on the morning of February 18, 1853, in New York, presided over by one Reverend Dr. Bellows.

In giving Kate up—in almost giving Kate away, as her father had been dead since 1820—Henry allowed himself a warmer appraisal of her than he usually gave. Kate, he wrote,

> has always been a most loving and provident husband to Mary, a most considerate and devoted wife to me, and an incomparable father and mother to our children. She has paid the servants' wages over again by her invariable good humour and kindness, and has been the sun and stars to us whenever our skies have been overcast by dread, or the night of any great sorrow has threatened to shut us in.

Henry's appraisal rang with peculiar contradictions. Was it odder that Henry saw Kate as a wife—or that he saw Kate as Mary's husband—a role that he himself ought to have played? Henry partly poked fun at Kate for assuming roles that transgressed his notion of women's sphere. But Kate's strangely androgynous function as both husband and wife had, surprisingly, articulated the very ideal of a Victorian family.

Henry recognized, anyway, just what a complicated and indispensable role Kate had played in the family. For all their "sub-antagonism," Henry appears to have missed Kate, his second "devoted wife," when she left his house.

For their honeymoon, Kate and her new husband set sail for six months in Europe, beginning in October 1854. Henry no doubt envied Kate her transatlantic ticket. As long before as 1849, Henry had contemplated European travel as an alternative to expensive enlargements—"so numerous has waxed our family"—to the cramped Fourteenth Street house.

"Looking upon our four stout boys," Henry wrote Emerson (conveniently forgetting about Alice), "who have no play-room within doors, and import shocking bad manners from the street, with much pity, we gravely ponder whether it would not be better to go abroad for a few years with them, allowing them to absorb French and German and get a better sensuous education than they are likely to get here."

Henry was itching, once again, to travel.

❧

IN AUGUST 1854, Henry snatched his ten-year-old son Harry from the family's veranda-ringed summer hotel on Staten Island, stowing him onto a steamer headed across New York Harbor. Then, with "headlong impatience" to keep this surprise a secret from his wife, he hurried his son into a daguerreotype studio on Broadway in lower Manhattan.

For this little excursion, Henry didn't choose just any studio. Photography, an infant technology, had hardly taken hold or spread very far, and thus Henry's idea was all the more daring and unconventional. Ever cutting-edge, Henry consulted a new practitioner of a new art: a fellow Irish-American New Yorker named Mathew Brady.

By that year, Brady had already toted up quite a bit of celebrity. He'd mounted an ambitious gallery of daguerreotypes, "Illustrious Americans," to excite interest in this brand-new medium, to scare up fresh business. These portraits included such illustrious figures as Daniel Webster, the Massachusetts senator famous for his brilliant oratory; and such obscure ones as the failed Illinois politician Abraham Lincoln. ("Make no mistake, gentlemen," Lincoln later quipped, "Brady made me President!")

For popular appeal, Brady also snapped celebrities like Jenny Lind, the "Swedish nightingale," who'd toured the United States in 1850 under the management of P. T. Barnum; and "General Tom Thumb," Charles Sherwood Stratton, the little person rendered a household phrase by this same relentless, ingenious, wild-haired showman. Later, in the 1860s, Mathew Brady would earn lasting respect for his stark and testifying portraits of Civil War battlefields—some of the most moving photographic documents of American history. But with this national agony still seven years away, Brady's portrait of the double Henrys testified more to his fascination with Barnum's sideshow curiosities.

In Brady's now-famous portrait, the elder Henry poses himself, one hand gripping the cane he often needed but was generally too ashamed to use. The father's amputated leg evades the portrait. But this unseen trauma underlies Henry's slightly pained posture. His beard-rimmed face comes across as thoughtful, mild, bespectacled, a philosopher's bust. He hardly looks like the epicenter of obscure passions and argumentative bombast that he is, the prime mover of his family's dislocations.

Beside him, the eleven-year-old Henry Junior resembles a scaled-down copy of his father and has the same enigmatic gray gaze. Yet though a summery white hat hangs from his small hand—appropriate, almost, for an Atlantic voyage—the child looks strangely stiff and hemmed in. He wears his "little sheath-like jacket, tight to the body, closed at the neck and adorned in front with a single row of brass buttons."

The meticulous Harry later felt "not so adequately dressed" as he'd have liked. He'd later blush at being nicknamed "Buttons" by the English novelist William Makepeace Thackeray, the author of the 1848 comic masterpiece, *Vanity Fair*. The epithet of "Buttons" teasingly spotlighted Henry Junior's curiously urchin- and sailorlike appearance. The creator of the ruthless social climber Becky Sharp, Thackeray would wield a cutting wit during his future teatime visits; such was the caliber of European to whom Henry Senior would soon introduce his children.

But young Harry had other reasons to fret on the day the daguerreotype was taken. The child dressed casually, in fact, because he got no warning. Nobody guessed in advance the photograph would be taken. The idea had occurred to his father as a freak, a caprice.

On this occasion Brady, with his dwindling eyesight and his painstaking long-exposure art, found himself drawn into a James family prank. Henry loved to spring surprises and to astonish everyone he knew, especially his wife. To this end, he involved his children in "common conspiracies against her." These intrigues amused the young James children—and they often appreciated their father's wit. But the jokes also "compromised" the whole family, and in increasingly dramatic ways.

✎

IN THESE FINAL years in New York, Henry's sense of humor and desire for novelty veered toward the "explosive," according to Harry. He'd thrown a few firecrackers in the summer of 1854 with the surprise daguerreotype. But in the summer of 1855, he let off a bomb. In a shock to his wife, his family, and his friends, he proposed a complete change of continents. He'd been threatening such a move for years. And even if he had now given up drinking, he was as restless and quixotic as he'd ever been. He'd complained about the bad manners his sons were picking up the New York streets, and he'd longed for his children to learn French like young aristocrats.

Even before this news hit them, the young Jameses were no stranger to upheaval. At home on Fourteenth Street, in the upholstered splendors of Victorian domesticity—with a marble bust of a Bacchante anchoring the room and a huge painting by Thomas Cole filling one wall—the James children had mostly felt rootless and ill-defined.

Already, they had grown up with few of the reference points that many well-to-do nineteenth-century children took for granted. For one thing, the James children couldn't tell their friends what their father did for a living, as Harry's biographer Leon Edel observed. "Say I am a philosopher," Henry prompted them, "say I'm a seeker after truth, say I'm a lover of my kind, say I'm an author of books if you like; or, best of all, just say I'm a Student." This statement, clearly, would have branded his children as "ridiculous" in the eyes of their playmates.

"What church do you go to?" was another question the James children heard in the street, and it often distressed them. Religion pegged people in nineteenth-century America, with its rival Protestant sects. Sectarian tags provided adolescents with badges of pride and identity. Association with a church—Episcopal, Methodist, Congregational, Baptist, Lutheran, Quaker, Unitarian, Dutch Reformed—furnished children, as well as their insecure and bullying adversaries, with a convenient résumé of their neighbors' class, ethnic, and regional associations. The Jameses were Presbyterian by background, but their parents had disclaimed the association. Threatened, curious, the young Jameses' neighbors teased them about what Harry later good-humoredly called their "pewless state."

With his usual detachment, Henry Senior gave his children cloud-high advice. He explained that they "could plead nothing less than the whole privilege of Christendom and that there was no communion . . . from which [they] need find [themselves] excluded."

The young Jameses' education, too, had amounted to "small vague spasms of school," as Harry later appraised it. They'd suffered through an avalanche of home tutors, dame schools, and day schools—selected by the ever-changing whims of their father. Harry remembered "dispensaries of learning" whose numbers astonished him. "We couldn't have changed oftener," he recalled.

And now Henry Senior's hunger for experiment, for the "supposedly supreme benefits of Swiss schooling," threatened to take a momentous new turn.

❧

HENRY HAD HELD off on his threat to travel long enough to give his family six years of upholstered and highly domesticated life in New York. But the "solutional 'Europe,'" as Harry called it, remained obsessively fixed in his mind, narcotically soothing to his restless nerves. Europe looked attractive especially when his crowded house, his unruly boys, and his children's proper education persisted as problems for him and Mary. And he added to these motives his own embarrassing overexposure in America as a free-love radical and as a barefaced advocate of divorce.

Then, in October 1855, as the Jameses began to pack their respective trunks with Swedenborg, with Dickens, and with Mary's long parade of clothes, Kate unexpectedly and dramatically reappeared among them. To their astonishment, Kate was determined to travel with them as she'd done before.

In fact, Kate came back to her sister's household having left Captain

Marshall outright. She'd made a "frightful mistake," as Henry phrased it in a letter to Emerson. Kate's husband's "character hid itself from an intimacy of years, and only disclosed itself in the penetralia of home, as made all the grinding littlenesses and coldnesses that are effectual and wearing out the human heart."

The echo of Kate's voice survives in this unburned letter. To someone who valued "affectional" warmth as much as she did, Captain Marshall had, disappointingly, provided only "spiritual isolation and iciness which left no green thing alive." Coldly, he'd "banished smiles and tears, laughter and all human sympathies to the other hemisphere"— Kate's worst nightmare incarnate.

In comparison to a marriage in which she "might have died," Kate found her home with Henry and Mary a warm and secure alternative. For all of his irritating theories and masculine bluster, Henry qualified as a warmhearted man who'd worked hard to create a more caring household than his father's cold and authoritarian one in Albany. Kate chose to return to this happier environment, to be, as Henry put it, "our sweet and stainless 'Aunt Kate' again, the refuge of all hearts, and the solace of every wear hour." In calling Kate "stainless," her brother-in-law not only welcomed her back but also defended her honor in an era when a woman leaving her husband was bound to raise censure.

For her part, Kate had acted with energy and courage to extract herself from a bad marriage. When the captain had suggested a separation "in the way of menace"—as a threat to a helpless and dependent woman—Kate had seized on the idea as a means of escape.

Strikingly, Kate had needed none of Henry's theories to execute her own version of divorce. As her cousin William Walsh later remembered it, the matter was quite orderly: marriage hadn't been "productive of happiness to either party," and the determined woman had simply "retired from his house," though the couple never legally divorced. That seemed to be enough for the Walshes, and little else is recorded as having been said.

Kate returned to the James entourage with the hybrid name of "Mrs. Walsh"—a dignity that, without ever returning to Captain Marshall, she carried with her to Europe and for the rest of her life. And though her marriage had failed, Kate had tasted an extra dose of international adventure and defined her future role as one of grand and foundational solitude.

Kate's example remained before the James children—as they began their new European life. Subtly, like a faint shadow on the wall, it provided a penumbra of unconventionality, independence, and escape.

· 5 ·

HOTEL CHILDREN

n Monday morning, July 9, 1855, the James entourage, three
adults and five children, crowded out of their train at Euston
Station in London. The terminal's formidable Great Hall, finished in 1849, welcomed them with an echoing classical cavern, a cof-
fered ceiling, columned facades, and high windows that streaked the
dark interior with the dim sunlight of a London summer. Out in front
of the station, the massive columns of the famous Euston arch formed a
gateway for American travelers who had landed at Liverpool. And for
the Jameses it was a welcome portal, as they had left their Fourteenth
Street townhouse in Manhattan some ten days before, weathering sea-
sickness and airless cabins during their voyage on the sumptuous Collins
steamship *Atlantic*.

For convenience, the Jameses put up at the neighboring Euston Hotel. With so many trunks and bags, with children ranging in age from
thirteen to six, Mary may well have insisted on the most practical possible alternative, especially since Henry planned to spend only a few days
in London. Thus the noisy precincts of one of the world's busiest railway depots would provide the children with their first real taste, and a
coal-smelling one, of the Old World.

When the Jameses forged out into the city, they wouldn't have hailed
a trim two-wheeled hansom cab but instead the roomier Clarence carriage. A "growler," the Jameses found, was an unwieldy vehicle that at

the best of times qualified as a rollover waiting to happen. Top-heavy, it tended to list dangerously if trunks were lashed to the roof. Even without such burdens, the interior was cramped, with Henry, Mary, Kate, and the three youngest children stuffed inside a nearly windowless compartment. (Sometimes, it's true, the family party needed "two throbbing and heaving cabs" for one of their excursions.) Growlers could get them places, but these lumbering vehicles didn't offer the famous open views that hansom cabs did.

But thirteen-year-old William and twelve-year-old Harry, perched up beside the lanterns and next to the driver, had a "coign of vantage," as Harry remembered it. Their four-wheeler rumbled forth, and the two young teenagers saw London "for the first time since [their] babyhood." Vast, imperial vistas opened up before them—squares, mansions, banks, hotels—all of them spiced by the boys' life-threatening seats beside a London cabby. The city of their idol Charles Dickens, spreading like a brick and stucco labyrinth in its smoke, hinted that even a whole lifetime might not provide enough time to explore it. London was also the city of William Makepeace Thackeray, author of *Vanity Fair* (1848), a friend of their father's who had visited their Manhattan house in 1852; their father had crossed the Atlantic to mix with the likes of Thomas Carlyle and Alfred Lord Tennyson—as well as scientists, politicians, aristocrats, and social radicals, the titans of the midcentury Victorian world, whom his young children could hardly as yet even imagine. As yet, the young James children were "but vaguely 'formed,'" as Harry would later put it, and they would deeply absorb this rich new world.

For Harry, the mere spectacle of the streets teeming with carriages and wagons and seething with crowds in all gradations of dress counted as glorious. But William looked at the high corniced houses and great parks of the world's largest city with a more jaundiced eye—the eye of a sardonic, assertive adolescent and a partisan of New York. London, he calculated in a letter to a friend back in Manhattan, was six times the size of New York. (In 1855, the English metropolis was actually nearer to three times the size of the Jameses' hometown.) But bigger didn't necessarily mean better, and the city struck the proudly biased William as "much too big to be agreeable." He could only regard London as "a great huge unwieldy metropolis with a little brown river crawling through it"—hardly a ringing endorsement.

Paradoxically, William's love of irony could partly be traced back to Dickens—himself a product of this restless London scene. But the boy's sarcasm also sprang from his own displacement, from his and his siblings' unfolding experience as what Harry would later call "hotel children"—children of transience and transit. Their father had his own business; he went to Chelsea to refresh his acquaintance with the irascible Carlyle (whom he cleverly pronounced to be "the same old sausage, fizzing and sputtering in his own grease"). But the children—between glorious cab rides—embarked now on their new career of exploring "the great bleak parlours of the hotels."

FOR NOW, HARRY saw less of hotel lobbies than his siblings. Shortly after his arrival in London and his outing beside the lanterns of the growler, he came down with a high fever that kept him in "the great fusty curtained bed" of his hotel room. A few days later, as the Jameses prepared to leave London for the Continent, Harry's illness blossomed into the chills and night sweats of malaria. Henry and Mary theorized that Harry had caught the "dull seed" of this disease a year before at the family's vacation hotel on Staten Island. But the typical incubation period of malaria is ten to forty days, and a Manhattan mosquito may have in fact been the culprit. It may have bitten Harry in his old bedroom, a few days before the departure of the *Atlantic*, while he was dreaming of future empires.

In the mid-nineteenth century, during the infant years of immunology, many physicians still thought malaria was caused by "bad air"—the meaning, in fact, of the disease's name in Italian. Accordingly, the Jameses may have worried about staying in London, with its infamously soupy and unbreathable atmosphere, during Harry's convalescence.

At any rate, Henry and Mary decided that their boy was well enough to travel. They also hired a courier, a kind of live-in travel assistant, to help them handle the challenging many-stage trip to Geneva, where they would enroll their sons in the much-discussed Swiss schools. This "black-whiskered" Italian, named Jean Nadali, would help them to crowd into cabs, railway carriages, and Channel steamers—the eight Jameses and their "fresh-coloured, broad-faced and fair-braided" French maid, Annette Godefroi, freighted with them from New York.

To be a "hotel child" was to travel in an entourage, sick or well, no matter what.

∾

WHEN THEY REACHED Paris in July 1855, the Jameses put up at the Hôtel Westminster in the rue de la Paix, in the heart of the old city—a hostelry that guidebooks recommended for families and described as "much frequented by English travellers." Henry later gave this hotel a sour review in the *Tribune*, but their balcony, the five James children soon discovered—as they leaned on it in the summer heat—overlooked the New Louvre.

At the time of the Jameses' visit, this fresh addition to the medieval palace of the Louvre had reached the imposing final stages of its construction. The new wing of the palace featured a grand wall of sculptured Napoleonic generals that immediately caught Harry's attention. Eagerly, the boy ran his eyes over this wall of generals and war heroes, and the achievements of the Bonaparte family struck deep into his consciousness.

Maybe Harry's fever magnified the impression; maybe the stimulating summer lights and scents of France worked their magic. But Henry, not previously disposed to favor warfare, marveled at the Louvre and its generals, at "such a galaxy as never was or should ever be again." He gloried in the "shining second Empire, over which they [the generals] stood aloft and on guard, like archangels of the sword."

This new extension to the Louvre marked the high ambitions of the French Second Empire, a dictatorship of Napoléon's nephew Louis Napoléon—an "empire" that had been founded by a coup d'état four years before, in 1851. The return of Napoléon's family, to be sure, had given birth to a peculiarly reactionary government for reform-minded Americans like the Jameses to admire, and the mercurial Henry gave this new emperor mixed reviews. His children would be both fascinated and repelled by the new leader—once thought to be a liberal reformer, as their own father claimed to be. They were also riveted by his wife,

Empress Eugénie—the former Spanish noblewoman Maria Eugenia Ignacia Augustinia de Palafox y Kirkpatrick, who, incidentally, was part Scottish-American, like the Jameses themselves.

The children would also focus on the four-month-old Prince Impér-ial. Harry long remembered the prince's baptism at Notre Dame, the lucky baby ensconced "in the splendid coach that gave a glimpse of ap-pointed and costumed nursing breasts and laps." Beside the coach rode the "*cent-gardes* [imperial guard troops], all light-blue and silver and in-tensely erect quick jolt, rattled with pistols raised and cocked." It was theatrical stuff, and it stirred the astonished twelve-year-old deeply.

His balcony view of the Louvre had already made enough of an im-pression. As the family's few days in Paris passed and Harry's condition fluctuated, the boy continued to obsess over the New Louvre, this mon-ument to art and bourgeois empire. He plunged into a lifelong obses-sion with the Napoleonic dynasty, which he would consciously and unconsciously link to the upstart imperious Jameses themselves.

Later, Harry declared that the elegantly arched and gaslit windows of Paris had been revelatory to him. He hugged the "whole perfect Pa-risianism I seemed to myself always to have possessed mentally—even if I had but just turned twelve!"

When the dashing Italian courier the Jameses had brought with them from London took Harry and William to see the magnificent artworks of the Louvre Museum, Harry's enthusiasm for Paris only grew. The boy was having a good day with his illness, but still he hung "appalled but up-lifted, on brave Nadali's arm." This arm figured distinctly in Harry's memory of the scene, and Jean Nadali would provide Harry an early in-stance of the Italian cheerfulness he would love later in life as well as an instance of companionship and support he would long remember.

In the palace, Harry swooned over the flamboyantly gilded Louis XIV–style Galerie d'Apollon. The glamour of this grand salon struck right into his heart—though William was evidently less impressed by such French flourishes. "People talk about Paris being such a beautiful city!" William later wrote to a friend in New York. "I never was more disappointed in my life than I was in seeing Paris." As for his brother's more rhapsodic reactions, William had his own interpretation: "Harry sentimentalises, as usual."

But the deeper object of Harry's admiration—if a definable one existed—was already lost in a golden fog.

⊷

THE FAMILY SOON left for Switzerland, switching at Lyon from the fledgling state-run Paris-Lyon Railway to more sluggish horse-drawn vehicles. In 1855, the small, fractured railway companies of Europe—though spreading tendrils everywhere—hadn't reached as far as Geneva.

One cool, bright summer morning the James entourage set out from an "ancient inn," the Hôtel de l'Univers, journeying toward Switzerland in hired "post" carriages. These conveyances came complete with postilions—brightly costumed attendants who rode on the coach horses' backs instead of driving from the front of the carriage like British coachmen. These men "bobbed up and down," strangely military, as the carriages rolled.

Harry, still feverish, roosted on a padded plank slung between two seats, nested among the family's luggage. For him, at least in retrospect, this leg of the journey was to glow with "the romance of travel." The steep hairpin roads into the high hills of the Jura recalled the novels of Stendhal that Harry would come to love, *The Red and the Black* (1830) and *The Charterhouse of Parma* (1839), romances full of coach trips and mustached postilions. In a telling contrast, William preferred the buckskin frontier tales of Thomas Mayne Reid, the Irish-American forerunner of Western writers, whose popular plays like *Love's Martyr*, staged in 1848, had transfixed audiences in the Jameses' New York.

As the carriages rumbled on, the teetering Harry soaked in exhilarating sights. He took in ancient stone villages, white-bloused and red-skirted peasants in *sabots*, or wooden shoes, a ruined castle—and finally, after a long day of jolts, an inn that received them with the comforts "of abated illness and of cold chicken."

⊷

ONCE IN GENEVA, the Jameses moved their trunks into their first palace—or at least the narrow slice of a palace that Mary and Henry could afford. The Campagne Gerebsoff, or Gerebsow, boxy and classical, actually billed itself as a villa. For his *Tribune* readers, Henry described the house as "a stone's throw" from Geneva, amid rich and rolling countryside. The city the Jameses had chosen, French-speaking and gracious, also counted itself as the hometown of the severe Protestant theologian John Calvin (born Jean Chauvin in 1509), so that their new residence embodied a strange conflict that was endemic to many nineteenth-century Americans. Geneva mixed Calvinism, the strict demon that had sometimes scourged Henry's and Mary's past, with joie de vivre, the permissive demon that would taunt their children's future.

The villa's wide, lush gardens ran down to the junction of two fledgling Alpine rivers, the Arve and the Rhône. When Henry and his children flung open their new windows, they confronted the snowy crag of Mont Blanc towering over a grove white and fragrant with orange blossoms. Their apartments, shaded from the summer heat by huge spreading trees, contained five or six handsome rooms rented from an invalid Russian lady, the Countess Gerebsow, who provided them with ample meals. In the evening, she performed on the piano for them "the most exquisite *morceaux* [little pieces]." And she charged the family only ten dollars a week, "as if our tie was one of friendship instead of francs," Henry enthused.

Wilkie, the third James son, blossomed in this household, this warm yet stimulating transplantation from the Russias. Just ten years old, Wilkie made special friends with the Jameses' gentle hostess. He also made it his job to regale his sick brother with the countess's colorful history as the wife of a Russian cavalry officer, thus convincing Harry that the fun-loving and food-oriented Wilkie had a "superior talent for life."

Seven-year-old Alice, meanwhile, got a different view of the villa from a strict Swiss governess named Amélie Cusin. In Switzerland, with its Calvinist heritage, the raising of girls was an especially disciplined business, and the young woman kept a close watch over little Alice. In fact, Mademoiselle Cusin provided the whole family what Harry later called an "extrusive but on the whole exhilarating" personal presence. *Extrusive* is a geological term, pertaining to lava. Though it was Harry's word, it may well have captured how Alice, as a little girl, experienced her severe tutor.

In Geneva, Alice's brothers' education had a much more lenient character. Their new school, the Pensionat Roediger in nearby Châtelaine, initially boded well. William and Wilkie enrolled, full of both excitement and qualms; Harry, still intermittently suffering from malaria, stayed home for the time being. The boys' new institution (charging a tony $350 a year) offered a playground as large as Washington Square and came complete, Henry noticed approvingly, with gymnastic equipment and a "nine-pin alley." It showcased an international sampler of well-mannered boys, "amply fostered and directed."

When Henry and Mary visited the school, Henry painted a utopian picture of the new education he saw opening up for his sons.

> They go down every fair day to the Rhone to bathe, of course under watchful care; they go twice a week to a swimming school upon the lake to practice swimming; they ramble all about the delicious neighborhood, in short excursions with their teachers; they make long pedestrian tours in the Summer vacation across the Alps; they sometimes visit Italy, sometimes some German city; they invade the fastnesses of the Jura; they ride on mules and donkeys; they pluck the wild strawberries; they drink at the wayside fountains; they eat the bread and honey of the mountaineers as they pause to avoid the noon-day sun; they inhale all the day the untainted air of those grand solitudes; and they sleep at night in barn or chalet a sleep so sweet, I am told, that every angel who waits on health and innocence unquestionably conspires to minister it.

Such a "modern" and experiential school avoided the harsh and narrow methods that Henry abhorred. But was this the famous "sensuous education" Henry had imagined and had tailored for his children? Just what did Henry mean when he used this famous phrase? Did he want to educate his son's senses—or allow them some limited form of sensuousness? Tours and mule rides and wild strawberries abounded in both sensory and sensual experiences. Swimming contributed to the "health and innocence" that the school claimed to promote, even if it also involved a certain amount of bared flesh. Henry loved that the school fostered his children's imaginations and stocked them new experiences, even if he didn't exactly specify, himself, where such lyrical field trips were supposed to lead them.

Before the end of September, however, Henry had seen more of the school's flaws, partly through his homesick sons' complaints, and abruptly changed his tune. The quixotic father now reversed his former enthusiasm and pronounced the Swiss schools "greatly overrated." Nurture at the Pensionat fell short, he concluded, of what he and Mary could provide, and they could furnish it for a smaller cost.

Home schooling appealed to both of the exiled parents, who had very little else to do but focus on their children. The decision to yank the youngsters out of their new school was also a result of Henry's perpetual impatience, his boredom at the villa, and the toothache that the *bise*, the seasonal north wind of a Geneva autumn, had inflicted on him. The "glamour of the Swiss school" had indeed turned "stale"—and in record time. Henry, as his daughter, Alice, later remarked, essentially qualified, himself, as a "delicious infant," and one who was easily bored.

But another, less examined force probably worked to change Henry's mind.

⁓

WILLIAM, AT THE age of thirteen, had quickly tired of plucking wild strawberries. His growing adolescent discontent probably contributed to the transformation of his father's once-worshipful view of this experimental Swiss schooling. Henry may have soaked up William's attitudes, being highly susceptible to his children and their opinions. He was happy enough, he admitted, to have the children "settle" the moves that the family made. Both Henry and William, anyway, had similarly restive temperaments. According to Alice's later opinion, William closely resembled his father in his "entire inability or indifference 'to stick to a thing for the sake of sticking.'" And he didn't want to stick now, any more than his father tended to do.

William would remember Geneva as a "queer old city"—and as such a very mixed experience for him. Characteristically, he found the new areas along the blue lake beautiful, but the old quarters struck him as sinister and saturated with black. As for his school, William's judgment proved simple and peremptory. The "Swiss schools," he wrote a friend, "are all humbug."

Henry sometimes indulged his offspring's whims, but as often, it was his own moodiness that changed his children's daily routines, if not their whole universes. The young Jameses grew up borne on the shifting currents of Henry's emotions and desires, and buffeted by them. What he valued today he might despise tomorrow, and he had the power to turn his tastes into his children's entire world. Like some capricious Greco-Roman deity, Henry could build a city, fill it with treasures, and then wipe it out before their eyes. He could annihilate any friends they had made, as if with a thunderbolt. With only a moment's notice, he could carry them away to some mountaintop arising from his over-heated imagination.

✌

IN EARLY OCTOBER 1855, a post coach carried the Jameses back across the Jura hills into France. In Paris, they had trouble finding lodgings because of the Exposition Universelle, or World's Fair, of 1855. A heavy Gothic-style Palais d'Industrie, or Palace of Industry, had been built in the Champs de Mars, stocked with agricultural and industrial exhibits from thirty-four countries. Under the auspices of the emperor, Paris was attempting to compete with earlier world exhibitions in London and New York, but its only obvious superiority was a dazzling array of Bordeaux wines. In such an atmosphere, the Jameses no doubt felt like rushed, unwelcome travelers in this haughty and expensive capital.

Soon back in England, they happily took refuge in the old-fashioned and homelike Gloucester Hotel, at the corner of Piccadilly and Berkeley Street, on the edge of aristocratic Mayfair. There "a fatigued and famished American family found . . . a fine old British virtue in cold roast beef and bread and cheese and ale," as Harry recollected it. Such a meal reminded them more of home—and British cuisine would become a comfort food for Harry, obsessively, in later life. The ale no doubt stimulated his and William's adolescent intensity, already very much alive in any case.

In this early Victorian London, children like William and Harry were allowed to taste the ale, which perhaps helped in the savoring of what Harry later called the "thick gloom of the inn rooms, the faintness of the glimmering tapers, the blest inexhaustibility of fine joint." At their age, their father had drunk hard liquor, and both of his sons were potentially susceptible to enjoying such pleasures too much.

In the London of this era, such ubiquitous chophouses specialized in bland British dishes like boiled beef, snipe kidneys, steaks and chops served on metal plates, and of course turtle soup, made with imported sea turtles. (The later Victorian delicacy mock turtle soup, famous from Lewis Carroll's *Alice in Wonderland*, was made from calves' heads, easier to come by than the disappearing marine reptiles.)

Such grisly cookery accounted for why London, with its "colossal proportions," consumed almost a quarter of a million bullocks a year, along with almost two million sheep, an unknown number of turtles, and three million tons of coal. Smoke blanketed the city with a smoggy, cinder-flecked pall that disrupted astronomical observations as far away as Reading. London also had a record number of "gin-shops"—gin being a very cheap and accessible drink for the working class—but these establishments were frequented mostly by women, as Henry irately noticed in one of his letters to the *Tribune*. Yet to the Jameses this metropolitan monster, with its bland cuisine and desperate desire for gin, welcomed them and refreshed their hopes: "There's nothing like it after all!" Mary and Henry agreed.

Hopes for English education, however, soon faded. Put off by British snobbery and corporal discipline, Henry and Mary rejected English schools and once more considered home tuition, interviewing a host of odd-looking aspirants at their cramped temporary house in Berkeley Street before choosing a Scot, Robert Thomson, as a tutor. They then moved their whole party to a bigger house in St. John's Wood at the beginning of December.

Harry remembered the St. John's Wood area, just west of Regent's Park, as packed with "lumpish 'mansions.'" But the new house, at 10 Marlborough Place, had the advantage of standing just around the corner from Henry and Mary's friends the Wilkinsons, who, unfortunately, had no appropriately aged children to replace their New York playmates. But the Jameses' new home offered, Harry recollected, "a considerable garden and wistful view . . . of a large green expanse in which ladies and gentlemen practiced archery."

The Jameses enjoyed the Christmas of 1855 in the St. John's Wood house, "draped in December densities," as Alice remembered the time.

Henry wrote an account to the *Tribune* downstairs while the children manufactured what he called holiday "bobbery" upstairs. In his letter, Henry noted that European countries were full of whimsical Christmas customs. He hoped that "St. Nicholas, the merry old elf, crossed the water to us last night, and that we are in for at least five stockings full of overflowing jollification." Celebrations of Christmas involving colorful decorations and gifts stuffed into stockings were in fact rather new to America, where puritanical customs had discouraged frivolities. In Massachusetts, the secular celebration of Christmas was still illegal in 1855. But in this matter the Jameses, worldly New Yorkers, were characteristically ahead of their time.

In England, Henry adopted his own idiosyncratic method of marking the holiday. Alice remembered that their father "used to spoil our Christmases so faithfully for us, by stealing in with us, when Mother was out, to the forbidden closet and giving up a peep the week or so before. I can't remember whether he used to confess to Mother after or not," she added. Seven-year-old Alice felt guilty and "ungrateful." But she hated that her father wrecked the surprise: "How I used to wish he hadn't done it!!" But holidays weren't the only pleasures that these unorthodox, perhaps overinvolved parents dampened or policed.

As a Christmas present that year, William received a microscope—a nudge from his father toward a future scientific career. Less sensitive about spoiled surprises than his sister, William nevertheless harbored his own criticisms of his father and his father's European project, as his rebellion against Swiss schools had shown. William later confided to Harry that he found the family's London residence "a poor and arid and lamentable time."

In William's memory, he and Harry did nothing "but walk about together, in a state of the direst propriety, little 'high' black hats and inveterate gloves, the childish costume of the place and period, to stare at grey street-scenery . . . dawdle at shop-windows and buy watercolours and brushes with which to bedaub eternal drawing-blocks." But the two got more sooty London air than their little brothers and much more than their sister, who was most often stuck at home. The brother's bond grew stronger. In his younger years, Harry had often been paired off with Wilkie; now he was old enough to circulate with the superior William, who turned fourteen in January 1856. That the two brothers "walked and dawdled and dodged" in London completely charmed Harry; he idolized William and increasingly loved to spend time in his company.

At the same time, the archaic social pageant of English life fascinated Harry as it appalled the hypercritical William, the "queer old obsequiosities and appeals, whinings and sidlings and hand-rubbings and curtsey-droppings, the general play of apology and humility." Harry loved the whole spectacle of Victorian London:

> the postmen in their frock-coats of military red and their black beaver hats; the milkwomen, in hats that often emulated these, in little shawls and strange, short, full frocks, revealing enormous boots with their pails swung from their shoulders on wooden yokes; the inveterate footmen hooked behind the coaches of the rich, frequently in pairs and carrying staves, together with the mounted and belted grooms without the attendance of whom riders, of whichever sex . . . almost never went forth.

Such rich customs riveted the aesthetically inclined Harry, and later in his life, such "picturesque" images would prove for him the artistic superiority of the Old World—already giving him an identity distinct from William, who loudly sided with America whenever he could.

Many accounts have taken Harry's bond with Europe at face value. But the pageantlike scenes that appealed to him as a twelve- and thirteen-year-old also held a more personal and internal meaning, hinting at Harry's budding theatricality, his later love of costume and pageant, and his incipient sexual stirrings—the staves of the footmen here exciting him much as Napoleon III's gun-bearing *cent-gardes* had done in Paris.

Amid these strange and colorful scenes, the two eldest James boys had only each other—another telling factor in their development. They "knew no other boys at all, and . . . we even saw no others . . . save the essentially rude ones," Harry would remember. Their tutor, Robert Thomson (later to instruct Robert Louis Stevenson), kept them for only a few hours between breakfast and lunch. He'd been hired to teach them

Latin, but the James boys actually handled only one textbook, *Lamb's Tales from Shakespeare*, and received no stronger remonstrance for idleness than "Come now, be getting on!" in a heavy Scots burr. Thus the boys' education amounted chiefly to rambles in London, with each "sport[ing] a beaver," a hat of close-clipped fur, on his head. They argued whether they were going to refresh their art supplies at Rowney or at Winsor and Newton. They hiked long distances in the teeming streets in order to wolf down "buns and ginger-beer."

London could be glorious, but it was also chill and bleak, with plentiful hazards; it wasn't altogether the England they had imagined from the books they'd loved back in New York. Harry noted that in Europe there were "little boys in the streets who stared at us, especially at our hats and boots, as at things of derision—just as, to put it negatively, there were practically no hot rolls and no iced water." Even for Harry, Europe had its disadvantages.

William, a far less romantic character than his brother, assessed the drawbacks of Europe more quickly and critically than Henry did. In his letters to friends back home, he expressed irritation as often as admiration. William tallied up, in his annoyance, the ignorant views that Europeans held of Americans. He was surprised that they viewed Americans as exotic and fanciful creatures. "Few English boys know that the English language is spoken in the United States!!" William reported to his friend Edgar Van Winkle. Likewise, William was astonished that one otherwise intelligent shopkeeper wondered whether he "came from New York by the Cape of Good Hope." Another one "thought Americans had no beards"—a mix-up perhaps involving Native Americans, who generally grow little or no facial hair.

Harry's barber had asked him, unaccountably, "if it was not very muddy in AMERICA?" No news of America seemed to have reached England since the last of His Majesty's governors vacated. Dickens, on his earlier American adventure, hadn't minded the mud—though he'd execrated the widespread and equally viscous American vice of chewing tobacco, which necessitated sawdust on every floor and spittoons in every corner.

William heard a welter of critical viewpoints that bothered him, even if he admitted that "such ignorance is rare." These misunderstandings added to his personal sense—common to teenagers but acute in William's own case—of not being known or understood.

⁓

THE JAMES CHILDREN enjoyed the advantages of London but often, as isolated Americans, felt abandoned there. They had to figure out the complexities of English money, manners, and cookery, often without much parental assistance. No wonder they "breathed inconsistency and ate and drank contradictions," as Harry remembered. "The presence of paradox was . . . bright among us," he would later recollect. Paradox meant cultural confusion as well as family conflict, in their cramped temporary digs. Harry judged their exposure to foreign complexity as "wholesome." But European cosmopolitanism, not to mention the intensity of their family life, would in fact complicate their young lives with unexpected frustrations.

Seven-year-old Alice didn't get to go out as often as her brothers; she saw more of improvised nurseries than European streets. Alice's features were a pixielike version of her brothers', but she shared with them even at this early stage a solemnity and intensity and light, piercing eyes. She was impressionable, being the youngest member of the family—one reason, probably, why she was absorbing more French in Europe than her just-older brothers Wilkie and Bob; she would come to talk like a native. In London, she remembered walks with the children's governess, the volcanically Swiss Mademoiselle Cusin, in the "grey dusk" of London. She especially recalled one visit to a hatmaker in the northern part of the city. Here decisions about a bonnet forced her to try to accommodate "the millinery point of view of Neufchâtel with that of the Edgware Road," but Alice, at seven, was cowed by the intricacies of bonnet design. The hat she ordered "came forth green shirred silk and pink roses," and she remembered, "My infant soul shivered, even then, at the sad crudity of its tone." Pink, then as now a signature color of little girlhood, didn't combine well with the other colors of Alice's imagination.

Such clashes built sophistication in the young Jameses, but they also caused distress and confusion. When upset, the children clamored to tell their tales simultaneously at the family dinner table at St. John's

Wood. Their mother and Aunt Kate, though sympathetic to their diffi-culties, remained pragmatically focused on holding the household to-gether, with Mary dismissive of foreign ways and more attentive to Harry than to the other children. Their father, though always most in-terested in William, tended to depart into worlds of his own—as he of-ten went to visit men of letters or of science. Increasingly the James children were left stranded on unfamiliar boulevards; they had to de-pend on one another to get by. Yet, often coming into conflict in their close quarters, they had to depend on their own intelligence even more. Braininess in the James family was becoming a matter of survival. And their household upheavals had only just begun.

BY JUNE 1856, Henry and Kate, scouting ahead, found the family a new pied-à-terre in Paris. Henry, eternally anxious and discontent, in-tended to settle his family in the city for two years—a veritable eternity in his calendar. Their first stopgap rental, at 44 Avenue des Champs-Élysées, overlooked a cobbled courtyard with a pump in it. It stood across the street from the Jardin d'Hiver, a showpiece greenhouse left over from the recent exposition, with its international crowds gaping at steam engines. This glassed-in winter garden sheltered tropical plants, hosted chamber-music concerts, and lit up the night with a grin-shaped swag of "little coloured oil-lamps."

Harry later remembered this "odd relic of a house," which belonged to an absent plantation owner from Louisiana. He recalled the glassy polish of the floor, the slick, steep staircase, and the "redundancy of mirror and clock and ormolu vase." It was the kind of house where a child could get lost or feel alone, on a summer afternoon, as the sun streamed down from the windows, hushing everything.

William, playing the critic in what was probably an admiring imita-tion of his father, penned a witty and hostile description of the place to his friend back in New York.

> Our house is furnished "à la française" . . . There are six gilt legged armchairs . . . Naked gilt babies all over the ceiling. Gilt stripes all over the walls; gilt sofas, gilt other chairs, gilt fender; huge gilt clock

and candelabra; gilt wood work; gilt every thing. There is a gilt clock in every room in the house except two—Every two weeks a man comes in to wind-up and regulate-the-clocks, which are not-one-like-any-of-the-others, and all wrong.

With so many shifts of scene, William's own life may have felt "all wrong," too.

William and his brothers now had a new tutor, one Monsieur Lerambert, who'd written a slim volume of verse and who spoke ten languages. At least William was now studying German, Latin, and arithmetic—and with his quixotic father on days when the tutor didn't show up. And finally William's French was improving. He boasted that he knew "about ten times as much French" as he did at home.

Better French, though, didn't brighten William's attitude, and he resisted admiring Paris. Most visitors in the 1850s and 1860s noted the vast modernization of the city, the "gigantic improvements" undertaken by the new emperor and his urban planner, the Protestant and Alsatian-born Baron Georges-Eugène Haussmann. As one guidebook of the era put it, "Many unwholesome purlieus, teeming with poverty and vice, have been entirely swept away, to make room for spacious squares, noble avenues and palatial edifices."

This gigantic construction project—Haussmann's widening of avenues, regularizing of facades, erecting of cast-iron lampposts—hadn't yet reached the shabby-genteel western reaches of the Champs-Élysées, where the Jameses had their rental. But even young William was aware of Louis Napoléon's recent order "that all the houses should be whitewashed"—whitewash, incidentally, being a mainstay of a dictatorship.

Ultimately, William admitted to his New York friend that the chalk-white city was "beautiful in some parts" and "wonderfully improved by the 'emperor.'" But still William put quotes around "emperor," remaining skeptical of Napoléon III's coup d'état as well as his urban planning. He found the Tuileries gardens "the ugliest place of the kind [he] ever saw." He approved, though, of the new and strange paving, "asphalte," on the streets—an innovation, actually, to keep the Paris mobs from building barricades out of uprooted paving stones, just as the widened avenues were to allow the emperor to bring artillery pieces into the city, to halt any protests by the city's famously insurrectionary inhabitants.

Soon the family moved to a "wide-faced apartment" in the rue d'Angoulême-St.-Honoré (later renamed the rue de la Boëtie), near the recently refurbished rue de Rivoli, where American tourists now thronged in cafés, and the expanded Palais Royal, built by Cardinal Richelieu in 1624 but now lined with commercial arcades where these same Americans shopped for chocolates, perfumes, and florid antiques. With fountains, palaces, and squares all around them, the Jameses had seldom lived in so fashionable a neighborhood.

After their New York and St. John's Wood row houses, William felt that a French *appartement* was a "queer way of living," with the family "all huddled up together on one floor." Here the Jameses once again found themselves almost literally on top of one another, scrimping their way in tight quarters because Mary found Paris so outrageously expensive.

Mary worried about costs because the quality of her family's home life mattered to her, especially during this exile. Especially with Kate as her frequent companion, she carried her own spruce model of an American household on her travels with her, finding French morality and domesticity beneath her contempt. Even so, her sons made their own arrangements at a nearby café and began the day with "softly-crusty crescent-rolls" and weak café au lait that Harry savored and remembered. Second Empire Paris offered many odd and luxurious dishes: chateaubriand (beefsteak), pigs' pettitoes exposed in shopwindows, *perdix aux choux* (partridge with cabbage and sausage), and *canard aux navets* (roast duck with turnips), a "popular dish." It was all a long way from their mother's simple and sensible fare of brown rolls.

If they tired of Paris, the family could take a carriage excursion to airy, elegant Passy (where Benjamin Franklin had lived), its sister mansion-district of Auteuil, or to the brand-new Bois de Boulogne (opened in 1852), a crescent-shaped park of lakes, *allées*, and woods on the west side of the city. Henry Senior, calling them "parvenus," sniffed at the young trees in this replanted royal hunting ground. Both he and William kept up a skeptical front, even when the family rambled through the improved center of Paris in what Harry, also ironically, later called "the blinding glare of the new Empire." One night, Harry plunged into the festival atmosphere of the rue de Rivoli, holding Mary's hand: "My mother anxiously urged me through the cross currents and queer contacts, as it were, of the great bazaar . . . rather than depending on me for support and protection." In a common but telling custom of the Victorian world, Harry tended to hang on the arms of his protectors, whether those arms belonged to the valiant Jean Nadali, the impatient William, or the worried Mary.

The family went everywhere together, and with tutors and governesses in the house, they didn't always separate even for school. Their involvement with one another, always primary, tightened to an almost incestuous pitch. In Paris, as in London, William and Harry were competitive daylong companions, and Wilkie and Bob, now eleven and ten respectively, squabbled with each other and pinched, poked, and otherwise tormented Alice, who would remember their hard "heels grinding into [her] shins" during one of the family's many carriage drives.

Meanwhile William, more subtle and verbal, but no less masculine in his impositions, now openly mimicked his father's trenchant speaking style and used it to persecute his siblings. He also offered his talents for family entertainment. Since the Jameses attended the theater more rarely in Europe (Henry and Mary didn't speak much French), William wrote his own "theatricals" for the drawing room. In these, he exercised his acerbic wit, exposing particularly Alice to sardonic ridicule. When not with her governess, Alice often sat with her mother and aunt, learning to sew. Her brothers, especially Harry, could sometimes be kind, she remembered. But as with William's teases and Bob's shoves, they often roughly vented their frustrations on her as an easy target.

Alice suffered, similarly, from a visitor the family hosted in Paris, the English novelist William Makepeace Thackeray. Having discomfited Harry by calling him "Buttons" upon seeing him in the Mathew Brady daguerreotype, the great man comically laid his hand on Alice's "little flounced person" and exclaimed in mock horror, "Crinoline?—I was suspecting it! So young and so depraved!"

Crinoline, linen stiffened with horsehair, was a material that had reached a height of fashionability in the 1850s; it provided support for spreading (and in this case "flounced") skirts, as a substitute for the layered petticoats of the past. Alice's costume showed that Mary had arrayed her daughter in the latest style—and one perhaps too adult for her seven or eight years. The novelist's witticism exposed Alice to yet another embarrassment, like the incident of the bonnet, on the sensitive female topic of clothes. In an era of feminine fripperies, Alice would be vulnerable to critiques of her appearance; at the same time, she wasn't sure how much she cared about the vestiary interests of her mother and aunt, when she was often more engaged with the books she borrowed from her brothers.

Like Thackeray, William loved to practice his wit on everybody around him, and he did so, as he did everything, with a fourteen-year-old's aggressive edge. Harry remembered William, since their New York epoch, as a "constant comic star." He assumed the role of family performer as a way of acting out his own feelings. One of his favorite harangues was to make fun of his small sister. William's teasing, Alice later reflected, had made her stomach tremble, and she had felt herself "a cave of emotional borborygmus" under the brunt of his blistering monologues. But William could also be sweetly attentive to her. As Alice's biographer Jean Strouse has shrewdly observed, she was "an object of fraternal curiosity." William wrote "beautiful poetry . . . in honor of Alice," and even sang it out loud, with a strong effect. William also sarcastically pretended to be Alice's devoted suitor, gleefully mocking the sentimental trappings of romance. Alice knew her brother was clowning, but her sibling's obsession with the role of mock lover left Alice confused and uneasy.

Also, these very attacks hinted at William's own isolation in a landscape devoid of accessible girls. Such faux flirting illuminated William's increasing hormonal frustrations. In later years, courtship would prove one of the most agonizing possible endeavors for him—and partly because of this early family confusion. William was battering his way through puberty, and his adolescent sexual energy played out, as often happened in Victorian households, inside the family—and with complicated future results for himself and for Alice.

Harry's own admiration was most focused on his more confident brother William. Harry liked Wilkie, with whom he also spent quite a bit of time, but he worshipped William and felt honored by the distinction of his big brother's attention. Still, Harry didn't confide everything to the formidable William; he also had a private life he would continue to keep separate. Already, at thirteen, he was beginning to write plays and stories. His first extant letter, about a boys' theater club, is addressed to Edgar Van Winkle, William's friend from Fourteenth Street. The letter shows both Harry's thespian interests and his desire to be a part of his brother's world. "I was asked w'ether I wanted to belong here is my answer. I would like very much to belong."

❧

WITH THEIR DAYS in one place beginning to build up, the Jameses welcomed a getaway—although it was necessitated by economic conditions more than three thousand miles away—to Boulogne-sur-Mer in the summer of 1857. The family needed to cut costs, and they thought they had found a gracious solution.

A somewhat fashionable "watering place," Boulogne faced the English Channel near its narrowest point and housed a large British exile community. The town aspired to combine, with its seaside promenades and wind-raked gardens, "a certain amount of English comfort with French taste"—an attractive holiday package for the Jameses, who were unsure, as was characteristic of Americans abroad, whether to associate themselves with the bold, frivolous French or the staid and powerful English.

During one excursion in the summer heat, Alice received an impression of Harry as a different brand of boy than William. After a long dusty drive in the countryside and a dismal birthday party, Harry dangled forlornly on a swing. Suddenly he exclaimed, with new insight into a conventional phrase: "This might certainly be called pleasure under difficulties!"

The James family found "pleasure under difficulties" quite often in Europe. And for the first time, young Alice could appreciate the wit of her more gentlemanly and sympathetic brother; it marked the conscious beginning, as she later remembered it, of her deeper attachment to him and her appreciation of his quiet wit.

Fourteen-year-old Harry had his own difficulties in Boulogne that summer—life-threatening ones, in fact. He fell gravely ill with what he later dubbed "the malignant typhus of the old days." (Aunt Kate had a special horror of unclean hotels and of the lice that caused the high fever and pink rash of this sometimes fatal disease.) Harry lay for weeks on end feeling glum and envisioning "scant possibilities." Fifteen-year-old William, attempting to be jocular, noted the shaved head and "raw-boned" gauntness of the younger boy, who was suddenly receiving all of the family's attention. William could rib Harry as well as Alice, as the children jostled one another in their tight hired quarters.

Harry's illnesses (on the threshold of adolescence) must have been formative. Deadly contagious illnesses roved the Victorian world with impunity and, even when they didn't kill, scarred the lives of many a nineteenth-century child. Harry's high fevers tended to throw him into the care of nursing females and protective males—Jean Nadali and his brother William—at crucial points. In the future, Harry would battle fewer illnesses than most of his siblings. But time would also show that he could also appear stuck, as a number of biographers and critics have noticed, in a kind of adolescent innocence that both isolated him and filled him with longing, as though Harry were perpetually confined to a sickbed.

&⁓

SOON AFTER THEIR holiday in Boulogne, the Jameses found themselves moving there in the autumn of 1857—uprooting from their third lodging in Paris (in the less-than-splendid rue de Montaigne) to take advantage of the lower cost of living in the provinces. Mary always had to pinch pennies, or sous, in order to underwrite Henry's whims and changes of scene, but now a new financial crisis in the United States had further "imperilled or curtailed" the Jameses' income. The Panic of 1857, stoked by overspeculation in railroads and real estate, got "bluer and darker," in one observer's words, every day. Soon Wall Street was "blue with collapse" and mobs from the "dangerous classes"—such as Mary James could remember from the Panic of 1837 twenty years before—took to the streets. The Jameses' share in this catastrophe amounted to the drying up of assets. Perhaps in a kind of sympathy with their countrymen, the Jameses passed a glum, wind-blasted winter beside the Pas-de-Calais, in a house with big windows overlooking the town marketplace.

Boulogne's schools enjoyed a "high reputation," and at the Collège Imperial, where he studied a variety of subjects including science and literature, William soon was in a position to take advantage of the opportunity. He and his brothers didn't usually get much extended time in schools—barely a term or two, as had happened in Switzerland and in the Institution Fezandié in Paris, a Fourierist academy of languages; still, William shone as the most committed scholar in a family of imaginative but often reluctant students. With teachers who liked him and admired his talents, he thrived in algebra and geometry. Soon he was entertaining the notion of becoming a famous engineer, like Isambard Kingdom Brunel—the legendary English designer of tunnels and bridges. "An Engineer in the present state of society is far more glorious than a Naturalist," he observed—an adolescent half-truth, certainly, in the unfolding era of Charles Darwin and Thomas Henry Huxley, "Darwin's bulldog."

Yet William himself felt more attracted to natural sciences than bridge building. He put his Christmas microscope to repeated use, longing to return to America, to "go out into the country, into the dear old woods and fields and ponds." There, he'd make "as many discoveries as possible"—finds he could claim as his own. "I'll be kicked," he declared, "if it would not be more useful than if I laid out railroads by the rules which others had made." Already, William longed to nurture his own innovations, not to pattern himself after others or repeat what had already been done. In many ways, he seemed a more practical and durable version of his iconoclastic father, though he had also declared independence from that hovering, hesitant man who inflicted on him a few rules and many expectations.

As part of his rebellion, William wasn't sure he agreed with his father's educational program. When, in another bracing shift, Henry took his family back to London in the spring of 1858, William wrote a friend that after three years abroad he thought that "as a general thing, Americans had better keep their children at home."

In a keen evaluation of his father's method, William felt he had "gained in some things but [had] lost in others." He offered his New

York friend a canny list of the pluses (learning French) and minuses (not learning math) in his schooling. But the larger picture of the advantages and disadvantages for the family as a whole was, as usual with them, maddeningly complicated. The emotional as much as the educational results were profound, since more than anything else, the Jameses qual- ified as natives of their own family, as William would famously put it. Their pioneering had welded them tightly together, but it marked them too, especially the children, with "pleasure under difficulties"—these seemingly endless removals and relocations.

Never content with any one house or school, Mary and Henry united in sacrificing their health and peace of mind for the good of their children, as they saw it. They mutually quested for the right education, the right English or Continental setting. Family life became a mania, a fascinating long-running social experiment, and one in which they all participated—though the children primarily figured as the guinea pigs of different educational systems. Still, the family became everybody's preoccupation and everybody's problem—and its experiment would be- come the Jameses' lifelong vocation.

Though the household remained Mary's province, where she reigned with the vigor of an Eleanor of Aquitaine, Henry loved to meddle in it. As a father without a decided profession (in spite of his increasingly the- ological and hence unpalatable *Tribune* letters), Henry continued to vent his time and nervous energy on his family. Like some child in a sandbox, he formed and then destroyed version after version of his children, never satisfied with the results. And these sand children, these transient off- spring of hotels, would soon get tired of this manipulation.

❧

WILLIAM, BY THE time he turned sixteen during the winter of 1857–58, had become a tall, bright-eyed, trenchant adolescent with a bony, nervous face. He was now sporting, as he boasted, a "cauda virilis"—literally, a "virile tail"—a frock coat with tails that pleased his fashion-conscious mother. (With his minimal Latin, William showed no consciousness of any more sexual meaning to this sartorial expression.) William's increasingly assertive ways, however, alter- nately delighted and threatened his father, especially because he was increasingly adapting the European experiment more and more for his eldest son's benefit. In essence, William had become in his father's eyes the "gifted child" of the family, and he would inherit much of the grandiosity and depression that his driven father had also brought from a troubled adolescence.

A letter Henry wrote to his mother from Boulogne in the fall of 1857 gave a telling snapshot of his evaluation of his children and their prospects. In it, Henry was delighted to report that his favorite son engaged in the "scientific pursuits" of which he approved. William, he hoped, would "turn into a most respectable scholar." Privately, William, who had been drawing adeptly for years, had thought of becoming a painter, and not only because the family had encountered so many artworks in Europe and because his father counted a number of artists in his wide acquaintance.

Fourteen-year-old Harry, by contrast, was "not so fond of study, properly so called, as of reading. He is a devourer of libraries, and an immense writer of novels and dramas." Though he hadn't seen his son's private scribblings, Henry judged that his second son might have "considerable talent as a writer." But Henry Senior wondered, especially with his prejudice against literary men—though he himself had courted many of them—if Harry would "ever accomplish much." What could Henry expect from this illness-prone son who liked to read but showed little interest in his schoolwork?

Wilkie, Henry's twelve-year-old third son, showed a "talent for languages" and spoke French almost perfectly. But he had "more heart than head"—a real drawback, in Henry's eyes. In Europe, Wilkie sometimes teamed up with Harry, leaving the youngest two children in the care of adjuncts like Aunt Kate or the Swiss governess.

Bob, Henry's fourth son, now eleven, possessed "ten times the go-ahead of all the rest," his father thought. Bob figured as Alice's half-demon playmate, the unpredictable and all-too-precocious *l'ingénieux petit* Robertson [the ingenious little Robertson] of the domestic schoolroom," Harry remembered, "pairing with our small sister as I paired with Wilky."

Yet Henry had already relegated these second-tier sons to an inferior future, and made no secret of it. Even William had heard his father say that Wilkie and Bob were "destined for commerce." And given the family's dim view of such enterprises, the boys must have wondered how they'd earned such a fate—except that the family's income from the Syracuse businesses and railroad bonds (now dipping precariously in value) didn't seem to extend far enough to help them.

Nine-year-old Alice also spoke almost seamless French. But her discipline at "reducing decimal fractions," as Henry observed in another letter, only fitted her for a "high destiny" in a laughable sense—especially in a family where a woman's mind and professional future appeared negligible. As far as Henry was concerned, Alice's adept French didn't even fit her for the so-called marriage market, where a woman's knowledge of modern languages was sometimes considered a social grace. Henry wasn't grooming Alice to become a future ambassador's wife.

What's more, Henry's critical view of his younger children's potential would only harden over time. By 1860, he'd have arrived at the conclusion that only William had any real ability and that the rest of his children were "none of them cut out for intellectual labors." All that strawberry-gathering in the Alps hadn't paid off.

⸎

UNDER THE SPOTLIGHT of his father's complex expectations, the gifted William increasingly agonized over the direction of his career—at his age, a more immediate matter than ever. He scoured his soul for his true future calling. "The question of 'what to be' has been tormenting me," William wrote his faithful New York friend from Boulogne in 1858, "and as yet I have come to no decision." William was sixteen, and he hadn't decided on his future career? William's agonizing might seem comical by the standards of twenty-first-century middle-class teenagers, with their cornucopia of choices. But nineteenth-century youths, even when they didn't simply follow in their fathers' professions or enroll in apprenticeships while still children, often faced rigid professional futures at even younger ages than William's. William's indecisiveness prefigured the future when young people would be allowed a longer time—entire college and graduate careers—to find and prepare for their life's work. In the nineteenth century, teenage boys were often routed into professions, often their fathers', but Henry had less objection to open-ended development than most Victorian patriarchs.

Yet William's urgency also underscored his need for Henry's love and approval. Imitating his father, William resorted to philosophy to solve his problem, launching a long, pompous, and pained chain of reasoning with the Socratic question, "In the first place, what ought to be everyone's object in life? To be as much use as possible. Open a biographical dictionary. Every name it contains has exercised some influence on humanity, good or evil, and 99 names out of a 100 are good, that is useful. But what is use?"

With a nebulous profession himself, William's father defined *usefulness* arcanely, with a mix of post-Calvinism and Swedenborgian rationalism. No wonder William felt puzzled. In addition to his own genuine conflicts on the subject, he had to try to figure out and somehow please his contradictory and mercurial parent.

Henry Senior, as his second son later claimed, had no "marked prejudices" about his sons' careers. "I marvel at the manner in which the door appears to have been held or at least left open for us to experiment," Harry recalled. Henry, no authoritarian, didn't force his sons into professions. Yet Henry's experimental open doors, Harry admitted, had a "tendency to close," even slam, suddenly and bewilderingly—such as when he suddenly switched his children's schools, just when they were getting used to them and liking them. Harry recalled "repeated cases, in his attitude to our young affairs, of a disparagement suggested as stirred by memories of his own." Henry, that is, had hated several of his own career tracks—for example, his studies at Union College in the late 1820s—and his bad memories made him even more unpredictable with his sons.

At times, Henry favored a career in the sciences for William, though he preferred philosophy; he aimed his "disparagement" at art, one of William's strong interests. With his austere philosophical prejudices, Henry labeled painting as frivolous, as spiritually debilitating. William didn't give up his drawing, but he leaned toward science as more acceptable to his father, especially after his microscopic forays in Boulogne.

WITH WILLIAM'S COLLEGE education in mind—and still stinging from their financial losses—the Jameses determined to return to America.

But what looked like a homecoming would only prove another brief stage in their itinerary of hotels and steamers. Back in the United States in the summer of 1858, the Jameses found their difficulties multiplying. They couldn't reoccupy their New York townhouse on Fourteenth Street, thanks to its inconvenient tenants. They couldn't scare up affordable lodgings in Boston. Thus Henry and Mary settled on one of the few other "respectable" options: Newport, Rhode Island.

This New England town, with its long grass and picket fences, looked "rather disorderly" to William after his acclimatization to the trimmed lawns of Europe. Henry and Mary quickly made arrangements for a "very comfortable cottage with four acres of land." And here William excitedly prepared to enter his father's old alma mater, that onetime candidate for the Ivy League, Union College in Schenectady.

But soon Henry, "stirred by memories of his own," haunted by his own youthful dissolution upstate, slammed William's door of opportunity shut. All colleges, Henry fulminated, were "hot beds of corruption, where it [is] *impossible* to learn anything." He himself hadn't, so why would William? William, sixteen and a half, felt the sting. He declared his father's view "very unjust." But as much as he longed to go to college, he knew he'd have to abide by his father's decision. Still, he (metaphorically) ground his teeth.

Tellingly, William's frustration with his father announced itself in an incident that autumn with a dog, a thin-flanked greyhound the family had acquired. In the summer heat, William and his brothers played with the animal, but the sixteen-year-old didn't bother to curb the dog, and Henry blamed him for it. The greyhound devoured apple pies and soap lard; he climbed onto furniture and chewed it. "Willy, that wretched dog is on the bed again," Henry yelled; "Willy, the dog is tearing the buttons off the sofa." Henry lectured his son on the need for discipline. Perversely, William responded by beating the dog with what he jokingly called a "savage frenzy." That was hardly what his father had had in mind, and Henry, disappointed and with tears in his eyes, railed at him: "Never, never before did I so clearly see the utter & lamentable inefficiency & worthlessness of your character; never before have I been so struck with your perfect inability; to do anything manly or . . . good."

With adolescent bravado, William brushed off this slur on his masculinity as a comic incident, portraying it to his friend Edgar Van Winkle as an enlivenment to what he considered a "dreary" home life. If on some level his father's disapproval sliced into him, William brushed off his guilt with his humorous retelling.

Worried about the idleness in his sons that he himself had caused, concluding that America was "not the place to bring up such 'ingenuous youth,'" Henry threatened to haul everybody back to Europe only a couple of months after their return. Henry was worried about what he saw as extravagance and insubordination among American young people. Despite his own history of iconoclasm, Henry was especially unfriendly to insubordination, especially William's sparks of rebellion.

Caught in the limbo of his father's indecisiveness, William tried to make the best of it. While the family hovered in Newport, William studied art with William Morris Hunt, a "New Englander of genius," a Boston painter who'd studied with Thomas Couture and Jean-François Millet in Paris and had, like the Jameses, only recently returned to America. Hunt's star student, the dashing John La Farge, immediately impressed William with his urbanity and savoir faire.

But by the spring of 1859, Henry fretted that William felt "a little too much attraction to painting . . . from the contiguity to Mr Hunt." He and Mary decided to "break that up." Clearly, Henry still hoped that William would choose a "philosophical" profession. With the aim of separating William from his and Harry's young painter friends like Thomas Sergeant Perry and of keeping the seventeen-year-old boy under surveillance, Henry finally hit on the idea of hauling the whole family back to Europe once again, this time with a plan for more ambitious education.

IN THE BEGINNING, Henry's scheme involved installing William at the fledgling "Academy," or University, of Geneva. By October 1859, the whole clan, including Aunt Kate, who wouldn't be left behind, found themselves back on the blustery Atlantic. This time, the rolling decks of their perpetual transience belonged to the steamer *Vanderbilt*, Commodore Cornelius Vanderbilt's iron-hulled Goliath.

In Geneva, the winter clouds soon lowered on the mountains. The Jameses put themselves up at the Hôtel de l'Écu, a staid city residence south of the Rhône that they had sampled back in 1856. Their new home, not far from the leafy lakeside Promenade du Lac and the Jardin Anglais, qualified as both a well-established hostelry and as an *hôtel* (urban mansion) in the time-honored French sense. That was a different way of being "hotel children"—in this case, the denizens of mansions, if only temporary ones. The luxurious houses the Jameses rented helped shape their tastes, especially young Harry's.

A surviving photograph of Harry, in Geneva in 1859, shows him posing on a patterned carpet with a stone urn and a swag of drapery beside him, with an intent look on his face. What Harry really amounted to was a youthful American tourist on a photographer's set. But his dark coat, his light waistcoat, his tie, and his doffed hat—as well as his serious, languid expression, his hip swayed a little—hinted at the splendors to which he'd been exposed and to which he would increasingly aspire. Would the traveler's hotel or the aristocrat's *hôtel* win out with these young Jameses? One of the paradoxical secrets of Harry's future literary success would in fact depend on an American sleight of hand that grew out of his adolescent travels. His life was often transient, but he liked to imagine deep-rooted forms of security and permanence. He would increasingly try to pass off the ephemeral hotels of his own actual experience as the time-honored *hôtels* of a monolithic European past.

In any case, the Hôtel de l'Écu no doubt now struck William with a sense of déjà vu. The Jameses had lived in Geneva before, and now they were back to the starting point of their educational experiments. Obediently, William parroted his father's current opinion, that a residence in Europe—though *residence* hardly captured the Jameses' transfers from one city to another—had "enlarge[d his] experience and mind" and that "nothing could be more advantageous for a scientific man . . . than the knowledge of French and German." Science amounted to William's moderate assertion of will against his father: Henry didn't exactly approve of it, but he preferred it to the dubious world of art.

Back in school, William got to cut up a cadaver—a pursuit that would influence not only his future career but his future hobbies. William would later love to dissect anything he could get his hands on. At home, in the tightly knit James household once again thrown on themselves for entertainment, William pursued a different brand of dissection. He resumed his sarcastic theatrical career with spoofed love songs in honor of his sister.

> I swore to ask thy hand, my love
> I vowed to ask thy hand
> I wished to join myself to thee
> By matrimonial band.
>
> So very proud, but yet so fair
> The look you on me threw
> You told me I must never dare
> To hope for love from you
>
> Your child like form, your golden hair
> I never more may see,
> But goaded on by dire despair
> I'll drown within the sea.
>
> Adieu to love! adieu to life!
> Since I may not have thee,
> My Alice sweet, to be my wife,
> Ill [sic] drown me in the Sea!

When she heard William perform this poem, eleven-year-old Alice took this tribute "very cooly [sic]," her brother noted. William needled his sister partly because he was bored—as he often noted in letters to his friends. Alice, submissive and brown-haired, stood in for the women William liked to imagine.

Meanwhile their father, according to Henry's old European habit, tended to go on one impulsive junket after another. William missed him and felt that without his father the family dinner table seemed "almost desert." Alice would remember that Henry abandoned his family, every so often, for a few days at a time. In fact, certain Continental cities would be perpetually marked with the memory of his mercurial departures and his "sudden returns." Quixotically, fresh from some train or steamer, Henry could reappear "at the end of 36 hours, having left to be gone a fortnight." His children were surprised to hear his voice in the house, to accidentally meet him on the stairs. Then, reunited with his family, he sat, Alice remembered, "with Mother beside him holding his hand and we five children pressing close round him 'as if he had just been saved from drowning.'"

⁂

EARLY IN THE summer of 1860, Harry and William took a week-long walk together in the Alps near Chamonix. Harry, who had just turned seventeen, characteristically hurt his foot, so that William had to nurse him, prop him up, and help him along. William, equally characteristically, brooded about his future career. He agonized over his dilemma between the arts and the sciences. The next phase of Henry's plan for William—insofar as he had a plan or held to one—involved his boys' learning the nineteenth-century language of both science and philosophy.

For that purpose, the family abandoned Switzerland in July. Henry stowed William, Harry, and Wilkie in German households. Their new hosts in Bonn, Harry remembered, "guided us to country walks and to the swimming-baths by the Rhine-side, introduced us to fruit-gardens where, on payment of the scantest tribute, we were suffered to consume off-hand bushels of cherries, plums and pears; suffered us to ascend the Drachenfels and to partake of coffee at Rolandseck and in other friendly open-air situations." That much looked like a return to the strawberry fields, the "sensuous education" of the Pensionat Roediger. Victorian adolescents were brought up to focus their appetites on the bushels of orchard fruit—and baths in the Rhine—in lieu of anything that might be considered more erotic; "dating" in the twentieth-century sense was almost entirely unavailable as a pastime, except in the carefully monitored realm of courtship—not, in any case, an option available to adolescent males like William and Harry.

Harry rhapsodized about the views and the sweetness of the fruit. William, in contrast, prosaically noticed that "plums are now 50 for a groschen." But the summer proved idyllic for him, too, although in a different sense. For William, this stay in Germany was the first time he'd been allowed away from his parents—if still under the watchful eye of his two brothers and thoroughly warned by his father against moral dangers. Henry Senior dreaded what female temptations William might encounter when living in another household, what rosy housemaid or impetuous piano-playing minx. The father worried and preached. For someone who'd touted "sensuous education," for someone who'd championed "free love," Henry had set himself against anything like premarital sex for his sons with a Calvinistic severity reminiscent of his Presbyterian forebears.

William was now sporting a juvenile mustache that made him feel free and cavalier. For Victorians, such facial hair signaled incipient manhood, and growing whiskers counted as one of the few uses of testosterone available to a "respectable" young man keenly monitored by his family. These days, Harry bent much of his energy on his wardrobe, as had shown in his studio portrait in Geneva. William proudly focused on his mustache. The monumentally repressed nineteenth century provided brothels instead of dance clubs or drinks parties for its youth. But especially among the respectable bourgeoisie, the promenades also channeled sexual energies, decorously, by means of exquisite dress for women and conspicuous whiskers for men.

Even if he swaggered a little, William still had the insecurities of an adolescent and even the tender feelings of a child. A country away from his father, who'd installed the rest of the family at the appropriately named Hôtel des Trois Empereurs in Paris, William got a little twist of homesickness. He professed, "I never value my parents (Father especially) so much as when I am away from them. At home I see only his faults and here he seems all perfection." For William, it took at least that much distance to obscure Henry's paternal defects. William, in fact, eagerly imagined a whole cozy James-family home scene. He envisioned

> Alice [at] the [window] with her eyes fixed on her novel eating some rich fruit which father has just brought from the Palais Royal, and lovely Mother and Aunt Kate in arm chairs with their hands crossed in front of them listening to Father who is walking up and down speaking of the superiority of America to these countries, and how much better that we should go home.

Yet in spite of these protestations of loyalty, William was contemplating a spectacular bit of rebellion—and one that would paradoxically help the family go home to America, once and for all. In July 1860, as if in unconscious commemoration of Independence Day, William stood up to his father. William announced a dramatic decision. He now intended, he declared, to be a painter.

William's letter must have hit the Trois Empereurs—his three solicitous parents, including Aunt Kate—like an insurrectionary bombshell. "I confess," Henry confided to a friend after the incident, "I was greatly startled and not a little grieved, for I had always counted upon a scientific career for Willy, and I hope the day may even yet come when my calculations may be realized in this regard."

Immediately, Henry scribbled to William a lengthy paternal admonishment about the potential degradations of art, outlining the superficially of such a profession in comparison to the "moral" professions, especially philosophy, that Henry favored.

William boldly countered his father's arguments. All his father's prejudices, he insisted, "ought to be weighed down by my strong *inclination* towards art, & by the fact that my life would be embittered if I were kept from it." William had had an unaffected natural inclination to drawing since childhood, and he now held on to it as a distinctive piece of himself. Such at least was his present conviction, William hedgingly added, admitting that his preferences might change. Even in his rebellion, William left himself an out.

With William's uncertainty thus dangled in front of him, Henry acquiesced. He trusted William might soon see his error and veer back to science. But in accepting William's choice, Henry also acted out of his own convenience—if in fact, in spite of his many protestations to the contrary, he had ever done anything else. For Henry himself felt ready to go home to the United States; he was, after all, back to ranting about "the superiority of America" to his patient wife and sister-in-law. In Europe, as Harry later observed, his father's "isolation had been utter." After the demise of his *Tribune* letters, Henry had been cut loose from his old friends and colleagues and from the American intellectual scene—insofar as he'd ever belonged to it. The discontented Henry was eager to go home, and so he had his own reasons for accepting William's decision to be a painter.

Henry booked a passage back to New York on the *Adriatic*—a former Collins liner, the grandest yet. But two years before, with Edward

Knight Collins's bankruptcy in 1858, this trophy steamship, after only one voyage under the American flag, had been ignominiously sold to the British Royal Atlantic Navigation Company, also known as the Galway Line. If the Jameses had first arrived in Europe on the *Atlantic*, a symbol of American defiance and pride, they retreated from it aboard an embodiment (as contemporary American newspapers saw it), of "our national defeat and humiliation."

Still, William hoped now to elevate the James name to the pantheon of American painting, along with those of Benjamin West and Thomas Cole. At any rate, with this well-placed nudge from its headstrong eldest son, the family's exotic European expedition had come to a sudden end, and they were forced to turn their attentions toward a country that, on the brink of a national crisis over slavery, had, even in the twelve months since they had last seen it, been drastically transformed.

IMPLOSION

On the night of October 3, 1860, a week after the Jameses' return to the United States, a full moon beat down on Fifth Avenue and on long columns of jubilant young men parading past cheering crowds. The street's solid brownstone shopfronts and shut-tered plate-glass windows flared up in the "artificial daylight," as the fledgling *New York Times* called it, "of more than ten-thousand torches." Endless columns of the Wide Awakes—the partisans of the gaunt west-ern upstart, Abraham Lincoln—snaked through the city in drilled mili-tary formation, wearing caped uniforms and high-crowned glazed caps much like those that would soon litter the battlefields of the Civil War.

Under big, swaying portraits of Lincoln, under banners splashed with antislavery slogans, the Republicans marched to brass bands blar-ing "Hail, Columbia," "Yankee Doodle," and even the "Marseillaise." Their political-club regiments—a characteristic feature of highly charged, militarized political parties of the nineteenth century, but more stirred up and belligerent than usual—paved the avenues with thousands of torches that raised a red, smoky glow. Magic lanterns, fit-ted with slidelike glass-plate transparencies—a familiar medium by this time—threw fiery images and slogans on theaters and concert halls. As it progressed through the city, the parade squeezed between jam-packed lines of spectators whom the police strained to hold back. Gaudy, decorated wagons carried ladies in star-spangled robes or batteries of flame-throwing Roman candles. The columns thronged down Four-teenth Street, east of the Jameses' former New York home. They rallied in Union Square, where the grand procession of torches, banners, and colored lamps swept in a "patriotic war dance round and round the as-tonished statue of Washington," as the *Times* described it, before the rounds of stump speeches and fireworks began.

Yet, even in New York, the Wide Awakes' enthusiasm was far from universal. On Fifth Avenue, some of the big houses were brightly lit up, with anxious, applauding gentlemen looking on from grand front steps and "fair Republican Floras" throwing bouquets and waving handker-chiefs. But many of the marble mansions remained silent and blacked out. On Broadway, the mammoth St. Nicholas Hotel was crammed with "strangers from all parts of the country" who hung out of every window—including delegations that had come by rail and steamboat from Maine, New Hampshire, and Massachusetts. But the more conser-vative New York Hotel next door, the haunt of Southern planters, defi-antly kept its façade dark.

Such contrasts on the parade route underscored the deep fractures of a bitter four-way presidential race: Lincoln and Stephen Douglas vying for the North, John Bell leading in the border states, and the proslavery John Breckinridge dominating the Deep South. Though Lincoln was a moderate westerner—married, in fact, to a slaveholding Kentuckian, Mary Todd—seven Southern states, led by South Carolina, had made it clear that they would leave the Union if Lincoln's antislavery Republi-cans took power. The James family, for five years distanced from the politics of their home country, had returned just in time for one of the most divisive and momentous presidential campaigns in American history.

Perhaps to avoid this furor, the Jameses had already vacated the city to which they had so recently returned. By the night of the Wide Awake march, Henry Senior and Mary had moved on to Newport to open up the family's new rented house. Bob and Wilkie had traveled up the Hudson to visit a paternal uncle. Harry and William may actually have lingered in New York and witnessed this event—though it is likely that they escaped to Newport the previous morning. Harry claimed total ig-norance of American politics, which he forever associated with "the busy, the tipsy, and Daniel Webster." Harry was preoccupied with an impending reunion with his good friend Thomas Sergeant Perry. Yet he couldn't fully give himself over to pleasure; as was so often the case, he was also embroiled with his family and their perpetual convulsions: his "services as an able-bodied and willing young man" were required by a travel-worn family "almost riven in twain," he wrote his friend, with comic exaggeration. "I think nothing of heaving a 60 pound trunk over my head."

On the verge of young manhood, eighteen-year-old William and seventeen-year-old Harry were unlikely candidates to join up with the Wide Awake marches that were erupting all over the Northern states, from Wisconsin to Rhode Island. With a father who was antislavery in principle but hardly active in the abolitionist movement, the James children had grown largely out of touch with the United States, with the tensions developing in their absence. But they had not been able to ignore the situation, even in Europe. Four years before, in 1856, a Southern sympathizer had cudgeled Charles Sumner, a senator from Massachusetts, almost to death on the floor of the U.S. Senate. In Paris, young Harry had witnessed a partisan Northern lady who was devastated and "in tears over the news." A year later Sumner had dined with the Jameses in their apartment on the rue d'Angoulême. Harry, thirteen at the time, had felt disappointed that the famous wounds on the senator's head had healed up.

More recently, the James boys had become increasingly involved in the news from America as reported by the newspapers in Bonn or Paris. Still they were taken off guard, astonished really, by the dire situation to which they'd returned: a new, tense America, where provocative, defiant abolitionism was pouring out onto the streets of New York, Boston, and Chicago.

⤬

THE NEWPORT THAT greeted the James boys when they stepped off the steamer appeared to have eschewed the fury of the larger cities. The old Rhode Island town was tiny, a shrunken grass-grown port with weather-beaten, tightly packed clapboard houses built by Quaker sea captains in more prosperous days. The town seemed lost among the colorful autumnal woods and big ponds and lonely rocky promontories that surrounded it.

The Jameses' house at 13 Kay Street lay in the heart of the old town, only a few minutes' walk from the harbor. Chosen for its price and location near to schools, the family's latest residence also lay close to the root of Bellevue Avenue—a dirt road striking southward into the fields. By the 1880s and 1890s, this farm track would sprout the grandiloquent stone mansions of the Belmonts and the Vanderbilts, but the Newport of 1860 was a ramshackle country town, with picket fences and wind-bent apple trees, less than vibrant or exciting, even though the rustic landscape of stone walls and dilapidated barns would transform, during the next few decades, into a Monte Carlo of the superrich.

The James children found that Newport had changed even since the year before. The town was halfheartedly, perhaps unwittingly, transforming into a seasonal tourist resort. With its small cluster of new hotels and summer houses—spreading farther along the harbor every year—Newport was steadily growing in fame and already hosting well-to-do visitors from across the United States.

❧

ON THE BRINK of the Civil War, in fact, two Newports struggled for supremacy, and the Jameses, newly arrived as usual, rather quickly deduced that they didn't exactly belong to either one.

The first Newport was a money-crazed but democratic American resort that welcomed visitors to the gregarious porches of the huge hotels inland from the harbor: the Atlantic, the Ocean, and the Bellevue. There, well-dressed and fashionable mobs devoured five-course meals in the long-tabled dining rooms, promenaded on the gingerbread verandas, whirled to polkas in the steamy chandelier-lit ballrooms, and flirted everywhere.

During the season, from July to September, parades of carriages clogged the roads to First Beach. There under a white flag, in "mixed" swimming, men and women—heavily armored in neck-to-ankle nankeen bathing suits—frolicked from nine to noon. (Men swam nude, under a red flag, in the less fashionable afternoon.) In the evening, landaus, four-in-hands, and dogcarts jammed Bellevue Avenue, so that the fashionable and the curious could air themselves. Everyone wanted to see and be seen.

The Jameses had more in common with the other Newport of genteel "cottagers." Increasingly, these property-owning visitors from New York, Philadelphia, and Boston staked their claim to Newport in the summer. By 1860, their "cottages" were proliferating and, like ladies' skirts, ballooning to gigantic sizes. In 1851–52, Henry's friend William S. Wetmore had built a "cottage" called Château-sur-Mer. He would expand it by the 1870s into an ostentatious granite mansion with manorial oak paneling, a colossal four-story tower, and a daring French hipped roof.

The Jameses, though, weren't rich enough to commission such fantastical palaces for themselves. They weren't prominent enough to circulate with the new crop of outrageously rich New York nabobs like August Belmont and Erastus Corning. As intellectuals and radicals, they envied but avoided the ultrafashionable culture in which ladies were required to change outfits nine times a day—even if Mary and Kate, when younger, might have relished such displays.

With their European varnish and their limited means, the Jameses mixed more with bookish Bostonians than flashy New Yorkers. Knots of prominent Boston literati summered in Newport: the poet Henry Wadsworth Longfellow; the abolitionist Thomas Wentworth Higginson (friend of the utterly unknown Emily Dickinson); and the social reformer Julia Ward Howe—soon to become famous for writing the lyrics to "The Battle Hymn of the Republic."

Eager to mingle with this crowd, the Jameses had rented a house that was huddled close to the Redwood Library, an august Palladian structure designed by the luminous colonial architect Peter Harrison. There the elder James boys could indulge in their favorite pursuit of reading as well as pursue their artistic studies with William Morris Hunt a few streets away.

The Jameses had arrived in October 1860, at the tail end of the season, though a few cultivated visitors still strutted on Newport's boardwalks and promenaded through its rutted, elm-shaded streets. As the fall deepened and the night air took on a bite, the family watched Newport transform into an isolated backwater, an island cut off. They conducted their daily business around shuttered "cottages," deserted grand hotels, and cliff walks where the beach roses had matured into rosehips and where autumn winds cut with an edge. Newport might have provided them shelter, but it looked increasingly bleak, especially with the dire political developments of the winter of 1860–61. Harry later dubbed Newport "the barren isle of our return from Europe."

Yet it could be argued by those who truly knew them that Newport suited the Jameses perfectly, even though Henry would rather have found a house in Boston. This cosmopolitan village perpetuated the rarified existence the family had been living in Europe. Newport's resort-town detachment suited the Jameses' own. With its sophisticated and educated denizens, Newport had "its opera-glass turned for ever across the sea," as Harry later put it. It spelled another stopgap arrangement for them, another out-of-season "watering place" like Boulogne-sur-Mer—though the town's clapboard would have reminded the Jameses more of their old summer haunts on Staten Island than of European spas.

As this fateful election season unfolded, Newport proved detached, too, in other respects. The town was basically neutral ground between North and South—as much as any New England town could be—in deference to the many Southern visitors who had escaped here from the fierce summer heat since colonial times.

Because of this distinct Southern presence, Newport's boardwalks and unpaved streets were vulnerable to sudden encounters between Massachusetts abolitionists and South Carolinian planters. To make matters worse, in October 1860, the month the Jameses settled in, Northern abolitionists marked the one-year anniversary of John Brown's raid on Harpers Ferry—a volcanic subject for any Newport shop or drawing room. (The raid was an event that had had a "sharp reverberation" for the James family even when they had been on the other side of the Atlantic.)

Yet, being "natives" of their own family more than citizens of the United States, the repatriated Jameses would feel the conflicts among themselves flaring up as much as the country's angry, divided politics. If the Jameses were "almost riven in twain" by unpacking, they had seen only the beginning of the challenges and disruptions that would soon unfold. Henry bribed William with another microscope soon after their arrival, a further nudge toward a more suitable career. Harry would find his own distractions in art. With something more like a fixed home, the James family would soon see clashes between its protective and ambitious elders and its increasingly bottled-up adolescents itching to rebel against parental control. Even Mary's good sense and serenity would be taxed as she prepared, with Kate's help, to hold an increasing headstrong family together in yet another new town.

WAR LOOKED INCREASINGLY likely, but Henry's first priority was William, and he soon settled his son at William Morris Hunt's studio at his wood-framed house, "Hilltop," a few blocks away. The Jameses had come home not because of the national crisis but "to learn to paint," as Harry remembered the family saying—with their friends and neighbors staring or laughing at such a bald and simple-sounding statement. But for Henry Senior at least, the phrase was ironic. The sooner William had his way, his father reasoned, the sooner he'd see the emptiness of being a painter.

Defiantly, the nervous eighteen-year-old William, with watery eyes, a scraggly mustache, and a rather startled hangdog expression that shows up in daguerreotypes of the time, plunged into his dream of becoming a painter. William's childhood of scribbling and sketching—as well as his long and complex struggle with his father—came to a head in Hunt's studio. A second-floor extension on a carriage house, it was a cool gray space with north-facing windows for even light, surrounded by the big trees of old Newport. It provided the sort of quiet where a young man might actually distinguish himself.

In this setting, across from the Old Jewish Cemetery, William spent the dwindling afternoons of the autumn of 1860 sketching and daubing. With Alice stowed in a girl's school a few streets away, with Wilkie and Bob shipped off to Concord, William had only Harry—left to drift in and out of his own imaginings—to haunt him in the studio as he tried to work.

Along with Hunt's most advanced student, John La Farge, a Boston lady or two "hovered and flitted." Or so Harry recalled. Women were not often seen in such places, but Hunt, a radical Bostonian, believed that women could actually be taught to paint. Yet, as there were no regular students but the self-motivated La Farge, William had the "vivid and whimsical" attention of his teacher mostly to himself.

William Morris Hunt, a gaunt and mustached Don Quixote lookalike, was, in the eyes of the status-conscious Jameses, the only teacher for William. One of the most famous American painters of the day, Hunt was known for his lucid, powerful depictions of ordinary life (*The Hurdy-Gurdy Boy*, 1851, and *Girl at a Fountain*, 1857) as well as his portraits of notable Americans such as the Adamses and Shaws of Boston, a class who were increasingly choosing Newport as a summer destination. Harry remembered him as "all muscular spareness and brownness and absence of waste." He went on to describe the painter's bridged bony nose, heavy eyebrows, and discerning glare. As fond of European pleasures as the Jameses, Hunt had studied in Paris with Thomas Couture and Edouard Frère, two proto-Impressionist "Barbizon" painters. Also in France, Hunt had fallen under the influence of Jean-François Millet, whose bold, naturalistic depictions of peasants had inspired some of Hunt's early field-girl masterpieces. Now, at thirty-six, this gifted New Englander, the brother of the notable architect Richard Morris Hunt, had alighted in Newport to paint landscapes of the rocky seaside meadows.

To seventeen-year-old Harry, Hunt showed occasional but kindly interest. He may not have known what to make of the quiet young man. A photograph from later in the Newport years captures Harry much as he must have appeared during his time at the studio. In the shot, Harry looks every inch the dandy he aspired to be: he wears a smart English double-breasted coat, with one glove on and one glove off, and his half-interested gaze wanders away from the camera.

Harry secretly yearned to return to Europe, to visit luminous Italy and escape dull Newport. After five years abroad, Harry's tastes had been formed in the lush settings of the family exile—the castles, palaces, and museums for which he'd nourished his own private appreciation by way of the novels of Stendhal and George Sand. Like every one of the other James adolescents, he longed for independence and escape. He began to consider art his best hope for a more exciting life. At least the circle of students and amateur painters at Hilltop provided Harry with the cultivation and refinement he craved. Conversation was an art and a staple at Hunt's house, and it was served up with trays of wine and exotic Azores cakes provided by Hunt's wife, Louisa.

But despite his lively interest in Hunt's coffee-drinking social circle, and in the house stuffed with pictures and plaster casts of classical sculpture, Harry spent most of his time crouching in his elder brother's shadow. William, as always, was the better student, working at his studies with an inspired dedication that impressed and cowed his younger brother. "I also plied the pencil," Harry remembered, but not so "critically, rapidly or summarily" as William, who was always full of teases, jokes, and sudden inspirations. He seemed to have perfected the performances he'd debuted back in the James parlor-theater in Europe.

Harry himself hadn't enrolled as a regular student; one artist in the family was plenty for his father. Instead he read or daubed unobtrusively in the downstairs room of the studio while the superior William rubbed elbows upstairs with the impressively cosmopolitan John La Farge, who was destined to paint the ethereal landscapes and mythological pieces for which the nineteenth century would exhibit a preference. He would eventually make a career for himself as a decorator and an artist of stained-glass windows at Harvard (where his famous "Battle Window" is located) and at Trinity Church in Boston.

Harry, meanwhile, did his best to sketch Hunt's casts of famous sculptures. For him, these hours of absorption, as he latter commented, "hummed with promise." He hoped he would grow more adept at the work and felt particular pride in his rendition of the "sublime uplifted face" of Michelangelo's *Captive* from the Louvre. But, significantly, the high-strung young artist didn't attempt to render the dying captive's male nude body, even with its precautionary Victorian fig leaf.

In an atelier, though, the fig leaf couldn't always be counted on. One morning, Harry was drawn to the main studio upstairs, where William and the "serious" students were sketching a live nude. The model, red-headed and athletic, turned out to be the Jameses' handsome cousin Gus Barker, who had gamely volunteered to pose on a pedestal, as Harry long remembered, "divested of every garment." Harry found Gus "the most beautifully made athletic little person, and in the highest degree appealing and engaging," an intrepid youth who would afterward, in his Civil War service, glow with a "rare radiance" of dedication and self-sacrifice. The mere vision of what he called this "beautiful young manly form" threw the reticent young man into turmoil. Both his cousin's boldness and his brother's competency at sketching him overwhelmed Harry. To judge from his later account of the incident, the scene ignited the future novelist's fears and doubts about his own competency and masculinity.

Harry knew of no words to describe his fascination with his cousin's unabashed display. The word *homosexual* wouldn't even be invented for another couple of decades. In a time when sexual desire of any kind was largely a taboo subject, especially for a repressed and gentlemanly teenager like Harry, sensuality often expressed and legitimized itself through the safer and more sanctioned category of art, in which a nude could appear safely aesthetic rather than provocatively sexual. Characteristically, Harry understood this crisis not as an erotic but as a professional one; all his hopes of becoming a great or even competent painter crashed inside of him. He felt that he might "niggle for months over plaster casts and not come within miles" of William's deft handling of the naked young man. Their cousin's "perfect gymnastic figure meant living truth," Harry felt. Yet it was a sexual as well as aesthetic truth that Harry would spend much of the rest of his life trying to understand. At that moment, he could only cope with the encounter by turning away and pocketing his drawing pencil.

For Harry, the rarified space of the studio provided a different kind of education than his father or Hunt had intended. It was just one of the places where the James boys would confront some of their first measures of "manhood." In antebellum America, manhood provided a largely unexamined ideal reinforced by same-sex schools, differentiated dress, and stiff religious conventionality. The disabled, ultrasensitive Henry Senior, who constantly lauded "manly" virtues, hardly fit the mold. But his sons would ultimately negotiate with even more complex permutations of acceptable manhood in the years to come.

❧

HENRY SENIOR, WHO had argued about education and careers with all four of his sons, decided to enroll his two problematic younger sons in school at Concord. He wanted to do something definite with two boys who hardly knew what to do with themselves. In the yellow sunshine of the autumn of 1860, Henry took his young teenagers to Massachusetts—grateful to find himself, along the way, among American maples, oaks, and dogwoods instead of the "parvenus and comical" foliage of the Champs-Élysées and Bois de Boulogne. Henry was also buoyed by his reunion with Emerson. When the party arrived at the philosopher's tall-chimneyed white Federal-period farmhouse—called Bush, with its nine famous chestnut trees—they had to wade "up to [their] knees through a harvest of apples and pears" to find Henry's onetime mentor. Intoxicated by his harvest, Emerson greeted them as (Henry thought) "a cordial Pan . . . in the midst of his household, breezy with hospitality and blowing exhilarating trumpets of welcome."

At Emerson's recommendation, Henry was about to enroll Wilkie and Bob in an academy run by an abolitionist agitator named Frank Sanborn. Soon after their arrival, Henry and his sons discovered the members of this reformer's odd school throwing themselves into a theatrical celebration of Hygeia, the ancient Greek goddess of health ("hygiene"), in a local field. The scandal of this school—the reason that Henry considered it one of the "magnificent experiments" of American civilization—was that it daringly educated boys and girls together. Thus both sexes freely consorted in this colorful Victorian neopagan frolic. Henry seems to have been willing to experiment with his younger boys, but he apparently never considered this school for Alice, who was kept close to home in a more traditional girls' school at Newport. Though attracted as always by experiment, Henry hardly took the education of girls as seriously even as that of his two younger and more problematic sons.

An early trial balloon of coeducation, the Sanborn academy attracted the offspring of the progressive New England intelligentsia, including the son of the celebrated novelist Nathaniel Hawthorne and his wife, Sophia Peabody. Julian Hawthorne fondly remembered the school as an old red schoolhouse repainted gray, "surrounded by the great, fresh outdoors." Louisa May Alcott directed dances and theatricals. Henry David Thoreau guided the students on walks through the woods. The student body went swimming or skating on Walden Pond, held masquerades at the Concord town hall, hosted regattas on the river, and even sneaked off for "a week's encampment on Monadnock Mountain— boys and girls, judiciously selected . . . chaperoning themselves on horseback parties." The school glowed with the idealism and rebellion of Concord-group New England, and it presaged the shape of the liberal education for generations to come. It would offer young Wilkie and Bob a taste of liberty and luxury they had seldom been allowed— especially because, for years, they had been educated at whatever school had been convenient for William—or Harry, with whom Wilkie had often been lumped.

Frank Sanborn provided a dynamic model for uncertain adolescents like the younger Jameses. He struck one student as "a tall, wiry, long-limbed young scholar with brilliant dark eyes . . . beneath a great shock of black hair." Volatile and earnest, he delicately balanced "passion and self-control." Most of Boston knew Sanborn, though, for his passion— as a fiery antislavery advocate who had critically visited the South and had vocally supported the Underground Railroad.

A bosom friend of John Brown, Sanborn had been one of a handful of men informed about the raid on Harpers Ferry in advance. That same spring, in 1860, Sanborn was arrested and questioned, even though his sister stalked the streets of Concord armed with a revolver to prevent the deputies from kidnapping him. Sanborn welcomed at his school a daughter of John Brown whom Henry would meet on his visit to Concord. He described her as "tall, erect, long-haired and freckled, as John Brown's daughter has a right to be." Like many Northerners who could be described as abolitionists, Henry saw slavery as a moral problem for white people more than an injustice against blacks. He felt enough sympathy with the movement to want to kiss this child, inwardly, "between the eyes."

Henry privately worried that Wilkie and Bob would want to kiss the girls, too—that they would ruinously fall in love at school. Just as he had sat William down to warn him against the dangers of sex, he probably did so with his younger sons. Even as a former "free love" radical, Henry seems to have held views about sexuality that differed little from those of other Victorians: in his writings he emphasized the sanctity of marriage and the importance of moral discipline. Accordingly, he hoped the matronly Mrs. Clark would keep an eye on the "urchins under her roof." As the future would prove, both of Henry's young sons were tinderboxes of hormones.

Neither fifteen-year-old Wilkie nor fourteen-year-old Bob found much attraction to learning, even in these interesting new circumstances. Back in Europe, in fact, Bob had wanted to voyage home and open his own dry-goods store—a throwback to his ancestors, perhaps, but anathema in a family that prided itself on remaining genteelly untarnished by business. Bob, though, also leaned toward artistic pursuits. Like William, he had a yen for painting. He was musical as well. A portrait of him painted about this time by John La Farge shows a sensitive youth in concert dress, playing a flute, his face a chiaroscuro of worry and sensitivity. Yet he didn't apply himself, his father thought. Both Henry and Mary considered Wilkie easygoing and unmotivated and Bob moody and quixotic; besides being younger sons, they were seen as having less talent than William or Harry.

At home these younger sons had always been disadvantaged by the unique talents of their elder brothers, but both Bob and Wilkie made their own distinctive marks at the Sanborn academy. Julian Hawthorne singled out both young men as "perfectly delightful characters, though, of course, unknown outside their circle of personal friends." They impressed Hawthorne with exactly the cosmopolitan qualities that, in the James household, in close comparison to their brothers, they seemed to lack. Hawthorne found them "good-looking, open-hearted fellows, [who] had been at school in Switzerland and Paris, were at home in England, spoke several languages, put on no airs, but were simple and hearty as sailors on leave. They had the best manners and no unfortunate habits."

As the New England winter set in, Wilkie got crushes on a couple of the girls: Grace Mitchell and Maggie Plumley. And in the spring he made himself genially famous during a regatta, a splendid event like all the Sanborn rituals. Sanborn waved a flag, and the race commenced. Wilkie raised his oars, evidently feeling that rowing would come naturally to him as the most athletic of the James boys. He was dressed for the occasion in smart rowing whites, and he had a new and highly varnished skiff provided by his father. But he spectacularly lost the race for the simple reason that, for all his European travels, he'd never been allowed to row a boat.

Otherwise, according to Julian Hawthorne, Wilkie dazzled the other students with sartorial gifts that would have delighted his mother. He was "the glass of fashion and the mould of form, but never the least clothes-conscious or la-de-da; good-natured to the marrow." Hawthorne described Wilkie as the "best dressed boy in the school" but also engaging when he chose to speak. He saw the young man as full of the good humor for which he was already famous in the James household.

> [Wilkie] was of middle height, broad-shouldered and symmetrical, with a good head, well set, and a smiling countenance. Peg-top trousers were in fashion then; Wilkie's were the widest and most enviable [at Sanborn]. He was sixteen years old when he came to us [actually fifteen], but appeared older by two or three years, being self-possessed and having the bearing of a man of the world. In the company of the ladies he was entirely at ease, and devoted; they all loved him.

Hawthorne remembered Bob with more measured praise, as "robust and hilarious, tough, tireless as hickory, great in the playground, not much of a scholar." The youngest James son was "full of fun and pranks and audacities." But, the mannerly Julian Hawthorne hastened to add, Bob was still "a perfect gentleman in purpose and practice."

Although few realized it, both of the younger James boys were unhappier than they revealed, and neither was very interested in being a gentleman. In the summer of 1862, Bob refused to return to the Sanborn school—threatening instead to run away to sea. Though Wilkie did return to Concord, he soon missed his brother, who had gradually replaced Harry as his closest friend in the family. Wilkie would leave the academy, with true James impulsiveness, after only his second year.

With their easygoing charms, though, the younger James boys forged friendships with the sons of the New England elite more readily than their more self-conscious elder brothers had done so far. Wilkie even contemplated a buckskin trek to California with Emerson's son,

Edward. But Henry Senior's hovering solicitousness and Edward Emerson's frail health soon derailed the boys' adventurous project.

∽

ALICE, LIKE EDWARD Emerson, had patches of nervous illness herself, though little is known about her health in this early period of her life, except for mentions in family letters that she was ill. Thirteen years old in 1861, Alice had been relegated to the Kay Street house and the girls' school on nearby Church Street. At home, she was expected to shadow her mother and aunt, as the females did needlework in the parlor or discussed family matters, including her brothers' more glamorous doings.

Besides his son, Edward, Emerson also had two daughters, Edith and Ellen Emerson, who had also attended the Sanborn school and through their father had gotten to know some of the James children. In December 1861, at the ages of twenty-two and twenty respectively, these genial, intelligent young women decided that they wanted to take the much younger Alice under their wings. With the Christmas holidays approaching, they took the bold step of inviting her up to their father's estate in Concord.

Such companions might do Alice worlds of good, and the thought of these older girls' superior lives in Massachusetts seems to have filled Alice's head with new possibilities: the mere prospect of the visit threw this sensitive girl into an ambivalent state of excitement and panic. Initially her father, as he reported to a friend, gave her "carte blanche to go at any expense of health"—a reference to what her parents saw as her nervous fragility. Concerned, perhaps too much so, Mary worried if it would be possible, with so much overstimulation, to "reduce [Alice] to the ordinary domestic routine," as her father phrased it—to keep her happy in the sober household role for which her mother and aunt were grooming her.

With his view of women as helpmates, Henry believed Alice should not be indulged in too much frivolity; she should be brought up as self-sacrificing and morally responsible. Soon enough he felt he had to step in and stop the plans for Alice's Concord outing, disappointing his daughter's hopes. The Emerson house, he told Alice, somewhat patronizingly, wasn't heaven—only a "foretaste" of such delights. If she was good, she'd have a happier future, perhaps even a Swedenborgian heavenly reward. But Alice was disappointed and mortified. She cried herself to sleep in her room.

Awkward, sensitive, dressed in embarrassingly different French bonnets or plainer fashions concocted by her two mother figures, Alice was already a zealous, obsessive reader of novels and, since Europe, a speaker of near-perfect French. So serious and timid a girl could easily put off her classmates at her provincial dame school, whose pupils modeled their behavior on the expensive floral and sentimental pages of *Godey's Lady's Book* (founded in 1830), the queen of early American women's magazines.

Alice often languished in what her main biographer called the "enforced uselessness" of Victorian female adolescence. She evidently took to heart the lessons of self-denial inculcated in nineteenth-century girls; Alice suffered from the self-discipline her moralistic father and her efficient mother exacted from her. If she escaped for a walk—the customary Newport panacea for unhappiness—she often wandered alone along the short, wind-battered cliffs of Newport, wrapping herself in introspective gloom. Or so she later portrayed herself. Later, she didn't remember Newport parties or outings, but her desire to visit the Emerson girls shows that she had a natural youthful yen for novelty and companionship, and no doubt found some of this in a town where her parents and brothers found a good deal.

Alice's self-confidence was fragile, however, and it would be tested even further by the arrival of some other young women more apt than she was to defy what Alice would later describe as Newport's "artificial and sophisticated" manners. In Europe, she had at least been the only young female in the family and, as such, an object of at least some attention. But now, with the debut of her more self-assured female cousins, Alice would find herself relegated, ever more unhappily, to the quieter corners of a brightening Newport sociability.

❧

THOUGH MARY AND Henry claimed a wide acquaintance in Newport, some of their closest friends there were Edmund and Mary

Temple Tweedy—relatives of Henry's by marriage who combined both intellectual ambitions and private means. The Tweedys, like the Jameses, had traveled in Europe and had recently returned to live in style on nearby Bellevue Avenue. On visits they brought with them their wards, first cousins whom the James children hadn't seen in a while. And these cousins, now grown up, would soon catch the James boys' attention as never before.

The four Temple girls who now swept back into the Jameses' lives were daughters of Henry's younger sister Catharine, who, along with her husband, had tragically died of tuberculosis in 1854. The Tweedys had then adopted the six children, Mary Temple Tweedy being their father's sister. In previous years, the girls and their brothers, with their touching histories, had attracted much sympathetic attention. (For Harry, their orphan status gave them a kind of glamour.) But when they stepped onto the scene at Newport, these Temple cousins, blossoming into their teens, highly interested the James boys—though Alice didn't care much for them.

Katharine ("Kitty") Temple, Harry's age, added a lively, soothing female presence to the Jameses' parlor, usually stocked with talkative sons. William especially welcomed her and, in 1861, painted an expressive portrait of her—with all her clothes on—as she must have looked during these visits. In William's rendering, Kitty, seen in profile, bends over her sewing, her eyes lowered in modest contemplation, her rich dark hair drawn back scrupulously over her ears. William's rendering of Kitty's "very handsome" head and shoulders later struck Harry as worthy of Édouard Manet.

When Kitty wrote William a friendly letter in November of the same year, his reply, overflowing with his characteristic overstatement, betrayed his enthusiasm for his correspondent. All jubilance in his letter, William scribbled musical notes (marked "boisteroso triumphissimo") and exulted, all dance and acrobatics: "chassez to the right, cross over, forward two, and summerset." He was so overjoyed with Kitty's communication that he had to recover himself with "violent exercise" outdoors—a brisk walk being the Victorian equivalent of a cold shower. In a day when the marriage of cousins was considered desirable, William's ecstatic admiration for Kitty seemed quite natural and laudable.

But Mary Temple (known as "Minny") caused even more of a sensation. When she made her debut at Kay Street, she arrived "slim and fair and quick, all straightness and charming tossed head," as Harry remembered. Unlike her more sedate older sister, Minny dazzled the room with her forthright, unconventional conversation. Recently, the seventeen-year-old confided, she was forced to confront a fashionable young man named Dance in order to tell him that he was "the most affected creature" she had ever seen. She also spoke of having "bullied" her inanimate literature tutor, one George P. Bradford, out of impatience with his plodding teaching.

As Alice enviously noticed, Minny often searched for "delightful" social engagements; she had plenty of charm to expend on Newport's drawing rooms and balls—where the James boys were not to be found. Loving wit and lively company, she laughed out loud at comic sketches written by her friends, yet her streak of defiance sometimes attached itself to more serious concerns. After reading a letter Lincoln sent to the *New York Tribune* in August 1862, in which the president proclaimed that his aim was to save the Union and not to end slavery, Minny pronounced herself "highly disgusted" with what she considered Lincoln's "very very weak" position: "I don't at all like the way he looks at Slavery," she declared.

With her frank nonconformity, Minny fascinated both William and Harry, though their admiration of her differed in kind. William, always enlivened by attractive women, felt the power of Minny's beauty and magnetism. But her opinionated and rebellious character cooled his ardor. Harry, in contrast, approved of Minny's originality and, beginning to find it natural to forge bonds with women, conceived a deep and abiding affinity for her. He was at least as "dazzled," he admitted, by the good looks and charm of Minny's brother Will, who was to die at the Battle of Chancellorsville in 1863.

Harry found Minny a "young and shining apparition" whose nervous, shifting sensibility fascinated him. She was a character who compelled wherever she chose to appear. Harry observed that she was both promising and vulnerable, prone to "noble flights" of hope as well "touchingly discouraged drops." Minny, who was to inspire much in Harry's future writing, appealed to the young man like some strong-minded classical goddess. He saw in her the "very muse or amateur priestess of rash speculation"—his own rash speculation as well as hers. That is, Minny dared, contradicted, and cut through life in a way that left the more inhibited Harry breathless. Minny combined masculine daring (her "rashness") with feminine emotiveness in a unique manner that intrigued Harry, who at the age of eighteen could not summon her ease or imitate her iconoclasm.

A photograph from 1861 shows the object of Harry's interest leaning pensively on one hand and outfitted in a dark dress with puffy, theatrical sleeves. Her startlingly short-cropped hair makes her resemble a moody, slender Hamlet more than a demure chignoned young woman. Minny's hair had been shorn off because of an illness, but she seems to have made dramatic capital out of her damage.

On seeing this photograph, William comically blamed the "catastrophe" on Minny herself: "Was she all alone when she did it? Could no one wrest the shears from her Vandal hand[?]" Attributing madness to his cousin in his usual ironic way, he also revealed his deep discomfort with Minny's unconventionality. "I have often had flashes of horrid doubts about that girl," William wrote her more predictable sister Kitty; "occasionally I have caught a glance from her furtive eye, a glance so wild so weird, so strange, that it has frozen the innermost marrow in my bones." William was joking, of course. Minny could not have cared less; she confided to a friend that she actually gloried in her reputation for "insanity."

As for her own view of her cousins, the eloquent Minny returned both brothers' compliments. She stamped her cousin Harry "as *lovely* as ever" and judged William "the same strange youth as ever, stranger if possible."

❧

EDWARD EMERSON VISITED in Newport in 1860 and 1861, witnessing the congenial battlefield that was the James household, particularly since all four boys had reached their teens. It daunted even Emerson's son to stay, as he later put it, with this "brilliant, original, and affectionate" family. Mealtimes never failed to rouse competitive spirits. Whatever stocky and mild Wilkie happened to say, he was "instantly corrected or disputed by the little cock-sparrow Bob," Emerson observed. Then Wilkie would good-naturedly fend Bob off, with Harry also chiming in to deflect Bob's taunts. It was a fast-moving blood sport.

Bob, barely flustered, only ratcheted up his invective, bringing Henry Senior into the fray as a guardian of minimum civility. Eventually, he would be drowned out by William as well as the other three never-silent sons. Dinner knives swiped dangerously in gesticulating hands.

Mary James, "bright as well as motherly," took the shy Edward under her wing, laughed reassuringly, and said, "Don't be disturbed, Edward; they won't stab each other. This is usual when the boys come home." Alice quietly enjoyed this rough and tumble, "smiling, close to the combatants." But at least at this stage she didn't join in these high-spirited contests. Girls were supposed to remain decorous and not raise knives—or voices, for that matter.

Alice would remember her Newport coming of age as less joyful than her brothers. For her, young womanhood at a stylish resort didn't signal the entertaining flirtation and expensive dresses that many female visitors relished at Newport. Instead young Alice spent her time, she wrote years afterward, "absorbing into the bone" the lesson that "the better part is to clothe oneself in neutral tints, walk by still waters, and possess one's soul in silence."

In spite of a tendency toward painful self-denial, Alice had a style of dressing at the age of twelve or fourteen that wasn't restricted to the drab or neutral; her mother saw to that. But in spite of Mary's supervision, Alice didn't often appear as lovely as she had in Paris in 1857, wearing a neat Parisian dress and three-quarters coat with flared sleeves, her hair scraped back and crowned with a braid across the top of her head. She was a young woman now, with her own distinct if quiet opinions, and not simply a doll that her mother and Aunt Kate could dress.

Alice's father, uninterested in her wardrobe, cared deeply about what he saw as her moral development. As Alice remembered, he often "anathematized"—railed against—his daughter's shortcomings, as he saw them, which evidently included a headstrong streak. "Oh, Alice, how hard you are!" he lamented. Henry envisioned the adolescent woman as an adjunct to her mother and aunt—a patient, self-sacrificing component in his own emotional support system, who was expected to listen patiently to his visions, tirades, and obsessions. He couldn't understand why Alice, often confined to the house, was sometimes unhappy and disappointed; her mother certainly never did. Alice, unlike most of the women Henry had known, often feigned hard indifference to her parents' criticisms. Yet she was highly sensitive, and her father's words stung her deeply: "I can remember how penetrated I was," she later wrote, choosing her words carefully, as she had been taught, this complicated "hard core" still difficult to account for.

A photograph of Alice in Newport in 1862, at the age of fourteen, shows her in a plaid dress decorated with ruffled strips and puffy sleeves, but her expression has grown deadly serious; her face appears mature, plain, and bruised. The change originated, no doubt, in the "muscular circumstances," as she called them, of the increasing self-denial required by her father. "How I recall the low grey Newport sky of that winter of 62–3," Alice later wrote, "as I used to wander about over the cliffs, my young soul struggling out of its swaddling-clothes as the knowledge crystallized within me of what Life meant for me." That meaning would have to unfold covertly, in the shadows of her brothers' more approved and exciting lives.

Alice's brothers, it's true, also dealt with bouts of youthful gloom and discouragement. They also wandered the rocks and cliffs of Newport— one of Harry's favorite haunts being the grass-tufted ledges of the Paradise Rocks, where he sometimes trekked with his friend Thomas Sergeant Perry. Sometimes he roamed by himself, "lone and perverse even in [his] own sight." Harry remembered, "Nobody in those days walked, nobody but the three or four of us," so that the James pedestrians had to themselves a vast and roadless region of overgrown pastures and breaker-washed promontories to explore. Newport differed from the Yorkshire of the Brontë sisters. But to the novel-addicted young Jameses, it was just pretty, rocky, and stormy enough to allow for romantic brooding.

Yet the family's visitors almost always noted the dash, the wit, and the cheerfulness of the young Jameses, indoors and out. Ellen and Edith Emerson made a visit to Newport in the summer of 1862, when the

Jameses had just moved from Kay Street to Spring Street. The new house was ivy-covered, built of fieldstone jointed with a rough and rustic plaster, and ringed with pines and willows. Henry was expanding the third story, to created a view of the ocean and squeeze in a few more bedrooms for the crowded family, which still embraced the dedicated but hardly influential Aunt Kate.

During the Emerson sisters' visit, Wilkie and Bob treated them to a voyage on the bright blue of Narragansett Bay in their small, trim sailboat, which the two had christened, after their sister, the *Alice*. (Bob loved sailing, so William jokingly referred to him as "the honest Jack Tar of the family.") Back at the house, taking in the whole family scene, the twenty-three-year-old Ellen pronounced William "the happiest, queerest boy in the world" and Harry "the most lovely, gentle, and good." Wilkie was "equally queer and equally good," and young Bob impish and intriguing, with "dancing eyes." Though she had once tried to cultivate Alice's friendship, Ellen left no thumbnail sketch of the Jameses' daughter.

With the James family, every day was a "Carnival," according to Ellen Emerson. Comings and goings were continual in Newport, but one day in particular so many family members and visitors surrounded the dinner table that Mary James, always the keeper of the peace, lined up all five of the Jameses on one side of the table so that nobody else would have to crowd in among her firebrand offspring. Sizing up the five James teenagers, Ellen and Edith "contemplated the vivacious row with rapture." Bob, sitting beside his mother, also surveyed his siblings, down to Alice sitting beside her father. "Look at the five potatoes!" he piped up. And the visitors agreed that "it did look very funny to see the row of plates with a great round potato on each."

At these high-spirited meals, even potatoes could become the object of humor. Another young visitor, E. L. Godkin—the future founder and editor of the influential liberal weekly magazine the *Nation*—also recorded dining-room free-for-alls, which he proclaimed an "entertaining treat." When all the James boys were at home, pandemonium reigned. They all told bizarre and colorful stories, eloquently critiqued their favorite books, and hotly debated matters of taste; so determined were they all to make their points that they jumped up from their chairs and gesticulated passionately as they argued their points. The boys' disputes, in fact, frequently got so frenzied that they called down humorous curses on their father—a shocking impropriety for the time. One of these was a wish that "his mashed potatoes might always have lumps in them!" Each of the boys adored his father, but they also welcomed the chance to grapple with him, punch at him, and to take him down a peg or two with the wit he had encouraged in them.

FRIGHTENING EVENTS, MEANWHILE, had been unfolding across the country. Lincoln's election shortly after the Jameses' return to the United States had sparked anger and panic across the white South. On December 20, 1860, the state of South Carolina angrily dissolved its union with the United States. Through that winter, the Jameses read in the *Newport Daily News* and the *New York Tribune* about the rebel states' ominous convention in Montgomery, Alabama, where other Southern states joined South Carolina in secession. Soon afterward, the new Confederacy brazenly seized federal forts and arsenals across the South. Then, a month after Lincoln's inauguration, on April 12, 1861, the thunder of cannon fire rumbled across Charleston Harbor. The Confederate general G. T. Beauregard opened fire on the federal garrison, and the war exploded.

Charleston Harbor would figure in some of the family members' futures. For the time being, though, when the Jameses discussed these upheavals in their dining parlor, the Deep South seemed almost as far off as Troy.

In public, Henry Senior advanced a typically obscure and theoretical view of the conflict. Sidestepping the incendiary, he delivered in Newport a series of philosophic lectures, which propounded the view that slavery wasn't an American problem but was the last vestige of a European one. He claimed to believe in a new-dawning social equality, though; according to his arcane definition of *progress*, he found both the antislavery and women's rights movements irrelevant to that advancement. In this, Henry took a different course than two of the most dynamic social movements of his time and so came across to some of his radical friends as insensitive, out of touch, and even backward-looking.

Henry tended to be conservative, for a radical—and all five of his children would echo, in their own ways, his paradoxical mixture of the progressive and the reactionary.

Henry's opinions seemed to be growing odder as he grew older; he increasingly adhered to his overarching mystical Swedenborgian vision of the world, which for him dominated all social and political issues. His confidence in development of the "race"—he blithely focused on white men—lay in a highly abstract theory of moral progress that only a few could believe in. Still, his Civil War speeches soon drew crowds in Newport; many found Henry's rock-solid conviction of victory comforting, in the discouraging opening years of the war. But with his arcane preoccupations, Henry had a hard time making himself heard in a Union that soon had more urgent matters to attend to.

Henry's sons evidently felt the approach of the war more viscerally, especially after Lincoln's call to arms on April 15. William was nineteen, and Harry had turned eighteen on that very day. The two were natural candidates for recruitment, and they watched their cousins and friends hurry to enlist. With war fever seizing young men across the North, Henry wrote to a friend that he had to grip tightly to the "coat tails of my Willy & Harry" to keep them from joining up. No government was worth giving up what they might become, Henry told them. No American, he added, ought to risk death until he had "found some charming conjugal Elizabeth or other" to share his life with.

The eldest James boys, in fact, probably didn't really "vituperate" their father, as Henry claimed, for holding them back. William, it's true, may have felt some genuine eagerness to fight. After only a few months in the studio, he'd grown disillusioned with art. He never explained his decision to quit, but his father's continuing disapproval no doubt heavily influenced him. Enlistment offered an intriguing alternative if not a perfect one. William struggled with the painfully mixed feelings— whether to love Europe or scorn it, whether to obey or defy his father— which had characterized so much of his young manhood. He went as far as to sign up, on April 26, 1861, for a three-month stint with the Newport Artillery Company.

It remains unclear if William ever did much service in this Rhode Island militia unit, and he afterward sidestepped a more substantial three-year commitment to the Union forces. He acquiesced, in short, to his father's pressure not to fight. Henry wanted to keep his son safe and continued to envision a shining career for William—a future that by September 1861 William embraced his own way by enrolling in the Lawrence Scientific School at Harvard. Henry was relieved that both art and combat had been vanquished, but, despite all of his love for science in a Swedenborgian context, he looked down on the Scientific School—a rather experimental branch of Harvard founded in 1847 to offer a program of applied sciences such as chemistry and engineering. William showed no sign of regret at having compromised with Henry; he was enthusiastic about the possibility of living in Cambridge, Massachusetts, seventy-five miles away from home. Willingly or unwillingly, William dodged the "manly" option of war service, though he no doubt assuaged his father by adopting the pursuit, also manly, of what his brother called "Science, physical Science, strenuous Science in all its exactitude."

As for Harry, he felt what he later described as "a queer fusion or confusion" about his own willingness to enlist. A twist of fate, however, saved him some of the stresses of William's difficult debate on the subject. In the middle of the night on April 17, 1861, with "the smoke of Charleston Bay still so acrid in the air," Harry, perhaps stimulated by the atmosphere of excitement, pitched in with a crowd of young men who were fighting a fire that had broken out at the Newport armory.

With others, Harry strained to bring to life an old rusty pump in the stable yard. As he worked doggedly to draw water, he got crowded into an awkward position, "jammed into the acute angle between two high fences." Then something tore. In a spasm of agony, Harry did himself what he later called a "horrid even if an obscure hurt." Because Harry remained cryptic in his later memoirs, describing this mishap as embarrassing and "extraordinarily intimate," biographers speculated for a long time that Harry's injury was genital. Historical sources, however, confirm only a back problem—though aching backs were a family peculiarity, even for those who hadn't had accidents.

This "hurt" strangely mimicked Henry Senior's earlier leg injury. Both accidents occurred during fires in stables, both struck in adolescence, and both severed the men, father and son, from the ease of "normal" lives. Harry's accident, anyway, marked him as disabled in some way. The "hurt" amounted to a gash he'd carry not only through the Civil War but also on into his adulthood. This injury would linger, but it didn't prevent Harry from having to deal with the question of a career, increasingly urgent in his father's mind. Harry had always liked the idea of going to college, and with English literature not as yet a university subject, he grasped at the notion of law.

Meanwhile, with increasing desertions as the war dragged on, the Union decreed a compulsory draft in March 1863 with the First Conscription Act. Even then, wealthy Northern families could keep their sons out of the army by paying three hundred dollars or procuring a substitute—an inequity that touched off draft riots among poor Irish-Americans in New York City.

The James family, however, didn't buy themselves out of anything. Providentially, William's bad eyes and Harry's recent back injury did the trick. Disability exempted both William and Harry from war service. At least their protective father, with high futures in mind, made sure his sons made use of their disabilities to keep out of the Union army.

❧

BUT IN A startling contrast, Henry—an unconventional and unpredictable abolitionist—strongly encouraged his second-tier sons to fight. He had long been worried about what his younger sons were going to do for careers. Wilkie had refused to return to the Sanborn School after his second year there. Genial but indolent, he had rarely cracked a book. Bob had been moping around at home since the spring of 1861, toying with the idea of a naval life, tinkering with his sailboat, but otherwise mired in caustic fifteen-year-old "idleness" that exasperated his parents.

With these two sons adrift, Henry could combine convenience with idealism about the evils of slavery. Though reluctant with his older sons, he could urge his younger two to serve. The boys themselves seemed eager to do so. But by 1862, when Wilkie reached seventeen, the minimum age for service, enlistment fervor had died down, diminished by the reality of bloody and inconclusive battles like the first Battle of Bull

Run and Antietam, stalled campaigns in the East, and amputated soldiers streaming back into Northern cities.

With mixed emotions, the fifteen-year-old Bob watched the massive U.S. screw frigate *San Jacinto* coast into Newport Harbor, its white-haired commodore cheered by the citizens after his capture of two Confederate diplomats who had been trying to secure British aid for the South. (This was the so-called Trent Affair of November and December 1861.) But trailing behind this victorious ship, a hospital transport overloaded with wounded volunteers steamed up the bay, bound for the hospitals of Portsmouth and Providence, where many young men lay dying or screaming in pain. Hints of the war's brutality both appalled and stirred the younger James boys; suddenly it all seemed real and close to home. But, bored at home, tired of their father's sermonizing about their careers and future prospects, both Wilkie and Bob soon welcomed the chance for glory, novelty, and action.

WITH HIS FRIEND Cabot Russel, Wilkie enlisted in Boston on September 12, 1862. Within a few months, his Massachusetts regiment saw its first action in North Carolina, in chaotic farmland skirmishes with the rebels. During his first experiences in the battlefields, Wilkie proved as gifted a correspondent as his older brothers. He reported to his parents, "[Cabot and I] lay beside each other on our bellies on the shore of the river, each of us fancying we saw men in the trees, and pelting away whenever we had the chance." As a fresh and still-boyish soldier, Wilkie hoped he was "not inclined to make friends with bullets," but he longed to plunge into a more decisive battle.

After nine months of mud and malaria, Wilkie gamely signed up for even more service. Fatefully, Henry's abolitionist friends tapped Wilkie to serve in the first free-black regiment organized in the North, the famous Fifty-fourth Massachusetts. In an era of rank prejudice, black soldiers kindled furious controversy. The unit's sponsors feared riots in Northern cities and outraged retribution from the Confederate army. True, the all-white officers, handpicked from arch-abolitionist families, despised this "vulgar contempt of color." But even they expressed astonishment that the black recruits, who included a son of the writer Frederick Douglass, turned out to be both intelligent and courageous. Wilkie's idiosyncratic father, though, had raised him with an open mind. Soon, Henry observed, the teenage lieutenant grew "vastly attached to the negro-soldier cause; believes (I think) that the world has existed for it; and is sure that enormous results to civilisation are coming out of it."

During the regiment's training, Harry visited their camp at Readville, Massachusetts, at a strategic junction of rail lines just south of Boston. There he found "bright breezy air and high shanty-covered [fields] with blue horizons, and laughing, welcoming, sunburnt young men." The young officers, he noted, "bristle . . . with Boston genealogies." He admired them all, including their "tawny-bearded Colonel," Robert Gould Shaw, the blue-eyed, twenty-six-year-old son of prominent Boston abolitionists, who would soon lead his black regiment into battle. But even more, Harry envied Wilkie, whose sociable good nature had helped to transform him into an admired and respected soldier. To Harry, Wilkie glowed with such competency that his "state of juniority gave way." Harry, suddenly envious, and perhaps shamed by his own limitation, bowed to his younger brother's masculine superiority.

Henry Senior, who prized the special valor of men, also felt proud of Wilkie. To show his support, Henry risked the discomforts of a trip to Boston to see his son's regiment embark on May 28, 1863. From the doorstep of Oliver Wendell Holmes's house, leaning on Dr. Holmes's arm, the lame, spectacled philosopher awaited the exultant march of the black troops through the city. Both of these fathers had now offered sons to the war effort; young Oliver Wendell Holmes Jr., a future justice of the Supreme Court and good friend of William's, had already enlisted in the Union army and had been wounded at the Battle of Antietam eight months before, in September 1862.

With Wilkie bound for life-threatening battle, Henry must have watched this march with deep emotion and perhaps even regret. For many, the departure of the Fifty-fourth Massachusetts was one of the most stirring moments of the Civil War. Having disembarked from their train, the troops formed their companies in Park Square downtown and progressed through Essex, Federal, Franklin, School, and Beacon streets. Excited spectators hung from windows and cheered from balconies. As the black soldiers and their white officers marched past, to a band playing "John Brown's Body," female relatives and friends pushed into their ranks to kiss the men and present them with flowers. Colonel Shaw saluted his family by bringing his sword to his lips in front of the Shaw house at 44 Beacon Street.

On Boston Common the black volunteers drilled for the benefit of Governor John Albion Andrew and other dignitaries—many had been skeptical about black soldiers—who crammed the reviewing stands in front of the statehouse.

Among the many spectators, the black writer Frederick Douglass, leonine and white-whiskered, proudly saw off his sons Lewis and Charles—having helped recruit young free blacks for the cause with his stirring essay "Men of Color to Arms." Charles Douglass marched proudly that day, but his brother, Lewis, was too sick to parade and had also recently been beaten by white thugs, a victim of the racial emotions that were running perilously high in Boston. With intense emotion, Frederick Douglass's fellow escaped slave Thomas Sims delighted in the spectacle of free black men bearing arms in the city where he himself had previously been handcuffed and returned to slavery, under the Fugitive Slave Law of 1851. Along with them, the abolitionist writer William Lloyd Garrison and the Quaker poet John Greenleaf Whittier— the latter appearing at the march in spite of his pacifist convictions— also watched the columns pass and clamorously cheered the troops.

The biggest crowd in the city's history, both black and white, had gathered, and spectators packed Tremont Street and State Street, the route to the harbor. But not everyone felt exultation. Even in abolitionist Boston racial prejudice simmered, and squads of police massed behind the facades, braced to quell the expected rioting. Private racist remarks were recorded in a number of Boston diaries, and catcalls and boos sometimes rang out in the crowds. At Battery Wharf, as the regiment boarded the steamer *De Molay* for their transport south, street toughs tried to assault the soldiers, whose bayonets might have done them harm if the police hadn't quickly intervened.

Now living in Boston and studying chemistry at the Lawrence Scientific School, twenty-one-year-old William James also watched Wilkie's company from the parade route. Twenty-year-old Harry, having just finished an idle year at Harvard Law School, motivated by the lack of a better plan that would please his father, was in his boardinghouse across the river in Cambridge, sick in bed.

Perhaps, like Lewis Douglass, Harry was genuinely ill. Certainly, in other circumstances, he could enter into public shows of emotion; he had celebrated Lincoln's Emancipation Proclamation, earlier that year, with crowds at the Boston Music Hall. But, given the "obscure hurt" that had kept him out of the war, he no doubt felt guilty when he witnessed soldiers, especially Wilkie, heading off to the battlefields. There the staggering numbers of casualties—twenty-six thousand dead and wounded at Antietam in 1862, thirty thousand at Chancellorsville in 1863—outstripped all previous (and in fact subsequent) American losses.

⚜

AT FIRST, WILKIE'S return to the South probably seemed pleasant enough, as his slow steamer plied southward in clear, hot weather. Some of the recruits, unused to traveling on water, found themselves "hee-bin'" (heaving), as they told Colonel Shaw. One young man felt sick but just kept walking around until he felt "right well." Wilkie and the other officers sat under a shady awning on the quarterdeck, looking out for the flat shoreline of Cape Hatteras on June 1. As the transport slid past the blockaded port of Charleston a couple of days later, Colonel Shaw thought he saw the top of Fort Sumter off in the distance and the pillbox-shaped turrets of patrolling ironclads, before his men landed at Hilton Head, South Carolina, that same day.

In a little more than a week, Wilkie's regiment saw some of its first action. From its base camp on the flat, shell-paved St. Simons Island, the unit moved on to the picturesque waterside town of Darien, Georgia, on the Altamaha River. In conjunction with a black regiment from South Carolina, led by Colonel James Montgomery, the troops moved to shut down what was at the time the second-largest smuggling port in the Confederacy. "Our artillery peppered it a little, as we came up," Shaw wrote his young wife, "and then our three boats made fast to the wharves, and we landed the troops. The town was deserted, with the exception of two white women and two negroes." Some grapeshot had torn the skirt of one of these women, but Montgomery promised her that her house and property would be spared. However, much to Shaw's disgust, and to the later indignation of newspapers across the South, Montgomery looted the town and put it to the torch—a piece of destruction for which Shaw and his Massachusetts troops were afterward wrongly blamed.

Before long, Wilkie's regiment joined other units at Charleston Harbor, at the flashpoint of the Confederacy, the place where the opening salvoes of resistance had been fired two years before. Union commanders itched to capture Fort Wagner, a leviathan earth-walled fortification studded with cannons that had defended the city of Charleston even against the assaults of federal ironclads. The Union craved a conspicuous victory, especially because Robert E. Lee's incursion into the North had been halted, at the beginning of that July, only by the carnage (more than fifty thousand dead and wounded) of the Battle of Gettysburg.

At dawn on July 18, 1863, the Fifty-fourth Massachusetts, Wilkie's regiment, led the charge on the fort. To some, the front position meant "the post of honor." To others, the black troops, in their mile-long exposed rush, fell to Confederate guns because Union commanders considered them expendable—just as the United States paid "colored" troops only ten dollars instead of thirteen dollars and had originally proposed arming them with pikes instead of rifles. But the black troops didn't waver. They held their line even as Confederate cannons, rifles, and grenades cut down one man in four. It was one of the most costly and futile slaughters of the war. Only a few days before, Colonel Shaw had been entertaining friendly ladies to tea and dreaming of his wife back in Massachusetts, but now he fell with the state colors. Cabot Russel, Wilkie's friend, also dropped to the ground. The black troops, dead and wounded, piled up—thirty, fifty together—in the sandy ditches.

One bullet ripped Wilkie's side; another exploded through his foot. The young officer stumbled as the column of men surged forward then fell back, leaving him gasping and alone on the battlefield. Wilkie had to drag himself from the walls of the fortress to the water's edge, keeping out of sight of rebel sharpshooters. He crawled behind a dune for cover, leaving a blood-soaked trail in the sand. If he was captured, he must have been aware, he'd be summarily hung as a Yankee who had dared to arm blacks. He took shelter behind a knoll, where at last some ambulance men found him and heaved him into a stretcher. Wilkie, lapsing into unconsciousness, remembered only one more thing. A round shot from the fort blew off the head of one of his bearers.

When he reached the field hospital at Port Royal Harbor, Wilkie was still struggling to survive. Scarcely a doctor roamed the makeshift facility. Groaning soldiers lay exposed on the ground around him, covered with flies and dying of their infected wounds. To Wilkie's horror, a young Ohio man "with his jaw shot away," crawled over to where Wilkie lay, unable to move, and "deluged [him] with blood." The incident scarred Wilkie, haunting him through years of sleepless nights.

After days of torment, in a stroke of luck—and in a painful irony—Cabot Russel's father, looking in vain for his own son, discovered Wilkie among the dying. The Union had no system for informing families of war casualties. Henry's artificial leg made it hard for him to scour the battlefields, and William and Harry evidently never volunteered to do so. If Russel hadn't taken Wilkie back to Newport, the young man might well have died in the Carolinas.

As it was, Wilkie had to have the inch-and-a-half canister ball in his ankle dug out of the bottom of his foot, during his voyage to New York. Even at home, under the care of his mother and aunt, he couldn't immediately be shifted from his stretcher, Harry remembered. Wilkie mended only slowly, and the infected "pouch" in his side had to be cut open again—years before the invention of anesthesia.

While helping to nurse his brother, William made a touching sketch of him, lying on his side on a pillow, his lips helplessly open. Henry, who also sat by Wilkie's bedside and tried to give his son Swedenborgian solace, observed that during his long recovery Wilkie often cried out "for his friends gone and missing," and his father "could hardly have supposed he might be educated so suddenly up to serious manhood altogether as he appears to have been." Henry was deeply touched; Wilkie had earned his father's respect the hard way. He had achieved a conspicuous and bannered form of "manhood." But in a peculiar echo of his father's injury, Wilkie the war hero walked the rest of his life with a limp.

∽⍥

ONLY A FEW months before his wounded brother's return to Newport, Bob had signed up. In May 1863, he was still only sixteen, a couple of months shy of the minimum recruitment age; to his brother Harry, Bob was still *"l'ingénieux petit* Robertson" of the Jameses' home schoolroom, the impish playmate of Alice. But now he had been commissioned as a second lieutenant; he served first in a white regiment, then in another black regiment like his brother's, the Fifty-fifth Massachusetts.

In many ways, in fact, Bob's service echoed Wilkie's: recruitment in Boston, training in Readville, the experience of being a very young white officer in a contemptuously treated black unit. Then, only a few weeks after Wilkie's near-fatal charge—which moved Bob deeply when he heard about it—Bob also found himself in the mud and malaria of Charleston Harbor, helping to build an artificial island, an artillery position all-too-hopefully called the Swamp Angel. (This artificial log-pile island soon collapsed into the mud.)

As the siege of Charleston dragged on, though, Bob's experience diverged from Wilkie's, and partly because of his personal temperament. Though Bob served bravely, he didn't have Wilkie's sociable resilience. All too sensitive, Bob tended to fret, shaken by the horrors around him. Homesickness and depression often paralyzed him. Though few of Bob's Civil War letters have survived—burned years later by Aunt Kate, or put to the match shortly after their receipt by Bob's worried father— it seems clear from the few surviving documents that Bob also struggled with liquor and women, those persistent vices of nineteenth-century soldiers. Bob's brothers, almost completely inexperienced with women, remained chaste. Bob's father, though, had also been a teenage alcoholic and had long had a weakness for female charms, and he lavished his son with warnings about such weaknesses of character.

Bob, the youngest male James child, may well have been the first to try sex. Any particular circumstances of brothels or roadside dalliance have been lost, though surviving letters, mostly of Henry's admonitions, hint at unnamed transgressions, that Bob's conduct had not been "irreproachable" in his own eyes. "Cheer up then my dear boy, and be a man," Henry advised. "Keep yourself from vices that are in vogue about you." The morally strict Henry seems to have believed that Bob had strayed into temptation, especially when, after a serious sunstroke unfitted him for regular service, he worked as an aide-de-camp for General Adelbert Ames during later campaigns in Virginia and Florida. A handsome aide had more opportunities for whiskey and women than a battlefield soldier did.

Both of the younger James sons, however, convincingly distinguished themselves in the war, which marked the high tide of their youthful lives. Valiantly, after more than a year of on-and-off convalescence, Wilkie returned to the army. (He too had the intelligence and energy to work for a general.) Both men made the rank of captain for their exploits—Bob's moment of glory being at the Battle of Olustee near the manatee-haunted St. Johns River in Florida. Both, too, enjoyed moments of triumph. Bob's company finally stormed Fort Wagner in August 1863. And Wilkie, despite continued problems with his foot, helped the Union armies capture the rebel stronghold of Charleston in February 1865. Henry, perhaps because he had previously underrated these sons, was filled with pride. Exultantly, he embraced them and congratulated them on "so much manhood suddenly achieved."

Unfortunately, neither Wilkie nor Bob would find the challenges of ordinary life as stimulating as the dramatic, draining, and emotionally fraught experience of war. After the close bonds of soldiering and the heightened adrenaline of battle, these young men would find it difficult to return to lives where they were no longer heroes, where they in fact felt somewhat second class. Drama—emotional, psychological, or physical— was for all the Jameses a familiar, almost hospitable environment, as their European travels had reinforced, and these two men's Civil War successes would prove difficult for them to recapture or live up to in coming years.

❧

HARRY, MEANWHILE, COULDN'T help but confront various forms of battlefield "manhood." In spite of his exemption, something in him longed for engagement, and he was painfully drawn by the compelling suffering of the war.

Even before Wilkie's injury, Harry had boarded a steamer from Newport, in July 1861, to visit the huge army field hospital at nearby Portsmouth Grove. There, in one of his closest scrapes with the war, he met young men his own age, sick and mutilated young New England volunteers. Yet if he witnessed terrible pain or gruesome wounds—young mechanics or farm lads with their arms blown off or pocked with illness—such sights did not feature in his later autobiography. Instead, Harry afterward congratulated himself as having matched or anticipated Walt Whitman's famous visits to wartime hospitals, even if he, Harry, "hadn't come armed like him with oranges and peppermints." Walt Whitman, though, had gone beyond his pocket mints. The good gray poet had passionately nursed the soldiers, cleaned their wounds, heard their outcries, sealed their last letters to their families. Whitman's shaggy blood-spattered embrace was paternal, unafraid, and unashamed.

Harry believed (or hoped his readers believed) that he, like Whitman, had risen to "the pitch of the last tenderness of friendship." He found the Union soldiers "attaching and affecting" in their plight. But his visit to the hospital lasted only three or four hours. More distant and detached than Whitman, he saw them as "amusing figure[s] of romance"—dashing war heroes. Then again, it may have been impossible for Harry—raised to value the "manly," yet alienated through temperament and accident—to acknowledge his feelings. Filled with his own insecurities, along with the guilty conscience of a noncombatant, Harry approached the soldiers with a complex, probably defensive attitude.

Likewise, when Harry saw his cousin Gus for the last time in Cambridge, among his swarms of war-eager friends in Harvard Square, he stepped back from hailing him. In only a few short years, Gus would fight his way to the rank of captain in the Fifth New York Cavalry Regiment. He would miraculously survive Stonewall Jackson, capture and imprisonment, typhoid, and the Battle of Gettysburg. But in 1863 Confederate snipers would shoot him off his horse in the woods of Virginia. And Gus Barker would be carried to a plank church by the

Rappahannock River, where he would bleed to death in the middle of the night.

❧

WHEN SUCH NEWS came, it was shattering. The grueling wartime years branded all the James children, Alice included, with both visible and unseen scars that lasted for the rest of their lives. Their peculiar relation to the war sometimes distanced them from the full-bore suffering of Civil War America. But their mixed feelings also embodied a sometimes characteristic American love of peace and ambivalence about war itself. They all had moments of valor and of conscience that colored their own strangely modern experience of the national catastrophe.

In an era of masculine sweat and grit, Alice often felt even more detached from vital experience than usual. To busy herself and contribute, she worked with the Newport Women's Aid Society cutting out shirts and rolling bandages. Wilkie and Bob had their grisly and glorious war stories. But Alice had no such proving ground, no such road to praise, fame, or her father's approval.

For the sidelined William and Harry, the damage from the war was to prove more subtle and internal. The Civil War saddled the eldest James sons with a bizarre burden: they had missed what was perhaps the most important event of their times; somehow they had not fully engaged with or even witnessed this incredible passage of American history. Their war had all been ingrown, hypersubtle, and (in their own eyes) shameful.

As the war had unfolded, both William and Harry studied at Harvard, hundreds of miles from pickets, the gunpowder, and the bloodshed. Their father's care kept them safe in the grassy garden of Harvard Yard, canopied under its serene old elms. But their Harvard Yard was empty and eviscerated, cut down to only a few students, its Commons shuttered, so that the two young men had to shift for themselves ignobly in boardinghouses. Every day, in their studies that hardly connected to the national tragedy, they were reminded of their inadequacy. Even before Wilkie's injury, William had increasingly leaned toward studying medicine—though not so soon as to be able to treat any of the wounded men in the hospitals. Harry found law school ill suited to his talents and remote from the immediate crisis of the war. Harry's obsession with reading crime fiction during these years sheds light on his need for escape. It also hints at a morbid fascination with wrongdoing and guilt—stoked by some of Harry's own guilt, perhaps.

When the two young men, home from Harvard, sat in their family's Newport garden during the Battle of Gettysburg, in the sweltering July of 1863, the most William and Harry could "do" was to run to the local newspaper office to fetch the latest telegraph dispatches, and worry about Wilkie and the future of the Union. Otherwise the war unfurled around them, soundless, like a pantomime.

ATHENIAN EROS

L ate in the year 1863, before the Civil War ended, Henry James Sr., as Ulysses S. Grant had done with his western campaign, opened up a whole new front. With the strategic determination of a Civil War general, the patriarch of the James clan made a daring railroad trip across the ragged forests of southern Massachusetts, from Newport to the distinguished redbrick city of Boston.

Usually Henry traveled to Boston with Mary, and often to hunt for a house. Newport was limited, and he was, as usual, compelled by the possibilities of a different setting: he was determined to settle down in what was possibly the world's most bookish metropolis; he was convinced that Boston would suit him and put an end to his family's perennial moves. Any rumor of a house available in the sacred city hit the Jameses' Newport drawing room like a bomb, like war news. Electrified by an advertisement, Henry would scrawl a letter, and he and Mary would scramble to catch the steam ferry to New Bedford.

On this outing, though, Henry presumably left Mary behind in Newport. Much as he hated to travel without her, women weren't invited where Henry was headed. It wasn't a three-story townhouse he was chasing. He'd been offered, instead, a niche in the Boston pantheon. He, who had hardly ever belonged to any group or organization, had now been honored with a membership in that monumental and legendary brotherhood of New England intellectuals, the Saturday Club.

He would be the only new member inducted in 1863, but such a distinction was coming to Henry somewhat late in life. He had recently turned fifty-two, and he looked more like a philosopher than ever before, with his dark beard streaking white at his chin. With his children almost grown and, in spite of challenges, gaining measures of independence, he could no longer have felt like a young man. His eyes troubled him despite his black oval glasses; his still-troublesome peg-legged gait made travel painful, especially if he was alone. It had been an effort for him to climb aboard the steep-stepped passenger coach that day; it was hardly built with the disabled in mind, and it was only the latest in a lifetime of physical challenges increased by travel.

Yet today he was in a rare state of self-satisfaction. Exalted by this honor, Henry watched eagerly for the first white steeples to rise out of the woods. Already, he had emotionally laid claim to this old, distinguished city—the first of whose outlying wood-frame houses had begun to appear alongside the tracks. As soon as Henry's train reached the causeway that crossed the marshes, a view of Boston on its round hill opened up. More than two hundred years old, built on seventeenth-century cowpaths that had become its irregular network of streets, the traditional Boston of the Adamses and the Cabots rose up from the water that surrounded it, roof mounting above roof. The city as yet had no skyline except for church steeples. Well-ordered brick facades and chimneys climbed gracefully toward the glittering dome of the statehouse.

From the causeway, though, where two busy railway lines crossed in the reed flats, Henry witnessed a new and different Boston in the making. Cranes and dredgers stood out everywhere in the watery desolation of the Back Bay. The city that was familiar to Henry—the realm of straitlaced, long-winded abolitionists, descended from dour, utopian Puritans—was changing. The whole western flank of the city, the marshes along the Charles River, had erupted into construction, and on a titanic scale. To rival New York and London, Boston was transforming this mudflat into future domestic real estate, in the most enormous landfill construction project the United States had yet seen. Endless trainloads of gravel, hauled in on a specially built spur line, cascaded thunderously into the broad basins. Inch by inch, block by block, the groundbreaking, ground-making city engineers shored up solid earth. Beyond the well-tended flowerbeds of the Public Garden—once water-front property—Gothic spires and bay-windowed mansions were shouldering up on the landfill, filling out the future posh, gaslit, beaux arts neighborhood of Back Bay.

When Henry disembarked at the Boston and Providence Railway depot, near Park Square, it wouldn't have been easy to hail a cab in this crossroads of horsecars. The tightly packed commercial buildings of downtown rose in one direction, and the construction of Back Bay raised a clamor in the other. The city hadn't always seethed with the traffic of wagons and horse-drawn omnibuses that slowed his progress. He could still remember the place from his first visit there at the age of eighteen, during the winter of 1829–30. At the time, Boston was a fussy, rutted town of less than fifty thousand people, where cows grazed lazily on the Common.

Then a student at Union College in upstate New York, Henry had defied his father by running away from his studies. Feeding off his anger and defiance, he'd fled to Boston and earned his keep, humbly, as a proofreader. He'd roamed the rainy cobbles beside the city's new Faneuil Hall Market, beside the harbor, which provided views and sea air. When it came time to sleep, Henry took refuge in a snug, stove-lit room on Beacon Hill.

Henry's undergraduate escape prefigured, in a sense, his later jaunts to Europe—and his whole family's nomadic existence. In staid and upright Boston, it would have been hard for this terribly complicated young man to drown himself in alcohol, gambling, or women. The first American antialcohol organization, the Massachusetts Society for the Suppression of Intemperance, had been founded in Boston in 1813—although the association, a precursor of the temperance movements that would eventually transform Victorian habits of liquor, soon fizzled out in the hard-drinking 1820s.

Even now, Henry retained elevated memories of Boston, especially those of his crush on the young wife of an Episcopal clergyman, Sarah Maria Nott Potter. Mrs. Potter, he had enthused, embodied the beauty and innocence of the biblical Eve "before the fall." Henry became rhapsodic when he looked at this Eve and listened to her talk. He wrote, "[I am] apt (as often before I have said in regard to some other married ladies of my acquaintance) to wish with the Psalmist, neither poverty nor riches, but just such a wife as Mrs. Potter." Henry phrased a gallant and even scriptural sentiment—but one, after all, that referred to a married woman. And something like this very mix of innocence, daring, and rebellion would also flavor his children's complex but erotically motivated interactions with the Puritan metropolis.

Now, the city provided plenty of cold-water surprises as well as warm memories. As Henry climbed the hill toward the Park Street Church, he found that the sidewalks of Boston teemed with Irish immigrants, the children of the potato famine, still wearing their homespun woolens and rustic leather brogues, hawking scrap iron or cabbages from wheelbarrows. Henry, a man from an Ulster family, no doubt found these newcomers all too poignant. Like him, these outsiders weren't exactly welcome in Boston.

THE DINNERS OF the Saturday Club were held at the Parker House, a solid, staid hotel built in 1855 on the eastern flank of Beacon Hill. The Brahmins, the cultured old-blood Bostonians who dominated the club, had a flair for understated luxury. The second-floor room where they met was paneled in richly carved American oak, and its windows overlooked the distinguished colonial granite church of King's Chapel and the graceful white Second Empire–style city hall, under construction when Henry first visited the club (and completed in 1865). The rather dim dining room, with its northern exposure, sported an oil painting of Harvey D. Parker, the canny owner of the inn. His portrait watched the diners fixedly, while down below Parker himself managed fleets of waiters, "honest florid and ornate ministers," as William remembered them, who served a plush seven-course meal with its accompanying sherry, Sauternes, and claret (champagne and Apollinaris mineral water cost extra) at three o'clock in the afternoon on the last Saturday of every month.

The Saturday Club corralled the literary and scientific lights of Boston, or at least the male lights. Boston had been riled by the "Woman Question" in the 1840s and 1850s, but ladies were not admitted to this particular gathering. The graying, lion-maned Henry Wadsworth Longfellow, best-selling author of *Song of Hiawatha* (1855) and other epic and household poems, anchored one end of the table. (His wife, Fanny Appleton Longfellow, had recently died in a freakish but weirdly Victorian accident, a fire that broke out when she was sealing packets of her children's curls with wax.) Longfellow, though an erudite professor of Romance languages, had made a remarkable popular success out of literature, with his accessible poems such as "The Village Blacksmith," a verse that would be memorized by generations of American school-children.

At the other end of the table, the Swiss-born naturalist Louis Agassiz represented the surging new disciplines of science. He had conceived of an almost religious purpose for his ambitious pursuit of geology and zo-ology. Across the river at Harvard, he was forging a reputation by study-ing the history of glaciations and "refuting" Charles Darwin's theories, which had recently been brought out in Darwin's landmark book, *On the Origin of Species* (1859).

Between these titans of art and science sat Henry's loyal friend Emer-son, who was largely responsible for Henry's admission to this august club and who quietly held more sway than almost anyone else.

Beyond these three mainstays—this uneasy symbolic trinity—the be-whiskered members of the club ranged themselves strategically around the table. Twelve to twenty men shoved in on any given Saturday. It was astonishing what famous men could be met during handshakes through-out the room.

One brisk regular was Richard Henry Dana, author of the exciting sea tale and boy's book *Two Years Before the Mast* (1840). As a young man with Byronic curls, Dana had gone to sea as a common sailor on the brig *Pilgrim* to cure eyesight damaged by measles and strained by his heavy reading at Harvard. (A manly sea voyage, with salt air and hard work, was thought to cure the ills of sedentary intellectual life.) Ever since, Dana dined out on his youthful adventure sailing around Cape Horn to the then-Mexican mission settlements of San Diego and Monterey.

Another habitué, the bearded and well-connected James Russell

Lowell, another professor of belles lettres, or literature, at Harvard, had recently launched the brand-new *Atlantic Monthly* as its first editor. This publication would help shape the future of Henry's sons, but Lowell had his own aspirations for greatness. This gentlemanly "fireside poet" had just penned a rather stiff poem, "Memoriae Positum," honoring Colonel Shaw and his black regiment—praising the sacrifice of Wilkie James's company. (In so doing, he anticipated by a century a more famous elegy, "For the Union Dead," by another Lowell—Robert—who showed the power of these Civil War experiences on the Boston psyche even in the twentieth century.)

No meeting of the club was complete without the side-whiskered Oliver Wendell Holmes Sr.—"Dr. Holmes," as he was usually called, because he was a medical doctor, and to distinguish him from his later-to-be-famous jurist son, Oliver Wendell Holmes Jr. A few years earlier, Dr. Holmes had published some of his witty table talk in a volume called *The Autocrat of the Breakfast Table* (1858). A relentless observer of life, Holmes tended to lavish the club with bon mots: "Knowledge and timber shouldn't be much used till they are seasoned" (the Saturday Club was so seasoned it was peppery). "To obtain a man's opinion of you, make him mad" (after several wine courses, arguments could erupt).

Friendship and rivalry alike flourished in the rarefied cigar smoke of the club. Henry reveled in Dr. Holmes, who he said was "worth all the men in the Club put together." But Lowell liked to snub Holmes (the doctor took it philosophically) whenever possible. Longfellow and Agassiz, in contrast, "loved each other like David and Jonathan," as one witness remembered, even when they entertainingly sparred.

In this enclave of civilized antagonism, Dr. Holmes admired the irascible Dr. Agassiz, whom he likened to an encyclopedic collection of quotes or "extracts." "I cannot help thinking what a feast the cannibals would have, if they boiled such an extract," Dr. Holmes quipped. A British guest countered that the cannibals might well relish Professor Agassiz not for his wisdom but for his plumpness.

Such was the wit that flew at the Parker House, at the then-staggering price of seven dollars a dinner.

Henry James Sr. had his own credentials: he had published *The Social*

Significance of Our Institutions in 1861 and *Substance and Shadow; or, Morality and Religion in Their Relation to Life* in 1863. In spite of such ponderous titles (neither sold well), Henry was well-suited for the persiflage of the club, and already had a good deal of experience with it. At a dinner in 1861, he had met Nathaniel Hawthorne, also an outsider and a guest. Henry thought Hawthorne had the look of a "rogue who suddenly finds himself in the company of detectives." But he also felt anguished sympathy for the shy and nervous novelist, who hated publicity and who felt self-conscious in the sometimes barbed company of these formidable Bostonians. Henry himself found these Olympians daunting, but, much more than Hawthorne, he wanted to belong.

Despite the fact that he had known and associated with some of the members for years, Henry didn't quite fit the club—he never quite fit anywhere. With his Scots-Irish ancestry, the transplanted New York native looked like an exotic bird in comparison to the staid Anglo-Saxon Brahmins of Boston. Even his friend the banker Samuel Ward described him as "Henry James of New York"—Henry's wealthy father having been known as William James of Albany, like some rugged Scottish chieftain. Edward Emerson persisted in stamping Henry's odd opinions and flashes of temper as "Celtic." He pointedly remembered that Henry's father had only recently boated over from "Northern Erin." Such references to Ireland—even though, to the Emersons, Henry embodied what was "best" and most Protestant about the island—carried a social chill. After all, the clubmen worried about all those Irish immigrants, with their brogues and wheelbarrows. Rich Bostonians of the era employed Irish Catholic servants and workers but harbored vehement prejudices against them. (Even Mary James lamented the bad habits of her Irish cooks and maids.) As historians have emphasized, these Irish weren't even considered "white"; they were hardly allowed to be human.

At the club, James Russell Lowell flatteringly pronounced Henry the greatest talker in America. But Henry's visits were far from harmonious. He was often hounded by a miniature theologian named Frederic Hedge, an avid clubman who frequently grabbed a seat beside Henry at the Parker House, spoiling to quarrel with him over Swedenborg. With Hedge, it was Henry's anticlericalism that earned him an enemy. But as an outspoken eccentric, Henry was a little too much, a little too vivid, even for one of the most cutting-edge intellectual clubs in America.

∾

MANY A DISTINGUISHED minister or professor lived beyond the broad salt marshes of the Charles River estuary, in the city of Cambridge. East Cambridge, right across the Canal Bridge from Boston, smoked with the brick chimneys of glass and furniture factories, but the western part of the city still resembled countryside, an old New England town with church steeples, surrounded by a patchwork of orchards, fields, and woods. Along Brattle Street, gracious clapboard houses with long lawns, like Longfellow's, had views of the gleaming curves of the Charles River. Other big genteel houses clustered around a large square area of grass, shaded by elms and planted with modest redbrick halls, some of them nearly two centuries old: Harvard Yard. Harvard had been founded in 1636 as a theological college for Puritans, and the place, still notable for the training of ministers, was sleepy with age. (By the 1860s, Harvard was dominated by Unitarians, as Yale was by Congregationalists.) But this backwater would soon grow and flourish.

Harvard in the 1860s was beginning a sea change, and the transformation would involve the two eldest James boys, who had preceded their father into Massachusetts—William in the autumn of 1861, and Harry in the fall of 1862. The two of them would not only witness these new developments but, as self-educated cosmopolitans, embody the new ideals.

Initially, Harry actually experienced the old Harvard, even though he had come to Boston a year later than William and mostly kept, as usual, to his brother's shadow. Harry had mixed motivations when he arrived in the beautiful autumn of 1862, following not only his brother but also his friend "Sargy," Thomas Sergeant Perry. Harry, it appears, was more in love with the idea of college than the practice of it; that fall, as he long remembered, he drank in the vistas of big trees dyed scarlet and orange—the Norton woods, near Divinity Hall. Here Harry paid a call to a new acquaintance and sat on a window bench, in the friend's room, inhaling through the window the "vague golden November."

The atmosphere pleased him, especially the avenue of trees leading up to the place. But a divinity student named Salter, in spite of his smart beard and mustache, disappointed him, striking Harry as a "product of New England at its sparest and dryest [sic]."

Enrolled at Harvard Law School, Harry encountered an institution that had served the needs of an earlier patrician and provincial New England; he mixed with a class of young men who had been channeled into one of Harvard's three graduate schools: law, medicine, or divinity. The cosmopolitan and largely self-educated Harry found himself surrounded by "young types, or rather with the members of a single type" whose narrowness, after his European travels, surprised him.

These young men attended morning lectures with Harry at Dane Hall, but Harry held himself aloof. When he was persuaded to argue a case in a "moot-court," the public exposure shook the diffident nineteen-year-old. Some of these young men knew how to strut and to pose arguments, but they were the product of the constricted and cliquish system that dominated many American colleges. As undergraduates, they had taken about three-quarters of their classses together. Their studies had been dominated by memorization and rote recall, as well as by Greek and Latin authors and mathematics—a fusty nineteenth-century adaptation of the medieval university curriculum of the trivium (grammar, logic, and rhetoric) or the quadrivium (arithmetic, geometry, music, and astronomy, as a preparation for philosophy and theology). As William's future son would observe years later, such students "went to the same lectures and recitations, sat under the same examinations." As a result of such regimentation, the young men "became attached to each other by all manner of ties while they passed, in gang-like freemasonry, through four years of almost identical experiences." They carried this phalanxlike solidarity into their legal studies and indeed into a Boston social life that had long been dominated by the doctors, lawyers, and ministers produced by Harvard's three professional schools.

Harry hardly fit this mold. He loved modern, living literature, the works of English and French novelists, and he wanted to write as well as read it. In the 1860s, Harvard College offered no instruction in English literature more recent than the medieval poet Geoffrey Chaucer.

Although Harry enjoyed meeting the cheerful, baby-faced Francis J. Child—the college expert on Chaucer and folkloric ballads—he mostly encountered William's less interesting friends: "*his* people," as Harry later wistfully phrased it. Harry made few friends of his own, feeling that his law-school classmates resembled remote actors on the other side of the footlights. He himself felt "singularly alien."

He wandered the local fields and woods by himself. At his dilapidated Winthrop Square boardinghouse or in the college library, he read the contemporary French literary critic Charles Augustin Sainte-Beuve (1804–1869), who was fascinated with the lives and intentions of living authors. (Harvard College mostly scorned to teach modern languages; when Henry Wadsworth Longfellow lectured on French and Italian literature, he had to provide translations for his listeners.) In his straying away from a stifling institution, Harry unwittingly followed the strategy of many a bright Harvard student who had educated himself by reading on his own and discussing his reading with his friends. The old Harvard system may well have been inadequate, but it had after all produced (or produced by neglect or antagonism) Ralph Waldo Emerson, Henry David Thoreau, and other luminous and iconoclastic New England thinkers.

William, who made friends more easily than his brother, was having a different experience. Since the fall of 1861, he had been enrolled in that half-experimental and half-orphaned branch of the university, the Lawrence Scientific School. Founded by the Massachusetts textile tycoon Abbott Lawrence in 1847, the Scientific School taught practical subjects like architecture and engineering. Yet, more than a mere trade school, it hinted at a different and more modern kind of higher education that would broaden into what we would now call liberal arts. William first encountered this future of Harvard in the unlikely person of his first chemistry professor, a tall and lanky man of twenty-seven named Charles William Eliot.

The energetic Eliot had recently excelled as a member of the Harvard crew, even if he didn't have a rower's compact physique. He was rumored to have been responsible for the red silk handkerchiefs the young rowers tied around their heads in 1858—the reputed origin of crimson as the Harvard color. With his spectacles, sideburn whiskers, and sober clothes, the young man sometimes struck his students as a severe and somewhat icy teacher. He imparted knowledge of chemistry through relentless laboratory experiments; and though William acknowledged his teacher's doggedness, he confided to his family, "I don't believe he is a *very* accomplished Chemist." Eliot returned the compliment by doubting William's abilities as a student. After his first year, William switched to the study of natural science and took as his mentor Louis Agassiz, his father's Saturday Club colleague. Eliot, however, was at least a competent enough scientist to coauthor a textbook, *Inorganic Chemistry*, which dominated late-nineteenth-century college classrooms. But his real gift, it would turn out, was for educational reform.

As early as 1858, Eliot boldly proposed changes for the Lawrence Scientific School that would include instruction in "Mathematics, Chemistry, Physics, Physiology, Botany, Zoölogy, Physical Geography, Rhetoric, French, German, & Drawing." His inspiration for this broader curriculum came from European universities, which, Eliot believed, were "as much in advance of us in all that pertains to higher education, as they are in the fine arts, in architecture, or in the more delicate of the mechanic arts." In 1863, in fact, he had left Harvard, in some disgust, in order to visit and evaluate such superior institutions. In Paris, he made intensive investigations of the Conservatoire des Arts et Métiers, the École Centrale, and the Sorbonne; in Germany, he traveled to the university towns of Karlsruhe, Heidelberg, Hohenheim, Stuttgart, and Tübingen. Like the Jameses, Eliot was a globetrotter who brought back his knowledge, as well as his creative discontentment, to the United States.

By 1865, Eliot was once again in Boston, collaborating with William B. Rogers at the Massachusetts Institute of Technology, which had been founded in 1861. But before the decade was out, Eliot would return to Harvard—in the much more powerful position of president, at the age of thirty-five—and would take his place among other vigorous educational reformers like Francis Wayland at Brown and Frederick Augustus Porter Barnard at Columbia. In 1869, Eliot would wrest control of Harvard from the educational conservatives and help transform a hidebound institution into one of the world's most eminent and progressive research universities. His was the dynamic, magisterial Harvard that would figure so prominently in the James family's future.

❦

BEACON HILL DREW the would-be Bostonians Henry and Mary, who were delighted and relieved, in the late spring of 1864, when they secured a tall, narrow house, redbrick with green shutters, on Ashburton Place, a tiny side street two blocks below the statehouse. Curiously, the Jameses' new home, on the North Slope of the hill, stood nearer to the African Meeting House on Joy Street than to the Brahmin mansions several blocks away in Louisburg Square. The Jameses themselves, as self-educated outsiders, had something in common with free blacks as well as with wealthy patricians of Beacon Street, though they would hardly have seen matters this way.

Except for Henry, most of the talkers at the Parker House were old-blood Bostonians, impressively rooted, who lived within five miles of the statehouse. They owned redbrick townhouses on the hill or stone mansions overlooking the Common, with their characteristic lavender-tinged windows (a glassmaking mishap from the Federal period). Some of the Brahmins lived across the river in Cambridge, in big, tree-shaded houses near Harvard Yard or Brattle Street. The distinguished Concord minority—Emerson and his hangers-on—often had to rush from dinner to catch the last train out of the city.

Henry himself now had a relatively easy limp home from these dinners, and a distinguished one along streets of tightly packed mansions. The preeminent Brahmin neighborhood of Beacon Hill, built on high ground above the harbor, reflected John Winthrop's feverish seventeenth-century vision of the Puritan metropolis as a "city on a hill," a beacon to all the nations. Originally Beacon Hill had amounted to no more than a wasteland of boulders and blueberry bushes, topped only by a wooden lighthouse tower. But by the nineteenth century the Hill had been transformed into a social beacon—a Federal-period neighborhood highly groomed and bricked in, crowned at its summit by the delicate brick-and-column confection of Charles Bulfinch's statehouse. Bulfinch's dome, originally framed in shingle, had been sheathed in copper and painted gray. By 1874, it would be leafed with twenty-three-karat gold, reflecting Boston's growing splendor and influence.

But Beacon Hill had another identity—largely missing from the Jameses' own accounts and thus scanted by some of their subsequent biographers. Since the late eighteenth century, the North Slope of the hill, where the Jameses now lived, had hosted a large and vibrant free black community. These black residents had renamed Belknap Street, where they had built the African Meeting House and the Abiel Smith School, Joy Street. Both of these institutions were decades old by the time Mary and Henry moved into Ashburton Place; they testified to the continued determination and defiance, if not always the joy, of black Boston.

Certainly Beacon Hill had long been a stronghold of abolition—as the Jameses, with all their antislavery friends, knew well enough. Unfortunately, stubborn racial discrimination also thrived even in the most radical parts of Boston—and even, subtly, in a family like the Jameses whose two younger sons had enlisted to serve with black regiments. The two slopes of the hill typified the brand of racial segregation that would prove stubborn in Boston as well as elsewhere: the South Slope, which faced the sun and the grassy Common, was inhabited by wealthy whites; the colder and more labyrinthine North Slope, nicknamed "Nigger Hill" or even "Mount Whoredom"—in reference to the prostitutes who sold their favors for a quarter—housed freed slaves. Still, the narrow cobbled streets of Beacon Hill inevitably teemed with Harvard-educated white professionals as well as black teachers and craftsmen, a curiously stimulating mix for what was then, as it is now, one of America's most atmospheric neighborhoods.

With the war still dragging on, Mary felt grateful to reestablish her household, to gather her two eldest sons back to her from their temporary digs in Cambridge. Wilkie, who had fought his way through an excruciating recovery from his wounds, had gone south again to join Bob for the closing chapters of the conflict.

As Harry remembered it, Ashburton Place embodied "the very taste of the War ending and ended." The drawing rooms and rose gardens of Boston hadn't literally witnessed bloodbaths and town torchings, as the dark fields of the South had done. But by the spring of 1865, Boston was overwhelmed with what Harry called "a monster tide" of returning soldiers: "bronzed, matured faces and even more in bronze, matured characters."

Harry recalled scenting the far-off battlefields from "worn toggery put off, from old army-cloth and other fittings at a discount, from swordbelts and buckles." Soldiers, some of them one-legged men like Henry Senior, cropped up everywhere in Boston. And some of them must have been black men, from Wilkie's and Bob's old regiments— even though Harry, with his usual blitheness, selectively remembered the "bronzed" white soldiers. His telling term, "bronzed," suggested the glory and the masculine grit of a war he himself hadn't encountered firsthand.

One memorable day in April 1865, Harry ventured into Boston Common, a broad fall of parkland lit up with blossoming trees. With the streets around the Common warm and pulsing, Harry longed to drink in the warm weather. Today he was turning twenty-one years old, and he loosened a little, in his tailored English clothes, seduced by the seductive spring warmth. The soft air had made people restless, and, as he later recalled, "one's own . . . pulses matched."

But he also saw in the strained, emotional faces he met a terrible sadness at odds with the flowering lilacs. The city of Boston, he discovered as he questioned passersby, was reeling from devastating, almost unbelievable news. Everywhere, Harry remembered, he met a "huge general gasp." People's eyes met, but they were too shocked, too overcome with grief to speak. Harry later felt shame that his birthday, April 15, coincided with the day of Abraham Lincoln's assassination at Ford's Theatre in Washington.

❧

HARRY, NOT SURPRISINGLY, hadn't gone back to Harvard. The law wasn't for him, any more than chemistry really suited his elder brother. But the Jameses' new neighborhood offered the James children other kinds of education. Around the corner, or rather up the hill, the Athenœum beckoned. The first private library in America, its many-paned windows overlooked the Old Granary Burying Ground, with its patriot graves including those of Samuel Adams and Paul Revere. The Jameses climbed the hill, without hesitation, for books—they had often opted for homes near libraries. And the Athenœum also counted as a Brahmin club in its own right, a venue for advantageous encounters.

Beyond it, just past the Park Street Church, the Museum, as it was simply called, had even a headier appeal. This Tremont Street institution housed portraits by the early American masters John Singleton Copley and Benjamin West—as well as more dubious curiosities like P. T. Barnum's bottled "Feejee mermaid." But the Museum's name disguised its true nature. It was a jostling New York–style theater—a scandal in a town whose parochial inhabitants tended to equate plays with prostitution. The more cosmopolitan Jameses, born thespians, adored drama and patronized the Museum with every dime they could spare. Their love of theater, in fact, pointed to a New York and a European sophistication that otherwise the James boys often found hard enough to express either at Harvard or on Beacon Hill. Harry especially was never as happy as when he was in a theater—a taste that would eventually lead him to become a playwright.

In addition to these attractions, fifty-three-year-old Henry Senior sometimes hauled his children to a "certain door of importances," as Harry remembered it, on nearby Charles Street. Number 148, a graceful redbrick townhouse, belonged to the eminent Boston publisher James T. Fields. His wife, Annie Adams Fields, was already turning her Friday evening "at home" into one of the most stimulating literary salons in America.

In spite of his checkered past—some of it known or guessed—Henry glittered as a salon candidate. Besides having joined the Saturday Club, he could point to his recent book (published with Fields's firm, in fact, though at his own expense), a manifesto of his philosophy called *Substance and Shadow* (1863). The book proved a sleeper if not a soporific; disappointingly, hardly anybody bought or read Henry James Sr.'s difficult and abstruse book. Even so, Henry often made a splash at Mrs. Fields's gatherings. His "Celtic" temper caused him to flare up and lavishly insult his fellow guests. Though he had stopped drinking more than a decade before, Henry still struggled with the emotional volubility that alcohol had exaggerated. Still, he usually followed these memorable outbursts with abject, profuse, and tenderhearted apologies.

Henry's indiscretions weren't always public, and his biographer

Alfred Habegger has discovered an incident from this time that hints at the complexities of his relations with women. Always scrapping for a fight, Henry had been publicly defending his friend Caroline Dall, a Boston feminist, from an unspecified attack from another of his cronies, the transcendental intellectual (and founder of American kindergartens) Elizabeth Peabody. When Caroline Dall came to see him on April 25, 1866, he gave her not only moral support but also a parting kiss on the lips, which interrupted their final handshake and landed on her, she wrote in her diary, like "an electric shock." Dall described the kiss as "prolonged, steadfast, and compelling." She wondered if it had an intellectual or even spiritual purpose, as "a divine pity—seemed to stream from his eyes." Such was Henry's combination of eroticism and Swedenborgian mysticism. "I write this down," the married Dall remarked, "because no one ever treated me so before." The abolitionist minister Theodore Parker had once given her a "tender kiss" on her forehead, but Henry's move was much more daring: "Phenomenally it must mean something. A pretty steady will—on H.J.'s part I fancy." Henry may not have committed adultery, but his impulsive shows of sympathy, affection, or sexual interest evidently went well beyond permissible norms.

Mary may or may not have known about her husband's peccadilloes, but she was well acquainted with his emotional volubility, and his unpredictable public persona may have been one reason she herself shrank from the social rounds of Boston's best and brightest. Mary seldom went to parties on Henry's arm, as wives often did. She had nothing to say to her husband's high-strung literary friends—and had no driving passion to be a feminist book reviewer like Caroline Dall or the mistress of a salon like Annie Fields.

Alice took more notice of Mrs. Fields, of her dark crimped hair and long neck, her calm and elegant encouragement of her guests. Sixteen and shy in public, Alice was still impressionable when her father debuted her at Charles Street. But, raised as a James, Alice savored like a rich dessert the conversation she witnessed in those Beacon Hill rooms. Mrs. Fields consorted with many of the most recognized figures of her era, including Mark Twain, Alfred Lord Tennyson, and eventually a young journalist from Nebraska, Willa Cather. In later years, after her husband's death, Fields would live with a woman, the Maine writer

Sarah Orne Jewett, in a characteristically Bostonian fusion of respectability and nonconformity. Even in the 1860s, as a married woman, Mrs. Fields provided Alice an intriguing model of feminine achievement, even if the young woman remained too modest and self-doubting to believe that she would ever become a grande dame, a hostess of a salon.

On one memorable occasion, Alice watched her father and Mrs. Fields join forces to "dilate on the vanity of riches." The more pragmatic James Fields protested that *he* thought it would be nice to have some well-heeled aunt leave him a fortune. It was a sentiment that Alice, dependent on her parents' money, could readily echo.

MEANWHILE TWENTY-YEAR-OLD HARRY had his own plans for combining moneymaking and literature. For some years now, out of his parents' sight, he'd been scribbling. He'd been trying on wildly different forms and styles like exotic costumes. Only partly tongue in cheek, he forecast to his friends huge printings of his future books. He dreamed of literary alliances—"Shakespeare, Goethe and Charles Lamb"—on a scale unavailable in Boston, even to his club-going father.

Harry's bravado, however, covered his hidden obsessive work and his stark fears. He swore his literary confidants (outside of his family) to secrecy. He even contrived to have the *Atlantic Monthly* send its replies not to Ashburton Place but to a friend's address. For one thing, the enterprising Harry had approached Charles Eliot Norton, one of his father's Saturday Club enemies, in order to break into the *North American Review*. For another, Harry understood all too well what a low opinion his father held of fiction—a prejudice related to his dismissal of painters—and how his brother William could tease, at the drop of a hat. Harry's home teemed with critics. "I cannot again stand the pressure of avowed authorship," Harry fretted to a more sympathetic friend. "Do not speak to Willie of this."

In this early cast for independence, Harry combined his father's literary aspirations with his mother's pragmatic savvy. Toiling behind closed doors on Beacon Hill, he published (anonymously) his first short story, "A Tragedy of Error," in the *Continental Monthly* in February

1864. He came out with his first book review in the *North American Review* in October of 1864—arranging with its editor, the scholarly Italophile Charles Eliot Norton, to tackle a "lump" of books for this journal during the upcoming season. "I am frequently in the way of reading French books," he told Norton, dangling his as-yet meager credentials.

Harry's first signed story—signed Henry James Jr., that is—broke into print in the *Atlantic Monthly* in March of 1865. "The Story of a Year" was a melodramatic Civil War romance. In a genre then popular, the story featured overblown, stock characters playing out heartrending scenes of parting and return. Such a histrionic formula seemed "concocted" to Harry in retrospect. But his fascination with the psychology of the waiting character Lizzie (as opposed to that of Jack, the departing Union soldier) actually came near to Harry's own experience of the war. He, too, had been waiting at home, like the members of Alice's bandage-rolling circle, instead of treading the battlefields, like his younger brothers. "What an awful thing this war is! I mean for wives," Harry commented to a friend in 1864. Though perhaps limited to his own passionate, house-ridden point of view, his early stories had a surprising freshness that soon attracted attention in Boston. Readers liked these cultivated, delicate romances by an author whose name, in spite of Henry James Sr.'s long public career, most of them didn't recognize.

Fame, though, didn't count as Harry's sole motivation. He was also interested in money, which, for him, was the vehicle of liberation. When his first check arrived, he cashed it without delay. He gloated over "the very greenbacks, to the total value of twelve dollars" he'd brought home. In private ecstasy, Harry fanned out these dollar bills in his third-floor bedroom at Ashburton Place. Still, Harry wasn't mercenary; he cared about the quality, the well-made sentences, of his fiction. But he also loved to dream, scheme, and plan his future.

This money amounted to Harry's "first earned wage." With it, he could have bought two sumptuous dinners at the Parker House. But Harry harbored bigger plans, first aired in his letters to sympathetic old friends like Thomas Sergeant Perry, who was lucky enough to return to Europe shortly after the Civil War, filling Boston-bound Harry with envy. To some extent, Harry merely indulged, so far, in vague dreams, "the golden light of promise," as he later described it. This feeling came from a visit Harry made to Charles Eliot Norton's sunny, book-lined library at his house, called Shady Hill, in the leafy riverside country west of Cambridge.

More practically, the twelve dollars meant a tiny down payment on Europe. Money meant a portmanteau, a future of villas. Already, Harry dreamed of Italy—the legendary domain of Norton's own studies and those of Norton's mentor and friend, the much-read English art historian John Ruskin, author of the monumental and influential *Stones of Venice* (1851–53). For Harry's new patrons, Italy was the country par excellence of art. And their heightened, transcendent pursuit of glowing Renaissance Old Masters offered something superior—though as yet Harry hardly knew what—to the more solid sobriety of Beacon Hill.

FROM THEIR PERCH on the hill, Henry and Mary watched with both pleasure and foreboding as their sons plunged out onto the brick sidewalks of Boston, carrying their aspirations and confusions into the quickening pace of postwar America. Though not autocratic in the Victorian style, Henry and Mary practiced an involved, observant, and sometimes highly invasive form of parenthood. From his library, Henry monitored his sons' education and their intellectual progress. Busy with her mending, her servants, or her account books, Mary scrutinized her children's health, finances, and emotional entanglements. The two of them formed a solid facade of parental observation and concern. They had chosen Ashburton Place, in fact, partly out of a determination to keep watch on their two eldest sons, both of whose activities now centered on Boston and Cambridge.

The state of Massachusetts suited Henry's particular parental goals, priding itself on its intellectual caliber, on its many distinguished churches, colleges, and libraries. Boston and Cambridge embodied the sort of intellectual ambition that Henry had worked hard to instill in his sons. He himself had failed in college and theological school, but he still yearned for his sons to become notable scientists, doctors, or lawyers—an irony, since Henry had chosen more idiosyncratic and idealistic pursuits in his youth. Henry's present vocation, in fact, remained idealistic. It was also unremunerative, in comparison to the more practical careers he tried to press on his boys.

In any case, the attached cities of Boston and Cambridge surged with the young and the gifted. New educational institutions were sprouting up all over: Tufts University in 1854, the Massachusetts Institute of Technology in 1861, Boston College in 1863, and Boston University in 1869—making Boston then, as now, an overgrown college town. Some of the growth of new institutions in the United States after the Civil War owed to the Morrill Act of 1862, which provided for the founding of colleges for agriculture and mechanical arts, the so-called land-grant colleges. (Iowa State University in 1862 was the first institution to qualify for these funds.) In Boston, the newer institutions mostly had different origins, but they were conscious of being mere seedlings beside the centuries-old oak of Harvard.

∾

WILLIAM AND HARRY, now handsomely tailored and in their early twenties, increasingly seized pretexts to escape Ashburton Place. Their sharp clothes hinted at their sophisticated aspirations. The two young princes—William sporting a dapper mustache—snagged horsecars to Harvard Square and boarded trains and steamboats to Newport to visit their Temple cousins.

Still slender and candid, Minny continued to live fearlessly, and without the professional pressure her male cousins felt; ladies had both the advantage and disadvantage of leisure. Though her relatives hoped she would marry, Minny was happier laughing out loud over comic pieces in magazines. She freely speculated about the universe and gave devastating critiques of her acquaintances. When the James boys squired her on excursions to the Spouting Rocks, near Newport, she ran so fast along the rocky shore that anemic William couldn't keep up with her.

William remained smitten, though he feared she would outshine him. To him, she was a spirited, somewhat off-putting woman, a candidate for his affections. To Harry, hers was the most extraordinary performance of life he had encountered. She had mastered the art of presence; her engagement in the world never faded, even though things often seemed to move too slowly for her. Although an orphan, she resolutely refused anyone's sympathy. She preferred entertainment, crisply delivered. If boredom set in, she did not bother to conceal her advancing glower behind the tiny smile of a lady.

Home, by contrast, offered little of Minny's kind of vivacity or daring. There, the boys found themselves immersed in the deep shade of their narrow street, where there was no break from the routines their parents laid down. The two absorbed the studious afternoon silence of the household, with everybody retiring between meals to read and to reflect. Alice had joined a girls' school in Boston and was making important friends, but her education came more from the books her brothers passed on to her or left lying around than from the lighter fare of a female academy. Serious study attracted Alice and, like many young women discontented with fripperies of dress or domestic drudgery, she was forced to educate herself. But for her, as well as for her brothers, Henry's hard-reading house could be oppressive.

As the older James sons struggled to break away from home, finances were always an issue. Back in 1861, during his first college year, William had reveled in boardinghouse freedoms—and dreaded the inevitable interference from Newport. When visiting, Wilkie teased William about his spending: "[Father is] going to break your head for spending so much!" But William feared his "prodigal philosopher" father less than his other parent. "Tell mother," he wrote, "there is no need for alarm about the finances." Next month's bill, he promised, would be smaller.

In 1863, after two years away from home, William still had to approach his father in his "old character of a beggar," in the pettiest matters. "I am [in] very great want of stockings. Shall I get them here? Ask mother. Please send the money immediately." Even hosiery needed (perhaps rather humiliating) parental clearance. Finances proved a ticklish subject, as his parents could be impulsively generous and then stunningly cheap. They indulged their favorite sons but fretted over the family's finite investments, so that all the James children learned to feel anxiety about the "sacred" family funds.

Long before Henry and Mary moved to Boston, William felt pinned down by his parents' financial thumb. Henry Senior might have been allowed to choose his calling with only his own satisfaction in mind, but his children, whose share of the family funds would be smaller than their father's, had to bow to economic realities. If William had chosen science in spite of his father's misgivings, he still had to contend with his mother. She thickly hinted that to become a doctor would pay much better.

In 1863, William thanked Mary for her concern. But he warned her not to strangle his "higher nature." He tried to assert some measure of independence. "I want you to become familiar with the notion that I *may* stick to science however & drain away at your property for a few more years," he wrote her, boldly enough. He also floated the hope of winning a position at Louis Agassiz's zoological museum at Harvard, founded in 1859, stuffed as it was with dried and pickled animal species from his various expeditions. There, William told his mother, he'd receive a salary of four or five hundred dollars a year—and keep his soul.

Henry and Mary clung to the purse strings as though they represented a form of moral authority. Yet they also brandished sentiment and eloquence—increasingly, in letters—to influence their restless children. They expected warm and informative correspondence in return. "Don't let *more* than a fortnight pass without writing," Mary instructed William, "for it is a necessity to our happiness to know how you are getting on."

Mary's run-on sentences were usually full of family and neighborhood news, her chatty attention wandering from one domestic subject to another. Possessive about her children, she filled her letters with lavish terms of endearment: her favorite was *darling:* "My darling Hubby" (to Henry); "My darling Harry" (to her favorite son). She squeezed her graceful, somewhat spidery handwriting onto every inch of the paper and often wrote on top of it crosswise as well, in a paper-saving technique favored by earlier generations. In contrast, her husband scrawled largely over his handsome letter paper, leaving generous space and showing a lordly disregard for expense that his children always noticed.

Born correspondents, the young Jameses gamely rose to their parents' epistolary challenge, producing expressive, exhaustive accounts of their doings—official reports, almost. The young men's letters home would grow increasingly complex, strategic, and sly. In the coming years, their missives would erupt like small volcanoes of independence—and yet also betray their continuing attachment to home.

Alice, too, wrote letters (though few from her early life have survived), but usually from home, as she traveled mostly from room to room instead of farther afield. Like many young women of the era, she was expected to live with her parents until marriage, but a wedding anytime soon appeared unlikely. Serious-minded, sharp-tongued Alice had no admirers; the only things she had received that approach love letters were mock-ups from William. "Cherie, charmante [dear, charming]," William addressed her from Harvard. "That you should not have written to me for so long grieves me more than words can tell, you who have nothing to do besides." William, as usual, combined the bitter and the sweet when addressing his sister, who needed no reminder of her lack of vocation and housebound status.

In the James home, letters counted as public property—the parents' property, that is. Henry and Mary routinely slit open their children's mail, in spite of repeated protests against this invasive practice. Even if the children scrawled "private" letters to one another, they had to conceal them, as William and Harry sometimes did on into their twenties, tucking papers inside papers, conspiring to keep more "interesting" and intimate news away from parental scrutiny.

IN SPITE OF his work with Louis Agassiz, William failed to land a post among the pickling jars at the zoological museum. So in the spring of 1865, with vague dreams of winning fame as a naturalist, William signed up for an expedition. Louis Agassiz was planning a voyage to the Amazon. William, who'd been dissecting animals with Agassiz and entertaining Mrs. Agassiz at social evenings, caught on to the eminent scientist's coattails. Zoological expeditions simply didn't pay; William's father and Aunt Kate soon realized they would have to foot the bill. But still, just as his little brothers were witnessing the final collapse of the Confederacy, William found himself on an adventure of his own.

On April 1, 1865, William boarded the steamer *Colorado*, with a party of naturalists and their hangers-on, bound for the hitherto unthinkable destination of Rio de Janeiro. William had hardly anticipated that he himself would be joining a trek to the jungles—although the imperialist Victorian era abounded with voyages that would map the uncharted hearts of continents (David Livingstone would shake the hand of Henry Morton Stanley at Lake Tanganyika in 1871) and catalog the people, plants, and animals to be found in these exotic places. But more personally, William had embarked on an extrafamilial odyssey that would paradoxically connect him more with his brothers Wilkie and Bob than ever before. He'd soon plunge into the same kind of isolated mosquito-ridden swamps that his brothers had encountered in the war years.

During his voyage south into the increasing heat, though, William remained a drawing-room creature, often airing his characteristic jaded wit. From the slow-paddling *Colorado*, he wrote his parents that from his heavy reading of adventure books, he'd expected to find "a deep Prussian blue over a sea of the same color," spice-laden winds, birds of paradise, flying fish, porpoises, and moon-kindled phosphorescence in the sea at night. But (perhaps reassuringly to his audience), he'd found the tropics no more kaleidoscopic than his cobblestone-dull home.

As he walked the decks, William also began to doubt his father's friend Professor Agassiz, reporting that "his charlatanerie is almost as great as his solid worth." Agassiz, after all, had undertaken a five-thousand-mile voyage to the tropics to prove that glaciers had once covered Brazil. This unlikely ice cap was a feature of Agassiz's rather unsatisfying theory of the origin of species, one that he hoped would overthrow Darwin's postulations. Though Agassiz had done important work in documenting an ice age in North America, the professor's current expedition was motivated by gloriously wrongheaded thinking, and his overbearing bombast, more than his doggedly creationist theories, provoked William's distrust.

When the Harvard expedition disembarked in Rio, Agassiz paid his respects to the stout, full-bearded Dom Pedro II, emperor of Brazil. William, however, introduced himself to Rio less glamorously, with mosquito and flea bites. Languishing in the heat, he got ringworms on his cheeks and neck. Yet he warmed immediately to the city that spilled across its green subtropical cliffs. Rio's bookstores, cafés, and street life reminded William of what he playfully described as "sinful" Europe. By 1865, the city had grown into a teeming coffee port, but it maintained old ties to France and Portugal, so that steamers dropped off the latest Parisian journals like clockwork.

William and his companions had little to do other than watch the boats come in, or read. But to his family, he reported luxuriously bathing "in a marble sarcophagus," in a frescoed court with palm trees. With Jamesian grandiosity, he imagined himself in Pompeii. And as a matter of fact, Vesuvius was about to explode under him.

William contracted a high fever not long after his arrival, breaking out in red tubercles that dyed his face as red as "an immense ripe raspberry." Such symptoms boded worse than ringworm: smallpox killed half of the people it infected. William found himself mired in the local *maison de santé* (hospital), where at Rio's exorbitant rates for medical care he got only a straw mattress and bland portions of chicken and rice. Luckily, his case proved to be variola, a milder cousin of smallpox. Still, he told his mother, the attack left him with "neuralgic pain" in his left eye—and vision problems would in fact plague him for the rest of his life. With such setbacks, William understandably insisted that his forte was "speculative" thinking, not "exploring expeditions"—a prescient statement.

By the time Agassiz's party actually plunged into the Amazon, William had recovered, and in the blossoming and mosquito-ridden jungles, he gained some respect for Agassiz, who paradoxically fueled William's esteem by saying that he, his protégé, was "totally uneducated." William had sparse formal training, it's true, but his bright unconventionality would ultimately make him a more versatile thinker than Agassiz. "Genius, in truth, means little more than the faculty of perceiving in an unhabitual way," William would later write—a proverb that, embodying as it did the originality of the young Jameses, also appealed strongly to his sister, Alice.

Away from Cambridge, William ruggedly transformed himself, like the heroes from his boys' books, becoming a Jamesian Robinson Crusoe. "What would the blessed mother say if she saw me now," William wondered to his family, with a note of pride. What, indeed? William now wore nothing but a ragged shirt and trousers, and he'd shaved his head. He sported a stubbly chin and "hacked up" hands from making barrels for Agassiz's Amazonian fish. He'd grown pink and brown with sunburn, and in three months, he hadn't cracked a book. He'd entered a state that he described to his father, without a clear explanation, as "sensuality."

In August 1865, in the rubber boomtown of Santarém, near the miles-wide confluence of the Tapajós and the Amazon, William strutted out to a "ball," where, in a palm-leaf house with a packed dirt floor, a black man improvised on a lute. The assembled party poured Portuguese wine from a huge dark bottle, sharing two tumblers among them. Several "lovely Indian maidens," friends of William's landlady, offered themselves to dance the quadrille and the polka—the approved European dances of the day. The young women, so different from the staid daughters of Boston, intrigued him with their combs securing their soft black hair, which was adorned with aromatic white Brazilian flowers.

William's pidgin Portuguese made his acquaintances scream with laughter. But that didn't prevent them all from gesticulating madly in order to communicate; William was good at pantomiming. As the evening went on, the rather repressed William sidled up to one of these beauties, with all the courage he could muster. "Ah Jesuina, Jesuina, my forest queen, my tropic flower," he rhapsodized. Whatever else happened that night—and William's letters refuse to specify—the young man was soon picturing this beautiful woman walking an Amazon beach "with her long hair floating free." He fantasized about her, pining for his loss.

And this was only one evening, one party, one sexual brush—and one comically doctored for consumption by his little sister. William wrote a witty letter, perhaps edited, but still showing his intoxication with Brazil. Headily, William plunged into other exotic binges of "eating & drinking & dancing with the Indian maidens." During an era in America when sex was rarely mentioned, William hardly knew what desires had broken loose inside him.

The expedition was showing William that he wasn't cut out for naturalism, even if he was interested in the inner workings of animals. But he was much more interested in the inner workings of people: himself, his friends, and the Indian girls. With time on his hands in the languid rain forests, he found himself thinking about his own clouded future more than the supposedly glaciated past of the Amazon.

After nine months of Brazilian rhythms and time far away from his family, William turned back toward Boston with complicated and conflicted feelings. He wrote his mother about how bizarre American life looked to him from the hazy rain forests. The idea of people "study-ing themselves into fevers, going mad about religion, philosophy, love & sich, breathing perpetual heated gas & excitement, turning night into day" seemed incredible to him. In this description of the ills of Ameri-can society, William focused strongly on the pursuits of career-making and courtship that were often on his mind but that he had been able to set aside in the palm groves of Brazil. Previously, as a professional-minded Bostonian, *he* had been the one studying himself into a fever.

William found himself actually missing the slush and ice of a Boston Christmas, cast-iron stoves, French magazines, theaters, and other ac-coutrements of civilization—"even churches," he admitted. Given his fastidiousness and his European background, he was hardly a candidate for rough living, no matter how much the hedonistic freedom of the rain forests appealed. His mother's softly lighted, chintz-fitted domestic domain now struck him as "almost too good for this world." Still, after his rites of passage, after this sexual awakening, William found it less than easy to go back to buttoned-up Massachusetts and his parents' spruce, hypercivilized house.

But now that his hope to become the next Agassiz had fizzled, he braced himself to follow his parents' plans for him. He'd wade back into the feverish, career-mad world of Harvard; he'd become a doctor, after all.

❧

AS RELIEVED AS Henry and Mary were to gather the pocked and peeling William back, they didn't cling to all their children. Once the war ended in 1865, Wilkie and Bob had returned proudly home, where they had been lavishly embraced and lionized. For six months during William's expedition, they convalesced on Beacon Hill. But Henry and Mary were determined to make the younger boys earn their own way; they had to learn how to care for themselves. The younger sons couldn't draw—as William and Harry did so often—on the stretched family funds. They weren't special or promising enough, even if Bob irritably insisted he should be, like William, given a chance to study painting. "Bob has some artistic taste," his mother commented to Wilkie, "and not a little sensibility to beauty in nature and art." Yet Mary cautioned, "He exaggerates his enjoyments . . . and wants to give everything else up for it." Mary and Henry were ruthless in their evaluations of their children's talents and possibilities. They could not squander the family funds on investments that were only indulgence and which would never pay off. Or so they reasoned.

Bob posed a special headache for the family, having picked up a taste for liquor on the battlefield. Whether or not he was yet a full-blown, active alcoholic, he was accruing more problems all the time. His attraction to drink was apparent enough at home that Harry, with uncharacteristic cattiness, joked about Bob's weakness in public. With his addictiveness and unevenness of temper, Bob resembled his anxious, mercurial father even more than his siblings did. And like Henry, he was riddled with quixotic ambitions that seemed almost impossible to realize. After the war, Bob applied for many jobs in Boston, but he had no skills to boast of except soldiering and French. After months of Bob's idling irritably at home, his worried father acted. Henry tapped his Saturday Club friendship with John Murray Forbes, the Bostonian railroad entrepreneur, to secure Bob an entrance-level railroad job.

Inconveniently, the work was in Burlington, Iowa, where Bob traveled reluctantly, full of unwillingness, apprehension, and a confirmed easterner's scorn for all points west. His new home on the Mississippi River was, obviously, a comedown from culture-saturated Boston and the art world that Bob had grown to love. Without delay, Bob, still only nineteen, descended into homesickness. He hated his work as a railroad clerk and suffered acutely from the biting cold and isolating emptiness of the Great Plains. A James wasn't made for such conditions, and the Chicago, Burlington, and Quincy Railroad was even harder for Bob than coopering barrels in Brazil had been for William.

Fatefully, John Murray Forbes helped shape Wilkie's future as well. Forbes, an energetic long-faced man, mixed philanthropy and commercial enterprise—a particularly Bostonian combination. A deep-dyed abolitionist, he agitated to hire freed blacks on his railroads, mostly as porters—so that black porters eventually became a conspicuous fixture of American rail travel, competent and comforting features of luxurious long-distance Pullman coaches. Forbes also promoted the use of free black labor (with white management) in cotton-farming ventures throughout the devastated South.

For such an enterprise, Wilkie fit Forbes's aims admirably, offering a hardy, cheerful personality, abolitionist credentials, and a recent acquaintance with Florida, where he'd campaigned during the war. On the downside, he had no knowledge of vegetable gardening, let alone cotton planting. But by February 1866, Wilkie found himself in the pine country south of Gainesville, buying up land for a cotton plantation.

Bunking in a plank shack, Wilkie energetically set about making land deals—and then having his men, for the most part freed slaves, clear the woods for cotton planting. The area had hardly been developed and was pocked with alligator-ridden swamps and traversed by primitive dirt roads. In this rough, less than temperate country, Wilkie got a taste of the frontier hardship and land speculation that characterized the mid-nineteenth century in much of the United States, not just the more celebrated West, further opened up by the Homestead Act of 1862. Ever optimistic, Wilkie plied his parents with hopeful accounts, with edifying visions of political equality and education for blacks. Along with his father's idealism, Wilkie had inherited, more than the other Jameses, his mother's fearlessness and vigor. He kept his courage intact in the face of Southern hostility to his project and plummeting cotton prices.

Though Forbes cannily slipped out of the investment in a year or two, Henry sank more and more money into the speculative cotton plantation. Having turned his son out to make money, he still couldn't help but extend at least a little support. Henry had a horror of bad investments, and he had certainly never meant to invest thousands of dollars in his third son. But the Reconstruction utopianism Wilkie had adopted from Forbes—his desire to rebuild the South on a new and improved model—simply mesmerized the older man. Aunt Kate, too, contributed some of her carefully hoarded money; though she had never been particularly close to Wilkie, she couldn't resist his enthusiasm.

Soon, beginning in June 1866, Wilkie, perhaps starved for company, even accepted the dubious gift of Bob's participation in his venture. Bob had given up his railroad job; their mother didn't want her youngest son underfoot in Boston, and Henry had refused to bankroll his ambition to study architecture. So the young man duly traveled down to Florida that summer, joining his brother in a primitive country that must have seemed remote even after his exile in the Midwest. There certainly wasn't much architecture to study on Wilkie's remote plantation, and Bob—stowed like baggage out of harm's way—turned out to be the most recalcitrant correspondent in the family, once he arrived in Gainesville. Diverting or even cheerful correspondence must hardly have seemed possible in the dirty roughness of the brothers' shack.

Bob's bad frame of mind soon taxed Wilkie's strength, too, in spite of Wilkie's warm affection for him. If Wilkie saw his brother drunk or approaching inebriation, he didn't mention it to his parents. But he did mention Bob's "temperament," his tendency toward morbid introspection and emotional highs and lows—a set of characteristics that indicated a drinking problem. Bob, like his ex-alcoholic father, often lost his temper, insulted people, and then felt guilty, so that, his brother observed, he "groan[ed] for hours."

In spite of Wilkie's ingenuity and hard work, signs of trouble in Florida soon intruded even into the Jameses' sheltered drawing room. Alice was shocked in 1867 when a visitor showed her a sketch of her brothers' house. Their plank dwelling struck her as "the most deplorable looking place you ever saw," with no blinds or curtains to screen the sun, hemmed in by monotonous pines. That same autumn, Wilkie limped home with the "intermittent fever" of malaria. His mother was astonished to see her plumpest child "thin and sallow," though she hoped the tonic New England air would soon cure him. "The crops have been an almost entire failure this year," she admitted, "incessant rains and catterpillars [sic] have done the business."

But even a bumper crop wouldn't have helped. The price of cotton had nosedived from over a dollar a pound right after the war to only fourteen cents in 1867. Wilkie would scarcely eke out enough money to buy out Aunt Kate's interest, let alone to repay his father.

❧

HENRY AND MARY, meanwhile, embarked on other land deals closer to home, buoyed by the prosperity and optimism created by the end of the war. Though still living in their Beacon Hill rental, they chafed to buy some brick or clapboard parcel of Boston, to join the ranks of their propertied friends. In the spring of 1866, they were on the point of purchasing any number of houses, as far away from the statehouse as Concord. At one auction downtown in Union Square, Henry had strained to bid on a house he had never even seen ten minutes before—though Mary "frowned at him," and the home was knocked down to another bidder. Still, the Jameses were soon to find shelter in another Brahmin neighborhood, Cambridge, just across the Charles.

In the autumn of 1866, the Jameses moved into 20 Quincy Street, at the crest of a low hill on the eastern side of Harvard Yard. Elm-shaded Harvard, with its redbrick chimneys, was just across the street. The family's new home belonged to a librarian: the Jameses rented the house from Louis Thies, one of the Harvard library curators. Blocky, solid, with a mansard roof, the big wood-frame structure had four ground-floor drawing rooms with fireplaces (where Henry could write, and Mary and Kate could knit) and abundant bedrooms. But it had few of the flourishes—the porches or porticoes or cupolas—of the neighboring professors' residences (one of them belonging to the perennial Louis Agassiz). A long lawn sliced through the block, and a wisteria vine promised grape-cluster blossoms in May. In Boston they always pronounced the name of the Jameses' new street "Quinzy"—a Massachusetts peculiarity that clearly separated the initiated from the naive.

After the more restricted space of Ashburton Place, the family could sigh in relief. Their new neighborhood tempted them with an open and parklike air. Across the way, Harvard Yard, with its cluster of redbrick Georgian buildings, with their green shutters and tall chimneys, reposed under a canopy of tall and slender elms. Brand-new clapboard houses were rising up, but orchards and cornfields weren't far away. From the family's new upstairs windows, the arc of the winding Charles River was visible to the south, across the ridges of more tightly packed houses. In 1866, even nearby Harvard Square, though more bustling, retained a rural feel. The square was lined with brick shops and traversed by horse-drawn trolleys, shaded by the majestic spreading elms.

The family enjoyed an unobstructed view of the Gore Library, built in 1838 of pinkish local granite, just to the west. With its spires and buttresses and four pepper-pot towers, the library mimicked a church; it had been inspired, in fact, by the resplendent King's College Chapel in the English Cambridge. (The library would be torn down in 1912 in order to make room for Widener Library, the more massive classical building that is now the centerpiece of the planet's fourth largest collection of books.) But Gore Library, a Gothic knockoff, revealed Harvard's uneasy deference to Europe—though the university would increasingly imagine itself in the more "American" architecture of Revolutionary War Georgian. From his bedroom on the third floor, Harry contemplated a distant view, to the east across Cambridge, of Bunker Hill and the "eloquent dome of the State House," as he remembered it—two symbols of American autonomy.

But it was William's and Harry's own personal autonomy that preoccupied them more. Harvard had once promised independence, but no more. Just as Henry Senior had dragged all of them back from Europe for William to study painting in 1860, he'd now relocated the household to Cambridge for William's sake (and a little for Harry's). William, now a twenty-four-year-old medical student, had his mother to arrange his meals, supervise his laundry, and lament his messy bedroom. (Aunt Kate was often on hand to help care for her favorite nephew, even if she liked to spend weeks at a time in her native New York City.) But Mary could oppress William with her interference. Her "Vandal hand," as William teasingly called it, cleaned up his hobbies—such as, in one famous case, a pair of prize grouse wings. Mary had been known to "heave a beautiful sigh" when she entered William's chaotic room. The move to Cambridge had brought the young man's observant and invasive family, especially his parents, right to the doorstep of his work.

BRIEFLY, ON HIS return from Brazil, William threw himself into "social intercourse," squiring his glittering Temple cousins to balls and parties all over Boston. Sometimes he escorted Minny—who as part of a new generation of woman scorned stay-at-home pursuits. William still nurtured a sort of crush on her, although her bright unconventionality, so unladylike, continued to moderate his admiration. Back in the Jameses' parlor, Alice had little admiration to quash. She pronounced

Minny a chameleon, "so much influenced by the last person she has been with . . . that one never knows where to find her." Alice herself, though she sometimes appeared sweet and wrote sentimental letters in the approved feminine style, had a sharper, more perceptive mind, which she sometimes camouflaged for the sake of convention. Deep down she harbored the soul of an uncompromising critic, yet even Alice grudgingly admitted that Minny was "very pretty" and undeniably "fascinating."

During the spring of 1867, William also took a liking, though an ill-fated one, to a Boston belle named Fanny Dixwell, an intelligent, quiet young woman whom William rated "*A*1, if any one ever was." Unfortunately, the eligible Miss Dixwell had another prime Boston match already in view—and, as luck would have it, with one of William's best friends. She'd encouraged the attentions of Oliver Wendell Holmes Jr., the son of the quoteworthy Dr. Holmes of the Saturday Club, and she would soon marry him. As the future wife of a Supreme Court justice, Fanny, though somewhat shy, would eventually produce some unexpected bon mots. In 1903, she would amuse Theodore Roosevelt by remarking that Washington was "full of famous men, and the women they married when they were young."

For William, this resplendent Boston "season" soon faded. The James family's move to Cambridge hadn't marked his entrée into the Brahmin social scene but instead a period of disaffection and virtual house arrest. He even abetted his own isolation, his live-in family claustrophobia: at his parents' urging, he set up his laboratory at home instead of working at Massachusetts General Hospital, across the Charles River in Boston.

Though he kept up a jovial flow of letters (Mary had taught him a certain sturdy cheerfulness), William increasingly, a prisoner in his third-floor bedroom, complained of back pains and eye problems. Sometimes, it was true, he enjoyed his anatomical studies. (When a songbird that Bob had given the family died mysteriously, William performed the autopsy.) But his monotonous work, his long hours of reading and solitude, and his nonexistent love life continued to cause him great anxiety. As recently as 1863, a *Mrs.* William James had seemed a "not impossible she." But by 1866, not only the she but also the means to marry her seemed permanently out of his reach. He could not picture himself as a man who could acquire any of the satisfying conventional comforts.

Previously William had joked about the ennuis of living at home, shut up with his "aged parents." But beneath his compensatory wit, his spirits continued to suffer under the monotony of medical studies undertaken primarily for the sake of his parents. William himself still didn't know exactly what he wanted to do; his own desires—once so optimistically focused on painting or on naturalism—had been systematically squelched by his father's irate idealism and his mother's worried practicality. He didn't want to be a doctor, but that seemed to be his fate. Hating himself for not measuring up to his parents' demands, William was now definitely depressed.

Harry, William's fellow inmate on the third floor of the librarian's house, proved even more piquant in his complaints—and illustrated quite vividly the source of both brothers' torpor. At twenty-three, Harry also felt stagnant and locked into the tomblike confinement of home. He decried the doldrums of the family routine. An "exciting" Sunday morning stood out as typical. A raw drizzle falling outside. His mother answering letters. And "fishballs lying heavy on [his] stomach."

Even more than William, Harry was coming to hate Cambridge. Ironically, he didn't value or in any way acknowledge the social opportunities his parents had hoped to provide him, in the big clapboard houses of the Brahmins all around. "The undergraduates of course are too young," Harry wrote a friend in 1867, fastidiously, "the law students (in general) too stupid and common, the tutors and several of the professors too busy, and Longfellow, Lowell, Norton and co. (in spite of great amiability), not at all to my taste." The Saturday Club titans his father had cultivated—and who in fact were forwarding Harry's fledgling career—left him crankily dissatisfied. After all, Harry didn't like to visit the "best" houses—like Shady Hill, the spacious home of Charles Eliot Norton and his learned, silk-sheathed sister Grace—more than once every two or three months. In his mind a "rigid, frigid" winter in Cambridge, destitute of theaters and art galleries, didn't provide any social "relaxation." It was "only a ghostly simulacrum of it."

Harry chafed against a New England society that, especially as a conscious outsider, he found bookish, clannish, and mired in stiff, tiresome tradition. But his discontentment was rooted even more in his parents' Quincy Street household. Home he pronounced "about as lively as the inner sepulchre." Yet the parents who now exerted so much control were the same characters who had instilled the possibility of escape: Europe, more and more, served as a counterpoint to home for Harry. "Can Cambridge answer Seville?" Harry wrote to a friend who was enviably traveling in Spain. "Can Massachusetts respond to Granada? . . . Bedbugs? Methinks that I would endure even them for a glimpse of those galleries and cathedrals."

Tellingly, Harry branded the young ladies of Cambridge "provincial, common, and inelegant." As an antidote, Harry relished the free, ecstatic company of Minny Temple, whom he saw whenever he could, in Newport or in the White Mountains of New Hampshire. Minny continued to enthrall him, but she was often more engaged with her other male companions, some of them potential suitors. Her somewhat finicky cousin, with his intricate and rather French literary predilections, was often left waiting in line; he seemed to have no interest in other female companions.

Harry's aloofness hadn't gone unnoticed. He had gained a reputation as a "woman hater"—in both hemispheres, according to William. Certainly Harry didn't obsess about women as William did. (Mary constantly fretted about William's crushes). Harry remained emotionally cool around females. William caricatured his brother as "an epic self-contained," gazing at the most intoxicating women with an "undazzled eye."

In the winter of 1866–67, after months of grinding work and stultifying home life, it was surprisingly William and not Harry who convinced his parents to send him to Europe. William, who had absorbed his father's unspoken dictum that travel was always curative, the "standing remedy" for Jameses under stress, played the card of his worsening health. He argued that he could go abroad to polish his German—a useful language for medical study in the nineteenth century. But it was his condition that won the day.

As his "very cheerful" mother failed to understand, William, once the great hope of the family, was beginning to descend into a mental state that would parallel his father's own crisis in England in 1844, when Henry Senior had hallucinated a demon squatting on the hearth. For now, William would combat his "fear of the universe," as he later called it, by means of a mystical remedy the Jameses had so often resorted to: pilgrimage.

∽

WILLIAM'S SPIRITS HAD lifted by the time he wrote his sister from the huge gilded saloon of the steamship *Great Eastern*. Having sailed from New York Harbor on April 17, 1867, he found himself at mid-Atlantic surrounded by children who were enjoying themselves by sucking on oranges. Even this odd observation, reported in a letter to Alice, improved on the prison of Quincy Street: it was an image of people getting some simple pleasure out of life. William found it good to be free of the others at home, even if he had to brace himself constantly against the ship's rolling. The young man could now appreciate firsthand why the *Great Eastern* had become infamous for its rocking-horse motion. But it was still the best steamer William could travel on—the cutting-edge successor to the other blue-ribbon-winning liners the Jameses had patronized over the years.

The *Great Eastern* outclassed everything that had come before it, even in a century that lived to crack champagne bottles on the bows of maritime superlatives. A "Triton among minnows," as the newspapers called it, the British-built ship measured five times the size of anything else afloat. In fact, it outsized any ship that would launch for the next fifty years. It resembled a "great swollen hunk of a premature Leviathan," the press observed, with its five gigantic smoke funnels and its paddles the size of Ferris wheels.

A vainglorious and ungainly monster, the *Great Eastern* had captured the admiration of Walt Whitman. Even more thoroughly, it had fascinated the French fabulist Jules Verne, who wrote an adulatory account of it called *Une Ville flottant (A Floating City)*. Verne, in fact, shared the voyage from New York with William—William's voyage out, Verne's return. The Frenchman had made a career of writing science fiction based on the exciting leaps in transportation that he along with the James family had witnessed. In *Twenty Thousand Leagues Under the Sea* (1870), he wrote precociously about submarines; in *From the Earth to the Moon* (1865) about space travel. With his full iron-gray beard, this thirty-nine-year-old best-selling writer would have been somewhat conspicuous to his fellow passengers, though William evidently didn't notice him at all. But although the two men weren't acquainted, they no doubt passed each other on the broad avenues of the pitching decks.

Aboard such a vessel, William could well revive, believing he was sailing to Europe to finish up his education, to "couronner l'édifice" (crown the edifice), as he hopefully put it. But William also suffered from periods of idleness and dissatisfaction, even aboard this floating palace; he hadn't completely shaken off the self-doubt that had swamped him at home.

He landed at the port of Brest in France near the end of April. Taking the train on to Paris, he wrote his family that he gaped at the "alterations of our old haunts" by the two magnificent boulevards that had been opened up in the area around the grand classical church of the Madeleine, near where the Jameses had once resided. Reading the philosopher Georg Wilhelm Friedrich Hegel for pleasure, William then progressed by rail across the blossoming spring landscape of middle Europe, by way of Strasburg and the Rhine, to the German kingdom of Saxony. In pursuit of further education, William intended to base himself in a distinguished center of learning and art, then also rapidly expanding with industry: the city of Dresden.

A smoky, congested metropolis on the river Elbe, Dresden in 1867 hadn't yet built its golden, three-tiered opera house, though it touted a distinguished academy of the arts. He would appreciate the city's two "noble" bridges, its open spaces, its steep-roofed houses. He settled in for the spring, and the somewhat drab details of his lodger's isolation—his breakfasts of bread and hot chocolate, his tiny stick-burning porcelain stove—soon filled his letters home. Yet sometimes he felt genuine excitement: soon he would feel the romance of the "grand old language" of German. But before long, that would qualify as the second-greatest romance he would find there.

William was lonely to begin with. He didn't exactly hunger for artistic evenings out, as his brother Harry did from the distance of Cambridge. Only wanderings in the deep-green Grosser Garten, with bands playing marches and waltzes, broke up William's marathons of heavy reading. He was hard-pressed, in fact, to entertain himself socially at all. At twenty-five, William declared that the "heyday of youth is o'er" and pronounced his German excursion about as exciting as a trip to Chicago. (Such indifference to the splendors of Europe scandalized Harry.)

More than anything else, William probably craved the "sensuality" he had started to explore in Brazil. William may have lodged in the so-called Florence of the north, but he readily contrasted the high-minded aspirations of Harry with his own more basic yen for warm female companionship.

William may even have taken advantage of his distance from his watchful family to visit a prostitute—if he hadn't already done so in Brazil. According to a letter written years later to his friend Thomas Ward, William had plunged into an unspecified experience, brought on by "mere physical nervousness"—his idleness and pent-up libido. And after this mystery experience, William felt he'd "come of age," but he also saw his action as a lapse that had thrown him into danger: "Boys will make mistakes," he confided to Ward, a companion of his Brazilian getaway. "The tho't of what *might* have happened makes me shiver now." William's fearful language hints at some sexual experience that caused him remorse. But one of William's most recent biographers suspects milder indiscretions that raised severe fears. A prostitute might have crippled him with a disease, of course. But even masturbation in the nineteenth century was thought to inflict brain damage.

In spite of his explorations, William remained painfully shy. In Germany, he felt more "akin" to the blushing British than the womanizing French. Though he'd bought a telescope for scientific purposes, he angled it at the girls' boarding school across the street. Otherwise he mixed mostly with his warmhearted old landlady, Frau Spangenberg; with beer-garden acquaintances; and with a smattering of expatriate

Americans. In letters back to Cambridge, William enlisted Alice's "feminine system of espionage" to find out more about two Miss Twombleys, of Boylston Street in Boston, one of whom he found "exceedingly pretty."

More materially, during a later stay in Dresden, William linked up with a woman at his boardinghouse with whom he would cultivate a friendship: a sensitive, moody twenty-nine-year-old from New York whose piano concertos enticingly washed over him in the evenings. The appropriately named Catherine Havens—or Kate, as she was called— moved William in a new way. And significantly, he confided this romance to his personal diary, but not in his letters home.

Like William, Kate Havens had a troubled spirit that had goaded her to foreign travel, and the two homesick expatriates soon bonded. But they amounted only to boardinghouse sweethearts, if that. Their changes of scene would separate them before long—at least for the time being.

AT LOOSE ENDS, with his back plaguing him, William made repeated visits to Teplitz, a cure bath in Bohemia, in what is now the Czech Republic. Over heavy Teutonic meals of veal, beefsteak, or mutton, William met an array of nervous and intriguing *Magic Mountain* characters: a compulsive Polish liar who proved provocatively "attentive" to him; a young Englishman with "a gift of the gab" who'd written a travel book about Iceland; and a young and flirtatious Bohemian noblewoman named Anna Adamowiz. With such companions, William wandered the ancient stone town of Teplitz, where the sun never seemed to strike into the damp streets.

It was the grand epoch of European cure resorts, and a spa "cured" its patients as much with company as with hydropathy. At a sanatorium William tried later, at Divonne, in the hilly French countryside near Lake Leman, he attracted a ring of attentive females—almost a cure in itself. William, ever the jokester, sent home a "comic" drawing of himself besieged by the "listening fair," young ladies in pin-striped cottons and tilted bonnets, arrayed under the shade trees in various sentimental attitudes, listening to him hold forth. "The cold water cure at Divonne," William wrote on his drawing, "excellent for melancholia."

At Bad Teplitz, the more official treatments included hot baths and scalding mud-plasters. The merits or demerits of this cure filled William's letters to his health-obsessed family—especially to Harry, who'd also suffered chronic back troubles since his Civil War–era pump injury in Newport. For Harry's back, William repeatedly recommended "blisters"—a time-honored medical practice that involved raising blisters by means of various skin-irritating liniments. William studiously "applied" quarter-sized blisters, one every night on each side of his spine, "over the diseased muscles." But such misguided self-mutilation hardly helped the young man's condition; the blisters most often caused swelling and infection, without at all helping the original injury. Still, his pain at least distracted him, and the regimen gave him some illusion of mastery.

Harry, back home, resolutely refused blisters. He cherished his own cure methods, including ice—quite a rare and gemlike substance in the nineteenth century—and "having his back nicely tuned up every evening by a rural Irish youth." Massage had dawned as an American industry. Harry's experience hints at the sensual or even erotic element wrapped up in many of these cures. Even if nonsexual, touch can be powerfully erotic to those who have gone long years without it, and sometimes restorative.

Harry seems to have improved and thrived with William's mere absence from the house—sibling rivalry, along with parental interference, lurked in his own infirmities. And the family dynamic shaped the Jameses' illnesses. William saw his bad back as "a family peculiarity." But vigorous, hardworking Mary had no such aches, and even Henry Senior, with his artificial leg, suffered from few such symptoms. William's bad health actually suggested a "family peculiarity" in a psychological more than a physical sense. Whatever dorsal problems William and Harry had inherited, they suffered even more from the spasms of James family politics.

Even though William had interposed the Atlantic Ocean between himself and Quincy Street, he remained paradoxically attached to the household of his familial tormentors. The swarms of letters that the steamers carried back and forth kept him tangled up with everyone. William mock-flirted with Alice, continuing the faux-romantic badinage he'd inflicted on her for at least ten years. He also pompously criticized Harry's ongoing literary efforts. He judged his brother's stories *"thin"* even if the traveling American women he met in Germany were breathlessly following Harry's latest three-parter in the *Atlantic*.

William himself was dependent on handouts from his parents. He deeply envied the eight hundred dollars Harry had made over the past year (he demanded to know the figure) and wished he himself had "anything to write about." In his column of achievements, William could count only a few dry scientific reviews. And, adding to his other troubles, he had almost no income to wedge between himself and his father's checks.

As his year wore on, voluminous letters kept William abreast of all the family minutiae. To his mother, William wrote about the cut of his new suit. In the nineteenth-century equivalent of sending a color photograph, he even detailed to her his "neat alpaca coat, white damask vest, blue cravat, and a pair of splendid cinnamon colored pantaloons." (William was his mother's son.)

William kept up a tense and sometimes adversarial correspondence with his father, a scrappy epistolary debate. He jokingly referred to Henry's recent magnum opus, *Substance and Shadow; or, Morality and Religion in Their Relation to Life* (1863) as "Substance and Shadder," just as he'd once "illustrated" another of his father's books with a drawing of a man beating a dead horse. William's financial dependence proved to be a dead horse, too—and one that he himself had to beat again and again.

By going to Europe, William had repeated Henry Senior's history of running from *his* father, to that snug room on Beacon Hill back in 1829. Then, though, Henry had earned his own way; while in Dresden William was still hanging on to his father's tab. What's more, William still hankered for his father's blessing. The young man's continued attachment to his father's whims and moods complicated his recovery. William remained emotionally fragile, but he was gradually asserting an intellectual independence, styled after his father's bombast, which would prove surprisingly hardy.

In the fall of 1867, William picked an argument with his father's latest Swedenborg article in the *American Review*. William, Henry's favorite son, couldn't fathom his father's meaning—*that* must be a bitter pill, William thought, a sign of his father's "mental isolation." Henry countered that William was only showing his immaturity. In Henry's mind, William's trouble understanding arose "*mainly* from the purely *scientific* cast" of his present "puerile stage of progress." To the credit of his fledgling self-determination, William held his own in this dispute. Still, Henry could domineer, in his peculiar way, even from as far away as Cambridge.

William's leash, however, had strained to its limit. His time was running out. By the fall of 1868, Henry and Mary decided that William's health wasn't improving in these European spas. His mother longed to nurse him herself, instead of abandoning him as "a lone outcast among the unfeeling foreigners." And William himself had to admit to Alice that his sabbatical, in spite of its entertaining high points, amounted to "one of the emptiest years of [his] life." In the end, his eighteen months in Europe had increased his sense of loneliness and idleness instead of curing it.

From the safe distance of Germany, William could now indulge in nostalgia for his New England home. Remembering Harvard's impressive Gothic library, he could laud his parents' Cambridge home for hosting a "library of books in the house and a still bigger one over the way." He could paint a rosy picture of dinners in Cambridge, remembering rich holiday spreads instead of the more habitual fish balls. He saw a roaring wood fire and the family's favorite Irish servant, the always "clean" Ellen, passing the different courses. At the table he saw a loving mother and a lively if bald-headed father, regaling the whole family with horsecar anecdotes, conjuring up speculative visions of the cosmos. He imagined his brother Harry "dealing his snubs around." When he was away, William could picture Boston as a veritable Athens, crowded with gods of stimulation. In the lonely stretches of his German exile, William's imagination could "bump like a moth" against his parents' high windowpanes. From his European distance, he tended to envision the happier aspect of the James family—the house of wits, and not the "inner sepulchre." But he would recall, soon enough, what his siblings had never been allowed to forget. Quincy Street harbored a grim secret that Alice, the neglected girl and youngest child of the family, knew best of all.

· 8 ·

BOTTLED LIGHTNING

I n November 1866, with the frosty weather coming, eighteen-
year-old Alice packed her trunk with warm clothing, readying
herself for a winter in New York City. Although she was the
James child least likely to leave Quincy Street under any circumstances,
Alice could look forward to a railroad journey down the low, rocky
coasts, interrupted by river estuaries and marshes, of Rhode Island and
Connecticut. She had triumphed in her own small way, winning a rare
reprieve from her parents and her arrested girlhood. Still, she would
travel under the watchful supervision of her aunt Kate, now fifty-four
years old, with her iron-gray curls and what Bob described as her
"mandatory ways."

The two women left their train and ventured out onto the crowded
sidewalks of Manhattan—a metropolis that since Alice's childhood on
Fourteenth Street had grown considerably. The four-story houses of an
earlier day were being replaced by six- and ten-story buildings; familiar
church spires were getting lost among the new brick warehouses and offices continually on the rise. This was the glittering, chaotic city that Walt
Whitman would celebrate in his *Democratic Vistas* (1871), with its "splendor, picturesqueness, and oceanic amplitude," with its elegant office
buildings of marble and iron, massive stores, concert halls, and ever-
lengthening thoroughfare of Broadway jammed with the traffic of

carriages, horsecars, and bundled-up pedestrians—yielding a "heavy, low, musical roar, hardly ever intermitted, even at night."

On Broadway in the early darkness of November, Kate and Alice took note of the latest fashions in bonnets and muffs. They passed rich new shops that neither of them remembered from previous visits—although Kate more frequently spent time in New York and recognized gaslit restaurants packed with fashionable women sporting their winter furs. Lower Broadway was jam-packed with carriages, horse-drawn omnibuses, cabs, drays, and wagons; as the visiting French writer Jules Verne noticed in 1867, it was a thoroughfare where "sheds and marble palaces are huddled together." In this splendor and squalor, Kate radiated the confidence of a native: she looked the part of a steady middle-aged woman, impeccably dressed, who might accompany a niece to fashionable dances behind the striped awnings of Delmonico's on Fifth Avenue and Fourteenth Street. Alice's Temple cousins sometimes graced balls in New York as well as in Boston, but Alice's prospects for dancing during the winter would almost certainly be limited.

As her brother William would do a few months later, she was traveling for her health. Her parents had sent her to New York—not, of course, to Dresden—in order to treat her latest wave of stomach cramps and nerves. Sickness was a ticket to a place where she might get a breath of novelty, but with Aunt Kate along she would hardly have much independence.

Alice settled into a row house at Broadway and Thirty-fifth Street. For her treatment, she had rented a room in the home of Charles Fayette Taylor, a cutting-edge orthopedic physician whom her parents and Aunt Kate hoped had a good chance of addressing her case. Taylor's small residential practice stood near the future site of Herald Square—where famous department stores would one day stand. But Macy's would not open its doors in the area until 1902, and Gimbels would not appear until after 1910. In the late 1860s, it was a neighborhood of townhouses with steep steps, basement kitchens, and adolescent trees out in front, stripped in winter. A few shops straggled along Broadway, which higher in Manhattan was almost deserted. A couple of blocks farther north, in a modest row house on West Thirty-eighth Street, George Herbert Taylor, Alice's doctor's brother and colleague, had recently founded what he called the Improved Movement Cure Institute. Alice would go there for her "motorpathic" or "movement cure."

The Taylor brothers believed in the power of exercise to counter nervous problems, especially for women; the two had imported their medical techniques from England and from Sweden, where in the early 1800s Per Henrik Ling had pioneered Swedish massage treatments, versions of which have survived into the present day. Before the invention of the distinct field of psychology later in the nineteenth century—a revolution to which William would later contribute—doctors most often treated mental problems by physical means; the Taylors tried to cure what we now call depression by means of orthopedic manipulation, understanding such ailments as an imbalance between overdeveloped nerves and underdeveloped bodies. (For good measure, George Taylor also employed a spiritualist on his premises.)

After examining Alice, Charles Taylor located her trouble in her stomach and spine. He had seen such symptoms before. He had long specialized in the treatment of the nervous exhaustion that another New York physician, George M. Beard, described in the late 1860s as "neurasthenia"—a term covering a wide range of symptoms that would later be known as depression, anxiety, hypochondria, or neurosis.

Neurasthenia was diagnosed with increasing frequency in post–Civil War America, especially among women. To many doctors, it was an alarming modern ailment, brought on by the stresses of technological and social advancement. And Alice, though hardly as advanced or emancipated as some of the daughters of Boston, had all the signature proclivities of a "neurasthenic" woman: she suffered from lassitude and depression because (it was believed) she read and thought too much. She had absorbed many of her brothers' books in English and French and had amassed, even as early as her teens, a remarkable store of self-education. According to nineteenth-century medicine, mental activity literally poisoned women—or, as in Alice's present diagnosis, deformed their bodies.

Through the winter, she churned through exercises to straighten her spine and strengthen her limbs; that was her reward for having doggedly persisted in her private studies. Luckily for her, George Taylor had recently invented a machine that featured an apparatus for expanding the chest, limbering the pelvis, and kneading the abdomen. The Taylors' patients were also directed to follow a regimen of massage, baths, and special meals as they toiled to regain their health. Some of Alice's fellow patients suffered from more straightforward physical conditions, spine and hip-joint problems. For instance, Alice got to know a "pretty little boy" named Willy Wood, and she grew attached to the child and was terribly disturbed to hear about his death a few months later. ("I hope that the Doctor has not pushed matters too hard with him," Alice remarked, hinting at the rigors of the Taylors' treatment.)

Most of Alice's companions at the supper table or in the exercise rooms were older women who had entrenched complaints about their nerves, high-strung and delicate upper-crust ladies much older than late-teenage Alice. Among these bored women, forced by custom into genteel inactivity, both neurasthenia and hysteria—an even more characteristically "female" disorder—were the most frequent psychological diagnoses. And these diseases, suddenly, seemed to be everywhere. William, a chronic neurasthenic, took an avid interest in these emerging afflictions. Kate had forwarded him a copy of Dr. Taylor's book, *Theory and Practice of the Movement Cure* (1861); William had developed a passionate interest in the treatment. He and his sister, as sufferers from nervous problems, had many symptoms in common. But their style as invalids differed markedly. In Germany, William would make colorful acquaintances at the spas; in New York, Alice made no lasting friends. She was painfully shy, perhaps bored or mystified by more ordinary people. Kate's take-charge presence, too, made it hard for Alice to meet people on her own terms.

While William's sanatoriums would boast mineral springs or airy mountain views, Alice's small room was urban—fretted by streetlights at night, the rumble of horsecars on Broadway during the day. But New York had its own attractions for her and her fellow invalid ladies. Alice took in the discordant, colorful pageant of the streets that her mother had admired thirty years before, keeping an eye out for the styles of dresses that William told her he wanted to hear about: intricate black bonnets with lace chignons; matching dresses without waistbands, gathered at the neck.

Christmas approached, but Alice stayed on in New York, now laced with snow and decorated with evergreen wreaths: she couldn't interrupt her regimen to come home. To soothe his sister, William entertained her with a description of a green brocade gown with organdy trimmings that their mother was hoping to acquire. "You've no idea how *delightful* your letters are," he told her, encouragingly, as if surprised by the flair of a little sister to whom he didn't always listen. But none of Alice's own correspondence from this time has survived.

When they wrote to *her*, Alice's family was careful not to mention her illness beyond forecasting her recovery. Mary pointedly emphasized the "fine accounts of [her] blooming appearance" and relished the report of a New York cousin who had seen Alice looking "fat as butter." "We are delighted to hear such fine accounts of your improvement, the beauty of your character and so forth," Harry wrote her in February 1867. The family kept details of Alice's condition hushed, but her admirable behavior as an invalid earned her the attention from her parents that she craved. Her brother poked fun at "the beauty of [her] character and so forth," but an illness could in fact be a formidable asset for a nineteenth-century woman.

 ⁂

ALICE RETURNED TO Quincy Street in the late spring of 1867. She was ostensibly cured or at least weary of treadmills. William had found the stodgy ground-floor parlors a "weary & empty place" without her, he had written. But on April 17 he had escaped to Germany, and she and twenty-four-year-old Harry now shared the large cold rooms and their parents' sober routines. "Alice seems bright and is an immense joy to us," Mary reported to William. "Her presence is a perfect sunbeam to Father." A "perfect sunbeam" neatly described Mary's notion of a fulfilled daughter but would seem to have little to do with nineteen-year-old Alice. Mary evidently envisioned a different young woman who might arrive on the next fine day. This Alice would never appear; nor could she have survived in Quincy Street.

Alice did her best to entertain her father, but Henry, fifty-six, was preoccupied by his lack of success and suffering from eczema. His doctors traced this condition to his "head troubles," as Mary called them— his chronic anxiety and nervousness. But his moods taxed his daughter's patience no more than his words. When he went out to lecture, Henry continued to promote his view of women as mental nonentities and emotional nannies for men; he brazenly discoursed on the sacred importance of women's traditional roles in the home at the feminist New England Women's Club in December 1868. Women, he predicted, would never have a high place in public religion. Many women in his audience would have disagreed with him. That Alice didn't even mention her father's tirades, at the time, hints at both her detachment from his hurtful view and the internalization of her frustrations. She never confronted him; any unhappiness she felt, she simply took to bed with her.

Only years later would Alice actually protest, declaring herself "impatient for the moment when the knitting of a good stocking will be thought as 'worthy work' as the painting of a flimsy sketch." During her childhood, William had been indulged in his artistic aspirations. Alice's continual needlework, by contrast, remained unnoticed—like Alice, a nearly invisible parlor fixture, like an antimacassar or a lamp, year after year.

It was not long before Alice fell ill again. In June, only a month after her return from New York, at the house of her old school friend Fanny Morse, in the tree-shaded streets of nearby Brookline, Alice had one of her spells. Mary ("the admirable mother," Alice called her) hurried to her daughter's bedside and then fetched her home in a carriage. The circumstances of Alice's breakdown remained murky: neither she nor her parents entered into the details. Alice had simply had "one of her attacks," Mary reported to William, caused by a "little overexertion"— though how the young woman might have overstrained herself on a pleasurable visit to a friend remained undiscussed in the family.

But the setting of this "attack" was not accidental. Alice had been staying with her best friend; her young women friends as well as her family engrossed her emotions and set off her insecurities. Aside from her fellow Jameses, Alice's close confidantes in Boston—Mary Lee, Annie Ashburner, and Fanny Morse, the cultured, ribbon-wearing daughters of well-to-do families—played the largest role in her life. With no sisters of her own, Alice depended on these relationships for entertainment, companionship, and a sense of her own importance. Such intimacies gave her solace but also sparked emotional troubles and conflicts that as yet remained mysterious even to Alice herself.

Alice had met Frances Rollins Morse, the refined daughter of wealthy Massachusetts mill owners, at Miss Clapp's school in Boston a few years before. Fanny was two years younger than Alice, and Alice often spent happy intervals away from Quincy Street with Fanny, her mother, and her younger sister, Mary. One Sunday after such a visit, Alice scribbled a note to her friend while she was in the middle of doing up her hair for the night. She balanced her letter paper on her knee—"in the most improper way," she acknowledged, remembering perhaps the manners she and her friend had been taught in school. Her note had "no purpose," she apologized, except that she wrote fervently to tell Fanny "how much I wish I could see you oftener—in short that I love you very much."

Such tender sentiments were sanctioned by the Victorian cult of female friendship. Young women were encouraged to cherish one another, often quite sentimentally. Yet Alice's strong attachment to Fanny comes through distinctly in her letter and suggests an emotional intensity that may have later flared at Fanny's home. "I feel myself to be a more respectable human being when I consider I have you for a friend, & I have you, haven't I, notwithstanding my sins," Alice wrote to her friend. "You seemed so sweet the other day that my heart has been full of you ever since."

ॐ

SHORTLY AFTER HER "attack" in Brookline—and maybe to recover from it—Alice and her mother traveled into Boston to buy one of the first mass-produced domestic appliances available in the United States, a Florence sewing machine. Isaac Merritt Singer, a New York entrepreneur and showman, had begun improving and manufacturing sewing machines in the 1850s, eventually founding the Singer Sewing Company. A Florence was a rival model—assembled, beginning in 1860, at a steam-powered silk manufactory in Florence, Massachusetts. Mary James considered a Florence a superior apparatus; she insisted on the best.

With the sewing machine set up at home, Alice felt excitement or at least professed it. "By the time you get back," she wrote William in Germany, "you will probably find Harry and father dressed in suits made by mother & me." Such chores, however, suited her mother more than Alice herself, with her interest in French novels and history. Mary herself was tireless. During one of her rare illnesses, she put up with her indisposition "like an angel," William noticed. Mary was clearly, as her favorite son, Harry, put it, "the perfection of health as of everything else." Even then she hardly slackened, "putting up cornices and raking out the garret room like a little buffalo." In Mary, Alice had a mother whose relentless housekeeping frequently galled her children.

Blocky and pleasant, with its fireplaces and bone china and comfortable meals, the Quincy Street house appeared an unlikely chamber of horrors. But it harbored something ineffable that the James children couldn't stomach. At least one visitor, Lilla Cabot Perry, later described the James home as the "stiff stupid house in Cambridge," with its "poky banality." Henry she allowed to be "genial and delightful," but Mary and her sister came across as anything but charming. Lilla Cabot branded the Walsh sisters "large florid stupid-seeming ladies." Mary was "the very incarnation of *banality*," and Kate wasn't much better. Most shocking was that Mary appeared to rule the roost. The future Mrs. Perry had scant sympathy for Alice, whom she called "clever but coldly self-absorbed." Retaliating in kind, Alice noted Lilla's "solid proportions"—so much in contrast, Alice quipped, to her slim income as the future wife of a struggling painter.

As the visitor had noticed, Mary indeed enforced her own rules in the house; according to the Cult of True Womanhood, that credo of domesticity, such was her privilege. For their part, the James children never critiqued their authoritative mother (or their "mandatory" aunt) openly. On the contrary, the younger Jameses normally imitated their father, who cheerfully spent his fireside hours "ringing the changes upon the Mother's perfections," as Alice remembered—lauding her "extraordinarily selfless devotion" and crowning her, with the hyperbolic sentimentality of the Victorian age, "the unconscious essence of wife and motherhood."

Alice exchanged knowing jokes with her brothers about their mother and her ways. She reported to William a characteristic exchange between Harry and their mother at the dinner table. "May I have some of those brown-rolls that were left this morning at breakfast[?]" Harry had asked. "Yes, certainly," Mary replied, "but do you wish to eat them with your soup[?]" "You can't certainly expect me to minutely explain what I intend to do with them," Harry responded. Mary, among her other uses, acted as comedic straight man, but perhaps her children's teasing was their only defense against her interference.

Sometimes, Mary's calm surface erupted unexpectedly. During Alice's convalescence, her outbursts perhaps betrayed her own buried discontents. Like her husband, she could be surprisingly barbed, even rude. She could also become biting about Henry himself, with her children—such as when she referred, mock-reverentially, to "your Father's immortal work." To the credit of her good sense, Mary hadn't lived with a mad theologian for twenty-something years without being aware of his personal limitations. She rolled her eyes. She wasn't perfectly patient. Like many a long-suffering wife, she fostered some hidden resentments.

Mary's jabs sometimes landed in surprising places, as Alice closely observed. That summer, the family, lounging on the "piazza" beside the house (having dragged out drawing-room furniture, lawn furniture being as yet unknown to the Jameses), received a visit from the diminutive Ohio-born assistant editor of the *Atlantic*, William Dean Howells. Henry asked for a description of some mutual acquaintance, and Howells approximated: "He is about my size." Unfortunately, Howells had slumped "all doubled up in a deep arm-chair, looking smaller if possible than ever."

Mary couldn't resist such an opening. "Ah, then he is a *small* man," she said, in what Alice considered her "inimitable manner." The result: "Mr. Howells for about five minutes was quite invisible, in fact mother was for some time the only person in existence." The family stifled spasms of laughter, fighting to regain composure. No wonder William missed his father's "energetic expletives" and his mother's "cool remarks," when away. But Alice wasn't always equal to handling these complicated personalities on her own.

On another occasion, Alice read out loud from a column in a Paris newspaper, about a paperlike material that could be eaten after it was read—so that its contents could be "well-digested." Mary replied, in the blank and blunt way that both irritated her children and sent them into paroxysms, "Why, that's very true, isn't it?" When she observed that love letters were "meant for one eye," her husband made humorous hay out of the remark by saying that "he supposed the other eye winked at them."

Their mother, Alice observed, constantly made such "delightful re-marks." Presumably these one-liners entertained the children because, in comparison to their own cleverness, their mother appeared obtuse, even slow-witted. But the James children also relished their mother's deadpan humor, which came from a literal mind they both loved and dreaded.

Mary, now stout and matronly, turned fifty-seven in 1867. Square-faced, light-eyed, she wore a serious and almost grim expression under her chaste white household cap. To judge from later photographs, she clothed herself in a commanding, no-nonsense mien that corresponded to her frilled, stiff, and fortresslike gowns. Her firm manner put off some of her more refined, ladylike Cambridge visitors—and a few of the gentlemen.

❧

IN OCTOBER 1867, Alice received a flattering invitation to join the Cambridge "Bee" from Susy Dixwell, the charming sister of Fanny Dixwell, who had earlier caught William's eye and who would marry his friend Oliver Wendell Holmes Jr. in 1872. Flattered and excited, Alice, who had been sick and depressed of late, was elated by this unexpected social distinction. The "Bee" was a sewing society formed in Cambridge at the beginning of the Civil War (Alice had belonged to a similar ver-sion in Newport) and now perpetuated to help the poor. The young women handcrafted items and sold them for charity, but the club had its more frivolous side. All of the "Cambridge misses," the daughters of Brahmins, attended the Bee, and Alice knew she could collect plenty of local gossip to forward to William in Germany when she went to one of their gatherings.

By fall, Alice noted that marriages were the Bee's fixation, and practically all the muslin-clad young ladies could manage to consider as they stitched and chatted. With memories of the war receding and normality returning to Northern cities, former Union soldiers made proposals under the Harvard elms or along the river walks in Cambridge. The Civil War had created a shortage of young men, but for most of Boston's belles this was hardly a problem. "There is the longest list of engagements and weddings," Alice wrote William, "and all the world seems to be getting married." Yet Alice, approaching the prime age of twenty, couldn't yet list any suitors.

During March 1868, still in the capital of the hilly kingdom of Saxony and largely unconscious of his sister's increasingly fragile state of mind, William continued to ply Alice with the relentless mock romance he'd used on her for years. If anything, he had increased the pitch of his *billets-doux* as Alice grew more womanly and as his own sexual frustrations at spas and boardinghouses mounted. In Dresden, on the riverside promenades, William—a dashing stubble-faced suitor wearing a rakish felt hat and a crimson scarf with a golden pin—drew the eyes of young women out sporting spring dresses. But, he comically claimed, he remained true to Alice, muttering only *her* name under his breath: "the peerless child of Quincy Street, *i.e. Thou!*"

Alice understood her brother's addiction to farce too well to toss "sleepless upon her couch," as he humorously imagined in his letter. She had long admired him with a little sister's devotion, but as she grew into a young woman, her affection for him increasingly veered into fear and distaste. Since her childhood, when his remarks had both elated and deflated her, Alice had been squeezed into a particularly maddening vise, one that had her in contortions by the spring of 1868. It seemed he planned never to let up, even now that romance was really a thorny issue in her life. Heedless of her insecurities and her loneliness, he continued to perplex his sister, via letters, from across the ocean. On one hand, he teased and dismissed her, describing her as "that idle & useless young female" whom the family had to feed and clothe. He wrote her that his life was "too serious for much letter writing to one's childlike sisters." Alice absorbed his cheerful denigration, signing herself "Your loving *idiotoid* sister."

At the same time, William kept up his steady stream of erotically tinged endearments. "You lovely babe," he'd begin, or "Cherie de Balle!" Once he'd joked that if he didn't hear from her, he'd "go *mad*, mad, MAD!" A year earlier, when she was in New York, William had pined to have her at home. If she had only taken the pills he had given her, he teased, "[You would be] at home sitting on the sofa, with my arm around your waste [sic] & rich tones of my voice ringing in your ear." Now from Europe he craved to sit with her and have her "sass" him as she'd done in earlier times.

William even had the nerve to dispatch big-brotherly advice to Alice on how to attract men. Alice wasn't a flirt—and wasn't even sure what she wanted from a man, if anything. Be "clinging yet self sustained, reserved yet confidential," her brother instructed her. In his eyes, she had to ignite the flame that would attract a male moth; she had to play the part of a lamp, beaming with earnest beauty, glowing with modest delight. He granted her the right to exhibit a "soul *with wings*," but he stipulated that her soul should take only brief flights. If she glided or soared, he worried, she'd scare off the men; to lure them, Alice had to keep her light *and* her wings adjusted; she had to make sure her gestures remained graceful and her voice mezzo-soprano and musical. Once again, as with her mother, Alice was receiving images of female perfection that diminished her hopes of ever pleasing anyone.

Alice didn't actively resist William's tampering, though she might have told *him* to be a little more understanding of women, if he wanted to win one. But she did sometimes "sass" her older brother. And she cared enough about William's Dresden romances that she anxiously monitored at least one of his boardinghouse intimacies. This Fräulein Smith, Alice judged, must be a "bold-faced jay." Alice reacted acidly to many women, and she had her own prejudices about female deportment, as well her own vulnerabilities to William and his crushes.

❦

WITHOUT WARNING, IN the spring of 1868, at the age of nineteen, Alice shocked her family with her most serious and spectacular breakdown to date. Alice plunged into fainting, phantom pains, attacks of "nerves," listless prostrations, and even compulsions to kill herself. Her body went into revolt. Down deep, Alice was sick of being modest, quiet, and overlooked while her brothers monopolized all the attention. She was bone-weary of "being 'good.'" Years later, she wrote that she longed to "burst out and make every one wretched for 24 hours," to abandon herself and "embody selfishness." Waves of pent-up feeling evidently convulsed Alice as never before; more than two decades would pass before she would write about the extremes of that spring. But from hints dropped in family letters and from Alice's own account, written in 1890, it seems clear that the young woman had advanced from quiet "neurasthenia" to something more dramatic and desperate. Doctors labeled it "hysteria"—a passionate loss of control, originating from what was seen as women's deeply emotional and irrational nature. "Falling into hysterics" could mean kicking, shouting, gibbering, throwing a fit something like a seizure—and Alice's behavior may have been something like this. Such "fits" occurred involuntarily, but much of her "hysteria," to judge from her later account, was more private and interior, amounting to a "violent revolt in [her] head."

With Alice's parents shielding her and, as usual, guarding family privacy, the Quincy Street neighbors would never have guessed that anything was amiss, but the big, boxy half mansion must have simply seemed all too quiet, with the wisteria vine that coiled up one side of the house dropping its sweet-smelling lavender flowers.

Alice spent days in bed or at best on a sofa in one of the four book-lined drawing rooms on the first floor. Her sofa—an ornate and curvaceous Victorian sofa, that asylum of Victorian females, with its horsehair and silk, its bolsters and pillows—might have seemed a pleasant prop for unhappiness. But Alice didn't languish there out of love or despair. She wasn't a lovesick maiden of the sort that nineteenth-century American audiences met so often on the stage, though she sometimes appeared as powerless as a melodramatic heroine. But she was far too intellectual and reserved to mimic such overblown despair. She had absorbed and carefully considered serious female writers such as George Sand (in the original French) and George Eliot. Ever studious, Alice counted herself, especially in scholarly matters, her father's daughter. But she had inherited his nervous temperament as well as his philosophical interests, and twenty-four years after Henry Senior had witnessed a demon on the hearth at Windsor, young Alice was following in his footsteps. For Henry and William, the horror of the world had inflicted paralysis and deep depression. For Alice, it now brought on an equally formidable array of problems, but magnified and exacerbated by her second-class status as a woman.

The possibilities of serious illness both terrified and stimulated Alice. She wept, she ranted, and she fainted away, indulging in an Ophelia-like performance—more or less involuntary—at which she could excel. Through her suffering, she could and did steal the show in the James family theater. And yet she played her new role excruciatingly, unconsciously, and in deadly earnest. As she later described it, she was pitted in a "never-ending fight" between her strong Jamesian will and her aggressively female body—a conflict that her body, she felt, would ultimately and catastrophically win.

The revolt of a woman's body, as the nineteenth century understood it, was the very definition of hysteria. Alice increasingly experienced fits, mood swings, bursts of ungovernable rage. She toyed with dark impulses to injure herself or others; she lashed out with raw hatred and anger. Still, she went numb with the fear that her "constabulary" moral restraints would weaken and she would commit the acts she was fantasizing. With waves of what she later called "violent inclination" mounting up inside her, she could barely keep herself from hurling herself out a window and into the hazy Cambridge spring. She lived in constant fear that she'd have to "abandon it all, let the dykes break and the flood sweep in."

Between the surges, Alice took her "women's" madness like a woman, displaying angelic resignation and patience that impressed the family members, including Mary, who expected nothing less from her daughter than polite, uncomplaining resignation. Henry had also instilled a sort of heroic self-control in his daughter; it was part of the Jamesian code of honor. Reflecting on this period years later, Alice wrote, "The only difference between me and the insane was that I had not only all the horrors and suffering of insanity but the duties of doctor, nurse, and strait-jacket imposed upon me, too." Alice was expected to monitor herself, though her state of mind—"luminous and active and susceptible to the clearest, strongest impressions"—made this excruciating. And yet she adroitly used her own breakdown to escape. As she later theorized, she did her best to "abandon" the self-control and self-denial she'd taught herself during her teenage years on the solitary cliff walks in Newport.

Still, she couldn't abandon her self-control entirely. Out of exhaustion, out of moral duty, she held herself together by force of will until she exploded. Such fits were a "degrading" form of release, she later judged. But ironically, because her outbursts had been involuntary, apparently not her fault, she found those surrounding her clumsily praising her for being "amiable" even in her distress.

Even when not in extremis, Alice tied herself into knots. As friends in her Cambridge sewing circle knew, Alice could be sharp, agonized, and charming by turns. She approved of how William had once teasingly described her, culling the expression from a crime story in a Boston newspaper. Alice, William said, was "bottled lightning." And now the lightning had burst the glass.

❧

THROUGH THE SPRING of 1868, Alice showed little improvement. She had always gotten better before, but now her parents didn't know what to do. The family was exhausted from the task of nursing her. It hardly helped that the Jameses could afford to consult fashionable doctors and their cutting-edge theories; Alice remained a conundrum to her father, her mother, her brothers, and to everyone else. Instinctively, they sought to cure her by rest, planting her on the sofa, screening away distractions and excitements, and trying to soothe her by means of house arrest.

In this method Henry and Mary anticipated the famous "rest cure" for hysteria that the Philadelphia doctor S. Weir Mitchell developed and promoted in the United States and England in the 1870s. To effect his cure, Mitchell locked his mostly female patients away—the more quiet and remote the room, the better. Women were deprived of all stimulation and forced into a coma of extreme inactivity.

Such a rest cure risked the horrors exposed three decades later by

Charlotte Perkins Gilman in her masterly gothic short story "The Yellow Wallpaper" (1892). From her own confinement, Gilman conjured up a sickroom of barred windows, a gnawed bedstead, and swagged and stained sulphur-colored wallpaper behind which, her fictional patient imagined, phantasmagoric female prisoners writhed to break free from their chains. As an intelligent woman smothered by domesticity, Alice James had much in common with Gilman, whether or not the Quincy Street wallpaper was yellow.

Family letters soft-pedaled Alice's condition, disguising its horrors. During June 1868, William did his best to comfort her, from Germany. "Beloved Sisterkin," he wrote her, "I take my pen in hand to waft you my love across the jumping waves of the Atlantic and to express the hope that you are better." And again, even more jokingly, as if his teasing would cure her, "I earnestly hope you get better and that lying about in the shade like amaryllis this summer will tune you right up. Keep a stiff upper lip & snap your fingers at fate—read as much comic literature as you can, and your sickness will wear itself out as it most always does."

At least Alice still had her books, and that was truly lucky. Rest cures often deprived women of the reading material that was considered so injurious, but Henry Senior had chafed against this prohibition on books during his own breakdown in the 1840s and evidently thought better of depriving his daughter. When her strength permitted, Alice went right on with her reading. Books, at least, gave her a sense of dignity and intelligence. With her family, as Alice later joked, "What I have always maintained against strenuous opposition, [is] that my Mind *is Great!*"

Yet the same books must also have reminded Alice of all that her brothers were allowed to do and she wasn't. When surrounded by books, Alice suffered some of the worst inner convulsions of her breakdown. As she lay on her sofa in her father's library, trying to make headway in a novel or a volume of letters, she tinglingly felt "waves of violent inclination suddenly invading her muscles." She physically clenched to keep from pitching herself out the window.

That was not the end. Alice would encounter an even more chilling impulse, one that revealed her pent-up rage against her father. As she later remembered the incident, she watched her father, her "benignant pater," sitting "with his silver locks, writing at his table." Overwhelmed by rage, she stifled the compulsion to knock off his head. The murderous impulse horrified her; she deeply loved the old man even if, down deep, she violently resented him.

Alice mended only slowly. By November 1868, she knew William had disembarked from the *Ville de Paris* and was on his way home. He arrived in Cambridge in time for Christmas, a dismal holiday given Henry Senior's lack of interest in conventions. William spent the day writing a letter to the elusive Kate Havens, focused on his distant friend rather than his nearby sister, though he was seeking treatment at the time for his own nerve and back ailments.

Harry was also ailing, but he didn't want to hazard the James family asylum. All during William's travels in Germany and Alice's illness, Harry had been living at Quincy Street, sequestered in his room, absorbed in his writing. Alice's paroxysms had worried him, but his own anxieties were also intense and compelling. He dreamed of escape.

⁂

IN FEBRUARY 1869, Harry, now almost twenty-six, swayed along in a railroad carriage traveling down the storm-buffeted coast of New England. Winter was rigorous in this climate and discouraged travel, even in the coal-fired age of steam, but Harry, despite his recent health problems, was determined to get to Pelham, just north of New York City. Minny Temple was there, among the black woods and snow-paved fields of Westchester County, the houseguest of her married sister Kitty and her sister's much older husband.

On his arrival, Harry burst into the house in his overcoat, tearing off his gloves. He'd scored a small victory at home, and he carried happy news. He'd wrested a letter of credit for a thousand pounds sterling from his father, he told Minny, and he was sailing for Liverpool on the steamship *China* before the end of the month.

Minny received her cousin in an old-fashioned parlor, the kind of stiff nineteenth-century room in which the ticking of a big gilded clock could easily be heard. Glad of his visit, Minny glided to her cousin, laughed, and welcomed him warmly, delighted by Harry's good fortune. Twenty-three years old in 1869, Minny stood erect, slight, and pale in the winter sunshine drifting through the windows. When she laughed, which was often, Harry noted the "free disclosure of the handsome largish teeth that made her mouth almost the main fact of her face." He found her expressive slenderness "becoming," but it was also a symptom of tuberculosis. Harry knew about Minny's illness, but he didn't quite understand, or wouldn't let himself understand, its extent. Maybe she disguised it or ignored it. Maybe he was too absorbed by his grandiose plans to notice.

Minny carried an illness differently from Alice. Minny had no use for a sofa. That winter she had been dashing around snowy Westchester in a small sleigh, snatching the fresh air and the sunshine, evading darker fears. She'd even been to a ball at Delmonico's in downtown Manhattan— that four-story resort of upper-crust pleasure with its huge florid pediment and cast-iron railings, familiar to fashionable New Yorkers; the ball had been thrown by a Mrs. Gracie King for her very pretty décolleté young daughter.

At this heady gaslit extravaganza, Minny had spearheaded a "raid" of "thirteen Emmets [her sister Kitty's in-laws] and a moderate supply of Temples," as she wittily reported. After a short review of dance partners, she'd pronounced the young society men of New York "feeble-minded boys." During the ball she instead escaped the press of dancers with a man of thirty-five, a Mr. Lee, whom she pumped for details of his European prowlings, his sisters' marriages to minor and epauletted German princes with crumbling castles, pinewoods, and vineyards.

Before this outing Minny hadn't attended an assembly in New York for two years. She'd been having hemorrhages, bloody eruptions from her lungs. One week she brought up seven big blood clots and even more small ones. Her cough foreshadowed the worsening tuberculosis that had killed her parents. (In 1854, Harry had witnessed Minny's mother, his aunt, racked with grief over her husband's looming death. Henry Senior had persuaded her to quarantine herself from her dying husband, and her sad cries of protest would haunt Harry for the rest of his life.)

At Pelham, Minny tucked her bloodstained handkerchiefs out of sight. She had been thoroughly examined by doctors in New York, and some of them had insisted that her lungs were "sound"; those were the ones she chose to believe.

Minny told Harry she hadn't been able to sleep, but the two cousins didn't really discuss her health. They instead talked excitedly about the English novelist George Eliot, whom Minny admired for her unconventional choices. (Eliot shared a house with a married man, George Henry Lewes—an exponent of free love whose unbalanced but undivorceable wife had borne several children to another man.) Minny felt "a desire to know something about her life—how far her lofty moral sentiments have served her practically." Harry had a good chance of meeting the renowned author in London.

He apologized to his cousin for his good luck; he found it "wholly detestable" that he should voyage off without Minny, and felt that travel would be "the right thing for her." Medicine at the time offered few other remedies for tubercular men and women besides trying different "air," faraway locations and climates. For those who could afford to travel to mountains or to Mediterranean shores, such cures sometimes "worked"—though the sanatoriums for consumption, whether in the Adirondacks or the Swiss Alps, often amounted to hideous, unsanitary death traps, full of feverish and slowly dying patients for whom bloodletting or exposure on glaciers did no good at all.

Minny gaily trusted she'd meet Harry next winter, in Rome. They'd live out an Italian idyll, a highly colored lithograph of reunion, there among the Aleppo pines and weathered ruins. When Harry snatched up his gloves and left, Minny generously hoped her cousin would enjoy himself; she knew that was his aim. She knew how bent he was on developing a career in literature, studying art, and residing in the lush European settings he remembered from the family's earlier travels. She knew how unhappy he had been in Cambridge, with its sober tea parties and harsh winters. She rejoiced for his escape, genuinely. But she felt sad, too. "I don't expect to see him again," she wrote a friend, "for a good many years."

❧

ONLY A COUPLE of weeks later, Harry signed in at the famous Morley's Hotel, beside the noble stone spire of St. Martin-in-the-Fields. He was ecstatic to command a grand smoky view westward over the cobbles of Trafalgar Square. He could reflect on the strange twists of fate that had brought him back, that dim and rain-soaked March, to London. He hadn't budged his stern parents by talking up a literary career that so far hadn't advanced beyond a few short stories and reviews. Henry Senior abhorred fiction, and Mary hardly considered writing would earn her dear son a living. Like his siblings, Harry had had to throw down the health card and capitalize on a back increasingly jangled and "in a queer condish," as William described it. With such an argument, victory was assured. A bad back couldn't be cured locally but only—in the mythology of the day—at a distant sanatorium, under the orders of a distinguished foreign doctor.

But Harry had also earned his ticket to Europe with a more embarrassing disorder: constipation. Like Alice, Harry suffered from his own version of bottled lightning—another symptom of the anxiety of living at home, under pressure, at Quincy Street. Though bound for a cure spa, Harry lingered for a long time in London, braving the raw weather that turned out "horribly damp and bleak, and no more [like] spring than in a Boston January." In order to dig a stronger foothold in his adored Europe, he soon commandeered bachelor-shabby lodgings on Half Moon Street. Even at this early stage, Harry strained to establish an expatriate and extrafamilial pied-à-terre. Yearning to pass as a native, he claimed he felt as if he'd haunted the teeming city for a year. In fact, though, Harry hadn't lived in London since 1856, when as an overdressed top-hatted thirteen-year-old he'd perched up beside the cablamps along with his brother William.

Harry remained under the watchful supervision of Charles Eliot Norton, his patron from the *North American Review*. The future Bostonian art historian, forty-one years old, bony-faced and with a scraggly mustache under his Roman nose, treated Harry as a protégé. Luckily, the Norton family party also included females with whom Harry felt more at ease: Charles's neat, delicate wife, Susan (and her sister Sara Sedgwick), as well as Charles's two formidable sisters, Grace and Jane, who were renowned for their learning. Harry called them the "invaluable" Nortons. But though he lounged with the ladies, charming them with his talk and his newly bought London gloves, he found himself not "much *en rapport* with Charles."

The Nortons swept Harry off to lectures, exhibitions, and private drawing rooms. To them, he figured as a conspicuous asset; he was, after all, twenty-six, handsome, dapper, well-spoken, the author of well-crafted stories. Jane Norton squired Harry to dine with the literary critic Leslie Stephen, the father of the future Virginia Woolf—a novelist not to be born for another thirteen years. Afterward, Stephen treated them all to the Regent's Park Zoo, by way of the newly bored tunnels of the London Underground, which Harry found "a marvelous phenomenon, ploughing along in a vast circle thro' the bowels of London."

With the intrepid Nortons, Harry also heard the monumental art critic John Ruskin lecture, peeped into his home in Denmark Hill, just south of London, and eventually shook hands with the internationally famous *"grand homme"* (great man) himself. Harry noted the two young nieces who lived with Ruskin, one a young Irish girl with a "rich virginal brogue," and the other a "nice Scottish lass, who keeps house for him." Ruskin liked fresh-faced girls—a taste he shared, as a matter of fact, with Charles Eliot Norton. Harry may or may not have scented such irregularities, but in his fiction he would increasingly explore the dim erotic secrets of respectable Victorian households.

One late-spring afternoon, the party came together in the quiet precincts of Queen's Square, Bloomsbury, at half past four, to meet another great man. The tireless Nortons had arranged a tour of no. 26, the workshop of William Morris, the now-famous poet and designer of the British "arts and crafts" school. Morris, "short, burly, and corpulent," as Harry described him, genially showed the Americans around his small-scale home manufactory. He explained his intricate, richly colored handiworks in a loud voice and with a nervous, restless manner. Harry's jaw dropped at Morris's creations, the exquisite display of "stained glass windows, tiles, ecclesiastical and mediaeval tapestry altar-cloths" that Morris had crafted there, piece by piece and stitch by stitch, with the help of his wife and young daughters.

Jane Burden Morris, the artist's wife, hosted the party for dinner. Mrs. Morris entertained her guests sheathed in a dull purple dress, without any of the customary hoops of the time, necklaced with garlands of outlandish and archaic semiprecious beads. Especially in this Arthurian regalia, Jane Burden radiated the iconic Pre-Raphaelite—an English school of art that appreciated her look: she had heavy brows and dense, wavy, dark hair bunched on either side of her sad-eyed, dreaming face. She struck Harry as a woman "cut out of a missal," a medieval prayer book, as he reported to Alice.

This stable hand's daughter had made an impression not only on Harry but also on the painter and poet Dante Gabriel Rossetti (whom Harry also later visited in his studio, a "delicious melancholy old house" on the river at Chelsea). Rossetti sketched and painted numerous portraits of this moody beauty—one showing her arrayed in a deep-blue dress, cradling lilies. The painting struck Harry, he wrote his artist-friend John La Farge, as "almost" a great work.

The "almost" illustrated Harry's tendency to hang back even from what he admired. Harry's appreciation of Jane Burden Morris, unlike Rossetti's, remained safely aesthetic. Still, his "art" obsession kept him hovering on the fringes of other people's more scandalous sexual lives. But at the moment Harry had other troubles on his mind besides sex.

FOR THE TWENTY-SIX-YEAR-OLD invalid, there was still the matter of his health, not to mention his work. In spite of his long jubilant letters home, Harry hadn't been able to write any stories. (He'd had writer's block at home on Quincy Street, too.) He'd been dogged by "loneliness and gloom" in addition to his chronic physical symptoms. In spite of its splendors, England hadn't alleviated the deep-seated unhappiness, loneliness, and self-doubt that had made him hate Cambridge but that he in fact still carried with him. When he arrived at his cure in the lush, sweeping pastures of west-central England, he found himself more depressed than ever. He wrote to the dignified Grace Norton, whom he was trying out as a bosom confidante, a "letter of darksome blue."

The boardinghouse cure establishment at Great Malvern crouched at the feet of soaring hills that commanded a panorama of the surrounding orchards and fields, now tingeing green with the advent of April. The patients could walk or hire donkeys and pony traps to explore this wet paradise. Otherwise, Harry observed, they did nothing but "bathe and walk and feed and read the newspapers and gossip from morning till night." Harry himself sketched smudgy charcoals of landscapes; nearby

Tewksbury Abbey inspired one dark, rather gloomy composition. But the company at two o'clock dinner stifled Harry after his exposure to London's leading lights. Even the bathing cure (Harry asked his brother about the "douche rectale" William had tried at Divonne) hardly did him much good. Feeling stuck and trapped, Harry wisely opted for more strenuous physical movement: tourism.

Once he got into a carriage, once he began to swan around the budding countryside on his own volition, Harry livened up. In Oxford, in the green gloom of April, he fell in love with the twilit botanical gardens and the dim stone quadrangles. He also stared at the towheaded and muscle-bound undergraduates afloat on the river, "the mighty lads of England," as he put it, clad in brisk blue and white flannel, "lounging down the stream in their punts or pulling in straining crews and rejoicing in their godlike strengths." As an invalid barely escaped from a sanatorium, Harry poignantly admired and envied these handsome examples of athletic Anglo-Saxon masculinity.

A chemist acquaintance of the Nortons guided Harry around the Oxford colleges and hosted him to a sumptuous many-course dinner in the cavernous hall of Christ Church College. Under the high vaulted and timbered roof, Harry counted the paintings of famous men that gazed down on him from between the resplendent stained-glass windows. He smugly noted to his family that he'd landed himself a seat at the high table, "at the right of the Carver." Harry was questing after a sense of his own importance, but he didn't always come face-to-face with the famous men of his time. As he drank strong ale tasting of hops from a silver tankard, he may well have unknowingly shared his meal with a mathematical fellow at Christ Church, Charles Dodgson, who, in his rooms on the northwest corner of Tom Quad, had been writing a revolutionary children's book called *Through the Looking-Glass*, soon to be published under his better-known pseudonym of Lewis Carroll. Here was another example of the unconventional Victorian sexual fringe, if Harry had known it. Like Ruskin and Norton, Dodgson too had a fascination with young girls.

Harry's tastes, though unclear even to himself, were definitely different. His brushes with undergraduate youth and glory at Oxford did him ineffable good after the stagnancy of home or a bogged-down spa. He reported to William, increasingly his medical confessor, that he'd had "a movement every day," and two daily in Oxford. "*Never resist a motion to stool* no matter at what hour you may feel it," William advised, in reply. "I blush to say that detailed bulletins of your bowels, stomach &c as well as back are of the most enthralling interest to me." Their health was a private and intimate interest the two brothers shared, in a curious fascination with each other's symptoms.

William advised Harry, though, to stash his medical reports on separate slips marked *private*, so that Alice—who could now again read letters and doted on Harry's—could freely read and cherish Harry's colorful travel accounts. The James family tended to keep mum about Harry's constipation, just as some later biographers have liked to portray Harry's 1869 grand tour as a glamorous literary romp, not as the headstrong escape from family and vexed cure odyssey that it also was. This trip would help make Harry into an author—and a brilliant one—without, however, as his letters subtly told, relieving the primary emotional causes of Harry's emotional blockage, the wanderlust and obscure hatred of home that had launched him into travel in the first place. "I am much obliged to you all for your good advice," Harry wrote his intrusive father, who had complained about his extravagance, "altho' I have been acting somewhat against the spirit of it."

With obstinate determination, Harry mixed personal and literary aims when he rounded back to London in May and secured a visit with George Eliot. As a teenager, Harry had loved her novels *Adam Bede* (1859) and *The Mill on the Floss* (1860). More recently, he had reviewed her rather flawed novel *Felix Holt* (1866) quite generously.

That Sunday afternoon, Grace Norton took Harry to what had been her childhood haunt of St. John's Wood; Eliot lived nearby at the Priory, North Bank. She was two or three years away from publishing her masterwork, *Middlemarch*—a thousand-page epic of provincial England whose treasure house of details would later influence Harry. In 1869, George Eliot was battling her own indispositions—excruciating headaches that struck her, unforgivingly, almost daily. Merely to see her involved delicate negotiations, as she'd receive visitors only if they were brought by her friends.

After introductions were made and Harry could sit down and look at the novelist more carefully, he found her "magnificently ugly—deliciously hideous." He noted her low forehead, her tired gray eyes, her prominent blobby nose, and her huge mouth full of crooked teeth set in an endless jaw and chin. Yet in these "massively plain features," Harry also discovered an irresistible charm—like that captured four years before in luminous chalks by the portraitist Sir Frederick Burton. George Eliot radiated "sweetness and sagacity." Her quiet, rich voice struck Harry of that of a "counseling angel." Fatuously, Harry afterward phrased his admiration as a (safe) crush: "Yes behold me literally in love with this great horse-faced blue-stocking," he wrote Henry Senior. But he also concluded, more fittingly, that Eliot had a magnificent mind, of "a larger circumference than any woman [he had] ever seen."

Harry described this visit enthusiastically to his father, to help justify the lavish expenses of his trip. (He also apparently dispatched an account to Minny, though that letter has been lost.) Harry later exulted that to take tea with one of the world's greatest novelists counted as a "fairytale of privilege." But such a pleasure was denied to two sufferers in America who had even stronger stakes than Harry in George Eliot's example of female intellectual achievement: Alice James and Minny Temple.

TO JUDGE FROM his surviving letters, Harry thought more about Italy than Minny as he breezed through Paris and lingered among the Alpine landscapes near Geneva. June 1869 found Harry resting at the mountain-hedged eastern tip of Lac Leman, beside the wave-lapped and white-turreted picture-book Château de Chillon. Near Vevey, at a hotel-pension that he'd later use in his most famous novella, *Daisy Miller*, Harry read John Stuart Mill's *On the Subjection of Women* (1869). He briefly noted this fact to William. But this revolutionary work didn't apparently prompt Harry to contemplate the predicament of the women he knew, such as his sister and his cousin.

A conscientious tourist, Harry took time to "do" Switzerland. Like many a rhapsodic postwar American traveler, he may well have snatched up an alpenstock and donned a feathered hat. But his deeper interest being historical and aesthetic, he veered resolutely southward. Not far away, over the glacier-guarded passes of the Alps, Italy baked alluringly under the summer sun. Charles Eliot Norton, John Ruskin, and others had taught Harry to enshrine Italy as the realm par excellence of art. The country was now Harry's consuming passion, and he embarked an aesthetic mania colored with the sterilized erotic impulses that "art" would often carry for him. Also, no James had yet crossed the Italian border. That golden realm of villas and ruins amounted to untainted territory—a Europe to which Harry could hold exclusive rights—unlike Germany, over which William had already thoroughly staked his own claim.

And yet Harry sensed that he wouldn't own Italy for long. Aunt Kate, now fifty-seven years old and still fond of travel, had also sailed from America in the spring of 1869, with her cousin Helen and another middle-aged New York Helen in tow. The Helens, complete with Harry's "insane" cousin Henry, loomed as an intricate and upsetting family entanglement—and as a complication to his solitary ecstatic immersion in Italy. Kate's itinerary weirdly shadowed Harry's, as if she were pursuing him but as if neither hoped very eagerly to meet up. "I am watching for Aunt Kate's arrival," Harry wrote his family, "but I don't expect to see her in some time." He made noises about wanting to join his aunt but did his best to keep well ahead of her. Though genuinely afflicted with a traveler's and a young man's isolation, Harry didn't rush to embrace his aunt's companionship, with its reminders of the household he'd worked so hard to evade.

But Harry had reached Italy first. To the housebound Alice, Harry detailed his extraordinary, Ruskin-style baptism into the country. "Down, down—on, on into Italy we went," he wrote about his descent from the Alps—"a rapturous progress thro' a wild luxuriance of corn and vines and olives and figs and mulberries and ches[t]nuts and frescoed villages and clamorous beggars and all the old Italianisms of tradition." This passage to Italy would prove one of the most important introductions of Harry's life, though one as yet free of human entanglements.

At Baveno on Lake Maggiore, Harry checked into a vast, cool, pink granite hotel that opened onto a terrace of orange trees beside the water. He dunked himself into a cold bath in a big marble tank, dined on fresh local delicacies, primped himself in his dim boudoir, and then, for his afternoon's outing, hired a sunburned Italian rower to pull him out toward two exotic islands, the Isola Madre and the Isola Bella. The Italian rowed, and Harry lounged, stretched out under a striped awning in the heat. The buttoned-up Harry had at last unbuttoned, a little. Coming down from the Alps, he'd writhed with stomach pains. He seriously needed to relax. But it remained unclear, as yet, if Italy could really loosen him up, if it could really cure him from twenty-six years of being a James.

Though awash in leisure, Harry envisioned many practical uses for this country he'd adopted. A studious tourist, an amateur apostle of Italian art, he wanted to pave his way to future assignments in travel writing and art criticism. As he traveled southward, through the sweltering groves of the Po Valley, Harry assiduously stocked up on settings and characters for short stories and novels. To his skeptical and expense-weary parents, Harry billed the "impressions" he was industriously gathering—and packing into rhapsodic letters home—as "a species of investment." He chalked it up as solid capital for a future writing career.

Harry also assured his worried mother that the winter he planned to spend in Italy wasn't just "recreation." On the contrary, he was piling up "serious culture"—a currency in itself, given the widespread worship of Europe in New York and Boston. He also played on Mary's maternal sympathies by arguing, "The only economy for me is to get thoroughly well and into such a state as that I can work. For this consummation, I will accept everything—even the appearance of mere pleasure-seeking." Harry bled with self-sacrifice.

Back in Cambridge, Henry Senior appreciated his son's talent enough to read Harry's letters out loud to visitors and to circulate them to the Emersons, who also enthusiastically savored them. "Your letters from Italy are beyond praise," William wrote his brother. "It is a great pity they should be born to blush unseen by the general public, and that just the matter they contain, in a little less rambling style"—he stipulated, big brother–like—"not appear in the columns of the Nation." Within a few years, the *Nation*—a "little" magazine founded in 1865 that circulated to cosmopolitan, liberal-minded New Yorkers, Philadelphians, and Bostonians—would be printing many of Harry's travel sketches.

Meanwhile, his expenses were mounting alarmingly. Traveling in grand solitude cost extra. And Harry's health (he argued) mandated luxury-hotel plushness; he just couldn't "rough it"—as William had done in the Amazon, as his younger brothers had done in Southern swamps during the Civil War. Before the end of his yearlong European trip, he'd in fact dropped two thousand dollars of the family's "sacred" funds, while Wilkie was toiling in Florida and Bob in Wisconsin to earn their livings. (With few other options and no family money offered him, Bob had gone back to the railroad work he hated in 1867.) As a point of comparison, the James family paid twenty thousand dollars in 1870 for the big solid librarian's house they'd previously rented. So Harry's extravagant cure tour cost a tenth of the price of the Quincy Street house—the equivalent of a fireplace-furnished drawing room and a bedroom, at least. No matter how strongly he protested when he wrote home, Harry was feathering his own future and not the family's.

HARRY ARRIVED IN Venice in the sunshine of September. He felt genuinely homesick enough to compare the city, though decayed and swamped with mosquitoes, to Newport. He found Venice "extremely like it in atmosphere and color; and the other afternoon, on the sands at the Lido, looking out over the dazzling Adriatic, I fancied I was standing on Easton's beach."

Still, reclining in a gondola while a boater-hatted gondolier poled him around, Harry toyed with other fascinations. In the tiny streets of the ramshackle city, Venetian men smelled bad (Harry preferred the English because they "love a bath-tub and they hate a lie"). But while swimming in the broad sunshine of one of the canals, the same men turned Harry's head with their frolicksome shoving, yelling, and paddling, "bare-chested, bare-legged, magnificently tanned and muscular." Yet these were not Walt Whitman's unabashed and sexualized waterhole bathers from *Song of Myself* (1855). Harry carefully categorized this beauty as "picturesque"—worthy of a respectable and tasteful painting. He also considered this cavorting something obscurely corrupt, in harmony with the refuse-strewn *canaletto*s and *campo*s, with the onceglorious palaces of the now-defunct Venetian Republic, which in 1869, with the Risorgimento (unification of Italy) still embattled, with the Italian economy derelict, stood "rotting and crumbling and abandoned to paupers."

Though his parents fretted about his expensive idleness, Harry hadn't in fact adopted the Venetian philosophy of *dolce far niente* (it's sweet to do nothing). Harry kept schedules, methodically worked his way through galleries, and spooned in chaste and solitary meals. Sometimes warmed to the core by the exquisite vistas of Venice, sometimes prone to napkin-daubing priggishness, Harry didn't know how to live out his impulses—or even, probably, what they were. Still, some foreign men with half-understood homoerotic inclinations, like Harry's future acquaintance John Addington Symonds, would come to impoverished Venice for sexual adventures with gondoliers, porters, and sailors; by the early 1870s, the city already sheltered a vibrant sexual underworld of which Harry was evidently, as yet, largely ignorant.

Shifting on to a blustery Florence in October, Harry hit an excruciating patch of isolation. To combat it, he even tried linking up with Charles Eliot Norton, whose party had also moved south for the winter. He joined Norton walking over a potential rental, a capacious villa at Fiesole, outside the city gates. Harry's spirits lifted in the entrancing autumnal garden, with its view of red-roofed Florence below and the violet, snowcapped Apennines beyond. He could fancy just such a many-roomed, tile-roofed villa for himself. But the Nortons themselves didn't satisfy a restless young man in Florence any more than they'd done in Cambridge—especially not the baleful Charles.

On an ordinary day, Harry spoke only to hotel servants and the custodians of churches. He made only fleeting and abortive acquaintances in the unheated Pitti and Uffizi galleries. He couldn't stand the bluntly obvious American tourists he bumped into there. He pronounced the postwar rush of midwesterners and social climbers "vulgar, vulgar, vulgar." To unburden himself of his "impressions," he craved his nimble-minded family, whom he sometimes longed to have with him in the autumn sunshine of Tuscany. At least he said he did. With the muttering sound of wind increasing the gloom of his lodgings, Harry pathetically warmed his fingers over his candle. Much like William's German sabbatical, Harry's dream tour had curdled into what he called the "bitterness of exile." With his bowels still plaguing him, Harry drew comfort from the odd idea that back home Alice and William were "getting better and locating some of their diseases in me"—a bizarre theory of family symbiosis that helped the Jameses explain why only one family invalid ever seemed to improve at a time.

❧

AT THE END of October, Harry switched to Rome—visiting the ancient city, now that the weather was cooling, for the first time, and not knowing how long his health would let him stay. Immediately, he adored the place. The city of weathered churches and half-buried ruins, spreading across its celebrated seven hills, made Venice, Florence, Oxford, and London appear, Harry thought, as "little cities of pasteboard." He went "reeling and moaning thro' the streets, in a fever of enjoyment."

Besides repeated sighting of Pope Pius IX, who fascinated him by resembling, with his raised benedictory fingers, a "dusky Hindoo idol in the depths of its shrine," Harry soon saw the requisite sights. He admired the simple and striking Pantheon, with its cool stone dome and its circular oculus admitting a long stream of smoky light. He swooned in front of the massive Colosseum—still filled with earth in 1869, a "grassy arena" choked with weeds and fringed with saplings. The ancient Roman arena hadn't yet been excavated, unlike the imperial palaces on the Palatine Hill that were being dug up and restored under the grandiose patronage of the tirelessly ambitious Louis Napoléon, emperor of the French.

In Rome Harry discovered a taste for antiquity—if that's what it was. He admired a bronze of an equestrian Roman emperor, contrasting this monumental figure to the effete pope who revolted Harry as a "flaccid old woman waving his ridiculous fingers." "As you revert to that poor sexless old Pope enthroned upon his cushions, then glance at those imperial legs swinging in their immortal bronze, you cry out that here at least was a *man!*" Such observations teemed with sexual, barely disguised genital metaphors. Harry's "obscure hurt" from the early Civil War period may not have caused him a genital injury, but his bad back—and now his other debilitating health problems—led him to envy and fetishize masculine potency.

Given his own financial dependency and chronic illness, Harry longed to identify with manliness and yet often saw himself—mirroring his character Clement Searle in his short story "A Passionate Pilgrim" (1871)—as sickly, nervous, and generally inadequate. In his letters he approved of his younger brothers, Wilkie and Bob, for taking up rowing for their muscular development. (Bob's chest had always been well developed, Harry noted.) He admired emperors astride their war horses, ogled sun-browned Venetian swimmers, and lionized the sword-bearing, bare-phallused statue of Benvenuto Cellini's *Perseus*, which he'd seen in the Piazza della Signoria in Florence and evidently greeted with envious or possibly homoerotic longing.

In Rome, with its reputation for brutality and sensuality, Harry's interest in representations of maleness intensified. He was drawn to the Roman imitators of the Greek sculptor Praxiteles (Harry gaped in front of the bare-torsoed *Antinous*) and fell in love with the Renaissance artist Michelangelo Buonarroti (Harry liked the beefy, patriarchal *Moses*, originally sculpted for the tomb of Pope Julius II). To Harry in his present psychological state, even the weathered military bas-reliefs on the Arch of Constantine struck him with the same message: "*Manly!*" Rome as well as Venice concealed an underground world of sexual license, both homosexual and heterosexual, a forerunner of the risqué backstreets that would be plumbed and exposed by American writers like Tennessee Williams almost a century later. But for now, Harry stuck to statues, and prepared to receiving his traveling aunt and her party and to provide the pent-up, travel-weary ladies "a useful distraction from the unbroken scrutiny of each other's characters."

AS BOTH OF them had probably known deep down back in Pelham, Harry would never meet up with Minny under the umbrella pines of Rome.

In November 1869, while Harry was settling into his room at the Hôtel de Rome, Minny paid a weeklong visit to the James family in Cambridge. With no real money and continuing bad health, she couldn't make the journey to Europe, but she longed to get away from New York, to recuperate from her sister Elly's marriage that October to a man twenty-eight years older than she was, Dr. Christopher Temple Emmet. Both of her sisters, Kitty and Elly, had wed "bald-headed" Emmet men old enough to be their fathers.

No wonder Minny had burst out that "if all other women felt the eternal significance of matrimony" as she did, nobody would get married, and the human race would grind to a halt. Quite apart from the aspersion cast on her sisters, these were fighting words in 1869. Kitty and Elly, previously Minny's orphaned allies, retaliated by telling Minny she was "queer" and that "they wouldn't be [her] for anything." If Minny had hoped for her relatives to empathize and understand her, she met with the opposite reception.

Henry bristled with his patent Swedenborgian advice, but Minny found her uncle's ideas "neither reasonable nor consoling." Nothing Henry said seemed actually to apply to her and her predicament. Irritated by his presumption, his low opinion of women, Minny did what almost nobody else dared to do—not the Saturday Club, not Henry's family. Minny lashed back. She roundly dressed Henry down. Pointblank, she declared her uncle's ideas were "not only highly unpractical, but ignoble & shirking."

Henry, shocked to be contradicted, accused Minny of *"pride & conceit"*—strong condemnations especially for a Victorian young woman. Minny suspected that her uncle hated her—disliked her at the very least. But she'd spoken, as she always did, straight from her feelings. She had a taste for justice, and she didn't back down.

Mary, who'd never approved of Minny's grit, shared Henry's hurt astonishment. She rallied loyally to her husband. And though Alice had her own reasons to resent her father's nettlesome bravado, she didn't sympathize with Minny any more than her mother did. Alice harbored a vexed, long-standing ambivalence toward her cousin.

In contrast to her brothers, Alice had often found herself sardonically "amused" by the " 'pride' and aristocracy and 'spirited nature' " of the Temple girls, which she contrasted with their habit of living off their guardians the Tweedys and others. " 'Noblesse oblige,' " Alice acidly observed, "doesn't seem to be the performance of noble deeds, but doing the ignoble ones with impunity and with an increase personally of your snobbish pretensions." And that may well have been Alice's interpretation of Minny's defiance of Henry Senior—as much as Alice herself may have longed, deep down, to defy her father. Whatever her motives, Alice spent the first part of her cousin's visit trying to "snub" her. But Minny forthrightly asked Alice to stop; and Alice, gamely enough, desisted.

Alice, it's true, had crankily bounced back from her breakdown. The month of Minny's visit, William evaluated his sister as "first rate"— especially in comparison to himself. From across the Atlantic, Harry rejoiced, jokingly, that Alice had dropped her "elegant invalidity," and hoped she'd stick to the "propriety" of good health. But the family's mere insistence on Alice's improvement—and their relentless catalog of her "healthy" doings—evenings with her women friends from the Bee, her theater outings, and her overnight slumber-party visits—betrayed their fears. Was Alice really well? Alice's brittle china-doll persona concealed, her family knew, explosive forces.

Meanwhile, Minny's visit at Quincy Street verged on disaster. Only William shone as a bright spot. He found his cousin "delightful in all respects." Around him—though he noticed she'd grown very thin, visibly ravaged and emaciated by her illness—Minny streamed with her characteristic fearless beauty, brimmed with her natural cheerfulness and humor. "I am conscious of having done her a good deal of injustice for some years past," William admitted to Harry. He now pronounced his cousin "a most honest little phenomenon." If William knew about her altercation with his father—and Minny no doubt frankly informed him—he respected her for her courage in keeping "true to her own instincts." He also pronounced her "more devoid of 'meanness,' of anything petty in her character than any one [he] kn[e]w, perhaps either male or female." Only the winter before, William had energetically abused Minny to Harry—his own thwarted attraction to his cousin probably heightening his critique. But now he honored Minny on her own terms.

But William was sinking down under his own burdens. Since his return from Germany a year before, he'd been sucked into bog after bog of depression. The "azure demon" had stalked him for months, his uncurable back troubles alone rendering him chronically "sick of life." That past summer—in spite of many enforced halts in his studying—he took and passed his medical qualifying exam. Now he sported the title of M.D. But as the autumn wore on, William felt himself "steadily deteriorating in all respects," unable to study, and desperately welcoming electrical shocks from a "galvanic disk" he wore strapped to his ribs in order to "cure" his back. But his back wasn't his only problem. His "stomach, bowels, brain, temper & spirits," he observed, all dragged him to new lows. In a time before psychological help was yet available, William prescribed himself chloral, a strong narcotic, in order to sleep.

Minny found Quincy Street as crippled as a plague ship. Besides William and Alice, the youngest James sons had made their own contributions to the James family asylum, though from a distance. Wilkie had spent part of the summer of 1869 at the family hospital in Cambridge, nursing the remnants of his malaria. He'd now shipped cheerlessly back to Florida, where the winter rain crashed down, in order to try to sell as much of the failed plantation, that bottomless pit of an investment, as he could.

Bob, toiling on his railroad job in Milwaukee, struggled even more than the iron-willed Wilkie. Harry grasped the painful irony of his brother's plight: "It fills me with wonder and sadness that [Bob] should be off in that Western desolation while I am reveling in England and Italy."

Bitterly lonely, craving his own form of distinction, Bob contracted a secret engagement with his cousin Kitty—not Kitty Temple, but Kitty Van Buren, the granddaughter of the former president of the United States (and like Minny Temple, Henry Senior's niece). Bob had probably consorted with Kitty during a visit back East in 1868, though details of the affair have not survived. Kitty, however, had a weak back, and as soon as he found out about this would-be marriage, William wrote a long bigbrotherly letter to urge Bob strenuously not to compound the "dorsal insanity" of the family, not to risk generating unhealthy offspring. William himself wouldn't marry anyone, even someone as "healthy as the Venus of Milo," if it meant passing on his bad back. Henry and Mary also disapproved. Telegrams flew. The family argued Bob back from the edge, and he testily broke off the engagement—though he stole another visit with his cousin in New Haven, Connecticut, in 1870.

Surrounded by such battles, Minny no doubt rejoiced to escape Quincy Street. She had, in any case, a voyage of her own to look forward to. Her sister Elly was taking her by steamer to San Francisco. Though Minny dreaded the storm-ravaged passage around Cape Horn, California goldenly beckoned. The bright cold Pacific air would work wonders on her lungs.

❧

BY FEBRUARY 1870, Harry had once again committed himself to Great Malvern and its cure bath. He'd meandered back across the Continent to England, having "hardly exchanged ten words with a human creature" in the inns and hotels on the way. The raw winter spa wasn't much better, though he built a fire in his dingy bedroom and wrote homesick letters, in which he imagined, across the miles of wintry ocean, his family gathering in the dusk for a Cambridge-style tea.

He had tea enough at Great Malvern, where he soon plunged into running sitz baths up to his chin. Otherwise, he was stuffed regularly with a monotonous British diet: breakfast a cold mutton chop, toast, and tea; dinner a leg or shoulder of mutton, potatoes, cold rice pudding; tea was cold mutton again, toast, and (of course) tea. With such a regimen, no wonder Harry suffered from constipation—as he himself understood. To relieve his bloating, Harry longed to live a year on vegetables: "unlimited tomatoes and beans and peas and squash and turnips and carrots and corn." Harry fantasized nostalgically about his mother's American meals, the "amber-tinted surface of the scalloped oysters—the crimson dye of the tomatoes—the golden lustre of the Indian pudding—the deep dark manes of the charlotte of apple and of peach."

Harry choked not only on the endless mutton but also on the mediocre company. To avoid home and its pressures, Harry spun wild plans for more travel. In spite of his homesickness, his love for Minny and colorful American dishes, he'd latched onto the Old World, especially England. In the middle of March, to see the countryside and get some exercise, he made the seven-mile hike to the cathedral city of Worcester—through elm-dotted meadows, over sheep-cropped greens, past half-timbered farmhouses and lodge gates to distant manor houses—feeling all the way "as if I were pressing all England to my soul." His deep affinity to tea-drinking, buttoned-up England would soon find print. But Harry's euphoric touring plans were about to suffer a check.

⌁

A WEEK AFTER this walk, on March 26, 1870, on a damp Saturday morning at Great Malvern, Harry got the latest steamer mail. The envelope of familiar stationery contained a closely written letter from his mother and a scrawled note from his father. They jointly announced some devastating news about "dear, bright, little Minny," as Mary called her. On March 8—the very day that Harry was musing on her American superiority—Minny had died.

Minny Temple's escape to California hadn't materialized. Her sister Elly and her husband hadn't gone out to the West Coast, after all. Minny had been trapped in frozen Pelham, ravaged more each night by her cough and her insomnia. She'd struggled alone with thoughts of death. Haggard, she'd nakedly faced the universe. Unable to sleep even with the chloral William had given her, Minny again consulted medical men in New York. Her usual doctor mechanically reassured her. But an eminent physician, a Dr. Taylor, visited her in Manhattan one evening just as she was going to bed. He sounded her lungs and then spoke to her very solemnly.

"My dear young lady," he said, "your right lung is diseased; all your hemorrhages come from there. It must have been bad for at least a year before they began. You must go to Europe as soon as possible." Minny quaveringly asked him how long she'd live. "Two or three years," he said—and Minny cringed, completely unprepared for such a death sentence. But she replied, "Well, Doctor, even if my right lung were all gone I should make a stand with my left." And then, as she charmingly reported the conversation to a friend, "by way of showing how valiant the stand would be, [I] fainted away."

Having received a hint about Minny's serious illness a week before, Harry had promised his parents to write her a letter. (They had corresponded frequently, and Harry had last written her a homesick letter, in January, from Florence.) But he'd felt that Minny's "immense little spirit" couldn't be extinguished, no matter what New York medical authorities might say. To him, Minny remained too dogged, too real, to disappear. He saw her with a whole life to live out. After all, Minny was only twenty-four years old.

The unexpected news crushed Harry. In page after page written home to his family, he mourned Minny. "It comes home to me with irresistible power, the sense of how much I knew her and how much I loved her." He reproached himself that he hadn't spent more of Minny's last hours with her. He pumped his family for details of Minny's last days. He agonized that he'd abandoned her.

And yet Harry also—strangely and fatefully for his future—began to transform Minny into a heroine, a symbol, a muse. "Minny has lost very little by her change of state," Harry wrote William, consoling himself almost too easily. "She lives as a steady unfaltering luminary in the mind rather than as a flickering wasting earth-stifled lamp." When he'd seen her a year before at Pelham, Minny hadn't been able to sleep. In Harry's mind, she'd gone on "sleeping less and less, waking wider and wider, until she awaked absolutely!"

❧

DURING HIS LONG musings about Minny's death, Harry also stomached his parents' summons home. He hadn't healed in Europe, and he'd spent a big chunk of the slender family fortune. Conveniently, Aunt Kate was catching up to him again, commissioned now to fetch him home by means of the cramped staterooms of the Cunard steamship *Scotia*, one of the last of the paddlewheel steamships left on the Atlantic. "Such a burden has been taken off my heart by Harry's decision to come home," his mother had confided to Alice. His father was relieved, too, but he had kept his worry about his son quiet, "not wishing to add to my anxiety," Mary remarked.

To Harry, going home had an entirely different feel; the necessity struck as another loss, compounding his cousin's. "It's a good deal like dying," he wrote his friend Grace Norton. He envied Grace's staying on when he couldn't: "Farewell, beloved survivors," he gestured, melodramatically.

The America to which Harry would return in 1870 was turning a corner in its Civil War recovery. In the South, the ideal of Reconstruction was already running out of steam, as Wilkie had been finding out at his imploding, impoverished plantation in Florida. But in the North, where the first black senator, the Reverend Hiram Rhodes Revels, arrived in Washington from Mississippi, in response to the Fourteenth and Fifteenth amendments, social progress was in the air. And the technological and industrial development that the war itself had sometimes curtailed, sometimes promoted, was now gathering crucial momentum. Even in the Jameses' genteel neighborhood, near the sleepy precincts of Harvard Yard, this juggernaut was being felt. Harvard was transforming itself radically, as the ambitious university accelerated into a period of unprecedented architectural and intellectual expansion.

When Harry got back to Quincy Street in May, a heat wave welcomed him. Sitting beside a window thrown open, he regarded the red-brick walls of the Harvard president's *"palazzo."* Beyond the gray stone mass of the library, he saw the spire of the university church as a "soaring *campanile*" in the *"piazza"* of Harvard Yard. (Just to hear Italian names, Harry crashed lectures at Boylston Hall.) Like many a returned traveler, the young man was infected with Italy—but even more with his own discontentment. Sitting overheated in his family's house, he heard the tinkle of horsecars in the square and the carpenters hammering at Memorial Hall, the huge new Gothic edifice at Harvard, built to commemorate the Union dead.

With Minny gone, Harry's homecoming felt especially hollow. In later years Harry saw Minny's death as a stark milestone in his life. Both he and William felt it marked "the end of [their] youth." But the end of youth, for the Jameses, wouldn't mean just decorating the house with the handsome male statuettes Harry had picked up for Alice in Rome. It certainly wouldn't mean starting a family or settling down to a professional desk, as so many Bostonians did after a grand tour.

None of the young Jameses wanted to settle down, and William in particular had been fighting for his very life. As part of his medical training, he had visited one epileptic patient at an "asylum," a dark-haired youth with greenish skin who sat on a bench against the wall with his knees drawn up under his chin inside a coarse, gray undershirt. William wrote that he looked like "a sort of sculptured Egyptian cat or Peruvian mummy." His dark eyes moved, but he appeared almost entirely non-human to the young doctor in training. *"That shape am I,"* William wrote. "Nothing that I possess can defend me against that fate." Anxiety about his own worsening condition put "a horrible dread in the pit of his stomach," and he felt such a panic about his dark moods that he thought desperately about suicide.

Though he had not been raised as conventionally religious, William found himself grasping at scriptural phrases—"The eternal God is my refuge," "Come unto me, all yet that labor and are heavy-laden," and "I am the resurrection and the life"—to stave off what he labeled as insanity. But then, in the dark times following Minny Temple's death, William rediscovered a French idealist philosopher, Charles Renouvier, who insisted in the primacy of "free will," and this notion proved to be just what he needed. Suddenly more upbeat than he'd been in years, William declared that his "first act of free will shall be to believe in free will." This epiphany marked the turning point in his crisis—parallel to his father's discovery of Swedenborg thirty years before. William would later describe his own agonies (disguised as the experience of a French psychological patient) as well as this transformation in his book *The Varieties of Religious Experience* (1902). But William's recovery was gradual, and so was his sister's.

Still, two springs after her breakdown, Alice too felt gusts of hope and made plans for escape. And Harry, closing his eyes, could imagine his window opened not on sweltering Massachusetts but on radiant Umbria. "Florence is within and not without," Harry wrote to Grace Norton. He hoped to wander Florence again in ten years. But the heavy clocks in the house were ticking. All the Jameses worked faster than that.

· 9 ·

HEIRESSES ABROAD

I n the July heat of 1870, the great ballroom of the Grand
Union Hotel in Saratoga Springs felt especially stifling. The
huge room—nearly empty as yet—blazed with hot gaslight
from wall sconces and chandeliers. An orchestra thundered out a magnificent Viennese waltz. At the entrance, at the foot of a flight of
wooden steps, a man in a linen coat and a straw hat collected tickets
from the guests. Harry, who had just arrived and who hovered expectantly around the doorway, noted that the ticket taker wasn't wearing a
waistcoat or a necktie, as his European counterpart would have done.
Here in this small town on the edge of the Adirondack wilderness in upstate New York, social life had unexpected idiosyncrasies. Only a few
weeks after his return from more mannerly English spas like Cheltenham, twenty-seven-year-old Harry was spending a month in the
scandalously luxurious resort of Saratoga, writing for the *Nation* as well
as drinking the local water for his health. He could expect to glimpse, at
this ball or at the nearby Congress Spring—where black servers ladled
out cups of curative mineral water for the well-heeled summer visitors—
Vanderbilts or Belmonts, General Philip Sheridan or General William
Tecumseh Sherman.

Below the ballroom stairs, in a basement, Harry had just caught sight
of a red-faced auctioneer bellowing against the strains of the waltzes
above. He was selling "pools" on the Saratoga races to a crowd of what

Harry described as "frowsy betting men." Especially since the end of the Civil War—when in fact horses of any kind had been scarce—Saratoga's races, held regularly at its new oval track just off Union Avenue, had drawn enthusiastic crowds of both spectators and bettors.

All manner of gamblers, cardsharps, sportsmen, and high rollers also congregated at a nearby Saratoga casino run by John Morrissey. Called "Old Smoke," Morrissey, the son of Irish immigrants, sported a bristling beard, a brawny physique, and a long criminal record. His popular "Club House" hinted at the darker side of Saratoga—its prostitutes and its huge gambling racket. But the casino's plush halls, all cigar smoke and chandeliers, attracted fabulously wealthy moguls of industry and even slightly wayward U.S. presidents like Ulysses S. Grant. For his part, Harry took Morrissey's reception rooms in stride, with his usual watchful composure. He actually preferred the casino in faraway Monte Carlo—the "blue Mediterranean," the silver-green olive groves, and the wooded cliffs of the Italian Riviera across the bay.

But the Grand Union "hop," as it was called, fascinated Harry much more, although the fashionable gathering was slow to start. Finally, a musician went to the top of the steps and "blew a loud summons on a horn." Two young ladies arrived alone, arm in arm, sporting white gloves. A fashionable couple appeared—the man clad in a railroad "duster," a loose casual overcoat; the woman exquisitely dressed, dashing up the steps with "satin-shod feet twinkling beneath an uplifted volume of gauze and lace and flowers." Soon others came with children—boys presenting tickets at the door, girls elaborately frocked. The ball began with mostly children dancing together, solemnly but boldly, as if to encourage their elders. After that, couple after couple took to the floor. A shortage of men forced many women to wait on the perimeters or else to partner each other, their cool silk dresses, buoyed up by petticoats, fanning out as they danced. The Civil War had created an imbalance between men and women that would take years to correct.

Instead of dancing himself, Harry mentally took notes—or at least that's how he portrayed himself in the charming article on the resort and its manners that he was writing for the *Nation*. At other times, on the long veranda of the arcaded brick Grand Union, with its three-story iron pillars overlooking the carriage-thronged thoroughfare of Broadway in

Saratoga, he simply observed the summer crowds. In the huge parlor just behind this "piazza," he wove in among the knots of couples and families who clustered around rocking chairs and small tables set with pitchers of ice water, refilled by fleets of black waiters. The male guests tended to lounge around the front steps of the hotel, puffing on cigars or chewing on toothpicks. Elsewhere, with their families, they tilted their chairs backward and their white hat brims forward, in various postures of repose. Many were gaunt Yankees, but they came from all over the country, Harry thought, from "San Francisco, from New Orleans, from Alaska." Women greatly outnumbered and outdressed them, exerting themselves to display their "diamonds and laces"; "at any hour of the morning or evening," Harry observed, "you may see a hundred rustling beauties whose rustle is their sole occupation." In particular, Harry shadowed one married woman who appeared with her husband, every evening, in a different exquisite outfit. He observed that she embodied a glittering contrast to the "dusty clapboards" of the hotel, "with her beautiful hands folded in her silken lap, her head drooping slightly beneath the weight of her *chignon*, her lips parted in a vague contemplative gaze." Harry appreciated female beauty and thought there was nothing prettier than a well-put-together woman sitting in a shady spot, focusing on her embroidery or a book.

Ever elusive and imaginative, Harry tended to prefer such still lifes to actual human interactions. It didn't matter to him that the Springs were famous for flirtation. Fast women mixed freely with the garrulous crowds, but respectable married ladies also tried their hand at playing the field. Harry, though, maintained the cool aloofness that William had observed in him years before. Saratoga women, anyway, weren't Harry's preferred type. They had the "vacuous grandeur" of the place and registered to him only as "money and finery and possessions."

At Saratoga, despite his seeming lack of interest, Harry found his predilection for the company of American women over that of their fathers, brothers, husbands, and sons was increasing. In Europe he had felt the opposite, preferring the aristocratic or artistic men he had met there. But back in America, he observed that the men pursued their hardheaded business interests, and only the women embodied the delicacy and richness of "culture." He could picture such women on the terraces of English castles, overlooking great private parks, in conversation with ambassadors and dukes. And, with a sensibility that would define his career, he would increasingly represent such exquisite American heiresses in his fiction.

❦

AT HOME IN Quincy Street, life was not so exquisite, as Harry found when he returned from his summer travels around New England in September 1870. When oppressed by his mother's regimented household, he devoured the sepia-tone photographs of Italian cathedrals that his friends brought back from Italy. He avidly monitored the Prussian occupation of Paris during the autumn of 1870 by means of telegraphed reports in newspapers, as if he himself were a cane-wielding bourgeois Parisian on the boulevards. As his European *Wanderjahr* of 1869–70 faded, he dreaded that his "European gains" would sink out of sight, smothered by his more mundane and scrappy Yankee life. But, even as he pined for Rome, he consoled himself with the greater misfortune of his brother Bob. Harry's life might be worse: he "*might* be lodged in one of the innermost circles of the Inferno—in Wisconsin."

To Bob, it may or may not have been hell, but the youngest James son had in fact been obliged to settle in Wisconsin. Every day, a thousand miles from Cambridge, he plodded the rough but growing city of Milwaukee, where he earned his way in life as a payroll clerk for the Chicago, Milwaukee, and St. Paul Railway. Since his romance with his cousin Kitty Van Buren had been squelched, Bob had increasingly turned inward—almost no letters from him during this time have survived—although William mentioned in his correspondence his brother's problems with his eyes and his back. Bob loathed the unimaginative work of bookkeeping, his unfortunate lot in life. But he had it better than Wilkie, whose Florida plantation had utterly collapsed into financial ruin—dragging down the family investments and transforming them into pure losses that his parents resented. Wilkie was unemployed now, staying in Cambridge but hoping to travel west with the Emersons during the coming spring.

Two more James children still boarded at Quincy Street: William and Alice. In the stolid parlors and drafty bedrooms, the three or four stranded siblings struggled with a strangulating "quiet, stay-at-home life," as Harry phrased it. They had to content themselves with an all-too-familiar household routine, with predictable rounds of mediocre coffee and rolls: "When one sits down to sum up Cambridge life *plume en main* [pen in hand]," Harry wrote a friend, "the strange thing seems its aridity."

Though Harry still hated Cambridge, he had the advantage and the distraction of an incipient career, regular sketches and stories appearing in national magazines. At about this time, William noted that Harry had sold one story, "Travelling Companions," to the *Atlantic* for the respectable sum of $150.

Harry's success, such as it was, appeared to needle his elder brother. William would cross the Rubicon of thirty that winter, in January 1871, and was earning nothing at all. His younger brother's literary fortunes must have both pleased and galled him to some degree. William had considered himself the great hope of the family, the son groomed for success. Quiet, romantic Harry was always secondary, and not quite of this world. But now the tables had turned, and Harry's financial marketability was thrust on William, day after day. It was hard for him to hate the kindhearted Harry. It was easier to hate and blame himself—something he had, in fact, grown quite practiced at doing.

Twenty-nine-year-old William now spent much of his time, as he would later confess to Harry, "shut up face to face with [his] impotence to do anything." He had earned a medical degree, but he had never really wanted to practice, so he drifted, battling the depression that made him dread the approach of evening and the twilight over Harvard Yard. To stay afloat, William forced himself to dine out—more than the solitary Harry could be coerced to do. Obsessively, William monitored the infinitesimal fluctuations of his health; he himself was his most engrossing patient. Reading the French philosopher Charles Renouvier had recently given William new motivation, but it remained doubtful if any of the philosophical, psychological, and self-help books he was devouring would ultimately do him any good. Even with his overstrained eyes, he read so voraciously that Alice said he had already "glanced" at and quickly sized up anything she considered starting. William was deepening his already formidable erudition as well as passionately engaging with the problem we would now describe as living with depression. He would increasingly be able to confront psychological problems as an original, compassionate thinker.

∝⧢⧢

AT THE MAIN station in Chicago, on April 18, 1871, a deluxe private Pullman car, christened the *Huron*, awaited its distinguished passengers. The Pullman was a mansion on wheels; since 1862, the Pullman Palace Car Company, headed by the entrepreneur George Pullman, had manufactured luxurious sleeping cars whose fittings—plush upholstery, drapes, and carpets, card and dining tables—recalled the finer fittings of nineteenth-century parlors. John Murray Forbes, the philanthropic tycoon to whom this particular car belonged, insisted that while they jolted westward he would be able to serve his guests the sumptuous many-course meals they might have enjoyed at the Parker House Hotel in Boston, where the Saturday Club met.

The guests soon assembled and boarded the car: the distinguished white-haired Ralph Waldo Emerson with his daughter and her husband; the rest of the Forbes family (including Mrs. Forbes and three daughters, Alice, Sarah, and Mary); two Bostonian Thayers related to the Emersons; and one plump, mustached young man in his midtwenties who walked with a slight limp: Garth Wilkinson James.

Wilkie was in luck, for a change. Partly through his old friendship with Edward Emerson—who was actually too ill with smallpox for this expedition—Wilkie had now joined an excursion that even his well-traveled brothers might have envied. He would accompany the aging Emerson on a tour of the remote West only two years after the golden spike had been driven in at Promontory Point, Utah, in 1869, to complete the first transcontinental railroad. An epic journey across the United States by rail was now actually possible.

As genially fond of travel as any James, Wilkie would cross the Missouri at Council Bluffs, traverse the Great Plains, and climb into the dry, sage-carpeted high country of Wyoming, with its vast herds of antelopes. During a brief stopover in Salt Lake City, Wilkie saw the famous tortoise-shaped Mormon Tabernacle; its elongated shingled dome, perched on sandstone piers, had been finished in 1867. Wilkie also met the shaggy seventy-year-old Mormon prophet, Brigham Young, who struck Emerson as a "burly, bull-necked man of hard sense." Later, after crossing the Nevada desert and the High Sierras, Wilkie's party toured Yosemite and the redwood forests with the soon-to-be-famous amateur naturalist John Muir. In San Francisco, Wilkie walked the streets of Chinatown before starting back East in mid-May, via Lake Tahoe.

Despite his moving Civil War letters, Wilkie had never been as much of a writer as other members of the family. He left no record of this colorful excursion; at least, no letter back home has survived. It was up to another member of the party, James Bradley Thayer, to take notes on the trip and write them up into *A Western Journey with Mr. Emerson*, a book published after Emerson's death, in 1884. Once again, as during the Civil War, Wilkie had passed through some of the most vivid scenes of his era without leaving or troubling himself to leave, as his brothers did, a literary trail. He had always been the most jovial and least intel-lectual of the Jameses, but for this too he would pay a price. The rest of the Pullman party returned to Boston in June, but Wilkie stopped in Chicago. He still had to earn his living, as his father continued to make clear to him. With John Murray Forbes's help, Wilkie settled for a job as a payroll clerk with Bob's railroad—a career path that Bob himself could hardly recommend. But Wilkie had few options. His father wrote to him that the family's sympathy for him was "acute and constant." But everyone knew his new life would be, in his father's warning phrase, "barely remunerative." He would earn scarcely enough to live on.

✧

TWENTY-EIGHT-YEAR-OLD HARRY, MEANWHILE, was gradu-ally making both money and friends. One Monday night in April 1871, about the time that Wilkie was traveling west, his brother dressed for dinner with particular care, choosing the color of his vest carefully—as he habitually did—and meticulously knotting and straightening his bow tie.

Harry had been invited to dinner by Elinor Mead Howells, the wife of William Dean Howells, the incoming editor of the *Atlantic Monthly*. This increasingly prestigious Boston magazine had just published

Harry's short story "A Passionate Pilgrim" in its March and April issues; in consequence of such publications, the young man was growing into a literary personage. He made sure he looked the part: though short-sighted and beginning to go bald, he customarily rigged himself out in spotless linen, polished boots, and lavender gloves. Even Harry's life, it's true, had its more quotidian side: his mother sewed his ample Victorian underwear. But still he dressed as dapperly as his small magazine income would allow. Arriving at the Howells' lamplit home nearby on Berkeley Street in Cambridge, he shook hands with an even more celebrated young author, the thirty-four-year-old Californian Bret Harte, who had just published "The Luck of Roaring Camp," his depiction of the mining settlements of the 1849 gold rush. He appeared in the Howells' parlor in order to be lionized. Perhaps envious, Harry privately called Harte and his wife "marvelous creatures," with a jab of irony. In 1871, the *Atlantic* paid Harte ten thousand dollars for twelve stories. These were astronomical fees, far above the rates that Harry himself was earning.

Harry considered that meeting Harte marked an opportunity "not lightly to be thrown aside." In order to dine with such a celebrity, Harry had turned down an invitation for that same evening from an equally "marvelous" creature, a former friend of Minny Temple's, Elizabeth Lyman Boott, a petite Bostonian heiress who was staging a party at her nearby "*atelier* and *salon*," as Harry called it. Lizzie was a painter, and she thought Henry would mingle well with her art-loving friends, most of them well-traveled Bostonians. Along with Howells, Lizzie admired Harry's "Passionate Pilgrim," his fable of a delicate and sickly young American longing to claim an English estate. It was an early example of Harry's "international" fiction, his pitting of the New World against the Old.

Of all people, Lizzie could sympathize with Harry's transatlantic themes. A cosmopolitan globetrotter, she had been expensively educated in Switzerland and Italy; she spoke ready French, Italian, and German. She had been brought up to play the piano and sing. At the age of ten, in Florence, she'd been taught drawing by Giorgio Mignaty, a Greek-born history painter. More recently, she'd studied art with William Morris Hunt, William's old teacher, with a circle of well-to-do women aspirants that he'd assembled in Boston after the end of the Civil War. Steeped in refined culture and with an income ample enough to rent villas and grand staterooms on the steamships, Lizzie and her father frequently crossed the Atlantic, as, much to Harry's envy, they would do later that same year.

Harry had a fascination with subtle, sophisticated heiresses like Lizzie. He had a use for such women—a watchful, feline, distant use. He wasn't interested in marrying a rich young lady, as he had repeatedly declared, but he sensed such women could aid his worldly advancement. As a first step, he was even now making literary use of an heiress: having written a number of short apprentice pieces, he was ready to write his first novel.

In the summer and fall of 1871, Harry's first long work came out as a five-part serial in the *Atlantic Monthly*. The influential magazine, with its salmon-colored cover, tended to be slipped into travelers' trunks on transatlantic steamers and was also a regular item on the reading tables of Quincy Street, where the magazine-devouring Jameses eagerly read and appraised Harry's debut novella, a somewhat odd piece of fiction that he had alliteratively titled *Watch and Ward*.

Harry's story traced the career of a young bachelor dandy who, having failed in love, concocted the perfect plan for winning a wife: he'd adopt as his ward a twelve-year-old heiress and marry her at the first opportunity. But the girl—blushing, chestnut-haired, blindingly rich—also attracted a host of other suitors. These rivals included the bachelor's clergyman cousin, the girl's own cousin, and a whole inbred gang who preyed with intense Victorian repression on the young woman.

This child heiress figured as yet another example of the Victorian arts' at times prurient obsession with pubescent girls. To be sure, the beribboned innocents in the fiction of the era harbored multiple dark paradoxes. In one sense, young girls embodied a melodramatic innocence and vulnerability—Harry's bachelor met the girl first at night in a hotel where she was standing in her nightgown over her suicidal father. In a different sense, girls incorporated everything Victorian men craved: beauty, sex, financial capital, security, even philosophical or metaphysical meaning in an intellectual world recently destabilized by the theories of Charles Darwin. And though Harry was personally less entranced by young girls than were Lewis Carroll, John Ruskin, or Charles Eliot Norton, he instinctively understood the power of the demure nineteenth-century Lolita. For many Victorian men, the most perfect wife (besides a helpless moneyed cousin) was a daughter they had raised themselves.

To his publisher James Fields, Harry hopefully joked that *Watch and Ward* would be "one of the greatest works of 'this or any age.'" But for all its rank Victorian sensuality—nocturnal scenes of grown men heatedly groping the girl's locked pocket watch with all-too-Freudian keys—the story didn't catch the spirit of the times. And it just didn't work. Friends like Grace Norton loyally championed it, and so did William Dean Howells. But Harry himself increasingly found this "slight" Bostonian novel of manners embarrassing and too revealing. It wasn't the monumental novel he'd itched to write, and before long he fiercely repudiated the work.

Both William and Henry Senior admired his "light" writing with cool reserve: travel sketches, art reviews, and dribbles of fiction didn't suit their "manly," philosophic minds. Harry's novel silently confirmed their opinion. Mary beamed when mentioning his work; but she was, after all, his mother, someone rarely credited with any taste or judgment. And so in the view of his family, Harry hadn't achieved success. Like his fictional hero in *Watch and Ward*, he was also beginning to feel like an "under-valued man."

IN THE FALL of 1871, the idle William began to spend more time, informally, in a starkly furnished room next door to the Massachusetts General Hospital in Boston. These were the modest facilities of the Harvard medical school, recently known as the Massachusetts Medical College of Harvard University, which had been founded back in 1782, but whose quarters were still minimal by modern standards. William knew them from his studies in the 1860s, but his classmate William Pickering Bowditch, a physiologist, had recently returned from Germany with cutting-edge German scientific equipment, and he had set up a laboratory in this bleak house on North Grove Street. Dissecting had previously fascinated William, and he now rediscovered his interest in anatomy.

William confided to Bowditch that his father was pursuing different scientific interests and had declared to Louis Agassiz, that same year, that he, Henry, had visited "every whorehouse in Boston" out of social curiosity. "I admire the old fellow," William remarked to his friend. Of course, William had his own strong scientific interests, some of them almost as unorthodox, which his fellow doctor now encouraged, both at the medical school and at his home, where Bowditch often invited the directionless William to spend an evening with him and his wife.

William, who was increasingly fascinated with the quirks of the mind, also explored his ideas outside of the dissecting lab. With years of reading in his head to draw on, William founded a "metaphysical club" with his Boston friends Oliver Wendell Holmes Jr., Chauncey Wright, and Charles Sanders Peirce, in the winter of 1871–72. Holmes was a jurist, the editor of the *American Law Review*; Wright an empirical and scientific philosopher; and Peirce (pronounced "Purse") was a physicist and logician. Collectively they combined a formidable range of intellectual perspectives that would do much to stimulate William's own emerging medically informed concept of the human psyche. For his part, Harry thought the "long-headed" members of this club would only "wrangle grimly" and struggle endlessly through brambly philosophical questions— a prospect that pasted the more fanciful young novelist with a headache. But still Harry envied William and his friends their bonhomie, as he himself had "not great choice of company either to wrangle or agree with."

While staying in the picturesque clapboard village of Bar Harbor, Maine, during July 1872, William got some heartening news. On one side of the bay were imposing granite cliffs, over which the greenish Northern Lights wove their patterns during the night. William had been out on the broad, ink-blue Atlantic, rowing the sisters Theodora and Sara Sedgwick; he'd also driven them out to see the famous spouting rock, caused by incoming breakers, on the rocky western shore of Mount Desert Island. In such a lyrical setting, William slit open a letter from Bowditch. His friend asked him to take his place in some of his teaching at Harvard. In the coming spring of 1873, William was invited to teach the physiology portion of Natural History 3: Anatomy and Physiology, fifty hours of class time for three hundred dollars.

Immediately, William wrote to Alice. A job was "just the thing to work my salvation in every respect if Eliot consents to it," he told her. The ambitious Charles W. Eliot had taken over the presidency of Harvard in 1869. In a small-scale but fateful decision, the scientific-minded Eliot *would* consent—thus starting William off on his important professional association with the most dynamic university in the United States in one of its most dynamic periods. William's substitute-teaching position would be depressingly lowly: Eliot himself when he was a chemistry professor in 1860 had complained about the "smallness of College pay" and the laboratory work that pushed "up to the very limit of physical endurance." But the job would focus William's energies, cheer him, and give him—at the age of thirty—his own source of income. The teaching assistantship was a real windfall. Living across the street from Harvard Yard for almost a decade had finally begun to pay off, for at least one of the Jameses.

&⪦

ALICE'S PROSPECTS, TOO, were looking rosier by the late spring of 1872. The Cunard liner *Algeria*, a fast screw steamer with one funnel and three masts, glided out of New York Harbor on May 11. The tiny staterooms of the *Algeria* accommodated two hundred passengers whose lorgnettes and opera glasses would almost certainly be trained on the increasingly jagged brick and marble New York skyline as it receded. And three of the names enrolled in the manifest were Mr. H. James Jr., Miss James, and Mrs. Walsh.

Alice had just turned twenty-three, but her face beneath her braided chignon was pale after long periods of seclusion in her father's library. Yet once the ship had sailed out beyond Fire Island, the Atlantic breezes added color to her cheeks as she stretched her legs on the deck. Down below was her trunk of highly ruffled frocks whose neat folding her fastidious mother had engineered and closely supervised. The tossing of the ship, which was "decidedly a roller," would make it inconvenient for Harry to write her anxious parents an account of her, though he would spend his time "scribbl[ing] on the tumbling washstand in the malodorous stateroom."

Alice, resplendent now with new courage, spent as much of the voyage as she could in the open air. She hadn't seen Europe for eleven years, not since she was a twelve-year-old in the care of a Swiss governess. Since that time, William and Harry had indulged themselves in grand tours, educational residences, and long basks in European spas. But finally, against the odds, her turn had come.

For once, this voyage was *for* Alice, whose concerned father had even contemplated selling some of his Albany property in order to send her abroad. With a wide and watery horizon tumbling around her, the young woman must have felt strangely privileged after her long confinement at home. But if, at last, she'd become a debutante worthy of travel, she still had to voyage out under the watchful care of her two protectors. Yet to travel with Harry counted as a privilege, and he and his sister were perhaps the two most compatible of the Jameses; Alice later noted that the pair of them could often laugh together about the foibles of the rest of the family. Harry instinctively sympathized with Alice, and she adored Harry, glowing with happiness in his presence and, as she later put it, wanting to "cry for two hours, after he goes."

Harry, who'd joined his aunt in lobbying for his sister's grand tour, had motivations beyond Alice's pleasure. He genuinely fretted about her health, but he had concocted his own plan, in fact, to reclaim Europe—and not just for the five months allotted to Alice. Harry hoped that his own odyssey abroad would stretch out for months or even years.

Before they had all sailed, Harry had arranged to write travel pieces for the *Nation*. In an early version of the sort of glossy travel features that would become so popular a century later, the *Nation* and other high-culture magazines or popular newspapers of the 1870s offered letters and "notes" from breezy foreign correspondents in Paris, St. Petersburg, Istanbul, and other far corners of the globe. Though the phenomenon of travel writing was hardly new—Henry James Sr. had offered rambling foreign letters to the *New York Tribune* back in the 1850s—such accounts claimed a new prominence in increasingly affluent post–Civil War America, as tourists boarded transatlantic steamers to "see" and "do" Europe. (Even a yokel like the young Samuel Clemens could now lark through Europe and write about it for an eager public, as Clemens did in his hotly selling *Innocents Abroad* in 1869.)

During the Jameses' European wanderings in the 1850s, travel guides had barely existed. (The English Murray family had started publishing "handbooks" in 1836, and John Murray had come out with the first blue-covered guide to London in 1856; the German publisher Karl Baedeker had issued his first crimson-covered guide to Switzerland in 1863.) An earlier generation of genteel travelers, Harry knew, had arrived in Europe armed with "introductions, photographs, travellers' tales and other aids to knowingness." But with fast locomotives and palatial grand hotels promising a modern age of middle-class tourism, meticulous and exhaustive guidebooks had exploded onto the market, with droves of travelers routinely buying and packing these thorough, beautifully printed tomes. These days, no one thought of voyaging without a pocket vade mecum.

Characteristically, the old-fashioned Harry felt nostalgia for "the poor bewildered and superannuated genius of the old Grand Tour, as it was taken forty years ago . . . [before] the eternal telegraphic click bespeaking 'rooms' on mountaintops." He scorned the "vulgar" tourist hordes but planned deftly to exploit the new American craze for European travel as a means of securing his reputation and financial independence. He didn't plan to author travel guides per se; he planned to achieve his ends with a more sophisticated form of reportage.

At the same time, Harry didn't shy away from the duties of tour guide: as soon as the three landed in England on May 21, Harry assumed the authoritative and slightly patronizing role of Alice's cicerone. (He was, in fact, a born guide, and it was a somewhat loftier guide's voice that he adopted in his European travel essays.) Characteristically, he judged the view of cottage gardens during Alice's first railway journey out of Liverpool, where they had disembarked, as an excellent "introduction to English verdure." (Harry had evidently forgotten that Alice had seen plenty of English roses in the 1850s.) More roses, it seemed, lay in wait.

Soon the party established themselves at a garden hotel in the redstone cathedral city of Chester, the nearest beauty spot to the smoky wharves of Liverpool. Harry made sure to scout ahead, snatching "a quiet stroll through the town" to get pointers on the main sights, in order to qualify as a true *"valet de place"* (hired guide).

For her older brother, Alice—whom he affectionately sketched for the family as she wrote at a table beside the hotel's ivy-fringed bow window—amounted to a pleasant responsibility. At times, however—to judge from the tone of his letters home—he treated her a little like a child he was babysitting. He never failed to pass on detailed accounts of her: "The country has no disappointments and Alice no *défaillances* [lapses]," he wrote. "She passes from delight to delight with daily growing strength and has enjoyed a week of those rare first impressions which remain forever memorable." Harry went on to report that Alice was thriving visibly, that she had filled her tourist's schedule with visits to the quaint old town and its small, neat cathedral. "We of course interpose large opportunities for rest," Harry was careful to add, also remarking that his "[d]ear house-cleaning mother" would approve of their spruce, briskly run English hotel.

Harry treated his sister and aunt (as well as his absent mother) with high courtesy—he shone in the role of his mother's "angel." But, though he sometimes cherished Alice, sometimes patronizingly saw her as an invalid, Harry found that his sister added to his trip in surprising ways. In spite of his protracted pining for Europe—and the brief euphoria of return—Harry soon found himself unmoved by the "show region" of the rocky, turfy Derbyshire Peaks through which the party soon roved in their open carriage. As he and the two ladies bumped their way through these windblown and stony landscapes, Harry absorbed the watery blues and greens, he reported, "without heart-beats or raptures or literary inspiration of any kind." If it weren't for Alice, he wrote Charles Eliot Norton, he'd have abandoned these *Pride and Prejudice* moors altogether, and taken a train direct to "London, mankind and the newspaper."

When, still in Derbyshire, the tourists sampled the terraced Elizabethan rose gardens of Haddon Hall and the gilded Restoration-period staterooms of Chatsworth House, Harry found his writerly inspiration still remained "cold and dull," still resolutely dead. Alice, though, brimmed with more "generous" reactions at each of their stops. Harry needed her enthusiasm in order to appreciate the well-trampled English attractions he was hoping to write up for the *Nation*. "I have been playing at first impressions for a second time," he told his readers, "and have won the game against a cynical adversary" (that is, himself). But it was Alice who helped him win.

Alice didn't just furnish Harry with his pretext for returning to Europe (and family funds for him to live on). She also transformed herself into her brother's travel-writing muse. Consciously and unconsciously, Harry made multiple uses of his sister, who became a sounding board, a female alter ego, a model (intelligent though she was) of a "naive" and excitable traveler. She also represented a wide and growing audience that would increasingly form the foundation for Henry James's success.

Harry zeroed in on the reader of the *Atlantic* or *Nation* back in New England (where Alice most often was), envisioning an "unsophisticated young person . . . reading in an old volume of travels" in a quiet room with a chiming Yankee pendulum clock. And he no doubt found it convenient to conjure up this usually female reader in the undemanding form of his sister.

Henry's sketch about Haddon Hall reported a "companion"—was it his aunt or his sister?—who observed how "Elizabethan" the place was. (The house was a paneled one with terraced rose gardens where Shakespeare's Countess Olivia might have listened to the sententious Malvolio.) Alice probably coined observations like this regularly, to judge from the family's praise of her letters home—though none of these have in fact survived. Or rather they have survived under Harry's name since, as Alice observed years later, Harry made a career out of appropriating her material: "embedded in his pages [are] many pearls fallen from my lips, which he steals in the most unblushing way, saying, simply, that he knew they had been said by the family, so it didn't matter." Harry snapped up both her experiences and her bon mots and incorporated them in his pieces—without thinking to give Alice any credit and steadily writing her out of his travel pieces.

The trio reached Oxford in early June. Alice was already proving herself a "capital traveler" in her own right—somebody who observed, relished, and recounted with brilliance. As is clear from letters written at other times in her life, she was writing her own accounts in her own style. A few of her observations in Oxfordshire made it into Harry's letters. She loved the Blenheim Palace gardener who called his bushes "rhosy-dendrons," adored this great golden-stone house of the dukes of Marlborough, with its huge ivy-smothered oaks, its bridged lake, and its long vistas of lawns. Like Prospero's daughter waking up to a brave new world, Alice was charmed by everything she saw—or at least that's how her solicitous brother understood her. (Alice's own observations, in her lost letters, would probably have sounded more pungent than Harry's.)

From the distant and less glamorous perspective of Milwaukee, Bob also enjoyed the letters and travel accounts Alice was writing, as forwarded to him by the family. Dazzled by his sister's descriptions, he even thought his childhood playmate might turn out to be the "genius of the house," after all. Even the overcritical William was enough impressed by his sister's writings to claim, only a little teasingly, that Alice had earned "the epithet of Mme de Sevigné," the famous seventeenth-century French epistolary genius. William apparently envisioned Alice's European travels as a springboard into a brilliant maturity "undreamt by any of us." Once back in Cambridge, he hoped, Alice would transform herself into the "lioness" of the next social season—if not into the next Louisa May Alcott or Harriet Beecher Stowe, those widely read New England women authors of the 1850s and 1860s.

If Alice wrote such entertaining letters, why didn't she author her own travel pieces? In the nineteenth century, to be sure, many educated American women kept diaries of their raptures and insights when traveling. In 1872, the very year of Alice's escape, in fact, another literate New England woman also traveling for her health was poised to make good, under her gender-neutral pseudonym of "H.H." Helen Hunt Jackson kept notes on her travels in Colorado and California, publishing them as *Bits of Travel at Home* in 1878. Later, in 1884, she used these impressions to enrich her novel about Native Americans, *Ramona*. (Jackson flabbergasted her childhood friend Emily Dickinson by becoming a best-selling poet, novelist, and travel writer.)

Harry, usually sympathetic, never envisioned his sister writing for a living. Though many nineteenth-century women published their European travels, Harry would lampoon such efforts. The fictional journalist Henrietta Stackpole, in his future novel *The Portrait of a Lady* (1881), would provide one example. Henrietta Stackpole, it's true, would more resemble Harry than Alice—being "thoroughly launched in journalism" and writing travel sketches about Newport before tirelessly crossing the Atlantic to cover Europe. But as a woman and a "radical," Miss Stackpole had, as Harry framed her, an "obvious" and hackneyed bent, including a deplorable talent for knowing "what the public was going to want." (Harry rarely had this knack, though Helen Hunt Jackson had it in spades.) Such an indefatigable travel writer was, at best, a good-natured comic figure; at worst, a vulgar hoyden who published her impressions for money. She was a figure Alice herself would find flimsy and instinctively dislike.

Even so, Alice knew her father and brothers never expected her to publish, in any form. They never expected her to forge any kind of career for herself, and she didn't yet have the self-confidence to prove them wrong.

∽

THE PARTY ARRIVED in Paris on June 26, and Harry soon treated his sister to the great art collections of the Louvre. But just to the west of the great palace, the charred stone shell of the Tuileries Palace stood starkly out. Hollow tiers of blackened arches looked down on the rue de Rivoli, the Pont Royal over the Seine, and the elegant old courtyard, with its cluster of trees, of the Palais du Louvre.

In their earlier childhood visits to Paris, the young Jameses had known this grand stone Renaissance palace, begun by Catherine de Médicis in 1564, in its mature splendor, with its tall chimneys and square, steep-roofed towers. But this old royal residence—where Louis XIV had stayed while Versailles was being built—had recently fallen victim to the latest round of upheavals in France. The Prussian siege and occupation of Paris from 1870 to 1871 had hardly damaged the French capital, but the subsequent era of the socialist Paris Commune had caused riots and running battles through the city. On May 23, 1871, a year before Alice's visit, during the so-called Semaine Sanglante (bloody week), Commune extremists had doused the palace with tar, turpentine, and petroleum and set it alight. Seen by some as a symbol of monarchical oppression, the palace would never be restored and would be demolished, in 1883, despite the protests of many French artists and architects. But for twelve years, the burned-out hull of the palace reminded American tourists that France had a turbulent political life as well as an exquisite cultural patrimony—and in 1872 that memory was especially raw.

Harry, who had followed these developments in the newspapers, warned his sister to expect a changed, scarred Paris. But his protectiveness was hardly necessary. Alice showed herself delighted to be in France again, relishing an evening at the Théâtre Français, lingering at outdoor cafés in the warm weather, reveling in a day visit to the Nortons at St.-Germain-en-Laye. Harry resolutely found Paris, he wrote his family, the definition of perfection. But his sister had an even more dramatic and visceral reaction to the city.

On the brash boulevards of Paris, Alice prowled with more vigor and brilliancy than her brother had ever seen in her. When she wrote home about her enthusiasm for Paris, her mother exclaimed, in some shock, "My daughter a child of France!" Mary suspected that the young woman had been dizzied by Parisian shopping and dining, by the "mere delights of eating and drinking and seeing and dressing." But this appraisal showed how little Mary understood her daughter. Alice loved millinery (her own mother's passion, after all), but she flared to life in Paris because of her excellent French, which was now actually useful, and her newfound sense of freedom.

"What has become of that high moral nature," her mother lamented, "on which I have always based such hopes for her, in this world and the next?" To judge from her later writings, her nature was just beginning to unfold. For one thing, she had an un-James-like interest in politics, as her later sympathy for rebellious politicians like the Irish patriot Charles Parnell shows. In Paris, Alice may well have harbored some fascination for the recent turbulence, which had involved an antipatriarchal feminist movement and such vivid figures as Louise Michel, the "Red Virgin of Montmartre." Alice never described herself as a feminist, and her resistance to authority was more delicate and interior, but something in her always appreciated a good assertion of defiance. She would soon enough have to summon her own version if it.

In late June, the party set off by rail for the Swiss Alps. At Montreux, on the eastern end of the blue Lake Leman, the excited Alice commissioned a French-inspired confection of a dress (afterward known in the family as the "Montreux dress"). At Villeneuve, a quaint little harbor town at the eastern end of the lake, the three settled down at the Hôtel Byron, a modest hostelry in spite of being named after a flamboyant Romantic poet. Alice found the place a little quiet for her tastes, after Paris, even with day trips through the woods and vineyards to Harry's favorite local beauty spots like the Château de Chillon, on its rocky island, and the ruggedly beautiful Gorge du Trient. But a new distraction was imminent. Previously the party had thrived as a threesome whom strangers sometimes mistook for a married couple traveling with their aunt. But this intimate and comfortable triad was about to expand.

During their two-week stay at Villeneuve, Harry linked up, fatefully, with the James family friends Francis and Lizzie Boott. Top-hatted and armed with a cane, Francis Boott, the patriarch of this family duo, was an expatriate Bostonian—a starchily proper composer with private means who prettily set Longfellow's poetry to music. He almost always traveled with his cherished daughter. Like many an émigré Bostonian of his era, he knew Europe in exquisite detail.

His dark-haired daughter, Lizzie, two years older than Alice, had returned to Europe with her father to advance her painterly aspirations. She was now implementing her recent Boston training by daubing whimsical landscapes, portraits, and floral studies. With a private fortune and distinguished cheekbones, Lizzie radiated an "amiability & sweetness," as Harry described it, that Alice sometimes lacked. With her melting voice, Lizzie performed songs on the inn piano, to much admiration. No doubt the young woman's many "accomplishments" grated on Alice, who had so few achievements and prospects of her own. But for the time being, Alice didn't bear any animosity toward this rival for her brother's attention, as she'd done in years past, more overtly, with her cousin Minny Temple.

Still, the trouble simmered while the Bootts hung on. It seemed the party would tour all of Switzerland together: Bern, Interlaken, then finally, as the summer took hold, Grindelwald, where the elevation was higher and the air cooler. Like other sightseeing parties in the Alps, the five companions devoted themselves to the admiration of nature. They set out on vertiginous mountain walks from their glacier-hemmed resort. Alice stayed back at the inn when she could. She enjoyed the broad vistas of layered mountains, seen from a coach or a railway carriage. But rough expeditions on foot (for Alice or for Lizzie) were another matter.

Alice found she abhorred the Swiss tourist round of tables d'hôte (fixed menus of local cookery). She loathed the endless fresh-air walks, with alpenstocks and feathered caps, to gawk at massive glacial vistas. Nor did she share Harry's taste for the physiques of "various thin-flanked Englishmen with par-boiled faces, fresh (if fresh it can be called) from the Wetterhorn & the Eiger." To make matters worse, she was juxtaposed, day after day, at the breakfast table and in the evening parlor, with the panoply of Lizzie Boott's gifts.

Evidently, Alice suffered in silence. At last the party split up. Tired of her secondary status, she was all too happy to see the well-tailored backs of the Bootts. Then she and Harry—that harmonious-seeming, married-looking pair—could head, with their aunt, onward toward Lucerne and Andermatt.

But, still higher in the mountains, the aftermath of these brewing tensions took its toll. The crisis happened at a steep-roofed village in a sunny spot deep in the mountain valleys, at Thusis. Now that she was free of Lizzie and restored to her importance in their party, Alice grew even more restless, nervous, and unhappy. The worried Harry tried to help. He took his sister on a sudden three-hour drive to the nearby town of Chur, at a lower altitude. There, in the more urbane capital of this rugged mountainous Swiss canton known as the Grisons, he hoped for the beneficial effect of orchards, vineyards, and a Stadt theater to lift his sister's mood. But this day trip did little to soothe or stimulate Alice. She soon took matters into her own hands. Back at the inn at Thusis—much to Harry's and Kate's alarm—Alice broke down.

As usual—in contrast to her brothers' more frank reporting of their own ailments and depressions—no account of Alice's particular symptoms has survived. Harry in fact hid from his parents that she'd had any trouble at all until well after her symptoms had passed. Even then, he was too protective and gentlemanly to cite unseemly details like stomach cramps, hysterical fits, or tearful tantrums. But Alice must have had a serious nervous attack. Writing to his parents as she was recovering, Harry blamed the crisis not on Alice's deep psychology—much as he must have been acquainted with at least some of it—but instead on "over excitement" caused by the high mountain "air." The climate disagreed with Alice, he theorized; the Alps simply excited and disturbed her too much. "Her verdict," he wrote his parents, "is that there is such a thing as being over stimulated." Actually, the opposite state—understimulation—was probably Alice's problem, and "air" had little or nothing to do with it.

Coincidentally, "air" was one of Switzerland's main natural resources and tourist attractions. The higher the altitude, the more germ-free and curative the air was supposed to be, even for "neurasthenics" or "hysterics" like Alice. For this reason, the most expensive resorts—Zermatt, St. Moritz, and Davos—were often situated high on passes or peaks, or else beneath the tongues of glaciers. But Alice disproved this factitious theory in a stroke.

"Air," the nineteenth-century superstitious scapegoat for mental and physical health complaints, merely camouflaged Alice's deeper frustrations. She missed the urban liberties of Paris, and she was evidently still raw from her long exposure to Lizzie Boott. What better than a breakdown to rush Alice back to "the center of the stage," which the young female painter had stolen?

Clearly Alice had stumbled, collapsed back into her old pattern. Harry and Kate hurried their invalid down into the "air" of Italy—late summer air, which, when they reached Venice, frothed with mosquitoes. The nets over their beds, even with the help of foul-smelling pastilles burning, hardly kept the mosquitoes off. On the Lido, though, the James party braved the open air and the insects: the three dined alfresco on a platform overlooking the Adriatic Sea, Harry with his eyes straying to the bathers on the beach. Later, during a breezy expedition across the lagoon to the lace-making island of Torcello, with its rich Byzantine mosaics, Harry gloried in the open air as well as, characteristically, the gondoliers who muscularly rowed them.

Alice seemed to appreciate this Italian "bath of light and air—color and general luxury," as Harry described it. But she didn't fall in love with Italy as her brother had done. Italy belonged to Harry, not to her. Here he was in his element, in a country he continually transformed into charming letters and handsome travel pieces. His "impressions," unlike hers, had market value; they could be turned into paying literary copy—"enough to support [him]self in affluence," he hopefully re-marked. Alice's travel experiences, like the sepia photographic postcards she was amassing, weren't supposed to translate into literature. Her sto-ries were only meant to bore her social circle and serve as keepsakes for the coming tedious winter evenings back at Quincy Street.

In September, the party struck north again to Paris, and Alice braced herself for her imminent return home. Though laden with "delightful pictures and memories," as her brother somewhat patronizingly put it, she no doubt wanted more concrete mementos of her tour. Sometimes with Harry in tow, she and Aunt Kate visited dressmakers and ransacked the galleries of the Bon Marché, a sumptuous domed department store (complete with a library, a refreshment hall, a gaslit room for scrutiniz-ing the colors of fabric, and an atrium with an ornamental footbridge) that had opened its doors on the rue de Sèvres that very year— department stores themselves being a cutting-edge invention of the de-cade, and one that thoroughly bewitched Alice. Anticipating the coming winter in Cambridge, Alice commissioned a cold-weather bonnet, a hat meant to slay her friends back home: "'*Ah Monsieur, sur des jeunes têtes, c'est divinement beau!*' [Ah Sir, on a young head, it's divinely beautiful!]," the milliner assured Harry. While Harry memorialized their trip with exquisite travel essays in the *Nation* and the *Atlantic*, Alice had to con-sole herself with headgear.

Having had her five-month fling, Alice sailed home with Aunt Kate on the lurching *Algeria*. She arrived back at Quincy Street just when the elms in Harvard Yard were beginning to turn yellow. Her tour, seen by the family as an extravagance, had cost $2,400, even more than Harry's earlier trip. (Hers had been a shorter tour than his, but there were more travelers to be paid for.) Like many genteel Victorian families, the Jameses usually saw travel as an investment, in education as well as amusement. For the outlay, the family hoped Alice had grown "older and wiser," hoped she'd squirreled away "innumerable delightful days and hours and sensations." And upon her return in October 1872, they expected this phantasmagoria to satisfy Alice, permanently.

But far from contenting this interesting young woman, Alice's Euro-pean tour only whetted her appetite for movement, stimulation, and free-dom from parental interference. Harry actually understood his sister best when, in November 1872, he imagined Alice back in Quincy Street, feeling, glumly, as if she'd never been away. "The dresses are un-packed, and the photographs, and the stories told, and Alice is ready to take ship again." But for the Jameses' spinster daughter, there wasn't a ship to take.

❧

HARRY, MEANWHILE, CONTINUED to relish the Paris that his sis-ter had to imagine from many miles off. After a stint in murky London, he delighted in what he called the "glittering bauble" of the French cap-ital, where he spent his days basking in a leisure free of family females— "walking, strolling, *flânant* [idling], prying, staring, lingering at bookstalls and shop-windows." A trifle homesick in the November gloom of 1872, Harry visited an unabashedly Anglo-Saxon restaurant on the Boulevard des Capucines and dined on *rosbif saignant* (bloody roast beef) and pints of English ale. Without his sister and aunt, he had only the waiters for company—though he walked through the Louvre with the white-haired and "serene" Emerson, now on his way to see the Pyramids.

In Paris, Harry also "struck up a furious intimacy" with another older man, the grizzled but richly bearded poet James Russell Lowell. Lowell would become the first in a long line of literary father substitutes. He was fifty-six and Harry twenty-nine, but they scrambled once or twice a week over the old quarters of the city, looking for the "queer places," the old streets and other curiosities of the preboulevard Paris that Lowell had unearthed. But Harry, as was his custom, pre-ferred to keep his distance from Lowell, to wander, often luxuriously bleak and unattached, in the twilit streets made infamous two decades earlier by Charles Baudelaire's *Fleurs de Mal* (1857)—though Harry hardly consorted with prostitutes, as the syphilis-riddled Baudelaire, who'd died a few years before in 1867, had famously done. Yet even for the less adventurous Harry, the temptations and liberties of Paris could not be ignored. Enjoying a reprieve after his family entanglements, Harry cultivated a bachelor's luxuries, but he'd also increasingly adopted the cold, detached, modern urban vision of a traveler, an expa-triate, and a perpetual orphan.

Harry had grown, however, into a shrewd magazinist. He'd become a literary workaholic who cultivated the air of an insouciant young man of means, an heir living graciously abroad. That was exactly the pose he struck in his travel pieces. He later claimed, with a snobbish affectation of aristocracy, that no member of his family had been "guilty of a stroke of business" in two generations. (He counted himself and his father, that is. His grandfather, after all, had struck it rich as a shrewd Irish immigrant entrepreneur and had been bathed in commerce.)

Harry stoked and stroked his own business. Though he could genuinely claim to be an heir to various family-owned commercial properties in upstate New York, he would have been more accurately described as a hardworking, scrappy journalist clinging to a financial shoestring. Calculatingly, he looked forward to the "realization of [his] investments"—the European train pilgrimages that he was spinning, Rumpelstiltskin-like, into gold.

≪≫

THE SUNSHINE WAS cold but the shadows even chillier, as Harry walked into the deep narrow streets of the old city Rome, from his room on the Corso, on Christmas morning 1872. He wished that he'd unpacked his overcoat from his trunk before setting out to climb the many curved flights of the magnificent Spanish Steps.

From the top, under the church of Trinità dei Monti, he looked out on a stirring panorama. Rome in such clear weather resembled the ancient red-roofed city, in pale-golden travertine, that he had first visited two years before: the tolling of church bells, the rattle of black, baroque cardinals' carriages in the streets, the blue winter sky outlining the hills crowned with churches, ruins, cypresses, or villas. But Rome had changed, too. Harry noted with dismay the resulting "modernized air in the streets, a multiplication of shops, carts, [and] newspaper stalls."

Winter had fallen elsewhere in Europe, with fogs and crusts of snow. Living in Italy would warm Harry's bones and cost him half the price of a dismal wood-frame boardinghouse in Boston. (Many expatriates clung to Europe because living there remained alluringly cheaper, through much of the nineteenth century, than in the United States.) And Harry calculated that though the *Nation* already commanded a Paris correspondent, it hadn't yet contracted one for Rome; he hustled to "nail" the position. Harry chose Italy because the country and its art treasures had recently blazed out as the ne plus ultra of the nineteenth-century intellectual establishment. Writers like John Ruskin and Charles Eliot Norton had fueled the burgeoning late-Victorian vogue for Italian art, history, and architecture. Increasingly relevant to American aspirations to high culture, Italy provided the ideal venue for the kind of writing Harry longed to do: art criticism, art history, and upscale travel writing. The increasingly sophisticated readers of the *Atlantic* and the *Nation* were hungry for the new Italian-inspired aestheticism. Consequently, Italy had become a sunny, dirt-cheap, artifact-ridden country where bright young Americans, Englishmen, and Germans idled in Latin splendor while carving out lucrative careers for themselves in the arts— cataloging painters of the quattrocento or advising American robber barons on their accelerating acquisition of Italian pictures, statues, and villas. The century, as it went on, would become the "age of Mrs. Jack," as Harry would describe it—the golden age of aggressive American collectors like Isabella Stewart Gardner (Mrs. Jack Gardner) of Boston, a regal figure descended from Scottish royalty whom Harry would come to know before the decade was out.

Harry settled into the now-familiar Hôtel de Rome on the Corso in a sun-drenched fourth-floor room. Later in the spring, the heat would grow suffocating. Roman tourists like Harry didn't dare open their windows at night, as *mal aria* (bad air) was thought to cause the eponymous disease of malaria. Mosquitoes, actually, carried this disease, though nineteenth-century doctors hadn't yet figured out the connection. (The common Roman experience of malaria, though, would later play a leading role in Harry's smash-hit novella *Daisy Miller*.)

So, in March 1873, sick of the hotel life to which he'd been condemned for ten months running, Harry moved into lodgings filled with the supposedly salubrious "air" of the middle Corso. His new apartment had two rooms—"one upholstered in cobalt and the other in yellow— with magenta *portieres* [curtains] in the doorways"—on a fourth floor with a balcony. In his new home, Harry commanded a middle-aged Roman maid whose cleanliness he thought would satisfy even his mother. Harry's landlord ran a little shop crowded with religious images in the basement; the unfortunate man huddled with his numerous family in a cramped alcove off Harry's vestibule, while Harry basked in sun, air, and space.

To Harry, this living situation amounted to a "pathetic old-world situation," a sample of *"moeurs Italiennes"* (Italian customs) that sometimes brought on a twinge of guilt. But Harry was no socialist, as his father had nominally been, and he didn't invite the family into his rented space to air themselves. Altogether, actual Italians, even when they furnished Harry with storybook quaintness, didn't interest him much. He hadn't come to Rome for their benefit, and he scoured the otherwise handsome city, vainly, for "interesting or 'cultivated' native society," as he'd found in Paris. But he discovered that everything Roman not imported and/or found in a museum disappointed him.

The older Rome Harry loved was growing ever harder to find amid the swarms of "sight-seeing barbarians" that Harry so detested. There was also the problem of "Cambridge on the Tiber," the number of Bostonian expatriates in the city. Harry hadn't crossed the Atlantic, he declared, for "Cambridge tea fights." His entanglements with American Rome painted the "dark side to a brilliant picture."

Nevertheless, the Eastern Seaboard had firmly entrenched itself. On his arrival, Harry spent Christmas 1872 in the company of his "aunt" Mary Tweedy, the former guardian of Minny Temple. This vigorous and sharp-tongued middle-aged lady was living high on the Pincian Hill in a bubble of Anglo-Saxon propriety, with an English butler named Cox and a pallid invalid husband. She took possession of Harry—so that the gallant young man felt himself called upon to serve as her *"caro sposo"* (dear husband) when they drove to the Vatican in her trim, blue-upholstered coupe. Aunt Mary, who wouldn't take no for an answer, frequently treated Cox to a spirited tongue-lashing, but she lavished Harry—thanks to his knack for handling women—with "all her sweetness."

Harry turned up his nose at the American colony in which he was immediately snared, dubbing it "a very poor affair indeed." But American Rome also lured Harry with glittering cosmopolitan trappings not to be found in the dour clapboard manses of Cambridge, Massachusetts. Soon Harry was dining out gloriously at a Roman palace on the Quirinal Hill. Liveried servants bowed him through a chain of cavernous and candlelit anterooms before he was "sonorously announced" into the lush bright heat of a reception room. This grand salon, Harry noticed, had a "*roof*, not a ceiling"—no doubt painted vaults and carved capitals studded with the heraldic suns and bees of the Barberinis, a papal dynasty who had once ruled Rome. Harry savored the honey of these historical bees: he'd penetrated the Palazzo Barberini, a massive white baroque palace whose grand Roman arches had been designed by Carlo Maderno and Gian Lorenzo Bernini in the seventeenth century. Harry's host, the master of this fifty-room slice of the past, was William Wetmore Story, one of the luminaries of American Rome, a leading sculptor and a cosmopolitan.

Story, a flinty Salem-born ex-lawyer, masqueraded as a Renaissance man. Besides sculpture, Story had dabbled in poetry, music, and torturous German translations. Initially—dazzled perhaps by the borrowed splendor of the Barberinis—Harry judged Story to be "friendly, humorous and clever" (the man fared better than his wife, whom Harry summed up as "fair, fat, and fifty"). But Harry soon modified this opinion and appraised Story as a case of "*prosperous* pretension": "His cleverness is great, and the world's good nature to him is greater." The problem was that Harry didn't much like Story's painstaking, icy, half-draped marbles and thought his wide reputation less than deserved. Story's lucrative Muse amounted to a "brazen hussy," Harry joked to his family. But the classical and historical hussies that Story liked to sculpt—Cleopatra, Delilah, the Libyan Sibyl, Medea—rolled out of his studio as anything but hussylike, resembling instead bland and pudgy Victorian matrons.

❦

ON THE QUIRINAL HILL, in the late-afternoon light of the winter of 1873, Harry communed with two goddesses. One was a moss-furred statue at one end of a delightfully decayed terraced garden. The other was his gloved companion, a strikingly handsome woman with rich dark hair drawn up in a simple classical style. Guided by this Muse incarnate, Harry scaled grassy stairways amid dark-green ilex and darker-green laurel. He and his companion gazed out over the rooftops of Rome toward the pale-blue Alban Hills and explored a ramshackle orangery whose citrus-loaded trees sprang up from monstrous terra-cotta tubs.

The Colonna Gardens, though they have mostly vanished from twenty-first-century Rome, struck Harry as timeless in 1873. These forlorn terraces with their weathered stone balustrades and benches were the haunted precinct of the Colonnas, another ancient Roman family whose history was riddled with papal intrigues. Such august associations created what could have been construed as a romantic setting. But Harry's first outing with Sarah Butler Wister was romantic only in the literary sense.

Sarah Wister, just under forty, came with the safety of a husband, a wealthy Quaker doctor from Philadelphia, and a reputation for cultivation. She swept out glittering *rondoletto*s on the piano, understood Italian paintings, and made it her business to encourage unknown young writers. Afterward, Harry would write uneasily to his mother, waxing both catty and gallant, that after such an afternoon "criticism would be graceless. A beautiful woman who takes you to such a place and talks to you uninterruptedly, learnedly, and even cleverly for two whole hours is not to be disposed of in three lines." Mary scented danger—a sign of how little she knew of some of Harry's motivations.

On some of her drives, Mrs. Wister shared a carriage with her mother, one of the nineteenth century's most fascinating celebrities. On the evening Harry met the legendary English actress Fanny Kemble, she was sixty-three, a year older than Mary James, and clad not in a sensible broad-shouldered cotton gown like Harry's mother's usual housekeeping uniform but instead in a magnificent evening dress of "lavender satin lavishly *décolleté*."

Fanny Kemble couldn't sing entrancingly, as she used to in her youth, but she had a long history of bringing whole rooms to their knees. At the age of twenty in 1839—then a dark-haired, pale, spirited beauty—she'd floored audiences at Covent Garden with her powerful portrayal of Juliet. A few years later, touring the United States to feverish acclaim, she stumbled into an ill-starred romance of her own, with a wealthy Philadelphian named Pierce Butler, who stalked her performances until she agreed to marry him. Only after her wedding did Fanny, an ardent abolitionist, discover that the bad-tempered Butler owned legions of slaves on two Georgia plantations. Hadn't he mentioned to her that he was one of the biggest slaveholders in the South?

After such a rank deception, Fanny struck back. She wrote a spirited exposé of slavery based on her visit (with her two small daughters, one of them the future Mrs. Wister) to her husband's plantation on Butler Island, Georgia. Following the resulting divorce, Fanny Kemble defiantly put on bloomers—an early version of trousers available to women—and otherwise took her life into her own hands. She embodied the caliber of woman Harry could safely worship. On meeting her, Harry plunged immediately into a memory of his childhood in St. John's Wood in the 1850s when he'd heard this stage legend read from *Midsummer Night's Dream:* he recollected vividly the actress's expressive face.

Fanny Kemble was a nonpareil, a phenomenal artist, safely mature, whom Harry instinctively loved and would cultivate in the coming years. But expatriate Rome was simply bursting with fascinating women—women who, incidentally, would have had a much harder time being fascinating in the domestic confinement of American (or English) homes. Such was Alice's own problem, as a matter of fact.

As the winter leaned toward spring, Harry found himself doing more than drinking tea and visiting dusky churches with such women. Mrs. Sumner and Miss Bartlett, two tireless riders, left Harry in the dust when they galloped out to the lush open country, where, as if traveling backward in time, they encountered gigantic aqueducts and shaggy-vested shepherds. Characteristically for a James, Harry got a boil on his behind and couldn't keep up. Otherwise, he claimed, he had a "tolerable seat" on a horse. But these women had better ones. Miss Bartlett, frank and unaffected, rated as an honorary boy, Harry thought, "an excellent fellow." Mrs. Sumner, née Alice Mason, patronized Rome as part of her decisive divorce of the well-known and once cane-beaten Massachusetts senator Charles Sumner. For his part, Harry could only boast that Mrs. Sumner had loaned him a horse. (Harry had felt baronial on his previous rental horse, but he couldn't really afford it.) He bragged to his family that five of the United States' most accomplished women wanted to go riding with him.

In the rarified community of Rome, other expatriate women

charmed Harry less than his horsewomen, and his relations with them hinted at his less public desires, fears, and aspirations. One woman particularly exposed Harry's telling dislikes. During an evening at the Palazzo Barberini, dining with the Wisters and with "the Marchese somebody," Harry encountered an extraordinary person who he thought looked like a "remarkably ugly little grey-haired boy" but who wore a chunky diamond necklace. Harry observed that this vigorous woman made colorful conversation but evidently kept most of her notions to herself—at least in so pompous and conventional a household as the Storys'.

Harry had faced off with Harriet Goodhue Hosmer, more informally known as Hattie Hosmer, a notorious local personality and a sculptor. As William Wetmore Story told it, Hosmer had come to Rome in the 1850s only to torch it. She'd set about shattering all the Victorian rules for women, boldly walking the streets without a male escort, riding out whenever she pleased, driving a carriage herself, sporting men's clothing, renting her own atelier to undrape models in—in short, giving the Romans notice that "a Yankee girl can do anything she pleases." For Harry as well as for Story, Hosmer no doubt appeared "too independent by half." Harry liked her sculptures even less than he liked Story's— though the otherwise staid Nathaniel Hawthorne, for one, had actually admired Hosmer's snowy, fluid classical figures. But Harry, characteristically, dismissed Harriet Hosmer primarily because she was a *woman* artist. Along with female sculptors such as Margaret Foley (1827–77) and Mary Edmonia Lewis (1843?–1911), Hosmer was a member of what Harry scornfully called "that strange sisterhood of American 'lady sculptors' who at one time settled upon the seven hills [of Rome] in a white, marmorean flock." He also reacted to her sexual unconventionality with stiff disdain that showed how far he himself was from such iconoclastic behavior.

Most often, in fact, Harry strongly disapproved of rule-breaking women. Though he appreciated spirited, unconventional, febrile personalities in the mold of his dead cousin Minny Temple, he drew a line at women's independence or artistic competence—not to mention the defiance of the conventions of gender. When he met the painter Luther Terry's stepdaughter, Annie Crawford, Harry found her fascinating but too outspoken—"hard as flint" and thus bound to repel admirers. Only a lion tamer could take her on, Harry declared. And unlike Miss Crawford's future husband—an adventurous and equally flinty Prussian count—Harry knew he hadn't been cut out to tame such lions.

His old friend Lizzie Boott, of course, didn't strike Harry as flinty—not even when she rode more expertly in the Campagna than he did. Because she was small-boned and refined—because she circulated in the shadow of her strikingly tall father—Harry judged Lizzie "mouse-like." But with her dark hair and eyes and her pearl-like cheekbones, Lizzie was at least half a beauty—and touching in her odd expatriate isolation. Harry would later pattern the childish Pansy, the daughter of Gilbert Osmond in his *Portrait of a Lady*, on Lizzie. He no doubt had Lizzie's exquisite refinement in mind when assigning her to the order of rodentia. That or her "women's" art of watercolors, floral studies, and genre pieces; Harry writhed critically when he considered his friend as a painter.

Nevertheless, Harry knew that Lizzie as an heiress outstripped him in her material advantages. When she and her father lived in Italy, for years at a time, they based themselves in a low, red-roofed, hilltop pied-à-terre in Bellosguardo near Florence called the Villa Castellani. In Rome, Harry envied Lizzie her studio, in her house near the Triton fountain of the Piazza Barberini—a square always awash with local models, trading on their picturesqueness. But Lizzie's work, Harry thought, amounted to a hobby, no more than a talent for illustrating books: "if she would only paint a little less *helplessly*, she would still go far—as women go." Clearly, when Harry rode out with Lizzie to the cork woods on Monte Mario, he was hardly in danger of falling in love with her. He was proof against her private money, her villa, and her cheekbones.

Sarah Wister, though, held Harry under a different kind of spell. The rides out of the Porta San Giovanni, into a wilderness of ruins, and the rides out of the Porta del Popolo, into sweeping fields toward the sea, impressed Harry deeply. Mrs. Wister made inroads, channeling as she did so much "fierce energy" in her slender body. Initially, Harry had skittishly told his mother Mrs. Wister was a "beautiful Bore." "Tell it not in Philadelphia," he added, "—where I don't believe they know it."

But by April and May, when the "season" was over and the American colony was dispersing, Harry regretted that he'd ever used such a "brutal phrase" about so fine a being. At the same time, as he told his father, he had no reason to regret that he wasn't Dr. Wister.

Harry's very ambitions, though, actually focused on women more than he probably knew. The sentimental alliance he'd forged with Mrs. Wister showed the shape of things to come and predicted Harry's upward future climb—at a time when women were commanding ever more importance as readers, as writers, and as promoters of writers. In the United States, these increasingly educated, increasingly traveled, increasingly ambitious women were making themselves the heiresses of literature and "culture" even more than of immense mercantile fortunes. In his past, Harry had bonded with women: his mother, his sister, and his cousin Minny. But his allegiances with influential women would shape his future even more.

❧

WILLIAM, BACK HOME in Cambridge and starting to teach his first Harvard course, worried about Harry's "exclusive diet of women." William's own would-be liaisons struck one wet match after another, and probably he envied Harry's intimacy with the "high sounding" names of Italian places and the fascinating women who inhabited them.

But beyond this, William's own touchy masculinity set off his worries about Harry. When William read Harry's high-strung travel pieces in the *Nation*—which most of Newport enjoyed—William thought their style "ran a little more to *curliness* than suited the average mind, or in general the newspaper reader." He advised his brother to cultivate a masculine "directness of style." Subtlety and ingenuity (those feminine qualities innate in Harry but also no doubt reinforced by Harry's artistic women friends) could be left to themselves.

Sometimes, it's true, William—a *literato* himself—could delight in the exquisite diction of Harry's writing. But he remained on high alert for anything "cold, thin blooded & priggish suddenly popping in and freezing the genial current." And nothing froze William's blood like a French phrase or a rhetorical flourish, the verbal equivalent (in his mind) of a ruffle or a piece of lace. Did William cringe when Harry addressed him as *"fratello mio"* (brother mine) in his letters—oddly reminiscent of the pretentious Mrs. Elton in Jane Austen's *Emma*, who called Mr. Elton her *"caro sposo"* (dear husband)?

For his part, Harry swallowed William's criticisms with admirable composure. He'd weathered many such rebuffs and corrections from his older brother—with the steadfastness and undimmed devotion of a Victorian wife. (He unconsciously used the model, really, of his mother's patient handling of his firecracker father.) Tellingly, in fact, William was shortly to feel, uneasily, when once again in close quarters with his brother, that Harry amounted to his "spouse," so glued together they were, so vividly and curiously did they replicate—in a way that might have fascinated William the future psychologist—the dynamic of their parents' marriage. But Harry's feminine forbearance (and William's irritability) were about to undergo a marital trial, and one that underscored the almost incestuous intensity of their relation.

During the spring and summer of 1873, while Harry left Rome and zigzagged northward over the Continent, leaving a pearl-like string of travel pieces in his wake, William brooded about joining his brother in Europe. During Harry's absence, William had fallen back into his chronic torpor. Cambridge was hardly exciting, with its Sunday dinners of "oysters and cold beef, tomatoes and apple-pie." His mother reported to Harry the whole "carte" of the meal, as there was so little other news to convey.

After fighting his way through the spring term at Harvard, William couldn't imagine incarcerating himself in the same formaldehyde-smelling classrooms in the fall. Sick of an emasculating "parasitic life" at home—when even his baby brothers were sweating out their own keep in Wisconsin—William initially contemplated crossing the Atlantic by hiring himself out as a private tutor. But maybe recollecting the spit-upon status of European tutors from his own childhood, William soon revised his plan—and borrowed one thousand dollars from Aunt Kate, to be paid back in installments from his six-hundred-dollar-a-year Harvard salary.

William crossed the Atlantic on the Cunard liner *Spain* in late October and raced southward to join Harry in Florence. ("A compliment to me!" Harry felt.) William, though, came sharp-eyed and prepared to be critical. He found Harry amiable, well-mannered, "wedded to Europe" (ambiguous praise), and he immediately sent his watchful family a full rundown on "the angel."

> He is wholly unchanged. No balder than when he quit; his teeth of a yellowish tinge (from the waters of [H]omburg [a German watering place Harry had visited in September] he says); his beard very rich & glossy in consequence he says of the use of a substance called Brilliantine of which he always keeps a large bottle on the table among his papers. His clothes good; shoes ditto he having just cabbaged from me the bast [sic] pair of gaiters . . . He seems wholly devoted to his literary work and very industrious. I doubt if [I'll] get him home in the spring. The "little affectations" of wh. mother spoke I have not noticed. He probably fears me and keeps them concealed letting them out when foreigners are present.

If this wasn't enough, William also observed Harry's fluent Italian, complete with theatrical gestures and arrogant manners toward Italians. Likewise he noted that Harry had become an "utter slave" to spirits and grew angry if a waiter didn't immediately bring him his wine—a hint that Bob was not the only James child with alcoholic tendencies. Especially, though, the observant William scrutinized Harry's absorption of foreign ways—Europeanness being a code for his growing distance from the family, his blithe independence, and (though William wouldn't have said so explicitly or have had much vocabulary for expressing it), his sexuality.

But William could be blunt. Now that the two closely involved brothers were reunited, William felt more comfortable in broaching the subject, over dinner or on a walk. He strongly advised his little brother to "look out for a wife." Harry, though, could be equally straightforward. He refused point-blank. As William complained in a letter to the more malleable Bob, his writer brother "positively refuse[d] to think of such a thing."

❧

IT WAS A cold, deep-blue autumn night, the half-moon erasing most of the stars. For Harry the night exuded rich Roman atmosphere; for William it was ungaslit and creepily "sinister." In the near darkness, the two made their way along what reminded William of a deserted, tree-hemmed country road—with mounds of rubble on one hand that Harry identified as the Roman Forum. Huge shapes of broken walls and ruins reared up; one particularly massive ruin, a whole hill of rubble, loomed up like a cliff. This was the famous Colosseum of Rome.

When the two clambered into the Colosseum's half-excavated center, like some desolate desert valley, William recollected the horrors of Roman gladiatorial spectacles and actually derived comfort, secular as he was, from an immense black crucifix that had been planted in that "damned blood soaked soil." If Harry hadn't been with him, William would have "fled howling from the place," as William later confided in his father. But William didn't howl out loud, just inwardly and to Henry Senior. So that Harry, besotted by his beloved Rome, believed he'd offered his brother a delightful moonlit walk. "I greatly value *his* impressions," Harry unknowingly reported to this same father, "they are always so lively and original and sagacious."

With such half-suppressed conflicts brewing, no wonder the two brothers soon separated to different quarters—Harry to his old lodgings of the previous winter, William to a couple of "sun-bathed" rooms at the Hotel de Russie.

William began his day, economically (he assured his mother), with a roll brought by a waiter "in wedding costume." He then bought a small paper of roasted chestnuts from an old woman in black on his way out to sample the sunshine—to prowl over the steps of broken thrones and the fallen columns of temples. Gradually, William revised his negative first impressions of Rome and found the blackened and crumbling limestone city increasingly beautiful. Soon enough he even claimed the blood-soaked and pagan Colosseum as his favorite place to bask in the sun.

But at midday, while he was idling in a café on the Corso, William knew all too well that his brother was scribbling furiously—and would soon appear "with the flush of successful literary effort fading off his cheek." When faced with Harry's sense of vocation, William hated his own idleness and yearned to be home working, making something (he still didn't know quite what) of his life. Italy might be delightful to "dip into," William wrote to Alice, but no more. The ancient Romans, after all, had gone about their own business. They hadn't, like Harry and his hypercultivated women, gaped at their grandfathers'—or their would-be and adoptive grandfathers'—tombs.

In the golden afternoons and warm Roman winter evenings, the two brothers relished walking around together. Harry in his old striped overcoat, William in his more dapper New England threads, the two shared the breathtaking view from the Pincian Hill over rooftops and domes and towers—over a Rome astride its seven hills, whose classic profile, in spite of its new gas lamps starring the shadowy evening, remained as yet largely unspoiled by the forces of modernity of which both brothers were unwitting agents.

The two Jameses could lean on the same balustrade, make fascinating conversation. And Rome, in spite of its illustrious history, had seldom witnessed such a pair. But really Harry and William—as their different visions of the Colosseum had dramatized—inhabited totally different planets, although their brotherly bonds were strong. When William came down with a case of "Roman fever" at Christmas, Harry unflinchingly nursed him—just as William, when Harry got sick a month later, became a "ministering angel" to an equally "angelic patient." But in spite of this fraternity, Harry and William couldn't bear to inhabit the same space for long. William soon chafed to leave Harry and Italy. "The strongest forces are not the most visible forces," William himself had philosophically observed.

Forces both subtle and strong seemed bent on dividing the brothers. Harry handily fit into the art-loving world of exiled heiresses. But the more straightforward William disliked Italy and the idle and aesthetic high-art pretensions of those who cultivated it. Unable to persuade his brother to return to America with him, William foresaw their future paths diverging even more drastically. The Jameses' success was starting to come out of their conflicts, out of their habit of defining themselves against one another. And their pitted rivalry, visceral beneath their angelic demeanor, hiked the already exorbitant price of their careers.

In late January, William caught a train north to Venice and then to Dresden, where, on one of the noble bridges over the Elbe he'd known a few years before, he struggled to reclaim and recapture his own life: "I expected to find Germany hideous after Italy," William wrote his old

Dresden flame Kate Havens, "but the effect was just the reverse. I enjoyed thoroughly the cloudy weather, the steep roofs, the earnest people and especially the grand old language." Kate Havens—an heiress herself, in a modest way—no doubt gave William a sentimental pang. William felt wistful, sad, and alone when he boarded a steamer from Bremen, bound over the rolling Atlantic for the United States.

Little did he know what kind of heiress was waiting for him.

· 10 ·

MATCHES

S he came from Milwaukee, Wisconsin, and her name was Carrie Eames Cary—an appellation with an unfortunate echo—though presumably she could have avoided the problem and gone simply by Caroline. This made it especially exasperating. Even a small irregularity in height, attitude, or politesse could decimate a woman's estimation in the marriage market, but she had overcome the stumbling block of her name by marrying Garth Wilkinson James and entering the James family. Yet in the course of her first visit to the Quincy Street house in 1873, the former Miss Carrie Cary made an even more serious error: she sported her diamonds—a lapse of taste, a faux pas of memorable dimensions. She wore two thousand dollars on her fingers, Henry estimated, and five thousand dollars—twice the cost of Alice's European tour—hung "pendant from her ears."

The bejeweled bride arrived with Wilkie during the bleak November of 1873, during William's absence in Italy. With only Alice at home to keep her parents company, Henry and Mary were in need of a distraction. They had looked forward, with curiosity, and not a small measure of skepticism, to their new daughter-in-law's debut.

Carrie materialized on the James family stage in an exquisite traveling dress. Her own sister-in-law back in Milwaukee had been married in a navy blue dress of the same cut, presumably for the sake of convenience. Midwestern women tended to be practical and, by eastern standards, straightforward. But the diamond earrings did not suggest an eye for necessary economy or an interest in the life of the mind.

Carrie was pale, slender, and twenty-two, with mousy hair of an indifferent shade. Though she'd been called plain, she was personable and met the Jameses with easy, ladylike manners that matched her exquisite trousseau. Of her impeccable outfits, Mary James ought to have approved, but on further scrutiny of the young woman, Mary recoiled. Henry Senior, always allergic to assertive women, thought he detected a certain self-importance in this sometimes restrained, sometimes impertinent woman from the Wisconsin prairies; there was, he thought, a hint of that pernicious flaw that marred many women, an "obstinate will." Carrie was agreeable enough, he later wrote to William, when she got her own way. But when she didn't, she revealed a "firm & energetic will," especially around Wilkie. This walking jewelry store, the family discovered, evidently had a flawed temper.

Carrie's diamonds glittered unceasingly in everyone's letters to Harry and William, who caught the chill and passed it on. The diamonds stuck in everybody's craw, almost as if they had been physically inserted into their flesh, just as Carrie herself had been physically inserted into the family.

Carrie's father, a self-made man, owned a chain of gentlemen's clothes stores in Milwaukee and a certain number of corniced, chunky shopfronts as well. Carrie wore the badges of the nouveau riche, and these distressed the Jameses—though, for all their gentility, they themselves owed their fortune to mercantile entrepreneurs. Yet in nineteenth-century America, an era of ramifying commerce and hastily accrued fortunes, such genteel hypocrisies abounded. The Jameses weren't alone in snobbishly looking down from one or two generations of wealth on people they called *arrivistes*.

Henry and Mary also feared that Carrie had imposed herself on their affable, gullible Wilkie. William worried that she was a "hard nonentity." As Henry Senior ruefully put it, "I cant [sic] for the life of me imagine why Wilky fell in love with her. He is in love apparently, deeply so, with an utter unconsciousness of its seeming a strange state to outsiders." Wilkie's choice, almost insolently different from themselves, bewildered his parents, who found themselves at a greater emotional distance from their second-youngest son than ever, even though they had recently made a trip to Wisconsin to visit. No one understood much about Wilkie's railroad work, though they knew he had recently chosen an outdoor version of it in Watertown, Wisconsin, over his old office job. "This is a crisis in Wilky's life when he is brought face to face the first time with the fact that he has got to stand on his feet, and provide for himself," Mary told Harry, with little empathy. Her son had made his bed, and there was little to be done.

A year later, in 1874—because of Wilkie's estrangement—no one in the family even really fathomed what Wilkie's new venture was all about. Wilkie left his railroad work to go into business with a man named Whaling, the son of one of the officials of the Milwaukee & St. Paul Railroad, whom no one in the family knew. He was going to sell iron locks and chains, mostly to the company for which he had formerly worked. "Wilky's fortunes seem to be brightening," his mother reported to Harry; "that is if he is prudent and all things work well," she added.

Carrie's cool welcome at Quincy Street had as much to do with Wilkie himself as his bride, as resentment still lingered over Wilkie's financial losses in Florida. In spite of the Jameses' high-mindedness, financial losses worried them. The family's distress over Carrie also reflected their uneasiness with what they themselves had allowed or even forced Wilkie to become—a midwestern businessman, something as foreign to them as Tierra del Fuego. Everyone had been fond of affectionate, hardworking, uncomplaining Wilkie. William and Harry, even more than their parents, repeatedly expressed nagging guilt over what had transpired with him. Out of self-reproach as well as affection, Henry and Mary hosted a big party for Carrie, with some sixty of Cambridge's finest circulating through their downstairs parlors. "Such flowers!" Henry Senior marveled. "Such meats and drinks!" Henry and Mary, to their credit, had tried to do much more than this.

◈

ON THE MORNING of May 30, 1872, the year before the bride's arrival in Massachusetts, Henry and Mary, having hastily packed their bags, had set off across the country. They had made a long and strenuous railroad journey—days and nights in a Pullman, across the greening flatlands south of the Great Lakes. Their mission was to shore up their two troubled sons in Wisconsin. Henry and Mary, now both in their sixties, remained tireless, loving, and interventionist parents—even when, partly out of favoritism and partly out of financial necessity, they had forced their younger sons into uncomfortable molds.

This intervention was the elder Jameses' first visit to the upper Midwest. Milwaukee, the setting of their two sons' exile, must have struck these genteel easterners as raw and recent, in comparison to places they knew. Even the rich growth of late spring wouldn't have much softened the angular buildings and straight streets of Milwaukee, laid out on the flat, windy shore of Lake Michigan. Milwaukee, incorporated in 1846, had been growing brashly for three decades, largely as waves of German immigrants had moved in. Most newspapers still published editions in German, in the foreign-looking Gothic lettering of the time. The city thrived partly from its huge brick breweries, run with imported German skill and expertise. (Joseph Schlitz had arrived in 1850, Frederick Miller in 1855, and Milwaukee brewers were creating beers that would become some of the most familiar in America.) Twenty-five-year-old Bob, already a serious alcoholic, would hardly benefit from this aspect of Milwaukee's fame—though beer, it seemed, was the least of his worries.

Henry and Mary had hurried west to keep their youngest son from breaking down. Bob was depressed and ill. He also had a private worry he evidently confided in William: though he was probably the most sexually experienced member of the family, he'd been suffering from impotence, perhaps when drunk. It isn't clear if the unmarried Bob had encountered this during masturbation or in relations with women. But with ready medical advice, William assured his brother that his troubles would cease when he got married and "sexual intercourse begins regularly." William sympathized with Bob's low moods and "mental troubles"—and probably with his worries about sexual performance. Henry and Mary were also sympathetic, though Bob probably told his parents less than William about such intimate matters. But he gave them an earful as soon as they arrived and all sat down together. He made it clear that he hated his railroad clerkship, loathed Milwaukee, and wanted to leave both.

Bob also had happier anticipations, as he could now introduce his parents to his new fiancée: a promising young local woman named Mary Holton. Henry and Mary met Bob's fiancée in the heavily furnished parlor of Highland Home, her father's showy house in Milwaukee. Immediately, they approved of this blooming, down-to-earth, unbookish Midwestern girl and appraised her as a good match. Mary grew attached to her identically named future daughter-in-law, approving the "economical talents" that would help this young wife survive on Bob's skimpy railroad income. Bob, despite his engagement, remained as colossally impractical and discontented as ever.

Miss Holton came from even grander local money and prominence than her friend Carrie Cary. Yet, more secure, she wore her money all the more lightly. Five months after the elder Jameses' visit, in November 1872, she would be married at her father's house, in the navy blue traveling dress that would later inspire Carrie's bridal selection. Mary, with her pleasant face and gentle waves in her hair, trimmed her gown with "a few natural flowers" instead of diamonds—though only Wilkie attended the ceremony, and he may not have noticed her restraint. The Holtons filled their house with flowers and fifty guests, who heaped wedding presents on the young couple.

Shortly afterward, Bob brought his new wife home, and at Quincy Street, Mary Holton James "won all hearts." William found this rose-pink young woman all "prettiness, amiability, vivacity, & modesty." A "dash of pluckiness" invited the white-bearded Henry Senior to spar a bit with her, as he had with his Boston flirts like Caroline Dall—as he'd loved doing with all his children in earlier times. Dinner, which over the years had grown more solemn, suddenly rang again with cheerful banter and laughter.

Alice sized up this new Mary, but Miss James refrained from her customary barbed evaluation. For her, the ice would break quickly. Alice, tough to please when she feared a rival, actually relaxed around this unaffected new Mary, warming to her dramatically. The two young women went around wrapped in each other's arms, sometimes pressing cheek to cheek. With her natural good spirits, Mary Holton captivated this subdued household. A year later, she even upstaged Carrie Cary by giving birth to a baby boy, Henry and Mary's first grandchild, only a week after Wilkie's wedding.

Even for Mary, though, it would require strength and patience to survive as a James daughter-in-law. Nor would it prove a simple matter to live with Bob, especially when he was drinking. The baby, William hoped, would steady his brother and provide him a "panacea for all his woes." But even naming the boy proved contentious, as both the James and the Holton patriarchs expected to be honored with a namesake. (Harry, in Italy, dreaded the creation of a third Henry, who would make him feel "queer, so sandwiched between infancy and maturity." William joked that Harry was worried that his nephew would go and "become a magazinist, and mix up the family articles more than ever.")

Bob resolved the conflict by supporting his wife's choice; his father-in-law in Milwaukee, after all, lived much nearer and barked much louder. The young couple christened the boy Edward Holton James—soon afterward shortening this ponderous name to a sawed-off "Ned." Bob's mother, however, blamed the younger Mary James for a lack of "conjugal sentiment"—such as Mary herself had always unfailingly bestowed on Henry Senior. This mother-in-law's rebuke would have stung, coming as it did from the acknowledged empress and arbiter of the domestic sphere.

Still, Mary adored her first grandchild from afar and demanded detailed descriptions of the baby. Wilkie couldn't provide one; all babies looked alike to him. But the child's Wisconsin grandfather delighted Mary by letting her know that the infant's skin was fair and his eyes blue, and that he looked like a James.

In spite of warm letters to Bob, Mary did not immediately go out to see this grandchild. One reason may well have been that Bob, still railing against his railroad work, had now moved out of a city he abhorred. At the end of their visit in 1872, Henry had offered his unhappy son refuge in Cambridge, but Bob, though perpetually hankering for more cultivated settings, had understood the limitations of his parents' hospitality. He'd taken a different path in order to cope with his unhappiness, moving early in 1873 to Prairie du Chien, a rough-hewn outpost two hundred miles to the west of Milwaukee.

The name of this place meant "Prairie of the Dog" in Bob's now-less-than-useful Parisian French, and might have seemed the last place anyone would expect to find a James, unless his first name was Jesse. (The famous outlaw Jesse James and his gang in fact robbed banks in Iowa during the early 1870s and often targeted money-carrying railroads like Bob's, the Milwaukee & St. Paul Railroad.) And in Prairie du Chien, outlaws weren't the only nuisance. The summers of 105 degrees Fahrenheit and the winters of 40 degrees below created a spectrum of weather that Alice wittily called more "arctic cold and torrid heat than was ever dreamed of by philosophers." There Bob, in addition to working long days in all weathers for his railroad, battled his low moods by cutting ice for his icehouse on the frozen Wisconsin and Mississippi rivers. Mary, he reported to his father, was hemming sheets and towels for their new house with a sewing machine that the James family had given her, and sometimes enjoying stormy carriage drives out across the "wintry levels" of the plains.

Back in Milwaukee, Wilkie was also struggling. His mother, monitoring the situation, grew even harsher on the subject of her less favorite daughter-in-law. "Wilky sends good news of his housekeeping," Mary reported early in 1874, after the couple had enjoyed three months of marital bliss. "His result is that he can live more cheaply as a married man than as a single one!—very like Wilky, who never looks accurately or rationally at any thing, when money is concerned.—Poor fellow! He writes *most affectionately* to me, a good sign that his wife has not weaned his love from his mother."

Evidently without qualms of regret, Mary could attack her son and his wife—especially on the subject of their household accounting, her own strong point. At the same time, she blithely exacted the full devotion that Victorian sons were supposed to lavish on their mothers. Mary's letter opens up a somewhat scary glimpse of this steely yet eager-for-praise woman, now in her middle sixties. No wonder the James children considered Henry Senior, for all his eccentricities, their milder and more indulgent parent. Mary laced her "sweetness" with grit—to the advantage of her offspring as well as to their horror.

Both James parents plagued their sons with their expectations. Mary expected them to marry daughters-in-law cut to her specifications. Henry, though impractical and unworldly, urged his sons, especially William, into careers that hardly fit them. Bob's and Wilkie's railroad jobs had proved disastrous, but hardly less than William's own medical career— now only slightly revived by his teaching anatomy part-time at Harvard. The only son whose vocation showed real promise was Harry, and he had carved out his own plans, in the face of his mother's worries about his unmarried state and his father's low opinion of fiction writing.

It is understandable that Henry and Mary wanted to keep a close eye on their children; they had all suffered depressions and other illnesses. To the parents, the children were vulnerable rare birds, easily knocked off course, navigating a hazardous world. Their children, they seem to have understood, hardly fit within the contours of conventional lives, and few outside the family shared or understood their moods and perspectives. But despite their sympathies, Mary and Henry could not ignore the fact that their hard-to-place offspring had to learn to manage their finances and careers, and so they tended to push, cajole, advise, and manipulate their children's lives.

In spite of such interference (or, perhaps, because of it), all the James children had taken their time to find their feet in the world. The family's cushion of investments, Henry and Mary's continuing solicitude and interference, and the young Jameses' warring aspirations and self-doubts conspired to stretch their childhoods on into their twenties and thirties. The younger generation's lofty passions combined with sexual awkwardness had also delayed their progress.

William, thirty-two when he came back from Europe in March 1874 and as yet unmarried, still lived in the same house with his parents and under their watchful eye. He was rarely far from the sound of their voices, and his letters passed through their hands. From Germany, he had brought a bearish fur overcoat made for him in Dresden, an exotic garment to sport in Harvard Yard, a reminder of the little freedoms he'd had in Europe. He'd enjoyed a smooth passage home and shipboard conversations with Julia Antoinette Kellogg, a Swedenborgian writer who in 1883 would publish a study of his father's philosophy. In spite of his father's limited fame, William had a hard time inching out from under Henry's shadow. Except for a few reviews of short scientific articles he had written, William himself was an utter unknown. The space that William had claimed for himself was limited to the dissecting tables and specimen-studded classrooms of Harvard. Once a wryly humorous lad with a microscope or a sketching tablet, he felt like a third-class academic drudge. And as for a future Mrs. James, how could he match what his brother had achieved with Mary Holton? His parents held even more stratospheric expectations for the son whom they still regarded as uniquely talented. He didn't know how he could ever satisfy them when he felt so often listless and fatigued, so rarely convinced of his own ability.

❧

IN THE OPENING months of the centennial year of 1876, in a characteristic moment of love and meddling, Henry Senior came home from the Radical Club on Beacon Hill in high excitement. He brought some sly news that he knew would rivet both his wife and his eldest son.

That spring, other people in Cambridge might be talking about Alexander Graham Bell's recent demonstration of his new communications apparatus to the American Academy of Arts and Sciences in Boston—the first telephone, which many still dismissed as only a toy. Henry, though, had an accomplishment that he considered no less wondrous to report. He declared, with playful conviction, that he'd just caught a glimpse of William's future wife. The radiant young woman in question, he announced, just happened to be named Alice.

How the existing Alice James reacted to this was not recorded. Nor is it certain whether this incidence of matchmaking intrigued or further depressed William, who actually had minimal experience of serious relationships or sex. At the threshold of thirty-four, William, who had risen to the rank of assistant professor of physiology, was working at Harvard for a mere $1,650 a year (though it was more than his previous salary), holding a post he thought was designed for "none but failures & invalids like myself." He faced a grueling round of teaching and laboratory work that he bitterly and colloquially described as "the 'last hair.' "

He may have sneaked in some guilty experiments in Brazil or Germany and halfheartedly pursued Kate Havens for years, but he judged himself to be not only a sexual beginner but also a genetic hazard to potential offspring because of his battery of emotional and physical complaints. He felt "strong longings" toward women, as he confided to Bob. But though marriage appeared "the normal state both for men and women," his hopes had been crushed by his bad back, eyes, and emotional state; he had even formulated a thought-out moral "resolution" not to marry.

As the 1870s wore on, Bob's and Wilkie's reports of marital satisfaction were eroding William's self-denial. But still he scorned run-of-the-mill women, plump pink homemakers bent on Victorian householdery, such as his old friend Tom Ward had married: "Were she mine," William told Bob, "I'd stifle her with a feather bed or bolster. I think she's stifling Tom fast with her tact and conventionality." At the same time, William felt ripe to be exploited by a nonentity—as he believed had happened to his brother Wilkie. He'd reached that pitch of desperation, and he knew it.

Before his father's announcement, William had frequented the Radical Club, an unlikely place to find a bride-to-be. The club wasn't actually very "radical" by the standards of the 1870s—even if it counted as one of the few intellectual Boston clubs that, unlike the Saturday Club or William's own Metaphysical Club, admitted women. It met alternately in two neighboring townhouses on Chestnut Street on Beacon Hill, in stiff and cramped old Federal-period parlors, and concerned itself mainly with the topics of religion and morality. Women were included for that reason; in the nineteenth century, females were often considered moral and religious beings, though still largely barred from being ordained to the ministry. Both sexes, though, could listen to or even present papers on many a thorny topic. As a matter of course, the reading of an address was followed by earnest discussion among the strong-minded members—a set of aging transcendentalist warhorses such as Bronson Alcott (the tireless educational reformer and father of the more famous Louisa May Alcott), and graying Unitarian firebrands like John Turner Sargent, one of the club's gracious sexagenarian hosts.

When his father originally described this future bride, William perhaps pictured a bluestocking, a formidable book-learned female in the mold of the late Margaret Fuller. The club welcomed bonneted intellectuals and social reformers like Elizabeth Peabody, Lucretia Mott, and Julia Ward Howe, the poet and suffragist. Recently, as a reaction to the Franco-Prussian War, Howe had floated the idea of a Mother's Peace Day—a notion that finally caught on, without the peace component, as Mother's Day. Still, in spite of her progressive views in favor of women as clergy, Howe remained conventional enough to regret that the Radical Club's explorations often strayed from Christianity—even though she pronounced the club a "high congress of souls, in which many noble thoughts are uttered."

It was just this brand of loftiness and piety that often amused or irritated William when he squeezed himself into the Radical Club meetings. So he must have been pleasantly surprised, during the winter of 1876, when he was introduced to Alice Howe Gibbens.

When William first shook her hand, Alice Gibbens had just celebrated her twenty-seventh birthday. With her lightish hair tucked up and curled in an attractive wave, some people called her handsome, though in the snug-necked gowns of the 1870s, she hardly put herself on display. Her eyes, however, engaged people with a frank, intense gaze—an expression that managed to suggest sympathy and acumen even in her posed studio portraits. Her lively, intelligent engagement with the Radical Club had already earned her at least one distinguished admirer besides Henry Senior: the sixty-nine-year-old Quaker abolitionist poet John Greenleaf Whittier, who'd kindheartedly offered to take notes for her on the club evenings when she couldn't attend.

Along with her younger sister Mary, Alice taught in a girls' school on the steep, narrow, lamplit streets of Beacon Hill. Women's education was becoming a growth industry, and not only in the gracious old neighborhoods of Boston. Alice had joined the countless young women who'd recently plunged into the profession—earning perhaps a third of what men earned as schoolteachers, but still augmenting, as happened in Alice's case, many a family's thin resources.

Alice's forebears sprang from respectable New England stock in Weymouth, Massachusetts, on the shore just south of Boston. But her mother, Eliza Gibbens, happened to be retiring and impractical. Alice, the eldest daughter, had grown up quickly and taken responsibility for her two younger sisters, and sometimes even for her mother, beginning at the age of sixteen in 1865. Then—as if the trauma of the Civil War wasn't enough—her father, an alcoholic who sniffed ether, had slit his throat with a razor in New Orleans during a business scandal.

Alice had survived by becoming a provider, a caretaker, a manager, a pillar. Although more intellectually engaged than Mary James, she reminded Henry Senior very much of his wife: she rated as the same kind of no-nonsense marriage prospect that Mary Walsh had been almost forty years before. Hence Henry's view that she was just what his son needed.

Alice also had more subtle attractions for William. Like the Jameses, she could claim to be a cosmopolitan. For economy's sake, she'd lived abroad with her family in Germany and Italy after her father's suicide. She even knew William's beloved Dresden, its bridges and churches, its autumnal fogs. (As a sign of her own romantic associations with the city, she'd had a photograph taken of herself, décolleté, draped with a jewel-crusted crucifix, in 1873.) No doubt the two Germanophiles compared notes—an early topic of common conversation. As she had lived in Dresden herself, Alice possibly borrowed some of the romance of William's heavy-yearning stay in that city—and unwittingly stole a march on Kate Havens, whom William had met during that same time. Here was a version of Dresden, or Kate Havens, who might actually be able to deal with William's up-and-down emotional intensity.

In March 1876, as one of her first acts of friendship, Alice sent William an unexpected package: a satirical poem about the Radical Club, a spoof based on Edgar Allan Poe's "The Raven," by one Katherine Sherwood Bonner McDowell. Some lines about a "young person with a patent costume" entertained William enough to turn his thoughts fondly toward the sender, who he was happy to discover had some taste for humor. William's own rare wit had been subdued in recent years, partly because of his unending residence in his parents' house and his thankless teaching of anatomy.

As 1876 unfolded, Henry Senior, now in his midsixties, became increasingly unwell. Henry had been attending clubs; he was laboring on another manuscript that would become his *Society the Redeemed Form of Man* (1879). But though his mind was as active as ever, the white-whiskered

James patriarch was definitely slowing down. Now in Cambridge for ten years, he was more happily settled than previously in his life; he increasingly avoided travel—the pursuit that had once beguiled him but which had never been easy for a family-bound, one-legged man. With age, his nerves had not stopped troubling him. He still suffered from his nervous depressions, though not as jaggedly as before; he was used to them, somehow, just as he was used, after almost two decades of apparently successful sobriety, to avoiding hard spirits.

Sometime in the spring of 1876—the Jameses routinely cloaked the dates of such events—Henry Senior suffered a stroke. The details remained private, with the inhabitants of the house themselves hardly allowing themselves to talk about it. But for weeks and weeks, the white-bearded philosopher sat in a strange listless state, tended by his wife and Aunt Kate, the woman he had called Mary's husband, who massaged his bare back with a towel. Henry's relation with his "other wife" had a touching intimacy, after more than thirty years of having her in his household, but Kate's loyalty remained with her kin, whether her sister or her New York cousins, and she had had many disagreements with Henry as well as with his children.

In the wake of his stroke, Henry was unable even to write a letter. His sudden "docile passivity" deeply upset William and possibly spurred him to think more of Alice Gibbens, and of a family of his own.

THE ADIRONDACK MOUNTAINS in northern New York State, rising some forty miles north of Albany, had long figured for the Jameses as a jagged, distant horizon. This blue-green, rugged range—a southern extension of the Canadian Shield, a vast uplift of billion-year-old rock carved into crags by vast glaciers—hardly seemed to belong in the state of New York at all. Its rocky peaks soared more than a mile above sea level. Its dark boreal evergreen forest, floored with bearberry and Canada mayflower, sheltered a near-pristine wilderness of waterfalls, streams, bogs, beaver ponds, and lakes. Moose foraged here, and eagles wheeled over the peaks.

By the 1870s, though, the Adirondack wilderness was under threat. Iron mines perforated the central mountains. Timber operations harvested hemlocks for tanning, spruce and fir for paper, pine for lumber, and practically every kind of tree for charcoal. Next door to the growing cities and factories of New York, the Adirondacks were on their way to being stripped and were only saved by a budding conservationist movement and, more ironically, by a brand-new industry: wilderness tourism. In 1871, Thomas Clark Durant supervised the building of a branch railroad line from Saratoga Springs to North Creek, north of Lake George and well into the peaks—thus inaugurating one of the great scenic train routes of the nineteenth century.

From Saratoga, the line ran northward and gradually climbed into high, wild country. Passengers thrilled as the train plunged in among ever-higher mountains and deeper, shaded valleys. From the remote rail depot at North Creek, stage coaches ferried visitors to the many mountain inns, cure resorts, sanatoriums, and wilderness hotels that had begun to spring up all over the Adirondacks. Lake Placid, Lake George, Schroon Lake, and Saranac Lake were becoming familiar and fashionable destinations, but the most famous wilderness hotel was probably the St. Regis House, founded in 1859 by a Vermonter named Paul Smith. The massive rustic clapboard hotel in the northern Adirondacks was renowned for its lack of bellboys or bathrooms (to preserve the wilderness experience) and patronized by such well-known figures as P. T. Barnum and Grover Cleveland.

In 1870, Harry had explored the region, from Saratoga Springs, only as far as an "unpainted farmhouse" surrounded by mountainous woodpiles. He'd gone to Moon's Tavern on Saratoga Lake, where he'd refreshed himself with an alcoholic beverage (unlike in "poor dislicensed Boston," he wrote—adding one more item to his dislike for the Puritan metropolis and hinting at his own enjoyment of a drink). In the summer of 1875, before he met Alice Gibbens, William had absconded on a fishing trip with some medical-school buddies to the northern Adirondacks, where the streams and lakes were still teeming with trout and black bass.

Alice James had been staying that summer with Aunt Kate at the Breadloaf Inn, among the steep woods and cool waterfalls of the Green Mountains in Vermont. On almost any junket away from home, Kate traveled with her as chaperone and sometimes nurse, even though Alice was now twenty-seven years old. As for William, he didn't want to board at a quirky hostelry that was destined to become in the next century a famous writers' retreat, especially not in the watchful company of his aunt and sister.

William and his friends put up at Beede's Boarding House, in the still wild and rough-hewn Keene Valley, just south of Lake Placid, in the shadow of the high peaks. They braced themselves for strenuous climbs, cold trout streams, icy swimming holes, and rude timber outbuildings. After all, they'd been overtaxed with Harvard intellectual life, with the urban "neurasthenic" pressures of horsecars and ten-story office buildings.

William and his friends encountered the mountains in the spirit of William H. H. Murray's recently popular book, *Adventures in the Wilderness; or, Camp Life in the Adirondacks* (1869). In short, everyone wanted to be "roughing it"—in the phrase made famous by Mark Twain's 1872 account of his frontier escapades in Nevada. Even in the age of the railroad (the golden spike had been driven at Promontory Point, Utah, only six years before), Nevada and the challenging wilderness of the West lay too far off, although William had trained out to Wisconsin in 1875 on a journey to visit his married brothers.

The unspoiled Adirondacks provided a convenient facsimile of the frontier, free of bison and hostile Indians. It was fit for grand masculine solitude or for the company of other men. Thus the genteel campers, refreshed by their exertions, chipped in to buy an abandoned cabin, known as "the Shanty," to provide themselves with a summer wilderness camp. In short, they instigated a modest variation of what wealthier men were building all over the Adirondacks: the so-called Great Camps, to facilitate wilderness recreation. Named after its Brahmin co-owner James Jackson Putnam, Putnam Camp, as it became known, lay deep in the mountain valley at Keene. It was a collection of weathered wooden buildings surrounded by weed-grown fields and clustering behind a plain clapboard roadside inn. For washing, only cold water was available. Beds were rudimentary, but after a night plagued by mattress lumps and wailing mosquitoes, the campers could fill their lungs with fresh air and their eyes with the profiles of ink-blue mountains. These rough cabins cheerfully facilitated a very specific nineteenth-century form of manly, wilderness leisure. Theodore Roosevelt would embody this ideal when he purchased two Dakota ranches in 1883–84; through ranching, hunting, and finally military service, he would transform himself from a small, bespectacled Harvard graduate with political ambitions to a frontier figure in a buckskin tunic.

At the beginning, Putnam Camp was an all-male hermitage where William and his friends could imagine themselves "leading a natural animal life & throwing all the vanities of learning to the dogs." William's repeated invitations to his old friend from the Agassiz expedition, Tom Ward, demonstrate how urgently William wanted to re-create the rough-and-ready slog that had built his confidence in the Brazilian jungle ten years before. William urged Tom to "break through [his] bonds and come": "I *depend* on Mrs. Ward to push you out of doors and keep you locked out for a fortnight." He promised Tom "pretty scenery, coolness, lots of walking climbing, fishing &c, and socially a most free & jolly time—altogether the most salubrious thing you can do—the most I ever did."

Far from being naturally rugged, William and his overcultivated chums counterfeited this form of frontier hardship. Their generation believed that such rigors had transfigured their fathers and grandfathers into commanding men. William must have been aware, of course, that William James of Albany had financed the Erie Canal, not dug it; and that Henry Senior had probably never chopped wood in his adult life. But that didn't injure the myth.

These younger eastern gentlemen probably understood that they were only pantomiming wilderness exploration. The joke on themselves added to their enjoyment. At the same time, these Harvard alums were actually pioneering a different and more authentic frontier—a new world of urban professionalism, whose demands would only intensify in the coming decades, as wilderness dwindled and as city stresses multiplied. With traditional male physical activities curtailed by sedentary work in the late nineteenth century, the trends of camping and wilderness adventure would in fact result in many narratives of renovated masculinity. One example of this phenomenon was Jack London's popular *Call of the Wild* (1903), in which a tame dog named Buck rediscovers the primitive "law of club and fang" and goes wild in the Klondike.

Men like William James were among the first to explore the antidotes for the stresses of modernity. William, of course, had been besieged by a lifetime of depressive episodes, but such concerns were not the exclusive domain of the James family. To cure neurasthenia and other "new" nervous ailments, William's friend James Jackson Putnam actually resorted to electric shocks at Massachusetts General Hospital; maybe hewing wood and hauling water wasn't such a bad prescription, after all. And, though wilderness camping was something of a fad, it authentically galvanized William in 1876—though he remained a first-rate neurasthenic, bogged down in his depressions and physical ailments. At least his vacations in the Adirondacks got him out of Cambridge, out from under his father's thumb. His share in the ramshackle cabins of Putnam Camp marked the first real estate William had ever owned.

IN THE SUMMER of 1876, around mid-August, Alice Gibbens warily came to stay next door to William at Beede's Boarding House. She came for mountain walks and camp suppers, to get to know William better while lodging, respectably, with family members, in the wholesome outdoors. As it happened, living so close to Alice caused William "seven weeks of insomnia," he later confided to her, but glimpsing her against mountain backdrops also intoxicated William and made him certain of his feelings.

By September, he had made up his mind. He declared himself to her, the woman his father had endorsed, in writing. He revealed his love in a hand-delivered note—a sign of his gentlemanliness, perhaps a way to prevent risking his feelings while looking into her eyes. "To state abruptly the whole matter," he wrote Alice, "I am in love, *und zwar* [it's true] (—forgive me—) with Yourself." William needed to use German for the same reason Henry sprinkled his letters and stories with French: to bolster his insecurity with a stamp of his European education. (German, at least, sounded scientific and "masculine" to the Jameses, while French was considered refined and "feminine.") German had earlier provided a bond between these two, and no doubt indicated intimacy; at the same time, Alice may not have required the language of Goethe in a love note. "My duty in my own mind is clear," William went on. "It is to win your hand, if I can."

For another, little more would have been called for. But William retreated into brambly paragraphs of stipulations and self-doubts: "It seems as if I were in a manner trying to force your hand," he wrote, "and convert an indecision about denying a proposal suddenly made and probably unthought of hitherto by you, into an explicit admission of the possibility of future acquiescence." He seemed to be saying he didn't want to compel Alice's love. That was why, he continued, he was withdrawing immediately to an inn twenty miles to the northwest, at Lake Placid. He wanted to give her due time.

Ever self-doubting, William was worried that Alice didn't care for him. His fears may well have been caused more by the phantoms of his own mind than by Alice's initial unwillingness. But with such labyrinthine reservations laid out in front of her, Alice began to entertain some doubts about William herself. She began to keep a certain cagey distance from him, both in the Adirondacks and when the two of them returned, separately, to their lives in Boston.

William's first love note to Alice had betrayed his romantic inexperience as well as his utter lack of self-confidence. Such handicaps underlay the turgid philosophical prose of his long letters to Alice during the fall of 1876. He considered himself "tragic" as opposed to "normal"; he speculated that his desire to marry might be a crime against nature or, in a rare religious reference, a sin against the Holy Ghost. These macabre gaslit communications ("scholastic and pedantic," as William himself called them)—which Alice later preserved and numbered, though with expurgations—hardly read like impassioned entreaties of a young man swept up in love. Well might William worry that his "general mania for theorizing at unseemly hours" might annoy or discourage Alice.

It seems that for William, love meant encountering his demons—the sort of demons that his father had so dramatically faced in his Windsor breakdown of 1844 or that his sister Alice had faced in her repeated collapses since the 1860s. To court Alice Gibbens was probably the hardest thing William had ever done—harder than coopering barrels in Brazil, sweating for his medical exams, or pasting curative blisters on his own back. William not only saw Alice as "self contained and self supported at a distance, not needing [him]," but also felt that he himself might prove fatally flawed. He worried that the "marriage of unhealthy persons" might be a "crime." The unhealthy person—that is, himself—might ultimately only have some lonely philosophical purpose in the world. (In his letters to Alice, William scarily echoed the prejudice of his crippled father. Though Henry himself had obviously had a family, he believed in a strange brand of social Darwinism, one that required sacrifices for the physical and moral development of "the race." Only "healthy" people should breed. Such ideas were a chilling dismissal of William's own worth, and his sister, of all people, would also later adopt them.)

Some men might cite their fitness to prospective wives. But William perversely authorized Alice's own hesitation. "My friend," he wrote her, "hold yourself perfectly free of me." Yet William's self-denigration also unfolded his generosity, his vulnerability, and his ability to understand Alice as an intelligent, independent being and not just a female annex of himself. William had come a long way since his sometimes irritable crush on Minny Temple in the 1860s. His open-mindedness boded well for a brand of modern marriage that would emerge in the late nineteenth century, along with women's unfolding legal rights to property and divorce as well as their personal rights to respect in marriage. In the short term, though, William's lack of self-confidence didn't serve him well during the shortening days of that autumn. Few details of the mechanics of this romance have survived (and none of Alice's own letters); the two of them, both hardworking teachers, probably communicated mostly through notes or perhaps met for walks in the drifting leaves. In any case, the laughter and German-speaking of their early acquaintance appears to have quickly evaporated.

Christmas 1876 came, and William, ever more isolated from Alice, hardly felt festive. Nosing about Harvard Square and the Boston shops, he found himself incapable of choosing a "Christmas token" for anyone, as he confided to Kate Havens. He bought only three presents—possibly for his parents and his sister, Alice. Even these he felt ashamed to give, they were so badly chosen and inappropriate.

Sinking back into the Yuletide torpor of Quincy Street, William considered his "delirious affair" with Alice Gibbens at an end. Had she dismissed the gloomy William on one of these walks, or had he renounced her? "She cares no more for me than for a dead leaf, nor ever will," he wrote Tom Ward, "and viewed in the light of my health since the fall, I must say that objectively it is fortunate that she does not." He urged Ward to "bury" the failed relationship and keep it secret. And, in spite of the affair's somewhat public inception via the Radical Club, William succeeded in keeping much of his romance secret from his family, confiding only in his ne'er-do-well baby brother, Bob. Bob had the advantage of geographic distance and also, as the first James son to marry, a certain masculine moxie. Significantly, William chose not to share his feelings with his brother Harry or his sister, Alice. That, of course, would have exposed him.

ALICE JAMES, ANYWAY, had found a romantic interest of her own. A year after her forced return from Europe, in October 1873, while idling with friends at Beverly on the North Shore of Boston, she met a good-looking, rich, and well-connected young graduate of Harvard Law School, Charles Cabot Jackson, a man who seemed to possess all the conventional attractions to women.

Usually Alice reacted coolly to the young men she met at Quincy Street, remaining reserved or becoming sarcastic behind their backs. Yet this time she was staying with her friend Fanny Morse, and perhaps the more relaxed atmosphere of the Morse household, surrounded by the autumn lawns and trees of Beverly, Massachusetts, inspired Alice to react differently. Also the temptation to confide in Fanny—and to write a long letter to her friend Annie Ashburner in England—evidently motivated Alice. In a rare lapse into schoolgirlishness, Alice reported to Annie that this young man had "the nicest face & the sweetest smile." Charley Jackson, as it happened, was at that time already rumored to be engaged. But his very unavailability fit Alice's own preference, as she betrayed to her friend: "I hope I shan't see him again," she admitted, "or I am afraid the illusion will be dispelled."

Alice, now twenty-six, was a neat, earnest, rather plain young woman, her hair worn in a braided chignon. Heading into her upper twenties, she seems to have craved an illusion of romance, perhaps even more than romance itself. As the 1870s unfolded, she agonizingly watched her women friends attract infatuated males and plan weddings. At the same time, she kept her distance from the motley parade of intellectual men her brothers brought through the house—a common means of accruing a suitor in the nineteenth century, and one that had worked out for Alice's own mother. These men, anyway, spectacled as they often were, took little or no interest in a shut-in and moody "bluestocking"—as Alice herself apparently understood.

In the marriage market of the time—and it was truly a market in every sense of the word, complete with dollar values attached to heiresses—Alice suffered from multiple drawbacks. She had a heavy, serious face and a somewhat old-fashioned wardrobe stitched together by her mother. "I can't get reconciled to the peculiarities of my clothes," Alice lamented in 1874; she had given up, she said, on her "features." But Alice also carried an admiration-killing reputation for ill health, oddity, and—even more toxic to a young woman's prospects—learning. Alice's serious reading—for example, Madame de Staël, the lively Swiss observer of the French Revolution—gave her a critical eye and a razor-sharp tongue that didn't conform to the feminine sugariness of the era.

A trip to Quebec with Aunt Kate in the late summer of 1873 gave Alice's sharpness free rein. Almost immediately, Alice took a dislike to her fellow travelers on a ferry. She declared that "all Canadians . . . are by nature several degrees lower than the lowest middle-class English, & art has yet done nothing for them." She judged Prince Edward Island, that cluster of rustic farms set in the stormy Gulf of St. Lawrence, to be a "dirty desolate hole," not the "Earthly Paradise" others had naively found it. Such an acerbic observer could not always be counted on for feminine delicacy. As she later put it, she found her own "company manners" preposterous to witness.

Yet Alice continued to believe or pretend to believe in marriage and lament her "tender and apparently undesired" affections. She joked that she would "elope with the handsome butcher-boy" if her female friends didn't rally to her side. The point, though, may have been to secure more attention from her confidantes.

As she put it more poignantly years later, Alice found it a "cruel and unnatural fate for a woman to live alone, to have no one to care and 'do for' daily is not only a sorrow, but a sterilizing process." In the mid-1870s, as her prospects for marriage dwindled, Alice increasingly directed her wit against her girlfriends' engagements and marriages.

"They seem to be such an impossible couple," Alice lashed out, on one occasion: the "they" being many a twosome who paid a conjugal visit to her house.

Alice found it ridiculous to "stay at home in a constant state of matrimonial expectation," she told Annie Ashburner. She knew men weren't "attracted by depressed & gloomy females." That was what she sarcastically felt the bookish spinster Jane Norton to be, even more than herself. In any case, Henry and Mary didn't seem to push Alice's marriage prospects. Even as a "forlorn failure"—or perhaps especially as one—their only daughter was actually indispensable to the household, and in a peculiar way. Alice had become the established family scapegoat, the family pet, the prime family invalid, the person who made the other ailing Jameses feel healthier and more competent by comparison. In her own way, Alice remained as vital to the family economy as the steady, cheerful, hardworking Mary.

Still, Alice didn't feel needed; she felt desperate for distraction. Though she saw him only "rarely"—and probably only at crowded Bostonian dinner parties—she made much of her unrequited crush on Charles Cabot Jackson. Charley was now, in any case, publicly engaged to a rich local beauty, Fanny Appleton. As for Alice, *her* closest and deepest connections were with her Bostonian female contemporaries Fanny Morse, Sara Sedgwick, and Annie Ashburner. These friendships offered her an intimacy of equals such as she had rarely felt at home with her overweening mother and aunt.

But having bitterly witnessed most of her girlfriends marry off, Alice cherished her nonromance with Charley Jackson for the next two or three years and trotted it out in her letters. In late 1875, Alice reported to Annie, after a dinner party at which she had seen him from afar, that Charley continued just as "beautiful & seductive as usual." "My passion grows," she insisted—though it must have been a peculiarly Victorian and repressed passion, to survive on so little; "it's fortunate I see him rarely for I am told that it wd. be altogether wild to nourish the faintest hope, Miss Appleton still reigning supreme in his affections." When Alice at last caught a glimpse of the more fortunate Fanny, in all her more prosperous finery and loveliness, she forced herself to admit that Charley's fiancée was "not bad-looking." Knowing herself to be plain,

Alice refused to look in a mirror for a long time after she got home to Quincy Street.

❧

ALICE GIBBENS DIDN'T belong to the Bee, Alice James's literary-minded sewing circle, but the two Alices in fact shared much more than their medieval name. Alice Gibbens, after all, was just a year younger than Alice James, and both of them—as unmarried women in their late twenties, lacking independent fortunes, traditional charms, and admirers—faced the same damning fate of spinsterhood. Both no doubt felt isolated, tagged as old maids in an era when women's marriages bequeathed both status and self-respect.

But neither Alice was really quite as singular as she felt. Neither late marriage nor spinsterhood, in fact, was actually as rare as the two Alices might have thought. Even in the previous generation, after all, circumstances had forced Mary Walsh to wait until she was thirty to be wed. Her sister, Kate, had married late and then opted for a dignified separation. Such women, relatively independent for long parts or the whole of their lives, were increasing in number in America. For centuries, northern Europe and the United States had exhibited at least two curious distinguishing features, unique on the planet: "(1) a high age at marriage and (2) a high proportion of people who never marry at all."

Women's late marriage had huge implications. As a number of historians have argued, this signature demographic can be traced back in Western culture as far as the late Middle Ages—and already, long before the 1870s, profoundly influenced the shape of "modernity" in northwestern Europe and the United States. Delayed marriage played out in countless ordinary lives, with a liberating tendency that had little enough to do with the parallel intellectual developments, for example, with John Stuart Mill's visionary manifesto, *The Subjection of Women*, published in 1869.

American women who delayed marriage in the 1870s had at least one advantage over their mothers and grandmothers and unmarried aunts: higher education. Neither of the Alices, to be sure, had benefited from the new attitudes: Alice James had had governesses and a few tutors, and a few years in girls' schools in Newport and Boston. But both Alices had inventively educated themselves—Alice James with her brothers' books and her European residence. Neither of their fathers had bought into the new rage for female academy education—to be purchased at places like the Mount Holyoke Seminary in Massachusetts, founded in 1837. (Such an omission was all the more insulting in Henry Senior, who nominally at least belonged to the New England reform circles where activists like Julia Ward Howe pushed hard for women's education.)

Females had graduated from Oberlin College and the University of Iowa in the 1850s, but the number of university women had swollen dramatically since the Civil War. Women's colleges sprouted up on the very doorsteps of the two Alices: Vassar in 1865, Wellesley and Smith in 1875, and Bryn Mawr in 1884—even the nearby "Harvard Annex" at William's institution, later to become Radcliffe College, as early as 1874.

Yet the two Alices made quieter but no less symbolic strides. Though humble in its way, Alice Gibbens's girls' school job on Beacon Hill highlighted a major shift in the late nineteenth century: young women in the Northeast had "started making teaching a women's field." More and more, careers outside of the home opened up for women in Boston, and Alice James—in one of her many differences from her mother—longed for one of her own. As she witnessed daily with her brother William living in the same house, a career could grieve as well as delight. But if a profession had translated into independence and European travel for her brother Harry, why not for her?

IN DECEMBER 1875, Alice's friend Fanny Morse persuaded her to make use of the erudition that Charley Jackson had apparently ignored in order to teach for a new women's correspondence school, the Society to Encourage Studies at Home. This school—the brainchild of Anna Eliot Ticknor, a daughter of Anna Eliot, an erudite Beacon Hill hostess, and George Ticknor, one of the founders of the Boston Public Library—aspired to extend the reach of Boston female braininess into distant parts of North America. Women who wanted education and weren't able to afford schooling or college training could, through letters, receive advice and tutoring from women who had had more educational advantages. It was an inspired idea, and the school caught on like wildfire after its inception in 1873.

Not everyone was convinced; Alice initially found herself "violently declining" the offer. But soon she "meekly succumbed"—or so she joked. In actuality, Alice James embodied the ideal recruit for the faculty. After all, she knew worlds about studying at home, having for years cultivated her own solitary and unappreciated life as a self-educated scholar. Tellingly, she was soon happily absorbed in her work. She taught the subject of history, working with the head of the history department, Katharine Peabody Loring, a vigorous young woman from Beverly, Massachusetts, and with mail-in students from Kentucky to Colorado.

Alice hemorrhaged with doubt about it all: "You can laugh and think me as much of a humbug as you choose," Alice wrote to her friend Annie, "you can't do so more than I have myself." Yet when her confidante picked up on Alice's self-denigrating cue and made light of the society, Alice promptly replied, "[I am] deeply hurt at yr. ridicule of my professorial character." She warmly defended her new endeavor: "I assure you it is not a thing to be laughed at." Someday, she added, Annie would be "only too happy to sit at [her] feet." Like her brothers, Alice could be alternatingly self-deprecating and grandiose, even at this relatively healthy stage of her life.

Her parents gave her a desk for Christmas in 1875, perhaps to facilitate her work. It was a promising gesture. But like Annie Ashburner, they may have largely dismissed Alice's tutoring. Neither thought highly of female education. Only William showed his sister respect, as he knew firsthand what hard work teaching could be. Also, he approved of a job for Alice in principle and had even tried to find her some work at the Museum of Comparative Zoology at Harvard. He honored Alice's new vocation by calling it a "historical professorship." To his credit, he rated it as an "immense thing" for her.

Alice also drew on the support of her fellow teachers, notably Katharine Loring, whom she had in fact first met a few years earlier. Alice had first encountered Loring in December 1873, at a North Shore lunch given by her friend Fanny Morse. And now that the Society for the Encouragement of Studies at Home had brought them together,

they found that they had more in common, as studious and neglected females, than they'd previously imagined.

The society didn't persist in Alice's life forever; her involvement pe-
tered out after a year or two. But December 17, 1873—the date of the
North Shore lunch—would in the meantime transform into an anniversary, "kept unknown to any." In future years it would turn into an "immense thing" for Alice in its own right.

HARRY CELEBRATED CHRISTMAS of 1875 in the "great fancy
bazaar" of Paris, with its gaslit streets and handsomely glazed shopfronts.
He probably bothered very little about his sister's new profession. For
one thing, he was completely absorbed in the French capital, where he'd
arrived in November. With a regal new wardrobe tailored in London,
he'd moved into a high, east-facing apartment on the quiet rue de Luxembourg (today the rue Cambon), centrally located minutes away from
his beloved Louvre and the cheerful, crowded cafés of the rue de Rivoli.
He reported to his father that he was now lord of a kitchen stacked with
firewood and outfitted with gleaming copper casseroles, a closet full of
French china that could turn his antechamber into a dining room, and a
parlor stocked with picturesque mirrors, clocks, and candlesticks. This
aesthetic bachelor's pied-à-terre was a step up from his lodgings in Italy,
and Harry imagined an even grander future.

He'd recently landed the position of Paris correspondent for the *New
York Tribune*—the same paper for which his father had penned letters
from Europe in the 1850s. Harry, with his tangled and diffuse prose,
would fail to captivate a newspaper audience, just as his rambling and
arcane father had failed to do. But he attracted refined readers; his
mother conveyed to him a compliment about a recent piece he had published in the *North American Review*: "Mr. James is always fascinating,
whether he writes a story, a sketch of travel, or a criticism." As a matter
of fact, Harry had now shored up the foundation of a literary career,
based on cultivated magazines like the *Atlantic* and three hefty books
he'd just seen through the press back in the United States: a collection
of his travel pieces called *Transatlantic Sketches;* a gathering of his stories
called *The Passionate Pilgrim;* and an ambitious novel he'd written mostly

in Florence, called *Roderick Hudson*, which would help pay for Harry's Parisian residence, after it won a "very charming notice," as Harry modestly put it, in the *Atlantic*.

Alice's educational letters looked flimsy, perhaps, beside Harry's critically praised tomes. Harry himself certainly didn't take his sister's work very seriously. He doted on cultivated women, like the many he'd followed around Rome, but he didn't encourage or promote women's education, really, any more than his father had done. Harry didn't at all favor women's "emancipation," as he later remarked, of the kind being debated at the Radical Club and increasingly talked up in Boston and elsewhere. In 1869, Julia Ward Howe and Lucy Stone had founded the American Woman Suffrage Association in Boston; that same year, Elizabeth Cady Stanton and Susan B. Anthony created the more radical National Woman Suffrage Association in New York, but these were not women who drew the eye of Henry James.

He had developed a taste for the luminaries of early Third Republic Paris. After New Year's, in late January 1876, Harry dressed for a reception of particular splendor. A colleague of his from the *Nation*, Auguste Laugel, had secured Harry an invitation to one of the great mansions, or *hôtels*, of the Faubourg St.-Germain, the aristocratic quarter on the Left Bank. The *hôtels* looked blank enough on the outside, hardly noticeable in the Latin Quarter's shadowy, narrow streets. Their courtyards, guarded by liveried porters and concierges, led to hidden palaces and gardens; their reception rooms, to which only a select few were admitted, sheltered a rarified realm of gilded mirrors, tapestries, and ancestral portraits.

Harry climbed carpeted stairs to a salon crowded with monocled ambassadors and members of the Académie Française. As his friends introduced him around, Harry was soon presented to an alert military figure with a twisted mustache and goatee, Henri Eugène Philippe Louis d'Orléans, duc d'Aumale. He was the fourth son of the former French monarch Louis-Philippe (1773–1850) and also a sort of national hero, the decorated and battle-hardened conqueror of Algeria in 1847. A writer on military and political subjects—a promoter of constitutional monarchy and empire—the duc d'Aumale greeted the young American writer in the "bosom of the Orleans family," as Harry later described the tableau to his mother. He was surrounded by his royal relatives, seated on silk sofas and posted beside marble mantelpieces. Only the so-called comte de Paris, considered by some to be the rightful heir to the French throne, was nowhere to be seen.

Moving through this faded royalist circle—"the skim of the milk of the old noblesse," as he called one fictional version of this coterie—Henry judged that all the Orléans women were notably "ugly." But he eagerly entered into a conversation with a princess of Saxe-Coburg, "old, corpulent, and deaf," who, though she had never heard of Harry's books, impressed him with her ingrained graciousness and affability. She embodied for Harry "what princesses are trained to [be]," and he would use her as a model for a plump duchess in a future novel, Madame d'Outreville in *The American* (1877).

These grandees would hardly become Harry's intimate friends; he regarded such types in his fiction as "prehistoric monster[s]" or at best well-preserved "specimens" of the past. With his excellent French, Harry was one of the few foreigners able to invade more intellectual salons like Gustave Flaubert's Sunday-afternoon *cénacle* (discussion group) of writers. Flaubert, the author of such exquisitely written and ground-breaking novels as *Madame Bovary* (1857) and *L'Éducation sentimentale* (1869), would, along with other inventive and iconoclastic French novelists, influence Harry's fiction.

For years, Harry had adored French literature. Now he was living it. *"Je suis lancé en plein Olympe* [I'm launched into an absolute Olympus]," Harry congratulated himself to Thomas Sergeant Perry, as his artistic and ducal connections multiplied. At the same time, like many an expatriate in Paris, Harry felt shut out of the intimate inner sanctums of French life. To judge from his letters, Harry was as lonely as William or Alice, and his special and complicated loneliness was proving even a harder nut to crack. William and Alice, at least, had yearned to find partners. But Harry had repeatedly declared, whenever the subject came up, that he didn't intend to marry at all.

In late November 1875, Harry climbed the hill of Montmartre to the rue de Douai, in order to meet the famous Russian expatriate novelist Ivan Sergeyevich Turgenev. The big-framed, hearty Turgenev, who received Harry arrayed on a sofa because of his gout, was fifty-seven years old (Harry was thirty-two), with a mane of salt-white hair and a neatly trimmed beard. Harry enthusiastically rated him "a magnificent creature, and much handsomer than his portraits." The two reveled in each other's conversation (in French or in Turgenev's stiff English), and Harry found himself compellingly drawn to this broad-shouldered, intelligent, gentle Muscovite, whom he symptomatically pronounced "manlier" than any other writer he'd known.

Harry in fact had a lot in common with this new father figure, who, unlike Henry Senior, thoroughly approved of his writing fiction. But, conversely, Turgenev resembled Henry Senior (and William) in his mistrust of "touches that are too *raffiné* [refined], words and phrases that are too striking, or too complete." Turgenev, Harry later self-deprecatingly remarked, didn't believe Harry's fiction was "meat for men," and he felt that it had "too many flowers and knots of ribbon." Still, though, it seems clear that Turgenev was taken with Harry and with his work. The Russian praised him, other friends reported, "in a way that he had rarely spoken . . . of anyone."

After one rainy winter afternoon of revelatory conversation with the author of *Fathers and Sons* (1862), Harry pronounced Turgenev to be an *"amour d'homme"*—a conventional yet oddly ringing phrase. Harry meant to describe Turgenev, with this detached French expression, as a sweetheart of a man, a man a person could love. But Harry's phrase also hinted at specific male love, a love between men—though in the homosocial nineteenth century, when homosexuality remained inconceivable, this phrase would hardly have caused a ripple of surprise. Men "loved" men as a matter of course—in a "manly" and innocent way— just as they unthinkingly linked arms when walking together in the street. The expression evidently didn't strike or trouble William, alert as he remained to Harry's other preciosities. But Harry was about to embark on an *amour d'homme* in a different sense.

❧

HIS NAME WAS Paul Zhukovsky—though in letters home Harry transliterated his name, in the French manner, as "Joukofski" or "Joukowsky." Harry resisted calling him Paul von Zhukovsky—a grand extension of his name the young man also used, a nod to his German mother and his Russian aristocratic background. At the age of thirty in 1875, some two years younger than Harry (though Harry simply thought him "about [his] own age"), Zhukovsky circulated in Turgenev's group as an aesthete and a painter—with charming manners and a fashionably full goatee. Zhukovsky was a "great friend" of Turgenev and so came ecstatically recommended.

The exquisite young Russian promptly riveted Harry's attention. His dark hair was swept back—to judge from a photograph of him taken in Paris in 1875—and his beard fanned in an operatic fashion; he wore well-tailored suits and signet rings on both of his small, neat hands. In his impeccable dress, heady conversation, and grand connections, the young man personified the refinement Harry deeply craved for himself. The painter's father, the poet and translator Vasily Zhukovsky, had counted himself an "intimate friend" of Johann Wolfgang von Goethe—and his son inherited some of Goethe's own drawings as a relic of this intimacy. The elder Zhukovsky had also tutored the young Czar Nicholas II, so that the infant Paul had partly grown up at St. Petersburg in the imperial Russian court, "dandled by Empresses"—as Harry excitedly reported to Mary. From his German mother, Paul had also inherited a "valuable background in Germanism," which no doubt fueled his enthusiasm for the avant-garde music of Richard Wagner as well as attractively shaping his "delicate and interesting mind."

All in all, Harry was snob enough, American enough, to envy Paul his stays in Venetian palaces and his coruscating Parisian circle of crowned heads and international divas. Turgenev called Zhukovsky *"l'épicurien le plus naïf que j'ai rencontré* [the most innocent epicurean I've ever met]," and Harry soon declared he was "one of the pure flowers of civilization."

That Paul Zhukovsky painted pictures also whipped up Harry's admiration. Since his adolescence of shadowing William at art school in Newport—and witnessing his cousin Gus Barker stripped naked on a pedestal—Harry had grown ever more obsessed with art and artists. In spite of his inability to paint or sculpt himself, Harry's art fantasies were taking on ever more intense colorings. And nothing showed the complexities of these longings more than his first significant novel, published the year before he met Paul Zhukovsky—that strange and evocative book, so foundational to Harry's life and career, *Roderick Hudson*.

It is possible that Harry gave Paul a copy; Zhukovsky apparently bestowed at least one painting on Harry, and this novel, even in its sober, stiff New England binding, would certainly have struck Harry as a fitting gift. Having just come out with a flourish, the book often served as Harry's calling card; it carried a certain cultivated celebrity among Americans in Europe. If Zhukovsky managed to wade through its hundreds of pages of Harry's finely turned English, he outdistanced Turgenev, who it was obvious by now had never pushed through much of Harry's prose.

Roderick Hudson, which Harry had started during a lonely winter in Florence in 1874, tells the story of a moneyed, Europeanized American connoisseur, Rowland Mallet, who desires something to complete his idle and lonely life. On a visit to his cousin in Northampton, Massachusetts, the thirtyish Mallet declines to be introduced to any marriageable "pretty girl." When his cousin replies, "I can at least show you a pretty boy," Rowland is delighted to encounter a statuette of a naked youth drinking from a gourd. The figure represents *Dipsa*, "thirst." But, the narrator says, "it might have been some beautiful youth of ancient fable—Hylas or Narcissus, Paris or Endymion."

Fascinated by the statuette, Mallet transfers his interest to the artist himself, who turns out to be a homegrown and untutored sculptor, twenty-four years old, a tall, slender young man whom Mallet finds "remarkably handsome." To Rowland, Roderick Hudson's features are "admirably chiselled and finished, and a frank smile played over them as gracefully as a breeze among flowers." Mallet finds the young man gifted and provincially misunderstood in a New England suspicious of art. He offers to take Roderick to Rome to give him an artistic education—and for less conscious or examined reasons: "Northampton is not so gay as Rome," as Mallet himself innocently remarks.

The novel entangles Rowland and Roderick in heterosexual romances—one of the reasons why it probably raised few eyebrows in the 1870s. Roderick is already engaged to his cousin, the plain and domestic and hypermoral Mary Garland. (Later Rowland also develops a secret though tirelessly chaste obsession for this same woman.) In Rome, Roderick also falls in love with the ravishing, intelligent Christina Light—arguably one of Harry's best fictional portraits—a discontentedly modern American heiress who doggedly delays marrying the impeccably courtly Italian nobleman Prince Casamassima.

For all of its richness of scene and characters, the novel resolutely centers on the friendship between patron and artist, between Rowland and Roderick. And this friendship ends only when Roderick, in the throes of an impossible passion for Christina and in the midst of an Alpine thunderstorm, slips off a cliff (or perhaps throws himself off, as the novel leaves it ambiguous) and dies. Many post-Freudian readers, at least, have wondered just what impossible passion mandated Roderick's grim end. In nineteenth-century literature, untimely death was often the obligatory punishment for transgressive passions, especially for women. What sin had really fueled the tragic ending of the novel?

Infatuated with artists (and chastely fascinated by women), Harry closely resembled his protagonist Rowland Mallet. In future decades, Harry would live out a Mallet-like pattern with a number of younger men, some fledgling artists. But Paul Zhukovsky now emerged as Harry's first opportunity to explore some of the longings he'd traced in the novel.

Unlike Roderick, Zhukovsky didn't qualify as a genius in the rough. About that, at least, Harry settled his mind right away. At the Paris Salon of 1876, Zhukovsky exhibited two ambitiously large pictures. But Harry, who had trained himself as an art critic, didn't think highly of them. Though Harry admired his new friend's cultivation, he blamed Zhukovsky for a "great deal of *mollesse* [softness] and want of will." "He lacks vigor," Harry reported to his mother, who was herself patently vigorous. Zhukovsky, Harry told his family, had inherited wealth and could afford to be "amateurish."

But in spite of his reservations, Harry's involvement with his "young Russian," his "dear young friend Joukowsky," swelled during the spring and summer of 1876. He "dined" with Zhukovsky in the restaurants and nightclubs of Paris and even in his own well-appointed flat—at last making use of the china in his closet. (In June, Harry invited his friend to the rue de Luxembourg to dine with the visiting Bootts. Paul found the crusty father *"extremement sympathetique"* (extremely nice), a figure straight out of Titian. Lizzie Boott was enchanted enough with Harry's Russian to trot out her best French, the fluency of which astonished her old friend.) Harry also visited Paul's apartment and studio, where Harry was transfixed by Italian art and "relics." Harry, unfortunately, found the Goethe sketches "awful." To put it mildly, Harry was a tough date.

In the blossoming "Parisian Babylon," Zhukovsky hosted a festivity at the Opéra one evening in June. (As an enthusiast of Wagner, Zhukovsky would design the costumes and four of the five sets for the premiere of Wagner's opera *Parsifal* several years later.) The grand new opera house of Paris had been opened with a gala performance only a few months before, in January 1875, a glorious landmark conceived by former emperor Napoléon III, supervised by his urban planner, Baron Haussmann, and designed by the architect Charles Garnier (in a grand neobaroque style that Empress Eugénie was reportedly gratified to hear described as "Napoléon III"). Dominating the vistas of the boulevard des Capucines and the avenue de l'Opéra in central Paris, the opera house was built for luxury; its 2,200-seat interior was swathed in plush velvet, encrusted with gilt nymphs and cherubs, and spectacularly lit by a three-tiered chandelier weighing over six tons. After the performance, the two friends joined Turgenev, whom Harry pronounced "jovial, prattlesome, and entertaining," though he was obliged to leave early. His exacting mistress, Pauline Viardot, expected him.

Zhukovsky more than made up for Turgenev's absence, introducing Harry to "all sorts of interesting Russians," including Princess Ouroussoff, a dark-haired, bright-eyed aesthete, the daughter of an industrialist who had married into the imperial family but now lived an artistic life on modest means. Harry found this Russian equivalent of Grace Norton "as easy as an old glove"—though all the more intriguing for being a princess. Her only fault that Harry could see was that she chain-smoked. But her haze of tobacco included the German ambassador, Prince Hohenlohe, and Paul's outing competently glittered with all the princely and distinguished splendors that Harry tended to crave. His infatuation with his Russian partly depended on these public trappings. But evidence has also survived of an intense personal attachment: the observant Turgenev tended to invite the two young men together, as a pair; and the two showed up as a telling "us" in Harry's letters home.

Mathew Brady's daguerreotype of Henry James Sr. and eleven-year-old Henry James Jr., taken in August 1854, a year before the family's departure for Europe. Henry Senior, who favored cutting-edge technology, commissioned this photograph as a surprise for his wife, Mary. *(By permission of the Houghton Library, Harvard University: MS Am 1092.9 [4597.6])*

William James's ink sketch of his family from a letter dated November 1861, showing Alice, Mary, Henry Senior, Wilkie, Kate, and Bob. This drawing is the nearest the Jameses came to a family portrait, but William teasingly described these figures as "more or less failures," especially Bob and Alice. *(By permission of the Houghton Library, Harvard University: MS Am 1092.9 [2501])*

Mary Walsh James in middle age, in the proper and elaborate couture she favored. Her children found her tirelessly cheerful, but her optimism hardly shows up in her photographs. *(By permission of the Houghton Library, Harvard University: MS Am 1094)*

Alice James in Paris at the age of nine, about 1857, exquisitely dressed by her mother. "Crinoline?—I was suspecting it! So young and so depraved!" William Makepeace Thackeray remarked. *(By permission of the Houghton Library, Harvard University: MS Am 1094)*

Henry James Jr. at sixteen or seventeen in the late 1850s, about the time he attended William Morris Hunt's studio in Newport *(By permission of the Houghton Library, Harvard University: MS Am 1094)*

The Jameses' cousin Minny Temple at sixteen in 1861. Her hair was cropped because of an illness, but she made theatrical use of the damage. *(By permission of the Houghton Library, Harvard University: MS Am 1092.9 [4597])*

William James in about 1868, at the time of his residence in Dresden and during one of the darkest and most depressive passages of his life *(By permission of the Houghton Library, Harvard University: MS Am 1092)*

ABOVE: Sketch by William James, probably of Alice James, from the 1860s, marked "The Loveress of W.J." *(By permission of the Houghton Library, Harvard University: MS Am 1092.2)*

LEFT: Alice Howe Gibbens in Dresden in about 1872, four years before she met William James *(By permission of the Houghton Library, Harvard University: MS Am 1092.9 [4598])*

ABOVE LEFT: Robertson James ("Bob") in 1872, at the time of his wedding in Wisconsin. He longed to be a painter, but to the family both he and Wilkie were "destined for commerce." *(By permission of the Houghton Library, Harvard University: MS Am 1094)*

ABOVE RIGHT: Sixteen-year-old Garth Wilkinson James ("Wilkie") in about 1861, two years before he volunteered for the Union army *(By permission of the Houghton Library, Harvard University: MS Am 1094)*

BELOW: Harvard Square as it appeared in the mid-1860s, when the Jameses moved to Cambridge. Horse cars provided the young James boys one means of escape from a household they found stifling. *(Courtesy of the Massachusetts Historical Society, Boston: Harvard College Class of 1864 Photographs, Photo 138.33)ß*

RIGHT: The Russian painter Paul Zhukovsky in Paris about 1875, at the time of his friendship with Henry James Jr. *(By permission of the Houghton Library, Harvard University: MS Am 1092.9 [4597])*

BELOW LEFT: The American writer Constance Fenimore Woolson in Venice, 1893, shortly before her death *(From Clare Benedict*, Four Generations *[1930]; courtesy of Widener Library, Harvard University)*

RIGHT: Henry James Jr. in the early 1880s, at about the time of the publication of *The Portrait of a Lady (By permission of the Houghton Library, Harvard University: MS Am 1094)*

Alice James in Royal Leamington Spa with Katharine Peabody Loring, 1889 or 1890. Their close relationship had inspired Henry James's *The Bostonians* (1886). *(By permission of the Houghton Library, Harvard University: MS Am 1092.9 [4598])*

Alice James as photographed in London in September 1891, six months before her death. With her customary self-denigration, she joked about her "refulgent beauty." *(By permission of the Houghton Library, Harvard University: MS Am 1092.9 [4598])*

Henry James Sr., approaching seventy years old, with his baby grandson Henry James III in 1879 or 1880 *(By permission of the Houghton Library, Harvard University: MS Am 1094)*

Henry and William James in late middle age, early in the twentieth century, when they lived for the most part on opposite sides of the Atlantic *(By permission of the Houghton Library, Harvard University: MS Am 1094)*

Harry praised Paul's sweetness, amiability, and artistic sensitivity—almost as if he were describing the virtues of a young fiancée. With his "picturesque" background and artistic delicacy, the Russian suited Harry. They had early on "sworn an eternal friendship," as Harry informed both William in April and Alice in June. Harry entertained the "most tender affection" for his new friend, whose noble connections occasioned an even more telling joke to William: "So you see I don't love beneath my station," Harry wrote.

That Harry shared this special friendship with his family, though, is also telling—especially in contrast to William's and Alice's secrecy about their relationships. (William replied, "I envy you the possession of the young [R]ussian painter's intimacy" and, oddly, asked Harry to "send Joukowsky's Portrait"—a common enough transaction in the late nineteenth century, but one showing some curiosity, and one the James brides had been going through.)

Given Harry's repression and fastidiousness, it's possible that he understood his relation as entirely "pure," just as he'd early on identified an "extreme purity of life" as one of Paul Zhukovsky's virtues. Harry's most authoritative biographer suggested that the novelist, with his extreme naïveté and inexperience, didn't even know that Paul was a homosexual until four years later, in 1880. Lack of sexual awareness was typical of the times. Another historian observed that Harry's "effeminacy, celibacy, and sublimation of eros can be understood as exemplary of nineteenth century sexuality rather than idiosyncratic."

Even among scientifically advanced Germans—and of course Zhukovsky, half German himself, knew the Teutonic model better than Harry—consciousness of a specific homosexual orientation had emerged only inchingly. Goethe and Schopenhauer had defended homosexuality earlier in the century, but it wasn't until 1886, ten years after Harry's Paris encounter, that Richard von Krafft-Ebing, the giant of the so-called sexologists, concocted a psychological (though pathological) model for homosexuality, in his *Pyschopathia Sexualis*. Another ten years would pass before the English-speaking world caught up, with Havelock Ellis's rather gothic *Studies in the Psychology of Sex: Sexual Inversion*, in 1897.

An earlier generation had dealt with homoerotic interests using terms like *male friendship*, *camaraderie*, or *fraternal union*—as, for example, Friedrich Nietzsche and Walt Whitman had done. Harry lived precariously in the twilight of a very peculiar Victorian sexual innocence—a complicated state, to say the least—and one that he loved to write about in his novels and attribute to American ingenues of both sexes. Such "innocent" terms, in fact, were exactly what allowed Harry to relate his affair frankly and yet unrevealingly to his family back in Cambridge.

Whatever the content of his feelings, Harry's relation with Paul Zhukovsky was pushing him toward intimacy, toward romantic engagement—his equivalent, at least, of William's long-running flirtation with Kate Havens. Yet the exact match for a James might still be hard to predict, and harder still to find in the world outside of their imaginations.

BOSTON MARRIAGE

When William boarded his steamship at the town of Fall River, Massachusetts, on the evening of May 30, 1877, he could hardly contain his elation. The tall white steamer, with its two tiers of observation decks, glided triumphantly out into Mount Hope Bay, threading among low-lying peninsulas and islands quilted with fields and woods. An imitation of an Atlantic liner, this upscale ferry carried William, newly liberated, into Narragansett Bay—that broad glimmering thoroughfare stretching toward the Atlantic and Newport, fifteen miles off.

Thirty-five-year-old William boarded with more energy than he'd felt in a long time, alert in his five foot eight inches. The Fall River Line steamers and their routes were familiar to William and all of the Jameses, and usually signaled a holiday and its corresponding uplift. The line connected both New York and Boston (via the Old Colony Railroad) to Newport's grand hotels and "cottages." Since the end of the Civil War, its steamers had increasingly catered to the wealthy and the well connected. For these passengers on the overnight to New York, there were luxury staterooms. For William on his shorter leg, there was a full supper in the dining room, with perhaps a glass of wine or two to celebrate the beginning of his summer vacation. The ship's interior featured majestic two-story columns, elaborately painted ceilings, chandeliers, armchairs, and potted palms—resembling the drawing rooms of mansions or the lobbies of hotels more than the parlors of the old Hudson River steamboats William could remember from his childhood.

He roved on deck later, drinking in the "soft strong air," realizing he needed to unkink. That afternoon he'd finished giving his final exams in psychology. Since 1873, William had been growing into his job as a physiology professor. When his charm and encyclopedic knowledge got the better of his darker moods, his energy could enliven a classroom. Still, the hard labor of the job had beaten him down this spring even more than usual. After his exam that day, he'd had to pay a visit to a distraught student who, in peril of failing out of school, had nearly resorted to suicide. William empathetically understood such an extreme state, and he'd been able to coach the young man, advise him, and "stiffen his backbone." Now, at least, it wasn't William who agonized about failure; it wasn't William's tortured backbone that needed straightening.

Decoration Day, the early incarnation of Memorial Day, had come. William pictured the sheaves of lilacs from the Quincy Street garden, which he might have harvested for Alice Gibbens and the decoration of war graves. "It was impossible," he apologized to Alice, regretting he hadn't been able to stay in town a few more days.

Alice had once more inched back into William's life. Although he'd given her up the previous Christmas, in one of his black fits of despondency, he hadn't really been able to let her go. The secret letters had trickled on. Alice's letters have not survived, and some of William's were later cropped and edited. But even more than a century later, these notes still echo with the urgent whispers of this love affair. "Oh thank you, thank you, for all you have written!" William wrote in the cold dark days of February. "*Somehow* interpreted, our relation must be immoral. I cannot say more, but am yours, yours."

In March, William attended a Chaucer lecture given by Francis James Child at the Lowell Institute, a philanthropic venture that offered distinguished lectures to the public. (Partially inspired by the Royal Institution in London, the institute became a branch of the Massachusetts Institute of Technology in the twentieth century and eventually gave birth to the famous Boston public television station, WGBH). Jostling crowds clogged the Old Corner Bookstore at School Street and Washington Street in Boston, where the tickets were dispensed.

William ran into Alice Gibbens at the lecture hall, which, with its dowdy seriousness, offered him a less romantic meeting than a garden or a beach. Again, their interests brought them together. Afterward, William wrote her with fresh enthusiasm—in a tone reminiscent of his father's letters, three decades before, to Emerson, after the latter's lectures. "Ah Friend!" William wrote. "To have you recognize me, to have your truth acquiesce in my better self, form hence forward the only possible goal of my conscious life. You *will* do it—you will value me, care for me." The affair between the professor and the schoolteacher again began to exhibit signs of life.

In April, during a brief getaway to the low granite cliffs of Newport, William dispatched this message: "Some day, God willing, you shall read the bottom of my heart." It all seemed more possible now. On April 21, William and Alice had taken a long drive together, and he returned "bowed down with solemn happiness." They hadn't pledged themselves to each other, in so many words, but a kind of fragile understanding was developing. "I will try to be a mate for . . . you," William ventured to promise, in notes that finally sounded more like love letters. He boldly signed himself as Alice's "friend & lover."

Earlier, William had suffered from doubts about being able to father healthy children. He was still fretting to Alice about his back and stomach problems, which he thought set him below a "standard of wholesomeness." To pass on his defects would also be a "crime," he wrote—repeating this harsh word once more. But he stepped off the Fall River Line steamer in Newport elated, ready to marry in spite of his former objections.

Since his days in the cool, charmed space of William Hunt's studio in the 1860s, William had only rarely returned to Newport, though he retained some fond memories of breezes off Narragansett Bay, or surf crashing on the Paradise Rocks. But, also like his siblings, William wrestled with melancholy recollections from the family's residence during his difficult adolescence. He had grappled with some of these on one visit earlier in the 1870s when he revisited the "old stone cottage" on Spring Street where the James family had weathered the Civil War; it was now dirtied and mildewed inside, with depressing wallpaper, half-lit by little low windows overgrown by Austrian pines.

Tonight his hopes were higher, though his desire for a family wasn't answered by the "new" Newport. Even from the deck, he could see the huge new villas that had sprung up everywhere—in old meadows and on once-wild coastlines—architectural confections in the more indigenous "stick" or "carpenter Gothic" styles, or the more imported faux-Tudor, faux-Elizabethan, or French Renaissance styles. Here were houses that embodied the fashion and excess of the time: granite, brownstone, and jigsaw-cut wood, bristling with ornate roofs and dormers and turrets and wraparound porches. Some of these grand villas had been finished so recently as to have no landscaping or only spindly saplings planted into the bare front yards; not until decades later would big, graceful trees shade Newport's gracious avenues. William didn't care for this building boom, though many of these houses would be treasured by future generations. He judged that this "restless striving after new architectural effects" had failed profoundly. In these new "cottages," he discovered "no look of domesticity," only "a prevailing commonness & rawness owing to the lack of trees."

Married men William's age and younger had built these houses; wealthy families like the Kings and Griswolds had grandly descended from New York, and the still-richer Vanderbilts would arrive on the scene and build palatial summer homes by the 1890s. Gilded Age Newport—with its marble mansions, regattas, and opulent parties—would rival even the French Riviera in splendor and style. William on his "little salary" from Harvard could scarcely afford a single room at an inn, let alone commission such a behemoth for himself.

He put up at Wilbur's Boarding House on "the Point" in old Newport—in a clean white room overlooking the water, calm as a mirror except when a fuming steamboat plowed across it. Three years before, a friend of his had boarded for sixteen dollars a week, boat included. William now went sailing, as his brothers had done years before in their small craft called the *Alice*.

William's mind was on the other Alice as the catboat clipped across the swells of the harbor. Later in his room, writing to her, he would adopt the intimate tone of an engaged man. Alice mustn't fret over his nautical outings. He only wished she could curl up in the boat as his passenger, to cool her cheek with sea spray, to enjoy the "rushing, slapping, and tinkling music of the boat, and the waving shores spread along the horizon in a vapory bloom of colour." For now, this idyll played out in William's head—every day on Narragansett Bay, he actually sailed alone. He foresaw only happiness for himself and for Alice Gibbens. The one possible complication was Alice's friend Katharine Hilliard— the "wicked" Katharine, as William regarded her—who was threatening to spirit Alice off to England for the summer.

Kate Hilliard was a staunch and forthright friend, ready to rescue Alice from an entanglement she wasn't sure her friend truly wanted. But Alice had an equally persistent William to reckon with. "Don't think either that you shall escape the future rides which it is your doom to take with me," he wrote from Newport, playfully. (Victorian engagements overflowed with all manner of rides.)

William couldn't wait to get back to Cambridge. But once he did, his confidence faded. William's moods, like his father's, shifted easily from optimism to gloom. From the first, Alice Gibbens had brought out William's vulnerabilities, and now she did so again: William fretted that his long, demonstrative letters from Newport had "embarrassed" her.

For her part, Alice worried about "a certain aridity & bleakness of mind" that she perceived in William. For every charming, high-spirited letter, he had also penned at least one riddled with doubts, health worries, and obscure intellectual reservations. Alice recoiled from his *"doctrines,"* his tortured views on his own fitness for marriage. A more modern woman than Mary Walsh had been in the 1830s, Alice showed less willingness to adopt without question a husband's peculiar dogmatism, especially one that could so strongly impact her future life. So she still hung back, worsening William's worst fears, and helping to create something of a vicious cycle.

The turbulent courtship, now a year old, had been riddled with agonized ruptures. "I renounce you!" William wrote, symptomatically, that July. "Let the eternal tides bear you where they will. In the end they'll bear you round to where I wait for you. I'll feed on death now, but I'll buy the right to eternal life by it."

William now tried to convince Alice to join him in the Adirondacks, but she bridled. To give herself breathing room, she contemplated an escape to cool Quebec. William begged her to reconsider, but in late July, he himself fled back to Newport. "We cannot separate so lightly," he wrote Alice in desperation. "You and I can never mean nothing each for the other." But Alice remained adamant about what William called "lonesome, dreary Canada."

William had no choice but to spend six weeks bracing himself up with the masculine life of Putnam Camp, the "physical renovation and invigoration" of trout fishing, rock climbing, and alpine walking. For more feminine consolation, William spent time with Alice's aunt and sister Mary, who were staying nearby. Alice's family, especially her mother, proved friendlier to William's overtures than Alice herself. To Alice's sister, William brought a baby chipmunk he'd rescued in the woods. Mary Gibbens kept the tiny creature warm and alive in her hands.

By September 1877, William had again relinquished hope. He wrote to his one confidant in the family, his brother Bob, that his love affair had once more fallen through: "I charge you to breathe no word of it, *ever*, to any one. The family knows nothing of it yet, and must not here-after. It is a painful business, but she is an angel incarnate."

IN NOVEMBER 1876, Harry attended a peculiar yet exquisite soirée in Paris. Beginning at nine o'clock in the evening, the affair was a "musical séance," held in the "enchanting studio and apartment" of Paul Zhukovsky. The young Russian's Italian relics and paintings gleamed all around, patches of color in the lamplit interior. Princess Ouroussoff smoked her endless cigarettes. Her sister, Countess Panin, a "ravishing young widow," accompanied her in her perpetual trail of smoke. During the evening, a small circle of émigrés listened raptur-ously to selections from Wagner's operas, dashed out by a talented young French pianist in their midst. Harry disliked such avant-garde fare. "I was bored," Harry reported to his father, "but the rest were in ecstasy."

Since the middle summer of 1876, Harry's letters to his family had been void of references to his "bosom friend" Paul, partly because Harry had followed the French custom of leaving Paris for the hot months. But now, in the autumn, he had rejoined his companion and the intriguing Russian bohemians to whom he'd become attached. "They are quite the most (to me) fascinating people one can see," Harry admitted, "with their personal ease and *désinvolture* [offhandedness]." Their curiosity and international experience opened up for Harry, as he described it, windows "all round the horizon."

Whether or not Zhukovsky's rooms literally opened out onto views of Paris, Harry had been entertained there before. In the novel he was writing, he described the slightly disturbing lair of a fictional French aristocrat, "an insatiable collector," whose

> walls were covered with rusty arms and ancient panels and platters, his doorways draped in faded tapestries, his floors muffled in the skins of beasts. Here and there was one of those uncomfortable tributes to elegance in which the French upholsterer's art is prolific; a curtained recess with a sheet of looking-glass as dark as a haunted pool; a divan on which, for its festoons and furbelows, you could no more sit down than on a dowager's lap; a fireplace draped, flounced, frilled, by the same analogy, to the complete exclusion of fire. The young man's possessions were in picturesque disorder, and his apartment pervaded by the odour of cigars, mingled, for inhalation, with other dim ghosts of past presences.

The American, in which this passage appears, would become one of Harry's best-known works; it started its serial run in the *Atlantic* in June 1876. A confident novel of manners with an international theme, *The American* would mark Harry's coming of age as a novelist, and it made shrewd use of a wide variety of materials drawn from Harry's heady, yearlong residence in Paris. The book's richly drawn characters and exquisite settings—opening with its famous first scene in the Salon Carré at the Louvre (which William, for one, thought exquisite)—would render this novel Harry's first critical tour de force as well as his first substantial financial success.

The American's richness partly grew out of Harry's deeply rooted love of French literature as well as his recent confabulations with French writers. While living in Paris, Harry had also penned critical studies of such giants as Charles Baudelaire, Honoré de Balzac, George Sand, and Gustave Flaubert, which he would collect in *French Poets and Novelists* in 1878. The so-called immoral subjects of such groundbreaking writers, all of them somewhat shocking to Bostonians, attracted Harry's interest in a complicated way. Though generally Harry steered clear of the self-consciously modern, he argued that Flaubert—the author of the scandalous *Madame Bovary*, which had gone through a high-profile obscenity trial in 1857—was in fact a "potent moralist." For Harry, who had inherited strong if unorthodox moral imperatives from his father, the key to success in fiction consisted in "the tale and the moral hanging well together"—a goal he seems to have achieved, unconventionally, in the twists and turns of *The American*.

Set sumptuously in Paris, Harry's new novel traced the romance between a rough, self-made California tycoon, Christopher Newman, and a charming and refined French aristocrat from an old family, Claire de Cintré. With such a pair of transatlantic characters, Harry developed a dichotomy he had previously explored in *Roderick Hudson:* the contrast between American "innocence" and European "corruption"—the elaborate, veiled artifice of an older, more decadent, sexualized civilization. "You're the great Western Barbarian, stepping forth in his innocence and might," one expatriate tells Newman shortly after his arrival in Paris, "gazing a while at this poor corrupt old world and then swooping down on it." This distinction between a powerful but naive America and a senescent but dangerous Europe set in motion a novel saturated with Harry's own indirect and disguised quandary about *sexual* innocence and corruption.

Harry's conflicts were long-running. Beginning with Minny Temple, whose provocative iconoclasm had obsessed him, the young novelist had been drawn by powerful sophisticates who defied conventions and ignited hopes, perhaps, for his own eventual "recognition." He had encountered many such complex and ambiguous beings in Europe. As the son of a stern moralist, he was intrigued by possibilities of self-portrayal that a more ambiguous and "sinful" Old World seemed to offer him. Yet there was no place, not even in Paris, where this internally directed man could freely discuss his conflicted desires. Only the empty white pages awaiting his words could hold such painful, coded confidences.

❦

CHRISTOPHER NEWMAN, THE protagonist of *The American*, radiated innocence. In the most obvious sense, Harry had little enough in common with his hero—an expansive, confident, mustached Civil War veteran and businessman who had made a large fortune by manufacturing and marketing "certain admirable wash-tubs." The most signal difference between author and protagonist was Newman's desire to find a wife in Europe: "I made up my mind tolerably early in life that some rare creature all one's own is the best kind of property to hold," Newman declares early in the novel. For his part, Harry had frequently insisted on the opposite, that he didn't want to marry. Still, the character of Newman also drew an undercurrent of subtlety and sensitivity not unlike Harry's own, and Newman's friendship with Valentin de Bellegarde, Madame de Cintré's handsome young brother, provides a little-noticed though vital subplot that throws light onto Harry's own Paris adventures.

In the novel, this friendship builds like a romance, but in the shadow of the main love interest. When Newman first visits Madame de Cintré in the Faubourg St.-Germain, he encounters a young man "sitting, bareheaded, on the steps of the portico, in play with a beautiful pointer," who meets him with excellent English and engaging manners. Newman notices that the young man strongly resembles the woman he came to visit; Valentin de Bellegarde, in turn, makes "a rapid inspection of Newman's person." On their second meeting, Valentin warmly greets Newman as "a friend already made." As the two begin to spend time together—more time, almost, than Newman devotes to the young man's sister—Newman recognizes Valentin's "free and adventurous nature" and for that reason predicts that they are "destined to understand one another."

Before much more time has passed, we are ensconced in an opulent apartment on the boulevard Haussmann: "Well, here I am for you as large as life," Newman says, extending his long legs, as they sit beside his fireplace. Eagerly Valentin replies that Newman has "interested" him without even making an effort. Valentin's open, engaging manner strikes the tycoon as "a long 'pull' dangling in the young man's conscious soul; at the touch of the silken cord the silver sound would fill the air." In return, Valentin "so fabulously!" admires Newman for "the flower of [his] magnificent manhood."

Harry and Paul Zhukovsky had also spent long evenings together, but the friendship detailed in *The American* had even more telling resemblances to Harry's friendship with Paul. Harry had noted Zhukovsky's *"mollesse"* (softness) and lack of vigor, decisiveness, and worldly ambition; he was so indecisive he couldn't even choose a pair of trousers for himself. Likewise, Valentin is charming and ineffectual, considering himself to be a "dead failure." In the novel, Newman and Valentin naturally "fell into step together" without "formally swearing an eternal friendship"; Harry and Paul, with an even more intense mutual attraction, did these two one better and actually declared an "eternal friendship," as Harry had written to his sister Alice in May 1876. Critics and biographers, including Leon Edel, have noted this strong resemblance without, however, investigating its deeper implications.

Valentin, whom Newman appropriately calls "Valentine," plays the part of a go-between and facilitator in Newman's courtship of Madame de Cintré. The young man often stands in for her—being more available than his somewhat cloistered sister, more actively and persistently attached to Newman, and more involved in his day-to-day life in Paris. In Victorian courtship, a man's friendship with a brother could in fact promote his pursuit of the sister, as Henry James Sr. had found through his friendship with Mary's brother Hugh Walsh in the 1830s. But Valentin's more obvious role disguises a second sense of a "Valentine" that operates more covertly in the novel and in fact reverses this logic, using the sister in order to cover a lively interest in the brother. Valentin de Bellegarde's central importance to this novel, hidden in plain sight, has not been fully acknowledged, but it is now possible to understand it in the light of our current understanding of how sexuality played out for repressed Victorians.

The relation between Newman and Valentin, as it unfolds, is riddled with ambiguous but unmistakable passionate intensity. It is love without a label. In repeated encounters, the two linger over late dinners, hold hands, and conduct many cryptic and suggestive conversations: "It's a pity you don't fully understand me," Valentin says during one fireside chat, "that you don't know just what I'm doing." Hinting darkly about his noble family, he takes Newman's hand and looks at him askance: "Old races have strange secrets!" he says fervently. The most literal secrets in the novel pertain to a Bellegarde family murder—of which Valentin is in fact unaware. But the young aristocrat's own secrets, equally as gothic, facilitate intentions, motivations, and passions that the novel cannot understand or express more directly.

Like Harry himself in real life, Valentin has sworn that he will not marry. "You're charming, innocent, beautiful creatures," he says to his sister and her suitor. "But I'm not satisfied . . . that you belong to that small and superior class—that exquisite group—composed of persons who are worthy to remain unmarried. These are rare souls, they're the salt of the earth."

"Valentin holds that women should marry and men should n't," Madame de Cintré remarks. "I don't know how he arranges it."

"I adore some one I *can't* marry!" Valentin confesses. Here he appears to refer to a notorious flirt named Noémie Nioche; to defend this woman's honor, he will later be drawn into a duel. But, far from adoring this coquette, Valentin admits she is "really quite a bad bore." The challenge between Valentine and Stanislas Kapp, an Alsatian brewer's son, erupts at the Opéra Garnier, at a performance of that parable of sexual license, Mozart's *Don Giovanni*, and it has almost nothing to do with the vixen in question and everything to do with Valentine and Newman. For the latter, it becomes the occasion to declare his strong feelings for Madame de Cintré's brother: "the exposure, the possible sacrifice, of so charming a life on the altar of a stupid tradition struck him as intolerably wrong." Newman asserts himself as a protective older brother: "See here . . . if anyone hurts you again!" Both men are deeply moved by this fraternal pact, but Valentin is in fact doomed to perish in a duel—with more intense and impassioned scenes at Valentin's deathbed in Switzerland. After his passing, Newman will find himself helpless to reestablish his previous connection with Madame de Cintré.

At the Opéra Garnier, Newman had concluded that he "only knew that he did yearn now as a brother"—a telling phrase for the complicated nature of this "friendship." In the Victorian world, family sentiment was the touchstone of all other affections, and it was often confused and conflated with romantic feelings—as had happened before in the James family, when William wrote jokingly romantic letters to Alice. But though for Victorians a man might love his wife in some sense like a sister, it would have been more unusual for a man to "yearn" for his brother; and Harry's choice of words hints at the extraordinary intensity between these two fictional men as well as, perhaps, some of his fraught feelings for his brother William, which Leon Edel described as "psychosexual" and "homoerotic." With the introduction of the brotherhood metaphor, it is hard to know whether Harry identifies more with the protective older brother or the vulnerable younger one. But this fictional friendship drew on Harry's deep psychology, his long history with William, as well as the more recent adventures that, to judge from his letters and the hidden romance of *The American*, had deeply stirred and troubled him.

QUITE SUDDENLY, THE young novelist moved to London in November 1876. He didn't record his parting scene, if any, from Paul Zhukovsky. His last comment about his friend from Paris, in a letter to his father, was actually disparaging: he labeled his friend "a most *attachant* [attaching] creature, but a lightweight and a perfect failure." Still, he admitted that he would miss the émigrés (plural) more than anyone else: "My few Russian friends here are what I most regret," Harry wrote. (With his infatuation for Russia, Harry had shown such enthusiasm for a "Russian snow scene, with superb horses," that his rich friend Mrs. Tappan had gone out and bought it for seven thousand francs.) But aside from Turgenev, Harry was actually close to only one person who came from that country: Paul.

Harry now made a sort of getaway, leaving Paris in what one of his recent biographers, Sheldon M. Novick, has called a "curious temper." Harry now put the English Channel between him and his friend, but it was perhaps just this distance that enabled him to bear with this complication in his life. The two would continue to correspond; and Harry, ever kindhearted and useful to all his friends, would try to get Paul Zhukovsky's paintings accepted at the Royal Academy.

Harry scooted across a Channel that lay uncharacteristically "as smooth as . . . paper"—though winter Channel crossings tended toward storminess. Harry's move surprised no one in Quincy Street. He'd always kept England in his thoughts, through all his Continental wanderings. Harry had described himself as a virtual native of the country since his boyhood visit there with his family in 1855: "I must be a born Londoner," Harry reiterated in 1876. And if that wasn't explanation enough, Harry added others: he'd lost his lease on the handsome flat in the rue de Luxembourg; London was cheaper than Paris, as Mary James herself had found out in the 1850s; London furnished better "*fires*" (Harry had been dogged by a sore throat for much of his time in Paris); and, more reassuringly, London wrapped him in quiet, so that Harry could bury himself in his work.

In London that winter, Harry continued with his serialization of *The American*. Back in Boston, William Dean Howells begged Harry to contrive a happy ending for the book. Readers in the United States, especially, hungered to see Christopher Newman succeed in his courtship. But Harry would shock and disappoint his audience in May 1877, when the last installment of the novel hit the *Atlantic*.

In the end, Harry would have Christopher Newman fail, and he would confine Claire de Cintré to a convent. It was an unhappy conclusion that hinted at Harry's increasing unconventionality, and not only because of Newman's homosocial romance with Valentin de Bellegarde. The rupture at the end of *The American* also hinted at Harry's growing and modern skepticism about marriage, a skepticism shared by other cosmopolitan writers, notably Gustave Flaubert. On a more personal level, this outcome also tapped into a strain of self-denial or even masochism in Harry that was surprisingly parallel to William's. The ending reflected a profound conviction, perhaps drawn from Harry's own Paris flirtations, of the near impossibility of hewing viable emotional connections, matrimonial or not.

Harry spent a grimly "detached" Christmas in London in 1876. It drizzled; it sleeted. An "absolutely *glutinous*" fog spread over a city already emptied and darkened by the holiday. Anticipating Christmas dinner in a chophouse (if one were even open), Harry staunched his loneliness by writing a long letter to his "mammy"—as he called her,

folksy and homesick. But Harry would soon accumulate his own comforts in London; as it happened, they were of a distinct and telling kind.

Harry found rooms in Mayfair, an aristocratic quarter of London.
At 3 Bolton Street, just south of princely Curzon Street and just north
of Green Park, he could glimpse leafy treetops from his windows. Around
the corner was Piccadilly, with its monumental gentlemen's clubs and
coroneted carriages picking up and disgorging notables. His "excellent
lodgings in this excellent quarter" included genteel furnishings parallel
to those of his flat in the rue de Luxembourg. But his new rooms were
also clotted with a "dusky" English atmosphere that included a wood-
enly polite though grasping landlady and a dark-featured housemaid
with the resonant voice of a duchess, who stocked his breakfast tray
with tea, eggs, bacon, and "the exquisite English loaf." Harry had set
himself up to enjoy such blue-china comforts, often provided by
women, without the exorbitant entanglements of a Victorian married
household.

Harry intended to live the life of a "bachelor." He had landed bachelor digs and picked a district of London wedged full of unmarried men
of many stripes and conditions. Half Moon Street, two blocks to the
west, would later house the famous Edwardian bachelor Henry Higgins
from George Bernard Shaw's 1913 play *Pygmalion*. A few blocks to the
east, just beyond majestic Burlington House—the home of the bachelor-
sprinkled Royal Academy—lay an even more remarkable and distinctly
British institution called the Albany.

With its grand entrance sheltered by iron gates, the Albany housed a
veritable warren of bachelorhood. A labyrinthine mansion that had once
belonged to the Duke of York and Albany, the building, with its central
location in the West End and its easy access to gentlemen's clubs, had
been converted in 1803 into upper-class bachelors' chambers. The rakish poet George Gordon, Lord Byron—a notorious bachelor if there
ever was one—had stylishly resided in the Albany before his marriage.
So had a host of other celebrated historical dandies, misanthropes, and
confirmed celibates. These included the famously bad Victorian writer
Edward Bulwer-Lytton (who had actually opened a novel in 1830 with
the line "It was a dark and stormy night") and William Gladstone, the
once and future Liberal prime minister of Great Britain. Two decades

after Harry moved in a few streets away, Oscar Wilde would concoct an exquisitely hypercivilized bachelor from the Albany called John Worthing and place him in his brilliantly subversive satire of London metropolitan manners *The Importance of Being Earnest* (1895). Wilde's play indicated the degree to which West End bachelors—rakes, dandies, and aesthetes—would enter popular Victorian mythology.

The term *bachelor*—which described young knights in medieval times—had accrued many meanings by the late nineteenth century, ramifying into a convoluted phenomenon in the Anglo-Saxon world and especially in England. It carried a complex burden of generally unexamined lore. *Bachelor* was one of those words that everybody understood but nobody understood—since, after all, a bachelor might have any number of motivations for staying single. He might be a studious monk, a hopeless philanderer, a devotee of art, a misogynist, an impoverished younger son, or a man who loved men—almost anything—and still pass under this convenient and breezy term. Harry himself understood this range of meanings and, given his own subtle ruses, its expedient ambiguity: to Lizzie Boott in the 1880s, he emphasized the "civilizing part played . . . by the occasional unmarried man of a certain age. He keeps up the tone of humanity—he stands for a thousand agreeable and delightful things. People ought really to be ashamed not to feel better than that what one is doing for it."

For reasons usually unstated, people like Lizzie sometimes felt uncomfortable with bachelors. Same-sex love was considered unthinkable by many, even those aware of how the century's same-sex environments— schools, whaling ships, mining camps, convict barracks, gentlemen's clubs, and so on—could foster such relationships. For those later called homosexuals, "bachelorhood" had a particular use; for the intrepid, it facilitated their movements through London's already considerable if clandestine underground life. In Harry's case, there is no evidence of such bold intentions in 1876, though he had lived all too close to similar hidden coteries in Paris.

Back in Cambridge, Massachusetts, "spinsterhood" could be involuntary and devastating for Alice. But in London, for Harry, "bachelorhood" was a deliberate, empowering choice. "I'm too good a bachelor to spoil," he declared, and to his retinue of women friends he exulted, *"Non mi sposero mai—mai!* ("I'll never get married—never!"). The slightly risqué but time-honored category of bachelorhood allowed Harry to evade marriage (Mary still warned him against designing women) and let him conduct his career and his social life as he pleased.

As an unattached man, Harry would soon find himself in demand by the upper-crust hostesses of Mayfair and Belgravia. Such doyennes would increasingly open their high-ceilinged dining rooms and drawing rooms to him and keep him from having to eat out at chophouses. After all, in an era chronically awash with extra ladies, a bachelor was often an asset since he was readily available, at short notice, to even out the numbers of men and women at a dinner party—a crucial balance that any alert hostess was careful to preserve, especially since men and women processed in pairs into the dining room after the gong and sat down together at the hostess's elaborately laid table. But Harry's attractions included more than a warm male body, suitably scrubbed, tailored, and comme il faut. His growing literary fame from *The American* would also help facilitate his circulation. He traded, too, on the charming and intelligent conversation that he'd learned at his parents' dinner table and honed through years of delightful long letters home.

Now, in such letters, he mentioned lords, counts, marchionesses, and ladies in great numbers. "I dined one day at Lady Rose's," Harry wrote his father and sister, after one orgy of socializing, "a big sumptuous banquet where I sat on one side, next to Lady Cunliffe (Lady Rose is one of the easiest, agreeablest women I have seen in London). Then I dined at a banquet for the Literary fund, invited nominally by Lord Derby." But he coyly entreated his family not to believe the report provided by their Bostonian friend Sara Sedgwick that he went out all the time and to excess. "I lead a very quiet life," he protested. "One must dine somewhere and I sometimes dine in company, that is all." But that was far from all. The ambitious young novelist was using his bachelor's life to forge literary connections and to furnish his work with scenes and characters, just as he had done in Paris.

In the winter and spring of 1877, while he waited for his social engagements to heat up, Harry also turned to another bachelor's resource in London: the city's celebrated gentlemen's clubs. Obliging friends put Harry up for temporary memberships in these institutions, whose grand or sometimes self-consciously unprepossessing facades, usually marked only with discreet brass nameplates, concealed refuges for upper-class men—veritable warrens of leather-upholstered drawing rooms and paneled dining rooms, wreathed in masculine luxury, privacy, and cigar smoke. In his early months in London, Harry patronized, among others, the snug Savile and the diplomatic St. James's, around the corner from him in Piccadilly. He haunted the distinguished Travellers' Club in the regal stretch of Pall Mall; one of the club's prerequisites for its pith-helmeted members was to have voyaged at least five hundred miles from London, in a straight line—a qualification that Harry had met many times over. In such posh, gloomy, wood-smelling rooms, Harry could read a newspaper in a wingback armchair, dine elegantly at trifling expense, or (best of all) rub shoulders with famous personages.

Of all these settings, Harry preferred the Athenaeum, abutting the Travellers' in Pall Mall. The Athenaeum's high-powered members—notables of literature, government, and the Church of England—no doubt struck Harry as greater worthies than the still-formidable subscribers to the Athenœum in Boston, a Brahmin club that by comparison to the English one resembled a glorified reading room. In the spring of 1877, Harry settled in and wrote his family letters on the club stationery, regaling Alice with a description of five o'clock tea in the great drawing room of the club, "all the great chairs and lounges and sofas filled with men having afternoon tea—lolling back with their laps filled with magazines, journals, and fresh Mudie [lending-library] books, while amiable flunkies in knee-breeches present them the divinest salvers of tea and buttered toast!"

Harry insisted he wasn't taunting his envious sister, who received her buttered toast from a dour Irish servant, as the heavy clocks ticked in Quincy Street. He was considerate enough of his siblings to feel guilty when he heard about the continuing misfortunes of his brother Bob, whose grim life in Wisconsin made Harry's London luxuries, he admitted, "seem like a festering sore on the bosom of Justice." Since his school days, Bob had had a taste for art and luxury, though his rough adult life in Wisconsin hardly accommodated his cravings for poetry, painting, and architecture. Harry arranged to send Bob a subscription to the *London Graphic,* an upscale illustrated weekly newspaper founded in

1869. It was a well-intentioned but clumsy gesture that dangled sumptuous engravings of art openings and royal appearances in front of Harry's stranded and luckless brother—phantasms of the richness of Harry's faraway, exotic life.

❧

WILLIAM HAD HAD enough of bachelorhood himself, as he continued to ride the ups and downs of his courtship. More than almost anything else, he longed to marry. And, although he felt little hope by the fall of 1877, he still wanted to win the elusive Alice Gibbens.

For all their complications and disruptions—perhaps because of them—William and Alice had strong feelings for each other. William continued to write Alice agonized letters, and she rewarded him, presumably, with epistolary crumbs; even a note from Alice could kindle William's hopes or else throw him into a frenzy. One letter surviving from the difficult winter of 1878 shows William continuing to anguish about reproduction. Later, he labeled his health doubts as "a good many hypochondriac feelings about whether [he] was a strong enough man to face the responsibility of marriage." But at the time he felt the questions strongly, and his obsessions dogged him in letter after letter.

At times, William wrote deeply disturbed tirades, and Alice seems to have coped by destroying part or all of the relevant letters, occasionally copying out just one paragraph that, for one reason or another, she wanted to preserve. Yet that she kept the letters, or even passages of them, shows her attachment to her troubled suitor—one who repeatedly damaged his own case more than anybody else could. "Was ever woman in such humor wooed?" William wrote, quoting from Shakespeare's *Richard III*.

And indeed theirs had been a peculiar, tortured courtship—tailor-made for a James—markedly different from the rose-framed mythology of popular romance. But their letters bear witness to something even more moving: the authentic encounter of two intelligent and battle-scarred people, manifesting all their grit and intensity.

On May 10, 1878, William persuaded Alice to walk with him under the leafy canopy of Boston Common. Beneath the delicate columned facade and golden dome of the statehouse, the Common spread with its big old trees, ragged lawns, and Frog Pond. In this lovely park, in the flush of the spring, Alice finally gave in. At last she agreed that they could simplify their terms; finally they could make their engagement public. Three days later, the two of them signed their names on a postcard they dispatched to William's friend Oliver Wendell Holmes Jr. The future groom scrawled only a single word: "Engaged!"

William's triumph occurred more than two years after he'd first met Alice; he was now thirty-six and she twenty-nine. They personified a seasoned example of modern "late marriage"—as ripe and mature an engaged couple as even the James family had seen.

Even so, their engagement sent waves of astonishment through William's family. Hearing the news, Mary Tweedy—as formidable and sharp-tongued as when Harry had chaperoned her all over Rome in 1873—flared up in indignation. She scolded her "dear delightful good for nothing nephew" William for dropping such a "bombshell" on the family. Her letter hilariously dramatized the indignant surprise that William's secret stirred up.

> Imagine us all in a state of bewilderment—*who* is she?—*where* is she? *what* is she? Do write & relieve our minds, or we will all be in the lunatic asylum—I drove all over town to find some one that could enlighten us—but in vain—I shant [sic] congratulate you until you let us know all about her, so the sooner you do it, the better, if you wish our blessing.

Other members of the family offered warmer, calmer, and more conventional responses. Wilkie wished his brother "contentment and happiness." Writing from Milwaukee, on the stationery of the North Chicago Rolling Mill Company (a firm with which his bolt business had apparently had dealings), he called the announcement "the greatest piece of news you have ever inflicted on the world and I suppose the greatest event that has ever transpired in the family." Except for the edgy word *inflicted*, Wilkie was ready to lavish his big brother with praise and well wishes.

Henry Senior and Mary exhibited a mixture of Aunt Mary's astonishment and Wilkie's heartfelt satisfaction. "We are delighted beyond our power to express in the good news," Mary wrote "Miss Alice"—promising to drop the "Miss" as soon as possible. "I must confess to have always been proud of him; but I shall now be prouder than ever, since he has been able to secure your affection and bring into our family one whom I know we can so truly honor and love."

William's choice of wife flattered both of his parents. Henry Senior had the triumph of having discovered Alice first. Mary could flatter herself that the young woman looked like a spouse in Mary's own image. After all, William had chosen her, as he told his brother Bob, "for her moral more than her intellectual qualities"—though he underestimated this former schoolteacher's sharp intelligence, which in the coming years would avert more than one family disaster.

Harry's reaction to it all was more nuanced and harder to read. On the surface, his letter flowed with politeness and graciousness. But it contained some buried barbs. Harry sent his "blessings" to the unknown Miss Gibbens, instead of to his brother, "as she will need it most." He jokingly implied that William—as he knew from his own career of spousal forbearance—could fray anyone's patience.

Harry subtly blamed William for not confiding in him: "of Miss Gibbens and your attentions I had heard almost nothing—a slight mention a year ago, in a letter of mother's that had never been repeated." Harry complimented William on the apparent wisdom of his choice but still demanded a photograph of Alice or a sketch of her "from another hand than your's [sic]—father's, mother's and Alice's." It was as if he needed some independent, objective proof of his brother's good judgment. And William understood his brother well enough to read the hurt between his superficially complimentary lines.

Unlike Harry, Alice had actually enjoyed a longer acquaintance with Alice Gibbens than her brothers had. On Alice Gibbens's first appearance, as a friend of William's and not yet as a declared fiancée, Alice James had greeted the newcomer politely and with a show of amiability. On her second, Alice James had conceived a dislike of this replacement Alice—a hostility that evidently surged up in her, against all her attempts to be civil, even before William broke his shattering news. If Bob's wife had seemed like a companion to Alice, William's looked more like a rival, and not only because the two spookily shared the same name. (Now, in his letters, William would have to call his sister "Alice J." or otherwise distinguish her. The family would call William's future wife "Mrs. Alice," "Mrs. William," or "William's Alice," but they never found a single distinction that worked.) For years, William had lived at home with his sister; for years, he was one of the brothers who had treated her with distinction—even if that distinction, in his playful odes and love notes, was often ironic. Now this woman had stolen her name, one of the few things that was hers, and was also taking William from the house.

William hadn't confided at all in his sister, as some Victorian men did during romances. She had been excluded from his thoughts and plans, and she now resented them. When Mary wanted to make a congratulatory visit to the future bride in Boston, Alice reacted viscerally. "I am greatly disappointed in not being able to go in to see you this morning," Mary wrote her future daughter-in-law, "and Alice much more so if that be possible, but she is too unwell to make such an effort herself, and also too unwell for me to be willing to leave her." Over two years, Alice Gibbens had come to know some of William's insecurities, but she was about to come face-to-face with those of the rest of the family.

A LITTLE BRICK row house, sweltering in the summer heat beside the grass-grown graves of Boston Common, hosted a wedding that would prove strangely short on Jameses. On the high-summer day of July 10, 1878—two months after William dropped his "bombshell"—Alice Gibbens slipped into her wedding dress at her grandmother's house across Boylston Street from the Common. Almost certainly, her sisters Mary and Margaret worked together to help her reach "the pink of perfection," in William's phrase, for the ceremony. Unlike the more sensitive William, who felt "heavy lassitude" in the summer, Alice could put up with the heat and was likely to have appeared cool and self-possessed. Maybe Alice wore white, a color made popular by Queen Victoria's wedding in 1840 (and three hundred years before by that of Mary, Queen of Scots). Victorian women frequently chose other colors, avoiding only black (mourning) or red (sexual license). But no description of Alice Gibbens's appearance, her dress, or any of the other decorative arrangements of the wedding has survived—and partly, as will be seen, because of Alice James.

The public period of the engagement had proved short—almost hasty, by the standards of the era. The lovers had originally discussed a fall date, gravitating perhaps toward a mellow season that matched their own sensible maturity. But for reasons he didn't divulge—and as the surprised bride-to-be reported to her Radical Club admirer John Greenleaf Whittier—William suddenly wanted to get married expeditiously and also "very quietly."

The night before the ceremony, William wrote Bob with some last-minute qualms about sex. He'd had to cope with the "unwholesome excitement of an engagement," he wrote—inciting masturbation (that Victorian taboo) or conversely the impotence that Bob had sometimes faced? Whatever his difficulty, William imagined that two months with Alice in the mountains would make him "all right again." The nervous bridegroom had just come back from an invigorating solitary stay in the Adirondacks and hoped his sunburn would make him look "well" for the event, with "a fine red on [his] cheek."

Sober and simple, the nuptials were held on a convenient Wednesday, no doubt reminding Henry Senior and Mary of their own bare-bones wedding, nearly forty years before. In one obvious difference, a clergyman and friend of the families, Rufus Ellis, read the vows—possibly in deference to Alice's family's more conventional religious scruples. Otherwise, plainness seems to have prevailed. The wedding guests numbered few enough to fit without strain into the modest parlor of Alice's grandmother's Boylston Street house.

The couple would strike out on their honeymoon directly after the ceremony. Perhaps they were driven from the door in William's parents' new phaeton, a light four-wheeled carriage drawn by hired horses or else a mare borrowed from their friends the Putnams. The couple then started on their honeymoon by train: they traveled to New York City, then up the Hudson Valley to the Adirondacks to the one place that William actually owned: his weedy time-share at Putnam Camp.

The rough cabin in the rugged Keene Valley lacked plumbing—William had to haul water from the well. But in spite of William's misgivings, the place would prove surprisingly hospitable to what William called "hymeneal felicity" (sexual compatibility, probably) and "romantic and irresponsible isolation." *Isolation*, though, in the sociable and family-webbed nineteenth century, rarely meant privacy; the young couple enjoyed the company of the ubiquitous and irrepressible Miss Kate Hilliard, hitherto a potential impediment, staying at Beede's ramshackle inn next door to them.

Yet the two had achieved even more solitude, paradoxically, at their wedding. Hardly anybody had shown up. Alice's mother and her sisters Margaret and Mary had dressed up for the occasion, as had the proud and joyful Henry Senior and Mary James. But that none of William's siblings attended the wedding tells an even more dramatic story.

It's not surprising that Wilkie and Bob, ailing financially and emotionally, didn't travel from Wisconsin. Wilkie's rash venture in the iron locks business had been doing abysmally, and he'd been forced to declare bankruptcy in 1877. Bob, in spite of his hardy wife and heartening offspring, had now started a downward alcoholic spiral that would result in a serious nervous breakdown by 1881.

Harry's and Alice's absences from the wedding, though, speak volumes.

HARRY DIDN'T APPEAR for at least one simple reason: he hadn't actually been invited. Harry first heard about the July 10 ceremony from his mother. Thanks to the lagging steamship mails, in fact, he received her letter five days after the wedding had taken place. Hurt but solicitous, he immediately wrote to his brother, apologizing that the "abruptness" of the union had prevented his sending Mrs. Alice a wedding present. "As I was divorced from you by an untimely fate on this occasion, let me at least repair the injury by giving you, in the most earnest words that my clumsy pen can shape, a tender bridal benediction." Harry addressed his favorite brother warmly, generously, out of his deep affection. He strove to be as gracious as his family reputation demanded.

The unexpected word *divorce* painfully stuck out in his letter, especially in an era when divorce had become a nettlesome topic—was alarmingly increasing in frequency and painfully obtruding into American consciousness, as exemplified in William Dean Howells's novel of four years later, *A Modern Instance* (1882).

Harry, though, didn't forecast a "divorce" between William and Alice; he lamented one between himself and his brother. The word echoes the witty spousal vocabulary that Harry had adopted with William, especially during their days of living in close quarters. But even at a distance, in their warm and frequent letters, they had often duplicated the dynamic of their parents' marriage, in which Harry patiently listened to William's doings, sympathized, and supported him in his emotional crises, while William, like his father, felt free to criticize. But Harry was not his mother, and his professional achievements had complicated these matters by reversing the old dynamic in which his brother was the confident superior. Now, William's wedding had returned him to prominence in the family and once more sidelined Harry, especially since both the courtship and wedding had gone forward without the younger brother's knowledge or participation.

Even now that they were in their thirties and rarely saw each other, the brothers' relations continued to be intricate and intense, and the occasion of William's wedding would expose raw nerves and hidden jealousies as well as deep and steady affection. In his painstaking analysis of Harry, Leon Edel identified a psychosexual complex, a hidden and troubled "homoeroticism," in the novelist's intense bond with his brother. Such terms have been criticized as too Freudian, but they give useful access to the tensions that underlay this otherwise solid-seeming relationship. After all, theirs was a bond that had often thrived best at a distance; its intensity was such that in recent years only the Atlantic Ocean had helped make this complicated rapport tolerable. But although criticisms, conflicts of taste, and long periods of absence had characterized the men's adult relationship, it had not previously been tested by the threat, on either side, of a love relation that might supersede it.

Having combined suffocating closeness with stark isolation, the Jameses indeed tended toward incest—as deep-dyed natives of the family, "with no other country," as William himself later expressed it to his sister, Alice—figurative and psychological incest, at least. Harry's anguished and tangled feelings toward William on this occasion hint at such unconscious conflicts. But whatever his motivations, Harry genuinely felt wounded and betrayed by his brother's sudden wedding—

though incapable of doing anything, with his Freudian "clumsy pen," except to congratulate his brother.

If William had invited him to the wedding, it is hard to know whether Harry would have crossed the Atlantic to attend. His deep attachment to William might indeed have convinced him to travel. But those same deep feelings—resentment, envy, or jealousy—might equally have tempted Harry to deal William a snub. William himself must have anticipated this. With Harry's bachelor life in London reaching a new pitch by the summer of 1878, William knew his brother was in demand. To be sure, Harry complained to William that he was "painfully silent as to details" about the wedding—and indeed William gave nothing away. But Harry could easily have pretended to have little use for his brother's quotidian nuptials in Boston.

Having lodged in Bolton Street for a year and a half, Harry was beginning to make dramatic social inroads. His father had penetrated Brahmin Boston by joining clubs and working social connections; in a similar campaign, Harry was gaining entry into one of Europe's most snobbish and high-powered societies. About the time that William announced his engagement, Harry—as he reported to his father (and not to William)—actually joined a gentlemen's club of his own. Harry's English friends Frank Hill, Charles Robarts, and Sir Charles Dilke had recently put him up for the Reform Club. The club, in Pall Mall next to the Travellers' Club, and founded in the reform-minded year of 1836, housed progressive liberals, but less dowdy ones than the Boston progressives Harry tended to despise.

Harry loved the Reform Club's embossed letter paper, which he soon dispatched to all and sundry. Harry also enjoyed the "big tranquil library," with its view of the well-kept gardens of Carlton House Terrace, and the cheap lunches (he was his economical Scots-American mother's son). That he'd been elected to the club relatively quickly reassured him, made him feel "strangely and profoundly at home," as Harry told his father. As a Jamesian outsider eager to find a place where he could be recognized and acknowledged, Harry declared that this new membership doubled his personhood (it was his outsider father's phrase).

Yet this crusty English institution, even as it embraced Harry, also singled him out as a foreign "New Yorker." In fact, Harry hadn't lived in the city, except for a six-month stay in 1875, since his childhood in 1855. In the snobby Anglo-Saxon world, the Jameses never quite shook their stigma of being Scots-Irish New Yorkers. But the embrace of mother England—or rather stepmother, as Harry had almost no English ancestry at all, though he would factitiously lay claim to one Saxon grandmother—soothed Harry during the time of his upset over William's marriage.

Harry chased other distractions and consolations. Besides his dinner engagements during the London "season" in the spring and summer of 1878, he had entered a new flush of literary celebrity. His latest brush with fame came in the form of a short story just published in Leslie Stephen's English literary magazine, the *Cornhill*. Harry's short story, which would outstrip even the popularity of *The American*, and which he'd dashed off rather quickly and called a "study"—a preliminary artistic sketch—was titled *Daisy Miller*. In England, it had become, surprisingly and almost instantly, a "great hit." "Everyone is talking about it," Harry observed to William, with some surprise: "it has been much noticed in the papers." In the United States, it would also cause such a public stir, with its provocative portrayal of the "American girl," that two magazines, *Littell's Living Age* and *Home Journal*, would immediately pirate it.

The sudden popularity of this "light" story astonished Harry. He had evidently hit a nerve. *Daisy Miller* both scared and fascinated its Victorian readers with a crucial puzzle: was Daisy Miller, Harry's bold and free-spirited "American girl," an innocent or a flirt? Such questions about female sexual motivation preoccupied Victorian men, and the story played adeptly on the era's paradoxical attitudes toward women. Fears about women's sexual desire had grown all the more urgent with the advent of a more independent, forceful generation—to whom, by the way, the two Alices in America more subtly belonged. (Alice Gibbens had been at least as reluctant to marry, if not as iconoclastic or flirtatious, as Daisy.)

Victorian men, saddled with their own form of the virgin-whore complex, longed for women to embody both virtue and wantonness— though rarely the same woman at the same time. Daisy, who seemed to embody both extremes, inspired both the fears and the prurient interest of Harry's male readers. (Daisy fascinated female readers for other, equally complex reasons: the character was a restless, unconventional critic of the stultifying limits traditional Victorian manners placed on women.) Did Daisy Miller, as some critics argued, really represent the new American "type," the complex and confusing female of the future? Did she represent radical innocence—or, with her nocturnal trysts with an Italian at the Colosseum in Rome, a shameless and immodest young woman, unconstrained by the traditional strictures of society?

Harry had cadged his story idea from a female friend in Rome in 1877, from a piece of gossip that fell in his way. At the same time, Daisy was a more bumptious reworking of Christina Light, Harry's disaffected heiress from *Roderick Hudson*. But even more fundamentally, she was, as his finest heroines would be, a creature of Harry's own deep psychological conflicts about sexuality, his unflagging quandary about "innocence" versus "corruption."

In this sense, Daisy (with her many sources in Harry's life) also drew on Paul Zhukovsky—though few if any of the story's legion of critics have made this connection—a figure who in 1876 had profoundly stirred Harry's own conflicts about sensuality versus purity. Harry had wondered whether his Russian bachelor friend was "pure" or licentious. He'd evidently seen Zhukovsky again in Paris in September 1877, just before he'd traveled to Rome and found his idea for *Daisy Miller*, and the man would continue to inspire a sympathetic but mixed response in Harry that resembled the question he left his readers about Daisy's own inscrutable moral quality.

With *Daisy Miller*'s abrupt fame in England—and notoriety in America, where the story was received with some bitterness, as a blow to the national pride—Harry was astonished that the public had "comprehended" a story he considered "sufficiently subtle." William, though, disliked the tale, finding it "thin." Harry thanked him for his criticisms—William frequently sent his brother frank critiques whether he wanted them or not. "I don't however think you are always right, by any means," Harry objected. For example, he found his brother's objections to the final paragraph of the story "queer and narrow." But this contested last paragraph, significantly, treated not the mysteries of the

elusive Daisy but instead those of her bachelor admirer, Frederick Winterbourne, who, after her death, returns to Geneva, where there are "the
most contradictory accounts of the motives of his sojourn," where he
continues to study hard and to maintain his ambiguous interest in "a
very clever foreign lady."

William evidently perceived Harry's novella in serious moral terms,
"too much as if an artistic experiment were a piece of conduct," Harry
objected, "to which one's own life were somehow committed." Apparently William concentrated his doubts on his brother's fictional
bachelor—thus making Harry feel that his own behavior was being
scrutinized. As Harry no doubt intended, most readers focused on the
blossoming and tragically doomed Daisy Miller, the title character,
rather than on her admirer, the confirmed bachelor Frederick Winterbourne. Like many other mysterious bachelors in late-nineteenth-
century books or drawing rooms, Winterbourne had an alleged but
invisible love interest, the previously mentioned older woman in
Geneva, who supposedly prevented his fascination with Daisy from
turning into an actual romance. Yet this ambiguous character squeaked
by the critics of the time, so entrenched and unquestioned had the status
of bachelors become.

ALICE, LABELED A spinster, confronted a less fascinating and more
burdened life, but because she was the daughter of a privileged household, her unmarried state provided some advantages unavailable to less
fortunate women. In the late 1870s, she relished horseback riding in
Vermont with her aunt, managed a literary luncheon society she'd
founded for her bright women friends, and drove a little phaeton that
her father bought her. This open carriage, which may or may not have
been commandeered for William's wedding, gave Alice a taste of holding the reins—something her mother had enjoyed in London in the
1840s. She clipped down the dusty summer streets of Cambridge. Still,
as an unmarried daughter, Alice largely existed to follow other people's
rules. Mired at home, she felt she played only a "passive part" in her
own life. In what she called the "bare, crude blankness" of Quincy
Street, she found nothing to take her out of herself. And in spite of her

parents' indulgences, in the spring of 1878, Alice dropped from her long-running low-level Tartarus into a pure hell.

More than even her brother Harry's absence, Alice's abstention from William's wedding amounted to a dramatic protest. In April 1878, as William's as-yet-undeclared preference for the new Alice grew clear, Alice reacted. With pains raking through her stomach, Alice took to her bed. She suffered the most terrible collapse she would ever endure, which she later described as "dark waters" of an oceanic magnitude.

Though no one explicitly linked her breakdown to William's engagement, Alice's timing vividly declared her anguish. Devoted to her eldest brother, Alice suffered with her own form of an incestuous convolution, whose pitch matched or even outstripped Harry's. But William hardly qualified as an innocent bystander in her confusion. He'd continued amorously to tease his "sweetheart" and "beautlet" on into the 1870s. He'd habitually if unconsciously vented his many sexual frustrations on his live-in sister. Helped by the typically Victorian conflation of romance and family, he'd even addressed Alice Gibbens in one of his love letters as "My friend, my sister."

Alice, his blood sister, keenly felt William's defection to a woman who was, to add insult to injury, a "peerless specimen of 'New England womanhood'"—as even her ally Harry acknowledged. How could an unwanted, unadmired spinster compete with such a paragon? Alice's fragile self-esteem couldn't stand up to such a formidable "angel." It shamed her to be so spectacularly bettered and supplanted.

Love had transformed William, as he wrote years later in *The Varieties of Religious Experience*, as "sunshine transforms Mount Blanc from a corpselike gray to a rosy enchantment." For Alice, the impossibility of finding love loomed hideously as the reverse fate—turning her roses, such as they were, into corpses. One by one, her women friends had abandoned her by means of engagements and marriages. Now her brother, her perennial housemate-in-misery at Quincy Street, was likewise deserting her. Through her breakdown and its armory of symptoms, she could at least secure her parents' love and nurture, as they became wholly absorbed in her malady.

More sympathetic to his sister, Harry wrote from England that it seemed "inconsiderate of William to have selected such a moment for making merry." Yet William hardly flaunted his happiness; no doubt Alice's illness had suggested to William one of his reasons for marrying "very quietly." His sister's condition evidently hovered like a cloud over the wedding—preventing anyone from cheerfully recounting, as Henry wanted them to, its details of flowers or wedding clothes. For a neglected child and a self-confessed "failure," Alice had indeed stolen the show.

But for Alice, the "hideous summer of '78" meant far more than a ploy for attention. As she described the experience years later, "[I] went down to the deep sea, its dark waters closed over me and I knew neither hope nor peace." Her "patience, courage & self control" all abandoned her in a flash. She writhed in a "moral prostration" that, as the daughter of an ethicist, she found hideously shameful. She described her ordeal not as an assaulting demon—her father's metaphor for his 1844 breakdown—but rather as a recurrent deadening and withering of her essential being. Her soul, as she described it years later, shriveled down to an "empty pea pod." Her metaphor summons the physical and emotional barrenness that Alice must have felt when surrounded by warm, fruitful, and child-rich Victorian marriages, especially William's.

In August 1878, as Alice herself was so painfully aware, she would turn thirty. Her long succession of difficulties had begun much earlier, of course—as long ago as her self-torturing walks in Newport as a teenager. And she dreaded that her "attacks"—which manifested physically, wrenching her stomach in spasms or paralyzing her legs—would stalk her for the rest of her life.

In the depths of her misery, Alice spoke seriously with her father, perhaps finding him in his study, poring over his volumes of Swedenborg. She had an agonizing question to discuss with him, and the old man put his engrossing private thoughts aside to listen to her. Alice pleaded with her father, who'd been her constant nurse and confessor, for moral permission to commit suicide. (Alice never had such intense conversations with Mary.) Henry, who cried easily, who hated to witness pain, must have been deeply moved by his daughter's misery—as intense and hopeless as his own had often been. At least, in her suffering, he could perhaps understand her a little. With his odd and inconsistent broad-mindedness—he had no philosophical objections to suicide—Henry gave her his permission. But Alice had inherited her father's toughness as well as his susceptibility to pain, and she clung on.

❧

IN THE AUTUMN of 1878, when Mrs. Alice returned to Cambridge pregnant, she and William rented rooms on Harvard Street, around the corner from the parental house. Besides his Harvard teaching, William had contracted in June 1878 to write a college textbook on the emerging field of psychology for Henry Holt, a prominent New York publisher who'd planned a series of books on American science.

With his chronic eye problems, and with the turmoil of his recent courtship and marriage, William wrote Holt that he doubted he could finish the book before the fall of 1880. Holt replied that he was "a little staggered by the length of time which you think it will take to write the Psychology, and hope that your health will improve and your engagements admit of modifications so that the work can be done sooner." Still, Holt, a shrewd editor about William's age, chose not to replace William, even though the ambitious author, with his new domestic responsibilities, wouldn't in fact deliver his book—his answer to Harry's success with *Daisy Miller*—until eleven years later, in 1889. Even though he was married and finding his feet in the new discipline of psychology, William remained a tortured late bloomer. He still had more in common with his sister and her agonies than Alice probably thought.

Through the summer and fall of 1878, Alice's malady alternately worsened and brightened with the unpredictability of the Massachusetts weather—to judge, at least, from the fluctuating reports that reached Harry in England. Surprisingly, Alice coped with her sister-in-law's proximity in Cambridge well enough, once the couple returned from their honeymoon. But then Alice's illness didn't obviously react to specific events; her "hysteria" worked darkly and obscurely, even to herself.

Ironically, one of Alice's first letters written after her recovery in November contained a panegyric to Mrs. Alice, whom Alice claimed she had the "great joy" of getting to know better. "She is a truly lovely being so sweet and gentle & then with so much intelligence besides," Alice wrote. Yet it was just this cheerful marriage and this deserving bride that had plunged Alice into her self-blaming misery. She sheepishly lamented giving her "poor family an immense amount of trouble" and hoped she was "learning to behave [her]self better & better all the time"—a recipe, really, for more stomach cramps.

A better sign of Alice's recovery—a strong and growing factor in Alice's creeping convalescence—was a friend who mounted the Jameses' Quincy Street porch at least as often as Mrs. Alice did. Alice's colleague from her brief teaching career, Katharine Peabody Loring, called often to check on Alice. An intellectual, traveled, and pragmatic resident of Boston's North Shore, Katharine had weak eyes but "strength of wind and limb," which Alice lacked. So Alice reported to Harry in the spring of 1878, even before her breakdown, at which point she enthusiastically told her brother "all about" her new best friend. As always, Harry requested a corroborating photograph. If he got one, he saw an image of an ugly but kindly-looking New Woman—the sort of unapologetic feminist or suffragist who might wear a tie in the late nineteenth century—a light-eyed, gaunt-faced, stern-mouthed Bostonian, with biggish ears and hair drawn sharply back. In the coming years, this distinctive no-nonsense countenance would grow familiar to Harry and in fact to all the family.

Throughout Alice's long, hard recovery and after it, Katharine's firm, fearless friendship grew ever more indispensable. Katharine had an iron constitution as well as in-the-trenches experience coping with invalids, having long looked after her chronically "nervous" younger sister, Louisa—a fainting, "hysterical" creature who'd seemingly inherited none of Katharine's muscle or pluck. Katharine had her capable hands full at home. Even so, she was a burden bearer and gradually took over her friend's recovery from Alice's worried but worn-down parents.

The friendship, as it developed, also abounded in pleasures. In the summer of 1879, the two women even sampled what Alice called William's "panacea for all earthly ills" in the Adirondacks. There, Katharine plunged fearlessly into the cold and stony brooks, though Alice preferred to reserve her bathing for a more civilized tub. In William's shanty—Alice quipped wittily that it lacked "nothing in the way of discomfort"—Katharine calmly hovered over her charge. Much to Alice's amusement, she tucked a rubber blanket (scoutlike, Katharine came prepared) between the ironical invalid and her buggy, moss-caked bed frame.

Wilderness "roughing it," it seems, didn't work its wonders only for men. Alice detested the Keene Valley (the "air" once again didn't agree with her), but Katharine thrived. Alice thought her friend possessed "all the mere brute superiority which distinguishes man from woman combined with all the distinctively feminine virtues. There is nothing she cannot do from hewing wood & drawing water to driving run-away horses & educating all the women in North America." In short, Alice admired Katharine as a "most wonderful being" and a "most sustaining optimist." The other Jameses were relieved to see the improvement in Alice's health and spirits after the convulsive summer of 1878.

The other Alice, William's wife, enjoyed her own rewards. On May 18, 1879—a year after her acceptance of William on Boston Common— she gave birth to a son. The ecstatic couple regally and dynastically christened the baby Henry III, much to the deep if delayed satisfaction of both Henry Senior and Mary, who with their quiet, stay-at-home life were all too ready to welcome grandchildren who lived nearby, especially an eldest son from their eldest son.

Though her relations with her sister-in-law improved, Mrs. Alice may not have immediately forgiven her for marring her engagement and wedding. It is unclear if her perception of Alice James was more objective, or more resentful, than the rest of the family's. But Mrs. Alice strongly suspected and confided in her husband what no other James, used to secrets as they all were, dared conjecture: that Alice and Katharine were lovers.

· 12 ·

ABANDONMENT

The success of *Daisy Miller* in 1878 had emboldened Harry to begin an ambitious new novel. "I must try and seek a larger success than I have yet obtained," he informed William Dean Howells in July 1879. He would most likely call it *The Portrait of a Lady*, as he told Howells and his English publisher, Sir Frederick Macmillan. He hoped the new book would be an antidote to recent works (*The Europeans*, 1878; *Confidence*, 1879; and *A Bundle of Letters*, 1879), whose sales had been "not brilliant." Harry's sales mattered to him as a point of personal pride but also because, now, he lived on literature, without loans or supplements from home. His impressive, unrelenting production barely kept him afloat, even though his Bolton Street household was hardly lavish. Yet Harry cared still more for fame, for the kind of recognition his father and William also craved, and which they gave only sparingly to Harry himself.

"Look out for my next big novel; it will immortalize me," Harry exulted to his new friend, the Boston hostess and art collector Isabella Stewart Gardner, who, like Harry, liked to think big. But he made this claim to "Mrs. Jack" in a moment of bravado; mostly he worked slowly and painfully, fretting about the success of his manuscripts. His royalties sustained the vital independence that protected him from family intrusion; he had "always to keep the pot a-boiling."

But even when he was short on cash and longing for a more substantial version of his triumph with *Daisy Miller*, Harry found that his literary ambitions sometimes clashed with his social ones. In late June 1879, he left his writing desk to accept an invitation to spend a weekend at Twickenham, on the sweeps of the Thames just west of London, with Frances, Lady Waldegrave.

That Saturday, Harry got a lift from London in the fashionable gig of his friend Sir Charles Wentworth Dilke, a young baronet with a passion for politics and—to judge from a later scandal—a weakness for women. Dilke relished procuring glamorous invitations for his American friend, and this weekend ranked highly—though, with Harry's more conspicuous literary successes, he was increasingly easy to present in society. Many hostesses were curious to meet the charming author of *The American* and *Daisy Miller*, the subtle psychological novelist who could depict both sides of the Atlantic so vividly, and who could draw such fascinating portraits of women.

In the long-lasting daylight of late June, the two men drove up to an extraordinary villa—more of a palace really, bristling with turrets, towers, and peaked stained-glass windows, surrounded by lush lawns and well-tended gardens. This was the legendary Strawberry Hill, an early neo-Gothic masterpiece built in the mid-eighteenth century by the novelist and architectural enthusiast Horace Walpole, son of Prime Minister Robert Walpole, who would end his life as the Earl of Oxford. The Waldegrave family had since inherited the property, and the handsome and ambitious Lady Waldegrave, now fifty-eight years old and married for the fourth time, had grandly extended the house in the 1850s and had since that time transformed Strawberry Hill, with its fifty-eight rooms and forest of chimneys, into an eminent Liberal political salon.

The two young men arrived, as planned, for dinner with more than twenty members of the British peerage who were also staying at the house. Frances, Lady Waldegrave had begun her life as the daughter of John Braham, a famous Jewish early Victorian tenor. An outsider like Harry, she had become not only an insider but also a powerful social force. She entertained lavishly, and her guest list was especially impressive for a hostess during the frenetic last weeks of the London "season," that upper-class social calendar that ran from the first session of Parliament after Christmas till midsummer.

Harry had previously witnessed the New York social season: the winter dinners and balls at Delmonico's; the summer evacuation, during the hot months of July and August, to Saratoga Springs and Newport. The imperial British version, however, was altogether more elaborate: by the late 1870s, when Harry first dipped into it, the season was thoroughly awash with balls, charity events, gallery openings, receptions, and dinners thrown by prominent people—much of this activity designed as a marriage market for the gentry and the nobility, beginning with the ceremonial "presentation" of silk-gowned teenage debutantes at the royal court. Elegant gatherings both inside and outside of London had come to mark these six months of frenetic social exchange: sporting events like Ascot and the Boat Race between Oxford and Cambridge, horticultural ones like the Chelsea Flower Show, and artistic ones like the Royal Academy Summer Exhibition. Besides, there were endless offerings of theater, opera, and dance, at which private boxes would be teeming with ostrich feathers, tiaras, and opera glasses. Still, much of the season was still centered on London and the aristocratic mansions of Mayfair, Belgravia, and Kensington. Lady Waldegrave's grand villa at Twickenham was only one variation on a theme, and it competed with a peacock's tail of other offerings.

Thirty-six-year-old Harry arrived at Strawberry Hill stocked with his own social conquests. He had dined in town with David Graham Drummond Ogilvy, Lord Airlie, a seasoned Scottish peer who was also a political force. By mistake, the splendidly-turned-out novelist had "marched up" through the tall portico and into the grand drawing room of the neighboring mansion. He'd suddenly found himself at the party of another Scottish earl, John Hamilton Dalrymple, Lord Stair; "a rather awkward thing," he wrote his mother, "with a room full of 'smart' guests and a hall-full of flunkies witnessing each other's discomfiture." According to tallies he'd kept during the winter and spring of 1878–79 for Grace Norton, he'd dined out at least 107 times. That was "folly," he admitted, somewhat complacently. But he'd plunged into this strong current and so far succeeded swimmingly. He had an appetite for social distinction reminiscent of his father's in earlier decades, but Henry Senior had preferred intellectuals. Harry gravitated toward nabobs.

Holding himself high, Harry entered the Waldegrave dining room—a magnificent Gothic hall that her ladyship had designed. Here Harry mixed with the noble and royal *crème:* the crown prince of Sweden, the twenty-one-year-old Oscar Gustav Adolf; the Duchess of Manchester, a celebrated German-born beauty. With the duchess was the Marquess of Hartington, later the Eighth Duke of Devonshire, her noble admirer, who, though he had a wife and children, brazenly traveled with this married woman from one house party to another. Other notables surrounded Lady Waldegrave's vast dinner table, with its settings of sterling silver and expensive china, so that Harry had little enough opportunity to entertain his hostess. He didn't find her to be the "witty or clever person" he'd expected, but she was "kind, honest and genial."

For grandes dames, in any case, Harry preferred his other intimates in London, several fascinating and peppery old ladies: Fanny Kemble, the grand feminist actor who had become a steady friend since Rome; Anne Benson Procter, who had befriended Shelley, Keats, Byron, Coleridge, and Wordsworth and could tell gossipy stories about these now-deceased Romantic poets; and Mrs. Duncan Stewart, an alert, hard-edged, sometimes shocking old lady cut from a similar cloth. For his own reasons, Harry was devoted to such formidable dowagers— women as strong-willed as his mother but more worldly in their accomplishments—and not only because he could and did translate them into compelling fiction.

The next morning at Strawberry Hill, walking into the breakfast room, Harry met another beautiful old lady, sitting alone. She was absorbed in "doing sums on the table cloth." Sitting down beside her with his coffee, he engaged her in a long conversation; this was Maria, Marchioness of Ailesbury (called "Maria Marchioness" or just "Lady A." by her highborn friends), a famous beauty of the early Victorian age whom Harry thought "looked exactly the same forty years ago as she does today." But in spite of such fascinating and legendary company, Harry was so much in demand that he had to hurry to another social engagement that Sunday evening. He simply couldn't stay the rest of the weekend.

A few days later, scanning his morning newspaper, Harry received a shock. To the distress of fashionable London, Frances, Lady Waldegrave had suddenly died of a heart attack. Harry was stunned that such a robust woman could "drop out of existence so suddenly," he wrote Mary.

The unexpected loss perhaps brought back another from long before. Harry told Howells that he wanted to create "the portrait of the character and recital of the adventures of a woman—a great swell, psychologically; a *grande nature*—accompanied with many 'developments.'" So far he had written only one "aching fragment" of his new novel, inspired by the figure who had succeeded like an artist at creating herself. For a decade now, his memories had matured inside him, and now his beloved cousin was ready to emerge in fictional form. He was getting ready to give Minny the introduction to the splendors of Europe that she had never had in real life. He longed to revive her in the guise of an heiress—open, engaging, and receptive—whom he would name Isabel Archer.

HER ARRIVAL WAS difficult, again and again delayed. For another year, Harry made little progress on his novel for Minny. Other projects and aristocratic engagements intervened, and in June 1880, he was interrupted by a new family crisis. Out of the blue, William arrived in Bolton Street and took up residence in a flat downstairs from his brother—a married runaway on an extended trip to consult academic colleagues.

Harry was happy to see William again and evidently didn't speculate much about his brother's motives. Once again, it was the thick of the London season, and he had other preoccupations. Crowded drawing rooms in Belgravia and Knightsbridge were bursting with floral arrangements, champagne, and décolleté ladies. Among other stiff cards embossed with crests and titles, Harry propped on his mantelpiece an invitation to the Mayfair mansion of the staggeringly wealthy William Cavendish, Seventh Duke of Devonshire, owner of the resplendent eighteenth-century Devonshire House, which towered over Piccadilly with its magnificent wrought-iron gates and forecourt but which reserved its ducal garden, a trim green metropolitan oasis, for invited guests.

William was unimpressed by Harry's aristocratic conquests, even if he grudgingly admired or secretly envied his brother's riding masterfully "bestride the [B]ritish lion." He declined the opportunity to attend the Duke of Devonshire's reception. Like his father, William preferred thinkers, and he was traveling to consult medical men and philosophers—especially those involved in William's new passion, psychology. Harry's enthusiasm for "paying visits and going to dinners and parties" struck his brother as frivolous, given Harry's self-declared need to work on *The Portrait of a Lady*, slated to start its serial run simultaneously in the *Atlantic* and in the British magazine *Macmillan's* in the coming autumn.

William, now thirty-eight, brought plenty of suggestions for his brother. He scrutinized London through pale blue eyes sometimes described as gray—all the more piercing thanks to his distinguished iron-grizzled beard. He promised his brother "much interesting talk," even if Harry noted that he tended to "descant on his observations"—to talk his patient brother into the ground. Their bond had now been curiously renewed, even though both of them went to great lengths to live their separate lives.

Hungrily, restlessly, William was "knocking about London." He puzzled over the paintings of Turner at the National Gallery, wandered through Westminster Abbey, and flirted at dinner with the mesmerizing Polish-born actress Helena Modjeska (who'd recently gone ranching in southern California). He had plans to work his way up to the sunny vineyards of the Rhine and then ramble over the cool and craggy Alps. He didn't have much money—though a few months before he'd received a largish legacy from Alice Sturgis Hooper, a wealthy Boston friend—so that Harry, ever chivalrous and tenderhearted, would eventually pick up many of the bills for William's hansom cabs, chophouses, and even his lodgings.

Though none of the Jameses apparently batted an eye, William had left his wife and child behind in Cambridge. He had hoisted himself aboard the liner *Brittanic* in New York Harbor on June 5. He'd jostled in among a troupe of famous American actors, including the Irish-born Shakespearean performer John Edward McCullough, overdressed and "swellish looking people," whose bon-voyage floral tributes—arranged in the shapes of horseshoes and steamships—overflowed from the staterooms on board. William also shared his luxurious ship with a slew of nattily dressed Astors, Vanderbilts, and Le Roys.

The actors and the tycoons got a regal send-off, but in William's case, only the sturdy Aunt Kate, now approaching seventy and mostly living near her relatives in New York City, saw him off. As she kissed him good-bye, she offered her favorite nephew five hundred dollars, perhaps regarding him as chronically poor as well as chronically ill. William declined, but his aunt pressed him with a ten-dollar bill to cover his immediate expenses; ever scrupulous, he promptly reimbursed Mrs. Walsh (who like her sister kept sharp accounts) by mail.

Once on board, William bunked with a "buyer," a traveling businessman—a specter of the itinerant life William had now chosen. Supping alone on the rolling ship, William got a twinge of guilt. He pictured his wife wandering their lodgings on Arrow Street in Cambridge. William imagined her explaining to his tiny, dark-haired son, again and again, "Papa gone!"

He had arrived in London just in time to spend his second wedding anniversary alone in a dusky West End flat. He celebrated the occasion by writing to Alice to reassure her—appropriately, under the circumstances—that he didn't "repent" their wedding. With an all-too-male forgetfulness, William couldn't quite remember if July 10 actually marked "the date of that strange performance in Boylston Street." (Likewise, he couldn't picture the dress Alice had worn at their wedding.)

"I want to tell you how solemnly I feel about my duties to you & the young one," William wrote, referring to his son Henry III, who had now just turned one. To complicate the already tangled names of the Jameses, the child had been nicknamed "Harry." Little Harry shared his uncle's name. But it was a more convoluted matter that his father was sharing his uncle's bachelor life, more than three thousand steamer miles away—as if ready now, after the subterranean complications introduced by his marriage, to resume the old bond between them.

❧

LIKE HARRY, WILLIAM was supposed to be writing a book; he had his sprawling survey of psychology to finish, and it had engrossed him more thoroughly than he had expected. Psychology, a dynamic and emerging discipline in 1880, fascinated William with its promise of healing and of discovering deeper significance, and he was pursuing it as seriously as his father had done with theology and morality.

Yet, without a motive he could easily name, William had set into motion what he himself recognized as this "queerest repetition of [his] old bachelor outward circumstances." Having plotted this voyage for months, he had at first even contemplated spending a whole year in Europe but had ultimately found such a span "unfeasible," he'd told a friend. The expense was unfeasible, but he blithely didn't take into account the potential emotional cost. William had only recently established a domestic household for himself, but now he could leave it for long foreign sojourns.

Though he was too old to be footloose, William could catalog time-worn Jamesish reasons for his voyage to Europe. For his big book project, he wanted to consult with fellow scientists, many of them Germans, to "make psychological feathers fly"—and Germany, certainly, was a hotbed of the new science of the mind in which William was immersing himself. As usual, he also needed to shore up his sagging health in cure resorts: his variola-affected eyes still plagued him, so that he could scarcely read, especially after dark—putting him at a disadvantage in a profession that demanded meticulous midnight oil, hours spent poring over Teutonic scientific journals. And he craved a detoxification from yet another long year of teaching—a strain and a will-to-vacation that anyone who has taught can well understand. William's reasons, as far as they went, rang true.

But William didn't and probably couldn't tell the whole story. "My wife," he reported to the same friend, "will stay at home." William probably gave Mrs. Alice more of an explanation, but evidence from his letters suggests that he mostly sheltered complicated feelings behind the privileges, apparent in the flatness of this statement, to which married middle-class Victorian men felt entitled. In their husbands' professional lives, wives were second-class citizens; male vocations inevitably came first. But the arrangement, even if it was sometimes customary, also helped William ignore or conceal some of the bumpy complications in his family life.

William had initially found his marriage "an easy & natural state." After two years, he still claimed his Alice as "an enduring haven of refuge from the rocks of life"—even though he penned this particular tribute from an Atlantic steamship that was carrying him away from his wife at fifteen knots.

Yet the birth of William's son in 1879 had filled him with both joy and dread. William's sobriquets for the new arrival, indeed, betrayed both his love and uneasiness. He immediately adored "the little animal"—an endearing but curiously zoological phrase. He also called the baby, jokingly, his "domestic catastrophe." Already, in past years, William had proved himself an aggressively witty son and brother— insulting his father, teasing Alice. Now a father himself, he overflowed with ironic nicknames. Most curious was "Embry" (a derivative of *embryo*?); likewise "Kulturmensch" (civilized man)—a reference to a child who was promisingly "strong, intelligent, and rosy"? William's sense of humor helped him cope with this new dynamic, but fatherhood also involved repeated surprises and setbacks.

At other times, William reveled in his growing offspring. When his "bratling" reached six months old, William laughed as he watched little Harry rolling about with his feet in his mouth, delighting in "the fatness of his own body in the most unscrupulous way, as if he thorough[ly] relished the joke of coming into possession of such an advantageous bit of organic machinery gratis." Six months later, William affectionately dubbed the newly ambulant infant a "baby hobgoblin," quite "bewitching" as he toddled around the room.

Influenced, perhaps, by his own father's unconventional domestic presence, William prized home life enough to contemplate using most of his five-thousand-dollar legacy to build his family a house—right next to the big old family house on his father's Quincy Street lot. Describing his plans to Harry in London, William drew a diagram and "speciously," Harry thought, explained how he could do without a parlor. This "non-parlor" struck the more conventional Harry as one of the fatal flaws in William's plans: "It would be as awkward for him *in the long run* not to have a regular parlour as it would be for him not to own a dress-coat or a high hat." William's parlorless blueprints, in fact, would never translate into timber. Still, "concocting the design" for his new house kept William excitedly awake at nights; he discovered his inner architect as well as, to a lesser extent, his inner paterfamilias.

William, though, had found the "cares of a nursing father to be very different from those of a bachelor." They were especially so because, early on, little Harry suffered epic Jamesian stomach troubles. These intestinal squalls strained his mother and agitated his father, deepening William's perpetual guilt about the genes he'd passed on. "Farewell to the tranquil mind!" William wrote his brother Bob, now an equally nervous father of two. "It is replaced by terrible solicitudes about the colour of diapers, the meaning of all that 'galluping,' wonderings whether the darling is not either too hot or cold, anxiety about the mother overexerting herself and a thousand more perplexities."

In this latest resurrection of his seemingly inexhaustible neurosis, William wasn't writing his magnum opus, although he had managed to dash off reviews of scientific books (in the spring of 1880, Malcolm Guthrie's *On Mr. Spencer's Formula of Evolution* and Johnston Estep Walter's *The Perception of Space and Matter*). He kept up a brisk correspondence with many notable psychological thinkers of his time, including the British philosophers Herbert Spencer and Shadworth Holloway Hodgson. But to finish a more substantial piece of work seemed impossible. William felt sucked into "fussing about nurses, starting housekeeping, looking up country quarters and then looking up others because they seem to disagree with the baby." He threw up his hands, stashed his young family in Cambridge, and, even before his departure for Europe, bolted off to Maine or other places on his own. Consciously or unconsciously, he imitated his own father's junkets away from the family during their European residence in the 1850s; Henry Senior, too, had been compelled to tear himself away from his family, even when he had already uprooted them on a similar impulse. As for William, his departures seemed both to sadden Alice and to relieve her; at least it took one extra baby, a large bearded one, off her hands.

Yet Mrs. Alice didn't just passively accept William's erratic absences, as many Victorian wives had to do. Rather, she seems prudently to have collaborated in William's departures. True to Henry Senior's early impression of her, Alice was as practical as Mary James had been. But in the particular of travel, Alice pursued a different strategy. Back in the

1840s and 1850s, eager to see the world herself, Mary had boldly faced the turmoil of steamships and hotels, with her small children in tow. She had remained glued to her husband's side whenever she could. Out of the same loyalty, incidentally, Mary had not now traveled abroad in years, apparently with equal contentment. At home on Quincy Street, she stuck to Henry Senior like the helpmate she'd always wanted to be, nursing him through his continuing moody ups and downs with almost superhuman stamina.

In contrast, Alice Gibbens James—ever William's "Guide," as he addressed her in his letters with their exotic postmarks—sacrificed some of her husband's company in order to provide a safety valve for him and stability for herself and her child. She was all too familiar with William's continuing depression and restiveness. These were the reasons she'd worried about accepting him in the first place. In her own family history, she'd tasted nomadic family life in Germany during her adolescence and intimately knew its bleak and hired inconveniences. From the same challenging experience, Alice had learned to value an all-female household made up of her mother and two sisters—which, in William's absences, she replicated. Sometimes she summoned her sisters to stay with her (as Mary had done with Kate) on Arrow Street in Cambridge. Sometimes she went away to stay with her mother in Boston or in Petersham, Massachusetts.

The return to a well-worn pattern might have comforted Alice. But at the same time, William's absences may well have resonated with the loneliness and loss that had followed the suicide of Alice's father when she was a teenager. Alice's letters from this period have not survived, but even William understood how her "noble trustful helpful heart . . . had to bear a heavy burden." But self-sacrificing nineteenth-century wives were supposed to bear burdens without complaint, and, in true Victorian fashion, Alice had in fact married her missing father, and William his martyr mother; they drew their modus vivendi, anyway, from their unstable pasts.

William traveled, as Henry Senior had, to avoid the humdrum depression of everyday life as well as the stresses, for him, of intimacy and family. But to avoid was not to escape; before striking off on his Continental tour, William rediscovered some of his own past sufferings.

London poignantly brought to mind, he reported to Henry and Mary, the adventures of his young father and mother in the winter of 1843–44, "coming to live there as a blushing bridal pair, with most of [their] chil[dren] still unborn, and all [Henry Senior's] works unwritten." He felt "a new kind of sympathy, especially for the beautiful, sylphlike and inexperienced mother." No doubt William thought of his own Alice, in her current role as a young mother. And he contrasted Harry's fashionable life in Mayfair to the "monotony" of St. John's Wood, in order to feel how much his parents, during his own childhood in the 1850s, had given up such glamour for their children. From a new and sympathetic perspective, he could now vividly picture the fresh-faced Henry and rose-cheeked Mary standing up against "the great roaring foreign tide," worrying about how best to nurture their small offspring and prepare them for a changing world.

"Better late than never!" William noted, with a new appreciation for his parents. In his letter home, he expressed what seemed a heartfelt wish that, in spite of all his "afflictions" and impracticality, he could have been a better son. He longed, now that his father had grown fragile and faltering, to be "more of a comfort to [his parents] in [their] old age than [he had] been in late years."

During his Continental escape, William would encounter other moments of emotional revelation. Later that summer, in the shadow of the Rhône glacier in the Alps, he wrestled with the sadness and guilt of his absence from home. He lay awake all night at his inn, raging at himself for his "unmanliness" in having left his family on a compulsion that perhaps he himself only partly understood. He'd cried only three times during his marriage, but now he broke down once again, "rolling down hill" in his grief. He contrasted the pristine Switzerland, with its clean water and its mountains—strong and good and "*honest*"—with what he saw as his own more selfish and tarnished life.

Yet neither of these epiphanies resulted in an early steamship home.

∽

HARRY REMAINED IN London, playing the part of the exquisitely tailored Mayfair bachelor. For props he had his canes and hats, his fashionable beard and his retreating hairline, and his swelling literary reputation. But his prosperous and increasingly plump appearance, in his later thirties, concealed equally agonizing conflicts, the "terrible algebra," as he put it to his friend Grace Norton, of living and loving. The very month that William came to board downstairs at Bolton Street, Harry had just returned to London from a visit to Italy, and from one of the most bizarre and formative episodes of his life.

In early April 1880, Harry had traveled to a rocky peninsula in the Bay of Naples, about an hour's carriage ride west of the run-down, over-crowded port of the same name. From Naples, Harry had ventured along the rough northern coast of the azure bay to Posillipo, with the accent on the second syllable—a picturesque village on an outcrop of yellow tufa cliffs. There he found small fishing boats beached picturesquely on the stones and sprawling golden villas sheltering among the umbrella pines. In ancient times, this golden headland was dominated by the sumptuous imperial Roman villa of Pausilypon—Greek for *sans souci*, or "without care." From his equipage, Harry would have glimpsed the ruins of this villa's theater, odeon, and baths nudging up among the lemon groves and gardens.

Paul Zhukovsky met his carriage. The Russian, who had long known the neighborhood, could have told him that near to Posillipo there lurked a nymphaeum—a cave dedicated to a female fertility spirit. This was just one of the exotic sea grottoes that dotted the area. These subterranean haunts (such as the famous eerily lit Grotta Azzurra, or "Blue Grotto," of nearby Capri) were favored by the painterly, swooning, and romantic tourists who wandered through Posillipo in the springtime. In 1880, the crown of Posillipo was the magnificent Villa Angri, with its unparalleled view of the bay, and the jewel in that crown was its current tenant, the German composer Richard Wagner.

The charismatic, square-jawed Wagner, with his side-whiskers and beret, was now sixty-six and had reached a pinnacle, having premiered his staggering *Ring* cycle at Bayreuth just four years before, thanks to the lavish patronage of Ludwig II, the king of Bavaria. In Posillipo he was touching up what would be his last opera, *Parsifal*, seeking visions for the staging of this Arthurian epic among the antiquities of Italy. His entourage included his formidable beaked wife, Cosima, as well as the couple's ten-year-old son, Siegfried.

Young Siegfried's tutor also traveled and lodged with the Wagners; he was a handsome young Thuringian poet and nobleman named Heinrich von Stein, who, "slender and blond," looked to Wagner "like a German youth out of Schiller." Another young protégé, the twenty-six-year-old mustachioed opera composer Engelbert Humperdinck, had also recently paid a call. Wagner often mesmerized his young acolytes, as his friend the black-eyed, mustached Friedrich Nietzsche later complained: "Ah, this old robber! He robs our youths, he even robs our women and drags them into his den."

Among the young men devoted to Wagner was Paul Zhukovsky, who was staying a picturesque twenty-minute walk away from the Villa Angri. Paul had invited Harry to spend four or five days with him at this villa. Harry told his father the visit was "long-promised." One surviving letter from Paul Zhukovsky, from September 1879, contains a warm invitation to visit. Paul had advertised *"bonne cuisine, excellent vin, vue paradisique, air excellent"* (good food, excellent wine, paradisical view, excellent air). But in this warm letter—one of two extant in the James papers—the young Russian, himself discontent and at loose ends, also warmly offered his hand and his heart to Harry; he said his friend was *"présent"* (present) in his thoughts every day, and as dear as before. Perhaps this kind of pressing warmth, although phrased in the respectful *vous* form, bothered Harry to the extent that he explained to his father that he had put off a visit to a connection that he increasingly regarded (and the single word spoke volumes) as "peculiar."

Paul also lured Harry to Posillipo with the bait of Wagner, whom he himself had just met. The Russian painter, now in his midthirties, was delighted to be able to claim his artistic hero as an actual friend. He had left Paris and was feeling lost and purposeless, but he had quickly insinuated himself in Wagner's inner circle; he was now designing sets for *Parsifal* as well as visiting picturesque local beauty spots like Amalfi and Ravello with the master and his hangers-on.

But from the moment of his arrival, Harry perversely backed away from meeting the celebrity he sarcastically dubbed "the musician of the future." He did everything he could to avoid an introduction at the Villa Angri. Like the rest of the Jameses, Harry had little ear for music—and certainly little fascination for this new style of opera that his era regarded as brash, risqué, and avant-garde. Also, Harry spoke no "intelligible" German, and Wagner spoke nothing else.

Harry's intransigence evidently proved a bone of contention between the two friends. Because the novelist appreciated famous and seasoned women, Paul tried to entice his friend by enumerating the charms of Cosima Wagner. Cosima, he reminded Harry, was the love child of two famous artists of a previous generation. Her father was the Hungarian pianist Franz Liszt (once a long-haired composer of rhapsodies, now in 1880 a tonsured Franciscan monk and music teacher). Cosima's mother was Lizst's onetime mistress, Countess Marie d'Agoult, a firebrand free-thinking feminist who'd written sympathetic accounts of the 1848 revolution under the male pseudonym of Daniel Stern.

Still, Harry dug in his heels and refused to meet the Wagners. The kind of celebrities who had interested Harry in Paris now left him cold—especially because the Wagners' revolutionary and bohemian background smacked of rank disreputability. He would have known the gossip that Cosima had borne Wagner his first daughter, Isolde, while still married to her former husband—during an affair that had unfolded when Wagner himself was still married to his former wife, the singer Minna Planer.

In England, Harry had had no problem mixing with many disreputable and even scandalous figures of every variety, including the Marquess of Hartington and the Duchess of Manchester—not to mention his good friend Charles Dilke, though the latter's involvement with a married woman in the so-called Crawford Affair would not ignite a scandal until the mid-1880s. But sexual indiscretions came in different forms, and Harry's rejection of Wagner was clearly a reaction against Zhukhovsky's now more open homosexuality.

Harry's discomfort focused on the atmosphere of Paul's Russian and German friends, a flamboyant group whose "manners and customs," loosed in the warm Italian spring, shocked Harry profoundly. It is unclear if Harry objected to what he afterward called their "aesthetics"—perhaps their boldness and unorthodox tastes—or else their "immoralities," as he put it. Homosexual expatriates of the era may have abandoned themselves, in their private Neapolitan setting, to freer expression or activity; but "immoralities" would not have had to be sexual.

Harry evidently disliked the fashionable nihilism of the Wagner group. Writing to his straitlaced and spinsterish friend Grace Norton, of all people, Harry insisted that any details about these Russians would "carry [him] too far." He didn't want to be carried into a grotto, Wagnerian or not.

To keep away from the villa, he fled to the nearby Naples Museum, where, alone in the echoing galleries, he contemplated a damaged piece of classical statuary representing the mythological princess Psyche, the troubled paramour of the Roman love god Cupid. Harry, who loved sculpture, gazed with growing emotion at this delicate, damaged girl, who beckoned to him with a touching fragility. The graceful little figure had lost her crown, and her "lovely" face was lowered in grief; it was as if the nameless Roman sculptor had caught her at the very moment of her separation from Cupid, at the beginning of her sorrowful quest to the underworld, as described by the second-century Roman writer Apuleius.

Moved by this image, Harry called her "the mutilated Psyche" in his letter to Grace Norton, without apparently absorbing the relevant irony. Harry's own psyche was "mutilated" enough, as were those of the other Jameses, all of whom seemed bent on running away from the people they most loved. The "mutilated Psyche," in fact, might have described the emotionally crippling Victorian era itself, as Sigmund Freud would brilliantly diagnose it a couple of decades later—and as William himself as a psychologist would eventually confront in more positive, hopeful terms. Freud's theories, after all, would emerge from his observation of the late-nineteenth-century breakdown (in more than one sense) of its strict sexual mores. Repression and redirection of erotic energy would become central for Freud's theories in such seminal works as his *Studies on Hysteria* (1895), *The Interpretation of Dreams* (1900), and *The Psychopathology of Everyday Life* (1901), as well as his much-criticized theory of Oedipal childhood psychosexual development, to be fleshed out in such works as *Three Essays on the Theory of Sexuality* (1905).

In any case, Harry's sexual psychology wasn't simple and would elude even the more sophisticated sexual theories of the next century. To be sure, Harry didn't consciously "love" his former bosom friend at this point, if he ever had. He'd increasingly found Paul a "ridiculous mixture of Nihilism and bric à brac," as he confided to Alice, scoffing at the Russian's Wagnerian infatuations and declaring him "always under someone's influence": first Turgenev's, then Princess Ouroussoff's, then Harry's own, now Wagner's. In his letter, Harry listed himself, "H.J.Jr. (!!)," followed by exclamation points, as if he couldn't quite believe that he himself could be admired.

It is not completely clear which of Harry's feelings were operative, but a victor soon emerged. He abandoned the villa after three days instead of his intended five; he didn't record the scene for his family or friends. Posillipo fell into what seems a complicated silence. In her theory of the "epistemology of the closet," Eve Kosofsky Sedgwick argues that silence functions as a crucial element of Victorian same-sex desire, carrying many essential meanings. An enforced wordlessness, Sedgwick suggests, stands in for what cannot be articulated, discussed, or morally allowed—Henry James being one of Sedgwick's silenced and closeted Victorians. " 'Closetedness' itself," Sedgwick asserts, "is a performance initiated by the speech-act of silence." And it was under a seal of silence that Harry placed his involvement with Paul Zhukovsky. When reflecting on the young Russian a year and a half later in his notebook, Harry wrote—significantly in Italian, the language of this poignant Neapolitan episode—*"Non ragioniam di lui—ma guarda e passa"* (Let's not discuss him—but look and move on).

Having collected himself and fled, Harry spent a couple of days alone in nearby Sorrento. Across the "vast pale-blue floor" of the Bay of Naples, streaked with fantastic paths and currents, Posillipo stood out as clearly and as starkly as the smoking cone of Vesuvius some distance to the right of it—"wonderfully distinct in the clear still light, and I can almost see the shapes of the villas, and the boats pulled up along the strand." It was a poignant reflection, as if Harry was straining to see back into the world he had lost.

Harry's sad view across the Bay of Naples was particularly resonant, given the letter he'd received from Paul nine months earlier, in which the young Russian had advertised a similar view and connected it to his and Harry's relation. He was surrounded by the *"adorable"* gulf, he had written Harry, as by the arms of a true friend; every time he turned to this friend, it comforted him. *"Et votre bonne et chère figure ressemble à mon golfe aimé, cela m'a été bien beau de la revoir et je vous en remerci,"* Paul had written in the language they shared. (And your good, dear face resembles my beloved gulf, it was good to see it again, and I thank you.)

He moved on to Frascati, a town of magnificent sixteenth-century villas at the base of the Alban Hills near Rome. Here he stayed with his courtly and decorous friend Somerset Beaumont, an Englishman whose "admirable, honest, reasonable, wholesome" character Harry contrasted to the "fantastic immoralities and aesthetics" of the homosexual Russian group he had just left.

Harry had recoiled, but whatever dislocation his removal had caused, he wasn't finished with Paul Zhukovsky. Though many details of their relationship have been obscured, possibly by Harry's destruction of their correspondence, a friendly letter from Paul to Harry, from 1898, has survived in the James papers; in it he recalls fond memories and updates Harry on his doings. Even eighteen years later, the Russian could address Henry James as *"Mon bien cher ami!"* (my very dear friend).

But Harry evidently required even more distance between himself and those who had stirred his discomfort. Traveling north to Florence, he settled into a hotel near the perennial Bootts, Lizzie and her father, Francis, in their airy hilltop villa at Bellosguardo. In this flush spring setting, Harry began to write his novel in earnest, reworking the troubled opening he'd started some time before—introducing, on the pristine lawn of an English country house, his fascinatingly contradictory character Isabel Archer.

"She was looking at everything," Harry wrote, "with an eye that denoted quick perception,—at her companion, at the two dogs, and the two gentlemen under the trees, at the beautiful scene that surrounded her. 'I have never seen anything so lovely as this place,' she said. 'I have been all over the house; it's too enchanting!'" This was perhaps Harry's most arresting character to date, soon to storm through the pages of the *Atlantic Monthly:* Isabel Archer was an ingenue with the exacting observation of a novelist, a naive Miranda facing a brave new world who nevertheless had her own strong "independence" of spirit—a woman, in short, who represented the conflicting aspirations of American women in the 1880s but who also reflected Harry's own psychological paradoxes.

After the debacle of Posillipo, the *Portrait* acquired a new urgency. Writing the novel allowed Harry to recapture some of the freshness of his pre-European youth through memories of Isabel's inspiration, his dead cousin Minny Temple. Harry needed Minny right now—to give him some reassurance. His female character, unlikely to be mistaken for himself, seems to have provided Harry with an opportunity to transfer his own feelings. With Isabel commanding attention at the center, this new novel would allow him to brood once again on the fragility of innocence and on the insidious modes of Old World corruption that had recently been operating in his own life.

As a psychological portrait, the novel revealed as much about Harry as anyone else, as many twentieth-century critics have asserted. Harry richly supplied his "lady," anyway, with many of his own experiences and perspectives—including his own early childhood memories of his grandmother's peach trees in Albany. Isabel was more untutored than Harry, as befitted a young woman who hadn't previously traveled in Europe. She would acquire an independent fortune that Harry, except for small installments from his parents, had never enjoyed. But her journey into a European world of obscure attractions and temptations would parallel Harry's own recent experiences with attractive and ambiguous European friends. One biographer, Sheldon Novick, has gone so far as to argue that the selfish, overrefined man Isabel disastrously marries, Gilbert Osmond, is based to some degree on Paul Zhukovsky.

Corruption was so pervasive in Harry's new novel that he could even impose it on what he called the "pure-minded" Bootts themselves, those world-wandering naive sophisticates. In spite of all their Bostonian proprieties, the Bootts would also become models for the depraved Gilbert Osmond and his (less-depraved) daughter, Pansy. In *The Portrait of a Lady*, lost hopefulness persisted as a theme that Harry couldn't shake off, as an essential obsession for him, as his most heartfelt novel to date opened up before him at his cubbyhole of a writing desk at the Hotel d'Arno.

In Florence, though, Harry didn't spend all of his time alone, or at the "tea-parties" of the Bootts or other uprooted Bostonians. Instead, he linked up with a new acquaintance, and one who came from an unusual quarter. Generally, Harry hated those persistent Americans who brandished a letter of introduction from some well-meaning friend (though Harry himself had spent his young career meeting celebrities by means of such flourishes of the quill, the nineteenth-century precursors to letters of recommendation). Now, just such an odious letter had been written by Harry's cousin Henrietta, Minny's sister. It had been written for an especially persistent suppliant who for months had been doggedly "pursuing [Harry] through Europe."

IN THE LUSH Tuscan April, a forty-year-old American writer named Constance Fenimore Woolson arrived at the dark and sooty central railway station in Florence. This modern terminal was squeezed into the old city, only a few streets away from the magnificent Duomo, with Filippo Brunelleschi's great golden octagonal dome and its mosaic jewelbox facades of white, pink, and green marble. Alone in the busy terminal, at the gates of the splendors of Florence, this small, delicate American woman was traveling on her own; hers was an intrepid undertaking for any unattached female in 1880, especially in Italy, infamous at the time for both banditry and overattentive men. But the lady faced the unfamiliar crowds resolutely; she was not easily daunted. Without as yet speaking much Italian, she ordered her luggage sent to her modest hotel in the Lung'Arno, the sunny riverside embankment from which the spires and towers of this glorious red-roofed city could be taken in.

In more ways than one, Miss Woolson had traveled an impressive distance. Born in New Hampshire and raised on the shores of Lake Erie, she was already a seasoned traveler and author of collections of "local-color" short stories about two American regions she had come to know: *Castle Nowhere: Lake Country Sketches* (1875) took the Great Lakes as its subject; and *Rodman the Keeper: Southern Sketches* (1880) surveyed Florida and other locations in the Deep South. During the 1870s, Miss Woolson had wintered in St. Augustine with her aging mother; the death of that mother the year before, in 1879, had allowed the unattached writer to cross the Atlantic for the first time in her life that winter and to pursue the acquaintance of a writer whose books she had anonymously and admiringly reviewed in the *Atlantic*'s "Contributor's Club." She idolized Henry James and was eager to see his London haunts. Not finding him there, she had pursued him (along with the warmer weather) southward across the Continent.

Harry called at Miss Woolson's hotel with some trepidation, prepared to recoil from an enthusiastic old maid some two years older than himself. After all, she was a woman scribbler who might seem to display the forwardness he so often disliked and was in fact parodying in his current novel through the character of the eager female travel journalist Henrietta Stackpole. But to his surprise, the door was opened by a neatly dressed, respectful-looking lady with narrow braids wrapped gracefully around her chignon. Her gentle face and thoughtful eyes struck him immediately as "amiable." The only drawback he could discern was that she was "deaf," he wrote to his sister, "and asks me questions about my works to which she can't hear the answers." As a matter of fact, Miss Woolson was stone deaf, but only in one ear. Once Harry had learned how to talk to her good side, he found her a willing and receptive companion.

Harry soon learned that this modest "local-color" writer had a grand family connection, one that was mirrored in her three-part name. Her great-uncle had been James Fenimore Cooper, the early American writer of pioneer and wilderness romances including *Last of the Mohicans* (1826) and *The Deerslayer* (1840), which had never engaged Harry in the slightest, but which William, the lover of "boys' books," had admired. (Harry later dubbed this bright, pertinacious, resourceful, lonely woman "Fenimore"—an oddly masculine nickname. Harry, who like William enjoyed playing with monikers, would try other "code names," such as he devised for many of his women friends: "The Costanza," "The Littératrice." No doubt he resisted calling her Connie, as her sisters back in America did.)

As fellow writers, the two bonded naturally, more than Harry might have expected. Harry was a meticulous worker, but Fenimore herself was cut from a similar cloth: she painstakingly crafted insightful sketches and stories—though it's unclear if Harry had yet read any of them—and had managed to secure herself a trickle of income to travel on. She now aspired to add Europe to her literary portfolio; it was flattering that she wanted not just any Europe but Henry James's version of it—the Europe of loaded heiresses, exquisite art, and imperiled innocence.

What's more, this acolyte writer—one of the first who construed Harry as a model, a master—came to Florence overflowing with high regard for him at a time when his former Russian companion's admiration, whatever its content, had wandered elsewhere or had proved unacceptably fervid. The attentive Fenimore may not have looked as safe as the seventyish Fanny Kemble or the relentlessly daubing Lizzie Boott—now in any case infatuated with a Europeanized painter from Cincinnati named Frank Duveneck, whom she would fatefully marry in 1886. But Fenimore must have felt safer to Harry than Paul Zhukovsky.

As their acquaintance progressed, Harry and Fenimore graduated from hotel teas to museum excursions: Florence offered a superb array of art at the Uffizi, the Accademia, and the Bargello (a former prison that had been turned into an art collection in 1865). Constance proved herself a good student as they roamed the galleries with an unchaparoned frequency that would have verged on impropriety if their friendship hadn't embodied primness itself.

One day, when they'd been gazing at statues in one of the vast Florentine museums, Harry said, "Of course you admired those grand reclining figures."

"No, I did not," Fenimore replied, trying to be honest. "They looked so distracted."

"Ah yes," Harry said, tasting the word and trying to translate it into something better, "*distracted*. But *then!*"

At a loss for words, Harry darted away, absorbing himself in a nearby fresco. Constance displayed quite a bit of homegrown American innocence, after all. She didn't like looking at the naked statues, being "not sufficiently acquainted with torsos, flanks, and the lines of anatomy, to know when they are 'supremely beautiful' and when not." Such naïveté amused Harry and allowed him to feel superior. But it also probably soothed him after his racy and upsetting Neapolitan episode. At the least, Constance endorsed Harry's own discomfort with nudity and its implications.

Harry had retreated to his safe old habits of cultivated females, lofty aesthetics, and echoing, cavernous museums. As something of an "old maid" himself, he'd unconsciously adopted his sister Alice's strategy—and pounced on a fellow old maid as a companion. But Constance

Fenimore Woolson would not be so easily dismissed, and neither, for that matter, could Alice and her friend Katharine.

❧

DURING THE INTERVALS of warm weather in 1881, Alice began to raise a "cottage" on a rocky promontory called Proctor's Point. Her site lay beside the Atlantic north of Boston, a mile and a half from the neat North Shore fishing village whimsically styled Manchester-by-the-Sea. She had chosen a plot on a flat, unspoiled coast pitted with small coves and guarded by low islets of pink and gray granite. The four thousand dollars Alice had paid for the land had to be borrowed from her father, and William blithely continued to call the place simply "Father's." But at Proctor's Point, or Point of Rocks as it was also called, Alice was turning herself into an architect and master builder, growing more active and vital than her family had seen her in a long time. And her plans, unlike William's previous parlorless utopia, were resulting in actual foundations.

Near Alice's land in Manchester, Massachusetts, a general flurry of building was going forward, with many new "cottages" rearing up. Henry Senior's Saturday Club friend Richard Henry Dana had built a summer house hereabouts back in 1845. But by the 1880s, the town, some twenty miles north of Boston, had begun to rival Newport. It boasted sprawling genteel summer homes, clapboard or shingle mostly, but sometimes built of more monumental stone. In the hot months, this surf-lashed shoreline, with its boulders and cormorants, was heavily trafficked by "summering" Brahmins. Alice, Henry, and Mary often ran into someone from Cambridge, some chatty acquaintance in a grand straw hat, on their drives or train journeys up. Alice also made the journey herself, traveling only with her friend Katharine.

Henry and Mary noted that Katharine was increasingly replacing Alice's other female friends—most of them married, anyway, or living at a distance. More and more, Alice had attached herself to the loyal and indefatigable Katharine, who had almost singlehandedly carried her through her 1878 breakdown and had since opened up wide, fresh horizons for her. ("Miss Loring has been a real savior to her," William noted to Alice's old friend Fanny Morse. "I don't know how Alice c[oul]d have got through this year without her.")

Katharine was always bounding up the front steps of the Quincy Street house to take Alice away on junkets all over New England: to Newport, the Maine coast, and the White Mountains of New Hampshire. This wiry, redoubtable Bostonian, indeed, like the new generation of woman to whom she proudly belonged, lavished Alice with all the best features of both a man and a woman, as the nineteenth-century construed them. She united, as Harry all too gallantly put it, "the wisdom of the serpent with the gentleness of the dove." In the starker words of Alice's biographer Jean Strouse, Alice had found someone, now, "who could be everything to her—man and woman, father and mother, nurse and protector, intellectual partner and friend." What it all meant, nobody in the family was sure. They only saw that Alice was more vigorous than she'd been in years.

The pair often drove out to Proctor's Point to supervise the workmen. The two women in their thirties, strolling around the lot, worked as equals, as they'd done during their stint of tutoring a few years before. At the same time, the wiry, alert Katharine visibly watched out for the more fragile Alice, lest she should overexert herself. Such vigilance had earned Katharine the James family's gratitude; as Harry had hyperbolically put it, he hoped his sister had "built a monument somewhere of forest leaves (or rather of New Hampshire granite) to the divine Miss Loring." Such a "wonderful being," as Alice called her friend, really did merit a monument. But that, in a sense, was what Alice was building.

As it rose, the villa stood out like a beacon. William came up to look at it, and he saw that it was a "conspicuous object" on the flat and rocky coastline. Alice's acre-and-a-half lot included access to a pier and a vista of rocky islets out in the white-capped Atlantic. Its half-wild setting rated as "delicious," William felt. Later, Harry too would see the place and also be impressed: the summerhouse had "the sea close to the piazzas, and the smell of bayberries in the air." (The limpid marine setting, in fact, proved heady enough to inspire Harry to use it, transposed to the more "Italian" Cape Cod, in his future novel *The Bostonians*. In this novel, too, he would explore his deep uneasiness with the brand of domesticity that Alice would practice there.)

All the Jameses would eventually gravitate to the house, really Alice's first home of her own. Proctor's Point had a pleasant influence, and it tended to relax and open the otherwise claustrophobic Jameses' family life. The house on Quincy Street had always been dominated, literally and metaphorically, by the spires of Harvard (as well as by the ambitions that a place like Harvard increasingly represented). Since the 1870s, the James house had enjoyed a view of "great bristling Valhalla," as Harry would later call it, of Harvard's Memorial Hall, a Civil War monument–cum–dining facility built by the architects William Robert Ware and Henry Van Brunt to honor the Union dead. (Memorial Hall simultaneously dispensed, as Harry wittily put it, "laurels to the dead and dinners to the living.") Alice's summerhouse, quite a different sort of place, opened itself up to the bare ocean and sky. But its greatest advantage, for Alice, lay in its location; it was perched only two miles up the coast from Katharine's own house at Pride's Crossing.

Alice probably looked proud enough as her house took shape; she had dreamed, schemed, and worked hard to create it since at least the spring of 1879 when she was still recovering from her breakdown and enjoying the happiness of her growing intimacy with Katharine. From descriptions he received, Harry pronounced her plans "very graceful," and a "great credit to her intellectual audacity." Yet he comically imagined Alice and Katharine naming the cottage, in the mold of sentimentally christened Victorian villas in England, "Alice's Whim" or "Sister's Suggestion."

Clearly, Alice had built her vacation house to be near Katharine, but she might have been still bolder. Hungry for experience and self-determination as she was, she might have extended her long vacations with Katharine into a domestic arrangement, liberating herself at last. No one, after all, had suffered more in the Quincy Street house than this daughter and youngest child, always kept on hand, always underestimated, always considered latest and last.

But although her "cottage" granted her a rocky acre of independence, she continued to live primarily with her parents. Partly, she still hungered for their nurture and support, even with the addition of Katharine. She also stayed out of habit and from the domestic ideals her mother and aunt had ingrained in her. Alice did the best she could, dividing her time between her white-haired parents and her dark-haired Katharine, herself embroiled in family concerns.

Alice could observe around her pairs of women who handled their lives differently. It was the heyday of so-called Boston marriages, and many pairs of women were choosing to live together. Mark DeWolfe Howe, a Bostonian writer and editor of the *Atlantic* in the 1890s, knew many such women and affirmed that their relationships were "unions." As Alice tried to find a footing for her "romantic friendship" with Katharine, she probably wasn't short on models. One of the most conspicuous was provided by the Jameses' friend Annie Adams Fields, the Boston hostess whom Alice had admired since her late teens. Mrs. Fields, after a long and affectionate marriage, became a widow in 1881 and wore black or purple widow's weeds, including a veil, for the rest of her life. But soon after her husband's death, she began to share her redbrick Federal-period row house on Charles Street with the unmarried Maine poet and fiction writer Sarah Orne Jewett.

The plump, light-haired Jewett had just produced a rather decorative volume of poetry called *Under the Olive* (1880). In a few years, she would reach more serious and psychological depths in her novel *A Country Doctor* (1884), an exposé of the conflicts of a woman physician. The love letters of Fields and Jewett, long suppressed, would eventually unfold the fascinating tale of the complicated relationship between these two passionate and intelligent women, who would increasingly become close friends of Alice and Katharine.

"Boston marriage," an ambiguous and protective category, paralleled in some ways "bachelorhood" for men. Some women who lived together were friends saving on rent or enjoying simple companionship; others were what we would now describe as lesbians. With the marginalized status of women's lives in the nineteenth century, these middle- and upper-class women founded long-term households without attracting very much censure or, for that matter, notice. If females, after all, lacked sexual drives and desires—as the Victorian world wanted fervently to believe—their ménages could harbor no amorous or sexual complications. What "improper" interest could two genteel spinsters past marrying age possibly have in each other?

Alice Gibbens James, for one, understood that women actually did have sexual desires. At least she was the sole member of the family who raised the possibility—in secret, to William—that Alice and Katharine might be lovers. This cannot conclusively be proved or disproved by the surviving evidence, and such ambiguities commonly featured in "Boston marriages." "Whether these unions sometimes or often included sex, we will never know," the historian Lillian Faderman writes, "but we do know that these women spent their lives primarily with other women, they gave to other women the bulk of their energy and attention, and they formed powerful emotional ties with other women."

Alice didn't understand herself as a lesbian—the term dated back to the seventeenth century and was only occasionally used in Alice's time. (Sexologists of the late nineteenth century were inventing or adapting diverse terminology: *Uranians, Sapphists, inverts,* and *female homosexuals.*) The lack of a more precise term probably served to protect Alice. Her relationship with Katharine was obvious and public, but Alice seems to have guarded her private feelings for Katharine warily, or else couched them in phrases (for example, Alice's appreciation of Katharine's androgyny) that, though loaded for us, tended not to draw the notice of her contemporaries. At the same time, Katharine was "one of the happy ingredients of her life," as William had observed. After years of being discounted and neglected, Alice had finally found someone who really wanted and needed her. Katharine counted as Alice's first and so far her only lucky break. That May of 1881, the two women would even cross the Atlantic together.

ALICE JAMES HAD hardly had an easy life, but her dream cottage at Proctor's Point amounted to a sun-struck Mediterranean villa beside the more troubled houses and households of her two Wisconsin brothers. In the spring of 1880, Wilkie inherited a house big enough to accommodate himself, his wife, and his two children. It had been his wife Carrie's childhood home in Milwaukee and was bequeathed to them by her father, who had made his money on haberdashery and had boarded with Wilkie and his wife since their wedding. But the once proud Carrie, now the mother of one son and one daughter (inevitably named Alice James), wasn't sporting diamonds any longer. Wilkie's bankruptcy in 1877 had saddled the couple with more than twenty thousand dollars of debt—a scandalous sum. Mary James was, not surprisingly, especially upset; she rued Henry Senior's having to liquidate railroad shares to keep Wilkie afloat.

Though warmhearted and agreeable, Wilkie hadn't grown any shrewder as a businessman since the days of his disastrous Reconstruction plantation in Florida. He'd tumbled through a "rude career," as his brother Harry put it. Ever since he'd come home from the Civil War, he'd remained a veritable sink for the James family money.

Extraordinarily bad luck had played a part in Wilkie's failures. Caterpillars and plummeting cotton prices had ruined his Florida venture. Then the Panic of 1873, resulting from runaway railroad speculation, wrecked his iron bolt business. The economic depression of the 1870s fueled wide unemployment in New York and populist rage as far away as the bone-dry Dakotas, bludgeoning many a worker's, farmer's, or entrepreneur's hopes. The Panic certainly leveled Wilkie's aspirations. By 1878, the usually optimistic thirty-three-year-old had to give a "sorry account" of his iron locks enterprise; after declaring bankruptcy, he had to scrape to find a (low-paying) clerkship. He just couldn't get on the right side of the boom-bust cycle.

Wilkie also suffered increasingly from deteriorating health. With his wounded foot from the Civil War plaguing him, he could be seen limping around the streets of Milwaukee on crutches, a picture reminiscent of his disabled father. And lately Wilkie had developed the symptoms of liver and heart problems for which Aunt Kate, always mindful of health and up-to-date on medical matters, had dispatched Blair's Pills—a patent remedy that did about as much good as the clover tea she also prescribed.

Bob, who turned thirty-two in 1878, was also living on the flat shores of Lake Michigan and struggling with a clerking job he hated. He was faring even worse than Wilkie, drinking more and more heavily and behaving badly, losing his temper at home. Even his resilient wife, Mary, noted that Bob was "cross" and had many a "bad day with liquor." On Christmas Day 1877, Bob's celebrations veered out of control into an outburst of rage, ruining the holiday. Bob had struggled with drink since the Civil War; from time to time his father, who had given him his genetic predisposition to alcohol, had tried to advise him. But Henry Senior was mostly too frail now even to give his son his patent sermons on restraint, although Bob was one of the few children who actually took his father's stark theological system seriously. Bob's studies of his father's idol, Swedenborg, didn't really uplift him.

Mary Holton James prided herself on being a patient, traditional wife, but she also qualified as a self-respecting woman who was growing fatigued with Bob's "selfish tyrannical turbulent spirit." Something had to change; there were children in the house. But Bob's household fell into even more disarray by early 1881. Bob already gave the impression of changing houses as often as he changed his coat—he'd recently taken his seven-year-old son, Ned, on a trip to scout out a newspaper job in Colorado, to escape his hectoring father-in-law—and the Jameses never knew where to address his letters. Bob finally returned to his railroad job but soon, choked with the soul-killing ennui of such work, picked a fight with his supervisor. As a refuge from these horrors, he buried himself still more in drink. Then, one day during that raw Wisconsin winter, Mary snapped. She finally stood up for herself and took her husband to task: she reproached Bob for hurting his family. Immediately plunging into deep remorse, Bob tipped over the edge so that he needed, as William diagnosed it, "asylum treatment."

Having returned from Europe, William caught a train to Milwaukee to help his alcoholic brother. William had a strong sense of family responsibility, in spite of his evasions (or perhaps underlying them). Over the years, William had written Bob dozens of big-brotherly and physicianly letters, taking over Bob's paternal upkeep from the fragile and exhausted Henry Senior. Even so, the squalid scenes that William witnessed in Wisconsin made him feel he had "no duty to these other folks at all." He praised his own "orderly" Alice in contrast to what he probably unfairly described as his younger brothers' "less expensive" wives. All the James wives, including William's own—and not omitting Katharine Peabody Loring or Constance Fenimore Woolson—had a lot to put up with. Women in nineteenth-century America absorbed many of the costs of marriage—an enduring gender imbalance on which all of the Jameses heavily depended.

Only one solution seemed possible. Early in 1881, Mary moved back in with her father at Highland Home. Wilkie helped move her furniture, and William hauled Bob back to Cambridge, for a stint at the nearby McLean Hospital. Founded in 1811, this venerable institution had first used rural rest to cure mental illness. But, under the influence of the emerging science of psychology, in which William played an increasingly important part, the pioneering psychiatric hospital had begun to try more aggressive methods, including galvanic shocks. Yet it was hard to know what even such "modern" methods would do for the dysfunctional Bob.

When Bob returned to Quincy Street after his treatment, his abrasive personality overwhelmed and exhausted the three inhabitants. Mary noticed that her irritable son got no exercise and sat around the house, immersed in his drawing or else in his low moods. Alice, who had few fond memories of her bullying nursery-mate, hardly liked having the surly Bob in the household. Even if unconventional, she expected of Bob what he had somewhat satirically described as "upper middle class manners." If it weren't for the helpful William and his sympathetic wife living nearby, Bob would have proved an impossible burden. Bob, in his midthirties, still didn't know what he wanted to do with his life, continuing to speak unrealistically of poetry or painting, and shied away from reconciling with his wife and her hostile father. Bob was replacing Alice as the most desperate and discontented member of the family.

IN LONDON, HARRY continued to bask in his celebrity. He had resolved at least some of his disputes with his family—William's critique of his fiction, Mary's desire for him to get married—by putting the Atlantic between himself and his relatives. Likewise, he'd solved his own household problems in an equally stark way: by not having one. True, he still maintained his trim Mayfair flat with its deferential and well-trained underlings—a model he'd favor, in fact, for the next four decades. But when Harry wanted domestic fraternity, he mostly got it from other people's houses.

During the winter of Bob's breakdown, in January 1881, Harry wrote to his mother from a "bachelor house" close to the famous racetrack at Epsom Downs in Surrey. One of several houses owned by Harry's friend Lord Rosebery, "the Durdans," as it was called, had an impressive library and paintings by the eighteenth-century masters

Thomas Gainsborough and Jean-Antoine Watteau. Lord Rosebery, a great "patron of the Turf," had bought the place because of its access to the training stables and the jockeys of its racing neighborhood, where the hyperfashionable Derby had been established by the eponymous Earl of Derby a century before in 1779.

Lord Rosebery was governed by three goals: to win a Derby (he would first do so with a colt called Ladas II in 1894); to marry an heiress (his wife, Lady Rosebery, the former Hannah de Rothschild, had just borne him—"disappointingly," Harry thought—a second daughter); and to become prime minister of Great Britain—a dream he would realize, more precariously, fifteen years later in 1894–95.

Blue-eyed, sideburned, baby-faced, just thirty-three years old, Archibald Philip Primrose, Fifth Earl of Rosebery, naturally struck Harry as "a very delightful creature." In November 1880, Harry had been staying with Lord Rosebery at his still grander estate of Mentmore Park in Buckinghamshire, a turreted and heavily decorated stone Victorian manor that Harry described to his mother as a "gorgeous residence" with a correspondingly sumptuous "manner of life." The chairs were all "golden thrones, belonging to ancient Doges of Venice," brought to England by his wife's Rothschild millions, though Lord Rosebery had also started life rich. In this setting, the crimson socks that Alice had obediently knitted for Harry might have seemed humble and out of place. But red stockings made by a sister were in fact de rigueur, all the rage among the houseguesting gentlemen of the time. When a silent footman arrived to ventilate Harry's dress shirt and turn his fashionable booties inside out, for his convenience, Harry had reached, at last, his own form of heaven. And yet he tellingly kept to his room in order to write his "mammy." He craved an audience for his good fortune but also remained tethered to his plain Yankee family. The more he traveled, the more they clung to him, as his frequent letters home testified.

At supper one evening, Lord Rosebery told Harry, surprisingly, that his ideal happy life would be "living like Longfellow" in Cambridge, Massachusetts. (Longfellow, to be sure, lived in comparative splendor in his yellow clapboard manse on Brattle Street.) Never mind that he was a politician; Rosebery's aristocratic charm required him to tell such courteous whoppers. He may also have hoped to get on Harry's good side for his own reasons. After dinner Rosebery scribbled in his diary that his new friend wanted to write a great novel before he died. (Harry was currently putting out *The Portrait of a Lady* in installments on both sides of the Atlantic.) Rosebery also recorded that the attractively plump thirty-seven-year-old Harry—who, apparently in his mother's grand tradition, fudged his age, declaring that he was thirty-five—had "made up his mind not to marry."

A scandal that would erupt some fourteen years later sheds light on Lord Rosebery's possible interest in such a detail. In October 1894, the young Francis Viscount Drumlanrig died in a "shooting accident" that was widely understood to be a suicide. This handsome young Scottish lord evidently feared blackmail or the politically damaging exposure of his sexual relation with Lord Rosebery, at that point the foreign secretary. (Drumlanrig was the eldest son of the homophobic and pugilistic Marquess of Queensberry and the brother of Lord Alfred Douglas, the lover of Oscar Wilde.)

This tragedy—which incidentally didn't prevent Lord Rosebery from becoming prime minister the same year, mostly because he was the only Liberal candidate the crustily ancient Queen Victoria didn't abhor—lay far in the future in 1881. But for a man who'd sworn off doubtful homosexual company, Harry kept finding it.

Also Lord Rosebery, corn-fed and genial, strongly reminded Harry of a "successful and glorified" Wilkie, who'd gone to Eton and Oxford, inherited an earldom, and married a Rothschild. The resemblance arrested Harry. But it didn't hurry him back to the United States to embrace the actual Wilkie, the bankrupt who now hobbled on crutches because of his Civil War wound. There were different modes of embracing liberal causes during the nineteenth century, and Wilkie's hadn't paid as well as Rosebery's.

Harry felt for his brother enough to send Wilkie some money—just as he sent money to the indigent Bob, to help him during his hardships. Wilkie thanked Harry for his "princely" gift: "It is so long since I have had any money that I could call my own that the possession of this completely dazzles me," Wilkie wrote back.

Still, month to month during 1881, Harry put off a planned visit to the United States; he just didn't want to steam back to the country of his birth or lodge in his parents' house. He clung tenaciously to his privileged, distant position.

∾

MORNING COFFEE WAS a glorious business at the famous café of Florian's on the Piazza San Marco in Venice. At this time of year, in late March 1881, morning light flooded through the Piazzetta, between its two gated columns topped with symbols of the Venetian Republic's old empire in the East. (On top of one pillar, San Teodoro stood on a Nile crocodile; on the other perched the winged lion of St. Mark, whose bones had reputedly been brought to Venice from Alexandria in the ninth century.) The beautiful Adriatic light also struck the towering campanile and the arched facade of the squat, intricate cathedral of San Marco, encrusted with Eastern marbles and adorned with bronze horses looted centuries before from the Hippodrome at Byzantium. The cathedral had recently been restored and repainted; that, Harry scoffed, was like putting "*maquillage* [makeup] on one's grandmother." When Harry had his breakfast rolls indoors at Florian's, he could enjoy the paneled, gilded interior of this coffeehouse founded in 1720, which both Lord Byron and Charles Dickens had relished before him. When he sat outdoors in the piazza, he could see the pigeons flocking on the herringbone pavement; smell the fresh rain puddles, or watch Italian cicerones guiding parties of smartly dressed English, German, and American tourists, who sported straw hats against the sun.

Harry had hared off to Italy for the spring of 1881—avowedly, to avoid the "season" and its taxing small-talk. Finally he had had enough of the aristocratic game he had been playing every spring since 1877. Among other Italian pleasures, Harry fell in love once more with the crumbling architecture of Venice, which he visited now for the third time. "I adore it—have fallen deeply and desperately in love with it," he wrote Grace Norton—and Harry fell in love with cities as well as with safely married or elderly women. He arrived alone, reaching his hotel by means of a *vaporetto* (Harry called it a *vaporino*), an aquatic public bus on the Grand Canal. But in Venice, before long, he linked up with a handsome acquaintance—"a queer, but almost delightful creature."

Herbert Pratt, sunburned and stout and moneyed, was an old medical school friend of William's. As such, he carried a whiff of Cambridge, Massachusetts. But mostly he embodied homeless cosmopolitanism: he'd thrown over a medical practice in Denver to travel for years in Spain, North Africa, and the Middle East. As the two men roamed around Venice, Pratt infected Harry with his romantic orientalist "passion" and fired Harry with an intoxicating pheromone scent of "the sun, of the south, of colour, of freedom, of being one's own master, and doing absolutely what one pleases."

When the two men visited a "queer little wineshop" frequented by gondoliers and *facchini* (porters), Pratt entertained Harry with stories of his languorous, guitar-strumming adventures, his abandoning himself in the grass under the fig trees of Spain. If Pratt narrated sexual adventures per se, Harry didn't record them.

On another evening, Pratt invited Harry to his rooms on the Grand Canal, overlooking the Rialto Bridge. On a hot night with Pratt's windows thrown open, cries of gondoliers rose up from the great curving palace-flanked waterway below. Pratt read to Harry from old Persian books, exotic aphorisms and poetry. "A great deal might be done with Herbert Pratt," Harry reflected—in fiction, Harry meant. Eight years later, Harry would preserve Pratt in his novel *The Tragic Muse*.

While in Venice, staying in his rooms on the Riva degli Schiavoni, with his vista of the huge pink church of San Giorgio, Harry finished his final installment of *The Portrait of a Lady*. The last chapters of the novel had been dominated by Isabel Archer's marriage to Gilbert Osmond and its attendant disillusion. "After a year or two of marriage the antagonism between her nature and Osmond's comes out," Harry had written in his notebook, "the open opposition of a noble character and a narrow one . . . Isabel wakes from her sweet delusion." As his work drew to a close, Harry fretted that Isabel's story would be too "psychological" and internal for his readers to appreciate: Isabel's objections to her husband were not just that he had had a liaison with Madame Merle, the cultivated, scheming American expatriate who had perversely helped engineer the marriage. They were also that, through her marriage, Isabel had encountered not only the manifold corruptions of Europe but also the possible disappointments, as Harry saw them, of human intimacy.

For Harry, the novel expressed a vast, poignant disillusion with a rare, delicate beauty and a psychological realism that would resonate with the starker literary tastes of the late nineteenth century. The writing of *The Portrait of a Lady*, a work about crushed hopes, had been framed in Harry's life not only by hired rooms in Italy but also by his own unrewarding brushes with sensuality. Harry had dodged both familial and amorous intimacy. As children, the Jameses had at least traveled as a family, holding on to one another for company. In adulthood, Harry and William had adopted their father's old expedients and now mostly traveled by themselves.

❧

WHEN HARRY FINALLY returned to the United States in November 1881, he sneaked into the country "by the back-door" on the fashionable northern steamship route from Liverpool to Quebec. He camped at Quincy Street only briefly before checking into a hotel in Boston. He'd returned to America only because he'd needed to see *"les miens"* (mine)—that is, his family—and make a try at "entering into their lives." But after a six-year absence, Harry could only deal with the draining emotions of the Jameses in small doses, from the gaslit independence of a hotel room.

After a brief getaway to New York City, Harry returned to his parents' house for Christmas of 1881. Christmastime had never spelled much festivity for the Jameses, not since Henry Senior had loosed the strings on the gift boxes, spoiling his children's surprises. This year, sadly, Henry Senior didn't have the energy for much mischief. Brittle and withdrawn, seventy years old, he was photographed about this time wearing the pillbox hat, white beard, and abstracted expression of some ancient Eastern sage. Though Mary brightened when she embraced her favorite son once again, Harry discovered his mother "worn and shrunken," tired out from decades of nannying her impossible family.

Harry had actually seen Alice, though, more recently. Only the previous summer, after his return from Italy in 1881, he'd entertained his sister and Katharine in London, the two women having hurled themselves into a bold tour of the British Isles. They traveled extensively in the north of England, though none of Alice's letters from the period have survived. But their planned visit to Scotland had to be canceled because of an incident reminiscent of old times. In Kew, near London, Katharine had visited an aunt and uncle who were staying nearby. Suddenly, with Katharine's attention compromised, Alice retaliated with a breakdown, such as she'd had with her aunt and Harry in Switzerland in 1872, after the Bootts had unwittingly intruded on their cozy family party. Now, however, the target of Alice's nervous possessiveness was Katharine, not her brother.

For his part, Harry had felt "a fifth wheel to their coach"—he'd not even been required to see them off when, after Alice's recovery, the two sailed home from Liverpool. Alice, having coaxed a little money from her father and found a willing companion, didn't want Harry as a cicerone, if indeed she'd done so even in 1872. She wasn't Harry's confiding travel companion any longer. Harry had once loved to protect his baby sister. But with her forceful new ally, Alice wasn't as confiding and deferential as she'd been.

So, feeling strangely alone in a house full of Jameses, Harry took refuge at the back of 20 Quincy Street, in the memory-filled sitting room he and William had once shared. In the winter twilights, Harry sat in this dim chamber with "poor" Wilkie, who'd traveled all the way from Wisconsin, that Christmas, to see his brother, whom he hadn't clapped eyes on in eleven years.

Harry declared Wilkie "wonderfully unchanged for a man with whom life has not gone easy." He obviously wanted to appraise his brother generously and compassionately. He tried hard not to see Wilkie's ravages, his limp and his gaunt, creased face with its graying mustache. Once the healthiest of the James children, Wilkie was so stiff with rheumatism that he could barely negotiate the stairs of the old family home.

❧

WITH SUCH EMOTIONAL strains, Harry soon abandoned Quincy Street and hurried south, spending three days at his friend Sarah Wister's house in Philadelphia. He no doubt wanted to reminisce about Rome, about the marble palaces and the fleece-jacketed shepherds. But Mrs. Wister radiated gloom as she and Harry circulated among her more cheerful friends, the "sympathetic, expressive and effusive" ladies of that city. Sarah Wister was scheming a trip to Jamaica; the Jameses were hardly the only members of their caste mired in the Victorian bric-a-brac of social obligations and domestic miseries who turned to travel for relief.

Reaching Washington, Harry put up in hired rooms and continued his convenient household-borrowing habits by attaching himself to his old friends Henry and Clover Adams. A cosmopolitan like the Jameses, Henry Adams, bearded and balding, had lived encyclopedically abroad. But, refreshingly, both he and his wife counted themselves as some of the few "cultivated Americans" who actually preferred to live in the United States.

Also like the Jameses, Adams had rambled through a number of careers: in the 1860s and 1870s, he had been his ambassador father's secretary in Britain, edited the *North American Review*, and then professed medieval history at Harvard. Recently, though, he and his wife had settled into what Harry appraised as a "commodious and genial" residence in Lafayette Square.

Adams liked his proximity to the executive mansion as well as to the senators; he was, after all, the grandson of John Quincy Adams and the great-grandson of John Adams and his nimble-minded wife, Abigail. Appropriately, Adams had just anonymously authored a biting satire of Washington manners and politics titled *Democracy* (1880), which caused a stir in this increasingly sprawling city that, Harry soon observed, lived to converse about itself.

In her dining room in Lafayette Square, Clover (aka Marian Hooper Adams) also appreciated repartee. Harry was soon reminded that his old Cambridge acquaintance liked to deploy an acidic wit that hardly befitted her innocuous nickname. Having previously run an intellectual salon in Boston, she had now become an astute Washington hostess. Harry famously called Clover "a perfect Voltaire in petticoats," but William, even less tolerant of strong-minded women, referred to Clover Adams as a "cockatrice."

The bright, ambitious, troubled Clover was no cockatrice; with her multiple fascinations, however, she did in fact resemble the nimble-minded Voltaire. Intrigued by photography, for example, she nevertheless refused to have her own picture taken. In the early 1880s, her husband obediently photographed her with a straw bonnet drawn over her face, revealing only a somewhat chunky chin and a multiply exposed dog wriggling in her arms. But Clover suffered not only from camera shyness but also from deeper disturbances. More than Sarah Wister—more even than Alice James—Clover Adams was prone to deep depression. Three years later, in fact, at Christmastime in 1885, she would take her own life during an episode of insanity following the death of her beloved father. Her method was "cyanide of potassium," a chemical, ironically, that she had used to prepare her photographic plates. Her bereaved Henry would then commission a monument for her from the increasingly prominent American sculptor Augustus Saint-Gaudens, who would become famous for his tribute, first conceived in 1884 and finally cast and erected in 1897, to Robert Gould Shaw and Wilkie's black regiment from the Civil War. It would be a stirring memorial, a masterpiece of American art, sensitively treating the doomed black soldiers' faces.

As for a monument to Clover Adams, it was easier to commemorate war heroes than suicides, especially in the 1880s. But the cowled, draped, sorrowing figure that Saint-Gaudens titled *Grief*—to be erected on the Adams plot in the Rock Creek Cemetery in Washington—turned out to be a masterpiece of calm and contemplation.

But grief was evidently far from Harry's mind as he hurled himself into the gaiety of the national capital. For all his condemnation of the "season" in London, he still got a frisson of pleasure, stimulation, and gratification from dining out. As he wrote to an English friend, "The sky is blue, the sun is warm, the women are charming, and at dinners the talk is always general." In his enthusiasm for the cultivated friends of the Adamses, Harry pronounced Washington the only city in America not ruled by money and "business," a somewhat naive claim even in 1882.

Harry loved the "air of leisure" that hung over the capital's wide avenues. The city's well-dressed strolling citizens—out in their furs or many-buttoned winter coats in spite of Washington's relative mildness—appeared neither worried nor flurried. But the dome of the Capitol, finished during the Civil War, and the almost-completed shaft of the Washington Monument stuck out rather rawly, Harry thought. Compared to more seasoned imperial capitals like London, Washington struck Harry as "provisional" and provincial, "an immensely painted but unfinished cloth."

Though he qualified here as a "rank outsider" (Clover wittily called him an emigrant), Harry racked up his usual social trophies, and an especially splendid one crowned his visit. It happened at a "big and gorgeous banquet" held in the Washington townhouse of Senator James G. Blaine of Maine, a future Republican presidential candidate who had strongly supported African-American suffrage during Reconstruction, but he would also push the notorious anti-immigration Chinese Exclusion Act during 1882. For this dinner, the senator had handpicked his guests, favoring Republican warhorses. When Harry arrived, he mingled with the British ambassador, the governor of California, and General William Tecumseh Sherman. Most famous for his scorched-earth march through Georgia to the sea late in the Civil War, Sherman was now an aging dignitary and memoirist who would refuse to run for president in 1884.

But an even grander guest buttonholed Harry into a conversation: the president of the United States, Chester A. Arthur. Harry found the president's suit and whiskers well cut, his stature impressive, and his manners "personable"—though, as he talked about Harry's distinguished relatives in New York State, he just couldn't keep them all straight. Harry might have chosen to meet a more fascinating president, if he'd been given the option. Joweled, cigar-puffing Arthur was a Republican machine boss from New York who had once inveighed against bureaucratic corruption. Elected vice president in 1880, he had become commander in chief when President James A. Garfield had been assassinated a few months before, in July 1881, after the second-shortest term in American history, by a disgruntled office seeker. But his most memorable presidential achievement would be to hire Louis Comfort Tiffany, the famous art-nouveau designer of glass, to redecorate the White House.

⁂

OSCAR WILDE, A young visiting poet and drawing-room celebrity from Britain, had just arrived in Washington and was being profiled in Harry's breakfast papers. The twenty-eight-year-old was beginning his famous American "House Beautiful" lecture tour of 1882; eventually his itinerary would take him as far afield as Leadville, Colorado, where he would lecture to silver miners about Benvenuto Cellini, the famous sixteenth-century silversmith. When the miners asked why Wilde hadn't brought the man along, Wilde informed them that he was dead. "Who shot him?" a miner asked. Or so Wilde would recount. He'd been known to exaggerate for the sake of an anecdote, and already he was famous for his epigrams, racy stories, and quips. With this dramatic flair, Oscar Wilde knew how to win an audience in a way the more re-served Harry might envy.

Harry proved less than amiable when he ran into the Irishman at a Washington party. The slightly plump, languid Wilde wore long hair, knee breeches, many rings, and a bright yellow silk handkerchief; he ad-dressed his listeners with flamboyant mannerisms and Oxford hauteur. Harry promptly declared this self-promoting young man "repulsive and fatuous." To Clover Adams, after the party, he confided that he thought Wilde was an "unclean beast," an even more visceral and suggestive phrase. Harry probably disliked Wilde both because he was showy and, more subtly, because he was Irish. Wilde brazenly reflected at least two sides of Harry—his Ulster ancestry and his erotic interest in men—that the novelist worked hard to suppress. Wilde was free-spirited to the point of recklessness, no asset as far as Harry was concerned. But at least one lady at this party pronounced Oscar Wilde fascinating and Henry James a dead bore. Wilde's one-liner about Washington: "It has too many bronze generals."

But Wilde had told a Philadelphia newspaper that Henry James, who'd just published his *Portrait*, rated as one of the greatest living nov-elists. Strong-armed by Clover Adams into paying a call—and wishing to thank Wilde—Harry nervously tried to relate to this vivid Irishman by remarking how much he, Harry, missed London. "Really? You care for *places*?" Wilde quipped back. "The world is my home."

It was a puppyish snub, but Harry smarted as he prided himself on his internationalism. He also preferred to keep an even temper, at any cost. But Oscar Wilde lived to get everybody hot under the collar, and Harry left Wilde's hotel room implicated, steaming.

❧

HARRY INTENDED TO roam into the South. But he recollected his family enough to send $250 to the convalescent Bob, now back at

Quincy Street. Bob gratefully acknowledged the gift and sent Harry the news that their seventy-one-year-old mother had been in bed with bronchial asthma. Though the doctor had assured the family that she was not in any danger, Aunt Kate had arrived from New York to nurse her, and Harry trusted that his father and his sister, with such expert assistance, could manage. A couple of days later, on January 29, 1882, Harry wrote his mother that he hoped the "devotion of the family"— including his own, long-distance—would ease her breathing and soon stand her on her feet again. But that very Sunday evening, as he was dressing for a dinner at one Mrs. Robinson's, Harry got a telegram from William's Alice: YOUR MOTHER EXCEEDINGLY ILL. COME AT ONCE.

Back in Cambridge, some four hundred miles to the north, it looked like snow. Though Harry hurrying to his train could hardly have known it, in the "closing dusk" of that same evening, with Kate sitting at her bedside, Mary Walsh James died.

Henry rushed home from the Park Square railroad station through deep, heavy, still-accumulating snow. Even the fast-running railroads of the Northeast, plowing through a winter blizzard, hadn't delivered Harry to his destination in time, and even his long, worried hours on the snow-blasted trains hadn't allowed him to prepare emotionally for the loss of Mary. Harry arrived twenty-six hours too late to see his mother alive. He felt he didn't know how much he loved his mother until he "saw her lying in her shroud in that cold North Room, with a dreary snowstorm outside, and looking as sweet and tranquil and noble as in life." Even the most self-possessed of the Jameses was profoundly shaken. Harry had been his mother's favorite son, but as he would always recall, he had been socializing at the time of her final breath.

Mary's other sons arrived in the wintry silence. William, who had also been away, journeyed by train back from a grand Harvard Club dinner in Chicago. Wilkie hurried back East from Milwaukee. Bob, living in the house, had witnessed his mother's last days. Henry Senior and Alice, whom William described as "the two who presumably might suffer most," bore up as well as they could, stunned and wide-eyed. For Henry especially, her husband of more than forty years, Mary's death was a deep shock and a profound loss.

Fittingly, Mary's funeral brought all five of the James children into one room for the first time since the Civil War—and, as it happened, for the last time in their lives. To the end, Mary was the glue that held the Jameses together: "Without her," Harry wrote, "we are scattered reeds."

⤛⤜

BECAUSE OF THE deep January snow and the frozen ground, Mary couldn't be buried immediately in her final resting place, by the sweep of the Charles River, in the Cambridge Cemetery. Instead, the Jameses laid her in a temporary vault on a "splendid winter's day," with the sun shining and the blinding snowdrifts lying deep and high.

The Cambridge Cemetery abutted its more famous sister, the Mount Auburn Cemetery, which, founded in 1831, claimed to be the first landscaped, or "garden," cemetery in the United States. Earlier New England generations had buried their dead in austere churchyards or in grass-grown "burial grounds"—with thin tablets of slate as headstones, marked with birth dates and death dates, grim formulas ("Here lies the body of"), and winged death's-heads. The nineteenth-century middle class, though, preferred a more romantic and sentimental vision of death. The Massachusetts Horticultural Society in planning Mount Auburn planted the new cemetery with flowering cherries and lilacs, weeping willows and cypresses and boxwood hedges. This lush garden heralded a new style of cemetery that was about to take hold everywhere in the United States. Mount Auburn Cemetery gave floral addresses to the contemplative genteel family tombs set around lakes and hills. It also blossomed, by the Jameses' day, with sculptural angels, lambs, dogs, cherubs, and sleeping effigies—as though death itself were a park, a museum, or a Grecian temple set over a lake.

Next door, on the back of the hill, the Cambridge Cemetery looked more austere, especially in the dead of winter, with the snowdrifts engulfing the tombstones. Though it also accommodated Brahmins, the Cambridge Cemetery was a poorer municipal sibling of the grander Mount Auburn. Even in death, the Jameses hovered on the margins of Bostonian grandeur—a dusky edge that Mary in particular had known well.

Harry remembered his mother according to her most dulcet traits. "She was patience, she was wisdom, she was exquisite maternity. Her sweetness, her mildness, her great natural beneficence were unspeakable," he wrote in his journal, building his mother a monument in words as exquisite as the marble effigies in Mount Auburn. "She was sweet, gentle, wise, patient, precious," Harry wrote his friend Isabella Stewart Gardner (who would herself be buried in Mount Auburn, in 1924, in a grand gloomy mausoleum decorated with Greek keys), "a pure and exquisite soul." No doubt Mary qualified as one source of Harry's obsession with the idea of purity, close cousin to innocence.

"I thank heaven," Harry added, "that one can lose a mother but *once* in one's life." In short, Harry mourned Mary as the embodiment of "exquisite maternity" (Alice similarly called it "divine maternity"), a family tribute, borrowed from Harry's father, who'd always seen Mary in such lights.

On the one hand, Harry's appraisal wasn't mere eulogizing; he could cite chapter and verse for his mother's virtues. He knew how Mary for years had worked long hours to supervise the household, nurse her ailing children, and guard-dog the family's assets. Though she'd loved the "country, the sea, the change of air and scene," she'd spent her nights and days, Harry claimed, in "dry, flat, hot, stale and odious Cambridge," even if the place may not actually have been the hell for her that it was for Harry. She wouldn't leave Henry Senior's side or Alice's when she was sick. Mary, a Victorian "angel" of devotion, had personified family virtue—and not least because she remained until the day of her death the one James who never abandoned another James, under any circumstances. And that amounted to no small feat. Harry didn't exaggerate when he equated his mother with the Jameses' "house" itself.

Yet, as Alice and William knew well, Mary cast complicated shadows, just like the Quincy Street residence. The house metaphor, tucked into Harry's eulogy and hardly noticed by biographers, hints at a darker side of Mary that surfaces, obliquely, in the James children's hatred of their Cambridge home. Yes, Mary *was* the house. And, because it was difficult to resent their seraphic mother, the children displaced their frustration onto rooms, fireplaces, sofas. None of the James children, after all, could bear the stuffy parlors, the heavy drapes, the stifling emotional atmosphere of 20 Quincy Street, which figured in their imaginations not as a lilac-flanked abode of Victorian sweetness but almost as a haunted house—a burdened, deadened, nightmarish place of confinement.

That Mary, the presiding "angel" of that house, should have had nothing to do with this stifling atmosphere seems highly unlikely. As well as self-sacrificing and nurturing, Mary could also be controlling, passive-aggressive, moralistic, obtuse, conventional, and parsimonious. No doubt her domestic orthodoxy contributed to the "dry, flat, hot, stale and odious Cambridge" that Harry had so hated—and which he'd been champing to escape all these years. Maybe it wasn't the elm-shaded precincts of Harvard Yard, after all; maybe it was Harry's "pure" mother and her conventionality. Maybe it was her scrutiny, her disappointment, he was running from. As critics have noticed, harsh, controlling mothers abound in Harry's fiction.

As her death revealed, Mary left a convoluted legacy. In her will, she bequeathed all of her remaining property—the residue of the old linen fortunes of her ancestors, the financial remains of the porticoed brick mansion in Washington Square—to her daughter, Alice. Aunt Kate had urged Mary to do so. Though Kate had experienced her own frictions with Alice—and these had increased in recent years, especially since the advent of Katharine Loring, of whom she didn't approve—Kate well knew how impossible it was for an unmarried middle-class woman to live decently without such a legacy.

For Alice, this inheritance counted as a final instance of her mother's care. "The blessed memory of her beautifull [sic] spirit will never grow dim," as Alice memorialized her mother to one of her friends. But the gift also revealed her mother's appraisal of Alice as the most vulnerable James—as a female, an invalid, and an even more worrisome case than her bankrupt brothers. No one as yet knew how Alice would cope with the aftermath of their mother's death, and her brothers all worried.

Mary had, in recent years, not shown much confidence in William, either. While calling her death a "severe loss to all of us," he took her passing with apparent equanimity. After all, he'd boarded with his mother longer than any of his other siblings except Alice, often clashing with her on domestic matters (she'd hated his jumbled room and his interminable dissections) just as he'd butted heads with his father over his career. Mary and her oppressive household had probably also contributed to William's fear of marriage—the spooked domestic skittishness that had sent him running to Europe in the summer of 1880.

Yet Mary's death sent genuine shock waves through all the family, rat-
tling even William's composure. Harry had called Mary the "keystone"
of the family arch. Without her, that keystone, the arch—elaborate, antique, and architecturally unsound—looked ready to crumble inward.

Mary's role had sometimes been invisible, discounted, or unappreciated, but she had knit, monitored the Irish servants, passed the brown
rolls at dinner, and swept out the corners. Without her, the family was
once again, as they'd been in 1855, evicted. And now, as they fanned out
again into the world, they lacked someone to shepherd their luggage,
cap their spending, and medicate their collapses. Strange travels,
strange futures loomed. Without Mary, the family might well scatter
like reeds. The winds were already gathering.

· 13 ·

STEAMER NEWS

I n the spring of 1882, shortly after her mother's death, Alice and her father sold the Quincy Street house. The transaction was a quiet business, considering that the family had lived in Cambridge for the better part of two decades, since the end of the Civil War through the rarely uneventful unfolding of the children's lives. The large, heavy wood-frame residence—with its four parlors on the ground floor, four big bedrooms on the second, and further bedrooms under the wide mansard roof—was too labyrinthine and memory-laden for Alice and her father. Nor did it fit William and his small family (one toddler, one child on the way), although the place was more or less this eldest son's inheritance. William didn't want to take over a dwelling where he had suffered so much; he preferred to keep his own rented space nearby. (The home he had once discussed building on his parents' property had never materialized, though William would have a house built on Irving Street in Cambridge.) Harry didn't want the Quincy Street house, either, but he stayed close, delaying his return to England, in order to lend a hand in whatever way he could.

The weather of a New England spring tended to be uncertain for moving house. Boston and its environs were prone to long intervals of rain, when the mud of Harvard Square would be deeply rutted with wagon and carriage wheels. (Many New Englanders kept a mudroom to help deal with the mess.) For Alice, any delay in her departure must have seemed a punishment; she would certainly have looked forward to her liberation, whatever the untidiness and strain of their removal. She had helped persuade her father to relinquish the house where he had settled after his long years of anxious departures, returns, flights, and passages, where he had learned to cherish his unchanging vista over the elms of Harvard Yard and his place among the Brahmin professors with whom he had warred and conspired. He would go with Alice to a home she made for him, no longer exactly the master of his own.

When the movers came, the family possessions were removed, with varying degrees of care. One piece that would certainly be kept close was the oil portrait of Elizabeth Robertson Walsh, Alice's maternal grandmother, whose features reminded her all too much of her own mother. Alice's davenport, her ornamental writing desk, its drawers packed with old letters, came out the door to meet its fate, as did the chairs the Jameses had dragged onto their "piazza" in warm weather and the horsehair sofas that had cradled Alice during her breakdowns. If they hadn't been stored or sold before this, there were also the volumes of English lithographs that Harry had read as a child, and the carpets on which he had lain on his stomach, kicking his heels in the air as he leafed through them, in the family's old row house in New York. Many of these pieces were headed, eventually, for steamers; others were bound, more or less, for oblivion. And oblivion, too, would eventually enfold the house. No photograph of it would survive, and it would be torn down in the twentieth century to make way for what is now the Harvard Faculty Club.

At 20 Quincy Street, Alice had often experienced what she later described as her "stifled sense." Her mother's strict rules of domesticity had been hard on her: "Poor human nature can stand but a slight strain," she later wrote, "when it comes to tea-cups and salt-spoons." But as wider horizons opened up to her—literally, the vistas from her house at Proctor's Point on the North Shore—she faced considerable challenges. Even with the vigorous Katharine at her side, buoying her up, Alice hesitated. She wasn't sure she could adequately replace her mother as her father's nurse. More than anything else, Alice felt herself "haunted by the terror that [she] should fail him." But she'd sworn to "look after [their] father and take care of his house." Harry astutely pronounced Alice a "person of great ability" poised, now, to "exert" herself.

Surprisingly, though, Alice had coped so far. Contrary to her troubled invalid past, she had lately been mostly erect, composed, and decisive. Alice, it seemed, had only been waiting for an opening. She'd held up well enough during the recent ordeal of her mother's death, and she'd readily taken over the management of the household, ordering the family meals from the cook and overseeing the maids. A month after Mary's death, in February 1882, Harry noted that, partly due to Alice's efforts, his father had returned to a "tranquil" state. True, Harry equally credited his father's Swedenborgian philosophy for his acceptance; his father, he wrote, had "his own way of taking the sorrows of life, a way so perfect that one almost envies him his troubles."

Having tactfully withdrawn to New York, leaving Alice in charge, Aunt Kate found her niece's transformation remarkable. Kate insisted that "her Mother's death seem[ed] to have brought new life to Alice." Kate imagined Mary peering down from heaven and rejoicing. The Jameses understood this paradox as another eerie instance of the family's symbiosis; they had often remarked that one member of the family seemed to benefit from the absence, illness, or in this case death of another family member.

By May 1882, Alice had settled her father and his well-traveled, red-bound Swedenborgs into a new house at 131 Mount Vernon Street in Boston, on the "flat" between Beacon Hill and the Charles River estuary. A few fashionable row houses stood here, but mostly the area accommodated stables and carriage houses to service the mansions farther up the hill, on the sunny South Slope. Once again, the Jameses had settled on the margins of Brahmin splendors: their trim brick residence stood next door to a fire station. Yet the new compact townhouse offered its share of advantages, and for Alice there were fewer chores to do. For Henry Senior, he now had the proximity of the Athenœum, with its marble busts, as well as the bookstores of Charles Street, with their troves of erudite books. Even after forty years, Henry loved to soothe his nerves by trawling such shops, as he'd done as a young married man in London. Now the seventy-year-old no longer had to totter aboard the horsecars from Cambridge—hazardous transport for an elderly, one-legged man. In his new home, he deeply missed his beloved Mary, but he had two attentive women, thirty-four-year-old Alice and her friend Katharine, to supervise the Irish servants and listen to his musings at dinner.

⁂

ALICE TRANSPLANTED HER father to her "cottage"—now a rambling seaside compound, with stables and a long pier marching out into the Atlantic—at Proctor's Point during the summer of 1882. The big, barnlike, freshly framed house wasn't quite finished yet, but its plastered newness must have added to its atmosphere of openness and light. Right next to its "piazzas," the breakers of the Jameses' ocean, the chilly Atlantic crashed on the pink granite shoreline. Beach roses bloomed, fuchsia or white, beside the bayberries, whose scent, Harry noticed, mixed with that of the ocean. It was a good place for people to recover, and Alice set up a sort of hospital for ailing family members. Alice's mother had always glowed with angelic self-sacrifice as well as nursing skills, and Alice now undertook these burdens. She invited her thirty-three-year-old sister-in-law, still estranged from her husband, Bob, to stay in Manchester with her nine-year-old son, Ned, and seven-year-old daughter, Mary.

Alice had always liked her brother's wife, Mary Holton James, and now took compassionate charge of her. There beside the ocean, amid the weedy American "scragginess" about which Harry ritually complained, Alice could provide her guests with rest, coolness, and peace. Alice took them on "charming drives"—no doubt in her bouncing phaeton, with her or Katharine snapping the reins and chasing the best views over an Atlantic strewn with rocky islets.

Alice touchingly filled in for her missing brother Bob, who had sailed away on a quixotic voyage to the Azores. Some James was always setting forth; Bob was bound for Fayal, a lush volcanic island and sailors' delight planted in the middle of busy Atlantic shipping lanes, where ships called on the steamer route between Lisbon and Rio. In the Portuguese-speaking town of Horta, a small port in the shadow of the three-thousand-foot volcano of Pico Gordo, Bob calculated he had enough money to live for about three months. (Bob had little enough of his own, but his brothers William and Harry helped him out from time to time.) No doubt the exoticism of this island, famously planted with grapes as well as with blue hydrangeas, had appealed to him; so colorful a place may even have interested him as an aspiring painter. (A similarly restless Paul Gauguin would later travel to Tahiti in 1891, on his own more fruitful escape from civilization and its discontents.)

More likely, this small, steep island or its neighbor, São Miguel, could also have counted as Bob's Brazil—his sensual hazing, his antidote to Wisconsin. But unlike William two decades before, Bob wasn't pursuing anything even so practical as bogus zoology. And he no longer qualified as a carpetbag-toting youth who could simply hitch his way to happiness. A thirty-six-year-old married man, he himself couldn't explain why he'd turned his back on his children and braved a storm-raked ocean, unless it was for the famous Fayal wine or the local women, who were renowned for working lace and, by some accounts, for welcoming sailors.

Clearly, Bob had adopted the expedient of travel to which both his father and brothers had so often resorted. He was still struggling with alcohol, the family complaint. Yet even during his worst bouts of alcoholism and mental illness in the 1840s, Henry Senior had almost always kept his family with him. Bob's drinking had estranged him from Mary Holton, as Henry Senior had never been divided from Mary Walsh. Bitterly and chronically unhappy, Bob was a captious, trying housemate, as his more disciplined father had seldom allowed himself to be.

"For the sake of pleasing Willy I have tried hard to think it wise to go back West," Bob wrote Harry from his ship. But Bob regarded Wisconsin with "nothing but horror." He dreaded his hostile father-in-law and his former soul-killing clerical work. "It seems like a dark thing sometimes to be sailing away on this hazardous sea—away from you all, especially from dear father." But if he missed Henry Senior, he didn't mention his wife or his children, from whom, too, he had a compulsion to escape.

Alice, however, didn't run. Her "dear father," for whom she'd always had a deep affinity in spite of his drawbacks, remained in earshot, reading on the piazza with a blanket across his knees. Bob's children's voices filled the house. Yet in spite of having taken in her niece and nephew,

Alice continued to worry over her own abilities. It was as if, now at last beginning to walk upright, she might stumble at any moment, or so she felt. In September when she returned Henry Senior to their "pretty" brick Beacon Hill house, Alice fretted to her friend Fanny Morse that she wouldn't be "equal" to her new tasks. She had to concentrate on one day at a time, she confessed, in order to crowd out the "vague terrors" that continued to harass her. "I used to think I loved my dear Mother & knew her burdens," Alice concluded, "but I find I only knew half of them."

In losing her mother, Alice had paradoxically drawn closer to Mary than ever before. But the more critical and demanding Mary also lurked in the household, undergirding Alice's actions—watchful and exalted. Alice suspected she herself wasn't cut out to be a materfamilias. She wasn't quarried from travertine, as her mother had been; she wasn't sturdy enough to serve as the family's "keystone" or foundation. Alice had more intricate virtues, and more shadows.

BOB, MEANWHILE, WASN'T the only James son who had bolted. Harry, after the death of his mother, dutifully intended to hunker down in America for at least six months, in order to buoy up his sister and father, but he didn't know how long he could stand it.

He hired lodgings higher on Beacon Hill, at 102 Mount Vernon Street, where, in the neighborhood of his old haunt the dramaturgical "Museum," he tinkered with a theatrical adaptation of his most conspicuous hit to date, *Daisy Miller*, even entering into negotiations with the owners of the Madison Square Theatre in New York. Bent on pleasing their audiences, the Mallory brothers wanted the play to have more obvious action and drama; the novella *Daisy Miller*, like much of Harry's fiction, was highly psychological and internal. Harry gamely provided a villain (the Italian courier Eugenio) and a happy ending: Daisy Miller recovered from her malaria and married Winterbourne. But Harry was no Dion Boucicault (1820–1880), that wildly successful Franco-Irish writer of popular melodrama. Ultimately, no one really wanted to produce his somewhat awkward play, and he had to content himself with publishing it in the ever-obliging *Atlantic*—and reading it out loud to

Isabella Stewart Gardner. Harry remained "desperately homesick for London," as he confided by letter to his dapper friend Lord Rosebery. Henry Senior, who had been growing closer to his second son, noticed the problem. Witnessing his son's stifled misery, Henry insisted that he not make any "sacrifices" for his sake.

So in early May 1882, Harry claimed a stateroom on the up-to-date Cunard screw steamer *Gallia*. He had recently attended the Concord funeral of his father's Olympian friend, Ralph Waldo Emerson, but Harry was in an upbeat mood. It did him good to board a steamer bound for Liverpool and to resume his international privileges. The liner, incidentally, boasted three masts but only two bathtubs for the whole ship; there were no baths for the twelve hundred steerage passengers the *Gallia* could cram into its bilges. A Gilded Age steamship, for all that it seemed to embody progress and freedom of movement, was a microcosm of the stratified world that had formed Harry's sensibility: though not as rich as the Astors or the Vanderbilts, he and his family could and mostly did ignore the desperately poor immigrants with whom he shared some of his Atlantic crossings. But related hierarchies of privilege and deprivation also pervaded the James family itself, with its two pampered and its two penniless sons. There were even biting distinctions, too, and continuing struggles, between the two eldest.

When he sailed for England, Harry could regard himself as not only the most successful James son but also, in his father's eyes, the most cherished one. On the eve of Harry's sailing, the widowed Henry wrote his son a startlingly emotional letter. "My darling boy," Henry Senior wrote,

> I must bid you farewell. How loving a farewell it is, I can't say, but only that it is most loving. I can't help feeling that you are the one that has cost us the least trouble, and given us always the most delight. Especially do I mind Mother's perfect joy in you the last few months of her life, and your perfect sweetness to her. I think in fact it is this which endears you so much to me now. I feel that I have fallen heir to all dear Mother's fondness for you, as well as my proper own.

This late-breaking paternal hug must have gratified Harry, who had grown up as his mother's favorite, not his father's. Henry Senior had

always favored William's eggheaded male pursuits, medicine and philosophy, more than Harry's fascination with fiction. But now, though
the younger brother had followed his own desires, Harry had inched
forward in Henry Senior's esteem. The father's old ambition and desire
for public acclaim, which had led him to drive his children to succeed,
had not been silenced, and the role of favorite would go to the son who
most successfully burnished the family name. Harry was a public man of
letters in a way that Henry Senior himself had never been, outside of a
small circle of Concord-group intellectuals and antebellum social reformers.

Perhaps in response to this surprising blessing, Harry decided to
make a stopover in his father's ancestral country of Ireland. Harry had
also been pushed to investigate the "Irish question," the ticklish problem of the political status of Ireland, by his Liberal friends in England.
He would conduct his investigation by visiting the south, though the
kin of William James of Albany had actually farmed their acres in the
north, at Bailieborough in County Cavan. (The Jameses' ancestral
home lay in the Protestant-dominated northern province of Ulster, although Cavan was a county that the Irish Republic would eventually
inherit.) Later in his life, Harry would mythologize the visit his father
had made to Bailieborough in 1837; he would characteristically elevate
his father into a kind of homecoming prince, a local son (though Henry
had been born in Albany) who had made good in America. For his part,
Henry had made a substantial impression on his Irish relatives, fascinating them not only with his wealth and education but also with his
intelligent and charismatic black servant, Billy Taylor. In 1882,
though, Harry's own exploration of Ireland would prove much more
perfunctory.

Disembarking from his liner, Harry glided ashore at the busy sheltered
harbor of Queenstown (today Gaelically renamed Cobh, or "Cove"), near
Cork. Queenstown was a small, active maritime place, which catered to the
Atlantic steamships coming and going from Liverpool: an express train
bound for Dublin waited on the tracks to take any mail that came off the
ships. Situated on the lush, twisting estuary of the river Lee, the place also
abutted the big, smoky town of Cork and the poor, marshy farming dis-
tricts of the Irish county of that same name. Accordingly, Queenstown had

served as the departure point for a significant number of the Catholic Irish who had emigrated to the United States, beginning especially after the Potato Famine of the 1840s.

Harry had frequently seen the town's waterfront arc of row houses, with the great stone cathedral rising behind. His family's steamships had often anchored in the bay. But this time he was determined to go ashore and see more. Small fishing vessels from the town plied the harbor. Queenstown, sturdily built on its Great Island, was dominated by jetties and wharves and mobbed with seagulls as Harry landed. As he walked among the small shops and stone houses, he had the sharp, lively local accent of Cork, which substituted *t* for *th*, in his ears. The town had highly interested other observers, but to Harry it was (literally) beyond the pale.

Only a little way outside the town, he viewed "some very green fields and dirty cabins" and hastily turned back. With such images of poverty in his head, he wasted no time in taking ship again. The *Gallia*'s two baths proved better than an underprivileged place that appeared to have none at all. So much for the "Irish question." In spite of his Ulster ancestors, Harry hated the sight of shanties. He hankered instead for his old haunts in Mayfair, its aristocratic mansions and imperial gentlemen's clubs.

THE JAMESES WERE always running away from Jameses only to collide with Jameses again. When Harry returned to his Bolton Street lodgings after his six-month absence, bracing himself for the "whirlpool of the Season," he found the truant Bob lounging on his sofa. No doubt Harry's younger brother had just stashed a bottle of spirits behind it. At any rate, Bob looked "battered and depressed" to Harry, who thought Bob none the better for the torrid Azores and the strong island wine. And actually seeing Harry's sumptuous Mayfair pied-à-terre—that dusky, well-appointed bachelor's den a block away from St. James's Park—evidently hadn't raised Bob's spirits or his self-esteem.

But Harry coddled his own unremunerative addictions. Though he now claimed to dread "society," he wasted no time in amassing quantities of calling cards and dinner invitations. In his first three days back in

London, as he boasted to his friend Grace Norton, he greeted 350 people. What obsession had him tipping his hat like a marionette? Harry confided to his journal that his socializing served as his "old salve to a perturbed spirit, the idea that [he] was seeing the world." But his old enthusiasm was missing; he had to admit that the glittering splendors of the season actually provided him what he admitted was a "poor" world. A brocaded duchess could do very little for the essential loneliness gnawing inside him. "I have a certain fear that you miss me," Harry wrote Grace Norton, "or shall I call it a certain hope?"

BY SEPTEMBER 2, 1882, eight months after his mother's death, William had slipped aboard his own transatlantic liner bound for Europe. For a year in Cambridge he'd played the part of dedicated husband, engaged father, supportive brother, and hardworking Harvard professor—with apparent contentment and increasing success. But although he was now forty years old, his ingrained malaise was again asserting itself, in a familiar and yet unexpected way.

Around the *Parisian*, a chill night had set in, the sky clotting up with clouds. Even the gilded saloon, with golden flickering lamps planted upright on the tables, hardly cheered him. He dreaded, as he'd done before, the "wild" strangeness of "night falling and gathering about a lonely ship." He could hear the rush of the water in the portholes of the low-slung coal-reeking Allan Line steamer (whose up-to-date engines had recently made the front page of *Scientific American*) as it labored out into the Gulf of St. Lawrence at fifteen knots. Having polished off his lonely supper, with brand-new spectacles on his nose, William now sat down at a gently rolling table to write his wife. He confided to her that Cambridge and its "*terra firma* conditions of solidity" were scarily slipping away from him in the oceanic night.

William's most solid terra firma, of course, meant Mrs. Alice. But he'd cast off from Alice as much as from the quay at Quebec City. Already homesick, William enclosed a kiss in his letter—the word *kiss* wrapped in an ink circle, with a squiggle of lips scrawled across it. This papery hello was meant for his three-year-old son: "Cover Harry with kisses and tell him to say good-bye to Sandy"—the family dog—"& give him my love. I forgot the worthy beast." And Sandy wasn't alone in being forgotten. Besides little Harry and the dog, two others William had left behind had to share the kiss. One was Alice, who was once again playing single mother. The other was the couple's three-month-old baby, William—or, to distinguish him from his absent father, "Willyam" with a *y*, or "Billy."

Once again, William had vacated Cambridge shortly after the birth of one of his children. (The family put it differently: William had loyally *stayed* until the baby was born.) This time, he'd finagled a yearlong leave of absence from Harvard and intended to spend most of it away from his family. His huge overview of contemporary psychology was years overdue but still growing in scope and ambition. What started out as a textbook was becoming a monster monograph. Professional consultations in Europe again seemed necessary—William kept up an enormous correspondence and wrote trenchant articles and reviews on moral and philosophical subjects, some of which would later be incorporated into his magnum opus. (As small indications of his tremendous range and intellectual power, William had recently published articles called "Rationality, Activity, and Faith" and "On Some Hegelianisms" in the *Princeton Review*.) William wrote with mounting clarity and liveliness about the developing field of psychology, which was still largely dominated by his two separate fields of expertise, philosophy and medicine. But William's growing confidence as a psychological thinker contrasted painfully with the realm of his own fraught psyche.

Throughout the autumn in Mrs. Alice's household on Garden Street, a succession of paper kisses arrived in William's letters, for little Harry. The kisses took the form of scribbles, ink sketches of lips, or lips topped with a Williamish nose and mustache. The word *kiss* often fueled the gift. Sometimes William personalized the gesture with an inscription: "Kiss for Harry." Some of the endearments wound up a little smudged, as if a flesh-and-blood kiss had gone into the making of them—or had been implanted by the little dark-headed boy on the receiving end.

From Venice a month after his sailing, in October 1882, William enclosed for little Harry a graceful sketch of a gondola. A hatted gondolier navigated it with its single oar; a hatted father lounged inside of it. The drawing was William's attempt to convey Venice to a three-year-old. "Instead of horse cars & carriages & wagons," William wrote to his son, "there's nothing but boats,—big black boats called gondolas; and the people speak Italian, what you can't speak a word of. I will send you a little picture of Venice to keep."

But then William found himself explaining something else.

> Your poor Dad has got no home now, but just rolls around the world, sleeping in another bed almost every night. Sometimes he almost feels like crying to get home to Momsy & Culturmensch & Willyam & all. But he don't cry, because, because its [sic] an evil thing for men & boys to cry. Only women & babies can cry; because the babies can't help it, and the women are a kind o' soft. Sometimes your dear Momsy did cry. If you see her cry, I hope you will kiss her & make her stop.

This heartbreaking nineteenth-century baby-talk reveals as much about William's state of mind in the 1880s as his entire (slowly swelling) body of psychological writing. It reveals William's agonized conflicts about love and manhood—insofar as it was himself, really, he was urging not to cry. If he had asserted his male prerogatives by going away, if he had put his professional life first, he'd also radically undermined his own sense of masculine virtue by once again abandoning his young family.

William claimed he was traveling for his career, to consult with his European colleagues. But just what eminent professors of psychology were to be found bobbing around on the lagoon of Venice? And how did William's stalled magnum opus, his *Principles of Psychology*, benefit from the cracked washstands and creaky bedsteads of Italian hotels? In Germany, in various guesthouses as he traversed the country, sometimes actually in pursuit of experts, sometimes on more recreational junkets, William had been "peppered over" with bedbug bites. That much ought to have spurred him to some self-psychoanalysis about his own purposes for being away. But, as deeply reflective as he was, as conversant with mental and philosophical states, William couldn't always penetrate or understand motives, which were, after all, as the new Freudian psychology would begin to discover in the coming decades, largely unconscious.

In spite of his well-adjusted appearance and brisk professional life, William had earlier genuinely verged on a breakdown—and partly thanks to the burden of that very professional life, his voluminous writing and his heavy load of teaching at Harvard. President Charles W. Eliot had let William go and had even been persuaded to hire Josiah Royce, William's new redheaded friend from California, as a temporary replacement. Eliot understood the value of European travel and consultation from his own seminal survey of European educational institutions in the 1860s. But he had lost his wife, Ellen Peabody, in 1869, and he wondered how William could bear to "stay the winter" away from Mrs. Alice.

William insisted, though, that he needed a leave not only for matters of research but also for his health, for his strained eyes and nerves. But if such concerns had really been the reason for his trip, William could have headed for a sanatorium, as he'd done in the 1860s. It made less sense that he had passed right through the Alps and dropped down to Venice, where, in the received wisdom of the day, the "air" couldn't possibly be any worse. (The "air," indeed, boiling as it was with mosquitoes, eventually completely shattered William's sleep.) In spite of the heavy rains, why hadn't William stuck to curative Switzerland, with its multiple-altitude swatches of "air" to match every known malady of body, heart, or head?

To be sure, William's own future psychological researches would drive at least one nail in the coffin of this preposterous theory of air—the idea that health problems were caused or cured by different kinds of climates and atmospheres. Science would increasingly discover the bacterial and viral pathogens responsible for tuberculosis, malaria, cholera, and the other signature diseases of the era. But this cherished mythology of curative air would die hard even in the twentieth century—and partly because of the irresistible license it gave for rich invalids and restless spirits to travel. The Jameses had invoked this privilege again and again. Sometimes a change of scene, of course, could really cure. History had its examples of this. But somewhere down deep, William must have known he needed something besides air to set himself right.

At the same time, it wasn't clear to William what he was running from, and what, exactly, he hoped to find in Europe. His father had certainly never really known why he had itched to travel, for all of his protestations in 1855 about the value of Swiss schools. Though William was not an alcoholic or an ex-alcoholic, he was as troubled by his particular form of depression as his father had been. He remained uncomfortable with the intimate burdens of family life. Earlier in his journey, observing the stout and bundled peasant women of Germany, William had agonized about the "mystery of womanhood" and more specifically "the Mothers! The Mothers!" His wife and all the bonneted and kerchiefed mothers of the nineteenth-century world were all one, William concluded. He recollected his "own dear Mother with tears running down [his] face." As a man forbidden to cry, William had to travel quite a few miles in order to appreciate his wife and mourn his mother.

William arrived in the city of Venice in October, when the rain wet the worn-down pavements of the old city. In the lovely Renaissance church of San Zaccaria, William luxuriated in front of the Giovanni Bellini altarpiece, a blue-robed Madonna standing an infant Jesus on her knee. At the "exquisite little" church of San Giorgio degli Schiavoni, he had other Harry-like raptures while looking at the Carpaccios, which he found "as good as they can be, in spite of the fact that Mr. Ruskin likes them so excessively." William of course had once aspired to be a painter himself, though now the art world had become Harry's territory. Yet William contemplated trespassing on his brother's terrain even more: he imagined writing a piece about Venice for the *Nation*. He was only stopped, he wrote to his father, by the spirit of *dolce far niente* (it's sweet to do nothing), as observed in the penniless young Italian men lounging around the Piazza San Marco, grinning, with round caps on their heads and six-centime cigars clenched in their teeth. But William hardly admired any such "cad" or idler—especially because he himself, shirking his duties in Venice, had more or less become one.

William went to lunch at the home of his wealthy friends Daniel Sargent Curtis and Ariana Randolph Wormeley Curtis at the Palazzo Barbaro—in one of two adjacent palaces that shared this name, one medieval and one baroque, fronting the wide, watery, S-shaped thoroughfare of the Grand Canal. The Curtises' staggering Venetian rental, which they would purchase outright in 1885, featured "colossal dimensions" and a highly encrusted "grand style" that impressed even the jaded William. In cultivating such splendors, William had transformed his life into Harry's. Maybe William now wanted to be Harry even more than, historically, trailing his more confident big brother around London or the Newport art studio, Harry had wanted to be William.

At the Curtises', William had lunch with a hanger-on cousin of the family, the twenty-six-year-old painter John Singer Sargent. Sargent and his cousin Ralph Wormeley Curtis, his studio protégé, were scouring the city for picturesque Venetian genre scenes—Sargent had been coloring up canvasses of Venetian women glassworkers and bead stringers. But in 1882, the year of William's visit, Sargent also daubed a portrait of William's hostess, Ariana Curtis, that showed, against a sea of Spanish black, a formidable, strong-cheeked matron. Wearing pearls, a lace collar, and a lace cap to contrast with all her black, the Sargent-ized Ariana Curtis observed the world with languid, half-lidded eyes—a taste of the expatriate splendor that William had to "fall back upon" during those rainy evenings away from his wife.

The Curtises provided William with colorful excursions. On one outing to the Lido, William fell in love with the hulking steamships departing for exotic and far-flung ports. "I feel sorely tempted to cast reason to the dogs, & start for Bombay," William wrote to Mrs. Alice. "I shall never again have such a chance!" Mrs. Alice's heart may well have skipped a beat at the mention of India; it wasn't entirely out of the realm of possibility that William, on this impulse, might bolt like Bob or else morph into a vagabond like his itinerant friend Herbert Pratt. Victorian husbands sometimes turned into such castaways. More characteristically, William contemplated roping his brother Harry into a trip to Sicily—a family-romance honeymoon that (probably luckily) never materialized.

❧

AT THE TABLE d'hôte at his modest hotel, however, William faced a stronger, more subtle temptation. Mornings and evenings, he encountered a young woman who shared the inn's dining table with him—the graceful wife of a Prussian officer named von Oldenburg. Away from her husband, the lady was staying with her family. Her three sisters appeared at the table with her. Her youngest sister was plump but pretty;

the second sister had lovely brown hair and "*such*" eyes," William thought. They were all tall, healthy, and "ravishingly beautiful." Signora von Oldenburg was the eldest and perhaps the plainest, but she had an exquisite complexion and lovely dark eyes. From his chair at their shared table, William was intrigued.

As the days went on, he came to know the Italian family and found out more about their lives; they were pleasanter company than the Curtises and other grand and somewhat strenuous Americans in Venice. Their unaffectedness and warmth soothed the homesick William as, more and more, the four handsome sisters preoccupied his thoughts.

William evidently understood at least some of the twists and turns of his fascination. This Italian family drew his attention partly because they pantomimed Alice Gibbens's—looking as William imagined Alice and her two sisters had appeared ten years before during their own European lodging-house wanderings in Germany. Or so he explained it in his letters home. To the lonely William, the officer's wife resembled a younger and fresher Alice: "You & she are a regular pair of twins," William wrote to his wife. Yet the exquisite atmosphere of Venice was also apparently working on William; his window opened up on the Grand Canal, with its beautiful light and graceful water traffic. It was not long before he gave his wife the startling news: he, the forty-year-old father of two, was "rapidly falling in love" with this Italian.

Not that Alice had anything to fear, William hastily added. His table talk with Madame von Oldenburg, he reported, remained unintriguingly "grammar-school." And, according to William, Alice had "no right to resent [his] being in love with her," since he had "once" felt that way about Alice herself. Clearly, William knew how to shove his foot in his mouth—and inflict wounds far more hurtful than he realized. It was partly William's troubled history that made him callous. Ironically, he appeared partly motivated by his genuine if displaced love for the wife with whom he couldn't bear to stay at home. His long-squelched libido also played its part, as did his father's lifelong delectation of ladies—passed down to William, as Bob had seemingly inherited Henry Senior's alcoholism. On his previous European getaway from his family, William had flirted openly with the actress Helen Modjeska in London, among others. But this time the entanglement was longer-lasting and potentially more wounding to Mrs. Alice. To be sure, William had previously been insensitive in his life—cut off from reacting, empathizing, and relating to others' emotions. He'd sometimes proved brusque and unfeeling to both Harry and his sister, Alice. But here was a new and troubling development of an old character trait.

Whatever its root causes, William's hotel dalliance soon grew even stranger. When the Italian family invited William to inspect some Venetian glass they'd bought, William sidled up to Madame von Oldenburg, flirted, and plunged still deeper in love. "I would give millions of dollars—anything," William wrote his wife, "if you could be here to share it with me. She would then fall in love with you; and she and I would then have one serious subject in common." Such a triangle of displaced passions was worthy of Shakespeare, or of Freud, or of the James family; Harry especially had made such substitutions in his adult life, using one person to keep the intimacy of another at bay. For his part, William strove to reassure his "everlasting bride" that this infatuation didn't reduce his love for her but instead made it "shoot to an unexampled height." Even a pre-Freudian reader, especially a wife, had to wonder what *that* meant. It hinted at a sexual meaning, and it was almost as if William were fantasizing about using his wife as a pawn to get to another woman—while Mrs. Alice struggled with William's young children, on her own, back in Cambridge.

Victorian husbands had few qualms about flirting or falling in love at will. But untypically William reported his indiscretions, such as they were, to his wife. At least he was honest, in some fashion. But he was also playing with the feelings of a loyal woman who had borne his travels with real magnanimity. With something more like self-knowledge, William wrote home, "Alice, I ought never to have come abroad alone."

∽

BUT MRS. ALICE's Italian look-alike, in fact, didn't rank as William's first extramarital crush. A few months before, staying with his friends the Wards in the Berkshire Hills of Massachusetts, William had encountered a handsome young woman from whom he'd hoped "nevermore to be separated"—the thirty-three-year-old Jewish poet and writer, an early visionary of the Zionist movement, Emma Lazarus.

For most Americans, Lazarus would become most enduringly famous for her later poem "The Colossus" (1883), containing the well-known and moving lines "Give me your tired, your poor, / Your huddled masses straining to be free." Lazarus's poem was a tribute to the Statue of Liberty as a "Mother of Exiles," but in it, she distinctly valued these exiles above the "storied pomp" of the Old or for that matter the New World. Emma had the instincts of a litterateur combined with those of a political firebrand. When she wrote her poem the next year, of course, the Statue of Liberty didn't yet exist, though in 1876 France had given it to the United States as a present for its hundredth birthday. The mammoth copper pieces of the gigantic figure were being manufactured in France, by the sculptor Frederic Auguste Bartholdi and Alexandre Gustave Eiffel, the engineer of the eponymous tower. Led by Joseph Pulitzer, Americans were slowly raising funds for the granite pedestal of the statue. The copper colossus would finally rise and dominate New York Harbor only in 1886, ten years after the present had first been announced.

"The Colossus" (a poem actually written as a sonnet) would give Emma Lazarus lasting fame, but her other works marked a still-deeper sensibility and restlessness. She energetically filled both the American mainstream and Jewish magazines of her day with ambitious poems and verse narratives—at a time when Jewish immigrants, one of the groups of "huddled masses" arriving at Ellis Island, increasingly made their presence felt in the tenements, factories, and shops of New York and other American cities.

That July of 1882, William was staying in the Berkshires of western Massachusetts with well-heeled New York friends. The house had "piazzas" on three sides, running right into the grass and into the views of wooded hills. He felt "six years" younger—the age when he had first met Alice Howe Gibbens—and felt "the same fresh boy as then." When he met Emma Lazarus, who was staying with his friends the Wards, he promptly fell "violently in love" with her.

With a certain Anglo-Saxon nervousness, William felt that Lazarus "brandished the [J]ewish flag, phylactery, tabernacle, golden calf, or whatever the standard of the Nation may be, very patriotically." But he also more directly accepted this dynamic, strong, dark-haired writer. For one thing, the thirty-three-year-old Lazarus showed herself as highly literate; she'd actually read William's specialized intellectual works, his reviews and philosophical essays. William increasingly argued against various forms of stark and pessimistic philosophy that were fashionable in the late nineteenth century, for example, that of social Darwinists like Herbert Spencer (1820–1903) and skeptical philosophers like Arthur Schopenhauer (1788–1860). In his embrace of the potential for human goodness, William had won a disciple: Emma told William that his clear, positive, down-to-earth writings had "converted her from pessimism to optimism."

Also, as an intelligent devotee, Emma gave William a taste of the affirmation he so desperately craved. Like the other Jameses, he spoiled to be admired. Perhaps such hankerings even lay at the root of William's crushes. In any case, this affair evidently took place mostly in his head and in his letters to his wife. (Though it reveals crucial aspects of William's personality, it doesn't appear at all in most biographies of him.) In August 1882, he wrote "Miss Lazarus" a letter, praising her poetry: "I think the power of *playing* with thought and language that such as you possess is the divinest of gifts." He hoped they would meet again, and that she and his "dear wife [would] become acquainted." But there's no evidence that they ever did. Five years later, in 1887, Emma Lazarus died, probably of Hodgkin's disease. She was just thirty-eight years old.

BACK IN VENICE, William's new table d'hôte infatuation reminded him of Emma Lazarus as well as of Mrs. Alice. Like Lazarus, the young Italian defended the Jews in Germany, not believing in "one race hating another." How Alice liked this link to the bewitching *"Emma"* isn't recorded. But William hastened to smooth over a potential rough spot. "Dearest," he wrote, "you will get used to these enthusiasms of mine and like them." His crushes only confirmed, he argued, his loyalty to Alice—since Madame von Oldenburg reminded him of her. To his credit, William wrote his wife voluminously and intimately about almost everything that happened to him. But his repeated absences and headlong admirations conveyed a mixed message, to say the least, to his diaper-besieged spouse in Massachusetts.

Another member of the James family, though, felt Alice's pain. During the month of William's Venetian holiday, Harry—himself on a little tour of France that would become a delectable travel book—wrote Mrs. Alice that she "must feel rather bewildered and abandoned." Having met and got to know his likable sister-in-law while in America, Harry could readily sympathize with her, as he often did with women. "Abandoned by your husband," Harry continued, aiming at urbane commiseration but perhaps unintentionally rubbing it in, "you seem to me, dear Alice, very greatly to be pitied."

Harry's sympathy, to be sure, had a barb in it—some remnant, perhaps, of his rivalry with Mrs. Alice. Yet his own troubled past with his brother helped him appreciate the costs of "William's own doctrines." More than his professed philosophical beliefs, William's "doctrines" amounted to his quirky, skittish methods of human interaction. These often exacted sacrifices from those who loved him, as his entitlement to unlimited travel had definitely done. As for Mrs. Alice, her conspicuous self-denial crowned her as a good Victorian wife, but her acceptance of William's traveling perhaps also filled some unscrutinized need of her own. Having some distance from William may not have been all bad. At the same time, Alice must hardly have known what to tell her friends when she and her nursemaid wheeled her pram, unattended, into the autumnal walks of Cambridge Common. And those recreational moments must have been few, as little Harry was suffering from dysentery in October, the month of his father's sojourn in Venice.

William, for his part, learned to sympathize with his own inconveniences if not always with Alice's, on his travels. With so many changes of scene, he felt he understood what Harry called his "furies at temporary lodgings." "Never, never again, under any pretext whatsoever, however specious, shall I become the homeless outcast that I now am," William pledged—striking out telegramlike capital letters on a Caligraph, an early incarnation of the typewriter, to spare his eyes. His misery granted him a self-revelation, of a kind. But it focused on his own discomforts and not on the conflicted feelings that had driven him from home in the first place. And his insight didn't result in any immediate plans for him to return to Cambridge.

After rambling across Germany, William settled for a few weeks in

Paris in November 1882. There, he took himself to the theater in the evenings (he saw Molière's *The Misanthrope* and longed to hear Mrs. Alice's "soft chuckling" beside him). He also attended the famous sessions of the pioneering French neurologist Jean-Martin Charcot. At fifty-seven, Charcot was already famous for his work on hypnotism and hysteria, but his work on these popular nineteenth-century subjects was more exacting and scientific than that of most of his contemporaries. This rigor attracted William, who as both a medical doctor and a philosopher always looked for links between the physical mind and its more metaphysical functions. Charcot conducted his work mostly at La Salpêtrière, a sprawling domed charity hospital near the Gare d'Austerlitz. Once a gunpowder factory (hence its name), the hospital lay at the forefront of nineteenth-century psychiatry: a thirtyish Sigmund Freud would spend a year studying there with Charcot three years later, in 1885–86. What would the young Freud have thought of William as a colleague—or, for that matter, as a patient? William seemed to illustrate many of Freud's future ideas about the workings of the unconscious. But with similar training in a similar era, the two would espouse very different conceptions of the human psyche and its potential: William would be far more optimistic about human nature than Freud.

In the autumn of 1882, as it happened, Dr. Charcot had been treating Ivan Turgenev, who'd been suffering from strange and unsettling symptoms: his back plagued him, and he could scarcely walk. Harry had alighted in Paris to see Turgenev before William arrived there—in one of the characteristic near-misses of the brothers. Harry had paid an affectionate visit to his ailing mentor, whose big frame now slumped, emaciated, on his sofa. The brilliant Charcot would soon diagnose him with cancer of the spine. And before a year had passed, by September 1883, Ivan Turgenev, Harry's substitute father, would be dead.

᠅

TELEGRAPH CABLES, IN the early 1880s, first announced such deaths to the world. But it was still the transatlantic steamers that conveyed the details and substance of important events between Europe and America. With telegraphic communication between continents as yet rudimentary (reliably available across the Atlantic only since the Civil

War), the circumstances of the deaths of Charles Darwin or Giuseppe Garibaldi in 1882 awaited the mails and newspapers carried to New York by steamship. That winter, on their return journeys on their great-circle routes into the Arctic, these same ships brought photographs and accounts of the new Brooklyn Bridge, the longest suspension span on the planet, which had been under construction since 1870 and in the spring of 1883 would finally open to a flood of foot and carriage traffic across its high arc over the East River, through its two sets of twin Gothic arches.

But for the Jameses, it seemed, steamers now mostly traversed the Atlantic with delayed bad news: Mary's abrupt death had apparently opened a grim season for them. In early December 1882, at his lodgings on the boulevard St.-Michel on the Left Bank, William got a scary, delayed letter from his wife, Alice.

The day before Thanksgiving, Mrs. Alice had arrived in Beacon Hill to find that her father-in-law had suffered a debilitating "attack of nausea and faintness." Henry Senior lay in his bed, weakened but able to eat a baked potato and an orange along with some brandy and Apollinaris water. The doctor judged the elder Henry might live on for years. But serenely, Henry Senior, now seventy-one, insisted he was dying.

This picture of his bedridden old father in Cambridge jolted William out of his Parisian preoccupations. He immediately consulted Harry by wire and set off by train for London. William had left his father content, if frail, under his sister's care, but matters had rapidly changed, and he was now horrified to be thousands of miles away at such a crucial time.

Back in Massachusetts, Henry Senior's rapid decline—which soon enough had him refusing food and, in his long tradition as a moralist and social critic, railing against the manifold evils of the world—inflicted devastation throughout his family. Alice James could hardly bear to witness her father's decline. Though she'd seemed well the summer before, she now took to her bed and remained shut up in her room. If her mother's illness had energized her, her father's danger laid her low, hinting at the depth of her need for him. Alice couldn't bear to nurse the failing old man. So Aunt Kate, herself seventy years old and not in the best of health, had to travel up from New York to take care of her brother-in-law. As she had done so often in the past, Aunt Kate promptly supplied her "gentle vigilance," as Mrs. Alice approvingly described it. But the distraught Alice James was more familiar with the costs of her aunt's supervision; in recent years, Alice had kept her distance. She knew, for one thing, that Kate didn't approve of Katharine Peabody Loring. This was one reason that, in consultation with her friend, Alice decided they all needed the support of a male family member in Boston. And, poised to telegraph, Alice chose not William but her brother Harry.

It was a crucial decision. Alice made it, presumably, based on her own past experience with her two elder brothers. And strangely, she didn't stand alone in her preference. Her decision mirrored Henry Senior's own predilection—a growing preference for Harry, which his illness only made clearer. And this consensus for Harry even reflected the more conflicted wishes of William's wife herself. William's self-preoccupation was now coming back to haunt him. For years, Henry Senior had regarded William above his other children. But now, in what appeared to be his final days, his allegiances had starkly shifted, and painfully for William.

Now everything happened at the lightning speed of the Atlantic cables. Alice James wired Bolton Street on December 9, 1882. Harry immediately looked up steamships. Both he and William, who was now racing to London from Paris, could sail soon, Harry telegraphed back to Cambridge. But Alice fired back: "Brain softening possibly live months all insist Wm. shall not come." At this crucial point in the life of the family, fully half of Alice James's message was devoted to keeping William away. Alice's attitude toward her problematic brother had hardened. If Mrs. Alice was inclined to forgive her husband, his sister had years of slights and neglects to resent. At so vulnerable a time, she hardly wanted her moody brother on hand; she far preferred the calm and gentle Harry.

In London, after consulting with his brother, both of them in "great perplexity & anxiety," Harry determined to embark, by himself, at once. William wasn't fooled by the reference to his father possibly hanging on for months; he felt the slight of not being asked to come. "Harry & I were both ready to start," he wrote his wife, clearly hurt. "I wanted to get to see [Father] if possible before the end, & to let him see me and get a ray of pleasure from the thought that I had come. But the teleg[ram] suggest[s the] possibility of his not recognizing me or caring, and if so I would rather not see him but have my last memory of him as I bade him good bye."

Harry must have felt the distinction of being the one chosen. But he was no doubt delicate in his care for William's feelings during this crisis. At the same time, years of forbearance with William's frequent criticisms enabled him to understand why the family had now sidestepped William's company. They didn't suddenly hate him; letters from everyone in the family, especially Mrs. Alice, overflowed with affection and commiseration. But, apart from his recent desertion of his family, years of incidents had taught them how difficult William could be.

Harry squeezed onto the five-thousand-ton iron-hulled German steamer *Werra* in Southampton on December 12. The four-masted, two-funneled vessel, a brand-new Glasgow-built behemoth, could make an impressive seventeen knots and carry a virtual town of more than twelve hundred people—most of them steerage immigrants, only two hundred of them Harry's preferred ilk of first-class waistcoated loungers. Harry himself, as a last-minute emergency interloper, hoped for an officer's cabin (without an officer, presumably). Harry would make, as he called it, a "very rapid and prosperous, but painful passage"—"prosperous" seeming a strangely urbane appraisal of a voyage to a deathbed. For years the Jameses had booked fast ships. But now this one could not possibly run the Atlantic fast enough.

William, meanwhile, paced Harry's now-vacant Bolton Street rooms, sidelined, distanced, stuck in the smoky dankness of a London December. The dim streets of the world's megalopolis oppressed William like the "inside of [an] old church." As he lay at night in Harry's flat, William tenderly contemplated his "poor dear old father," whom he had both loved and resented during the Jameses' halcyon years in New York, London, and Newport.

Family letters cast "no clear light" on his father's case. The problem wasn't a shortage of information. Mrs. Alice wrote detailed, moving accounts of William's father, who, weary from his lifelong struggles with his demons and anguished to be without his wife, hardly wanted to hold on: "The dear, dear old man lies there, filled with this desire to die, and taking his life in his own hands lays it down because he has had enough." Katharine Loring also inserted dispatches, just as she'd wedged herself into the affairs of the family. Aunt Kate joined in the flood of letters when she could manage it. But all these thick or thin missives arrived late, arrested, fatally outdated.

In London as in Paris, William had suffered from the time lag that went along with his self-imposed exile: a letter normally took ten days or two weeks to cross the more than three thousand miles of Atlantic storms. Of course, William could receive the cryptic, clipped telegrams that pulsed under that same dark ocean, through one of several submarine cables ticking by the 1880s. But the one-line puzzles of telegrams remained as exorbitantly expensive as their much-touted wires had (historically) proved fragile. The first transatlantic cable, laid in 1858, had blinked triumphant messages back and forth for only three weeks before it fell silent. Queen Victoria had sent a telegram of congratulation to President James Buchanan, but her jubilation had been premature: a really successful cable was laid only in 1866 by the otherwise ill-fated *Great Eastern* (on which leviathan steamship William had afterward enthusiastically traveled in 1867). For fifteen years, the Atlantic had been wired; but this technology of connection now only underlined William's isolation from his family.

When trying to ascertain his father's condition and state of mind, William had to cope with expired updates, missed and crossed messages, and confusing replies to letters he hardly remembered sending. It didn't help that Mrs. Alice didn't trust her own judgment and, in the throes of wifely self-sacrifice, couldn't decide whether or not to reel her husband home. She had little enough leisure to think: her small children no doubt clamored for her in Garden Street while she tried to keep up with Henry Senior's condition and write William about it. She hesitated to call him back for another reason. An account of little Harry's sickness she'd dispatched three years before had "hurried" William home from Europe before he was ready. William hadn't liked that, and the incident was a piece of conjugal guilt that remained burned into Alice's mind.

But the regal husbandly privileges on which William had banked for four years had now run out. All at once, it seemed, his family had sided against him. It was now his turn to feel abandoned.

On Wednesday, December 20, before any family telegram reached him, William read in the London *Standard* that Henry James Sr., the philosopher whom some few might remember for his esoteric books, had died.

≈

HARRY GOT THE news at noon on December 21 when the *Werra* berthed in New York. Letters from both Alice and from her friend Katharine lay in wait for him at the dock. His sister's was tender and tearful. She was counting the minutes till her brother's arrival home. She added that the family hadn't been able to delay the funeral until Harry's uncertain arrival. Their father had been buried at the Cambridge Cemetery, again in its winter bleakness, that very morning.

Reeling from these tidings, Harry disembarked with a blinding headache. In the snarl of New York carriage, wagon, and omnibus traffic, he took a long time to reach Grand Central Depot, a big three-towered French palace of a railroad station, the precursor to today's Grand Central Terminal. This majestic structure, completed in 1871, was familiar to Harry from his short winter residence in the city in 1875 and from his more recent visit to the United States in 1881–82. But it was nevertheless a sign of how much New York, his family's old home, tended to change and rebuild itself whenever he spent time away from it. Because of waits and delays, Harry didn't reach Boston till eleven o'clock that night.

At the station, Harry ran into his brother Bob, another haggard traveler, who had caught a train from Milwaukee, where he was straining once more to live with his wife. He had come just for his father's funeral. He would have to disappear from Boston right afterward; his relation with his father, anyway, had been especially troubled since his recent alcoholic breakdown and family estrangement. Though he was temperamentally very like his father—and though he was the only child with much interest in Swedenborg—the old man had hardly summoned Bob to his deathbed.

When Harry finally reached Mount Vernon Street, the house lay darkened and hushed. Aunt Kate no doubt met Harry at the door, grim-mouthed but poised. Alice received her brother in her bedroom, where she lay drained and "very quiet."

Keeping their composure, the two women filled Harry in. Henry Senior's final hours had been "tranquil" and "painless." After a "series of swoons," he'd no longer been able to leave his bed. The philosopher, with his eyes raised to his rarer inner reality, had attracted "little of the sick-room" about him, Aunt Kate insisted. The "softening of the brain" about which Alice had telegraphed was "simply a gradual refusal of food, because he *wished* to die." Henry Senior had certainly endured enough pain in his existence: the sting of professional failure and obscurity, the burden of lifelong anxiety and depression, and the cares of a family he loved but who had also often disappointed him. Without Mary to console him, these burdens had grown all the more unbearable. At the same time, he felt a personal exaltation at having achieved, at the end, what he thought of as an exalted Swedenborgian "spiritual life." He appeared "perfectly cheerful" to the people around him.

But during her earlier agonized visits to her father's bedside, Alice had registered surprise that the old man, a James wit to the last, had popped out "the most picturesque and humorous things." Alice was in no state, however, to write any of these down. If she had been able to stay by his side, she might have heard words that were still more revelatory. But on the afternoon of her father's death on December 18, 1882, Alice lay prostrate in her own bed, kept limp by Katharine's doses of opium. It had almost killed Alice to watch the father she loved "fade day by day."

So it was Aunt Kate who, with the assistance of a hired nurse, kept a constant vigil at her brother-in-law's bedside. Her conflicts with Henry from the 1840s and 1850s were now ancient history. But though Kate had spent much of her adult life with this man, living intimately in the same house, she had never quite been in sympathy with him and in recent years had been much happier living near her New York relatives, savoring her matronly independence. Still, she had known Henry longer than anybody else in the house, and she had witnessed firsthand almost all of the triumphs and the disappointments of his life. She could listen to his repeated wishes to die, not without empathy, watching over him with calm eyes. As Henry's strength flagged—as he slipped under his own doses of opium—Kate heard him speak several times of his wife of more than forty years. "Mary—my Mary." And near the last, Kate also distinguished Henry's murmur: "Oh, I have such good boys—*such* good boys!"

These "last words," as Kate understood them, said a lot about Henry as a father—and revealed even more about him than the Swedenborgian higher realm to which he considered he was "going with great joy." He'd worshipped Mary. He'd lived for his four sons, especially Harry and William. But he had sometimes blanked that he also had a daughter.

Yet Alice suffered from her father's death more visibly than any other family member. After Henry's death, Kate was horrified by Alice's proposing a dissection of her father's head in order to settle the debate over the cause of his death. It was an unusual request, and it showed that Alice had become a little unhinged in her grief. Next, backing away from the idea of an autopsy, Alice exerted herself to have a cast molded of Henry's face for the absent Harry and William. This death mask would prove macabre enough, "terribly emaciated," Harry later thought, propped up on a chest of drawers and standing above the fissures that would soon rapidly spread through his family.

Aunt Kate pursued her own priorities. Left by Alice's illness in command of the house, she scoured Henry's study and bedroom. Over the grate of a December fire, she burned an unknown number of Henry's and Mary's letters. In a dramatic moment, Katharine Loring intruded on Kate and caught her in the act of laying papers on the flames. This discovery ratcheted up the tension between Katharine and Kate and even more between Alice and her aunt. Kate, who had never even lived at Mount Vernon Street, was taking liberties with Henry's papers—an example of her "mandatory ways" and of her high-handedness with the family she had helped to raise.

Why, anyway, would Kate want to obliterate Henry Senior's letters? Henry himself had already weeded out some of his papers before his death. He'd "tied [up] his manuscripts" for William, to whom he'd bequeathed all his philosophical books and manuscripts. Though somewhat out of favor, William still had more intellectual interest in his father's work than anybody else in the family, including Bob. But Kate burned with a single-minded mission. She skipped meals, as Mrs. Alice noticed, to prosecute her business, and for reasons that had their own complicated history.

As with her sister, Mary, Kate's cheerful manner covered a ruthless practicality—a grim determination that palpably emanates from the stiffly posed studio photographs taken of her late in her life. True, Aunt Kate had once been something of a rebel, marrying and divorcing at will, defying Henry Senior and his household fiats. But discretion and propriety had built up in Kate over the years. Now over seventy, and the stand-in matriarch of the shattered family, "Mrs. Walsh" acted in its best interests, as she saw them. She edited the past according to her own matronly dignity, shocked conventionality, and dynastic pride—if she concealed no more urgent personal reasons. Alfred Habegger, the biographer of Henry Senior, believes that Kate wanted to cover up her involvement with radical religious groups in the late 1830s. But Kate may well have had other youthful indiscretions, hers or other people's, to hide. Perhaps she had once, in the early days, had a crush on Henry Senior; perhaps Henry himself had had some minor affair that Kate wanted to cover up for her sister's dignity. In any case, Kate was successful in her work. With a poker and a quick eye, she plunged much of the early history of the James family into darkness. The sparks of her fire wafted extinguished secrets of the 1830s and 1840s up the chimney.

Had Harry arrived sooner, might he have saved some of his father's old love letters to Mary or others, if such existed? Probably not; he shared Aunt Kate's sense of the family's privacy or had an even greater sense of it. In time, he would prove a vigorous and paranoid letter burner in his own right—and on an even more massive scale.

With everybody distracted, nobody telegraphed William the news. Alice writhed with her stomach cramps in bed; Harry nursed his splitting headache in a darkened room, watched over by the death mask of his father; Aunt Kate relentlessly torched papers. So, as it happened, William learned about his father's death from the newspapers rather than from his family via the Atlantic cables.

Characteristically, though, Harry made up for his own part in this neglect by taking William, in spirit, to the graveside. He traveled out to Cambridge Cemetery on the final day of 1882. The winter air glowed, still and bright, over the denuded trees. Viewed from the high ground of the municipal cemetery, the Charles River hooked out toward the Atlantic that had so dramatically intervened in every one of the family's lives—and would separate the various members of the family more and more. Harry discovered his father's freshly grave dug, as he told William, "extraordinarily close to Mother." He stood by the two linked and frozen plots and read out the letter that William had written to his father from London on December 14, and which had arrived too late for Henry Senior to hear.

"Darling old Father," William began—with Harry's voice. William's tender letter declared both his devotion to his father and his independence from him. In it, William acknowledged the hell his "peculiarities" had given his father. But hadn't he, William, always been a "creature" alien to Henry, a surprising son who hadn't fit into Henry's plans? William only hoped—in a moment of self-knowledge, from his distant perch in London—to do better by his own sons, as his little boys grew up. It was a genuine and heartfelt wish, and one that would have future consequences.

"Good night my sacred old Father," Harry read out. "If I don't see you again—Farewell! a blessed farewell!" It was a torn good-bye from Henry's favorite sons, the two of them suddenly merged and indistinguishable.

❧

WILKIE HADN'T SHOWN up at his father's funeral. He stood out as the one child living in the United States who'd been conspicuously absent. Though he ranked as a less favored son, he would have hauled himself to Cambridge by train if he could. But that December, thirty-seven-year-old Wilkie could scarcely rise from his own bed.

Housebound in Milwaukee, Wilkie was racked with the rheumatism that had spread from his Civil War wounds and now engulfed his entire body. And Wilkie had other medical problems—heart and kidney ailments—brewing inside of him. His brittle wife, Carrie, who'd long since pawned her diamonds (though her now-deceased father had ransomed a few of them back for her), nursed her husband with broths and liniments she made herself. Their children, Joseph and Alice, both under nine, played quietly in the house over a frozen Christmas holiday while, far away, in a big eastern city they'd never seen, their grandfather died. By early February 1883, these unlucky children would themselves contract scarlet fever, a deadly strep-induced infection that spawned red rashes and jeopardized Victorian children's lives.

Such home miseries afforded Wilkie his only relief from his hated clerkship at Internal Revenue, the nineteenth-century incarnation of the IRS—although personal income tax, as such, didn't yet exist. Income taxes had been pioneered between 1862 and 1872, at a low rate by today's standards, but these levies had been highly unpopular and were repealed. Income tax would be reinstated only in 1913—a boon especially for the tycoons of the Gilded Age. In 1882, most of the government's income came from tariffs on alcohol and tobacco. In any case, Wilkie's government job was poorly remunerated; and if he didn't report to work because of illness, he wasn't paid at all. With his previous business failures in cotton and iron locks, he'd accrued many debts, both public and hidden. These galled him, now, even in his dreams.

Shortly after receiving the news of his father's death, Wilkie heard from Harry, whom Henry Senior had named the executor of his will. Henry's somewhat surprising choice of Harry showed how dramatically the old man had warmed to his second son. The choice also signaled their father's appraisal of Harry as the most competent of his children— a vote of confidence that the conscientious Harry now worked his hardest to deserve.

To Wilkie, as to his other siblings, Harry reported that Henry Senior's estate amounted to $95,000—a sliver of William James of Albany's robber-baron millions, but a striking sum at the time—most of it invested in three commercial "houses" in Syracuse, the rest in railroad shares. That much came as good news. But bad news crushingly followed: Henry Senior had completely cut Wilkie out of his will.

Henry Senior's brutal excision, to be sure, followed its own peculiar rationale. It factored in all the money the family had advanced to the hapless Wilkie over the years and lost—a carnage of railroad bonds, in itself. Carrie's much-discussed diamonds, though observed nearly ten years before, had also convinced the James family of her own flaunted wealth, on which Wilkie and his children could draw.

But Wilkie's exclusion from his father's estate also reflected a caprice—one of the many quixotic impulses the old philosopher had entertained during his long life—and one that happened to get set in stone, in his last will and testament. On an earlier whim, under Aunt Kate's persuasion, Henry had also toyed with the idea of leaving all of his commercial properties and railroad bonds to Alice. It was an offer that Alice, not wanting to bilk any of her brothers, had immediately refused.

In profound ways, Henry Senior's slap at Wilkie weirdly echoed and reenacted Henry's own disinheritance by his father in the 1830s—the paternal blow that had crippled Henry almost as much as his ragged teenage amputations. Old patterns died hard even in a family struggling for enlightenment and laboring to improve on the mistakes of previous generations, as William was now pledging to do.

But Wilkie could hardly be expected to appreciate this historical irony. Feeling betrayed, he poured out his rage to his brother Bob, his closest ally in the family. Bob, riding a rare moment of prosperity, lived nearby on a thirty-five-acre farm at Wauwatosa, Wisconsin, behind a "Grecian portico," as Harry described it, financed by his father-in-law. But Bob also suffered, though less obviously, from the harsh terms of Henry Senior's will: their father had "placed a limitation upon [Bob's] share of the estate," as Harry delicately put the matter to him; that is, he had assigned Bob less than a full share of his assets. "The more I think of this discrimination against both of us," Wilkie wrote to Bob, "the more unjust and damnable it seems to me." Their father had committed a "base cowardly act," Wilkie fumed, a "death stab" at the only two of his sons who'd fought in the Civil War—and the two who had struggled hardest since their young manhood to earn their own livings.

Bob readily sympathized. But then again, so did Alice and Harry. The three siblings soon agreed that, especially in view of Wilkie's sufferings, they had only one choice: to break the will. As Henry Senior and his own siblings had done a generation before, they would split the estate into equal shares.

Only William, surprisingly, hung back from this arrangement. His attitude remained obscure and complicated. As the lone holdout, William stipulated conditions on any share granted to Wilkie. William fretted, probably, about his own growing family. He also hated the idea, he said, for the children "to absolutely ignore" his father's will. William's intransigence, to be sure, didn't qualify as his most shining moment—and it came at a time when he was already not very popular with most members of the family. But, kept at arm's length in a soupy metropolis he hated, an ocean away from these happenings, he was battling his own troubles. He agonized about not working on his book. He carped that nobody in Boston seemed to want him or need him enough even to produce an available bedroom for him if he wanted to come back. With his brother Harry officiously running the show and advising him to stay where he was, William felt as if *he* had been disinherited.

Harry meanwhile hurled himself into this new paternal role—on which he bent his somewhat maternal talents. As much as he disliked the Midwest, he took a train to Milwaukee at the end of January 1883 to consult with Wilkie about the will. After he arrived, the blistering Great Lakes cold pushed the temperature down to twenty degrees below zero Fahrenheit. And inside the winter-battered house, Harry found his brother, the cheerful playmate of his childhood, "sadly broken and changed." The bedridden Wilkie appeared to Harry "pretty well finished." And to make matters worse, his sister-in-law's "imbecility," Harry judged, added to the squalor and helplessness of the household. Harry (diplomatically) "lectured and preached" household management to Wilkie and Carrie, as his mother would have done in his place.

Harry's well-meant advice may not have sat well. It evidently bothered Carrie, although the gentle Wilkie warmly appreciated Harry's "loving, tender, moderate and wise counsels." But Harry also worked tirelessly to persuade William—or at least railroad him—into a reapportioning of the estate that would soon grant Wilkie a sliver of material comfort. In the summer of 1883, Wilkie, his health rallying, took a trip to the East via his old failed plantation in Florida. He met his brother Harry in Washington, and—at Harry's and at his sister Alice's invitation—took refuge at the Mount Vernon Street house for a few restful months.

But, back in Milwaukee and back in bed, Wilkie only worsened. In late September 1883, he dictated a moving letter to his brother William. He revealed he had Bright's disease, a scourge of the kidneys. His heart problems and rheumatism had also returned, so that he couldn't sleep, now, without drugs. For months he hadn't been able to work, but he still hoped to "gain strength" if he could. At the same time, Wilkie understood that it might not be long before he'd "peg out"—a phrase touchingly echoing his father's language of lameness, in talking about dying. The father and son shared injured legs—in Wilkie's case a foot—which, even in their worst sufferings, even in their last estrangement, created a certain bond between them.

By this time William had come home from Europe and had taken over the tag ends of his father's will as well as the care of his own family. Harry had correspondingly, in the usual James square dance of complementary moves, shifted back to London. So it was William who now took the responsibility, who now made a flying railroad visit in October—though his Harvard term had already started—to comfort his suffering, nervously afflicted brother.

Shortly after William's visit, in the early evening of November 15, 1883, Wilkie died. Though once the most pink, cheerful, and robust of the Jameses, he hadn't lived to see his thirty-ninth birthday. He now left behind him a snarl of debts and two children under ten. His widow, Carrie, would inherit convoluted money problems. Though she would initially keep in touch with her husband's family, notably the check-writing Harry, she would soon want little more to do with the people at whose hands she'd suffered so many indignities. And she would urge her friend and sister-in-law Mary Holton James—whose estranged husband, Bob, had used his part of his father's legacy to buy his freedom and to stake out a new life of painting lessons in Arlington, Massachusetts—to keep her distance, too.

But distance had always figured in this family's drama of connection and disconnection. And the convenient distance provided by the Atlantic would soon, once again, and with a new intensity, shape the family's future. The James children, having lost their rooted parents, would soon split into two discrete transatlantic branches.

❧

IN THE MOUNT Vernon Street house, during the long winter days after her father's burial, Alice longed for escape. She suffered such "ghastly" loneliness, as she later wrote, that she sometimes wanted to run to the firemen next door to flee her isolation. "Alone, Alone!" had "echoed thro' the house, rustled down the stairs, whispered from the walls." And except for the Irish servants, Alice was often home alone. She had refused to board with Aunt Kate, especially after the recent tension between them. She couldn't always wrench Katharine away from her exorbitant sister's wheezing sickbed. Agonizingly, Alice had lain alone in the dark and counted the minutes and the hours.

Confronted with this postparental isolation, Alice played illness as her trump card. Not only did a breakdown provide Alice immediate human company—doctors, nurses, worried relatives, her friend Katharine—but it also provided her much-needed physical contact. Sickbeds in the Victorian era crackled with an erotic charge—in a period that otherwise sheathed middle-class Anglo-Saxons in layers of clothing that precluded physical touching. Some of the most passionate scenes in nineteenth-century novels took place around sickbeds—for example, Marianne's self-inflicted brush with death in Jane Austen's *Sense and Sensibility* (1811)—with high-colored heroines in feverish dishabille.

In May 1883, six months after her father's death, Alice checked herself into the Adams Nervine Asylum in Jamaica Plain, a leafy suburb south of Boston. There she spent three months trying to vanquish her "nerves" by means of an exacting diet, vapor baths, and massage, with a version of the notorious "rest-cure"—that sensory-deprivation regime designed especially for women by the Philadelphia doctor Weir Mitchell—in the quiet wooded environs of the recently established and freshly planted Arnold Arboretum. In seizing on such a curative vacation, Alice had perfected what one critic of Victorian culture has called the "medicalization of womanhood." Alice had imagined herself as a perpetual female patient, subject to the intrusive paternal male medicine of the era and yet, peculiarly, in command of it.

Though the fashionable galvanic shocks hadn't really advanced Alice's recovery, she tried to stave off another collapse, in the winter of 1884, by means of one of these low-voltage cures in New York City. Alice described her émigré doctor, William B. Neftel, as "a Russian electrician," who, though he had a "quackish quality," also nudged her back toward health with physical exercise. Neftel's fees were stiff enough to provide a kind of fiscal exercise in themselves. But Alice wanted finally to subdue her "hysteria"—or claimed that she wanted to. Still, her nervous illness—that exquisite involuntary performance that snatched her family's attention, that baffled and eluded all her doctors—remained her pièce de résistance (and, literally, a piece of resistance). It counted as her most potent assertion of self. Triumphantly, Alice had written a text, in her own body, that even her learned male doctors couldn't decipher.

Alice soon chafed, though, to leave her Manhattan hospitalization. The ever-expanding city of New York hardly suited Alice: she had objected to its "flimsy houses," ash barrels, and—in her own version of the knee-jerk anti-Semitism of the time—Jews. Though they were grandchildren of striving immigrants themselves, the Jameses usually mustered less compassion for the "huddled masses" of the 1880s than William's flame Emma Lazarus did.

With Harry and Katharine in Europe, Alice soon contemplated a bold measure: reverse emigration. And a year later, when Alice actually gathered her courage and sailed to England, she went as her family had always done: in pursuit of health, for an indefinite time. But more, she crossed the Atlantic in order to join her brother Harry. Aunt Kate continued to offer to come and live with her niece, as the two had so often traveled and vacationed together in the past. But Alice had grown independent enough, at least, to resist her aunt's interference. She now found Kate's company tedious and unrewarding. With Harry, she felt more stimulated and more content; the two had long shared an empathetic bond. They loved the same books; they both had literary talent, even if Alice's as yet showed up only in her conversation and letters. More and more, they also had in common their unmarried status. They were a "spinster" and a "bachelor"—although Alice had a companion, the dogged Katharine Loring, who came back across the Atlantic to fetch her, and with whom she landed at Liverpool in November 1884.

❧

CLARGES STREET LAY only two blocks away from Harry's flat in Mayfair but some three thousand steamer miles from Cambridge,

Massachusetts. Still, in the winter of 1884–85, a year after Wilkie's death, this narrow, bricked-in street, plunged into shadow for most of the short winter day, must have felt like a lost Atlantean world of its own.

From time to time a visitor—usually a trimly dressed American lady with a muff alighting from a carriage—rang at number 40. After the lady had stamped a bit in the cold, a servant appeared—dour, correct, and officious. The maid stripped the suppliant of her calling card but regretted to inform her that Miss James was unwell and wasn't receiving visitors.

This new housekeeper-maid, who deflected many a courtesy call after Alice James's arrival in London that late autumn, insisted on being addressed as Campbell. British tradition demanded a surname for an upper servant. (A butler, for example, existed as Dredge or Simcox, never as John.) Thus Campbell, on her dignity, didn't offer her Christian name for domestic use, as did the Irish Mary who'd preceded her in Massachusetts. Beaded and "banged," Campbell was an almost aggressive figure in contrast to the "soft mass of formless virtue" of Mary, who had formerly attended to Alice's breakfast table and bedside. Alice now missed her old servant and that woman's gentle ways.

At Clarges Street, in addition to her vigorous British servant, Alice commanded a pleasantly furnished little drawing room—whose windows, in the deep, narrow street, hardly soaked in enough winter sunlight for her to write a letter. She slept in what she called a "tomb-like closet" of a bedroom. But even this small flat tended to drain Alice's funds. The sole James daughter had little enough to live on, even though her brother Harry, in a characteristic gesture, had made over his fifth of their father's estate to his sister, in addition to her own share—and even though Alice had inherited (and now rented out) both the Manchester and the Beacon Hill houses.

But Alice had little enough to live on in a starker, more painful sense. She observed that Harry and Katharine amounted to her "only anchorages." She'd come to England to live near her favorite brother. Harry was about the only visitor who could charm his way past the barrier-like Campbell. Most other callers Alice refused. One exception proved to be an enterprising miniature expatriate widow from New York, a "pincushion of a woman," as Harry described her. Mrs. Van Rensselaer had inserted herself into the house and impressed Alice as "a little round ball that has rolled about in the dust all its life," as she wittily wrote her aunt and brother William; this visitor came stocked with stimulating tabloid stories of murder, plunder, and corruption.

Alice, though, craved other, more calming company. As well as to live near Harry, she had migrated to England in order to shadow her friend Katharine, who had been lodging in England on and off with her father and invalid sister, Louisa. These two chronically sick New England Lorings, in the usual genteel pursuit of "health," had most recently settled in the invalid-friendly spa city of Bournemouth, on the rainy south coast of England. The whole island of Britain, in fact, looked much friendlier to invalidism than America did. In England, Alice later wrote, she felt "not the least shame or degraded about being ill." England cultivated more of a "sense of leisure" than the more vigorous and businesslike America. And that Alice had considered, too, in her relocation.

On mild days, Campbell wheeled Alice into nearby Green Park in a bath chair, the nineteenth-century precursor to the wheelchair. Since leaving her stateroom on the *Pavonia* at Liverpool, Alice had versions of the physical ailments she'd had before: stomach problems, back problems, and general weakness. Though she insisted she wasn't suffering from nerves anymore—a doubtful claim—she had mostly been unable to walk for three months. She could only navigate, haltingly, around her bedroom. The more mobile Campbell proved an "excellent servant" to Alice. But she'd also, in the grand tradition of English servants, "brought the science of dawdle to perfection."

When not creatively lingering, Campbell lavished her mistress with commentary on her state of health: "You are indeed very delicate, Miss, & it is hard to be so ill," Campbell remarked, "but then you ought to be thankful that there is nothing repulsive about you & you have no skin disease." As long as she didn't have a skin disease, *she* would never complain. "Your illness is a very pleasant one, Miss," Campbell concluded. And then, as if to reinforce this happy idea, Campbell concocted an "elaborate coiffée" (hairstyle) for Alice to wear on her pillow. Alice, now thirty-six years old, felt essentially gaunter and more "mildewed" than ever. But she'd never, she gamely joked, worn such "varied & dressy locks" before.

In such a decorated condition, Alice received Alfred Baring Garrod, a specialist on gouty diseases who'd later in his career attend the corpulent and aging Queen Victoria. One of the many doctors Alice had consulted in her life, Garrod counted as at least the second physician Alice had seen since her recent landing in England. Alice wittily described him as a "round, genial ball of seventy." He bowled cheerily into her room, rolling with smooth courtesies, to inflict "percussing & stethoscoping" and listen to a history of her case. At this point in her career as a patient, Alice wished she'd just printed up "small pamphlet" describing her symptoms, she'd had to recite them so often.

Dr. Garrod soon gave Alice a familiar diagnosis. Gout (his specialty) wasn't really her trouble so much as "excessive nervous sensibility." For such a complicated condition, he hung back from prescribing diets, climates, or baths. But Alice didn't mind; she delighted in stumping her legions of doctors. Nobody could beat her on the subject of her own illness—as she amply showed in her cross-examination of this uninitiated expert. Could the trouble in her lower spine be caused by gout? Alice probed. "Oh! dear me yes," the old man replied, "I have seen people with their legs powerless for years from this cause!" But still he maintained that Alice had no "organic trouble"; her organs were simply disturbed in their functions—a somewhat baffling distinction, but one typical of this charming aristocratic doctor, a "gentlemanly-Punchinello type," as Harry later sketched him.

Inevitably, such Victorian semiquackery failed to fathom the deeper dysfunctionality (or functionality) of Alice's illness. Whatever its complex bodily and psychological sources, it filled the role of a career in her life. In the late 1870s and early 1880s, Alice had tried her hand at phaeton driving, house building, lunch-club hosting, and even housekeeping. Some of these activities had been hard-won, others thrust on her against her will. But none of them really seemed to give her lasting emotional satisfaction or to tap her intellectual abilities. And none of these masculine or feminine pursuits had brought her as much attention and solicitude as her long career as an invalid—a career in which she'd outstripped even her historically illness-prone brother William.

Now, as in the past, Alice's illness provided her with something to fill her hollowed-out time. Well-to-do nineteenth-century families thrust genteel inactivity on their wives and daughters as a mark of status—as the American sociologist Thorstein Veblen would famously and astutely observe in his *Theory of the Leisure Class* (1899). And the Jameses had followed this deeply ingrained fashion. Even Alice's elaborate wardrobe, her cherished excursions over the years to buy frocks and bonnets, was insidiously designed—like so much Victorian female clothing—to fit her for idleness, to decorate, encumber, and encase her. (Harry's own self-chosen wardrobe of tailored English suits had likewise buttoned him into his own form of repression and stultification—another instance of a "feminine" dynamic in his life.) This fashionable female leisure had an even darker side. A paisley design only looked like luxury; Paisley, Scotland, had been churning out imitation Kashmiri shawls for decades. But such ornaments enwrapped many a housebound and symptomatic Victorian woman. And such genteel inactivity had already proved particularly devastating in Alice's own case.

Alice harbored plenty of talents. With her own idiosyncratic wit, with her insights into human characters, she had some of the aptitude and promise of a Johnsonian essayist or a Dickensian novelist. (These trenchant and delightful sketches of the formidable Campbell and the genial Dr. Garrod come straight from Alice's letters.) As the daughter of a philosopher, Alice had grown up hearing intellectual insights and even, when her family would listen to her, coining them herself. She vented her observations, in her isolation, on doctors and on servants. She preserved them, sometimes, in her spirited letters to her family. But unlike her brother Harry she was unable to conceive of addressing them to a larger public.

Alice suffered from no aversion to writing in itself, as her residence in England would eventually prove. But she'd never really dared to entertain literary aspirations—hadn't been encouraged to foster any in a family where women's work was conceived as entirely domestic. She hadn't been raised to jostle with her brothers intellectually or to compete with them on that level. As a bright female she'd been allowed to read the highbrow journals of her time but hadn't been licensed to write for them. Her father had disdained lady intellectuals, and even her sympathetic brother Harry had inherited a good deal of Henry Senior's disdain and frequently exhibited similar prejudices against women as artists, writers, or thinkers. When Alice contemplated any artistic profession, she thrilled at the "joy and despair" of it—"the joy of seeing with the trained eye and the despair of doing it." Her "stifled sense," long cultivated in her parents' household, had paralyzed her, had stymied her from daring and doing.

Now freed from her parents' control, granted an independent income—akin to the five hundred pounds a year of free income that Virginia Woolf would decades later prescribe for women writers—Alice could presumably have tried something intellectual or literary. She might have voyaged to Europe in order to write, as her brother's increasingly close friend Constance Fenimore Woolson, and other women she knew about, had done. (During the previous winter of 1883–84, Harry had been spending quality time with Fenimore at "discrete intervals" in London; "Costanza," as he called her, had lived for several months near him, and the two of them had deepened their writerly and personal friendship, with Harry somewhat indulgently cultivating a carefully calibrated relation with a woman who clearly admired him and his work. "She is a very intelligent woman," Harry told William Dean Howells, a little patronizingly, "and understands when she is spoken to; a peculiarity I prize, as I find it more and more rare.") But Alice, unlike Fenimore, hadn't stormed the beaches in England in order to write. Instead, she'd washed up as a wreck. Her psychological inhibitions remained, even now that her practical circumstances had opened up some possibilities for her.

At the same time, Alice's new experience of emigration, padded and advantaged as it was, provided its own shocks. She had taken sick on the boat and remained so even weeks later when, having found Mayfair too dear, she joined Katharine, and their mutual friend Miss Mattie Whitney, in the invalid-haunted, bay-windowed terraces of Bournemouth. In this new spa town, it was unclear if Alice's new lodging-house life would start her on a fresh path or if it would only protract her career in neurasthenia. So far, Alice's raw English exile, an echo of every other James expatriation, didn't look like an exorcism of the past as much as a perpetuation of it. Though Henry Senior was now dead and buried, the family demons remained alive and well.

∼⧉∽

HARRY, MEANWHILE, TRIED not to flinch at Alice's arrival. When in the autumn of 1884 Alice proposed steaming across the Atlantic, Harry braced himself. Down deep he knew what his sister's arrival meant: family obligation. He had, after all, interposed the Atlantic between himself and his relatives, in part, so as not to be dragged into the James family bog.

And yet Harry was vulnerable; he had a fascination for this bog and his own affinity to it. Even at a distance, he remained "haunted by fears and anxieties" about Alice. And, just as he'd generously given Alice his share of the inheritance, Harry evidently believed Alice and her troubles, in a way, belonged to him. A fatal inevitability lurked in this new transatlantic realignment of siblings. Just as William had long looked after Bob as a special charge, Harry was poised now to look after Alice.

Yet even with Alice bearing down on him, Harry didn't contemplate taking her in. That much Harry could confide in his spinster friend Grace Norton, who'd appropriately annexed Mary's maternal role in his life. Though many Victorian brothers and sisters set up households together, Alice and Harry, with delicacy unusual to the other Jameses, respected each other's privacy. Harry had no more intention of housekeeping with his sister than he had of acquiring a "conjugal Mrs. H." And Alice lived in terror of imposing herself on her loving but skittish brother. But when Harry heartily declared his sister "un-dependent and independent" and liable to "*cling* no more than a bowsprit," having "her own plans, purposes, preferences, practices, pursuits"—he spoke more hopefully and rhetorically than otherwise.

Down deep, Harry didn't actually believe that Alice was independent but rather that she was weirdly and fatally dependent. And he wondered if Alice was going to "wreck and blight" his carefully arranged London life. Even when, after her first London stint, Alice moved to Katharine's sphere of Bournemouth, she barraged Harry with telegrams and required an extended visit (with the advantages, for Harry, of helping him dodge the now-hated London season and allowing him to cultivate the friendship of the tubercular and long-mustached Scottish novelist Robert Louis Stevenson). But, as he'd feared, Harry soon found himself mired in a "winter of infinite domestic worry, preoccupation, and anxiety."

When Harry came to stay at St. Alban's Cliff, Bournemouth, he flattered himself that Alice got better under the influence of his company. He also thoughtfully brought down from London a "lady-nurse, or companion," to help Alice's maid take care of her. Alice needed Harry partly because Katharine had been called away to care for her weak-lunged sister, Louisa, which upset Alice; she hated competing for attention. Alice cared acutely if her friend left her; she required much less from her oversensitive brother. In Katharine, Alice had found a true soul mate, someone who understood her mind as well as her illnesses. "No one understands what she has been & done for me," Alice had earlier confided to her friend Fanny. For his part, Harry needed Alice in order to feel wise and big-brotherly—that was his role, anyway, as a master novelist. All in all, Harry had invisible, convoluted, intricate ties to Alice—and unexamined rivalries with her close friend.

❧

THAT SPRING, THIS antagonism would go public. Harry's uneasiness with his sister's dramatic dependence on her companion manifested itself in his 1885 novel, *The Bostonians*, in which he drew an unflattering picture—much of it drawn from Alice's private experiences—of feminism, of "Boston marriages," and of the city of Boston itself. Beginning in February 1885, the serialization of this novel in the *Century Magazine* coincided with Alice's early residence in England and Harry's first long-term attendance on his sister—even though the bulk had been written in the previous year, soon after Harry had freshly observed his sister's "friendship" in Boston and Manchester, Massachusetts.

The Bostonians would prove Harry's weirdest and most lugubrious fictional cocktail to date—and one that soon crumpled the faces of Harry's American readers with its bitter flavor. Mark Twain for one would hold *The Bostonians* in particular abhorrence, ranking its tedium and sanctimoniousness on a level with John Bunyan's heaven. (Bunyan had described this heaven in his longwinded treatise, *The Holy City*, of 1665, and incidentally, the city of Boston had prided itself on shining out as a beacon since even before Bunyan's time.) For Harry, in contrast, Boston had always counted as an antiparadise. His was a dark and somewhat cranky evaluation of the city. When he gave it full force in his new novel, he didn't endear himself to his influential and reform-minded Boston audience, some of his most loyal readers.

Harry's novel traces the romantic fortunes of Verena Tarrant, an impecunious but gifted orator who catches the attention of a rich, pale, nervous, explosive feminist, a "female Jacobin" named Olive Chancellor. The imperious Miss Chancellor determines to annex Verena as a protégée and to involve her in decrying the wrongs done to women. As the two work together, Olive grows clingingly obsessed with Verena, while Verena develops an extreme dependence on her friend. But Miss Chancellor finds a rival in a jaded and reactionary Mississippian, Basil Ransom, who horns in on their women's friendship, scornful of their feminist causes. He schemes to marry Verena himself. A battle of the sexes rages through the pages of the book—which, eventually, the gaunt and chauvinistic Basil wins. Through it all, Harry portrays Olive's influence over the weak Verena as unnatural and sinister—an echo of Katharine Loring's power over Alice—but also spotlights Basil's own selfish machinations.

To be sure, *The Bostonians* is less a portrait of a "Boston marriage" than of a psychological dependency. The novel exposes a subterranean psychopathology of hidden motives and neurotic needs that only a member of the tortured James family could have exhumed. And like Harry's earlier novel *The American*, *The Bostonians* bludgeons and then buries nineteenth-century notions of romance and marriage. At the end of the novel, Verena and Basil's union proves "far from brilliant" and is stained by Verena's continuing tears—an ending that embodies Harry's deepening sense of the fragility and cruelty of human intimacy. Even in the 1880s, when "realist" fictions pushed bleak exposés of emotional relations and of industrial society, influenced by the emerging tooth-and-claw social Darwinism of the time, *The Bostonians* stood out as an incisive if monumentally depressing "modern" book.

More personally, the novel's devastating psychological triangle mirrored Harry's own ambivalences about Alice and Katharine's friendship—and his own tug-of-war with Katharine over Alice. Harry didn't exactly want to win this tug-of-war, didn't want to have his sister on his hands, all on his own. But still he didn't want to lose, either. If anything, Harry must have felt jealous of Katharine, who often shared Alice's household and frequently, to judge from her surviving letters, dominated her imagination. Though Harry had drawn a scathing portrait of Basil as a reactionary, he himself shared both his Mississippian's scorn for emerging women's freedoms and his desire to win and keep a woman—in this case his sister.

As he lived out his own version of his fictional triangle, Harry showed plenty of contradictions. When Katharine was unavailable, Harry had to "tremble" to think of what her absence would do to his sister. Harry well understood the "drama of [Alice's] separation" from Katharine, whenever it occurred. He rightly identified such partings as "bereavement[s]." But Harry also bemoaned the unhealthy effects he thought Katharine had on his sister: "As soon as they get together Alice takes to her bed." Harry discerned a dark symbiosis. He confided to Aunt Kate his fear that his sister had about as much chance of relinquishing Katharine—in another strange allusion to their father's amputations—"as of her giving her legs to be sawed off."

But Harry's novel treated more than his worries about his sister. *The Bostonians* acidly satirized the reform-minded Boston on which Harry had now decisively turned his back. His most detailed "social novel" to date, it showed that Harry had fallen under the spell of the realists; he even visited Millbank Prison in December 1884, just after Alice's arrival, to take notes for his new novel, *The Princess Casamassima*, even though he abhorred the self-consciously "social" settings favored by his friend William Dean Howells or his rival from the Paris writers' cenacle, Emile Zola. Harry's laboriously drawn vignettes of Massachusetts added to the heaviness of *The Bostonians*. But no doubt such passages, like the final drama of the novel at the Boston Music Hall, felt purgative to Harry on a personal level. Such paroxysms helped Harry lay his hatred of Boston—and perhaps also his parents and their Quincy Street world—to rest.

The Bostonians also allowed Harry to rant, as his father had done in the 1850s, against the women's movement, which, following in the footsteps of his father, he so disliked. Though he had once admired Minny Temple and her unconventionality—as well as her willingness to challenge his father—he had grown more like his father with age, and more resistant to assertive and outspoken women. (Even his many self-reliant women friends, like Fenimore, were chosen, in part, because they kept their feminism quiet, if they had such inclinations. He liked Costanza because she respectfully listened to him.) Harry got into trouble with his portrait of Miss Birdseye, whom everybody thought a dead ringer for Elizabeth Palmer Peabody, Nathaniel Hawthorne's sister-in-law, a vivid old abolitionist and reformer of the time. But as an antifeminist text, *The Bostonians* lashed out even more at Katharine Loring—to whom Harry always behaved chivalrously in person. Or rather it targeted the feminist agitation rampant in Boston, which Katharine only fitfully espoused and which Harry himself poorly understood. In the early 1880s, the issue of women's suffrage heated Boston drawing rooms and lecture halls. But Harry's novel hardly contained a recognizable or convincing portrait of this political struggle.

More tellingly, Harry took another subject in *The Bostonians*, one less obvious especially to nineteenth-century readers. Harry's treatment of the taboo subject of same-sex relations connected him to his old literary favorite, the French novelist Honoré de Balzac. In 1882, during his tour of the French province of Touraine, Harry had literally followed in Balzac's footsteps—to gaze decoratively at the gardens, marketplaces, and chateaux that had articulated Balzac's full-blooded portraits of provincial life. But in the mid-1880s, *The Bostonians* more subtly followed Balzac in a different sense, by trying out some of Balzac's famous (or notorious) sexual open-mindedness.

The Bostonians didn't discuss lesbianism openly—Olive Chancellor's attraction to Verena remained latent, suggestive, and characteristically ambiguous. But Harry's novel shadowed Balzac's 1835 novella, *La Fille aux yeux d'or (The Girl with the Golden Eyes)*, in which a man and woman battle over the soul and body of a young woman. Such a scandalous topic, by the way—even when sanctioned by Balzac—would certainly have found itself "banned in Boston" and not encouraged. Bostonians like the Norton sisters imposed their own form of censure: Grace Norton had famously given a copy of Michel de Montaigne's *Essais (Essays)* to a young bride "with the 'naughty' pages gummed together"—a piece of prudery that Alice James found "deliciously droll."

In 1885, the prim Grace pronounced Balzac's *Contes Drolatiques (Comic Tales)* "unmentionable," though Harry argued that these ribald stories counted as "magnificent, superb" and insisted, in a rare moment of masculine rebellion, that the "feminine point of view here is inadequate." At the same time, Harry hardly scorned feminine opinion or propriety by writing his new (and heavily cloaked) novel. "*Do* like the *Bostonians*, dear Grace," he pleaded, throwing in three exclamation points with Queen Victoria–like coyness, "it is something like Balzac!!!"

Indeed, as a reflection of Harry's own emotional life (or lack thereof), *The Bostonians* simultaneously marked both sheer daring and monumental cowardice. A few decades later, Balzac's *Girl with the Golden Eyes* would inspire Marcel Proust, another male writer, to obsess about women's same-sex entanglements as a deflection of male ones. But Proust's lesbians proved at least partly transitional, and *La Recherche du temps perdu (Remembrance of Things Past)* would gradually edge into Proust's own more familiar male homosexual realms. For Harry, though, *The Bostonians* functioned as a roadblock, not a road; once again he was *not* writing about the likes of Paul Zhukovsky (or John Addington Symonds, a homosexual acquaintance whom he claimed to William never to have met). He was bent on *not* letting himself turn into Oscar Wilde—a married man who would hide and deny his homosexual inclinations on into the 1890s but who would meanwhile adopt a risqué and flamboyant persona that Harry hated. Harry safely phrased *The Bostonians* as a study of other people's ambiguities, not his own.

The lived experience in *The Bostonians*, of course, really belonged to Alice, not to Harry. No one in the family remarked on the elephant in the room, the substantial and scandalous point that the "Boston marriage" in the novel reflected Alice's. What Alice herself thought of *The Bostonians* is far from clear. As an adoring sister, she might well have felt a tiny bit flattered that Harry would take such interest in her life. But she must have been more than a little resentful that he should make such a twisted portrait of it. Little evidence survives, and biographers have not wondered much about Alice's response, as if the novel just counted as another monument in Harry's rise to fame and didn't concern her at all.

Alice never definitively commented on *The Bostonians*—unless she spoke to Harry about it in private or wrote him a letter that he subsequently torched. Alice didn't assume the role of critic, especially with her cherished Harry. In her letters, she hardly even allowed herself to feel hurt by Harry in other matters; she represented him as patient and generous, good to her, a worthless invalid, when she really didn't deserve it. During the serial run of the novel, of course, Alice lay prostrate and housebound in a foreign country. And perhaps the novel's exposure, fictional or not, of Alice's intimate life rendered her even more shut in and ill. Alice might well have read installments of Harry's novel in the *Century* while lying incapacitated in Bournemouth, and his portrayal of her life must have grated on her. Even if she didn't allow herself to resent Harry overtly, she must have sensed that he had once again poached on her life—and unflatteringly—for his own purposes.

The Bostonians also showed that Harry had contrived a new use for Alice, even if she had found a corresponding use for him as a bedside visitor. Once again, as he had done during their 1872 European tour, Harry was swiping Alice's material—or what was potentially her material. He was distorting it and translating it into paying copy. He'd even drawn some of Olive's complaints to Verena from conversations he'd overheard between Katharine and Alice during his recent stay in Boston in 1883.

But Alice, prostrate as she was among her pillows, was preparing to make her own literary use of her sufferings. In time, a little book of her own would shake the author of *The Bostonians* to his foundations.

SPIRITS

I n late June 1885, on a farm in the hills of southern New Hampshire, William James, battling a nightmare, tossed on his rented mattress. Nearby in the woods, fireflies lit up; and on Chesham Pond, the mosquitoes drifted through the fine, warm night. Nearby, as well, the stark, isolated peak of Great Monadnock rose up under the summer stars. The mountain, far away from all others, ruled an island of surprisingly wild country, schist boulders and red spruce, where, in 1887, the last wolf in New Hampshire would be shot. Decades before that event, Herman Melville had used Monadnock to describe the hump of the sinister white whale in his novel *Moby-Dick* (1851). As for William, the mountain's great brooding presence—it was said to overlook all six of the New England states in its lonely majesty—seemed less portentous; mostly he was delighted with the warm, clean air of the countryside. But that night William dreamed that "the poor little Humster"—Herman James, his seventeen-month-old baby—had grown a "hooked nose." And then, in a horrifying twist of the dream, William imagined that his child was dying.

The next day, William wrote a single line, almost an afterthought, about this dream to his wife, Alice. As a psychologist—even fifteen years before Freud's *Interpretation of Dreams* (1900)—William probably grasped the meanings of his nightmare. The prominent nose echoed a family joke. William's third son, when first born in January 1884, looked, his father thought, startlingly Jewish. Did Emma Lazarus still linger in William's mind? Harry echoed this witticism from faraway Paris; he greeted his new nephew as the "little Israelite." As the newest James, anyway, little Herman apparently had in store for him a lifetime of family nicknames and witticisms. By the winter of 1884, when the child had started to crawl across William's Cambridge parlor, his father dubbed him the "human turtle."

The other half of William's dream—that Herman was "moribund"—would afterward seem a portent. But William's fear sprang from concrete circumstances. Back in Cambridge with his mother, little Herman was suffering from whooping cough. William had evacuated six-year-old Harry and three-year-old William to the remote hamlet of Pottersville (now Harrisville), New Hampshire, to escape this highly infectious and tenacious Victorian child killer. His sister-in-law Margaret Gibbens, a maiden aunt, was recruited to help him, as Aunt Kate had been. Margy Gibbens faced "a labor fit to break the back of Hercules." To complicate matters, little William had started to suffer from plugged bowels, resistant even to castor oil, in the grand tradition of his uncle Harry.

At night the rain crashed down. During the day, the heat hung in the fields and woods. For entertainment, William and young Harry bounded up a nearby hill to capture the view—the great stone-tipped mountain, three thousand feet of it, sprawling to the south. Little William ate like a horse and, under his aunt's frayed surveillance, slept "like an elephant." When big William impishly asked his little son to switch roles, to "play he was papa and I William," the little boy had a ready answer. "I want the whip, I want the whip," he chanted feistily.

High-spirited wit abounded in William's household, flourishing even (or especially) under duress. But William increasingly longed to bequeath his sons more security, support, and consistency than his father, with all his caprices and contradictions, had provided. William was starting to grow into the role of father. In future years he'd even be spotted shepherding his sons, unorthodox though he was, to the regular Sunday services at the Harvard chapel. And in this crisis summer of 1885, William had taken on the role of guardian.

These days, William chose to stay with his family instead of slipping away. But, ironically, he'd been "practically separated" from his wife, Alice, for the previous four months. That spring, in March 1885, Mrs. Alice had fallen ill with scarlet fever. The children had been spirited away to their grandmother's, and Alice had been quarantined in a room above William's study. The servants placed coal, food, and water outside of her door, and Alice took them in, William thought, "like an antique leperess."

Pink with the contagious flush of scarlatina, Alice had to incinerate in her bedroom fire any letters, newspapers, or books she'd touched. Yet for her, the leisure to read without "babies, callers, witnesses, notes to write, or duties to perform" felt like a vacation, and now her wandering husband pined to hear her "ladylike" voice through the door. At forty-three, William was growing into his marriage, too. He relished intimacy with Alice in person and not just in letters, from across three thousand miles of stormy ocean.

But he and Alice were about to encounter a severe test. In early July, a few days after William rejoined his wife in Cambridge, the parents' worst fears materialized. Herman James's whooping cough worsened into pneumonia. Doggedly, the infant struggled to breathe. For nine days he battled heroically. His "constitution proved so tenacious," William wrote to his cousin, "that each visit of the doctor found him still alive." Then on July 9, 1885, the baby died.

"Dear little Hummer! Dear little soul!" William wrote to Aunt Kate. His lost child had been the "flower of the flock," William wrote over and over again to friends and relatives. *The flower of the flock;* William repeated this curious mixed metaphor like a mantra in his grief.

The bereaved parents drove a buggy out to the Cambridge Cemetery. There, Henry's and Mary's graves, once winterbound and frozen, now sprouted roses, barberries, and an adolescent pine tree. William and Alice buried their child in a corner of the James family lot. For a coffin, Herman nested in a wicker basket of a cradle. William and Alice draped it with white canton flannel; they heaped the makeshift casket with pine branches, birch leaves, ferns, and July wildflowers. For William, at this summer burial, Alice became "aggrandized and illumined" by her maternal agony. Babies were "soft memories," Harry wrote from London, also feeling for Alice as a bereaved mother: "Alice will always throb to the vision of his little being." The parents found themselves grafted together by what William called a "taste of the intolerable mysteriousness of this thing called existence."

❧

EXISTENCE, FOR WILLIAM, had always hovered on the edge of what was tolerable, but still he continued to pursue its mysteries. At some point in the year 1885—probably in the shortening days of autumn, a few weeks or months after little Herman's death—he arrived at a tall brick townhouse on Pinckney Street, on the crown of Beacon Hill. He and his wife had made an appointment with a woman named Leonora Piper.

A so-called trance medium, the twenty-six-year-old Mrs. Piper had recently taken to hosting spiritual sittings for friends, neighbors, and their friends and neighbors. Mrs. Alice had given William a fervent endorsement of her inexplicable powers; her mother, Elizabeth Gibbens, and sisters, Mary and Margaret, had made the original discovery. The Gibbenses and the Pipers were linked by way of the underworld of Boston servants. Many an Irish maid or cook in the city, though she didn't attend parlor séances, pursued an avid fascination with the supernatural. The excited flush of downstairs hearsay had brought these gentlefolk together, and fatefully so.

William, ever the scientist, arrived at the house skeptical. He suspected his mother-in-law was a victim of the medium's trickery, and he had been playing the *"esprit fort"* (strong one) with the women of the family. But he was also intrigued. He became all the more so when he met Mrs. Piper, who had set herself up as a link to the world of the dead. The young woman was shy, not at all showy or pretentious. She had a neat arrangement of wheat-blond hair, a slender frame, and a gentle and self-possessed dignity—appropriate to her wholesome New Hampshire girlhood and her graceful Beacon Hill house. Leonora Piper didn't *look* like a medium, except that she had lucid blue eyes and strong, almost craggy New England features, which admirers perhaps euphemistically called "Grecian."

She greeted her guests cordially but omitted the customary introductions. William and Alice's anonymity was thought necessary in order to test the medium's powers; Mrs. Piper needed to come to them as a complete stranger, someone who couldn't use her knowledge of the family to manipulate them. There was the matter of the gossiping servants, but that was considered negligible, if it was considered at all.

Mrs. Piper invited the Jameses into an alcove of her house. Here she held her séances without the usual props of darkened rooms, draperies, levitating tables, or crystal balls—as William was relieved to discover. But still she was a trance medium, and her reverie gave her séance its hair-raising centerpiece. She didn't grow limp or passive like a hypnotized person; instead, she exhibited, as William later wrote, "great muscular unrest, even her ears moving vigorously in a way impossible to her in her waking state."

Mrs. Piper had first entered such a trance shortly after her marriage to a well-to-do Beacon Hill Bostonian, William Piper, in the early 1880s. In 1884, Leonora had attended a mind-cure circle on Beacon Hill that was run by a celebrated blind clairvoyant named J. R. Cocke. Unexpectedly, the young woman had found herself shaking with chills. She saw in front of her "a flood of light in which many strange faces appeared." Then, responding to the beckoning of a mysterious hand, she trance-walked to a table in the center of Dr. Cocke's parlor and picked up a pencil and paper. With these, she began to reel off lines of "automatic writing" (or "spirit writing") before awakening, in evident surprise, from her swoon. For a future medium, this performance marked a promising and provocative debut.

But Mrs. Piper could trace her psychical gifts, as the Victorian world described them, back to her childhood. At the age of eight, while playing with acorns in an autumnal garden, Leonora had been struck by "a sharp blow on her right ear"—a falling acorn or a spiritual slap? In the sibilance that followed, the child discerned the letter *S* and then the words "Aunt Sara, not dead, but with you still." Inevitably, it turned out that this same Aunt Sara, who lived in a far part of the country, had passed away that very day. The acorns *knew*. Or rather the spirits did, in Leonora's telling of the story, later preserved by her daughter; they knew about the death and also hinted to the little girl that she might have unusual powers.

Like many other Victorian trance mediums, Mrs. Piper employed a "control"—a trusty spirit intermediary whose job it was to find and fetch her sitters' departed friends and relatives. Early in her career, she had auditioned several such ethereal telephone operators. She'd tried a Native American girl with the improbable name of Chlorine, presumably accented on the second syllable to distinguish her from the chemical disinfectant. She had also summoned the irascible steamship and railroad tycoon Cornelius Vanderbilt, who had died in 1877. And she had even recruited the composer Johann Sebastian Bach, who had evidently mastered English during his centuries in the world beyond.

By 1885, though, Mrs. Piper had settled into a working relationship with a deceased French doctor named Phinuit (pronounced "Finney")— a bad-tempered entity formerly employed by Dr. Cocke, the blind clairvoyant, and also known around the astral plane as Finne or Finnett. Phinuit manifested himself, in Mrs. Piper's trance, with a deep, gruff growl that strongly contrasted with Leonora's own musical contralto. This control would especially interest the bearded, note-taking psychical researchers who would investigate Mrs. Piper and her alleged powers through the late 1880s. These psychologists, of whom William would be one, couldn't quite make out if Dr. Phinuit was an "actual historical person" or just a handy, if pushy, spirit-world go-between. Oliver Lodge, one of these investigators, theorized that Phinuit was "probably a mere name for Mrs. Piper's secondary consciousness."

Whatever her control's origins, Leonora had to struggle in order to enter her trance. She exchanged sharp words with the recalcitrant Phinuit to encourage him to contact the requested spirits. Then things would grow more relaxed. The gentle Leonora would give much sage advice to her clients, and she would modestly annex only one material power from her nonmaterial friends. She could (her adherents claimed) wither blossoms and render them scentless. It was hardly a useful or very constructive magical power; and it was not on show in the alcove where William and Alice James waited, anxiously, for spiritual information to emerge.

From the depths of her trance, Mrs. Piper fished up two names. One was Niblin and then the variant Diblin. To her listeners, these words corresponded to the name of Mrs. Alice's long-dead father (Gibbens), who had committed suicide decades before in New Orleans. The other name was Herrin. Mrs. Alice took that to indicate Herman, the child she had lost.

∽≫

MRS. ALICE HAD her own emotional urgency in consulting this medium: she longed for some reassurance that she would see her little son again. But William, though he shared his wife's loss, went to see Mrs. Piper with a keen desire to know if she derived her knowledge from clandestine sources, from the dead, or (as he increasingly came to believe) from some little-understood faculty of the human mind.

Even before Herman's illness and death, William had waded into the waters of so-called psychical research, investigating hypnotism, mesmerism, and telepathy. In the spring of 1885, at the Massachusetts Institute of Technology, he had gone to see a so-called materializing medium—a spiritualist who claimed to be able to summon up the spirits of the dead. He hadn't been impressed. Still, during 1885 and 1886, the urgency of his work intensified by the loss of his son, William tracked one such medium, Helen Berry. He attended twelve séances. (His friends and relatives logged twenty-three more on his behalf.) But, William wrote in a study he published in 1886, "No spirit form came directly to any one of us."

Still, William plunged on into the fringe world of mediums. His intellectual interest in spiritualism, to be sure, belonged to his broad, open investigation of the human mind and its powers. But he shared his fascination with many, many others from all quarters of life; "psychical phenomena" absorbed both intellectual and popular-culture circles of the time. By the 1880s, mediums were in high vogue, with their draped and blacked-out rooms, startling table rappings, and abrupt "materializations" of shrouded spirits. The new mania inevitably involved chicanery, and it attracted many of the confidence tricksters, so active in nineteenth-century America. Skeptical patrons sometimes exposed an apparition as the medium herself, swathed in thin muslin that she had smuggled into the séance. Such a gauzy spiritual accessory could be tucked inside the medium's underdrawers—fished out in the dark or in a cabinet, during noisy proceedings—and donned as the medium flitted around the room for added theatrical effect. Trapdoors, bribed servants, and pilfered mail (for inside "spirit" information) had also been exposed.

The machinery of séances looks bizarre in historical retrospect. It struck some contemporaries, such as Alice James, as preposterous. But the phenomenon had deep folkloric roots, wide appeal to both low and high audiences, and surprising relevance to the emotional needs of many increasingly secular Victorians, among them William James.

Spiritualism in the mid- and late nineteenth century, in fact, pulsed with the high voltage of a religious revival. It swept through Europe, where it remained a perennial and iconic feature of aristocratic eccentricity long into the twentieth century—as exampled by the clairvoyant and Tarot-reading Madame Sosostris of T. S. Eliot's *Waste Land* (1922) and the feckless Madame Arcati of Noel Coward's *Blithe Spirit* (1941). But, strangely enough, this "modern" spiritualism actually came originally from the United States—from the Jameses' own backyard and milieu. Another fiery product of the burned-over district, it began with the famous "Rochester rappings" at Hydesville, New York, in 1848. And it afterward burgeoned into a full-scale cultural fad—an irrepressible parlor entertainment, a vast snake-oil industry, and (as psychologists like William began to investigate it) a blistering scientific wrangle.

Mrs. Piper, though, didn't make use of vaudeville chicanery. Married to a well-to-do Bostonian, Leonora Piper hadn't seized on mediumship for money—though some were able to pay the bills by means of séances. William regarded Leonora Piper as a "simple, genuine, unassuming Yankee girl"; she was earnest as well as seemingly well informed about the people who came to her séances. In this, Leonora Piper resembled one of the most convincing and successful mediums of the 1850s and 1860s, an Americanized Scot named Daniel Dunglas Home. Home, with his wild raven-black hair and soup-strainer mustache, had dazzled czars and French empresses with his uncanny knowledge of their dead relatives. And he boldly held his sessions without fully dousing a room in darkness. "Light should be the demand of every spiritualist," Home explained. And Piper, whom William famously called the "white crow" of spiritualism (one white crow, he reasoned, could prove that not all crows are black), seemed bathed in light—honest, open, and willing to cooperate with scientific investigation.

Many people wanted to know what made mediums like Leonora Piper tick. By 1890, even Bob James found himself "preoccupied with spirit rappings." But in the mid-1880s, his brother William took a more measured scientific interest, focusing his scrutiny on the brain. His infatuation with Mrs. Piper—which his distinguished biographers have downplayed (and adherents of psychic phenomena have played up)— remained largely professional.

At the same time, William's enthusiasm was flavored with personal motives as well as with an idiosyncratic and hopeful credulity. His desire to believe in Mrs. Piper was reminiscent of William's father's obsession with Emanuel Swedenborg decades earlier. "I wish to determine a fact"—William wrote to one potential guinea pig, Elizabeth Blodgett, in 1888—"namely what is all this mediumship? And the admixture of knowledge & ignorance, and low passions and superhuman passions is what makes the problem so fascinating. I entirely believe in my medium [Mrs. Piper]. She fails however with about ½ of her sitters, or more."

William, for his part, increasingly loathed the "social side" of his psychical research. He recoiled from the sometimes tawdry parlors of mesmerism, séances, card readings, and spirit trances. To him, Mrs. Piper's trim Beacon Hill drawing room stood out as a lone oasis of respectability. At the same time, William remained deeply engrossed in the psychological implications of trances and other such extreme mental states.

Spiritualism, indeed, was only one of the pseudoscientific fascinations with the human mind that gripped the late nineteenth century. "Psychical research," as it was called, was only one of the lines of investigation by which William, an acute observer and a formidable theorist, was shoring up a philosophical reputation. Strangely enough, such probings of the mind's powers (or the mind's self-deceptions) would eventually help fuel the paradoxes of modern psychology. In the 1880s William was shaping his own version of this psychology—in his huge, still-unfinished "textbook"—even if his association with the Society for Psychical Research rated as one of his more bizarre professional links.

Still, William's professional embrace of Leonora Piper had its hazards, which went far beyond his encounters with cranky and vengeful spirits like Phinuit. Trickery and deception laced the world of mediums, and much of the "research" of the time actually concentrated on exposing hoaxes. The balding, assiduous Richard Hodgson, a legal expert who documented some of the most thorough, skeptical, and scientific case studies for the SPR, besieged Mrs. Piper and her husband with private detectives in the late 1880s, trying to unearth evidence of fraud. He was unable to find any. But psychical researchers always had to keep alert for what William's English friend and colleague Edmund Gurney wearily described as "fraud or simulation of fraud." Because dishonesty, in the twilight world of the mediums, lurked everywhere.

Plenty of William's colleagues shared his fascination with Mrs. Piper, but his two siblings in England shied away. Alice registered her skepticism dramatically. As Leonora Piper occasionally worked with props—mementos or material remains that presumably helped Phinuit locate spirits in the crowded afterlife—Alice sent a lock of her hair at William's urging in late 1885.

Alice soon confessed a "base trick." The hair sample belonged not to her but to a friend of her nurse's, dead four years. "I thought it a much better test of whether the medium were simply a mind-reader or not," Alice explained. She hoped William would forgive her "frivolous treatment," she wrote him, with a twist of irony, "of so serious a science."

THAT SAME WINTER, Alice had once more claimed rooms in Mayfair. With Katharine again away—their excursions on Hampstead Heath the summer before now just memories—Alice had settled in Bolton Row, just down the street from Harry. Here, as she wrote her aunt Kate, she commanded a view over low-slung backyard quarters of kitchen maids, grooms, and coachmen, a "vast sea of mews." She sat, or lay in bed, beside high windows that absorbed such light as could be squeezed out of an English winter. A Swiss-born landlady provided trays of potatoes—boiled, roasted, mashed, and baked—in a "larger repertory," Alice joked, than if the woman had been born British. Alice's fourth "keeper," or hired companion, slipped away to Sunday services piously fasting. But otherwise this Miss Ward hadn't yet revealed the "debased" human nature Alice had so often encountered among hired help.

Alice's legs remained frozen with her symptomatic paralysis. But Bolton Row would soon see the dawning of a "little modest day." As

spring came in and as her health allowed, Alice found that her prime location offered her a small oasis of mostly female sociability, including
the regal and aged Fanny Kemble and Constance Fenimore Woolson.
(Alice evidently liked Constance, though Katharine Loring cultivated
her friendship more actively.) Alice's guests gathered in intriguing knots
and combinations, which, she thought, tinted her brother Harry
"greenish," as *he* didn't always assemble such interesting groups. Alice
refreshed her callers, most of them family friends and connections, with
talk of Plato and Emerson. Luminaries gravitated to Alice for her intricate conversation and tart wit, not only because she was Henry James's
sister.

Alice had, without much effort, created what her distinguished biographer Jean Strouse has described as a "London salon." Alice herself
floated the term experimentally. To play the hostess of a salon, the important and sought-after "lady" of a metropolitan drawing room, intrigued her. Steeped as she was in French culture, Alice no doubt
thrilled to the allure and glamour of that traditional role for women,
drawn from the grand aristocratic and artistic circles of France.

Her extemporaneous gatherings connected her, if briefly, to a role
that many ambitious American women tried—in London, Rome, Florence, Newport, or Boston, during the middle and late nineteenth
century—with varying degrees of duration and aplomb. Annie Fields
had long ago shown her younger friend that a determined, intelligent
woman could assemble writers and artists—coax them, blandish them
into good humor, and subtly shape their endeavors. Some people called
such feminine involvement encouragement. Others identified it as the
power behind the throne.

Alice had formerly hosted a salon, or at least a ladies' luncheon club,
drawn from her Civil War–era sewing bee, back in Cambridge. Though
her resources remained slim, she had a little money to work with; her
income had, she observed, "the greatest capacity for diminishing itself
and yet still existing." Rents from family properties in Syracuse planted
her firmly among the "smug and comfortable," as she put it. She ranked
as an "heiress" if not a "bloated capitalist." With her private income and
her conversational savvy, Alice might have followed in the footsteps of
Madame de Rambouillet, the friend of Molière, or Madame d'Épinay,

the confidante of Jean-Jacques Rousseau. Alice's claims were much more modest, but from her sofa, she certainly conducted a "very considerable, social winter," Harry judged. Her sessions in Mayfair amounted, in fact, to séances of a sort—rare gatherings of personalities, evanescent manifestations of wit and insight.

But Alice hadn't really been cut out for the part of a hostess. Mediating among high-strung personalities strained her. Her sardonic wit drove discords into the drawing room instead of harmonizing its personalities; Alice had long scorned her own "company manners" and, down deep, cared as little for her visitors in their hats and afternoon dresses as her brother Harry, now in his forties, did for the pretentious flower-choked London season or tedious, fogged-in country-house weekends. Basically, Alice's universe had twin stars, Harry and Katharine. She didn't covet more elaborate constellations.

Though she'd return fitfully over the next few years, Alice abandoned the metropolis—and her fledgling salon—in May 1886. To stretch her income, Katharine helped her friend settle in what Harry disparagingly termed "the provinces," specifically Leamington—pronounced "Lemmington," as if in commemoration of the famous suicidally conformist Arctic rodents—deep in the turfy English Midlands.

Like the grander "watering place" of Bath, Leamington sported a Royal Pump Room for the quaffing of curative waters: the town had traded on its saline and iron-tinged chalybeate springs since the eighteenth century. But since the 1840s, the heyday of one Dr. Henry Jephson—who'd attended croupy notables like Princess Victoria, Florence Nightingale, and John Ruskin—Leamington had stodgily exemplified the quintessential Victorian health resort, its genteel terraced houses and solemn gardens teeming with walking sticks, lap rugs, and bath chairs. Bland bands blared from gazebos. A hospital of a town, Royal Leamington Spa, as it liked to call itself, offered itself as the perfect place for Alice to pursue her primary career, as she put it, of "trans-Atlantic neurasthenia."

No streams of notables freshened Alice's parlor here. Nobody visited. By the later 1880s, dry spells could last as long as six weeks, as Alice coped with the bleakness of Victorian lodging-house life. One rare visitor in 1889 asked Alice if she didn't get "awfully tired of read-ing." The visitor, Miss Percy, didn't read much herself. But she im-ported, briefly, a "round, bustling, cheery-in-the-morning" personality into Alice's more sardonic solitude. Besides Harry and Katharine, Al-ice's visitors brought "no excitements"; "occasionally a new old-maid adds herself to my circle," Alice self-deprecatingly wrote to William. A Miss Palmer, another specimen, sported a tumor and an income of ten shillings a week. But even such dispiriting spa friends didn't always rally back to Alice's bedside after their first viewing. They left Alice feeling even more alone—like a "Barnum monstrosity which had missed fire."

During 1886, Alice replaced "Wardy" with "Nurse," the young Emily Ann Bradfield, who had frolicked as a little girl in a Gloucester-shire village during the period when Alice, in Cambridge in the 1860s, had first broken down. It seemed odd to Alice that they'd thrown their lots together. This loyal young Englishwoman would eventually inspire Alice with a hope that "human good outweighs human evil."

But Nurse had a figure like a bookmark and a face like "a sheet of note paper," Alice noted. She initially looked like a poor companion for the intricate Alice James. Alice lamented how ludicrous it was for some-one who'd grown up with her father and William to be "reduced to Nurse and Miss C[larke, Alice's Leamington lady] for humorous daily fodder." At her worst, Nurse struck Alice as a "diseased jelly-fish." Even at her best, Nurse exemplified a provincial Englishwoman, as Alice saw the type, with "abrupt and arbitrary streaks of supreme intelligence tra-versing a bog of absolutely . . . passive imbecility."

Once, Nurse, poker-faced, was pulling petticoats over Alice's head. Alice flooded with the ironic richness of the scene. With her coruscating imagination, she felt surging inside what she called the "potency of Bismarck"—so different from her servant's contented mechanical blankness. Alice exclaimed, "Oh! Nurse, don't you wish you were inside of *me*!" "Inside of you, Miss," the young woman countered, "when you have just had a sick head-ache for five days!" And the two women laughed, relishing the high humor of the moment. Nurse had scored a point for Gloucestershire.

But when Katharine stayed away—as she did for weeks or months, nursing her sister Louisa—Alice suffered from loneliness. Harry noted that especially in Leamington Alice saw "*only* women, so far as she now sees anyone." Yet Alice wasn't really a "friendless wisp of femininity," as she jokingly referred to herself. She sallied forth in her bath chair. She formulated strong opinions about the powderkeg political situation of Ireland, as Irish self-government was being hotly debated. In England, the Liberals, led by Prime Minister William Gladstone, supported Home Rule for the island in 1886. But the Unionists—those who wanted to preserve the union with Britain that had been forced on Ireland in 1801—won the day.

Alice followed with fascination the drama of the Irish nationalist Charles Stewart Parnell—Parnell's clearing himself of the notorious Phoenix Park murders of two English diplomats in 1887 (a moment of triumph) and the revelation of his scandalous liaison with a married woman, Kathleen O'Shea, in 1889 (which ended his career). Alice's sympathy for the Irish and her defense of Parnell were probably especially provocative in a conservative Unionist enclave like Leamington.

In the late summer of 1888, chilling events heralded in the British newspapers gave Alice another cause, another occasion to draw on her strengths. Unsettling news accounts came of mysterious attacks on poor women and prostitutes in the East End of London, beginning with the murder of forty-three-year-old Mary Ann Nichols on August 31. Her body was discovered, strangled and brutally slashed, in front of a stable in Whitechapel. The night of Saturday, September 8, Annie Chapman, forty-seven, was killed in nearby Spitalfields. The murderer, whose removal of organs suggested surgical skill, remained at large throughout the foggy autumn darkness of that year. Britain was paralyzed with fear and revulsion as, over a period of several tense weeks, more victims— Elizabeth Stride, Catherine Eddowes, and Mary Jane Kelly—were found on weekend mornings, their throats slit and their bodies badly mutilated.

During the so-called Whitechapel murders in 1888, Alice grew so animatedly "*wüttend*" (furious) with the London police that her outrage charged her with what her brother described as "robust health." Faced with Jack the Ripper, Alice hardly cowered in her lodgings in the fashion of the despised and now-dismissed Wardy. She swelled with indignation against this anonymous (and never identified) killer of women.

☙

HARRY HOPED HE'D stay warm at the Villa Brichieri. That wasn't a given in 1886, especially not in the month of December. Heat wasn't guaranteed in a grand, draft-prone villa on the hill of Bellosguardo just outside Florence. One could get chilblains, bad for the scribbling of novels—although when incapacitated, all the Jameses readily resorted to dictating their thoughts to an amanuensis. In any case, Harry had been hard at work. Recently he had published *The Princess Casamassima* (1886), a realist novel in which he had resuscitated his character Christina Light from *Roderick Hudson*. In Bellosguardo he would undertake a novella about privacy, seduction, and literary fame that would become even more famous—and more revealing of his own deep sense of isolation: his remarkable *Aspern Papers*, which would be serialized in the *Atlantic* in 1888.

A villa bettered an "insanitary Florentine hotel," but hired quarters in a crumbling patrician residence inflicted other hardships. Some Americans, such as Charles W. Eliot, didn't think highly of these rentals, which were built solidly of brick or small stone and plastered yellow, the prevailing color on the hill. "The word villa," he had observed, "is deceptive." The floors were made of brick, a dirty rope might serve as the handrail on the stairs, and the door fastenings reminded Eliot of the hooks and bolts used on New England barns. Eliot noticed flies eating uncovered sugar on the sideboards, linens spread out on the billiard tables, and a "young lady's room look[ing] as if a dirty-clothes-bag, drawers, closets and wardrobes had no existence."

These villas, two or three hundred years old, hadn't always been well maintained, in the eyes of modernizers like Eliot. But Harry loved Bellosguardo for its age-old atmosphere, even if that meant chilly rooms. In any case, he rested assured that his "landlady," as he called her, would have stocked ample firewood for him. In fact, she had piled it high with her own fair hands. For Constance Fenimore Woolson *was* Harry's landlady, and she proceeded to lavish him with devotion *"sans bornes"* (without bounds)—or so he claimed. His own devotion, Harry gallantly added, matched hers.

For his escape from smog-choked London, he and Fenimore had struck on a practical, cozy arrangement. Constance had leased a "roomy and rambling" apartment in the Villa Brichieri for two years. But, not yet ready to move there from the nearby Villa Castellani, she allowed Harry to sublet the villa's seigneurial high-ceilinged rooms, its "big wood fires," and breathtaking views out over the smoky rooftops of Florence.

On Christmas Eve 1886, Harry hunkered beside the glow of a crackling fire, penning ecstatic letters. But he may not have sat alone; even if Constance wasn't yet with him, chances were that she would come to dinner that evening—ready to lavish on Harry the cheerful Christmas companionship he hadn't even known during his haphazard childhood.

Constance and Harry's arrangement soon grew even cozier. Later that winter, Harry struck out on a junket to Venice—and promptly contracted jaundice. As soon as he could be moved, Fenimore—now living in the villa herself, though chastely in the upper rooms—ushered the ailing Harry back under her roof. Harmoniously, the two writers, both of them now comfortably in their forties, spent the exquisite months of April and May 1887 in the airy galleries of the villa and on its operatic terrace.

The friends who visited them, though mostly adroit cosmopolitans, no doubt raised eyebrows when they witnessed a ménage that in Boston or New York would have rated as racily improper. Henry James boarding with a woman? Had he actually found, at last, the romance that had so long been conspicuously missing from his life? Was the bright, devoted Miss Woolson, with her wound-up hair and trailing gowns, Harry's mistress? Or was she merely hoping to be?

The liaison certainly appeared promising. Even decades afterward, Leon Edel, Harry's monumental biographer, couldn't resist romanticizing Harry's clandestine visits to Fenimore in the 1880s—especially this particular blue-skied Florentine honeymoon. As he lyrically describes it, this Italian sojourn invites a parallel to E. M. Forster's later novel *A Room with a View* (1908)—in which a prudish Anglo-Saxon romantically and sexually awakens in the flush of a Tuscan spring. (Forster's fictional Lucy Honeychurch quasi-biographically traced Forster's own repressed homosexual yearnings while he was touring in Florence with his mother, just a decade after Harry's residence with Fenimore.) Harry's Italian passions were similarly inflated and lyrical, and perhaps had similar origins. But even after many years, Harry had evidently not experienced a full-blown Italian romance with any man or woman.

Harry's intense friendship with Fenimore, to be sure, hinted at the novelist's most plausible heterosexual romance. Leon Edel, dismissing Harry's own participation in such a liaison, construed a one-sided romance. For Edel, Constance harbored unrequited hopes for Harry's love. Edel framed a myth, as one of his critics described it, of "a lonely spinster who carries a torch for the icy James all over Europe." Such a fable, though, flattens the complexity of one of the most unusual American women writers of the late nineteenth century, as well as ignoring Harry's own motivations in the friendship.

Harry was comfortable with Constance, and she had managed to melt his sometimes chilly facade. That was an achievement in itself. But she did so with intelligent sympathy, not with erotic attraction. That April and May, Fenimore lavished on Harry her best company because, with what we now call seasonal affective disorder, she was at her best in the light and warmth of a Mediterranean climate, with its palm trees and early springs.

Constance had chosen Italy largely because of Harry. Through the 1880s, she had better chances of seeing him here than in Germany, where she also resided. Even in Harry's absence, Constance—basking in his literary visions of the Italian countryside—might feel as if she were inhabiting his imagination. To be sure, the often solitary Fenimore loved Harry's charming company. She enjoyed having him with her, as the servants brought them tea on their terrace. Though Fenimore certainly welcomed Harry's visits, she had plenty to do in his absence.

In 1882, she had published her previously serialized first novel, *Anne*—her answer, as at least one critic argued, to Harry's *Portrait of a Lady*. Her novel featured a lady, Fenimore's fictional Anne Douglas, who played out a more active role in her own drama than that of the tragically passive Isabel Archer, who listlessly conformed to the predominant "male culture." Fenimore's plucky book sold briskly in the United States. Among the ever-expanding crowd of female readers (among them Alice James and Katharine Peabody Loring), Miss Woolson's short stories and novels struck a chord. Women clamored for them at bookstores. And Constance, like Harry a self-made freelance writer, had to write and publish in order to support herself.

As he sat on his friend's terrace, Harry was careful not to mention Constance in his letters to William, as if he didn't want his brother to believe he'd come to Florence in order to pursue a dangerous liaison. But he opened up more to his sister, Alice, and to his sophisticated European friends, who understood his chaste liaisons with women better than William—always hoping for Harry to try matrimony—tended to do.

To be sure, Alice could note that Harry was sometimes to be found "on the continent flirting with Constance." But she also knew, when her brother fell ill in Venice in 1887, that Harry's friend Mrs. Katherine De Kay Bronson wasn't an amorous connection. Rather, Mrs. Bronson made a useful nurse, along with a good society doctor and, as Alice tellingly described him, "an impassioned Gondolier." This excitable Venetian boatman worked for Mrs. Bronson and attended the ill Harry. For reasons best known to himself, he burst into tears at the Venice railway station when Henry James departed.

All in all, Harry's affection for Constance, though genuine, hadn't actually spurred him to many visits. Before his arrival at the villa in 1886, Harry urged the perennial Bootts, from their cypress-ringed hilltop villa, to keep an eye on his "amiable friend" in his absence. "She is a deaf and *méticuleuse* [finicky] old maid," he wrote, hardly praising her to his friends as a lover might do. Constance was also "an excellent and sympathetic being" whose gentle goodness kept Harry attached to her.

In planning his stay in Florence, Harry had told Lizzie Boott that their "good" Fenimore had to be "worked in." Perhaps Harry feigned indifference for Lizzie's benefit. Maybe he wanted to fool himself. Despite his reputation as a painstakingly psychological novelist, Harry didn't always understand his own feelings. But maybe he saw Fenimore as a beloved but slightly trying obligation, as he did his sister, Alice. At the same time, he blithely assumed that Fenimore, like Alice, eternally yearned to see *him*. He assigned Constance "an immense power of devotion (to H.J.!)." But Harry probably flattered himself with his estimate of his transcendent importance to both women.

It was easy for Harry to read Constance's sweet, admiring manner as hero worship, especially on a warm Italian terrace. Flattering manners overflowed involuntarily from such a well-brought-up Victorian woman—a woman who, however, was growing away from her habitual reinforcement of male egos toward visions and itineraries of her own. Harry himself, after six years of knowing Constance, hadn't progressed as much. He still siphoned from Fenimore the admiration he'd once found in Paul Zhukovsky—whose onetime allegiance to "H.J.Jr. (!!)," incidentally, Harry had accorded *two* exclamation points in 1880.

Fenimore's few surviving letters to Harry give us a hint of the couple's possible conversations at the Villa Brichieri. Tellingly, these letters from the early 1880s read more like an exhaustive if friendly critique of *The Portrait of a Lady* than like lovesick missives. (But such subjects, indeed, hardly necessitated the mutual letter burning on which Harry nervously insisted.) "You know I have found fault with you for not making it more evident that your heroes were in love with the heroines, really in love," Constance wrote. She cannily pointed to her friend's deep standoffishness as reflected in his ambiguous, chaste bachelor characters like *Portrait of a Lady*'s Ralph Touchett. (Ralph supposedly loved his cousin Isabel but, being sickly—a frequent nineteenth-century metaphor, by the way, for "inversion," or homosexuality—never acted on his passion.) Constance both offered literary criticism and dropped a personal hint, although she probably knew better than to cherish hopes. But she felt kinship with Harry, perhaps, for an entirely different set of reasons.

Some possible explanations of Fenimore's motivations surface in her short story—her best-known piece today—"Miss Grief." In it, an unpublished writer named Aaronna Moncrief (nicknamed "Miss Grief") travels to Italy in order to haunt a well-established male writer in whose work she'd glimpsed authentic moments of passion or compassion—qualities that turn out to be poorly represented in the man himself. The Harry-like author recoils from what he sees as a middle-aged spinster dressed in rusty black. And he spurns her unusual writing. The story has sometimes been read as an exposé of Fenimore's romance, or lack thereof, with Harry. But Constance published "Miss Grief" in *Lippincott's* in 1880, before she'd actually met Harry. More profoundly, this story indicts Henry James less than the whole male literary establishment to which he belonged. In the late 1870s Woolson had wrangled with her Boston publisher, James Osgood, who'd failed to promote her books or even pay her for them. And she'd inwardly struggled for a long time with literary father figures like William Dean Howells and her own great-uncle James Fenimore Cooper. By befriending her, by gallantly trying to understand her writing (and including her in his *Partial Portraits* in 1887), Harry sometimes appeared to offer her compensation for all this institutional misunderstanding and neglect.

At the same time, Harry inflicted his own form of neglect, springing from his deep discomfort with women both as artists and lovers. Harry would write a stinging evaluation of Constance's fiction in 1887, shortly after his idyllic holiday with her. His essay in *Harper's*, "Miss Woolson," praised but also subtly dismissed her fiction. It amounted to what one biographer, Lyndall Gordon, has called "a calculated betrayal; it carried an armory of stings in its velvet glove." Harry's attack was all the more egregious because, as one critic argued, Fenimore may well have felt that Harry's writing was "competing with, even feeding off of, women's fiction, including her own, and achieving recognition at the expense of women authors."

"Miss Grief" also hints at an additional twist to Constance's odd alliance with Harry. Constance's sexuality gave indications of being at least as ambiguous as Harry's. In "Miss Grief," Aaronna Moncrief, a brashly forward woman who shatters the feminine bounds of propriety by both writing poems and pursuing the attentions of a male grandee, reveals that she lives with a woman named Serena. With her friend, Miss Grief had tried to learn to smoke—that unfeminine activity associated, in the late nineteenth century, with female "inverts," or lesbians. Surprisingly, however, Serena turns out to be only Miss Moncrief's Aunt Martha. Such a false lead exposes a "lesbian impossibility" in the story, as one critic has put it—a longing that is impossible to fulfill, as opposed to a more substantive day-to-day Boston marriage like that of Alice James.

In itself, such a shred of evidence might not amount to much. But Woolson's short story "Felipa," published in 1876, tells the story of an adolescent Minorcan girl who falls in love with a beautiful young woman named Christine. And her late novels *Jupiter Lights* (1889) and

Horace Mann (1894) also trace lesbian "impossibilities"—the latter featuring a pipe-smoking woman sculptor based on the colorful Harriet Hosmer and on Charlotte Cushman, with whom Hosmer conducted a high-profile affair in Rome between 1858 and 1865. It seems Harry wasn't the only admirer of Honoré de Balzac and his provocative lesbian fiction, *La Fille aux yeux d'or* (*The Girl with the Golden Eyes*).

Fenimore would write her novel *Horace Mann* during the early 1890s in Cheltenham, where, in the damp grayness of England, she dreamed of the lost color and warmth of Italy. Constance struggled with depression, isolation, lack of money, and lack of recognition—as well as a depressingly silent lodging house in an out-of-the-way town that seldom fell into Harry's itinerary. The provinces sufficed for anyone who wanted quiet. But Constance no doubt wanted something more. Cheltenham, like Alice's Leamington, looked like a waiting room on the margins of more exciting, empowered, and masculine worlds. Meanwhile, Harry was dining with bachelors at his club and writing entangled fictions that, even if they increasingly sold poorly, got positive reviews.

At Leamington in the summer of 1889, Alice noted this very contrast between her life and Harry's. That weekend, Harry was staying at Wilton House, the grand stone seventeenth-century palace of the Earl of Pembroke, surrounded by its vast park and water gardens. Back in 1873 during Alice's European tour, the two siblings had taken a carriage together with Aunt Kate from their lodgings at the White Hart, "humble pilgrims" in quest of their futures. They'd rambled through those same echoing galleries and halls. They had admired a handsome group portrait by Anthony Van Dyck—the silk-clad family of the Earl of Pembroke in 1630, posed in a rust-colored fog of classical grandeur. Did Alice think of her own family's portrait, nonexistent as it was? She certainly contemplated herself and her brother as contrasting pictures. To some people, Alice admitted, it might seem as if her "fall" since that day had been as great as Harry's "rise." Harry now slept as an earl's guest in one of the most glorious houses in England. Unlike her, he was cohabiting, at least for the weekend, with "that glorious object"—the sacred fire of art, the gold-tinged panorama of a lordly family. And yet from her solitary sofa, Alice insisted, she'd learned "wondrous things." And if Fenimore had her novels, Alice James had acquired something, by 1889, as compensatory.

꙳꙳

IT BEGAN IN December 1886 as a series of quotes in a copybook. Alone in her damp lodgings, Alice transcribed passages from the nineteenth-century Russian novelist Leo Tolstoy and from the seventeenth-century American theologian Cotton Mather. The copying filled time; it loosed Alice's fingers. But did this exercise doom Alice, placing her in a long line of genteel women who'd transcribed the works of great male writers in ornamentally bound collections, the "elegant extracts" scorned by Jane Austen in *Emma*?

At the age of thirty-eight, Alice appeared too old for such anthological busywork, the literary equivalent of the ornamental needlepoint she had always despised. But Alice longed to become more than a reader, and her notebook soon showed the range of French authors—Michel de Montaigne, Anatole France, Madame Roland, dozens of others—she admired. It was as impressive as Harry's roster when he'd written *French Poets and Novelists* in 1878.

But a deeper, more peculiar, more electrifying drama was beginning to unfold. Into her leatherbound notebook, Alice copied fateful verses from Edward FitzGerald's *Rubáiyát*; a description of the ill-fated Maggie Tulliver from George Eliot's *The Mill on the Floss*; soul-stirring passages from Carlyle, now five years dead. All these monumental Victorian writers, in fact, had died during the previous decade: FitzGerald in 1883, Eliot in 1880, and Carlyle in 1881. Alice wasn't performing some rote literary exercise; she was summoning, in a sense, her own spirits—auditioning, as Leonora Piper had done back in Boston, for a "control."

A startling voice broke out in Alice's notebook. "Renunciation remains sorrow tho' sorrow willingly born," said the voice. "The frightful separateness of human experiences," said the voice. As in one of Leonora Piper's spine-tingling séances, the voice erupted starkly out. But the voice didn't belong to a table-thumping spirit. It belonged to Alice herself, but it differed from the chatty, ironic narrator of her letters. It differed, too, from the household manager who had ordered her father's suppers back in Beacon Hill, or the invalid who'd repeatedly called out, in these damp lodgings, for Nurse's help. Now, on paper, Alice spoke in riddles. She spoke in aphorisms. She'd conceived herself—if only fleetingly, if only privately—as an authority, as an author, as a sage of the sofa.

Then, on May 31, 1889, alone in Leamington, Alice left the extracts behind. "I think that if I get into the habit of writing a bit about what happens, or rather doesn't happen," she wrote, "I may lose a little of the sense of loneliness and desolation which abides with me." Such was Alice's modest beginning: writing about what *didn't* happen. Alice only promised herself, with a twist of her usual sarcasm, a "written monologue by that most interesting being, *myself.*" But she also knew she contained, down deep, a "geyser of emotions, sensations, speculations and reflections."

Now, at the age of forty, Alice embarked, tremblingly, on her "first Journal!" With this exclamation point, Alice marveled at her own audacity—and started in.

SIGNIFICANTLY, ALICE INAUGURATED her diary two months after a grave family event. On March 5, 1889, after an incremental decline into paralysis, Aunt Kate died in New York City. Since the deaths of her sister and brother-in-law, Aunt Kate had remained "vigorous," Alice observed, but in her letters she betrayed worrying "signs of a loss of memory." Nursing her own ailments, Kate had hardly visited in Boston or in England.

William sometimes ferreted her out in Manhattan; otherwise Aunt Kate offered only epistolary filaments, her familiar letters full of cousinly doings and home cures. Unable to walk in her final months, she'd died at last in the house of her niece Lila Walsh, and not among the Jameses. She hadn't been nursed, as was the nineteenth-century expectation, by the niece she'd practically raised from babyhood. "I am devoutly grateful that Lilla has been able to fill my place so fully," Alice remarked, using her relative's nickname. She felt relieved that she and Harry had been spared the "contemplation" of their aunt's disintegration: "Poor human nature can stand but a slight strain when it comes to tea-cups and salt-spoons."

It wasn't as though Alice didn't miss her second mother. "A dozen times a day," Alice wrote in her diary, "I find myself saying, 'I'll write that to A[unt] K[ate].' I suppose I did so before; it only seems oftener now, when I have to pull myself up." Though she'd chosen not to live with her powerful, overshadowing, conventionally minded aunt, Alice acutely missed one of her few links to "farbackedness," her lost past. And yet the death of her last real link to her parents' generation freed her more than she herself perhaps realized. Now, instead of letters to Kate, she wrote in a private medium unmediated by her unbookish and conventional aunt, where no one could edit her, squelch her, or judge her production. With such privileges, Alice could even invoke a "poor Aunt Kate"—not only because Kate had died but because of the salt-spoon limitations under which the old woman had lived and against which conventions her niece had increasingly bent her sardonic strength.

Freed from Kate's expectations, Alice now gave a franker evaluation of her aunt's life than she'd been able to accord her mother. Looking back on Kate's career as a Victorian aunt, Alice appraised it as a "failure." Kate had been cut out for "independence & a 'position,'" Alice wrote to William—a more prosperous marriage, more voyages, children of her own. But she hadn't been able to achieve them and so, as a woman, had relegated herself to her auntish second fiddle, to her long dependent domestic embroilment with the James family. Even here, Alice thought, Kate had failed. Their aunt had longed intensely to "absorb herself in a few individuals"—that is, the James children. But she'd never been aware, and luckily, how much she'd missed the mark, "how much the individuals resisted her." To Kate, Alice's own rebellion had appeared "a great & ungrateful betrayal: my inability to explain myself & hers to understand, in any way, the situation made it all the sadder & more ugly." With her diary, Alice had determined to explain herself to someone, though as yet the audience of the diary remained a ghostly one.

For her part, Kate explained herself—as was the wont of the Jameses and the Walshes—through her last will and testament. Kate had amassed a surprisingly large estate. Like her sister Mary and her Walsh ancestors, she'd pinched pennies and stowed her profits away. But to the Jameses' consternation, Aunt Kate had left the bulk of her fortune not to the children she had raised but to some young female Walshes in Connecticut. Though she left her favorite, William, a legacy of ten thousand dollars, Kate largely cut off the other James children. She ignored the people "with whom her life had been passed," as William put it, those "with whom we had always considered her so united."

Kate's death, with all its twists and turns, left as profound and bizarre a legacy for the younger Jameses as the deaths of their own parents had done earlier in the 1880s. William wanted more resolution, and in November 1889, Leonora Piper made contact with Kate in the spirit world. Mrs. Piper's "usurpation by 'Kate Walsh,'" William wrote his fellow psychic researcher Richard Hodgson, rated as the most "strikingly personal thing" William had ever witnessed in a séance. First, Mrs. Piper's resourceful and gruff control, Phinuit, made cracks about Kate's failed marriage to her sea captain in the 1850s and impishly taunted her as an "old crank." Then Catharine Walsh herself seized hold of the medium, speaking with what William described as "much impressiveness of manner" and "great similarity of temperament."

Alice's own haunting by Aunt Kate would prove hardly less hair-raising. Though she hadn't chosen to be a medium, Alice often lived with what she called "ghost microbes." Some of these infested old family letters arrived in Leamington in 1890 from the United States in Alice's old davenport or writing desk. Most of Alice's heirlooms, in fact, would remain warehoused; Alice feared that lodgings qualified as her "highest attainable abode." But still, she admitted, "my fancy plays about the soup-plates & gravey [sic] boats as the nucleus of an impossible home."

Kate had once insisted on Alice's receiving all her parents' inheritance, but her attitude had changed, or soured. Kate's other legacies to Alice soon convulsed her with both amusement and indignation. Kate had bequeathed Alice some silver, but with only a "life-interest." If "theft, fire, or flood" should destroy this cutlery, Alice joked, she could never hope to repay the eventual heir. Likewise, Aunt Kate had left Alice a shawl with the same humiliating stipulation. "A life-interest in a shawl, with reversion to a male heir, is so extraordinary & ludicrous a bequest that I can hardly think it was seriously meant," Alice fumed.

Leonora Piper had correctly identified Aunt Kate as an "old crank." Her restricted gifts perfectly articulated the family's longtime practice of rating Alice last and subordinating her claims to those of the men in the family. Faced with such pettiness, Alice renounced all claim to these trinkets. Alice could laugh; but she also felt, as she told Harry, "publicly humiliated." With Harry, Alice could cry openly and bitterly. Kate had chosen to rob from her, in her "limited little helpless life, passed in one dreary room in a far-off country, the small luxury of devising *for herself* the disposal of the objects in question."

Alice had very little recourse besides Harry's ready sympathy. For he, too, had been cut out of Aunt Kate's last remembrance. Even in the midst of her own humiliation, Alice could regret, like the devoted sister that she was, that Aunt Kate hadn't left "some small personal possession to Harry who is always giving & never receiving."

HARRY HABITUALLY COMPLAINED to the more settled William, "[My own] wifeless, childless, houseless, classless, mother- and sister-in-lawless, horseless, cowless, and useless existence seems too spare indeed . . . in the lurid light of your fireside." But in January 1886, just before his spring cohabitation with Fenimore at the Villa Brichieri, Harry had moved from his cramped lodgings in Mayfair's Bolton Street to larger quarters in the still more "chaste and secluded" district of Kensington. Just how much more chaste could Harry get?

At 34 De Vere Gardens, just opposite the graceful green avenues of Kensington Gardens, Harry commanded rooms flooded with light "like a photographer's studio." He could "commune with unobstructed sky"—a luxury in the dark and built-over metropolis of London. He enjoyed an almost aerial view over the rooftops of South Kensington, similar to that which would be made famous a couple of decades later by a soaring and resolutely sexless Peter Pan, whose puckish statue would grace Harry's favorite walks in Kensington Gardens early in the next century.

At De Vere Gardens, Harry lived like a metropolitan nabob, in contrast to Alice's narrow boardinghouse life. He commanded a huge drawing room, which he hoped to convert into a princely, crimson library. He boasted a smaller sitting room, which he furnished in the rich yellows and blues made popular by the expatriate American painter James McNeill Whistler. In his new home, Harry also had the services of a pair of servants, the Smiths, a manservant married to a housekeeper. His "wooden-faced" cook presented herself to Harry heavily aproned for his "orders of the day."

Harry also symptomatically acquired a dachshund, which he named Tosca. The dog helped him get his exercise in Hyde Park and facilitated his encounters in the street with his neighbor, the aging Victorian poet Robert Browning. A generous brother, Harry invited Alice to take advantage of the "convenience" of his flat and partake of all this splendor during his long absences in Italy. When she arrived, what Alice chiefly noticed was the "furtive manners & scuttling motion" of Mrs. Smith, the housekeeper, whom she likened to one of her boardinghouse black beetles. "But never lisp a word to Harry," Alice urged Mrs. Alice, her confidante in the family; she didn't want to appear ungrateful for her brother's largesse. "Alice has kindly taken my rooms and servants off my hands," as Harry graciously put it.

❦

BACK IN THE United States, William and Mrs. Alice were also sinking roots in real estate and making once-improbable homes possible. In 1886, the year that Harry moved to Kensington, William bought a farm just south of the White Mountains in New Hampshire for $7,500. The property—on ninety acres of oaks and pines beside the tranquil Lake Chocorua—included a house, a brook, and a "splendid spring of water." A bristlingly wooded, rock-tipped 3,500-foot mountain (Mount Chocorua) reared up behind the property. The porous old homestead sported fourteen doors, William claimed, which swung open right into the fresh air. Such a big, airy spread—a family version, really, of Putnam Camp in the Adirondacks—appeared ideal for William and Alice. By 1887 they were expecting their fourth child.

In March 1887, William did Harry one better than his dachshund. "My live-stock is increased by a Töchterchen [little daughter]," William announced to a friend, with his usual paternal playfulness. He found her "modest, tactfull [sic], unselfish, quite different from a boy." (Now William's boys had started to talk back to him, as William had done to his own father before the Civil War. Little Harry memorably pronounced that *his* father was "more than a clown.") William and Alice named their baby girl Margaret Mary, the two ancestral Gibbens names also represented by her two maternal aunts. But afterward William and his wife, to keep clear of confusions, nicknamed their daughter "Peggy."

The arrival of a new niece thrilled Alice. A rustic property in the New Hampshire hills, on the other hand, left her cold. But Alice was moved that "he is a girl"—as the family joke went about the new baby. A girl, Alice declared, would "elevate the tone of the house and be some one for me to associate with in the future."

Knowing what it was like to be a James female, Alice longed to "protect the innocent darling before she is analyzed, labeled & pigeonholed out of existence." With such sentiments, Alice might have reestablished a household near her niece, in a manse like her erstwhile Manchester "cottage." She could have superintended her niece's upbringing as Aunt Kate had done with her—and do a better job of it than Aunt Kate had.

But Alice made no such move. Acutely, she felt herself only a haunter of the more luxurious homes of her brothers. She seems never to have seriously considered creating a more elaborate household for herself, and for a complicated set of reasons on which her remarkable diary, her one real home, would soon shed light.

ON JULY 18, 1889, Harry presented himself in Leamington, after what Alice thought was a longer-than-usual absence. He lunched with his sister at her lodging house, cheerfully enough. But Harry excelled at keeping secrets, and he didn't let slip what he was really thinking. At last, though, a "queer look," Alice noticed, stole across Harry's face. "I must tell you something," he said suddenly, as if to prepare her for a massive surprise.

"You're not going to be married!" Alice shrieked. The word Alice used in her diary was "shrieked."

"No," Harry said, "but William is here, he has been lunching upon Warwick Castle and is waiting now in the Holly Walk for the news to be broken to you and if you survive, I'm to tie my handerch[ief] to the balcony."

Harry's joke, like so much of the Jameses' signature wit, screened underlying worries on his part. He had dreaded this moment for two months and "looked white as a ghost," as Alice noticed. He was afraid the shock would trigger a breakdown—that the news of William's arrival would set off what Alice called her "large repertory" of hysterical symptoms.

William, who "somewhat dreaded" the encounter, hadn't seen Alice in five years. Harry had worried about Alice's lingering reaction to Aunt Kate's will, which he judged had "brought Alice pretty low." Aunt Kate's passing her over had seemed a "slap in the face"; William hoped Alice wouldn't blame it on him, since he'd received a large legacy himself. With everything else that his sister didn't have, did Alice need him, his pockets full of Aunt Kate's travel money, his head full of Aunt Kate's ghostly approval? Harry had protested that Alice *did* want to see her oldest brother; it would "distress her" if William didn't drop by. And yet William knew, as Alice did, how tangled his relation with his sister had become.

"Enter Wm. *not à la* Romeo via the balcony," Alice wrote in her diary. She alluded to the long painful joke of a family romance, or lack thereof, that she'd experienced with her brother—"the prose of our century to say nothing of that of our consanguinity making it super[er]rogatory." Alice had to swallow two hundred grains of bromides to remain calm. Yet she hardly blamed William; he was "simply himself," she concluded, "a creature who speaks in another language as H[arry] says from the rest of mankind and who would lend life and charm to a treadmill." Bringing into her dreary lodging rooms the heady James wit that Alice so appreciated, William also imported the "exquisite *family* perfume of days gone by." To preserve it—because William's visit was thorny and also brief—Alice memorialized it in her diary.

For Alice, William unconsciously flaunted his many advantages, and not only his sterling wife, his loving household, his charming little girl.

To top it all, he was soon to become a celebrated author. For many years, William had nurtured his own writerly ambitions—exhibited thus far in years of scholarly reviews and academic lectures. For eight or nine years, he had been working, in an obscurity reminiscent of Alice and her journal, on his "textbook." But in 1890, the year after this European jaunt when he shocked his sister—the same year, incidentally, that he and Mrs. Alice finished the renovations on their new townhouse at 95 Irving Street in Cambridge, which was to became their permanent residence; and the same year their fifth and last child, Alexander Robertson, was born—William finished and published this magnum opus. Titled *The Principles of Psychology*, this sprawling fourteen-hundred-page work was patently Jamesian, ambitious and intricate. Against the rules of textbook writing, William had inserted himself prominently into this "*biggest* book on Psychology in any language," as he called it. He had summoned and mediated the psychological authorities of his century with a Leonora Piper–like aplomb and marked the whole field with his strikingly individual voice.

When at long last his book came out, after its years of brooding gestation, William understandably gloried in its flattering academic and popular reception. At the age of forty-nine, he completely reversed his publishing catastrophe of 1882, when he'd edited his father's manuscripts and received an unflattering reception with his *Literary Remains of Henry James*. With his new authoritative monograph on psychology, William rose to prominence on both sides of the Atlantic.

Behind William's publishing success, incidentally—besides his own eclectic but dazzling grasp of world philosophy as it stood in the 1880s, besides Mrs. Alice's superhuman patience and support—lurked Sarah Wyman Whitman, a year younger than William, who ran her own salon in the 1880s, a philosophical and artistic club, in her studio and at her luxurious homes in Boston and in Beverly, Massachusetts. Mrs. Whitman, who had been trained in Paris, designed stained glass for Harvard's Memorial Hall and handsome flower-motif bindings for books by Celia Thaxter and Sarah Orne Jewett. But for William she did even more. Mrs. Whitman nurtured William through his hard times, propped up his ego, and fanned the flame of his genius—even helping out with the task of correcting his mammoth manuscript. With his now-perennial attraction to intelligent and sympathetic females, William found the enrapturing Mrs. Whitman "the best woman in Boston"—a piece of enthusiasm that may have rankled a little with both of the Alices in his life.

In many ways, Alice James shared in her brother William's triumph and even guarded it jealously; she deeply resented an "idiotic review" of the *Psychology* that appeared in the *Nation* in 1891, swelling with "disgust and indignation" on William's behalf. At the same time, it would have been easy for Alice to feel that everyone in the family had tasted success except for her.

Even Bob was getting into print. As far back as March 1885, he had published a poem in the prestigious *Atlantic Monthly*, the scene of Harry's early successes, titled "The Seraph Speech." His sporadic production of poetry since then hadn't exactly been distinguished; his work remained stodgily conventional and sentimental, as well as bogged down in his own version of his father's Swedenborgian mysticism. But in his paintings done in Concord, Massachusetts, Bob exhibited a talent competitive with William's in the early 1860s, and he even sampled some public success. Alice couldn't marshal anything of the kind.

Alice placed her one and only published work, a letter to the family's friend Edwin Lawrence Godkin, the editor of the *Nation*, in the summer of 1890. "For several years past I have lived in provincial England," Alice wrote. "Although so far from home, every now and then a transatlantic blast, pure and undefiled, fans to a white heat the fervor of my patriotism." In a few more lines, she described an incident at her boardinghouse, where a lady from the United States, on learning that an invalid was there, said it was just as well that the landlady couldn't offer her a room in the same establishment: "My little girl, who is thirteen, likes to have plenty of liberty and to scream through the house." Alice signed herself, anonymously, "Invalid," in wry appreciation of this anecdote and its illustration of the robust character of American females. But no doubt she craved "plenty of liberty"—if not to "scream through the house"—herself. After all, Alice hardly felt free to write whole lyrical articles, as her brother Harry had done, for the *Nation*.

In her diary, to be sure, Alice had found freedom and a voice. But if her private journal sometimes counted as her only home, her private world, her remuneration for a lifetime of neglect, it continued to appear

to her a modest and minimal one. As a diarist, as an exile, Alice reminded herself "of a coral insect building up [her] various reefs of theory by microscopic additions drawn from observation, or [her] inner
consciousness, mostly." Like her stifling room with its remnants of her
past scattered around, her old letters and her parents', her diary tended
to teem with "ghost microbes."

Like Emily Dickinson—another unappreciated nineteenth-century
American gentlewoman—Alice had chosen a private and secret form, a
"women's" form of literature. In future years, Alice would movingly
quote Dickinson's famous poem scorning publication—in the edited
and conventionalized version of this poem that was available in the
1890s.

> How dreary to be somebody
> How public, like a fog
> To tell your name the livelong day
> To an admiring bog!

The content of Alice James's unpublished diary, like the powerfully
iconoclastic work of Dickinson, stood out as strikingly "unwomanly" by
the standards of the time. Alice's writing showed the fascinating breadth
of her interests and often focused on politics, a realm the other Jameses
had hardly grazed. Surprisingly, Alice—though not a feminist—had
turned into an egalitarian and a radical, criticizing the English class system from a fiercely American point of view. In her contradictions of
iconoclasm and conservatism, she strongly resembled her father; she
carried a heterodox and sometimes conflicting burden of beliefs, which
her writing helped her flog out. In her diary, too, she reflected on her
own life as a James, and that allowed her to define her place in the family in a way she'd never done before.

Alice determined that her subject matter wasn't going to be "feeble
ejaculations over the scenery"—the sentimental stuff of many a Victorian woman's diary. Such was the tendency, if it came to that, of Harry's
early travel pieces to which Alice had willingly or unwillingly contributed on her tour of England with him in 1872. "The paralytic on his
couch," Alice wrote, "can have if he wants them wider experiences than

Stanley slaughtering savages." The well-informed Alice referred to Henry Morton Stanley, a British-born once-Confederate journalist who had wandered through Africa and ferreted out the source of the Nile. The explorer had greeted Dr. David Livingstone on the island of Ujiji with one of the most famous one-liners of the nineteenth century ("Dr. Livingstone, I presume!"). Stanley had kept his own diary, *How I Found Livingstone* (1872). And Alice's diary was as epic as Stanley's, if more secret and internal: "Let us not waste then the sacred fire," she wrote, "and wear away the tissues in the vulgar pursuit of what the others have and we have not." Alice maintained that "admitting defeat isn't the way to conquer" and asserted that "from every failure imperishable experience survives."

Alice must have sensed that if her diary could survive her, this "imperishable experience" might transgress the boundaries of death, much as Mrs. Piper's obstreperous spirits were supposed to do. ("I do pray to Heaven that the dreadful Mrs. Piper won't be let loose upon my defenseless soul," Alice wrote in her diary, acidly, late in her life.) At least Alice knew that in this private confessional she had seized the right to speak from the bedrock of her personal failure, from the acerbic wisdom that this very failure had given her.

But she couldn't know that soon, very soon, her diary would ramify into something even more impressive and hair-raising than that. As a colloquy with the spirits, it was about to offer her a stage for the most dramatic and spectral act of her life.

· 15 ·

CURTAIN CALLS

F rom the wings, in his meticulous and resplendent evening dress, Henry James watched with agitation as the drama of his youth unfolded before him on the stage. Handsome faces flushed with passion as well as rouge; gesticulating hands fluttered and momentarily touched. The painted backdrops and flaring gas jets conjured up a distorted, bigger-than-life Paris.

Harry had haunted this theater, the Winter Garden at Southport, since New Year's Day 1891. During the holidays, genteel winter visitors thronged the promenades of this would-be Riviera wrestling with the Irish Sea. The town lay only a brief railway journey north of Liverpool, with its warrenlike docks and unloading steamships. By contrast, Southport's wide sands spread vacant, bleak, and wind-beaten during this colorless, inhospitable season. Even its famous gardens lay frostbitten and bedraggled.

But Harry hadn't come to view exotic blooms in the Winter Garden greenhouses. On January 3, the day of his premiere, the well-known novelist had been unable to force even a mouthful of dinner at his stodgy hotel, the Prince of Wales. He'd hurried to the theater in order to hover about the waiting set. Once he was on stage, he'd dusted the mantelpiece, aligned the pasteboard vases, and turned down the corners of the carpets of this counterfeit French drawing room. It was the same fussy routine that Alice, far away in South Kensington with Katharine, had often observed during his visits. Yet at eight o'clock, when the curtain went up, Harry found himself as "calm as a clock."

Four decades had passed since, under the steaming footlights of Manhattan theaters in 1850s, the very young Harry had breathlessly watched the fleeing slave Eliza escape across a facsimile of the icebound Ohio. Back then, all the young Jameses, infant aficionados of the stage, had adored plays and jostled with one another to show their knowledge and enjoyment. But Harry—forty-seven now, bald, bearded, stout, and impeccably tailored—currently envisioned fresh triumph as a playwright. This ambition he felt with an urgency he hadn't recently experienced when writing fiction. Perhaps with an eye on William's recent success, he now awaited the verdict on his stage adaptation of his 1877 novel, *The American*.

William's two-volume magnum opus, his *Principles of Psychology*, had made a stir; Harry acknowledged the "mighty and magnificent book," but his own literary fortunes were swamped and sinking, in a reversal counting as another instance of the symbiotic ups and downs of the two brothers. Though in the past few years Harry had published *The Princess Casamassima* (1886), *The Aspern Papers* (1888), and *The Tragic Muse* (1890), his recent fiction, although critically acclaimed, had failed to reach a wide audience. Harry longed for more substantial notice, as well as to make more money from his inspirations. As he wrote to his friend the tubercular novelist Robert Louis Stevenson, "Don't be hard on me . . . I have had to try to make somehow or other the money I don't make by literature. My books don't sell, and it looks like my plays might."

Harry noted that even a frothy play at the Haymarket Theatre in London, *The Dancing Girl* (1891)—by the shameless Victorian melodramatist Henry Arthur Jones—might well rake in as much as ten thousand pounds during a yearlong run. (In the exchange rate of the day, that amounted to fifty thousand dollars, enough to buy two houses like the old family home in Cambridge, or six ramshackle farms like William's spread in New Hampshire.) But Harry hadn't fastened on the theater only for lucre. As long ago as 1882, when he had tried unsuccessfully to get his dramatization of *Daisy Miller* produced, he had longed to write for the stage; he thought he heard in drama the call of his literary destiny. His "pale little art of fiction," he told William, had only counted as a "limited and restricted substitute" for his one true vocation.

Harry had picked a heady time to try to write plays. Recently, theaters in England had posted new, foreign-looking names on playbills that advertised new and revolutionary productions. It was the age of Henrik Ibsen (1828–1906), the lion-whiskered Norwegian iconoclast, whose dark psychological dramas challenged prevailing bourgeois conventions about marriage, family, and material success. A belated English version of Ibsen's play *A Doll's House* (1879) had electrified London critics and audiences in 1889. A production of *Hedda Gabler* was slated for the spring of 1891, and this play would help revolutionize English theater even more. Harry, like many English speakers, had never seen an Ibsen play before this period; initially, he reacted negatively to what he saw as the "grey mediocrity" of these Scandinavian imports. But such grey mediocrity was just Ibsen's point, and plays like *Ghosts* (1881)— which left Harry shocked and disappointed—packed scathing moral critiques. Soon Ibsen would be joined by such playwrights as August Strindberg in Sweden and Anton Chekhov in Russia, whose inventive, starkly modern plays would break the mold of the popular Victorian farces and melodramas. By the 1890s in the English-speaking world, the young tigers of the theater were mostly Irish: William Butler Yeats, George Bernard Shaw, and Oscar Wilde, among others. Harry had an Irish background, too, but he hadn't tapped it to inspire his dramatic work.

Waiting for his premiere had agonized Harry. The suspense, he wrote his old theater partner William, threw him into a "state of abject, lonely fear." And Harry was genuinely "lonely." Alice hadn't joined him: with the worsening of her back and leg complaints, travel now taxed her too much, and she reclusively avoided crowds. As for Fenimore, her company at such a public event might well have fueled rumors or even sparked a scandal.

In Southport, Harry mainly had the company of his unofficial agent, the twenty-nine-year-old American expatriate Wolcott Balestier—a transatlantic personality whose sister would soon marry Rudyard Kipling. On the stage, the young English actor and director Edward Compton tackled the part of Christopher Newman, the California millionaire in Paris. An American actress named Virginia Bateman, who'd ominously been sick in bed for a week before this debut, played the role of the exquisite and charming Claire de Cintré. She would appear dressed in "all Liberty"—gowns from the famous Regent Street department store, which now furnished dresses as well as its signature fabrics. But it was "good Liberty," Harry hastened to add, in a moment of snobbery. In such contemporary costumes, these two enacted Harry's old romance between a rugged American and his aristocratic love—a clash between two cultures and two continents. Yet though the leads were actually married behind the scenes, the two doomed lovers in the play didn't resolve their differences now any more than they had in 1877. Claire de Cintré still retreated into a convent, and Christopher Newman walked away disappointed and empty-handed. The evening ended not with a wedding but a rupture.

Harry may have hoped that this less-than-happy finale might not bother audiences in this new age of Ibsen. *A Doll's House* had assailed the subjugation of Victorian wives. *Hedda Gabler* had again attacked bourgeois marriage. (Harry would call the play Ibsen's "queerest," although he would eventually appreciate its devastating ironies.) Thanks partly to Ibsen, broken relationships and fractured middle-class hopes no longer astounded even provincial audiences. In fact, under the auspices of the new realists, such outcomes were now enjoying a considerable vogue. Harry had reason to hope that the kind of modern dislocation that he had pioneered in the 1870s, with his intricate psychological work about the failure of romance, would make him a peer of Ibsen's in the 1890s, although it was equally possible that *The American* would simply be construed as bad melodrama. That's what had happened to Henry Arthur Jones, Harry's moneymaking model and the coauthor of the smash hit a few years before called *The Silver King* (1882). When Jones had tried to pen a heavier and more earnest work, *Saints and Sinners* (1884)—a play that confronted conventional religion in the English provinces—he'd been booed off the stage. Nineteenth-century audiences, low and high, judged their theater viscerally and took it very personally.

During Harry's premiere, the audience strained to catch all the lines in an irritatingly echo-prone house—and hence curbed their appreciation.

The silence ratcheted up the playwright's anxiety. As the Jameses had done all their lives, Harry was waiting nervously to be understood, accepted, approved, loved—as he had tried so hard to fit in, over the years, in English drawing rooms and clubs, obsessively adding famous names to his list of friends. Now, when Harry heard the roaring applause at the end of *The American*, he eased up. He "flushed with the triumph of his first ovation." The applause was deafening.

After a round of bows from the actors, the crowd clamored for the "author, *author*, AUTHOR!" The elated company, including Edward Compton and his wife, urged the playwright onto the stage. After the three bows in front of the thunderously clapping audience, Compton turned to Harry, seized both of his hands, and wrung them in a generous, theatrical gesture.

Harry more pompously remembered this moment.

> One (after a decent and discreet delay) simpered and gave one's self up to *courbettes* [bows] before the curtain, while the applausive house emitted agreeable sounds from a kind of gas-flaring indistinguishable dimness and the gratified Compton publicly pressed one's hand and one felt that, really, as far as Southport could testify to the circumstances, the stake was won.

Harry's demure yet convoluted language showcased both his high expectations and his ever-more encrusted "late style." This mode of expression was the sequel to the knotty language that William spent years trying to get his brother to give up. But Harry's prose was getting thicker (or richer) with age. And among many factors, Harry's involuted style would eventually thwart his hopes for large book or ticket sales.

In Harry's version of the curtain call, it was tellingly "one's" hand that was pressed, not Harry's own. Harry lived habitually in a protective shell of words, which, on occasions like this, projected an absurdity reminiscent of the humorist Max Beerbohm's later parodies of the "Master's" style as well as the otherwise admiring cartoonist's impish caricatures of Harry's increasingly ponderous profile. James Thurber, an American wag of the next century, had just Harry's brand of pretension in mind when he declared that the overuse of *one* made a speech sound like a trombone solo.

To Alice, who hung in suspense about the evening, Harry soon cabled: UNQUALIFIED TRIUMPHANT MAGNIFICENT SUCCESS UNIVERSAL CONGRATULATIONS GREAT OVATION FOR AUTHOR GREAT FUTURE FOR PLAY COMPTONS RADIANT AND HIS ACTING ADMIRABLE WRITING HENRY. The "late style," rife with ambiguities, now also apparently flourished in telegrams. Did the modest Harry mean that the "writing" of the author had rated as "admirable," too?

Between the third and fourth acts—when the relative quiet of the audience had upset Harry—the loyal and "wondrous" Wolcott Balestier, as Harry called him, had ducked out of the theater. He'd cabled "fifty vivid words" to the *New York Times* that would be "laid on every breakfast table" in Harry's ancestral city, or so Harry imagined. After the performance, Harry instructed Balestier to send William Archer, a famous dramatic critic, to his rooms at the Prince of Wales. When he arrived, Archer murmured some words of congratulation. But he added straightaway, "I think it's a play that would be much more likely to have success in the Provinces than in London." He then went on (as if on a "divine mission," according to Alice's account) to enumerate all the defects and flaws of the piece. In his celebratory dinner with the Comptons that followed this interview, a piqued Harry struck back. According to Alice, Harry served Archer up as "roast prig, done to a turn."

In spite of Harry's wit, though, the exasperating William Archer proved prophetic. Harry's play toured with some success in the provinces, Harry straining to sharpen it up during the many rehearsals. He made notes for Compton on how to speak with an American accent: *off* should be pronounced "awf." He witnessed a gratifying small triumph of his play at Cheltenham with Fenimore. But pieces of the production kept giving way like rotten planks. Before the play opened in London, Mrs. Compton, now pregnant, quit the cast, her illness in Southport no longer a mystery. Harry insisted that a young Kentucky actress he'd admired in *Hedda Gabler*, Elizabeth Robins, should play the all-important part of Claire de Cintré.

Harry's London premiere was at the Opera Comique on the Strand. This opera house was tall, narrow, and badly built; it and the adjacent Globe Theatre (nothing to do with Shakespeare's Globe) were known as the "rickety twins." The Opera Comique was so drafty that members of the audience frequently caught cold; but the American ambassador was in attendance, and other society grandees filled the steep seats. William was also present along with Constance Fenimore Woolson. (On such a gala evening, William got a mistaken impression of Miss Woolson's "gaiety.") The house, packed with Harry's friends and well-wishers, appeared to reconfirm the early approbation of Southport. Again the audience maniacally clapped; again the audience demanded the author. In response, Harry shuttled out and demurely bowed to the warm applause.

But the critics took away a more divided reaction. To some, Harry's play came off as curiously flat yet still melodramatic. Harry, adept at psychological intricacy, had perhaps broadened and amplified his light, ironic characters too much. Harry's forte was arguably neither passion nor action, those staples of fin-de-siècle drama—as his so-called late style broodingly illustrated. Deeper psychological drama was possible, but Harry had not, in fact, learned the lessons of Ibsen, such as they were. After its seventy-sixth performance, *The American* died, as the loyal Alice noted, an "honourable death."

Harry had hardly given up, though, on the theater. He had two more plays up his sleeve. Alice secretly suspected that Harry's *Mrs. Vibert (The Tenants)* would "only appeal to that limited public that suspects that art and subtlety exist." But in the meantime a more immediate drama was unfolding in Harry's and Alice's lives.

⁂

ALICE, PERHAPS HARRY'S most enthusiastic supporter, hadn't graced any of the performances of *The American*.

She'd kept as faithful to her own careers—her illness and her diary—as Harry had to his. In May 1891, during Harry's marathon rehearsals, Alice braced herself for the latest in a long line of doctors: Sir Andrew Clark—a well-connected Victorian physician who would later attend King Edward VII—alighted from his vehicle at 41 Argyle Road, just north of the fashionable height-of-the-season carriage jam on Kensington High Street.

When Alice had moved back to London that March, Katharine had braved "3000 miles of sea-sickness" to rejoin her. Relieved, her indignation at Katharine's long absence dissipating, Alice abandoned herself into what she called a "tangle of shawls." In London, in a gracious, quiet enclave of Kensington called Campden Hill, Alice's worsening illness had at last earned her something like the bay-windowed house she'd longed for—"a decidedly silly little house," as she put it. The house had a pillared portico and a bay window, and it glowed with whitewashed plaster. Katharine "had only to wave her magic wand," Alice wrote in her diary, in order to conjure up a substantial if extemporary late-Victorian establishment.

Their new rented townhouse included two servants. Mrs. Thompson, a cook, came as part of a package deal, presumably because nobody else wanted her bland sauces. And the "excellent Louisa," a bumpkinish Leamington import, provided Alice with an entertaining wide-eyed credulity. Was Kensington, Louisa wanted to know, the "Jack the Ripper part" of town? She hated to venture out into a neighborhood that she wrongheadedly equated with gristly fogged-over murder scenes from the illustrated newspapers. But Alice held high hopes of transforming Louisa from a cloddish "Slavey" into a nimble metropolitan "House-and-parlour-maid."

The loyal and tireless "Nurse," Emily Ann Bradfield, also clung to her position in Alice's retinue. But Kensington proved difficult for Bradfield, mostly because of the new cook. Mrs. Thompson, a low-church evangelical, frequently recounted a "beautiful dream" to Nurse, in which she was plied with questions. She answered them only by pointing heavenward, toward the Savior. Not surprisingly, Thompson was also a "strenuous" teetotaler who refused to pour wine into any of her sauces; how could she sample them, then, without sin? Alice and Katharine's table, therefore, hardly offered the gustatory temptations of Harry's London clubs, let alone the splendors of quail or trout dinners at Claridge's or the Savoy.

Even without such luxuries, Alice felt that Katharine and Harry had made her life "rich beyond compare." She judged that over the last winter she'd been "broadened and strengthened." The change had come partly via the "human comedy"—the phrase reminiscent of Balzac—that Alice had wittily observed and recorded in her diary. For years she had tartly construed her doctors as part of this human comedy. Sir Andrew, however, wore a serious face. Summoned by Katharine because she felt Alice was "going downhill at a steady trot," he imparted a sobering diagnosis. Alice had "cardiac complications," and the painful lump she'd had in one of her breasts for three months was a tumor. Even in 1891, that word sounded a knell. Alice caught her breath. It was more than even she had expected, and she turned to her diary to pour out her feelings.

"To him who waits, all things come!" Alice wrote, with surprising and seemingly perverse euphoria. "Ever since I have been ill, I have longed and longed for some palpable disease." Alice was partly ironic, of course, and that helped her cope with a staggering blow. At the same time, she felt genuine vindication as a career invalid who previously had little enough to show for herself beyond a "monstrous mass of subjective sensations" at which medical men had often scoffed. All in all, Alice took her death sentence with a detached scientific interest reminiscent of her brother William's attitude toward his explorations of the mind as well as with "pathological vanity," as she called it—her pride in her own invalidism.

Alice's grim diagnosis, incidentally, coincided with some of the earliest advances in the treatment of breast cancer, but these were probably largely unknown to genteel Harley Street doctors like Sir Andrew, whose credentials more often included testimonials from prominent patients than authentic medical skills. The Dutch surgeon Adrian Helvetius had performed the first lumpectomy and mastectomy in the seventeenth century, but more successful procedures for such surgery were being pioneered by the New York surgeon William Stewart Halsted in the 1880s and the 1890s. (Among other advances, Halsted introduced thin rubber gloves to surgeons who'd previously gone in bare-handed.) Also, Wilhelm Conrad Roentgen's discovery of X-rays in 1896 would lead to radiation treatment of cancer by 1899.

The Jameses had been exposed to cutting-edge nineteenth-century medicine (William's studies with Jean-Martin Charcot, for example), but they could as often wrap themselves in genteel obscurantism. Alice probably didn't believe the old chestnut that breast cancer emanated from melancholia—a time-honored classical notion. But in reacting to her diagnosis, significantly, she didn't order up a copy of the *New England Journal of Medicine*, which by 1891 was in its distinguished seventy-ninth year. Instead she resigned herself stoically to what she regarded as her fate.

As Sir Andrew's "uncompromising verdict" sank in, Alice faced even starker emotions. She might appear "picturesque" to herself, a "cameo" of terminal illness, but she genuinely worried about Katharine and Harry. They would "*see* it all, whilst I shall only *feel* it." The two most important people in her life would have to struggle with their grief. Harry, who poured out his feelings to William, chiefly noticed his sister's remarkable "*force d'âme*" (strength of spirit). She had risen to the occasion, gradually acquiring a serenity, he thought, that gave her comfort and stripped her of her nervousness and abiding horror of life. Katharine tirelessly cared for her and kept her house. Harry visited often, bringing his natural tenderness, now especially valued. Alice, citing the old James-family reference to Harry as the "angel," described both of her caregivers as "archangels" who looked after her with "infinite tenderness and patience."

As for William, Alice feared that his nervous sympathy would make him suffer too much; she vowed to keep her condition a secret from him until it was all over. But soon enough she changed her mind, regarding him as espousing a sober, stoical "philosophy of transition" similar to her own. So that autumn William boarded a steamer in order to take in Harry's London premiere and see his sister, Alice, for the last time. He found her face the same as he remembered. As he sat with her at Argyll Road, he thought her voice was weaker, even though she managed to show visible excitement about Harry's plays. William also found her fascinated with her own demise, her "mortuary attractions," as she put it. She could lie in only one position in her bed and seemed to "feed almost exclusively on poisons," he noticed. "Poor strange and wonderful little being that she is," William wrote to Mrs. Alice. His touching diminutive hinted at his deep compassion for his little sister as well as his utter incomprehension of her.

That September, Katharine talked Alice into being photographed. True to form, Alice resisted at first; she didn't like the "one-eyed monster" of the massive boxy camera of the 1890s. Such an ordeal would prove "woman's inhumanity to woman," as Alice teased Katharine. But the photographer came and went. When the photograph came back,

Alice joked, with her usual self-denigration, about its "refulgent beauty."

The photograph, though, is one of the most evocative taken of Alice in her life—along with her elfin childhood photograph from Paris in the 1850s. A month past her forty-third birthday, Alice reclines against a pillow patterned with arabesques, wearing a high-necked silk bed-jacket, as if the mysterious richness of her inner life had materialized at long last in the external world. With her hair brushed back and bound, Alice's is a recognizable James face, akin to her mother's, her father's, and her brothers'. But her slightly turned, abstracted eyes—in the clear James blue that comes out gray in the photographs—even more profoundly connect her to her quick-minded, brooding family. A philosopher of the sofa, of the sickbed, she'd at last transformed into a sibylline philosopher of the "human comedy" she'd so relentlessly observed and so tartly enjoyed. The photograph, like the diary, embodied Alice's mature self-expression—before the gauntness and the morphine-induced dreaminess of the next few months eroded it.

That winter, in the dusk of Alice's life, Katharine stood ready to administer a lethal dose of morphine if Alice needed it. Her loyal friend stuck to Alice's side, sometimes helping Alice with her diary by serving as her amanuensis. As usual, Katharine helped in any way she could, and Alice now accepted that assistance more readily. Previously, Alice had been known to roll her eyes about Katharine's sometimes obtuse practicality; she'd found Katharine "so excessive in the normal that she seems to me at moments to be barely a rudiment." Yet now, Katharine had become almost everything she needed. For Alice, that meant someone who could bring both of her parents back to her—who could embody the best features of both men and women. Though Katharine was attired in ample New England petticoats, she abounded in "certain male virtues": she didn't go into hysterics about mice or drunken men, as Alice's other nurses had done. Yet, as a tenderhearted woman, Katharine knew her way around a sickbed. Alice continued to laud her friend's "unexampled genius for friendship and devotion." Her crisis, in fact, only magnified Katharine's all-purpose virtues. Right down to her last diary entry, Alice mustered wry praise for her companion of almost two decades—quoting a visitor who'd called the gaunt, hardworking Katherine "the New England Professor of doing things."

Katharine would take care of many things, and after Alice's death she would take her friend's ashes back to the United States, to be buried next to her parents in the Cambridge Cemetery. (Harry, visiting Alice's grave years later, would be moved to tears when he saw the commemorative urn from Florence William had inscribed with lines from Dante's *Paradiso*: "One sank down on one's knees," he wrote, "in a kind of anguish of gratitude for something for which one had waited with a long, deep *ache*.")

Movingly, it was also Katharine who finished Alice's diary, describing her last conscious hours on the night of Saturday, March 5, 1892. Late into the night, Alice was still "making sentences." For the previous day, though she'd grown ominously weak, she couldn't "get her head quiet" until she'd dictated another phrase for her diary: "Physical pain however great ends in itself and falls away like dry husks from the mind." As she faced the "footlights of [her] last obscure little scene," Alice made sure Katharine wrote down precisely what was forming in her mind. A true James, Alice couldn't rest until she'd got the wording right.

❦

ON THAT COLD, bright Sunday afternoon in early March, Harry moved in and out of the room where Alice was dying. Having often been at her side over the past few days, he'd seen her sinking away, mouthing barely audible things. He'd watched her falling into a "perfectly gentle sleep." Toward the end—near the hour in the afternoon when her own mother had died—her breathing became a "constant sort of whistle in the lung." Her pulse flickered. "Her face then seemed in a strange, dim, touching way," Harry wrote William, "to become clearer. I went to the window to let in a little more of the afternoon light . . . and when I came back to the bed she had drawn the breath that was not succeeded by another."

In the final hours of Alice's life, to comfort her, Katharine read to her an Italian story by Constance Fenimore Woolson called "Dorothy." Perhaps Harry had brought it; perhaps Constance had sent it to

Katharine directly. The story chose for its setting the rich and castellated hills near Florence, a long way from the chill London room where
Alice was to die. But in this story, in a striking coincidence, the title character perishes from grief. Wanting to die, she pitches off the parapet of
a hilltop villa based on the Bootts' Villa Castellani. As a bright, nimble-
minded American woman, the story fancifully suggests, Dorothy might
almost have soared instead of fallen. This touchingly airborne character
betrays another bond between Constance and Alice. Both suffered from
deep depressions and suicidal impulses. Both women yearned, at times,
to die—though, in their writings, they longed for something more like
flight.

To staunch his grief, Harry ventured out to visit Fenimore in Oxford, in her sun-flooded eighteenth-century rooms, in the embrace of
her intelligent sympathy, a week after his sister's death. The day Harry
spent with his gentle, commiserating friend no doubt recalled the comforting intimacies, bourgeois or bohemian, of the Villa Brichieri and its
sunstruck terrace overlooking the red roofs of Florence. Yet in five years
the two friends hadn't revisited this cohabitation.

Did Constance expect, now that Alice was gone, for Harry to wax
"more attentive," as Harry's biographer Leon Edel put it? Edel's theory
about Constance's unrequited passion seems plausible enough in a
Harry-centered universe. As long as actual matrimony didn't threaten,
even Harry himself sometimes favored this flattering view of Fenimore's expectations, and his biographers have followed suit. Harry liked
to see himself as a charming, well-tailored, successful bachelor, who
might attract women; but such a self-image was only possible during an
era when these very qualities didn't as obviously shout "gay" as in later
times. As it was, Harry's front of bachelorhood was so successful that he
sometimes fooled even himself. But it's less certain that he fooled or en-
snared his old friend.

In July 1893, after two years in England, Fenimore moved her itinerant household back to Italy. She knew that Harry's charms weren't reliable. But those of Venice, the Serene Republic, boded well. Constance
took rooms in the Palazzo Orio Semitecolo, also known as the Ca'
Semitecolo, a fourteenth-century Venetian palace fronting the water.
Her new home warmed her with its pink brick, delicate balconies, and

galleries of windows that admitted light and air, each of them forming a distinctive Venetian peaked arch. Gondoliers moored their boats at posts sunk in front of the palazzo. She commandeered gondolas often—to pursue the slices of summer sun over the water, to scribble notes about the pink and golden palaces of Venice or on its sharp-smelling lagoon, as if for a future novel. In Venice, Constance was beautiful when she went out. A photograph of her from 1893 shows the novelist much as she must have looked pausing on the Rialto Bridge, or tugging at the doorbells of her American acquaintances. The portrait shows a serious-looking woman with a broad collar, a choker, and a chignon of wound-up braids—pale, slightly plump, with small, sad, serious eyes. The lady in the photograph almost resembles Harry's brisk and self-sufficient Fenimore: "free, independent, and successful—very successful indeed as a writer—and *liked*, peculiarly, by people who knew her."

But Constance, at the age of fifty-three, also quietly struggled with a sense of horror not unlike Alice James's. In her strong woman's solitude, she suffered increasingly from her deafness, her expatriate loneliness, and her deep-dyed inherited depression. Touchingly, Harry knew his friend well enough to understand that she counted as "exquisitely morbid and tragically sensitive." He was aware that she lived with "chronic melancholia and of the tendency to suffer and to insist on suffering, more than [any] being" he had met. And yet Harry didn't always thoroughly understand the causes for Fenimore's unhappiness, her discontentment as a neglected woman writer, her dread of darkness, as the meager light glimmered over the lagoon of Venice during the winter of 1894.

Early in the morning of January 24, 1894, Fenimore, lying ill with a bout of influenza, rang for some milk. A nun who was nursing her brought some, but Constance rejected it. She wanted milk from the *pink* cup, she insisted strangely, the pink cup in the dining room. The nun obliged, but when the woman came back into the room a few seconds later, she found the bed empty and the curtains raked open. Hurrying to the window, she spotted a white heap on the pavement below. Constance had—as newspapers in Venice, London, and New York were soon to report—jumped from the second-story window. The nun shouted for Constance's favorite gondolier, Angelo, who was asleep lower in the house. The doorbell rang; people bustled in the street. Somebody called a doctor. Soon enough, Constance was carried back up to her bedroom. One of the men at the scene thought he heard her murmur "some word which they thought was an Italian one for cold." Then Constance Fenimore Woolson died of her injuries from the fall.

Back in Kensington, Harry didn't hear the news all at once. The first word came in a cryptic Atlantic cable from Constance's married sister, Mrs. Clara Benedict, in New York. Fenimore, dead? At first, Harry evidently mistook the case and imagined that Constance had contracted some "fatal form" of influenza. He flooded with "ghastly amazement and distress," having not even heard that his friend was ill. But once he returned home from the offices of Cook's with railway reservations to Rome for Constance's funeral, darker rumors reached him. More agonized telegrams arrived, and lurid accounts cropped up in the evening newspapers.

"Constance Fenimore Woolson committed suicide," one of the stories read. She'd "jump[ed] from a window of a house in Venice where she had lived seven months. Death was almost immediate. Miss Woolson had suffered from influenza for four days, but she had been eccentric for a longer period."

"Eccentric for a longer period"! What kind of explanation was that for a cause of death? But the allegation of suicide cut Harry to the quick. Especially in 1894, especially to him, the notion of suicide was appalling. At first, Harry instinctively defended his friend's honor, though rather flailingly. He insisted Fenimore's fall must have sprung from "some misery of insomnia pushed to nervous momentary frenzy," "some sudden explosion of latent brain-disease," some "sudden *dementia*." But if such a feverish lapse supplied the only possible "hypothesis," why did Harry soon cancel his travel plans, as though he were suddenly worried about the stigma of suicide? Leon Edel suggests as much. But did Harry dodge Constance's burial at the Protestant Cemetery in Rome because he felt conventional scruples about suicide, or because he felt responsible for Constance's killing herself? In any case, he was simply, as he confided to Francis Boott, "too sickened with the news."

Fenimore herself had felt such restraints less. Though the mystery of her death has never been fully resolved—Harry's far-fetched and decoy hypotheses of Fenimore's unpremeditated madness have enjoyed an extraordinary longevity—one of Woolson's biographers uncovered documents, including markings in a volume of Stoic philosophy she was reading in Venice, that "suggest why she may well have committed suicide." After all, even before he suspected the worst, Harry declared that Constance "had no dread of death and no aversion to it—rather a desire and even a passion for it; and infinite courage and a certain kind of fortitude." As another Woolson biographer has noted, the windows of Constance's bedchamber had sills that it was difficult to "topple out of with ease in a dizzy spell. It could only have been a deliberate act."

Fenimore didn't leave a note. Whatever her motivations for hurling herself out the window, she didn't provide any explanation for Harry or for anyone else. Writer though she was—and in a poignant contrast to Alice James—she sealed her final hours in a sepulchral silence.

In April 1894, Harry had to face that silence in person. He conducted Fenimore's sister and her niece, the "poor helpless clinging" Clara Benedict and her similarly named daughter, Clare, to Venice. These overwhelmed New Yorkers needed all Harry's support in a country where they didn't speak the language. And as their strange mutual ordeal began, Harry had to buttress the "dolorous" relatives when the seals on Fenimore's apartment in the "sad death-house" were broken. Even self-possessed Harry was shaken to witness the scene of his friend's fall. He found that the house—in the style of his later gothic tales like "The Altar of the Dead" (1895) and *The Turn of the Screw* (1898)—"stare[d] down at one with unspeakably mournful eyes of windows."

Harry would board for five weeks in Venice, in Constance's former rooms at the Casa Biondetti. He didn't stay at the Palazzo Barbaro, home of his friends the Curtises—an exquisitely haunted treasure-house that he later would later re-create in his magnificent novel, so flavored by the deaths of both Constance and his cousin Minny, *The Wings of the Dove* (1902). On this stay, Harry's own hauntedness was quite concrete and immediate: he plunged into the "horrid predicament" of sorting through Constance's belongings.

His time in the palazzo has in fact spawned as much mystery and conjecture as Fenimore's death itself. Many writers have suggested that

Harry took part in this ritual in order to check up on his friend's vow to burn all his letters. Some have believed he dogged Constance's relatives to the Palazzo Semitecolo in order to destroy any papers "that might have been interpreted as incriminating"—that might have been too revealing about Harry's erotic identity, about his romance or nonromance with Fenimore. But it would have been ticklish for Harry to burn letters with Clara and Clare Benedict underfoot at the Ca' Semitecolo. They were as bent on preserving Constance's things as Harry may have been on destroying them. Still, during those cold days of an Adriatic spring, a "convenient" crackling fire was always burning. It was an antidote for the fear and moodiness that Harry described in his notebook as "one's eternal exposures, accidents, disasters." Harry was terribly private, very vulnerable, and he resembled his very Victorian aunt Kate in his passion to preserve his respectability—and to do so by eliminating letters. Before the end, he would destroy many of his own amassed papers.

To be sure, Harry had his prudish side, his starchy Victorian respectability. But more understandably, he rightly dreaded the lurid publicity of yellow journalism. One cautionary example sprouted up like a poisonous toadstool in the *New York Herald* a few years later. "The truth about Mr. James' bachelorhood is known to very few people," the newspaper gossiped; "the truth is his heart was buried nearly three years ago in the grave that covered all that was mortal of Constance Fenimore Woolson. For a long time he had been this author's devoted slave . . . And so long as Miss Woolson's memory remains green in his heart it may well be said that he is too thoroughly celibate to ever think of wedlock."

But even odder rumors would eventually surface about Harry's attachment to Constance and his activities shortly after her death. In a BBC broadcast in 1956, an ancient American lady named Mercede Huntington, who had known Henry James in her youth and his old age, reported a "strange story" the novelist had supposedly disclosed to her. According to this account, Henry James had gone out onto the lagoon of Venice at night in order to dispose of Constance's gowns—her signature black rusty gowns like those worn by "Miss Grief" in her 1880 story. The gowns refused to sink, their full sleeves and skirts ballooning up on the face of the water. He tried to beat them down, but they kept breasting the waters of the lagoon. The gowns wouldn't let him forget, wouldn't let him drown Constance's memory.

This ghostly curtain call has featured prominently in many accounts of Harry's relation with Constance Fenimore Woolson. It is unclear, though, how much of this nocturnal errand was fantasy—either Mrs. Huntington's, or Harry's late in life. Harry no doubt wanted to rid himself of Fenimore's gowns—those reminders of her body, her person. But presumably he could have found many easier methods, especially because the gowns might well have been exactly what Constance's sister and niece packed up in the trunks. As Clara Benedict reported, the loyal and decorous Harry "never left us until all her precious things were packed and boxed and sent to America."

Whatever really happened in Venice, it remains clear that Harry wanted acutely to forget about it. To banish his entanglement with the Benedicts, Harry wrote to Francis Boott, *"Non ragionam di lor!"* (Let's not discuss them—that is, the Benedicts). This phrase, oddly enough, almost exactly duplicated the words Harry had scribbled in his notebook more than a decade before about Paul Zhukovsky: *"Non ragionam de lui—ma guarda e passa"* (Let's not discuss him—but look and move on).

So easy and common an Italian phrase might have occurred coincidentally on both occasions, with no subconscious connection. But in 1894, significantly, Harry had again used these words to impose a seal of silence on emotions too conflicted for him to countenance. Were both injunctions to silence actually instances of what Oscar Wilde was to call, in the same decade of the 1890s, the "love that dare not speak its name"? Harry's love for Constance Fenimore Woolson, in the end, may well have been as "queer," as resistant to conventional nomenclature, and as stifled by silence as his infatuation for Paul Zhukovsky. Such phrases had ended both of these relations—and they had strangely bookended Harry's expunged love for Fenimore.

❧

WHILE ENJOYING THE pinks and golds of Venice in the spring, with darker shadows on the lagoon, Harry received a copy of his sister Alice's diary. Did he open this package in the Ca' Biondetti, in Constance's old rooms? Did he read it in the light of a gas lamp Constance herself had once trimmed and lit? Katharine Loring had arranged for four copies to be privately printed in Cambridge, Massachusetts, according to Alice's last wishes. Reserving one for herself, Katharine distributed the other three copies to Alice's three living brothers: Bob, William, and of course Harry. Harry unwrapped his own copy sometime during the weeks when he was wrestling with Fenimore's legacy.

This was probably the first Harry had heard that Alice had even kept a diary. Absorbing this new vision of his sister, Harry kept a long silence and only broke it to William in late May, once he'd escaped from Venice. By then Harry had alighted in nearby Ravenna—a city whose ancient, plain, sand-colored churches hid sumptuous azure and gold mosaics in their interiors. Alice's dim lodging-house life, Harry had discovered, had also concealed something fully as beautiful and surprising: her fiery internal life.

Writing to William, Harry acknowledged his receipt of "Alice's magnificent diary." He found it "rare—wondrous," he said. He strained to convey his "immense impressedness." But, he confessed, "[I have been] terribly scared and disconcerted—I mean alarmed—by the sight of so many private names and allusions in print." Harry went on to confess that he'd gossiped quite a bit to Alice, for her entertainment. He'd even embellished quite a few stories. He couldn't imagine why Katharine hadn't "sunk a few names, put initials . . . in view of the danger of accidents, some catastrophe of publicity."

Harry's anxiety about publicity makes some sense: he was famous enough to be targeted by the newspapers. He also felt some bona fide concerns about his touchy web of acquaintances in England; his noble or artistic friends might easily take offense. Yet Harry's morbid fears appear distorted in view of the mildness of Alice's admiring portrait of him in the diary. His sister had hardly written a scandal sheet, and it is hard to know what "danger of accidents" Henry might have been afraid of.

Surprisingly, in a bizarre reversal of the brothers' roles, Harry's horror stood in stark contrast to William's approval. William had read Alice's diary in March 1894 with a keen appreciation of its "unique and tragic impression of personal power venting itself on no opportunity"—an apt summary of the diary's cri de coeur. William relished his sister's "*deep* humor." Also, because of his complex history with the writer, he was filled with "strange compunctions and solemnity." William admitted that Harry must feel more familiar with its subject matter than he, who had remained in the United States, could ever be. But he was deeply enough impressed to feel that the diary "ought to be published." "I am proud of it," he wrote Harry, "as a leaf in the family laurel crown, and your memory will be embalmed in a new way by her references to your person."

But Harry didn't want his "person" embalmed or exposed. Evidently he destroyed his own copy of Alice's diary. It might have happened in an Italian fireplace, out of force of recent habit. Or perhaps Harry burned the book years later, just before his death. The copy that survived in the James papers was William's. And Harry's fears cast such a chill over the diary that, unlike the *Literary Remains* of Henry Senior, it remained in an archival deep freeze for decades. Already, Harry had elected himself the guardian of the James family reputation. As a writer, as the most famous James, he was in a position to manipulate the family image. Long after Harry's death, the diary appeared partially and with heavy edits in 1934, in Anna Robeson Burr's *Alice James: Her Brothers—Her Journal*. But a complete edition of Alice's one book didn't appear until 1964, more than seventy years after her death. Feminist critics would welcome Alice's diary as a moving, articulate account of a woman's suppressed life, but the diary would appeal to many audiences, with one critic declaring it "one of the neglected masterpieces of American literature."

Harry's draconian repression of Alice's diary hints not just at the light indiscretions of overcolored anecdotes but also at deeper and darker fears. One gigantic, glaring fact of Alice's journal stood out: her friendship with Katharine. True, most of the Jameses' contemporaries didn't much question this relation. The intense women's partnerships and cohabitations of the Victorian era were blithely construed as both natural and chaste. Ironically, Harry's very public *Bostonians* had cast such relations in a more lurid light than Alice's matter-of-fact, philosophical diary entries. But *The Bostonians* had been fiction, under Harry's authorial control. This new, less pretentious memoir by Harry's sister was actually more powerful, as a firsthand account, and it was more of a threat to Harry. For one thing, Alice clearly indicated how thoroughly Harry accepted her intimate life with Katharine.

What's more, Alice knew Harry as well as anyone; along with Feni-more, she had the potential to describe his private life. And just as Harry had been more sympathetic to his sister during her lifetime, closer to her than to other members of his family, he now feared the "publicity" of disclosures Alice's diary might make—about himself quite as much as about her. Harry's destruction of Alice's journal, though it appears cal-lous, amounted to just one of his many terrified efforts to keep his own unconventional interior life, as well as Alice's, private. It pointed to the magnitude of his insecurities. To the extent that Harry and Alice shared parallel covert desires, Harry must have worried that their tendencies would show—especially as, in the coming decades, his own same-sex fascinations became harder for him to keep secret.

Now fifty-one years old, Harry was increasingly susceptible to lone-liness; though beloved by many for his gentleness and kindness, he would soon crave more consequential companionship. Besides Alice and Fenimore, he had recently lost other comrades. His old friend Lizzie Boott had died from pneumonia in 1888, tragically leaving an infant son behind in her solemn old father's care. Harry's energetic young agent Wolcott Balestier had been "swept away like a cobweb," as Alice had noted, by a sudden illness in 1891. What's more, Harry's fellow writer Robert Louis Stevenson, who'd been warming himself in the South Pa-cific in an attempt to cure his tuberculosis, would succumb to that dis-ease in Samoa by December 1895. With such friends stripped away, Harry would sink into a deep depression. He had lost some of his most important intimacies, and they would be hard to replace.

WITHOUT ALICE TO encourage him and comfort him—without Al-ice fretting for a telegram from him, even—Harry premiered his second play. With much fanfare, *Guy Domville* opened at the St. James Theatre in London on January 5, 1895. Six months had now lapsed since Harry's punishing ordeal in Venice. But the feverish rehearsals for his play had rendered him, Harry told one London hostess, "too preoccupied, too terrified, too fundamentally distracted, to be fit for human intercourse." At the scintillating tables where he'd so often charmed, Harry now feared becoming "a death's head at the feast." Writing to William the day before this first performance, Harry enclosed a "florid 'poster'" of advertisement. He begged for some "Psychical intervention" from his brother's spiritualist friends like Leonora Piper. The advance tickets had sold briskly—not least to Harry's noble and artistic friends. The outcome of Harry's whole theatrical gamble hung in the balance.

Having distracted himself with another play, at the Haymarket Theatre down the street, Harry arrived at his own premiere late. By the time he arrived, a number of mishaps had already marred the performance. But as the curtain went down, applause went up—as it had at Southport four years before. Harry's many friends (or plants) in the audience then began shouting, as they had before, for the playwright. Harry ventured out on the stage, towed by his manager, the good-looking, wavy-haired late-Victorian director and producer George Alexander. His "extremely human and extremely artistic little play," as Harry saw it, had struck the gallery—the ordinary London theatergoers—quite differently than it had the swells. Against the "gallant, prolonged and sustained applause" of Harry's fans, "hoots and jeers and catcalls" went up. In disbelief and shock, Harry found himself booed off the stage.

How had such an outrage happened?

In the "weary, bruised, sickened, disgusted" days that followed, Harry fumed over his embarrassment and then, increasingly, agonized over his failure. Writing to William, Harry first interpreted the debacle as a confrontation of high and low culture, the "forces of civilization" facing off against the "roughs" who roared like the caged animals at the Regent's Park Zoo. Harry's subject, true, appealed to a lettered audience. A stylized historical piece, an "episode in the history of an old English Catholic family of the last century," didn't grip everybody. The play teemed with wigs, verbal intricacies, and moral convolutions. But the problem went deeper than the hardening high culture versus mass culture split of the late nineteenth century—as important as the new high culture fostered in universities and museums would prove for Henry James and his reputation.

Guy Domville simply hemorrhaged disaster. As a production, it was riddled with unfortunate mistakes, but even as a conception, the play was splintered by fatal flaws. To begin with, it was an artificial and old-fashioned melodrama, and that much soured a crowd of younger critics—George Bernard Shaw and H. G. Wells among them—who otherwise had sympathy for Henry James. Their objections were mild in contrast to the audience's. When Guy histrionically declared, "I'm the last, my lord, of the Domvilles!"—a Cockney wit in the audience shouted out, "It's a bloody good thing y'are." This heckle embodied the tensions of social class in Britain. Clearly, Guy Domville qualified as an upper-class fop. The play mystified and irritated the outraged gallery, who had paid good money for romance. Something was rotten in the state of Denmark, only it didn't play well on the stage.

Fatefully, *Guy Domville* featured an eponymous protagonist whose convoluted love problems defied belief. Guy Domville aspired to take orders as a Catholic priest. As a paid private tutor, he concealed a bizarre passion for his young student's mother. After an added fit of un-convincing carousing, after a self-sacrificing renunciation of his love on behalf of a buddy, Guy lost the audience's sympathy entirely. The char-acter, like the play, went nowhere, didn't resolve, and made no sense. Profoundly unsatisfying, *Guy Domville* not only died on the London stage but would prove completely unrevivable, even in high-art theaters of the coming decades that made it their mission to resuscitate almost any play.

Harry hadn't crafted good drama. But he was famous enough that he'd made *himself* into good drama. In the coming years, Harry's spec-tacular failure would inspire more than one writer with material for fic-tion and nonfiction. Guy Domville's trumped-up sufferings invited scorn. But Harry's own lacerations proved all too genuine.

The play Harry had seen at the Haymarket before his own premiere—Oscar Wilde's *An Ideal Husband*, a West End success—cast revealing light on his own catastrophe. Harry found the piece "so help-less, so crude, so bad, so clumsy, feeble and vulgar" that he felt deep dis-gust. Yet the crammed, ecstatic house had seemed to augur well for Wilde and badly for Harry's own play. Oddly enough, Wilde's drama looked fully as artificial as Harry's—if anything, it outstripped Harry's in absurdity. And like Harry's, it also showcased grotesque heterosexual romances, replete with ingrown Victorian convolutions. But unlike Harry's play, Wilde's set a "deliberate trap," as Harry unsympathetically but astutely described it. Like Wilde's other dramas, *An Ideal Husband* spoofed the conventions of Victorian romance and marriage. Wilde's nonstop irony—his "'cheeky' paradoxical wit," as Harry primly described it—comically assailed his audience with a relentless parody of their own foibles. While Harry's play smelled of stale air, Wilde's blew like a fresh breeze across the stifling late reign of Queen Victoria, since 1876 styled Empress of India.

Harry hadn't patterned his play on Wilde's " *'décadent'* and *raffiné* " (decadent and overrefined) wit. He also didn't want to imitate Wilde's unconventional and impudent curtain call, at the recent premiere of *Lady Windermere's Fan* in 1892, when the Irish playwright had appeared "with a metallic blue carnation in his buttonhole and a cigarette in his fingers." Wilde would soon pay for his own rash defiance of sexual mores. By the end of 1895, Wilde would stand convicted of sodomy, humiliated, ridiculed, and sentenced to two years of hard labor at Reading Gaol.

But Harry would also live under a sentence that would endure more years than Wilde's. Wilde's erotic life was secret and covert, but at least he *had* an erotic life. The fear that gay men lived with had driven him underground; publically, he had lived in Chelsea with a wife and two sons, indignantly denying the accusations of homosexuality, going so far as to sue his male lover's irate father, the Marquess of Queensberry, for criminal libel. But Wilde knew who he was, down deep; he could share his turbulent love for Lord Alfred Douglas with his confidants. Harry also lived in a prison of fear, but for him that prison was deeply internal as well as external. He himself dared not speak its name, to use Wilde's famous phrase. For most of his life, fear had walled Harry off from his family, his friends, and the possible objects of his affection.

~

WILLIAM'S PRISONS, SUCH as they were, looked much more cheerful in the radiant late summer of 1895.

That September at Putnam Camp in the Adirondacks, the nights already crackled with bracing cold. Having adventured out to the Colorado Rockies earlier that summer, William found himself, at the age of fifty-three—his shovel-shaped beard starting to show runnels of gray— more "alive" and eager to work than he'd felt in years. He was writing and collecting thought-provoking essays on tumultuous questions of religious belief, as seen by an empirical philosopher. These he would gather a couple of years later in *The Will to Believe* (1897), a book that would sell with Bible-like vigor.

Putnam Camp was filled with women and children—the spouses and offspring of the men who'd founded the place in the 1870s as an antineurasthenic resort, a place for effete professionals to regain their masculinity. Evidently the fresh air, the frigid stream water, and the wood chopping had worked. All the men—the Putnams and Bowditches and Lowells and Cabots—had reproduced. And they'd reproduced mightily, in true nineteenth-century fashion. The scene teemed with a pandemonium of children, nurses, wives, cousins, friends, and hangers-on. William actually found these crowds as bracing as the chill nights. The camp cheered William with its wholesome chaos; he gloried in strenuous mountain walks, plain grub, campfire songs, and makeshift outdoor theatricals. The compound rang with the noise of rosy Anglo-Saxon offspring—the big families that Theodore Roosevelt would officially encourage a few years later, to bolster the white European population of the United States.

William had once again chosen to spend some time away from Mrs. Alice and his four growing children. William and Alice had been married now for almost two decades; Harry, their eldest, had recently turned sixteen years old. But in the summer of 1895, Mrs. Alice had sunk into a depression. No doubt Alice could cite many causes for what her husband called her "groundless melancholy." In her discontentment Alice had plenty of female company; she shared her funk with many other married and unmarried women of the late nineteenth century: Sarah Wister, Clover Adams, Alice James, and Constance Fenimore Woolson, to name only a few. Her complicated husband and his behavior had to have played a significant role, even if William hastened to reassure her of his affection. When he looked back, he said, he could date his "normality" and "efficiency" to the beginning of his marriage. "I cannot *imagine* anything different or what sort of an alternative could be," he declared.

But William had actually penned this panegyric in response to an agonized inquiry from Alice. Had William *really* wanted to marry her?

Did he now regret it? "That's why I haven't answered your question—it is asking whether I am sorry or not that this planet is the earth," William wrote her from his boisterous camp. "I bless you day and night and my gratitude to you for all you have been and are to me, runs over and over. And it is the most absolutely literal of truths that you *never* stood as high in my eyes as this last year has made you stand." Lovingly and sincerely, William attempted to thank his stalwart, long-suffering wife; after all, he appreciated her virtues and cared for her deeply. But did he also protest a little too much? Did he apply his praise a little too readily? Perhaps in her "melancholy" Alice worried about William's regrets less than her own half-acknowledged doubts, accumulated over the years. All wasn't exactly well in this modern marriage, as much as these two people loved and needed each other.

In the rough beauty of the Adirondacks, William wasn't contemplating marriages and their nature; instead, he was obsessively reflecting on "falling in love, passing honeymoons and the like." He found himself "flooded" with exhilaration and "simmering with a happiness"—as he had been with Mrs. Alice, during what he called her "holy girlhood." (The Jameses used words like *holy* and *sacred* differently from other people—secularly and lyrically.) William amused himself replaying, in his head, his outdoorsy honeymoon. But he did so, significantly, without the benefit of the flesh-and-blood Alice.

Instead, William relished the flush September beauty of the Adirondacks with a fresh-faced twenty-one-year-old woman from Brooklyn named Pauline Goldmark. Pauline, clear-eyed and serious-minded, parted her hair straight down the middle and wore a pressed frock in a posed studio photograph from the time. In the mountains she roved in boy's breeches, her light hair wafting free from the severe pulled-back styles of the 1890s. William declared her an "up at sunrise, out of door, and mountain-top kind of girl." He reported to Alice that his young former Harvard student Dickinson Miller, who'd introduced her to him, showed symptoms of being "very sweet" on this "little serious rosebud of a [M]iss Goldmark." He added, "She climbs cliffs like a monkey in his company—it would be jovial if they contracted an alliance." But wasn't it William who'd gone "sweet" on Pauline?

At Harvard, William primarily taught indistinguishable hordes of young men. But he also nurtured a few bold and pioneering Radcliffe Annex students. One of these, the future modernist writer Gertrude Stein, studied with William before her graduation in 1897. Stein jumped at the chance to learn from a James; she afterward admired William's brother Harry as the "first person in literature to find the way to the literary methods of the twentieth century." Stein's friend and lover Alice Toklas would later write to Harry suggesting he adapt his novel *The Awkward Age* (1899) for the theater.

According to her *Autobiography of Alice B. Toklas*, Stein similarly "delighted" in William. One heady spring during the 1890s, Stein caroused at the opera late into the night instead of sweating through the readings William James had assigned. "Dear Professor James," Stein wrote on her exam, "I am so sorry but really I do not feel a bit like an examination paper in philosophy today." She left the rest of her paper blank and then waited, in some trepidation, for the consequences. "Dear Miss Stein," William wrote back on a postcard, generously, "I understand perfectly how you feel I often feel like that myself." He granted her the highest mark in his course. No doubt the free-spirited William approved of Pauline Goldmark in a related but more hormonal way. William found himself in a "happy, *happy*, HAPPY!" mood that contrasted strongly with his wife's bogged-down domestic ennui. Many a wife was unhappy in 1895—even if, with the so-called second wave of women's emancipation, the word *feminism* was now being used in Britain (and would arrive in the United States by 1910).

In an unkind moment, William could call Pauline "ultra simple in mind"; he praised her for her perceived moral fiber rather than her intellect. But, as he had so often done with women, William strongly underestimated his young friend. Pauline was no more a floozy than Gertrude Stein, Emma Lazarus, or other bright, determined young Jewish women coming of age in the late nineteenth century. Pauline's father, Joseph Goldmark, had been banished from the Austrian Empire because of his involvement in the revolution of 1848. When he arrived in the United States, Goldmark had used his skills as a chemist to found a munitions factory in Brooklyn and later to supply the Union armies during the Civil War. Pauline had nine siblings. Her sister Alice married Louis Brandeis, the distinguished jurist and groundbreaking first

Jewish Supreme Court justice; and her sister Helen wed Felix Adler, the philosopher and founder of the American Ethical Culture Society.

After graduating from Bryn Mawr, Pauline conceived herself as a "New Woman"—an emancipated female who could do important work and decide her own future. With her sophisticated intellectual and political background, she was less restricted than any of the James females. After the turn of the century, Pauline would undertake a career in social activism, in the muckraking vein of Jacob Riis. She found out how the other half lived by studying the longshoremen, delinquent boys, neglected girls, and working mothers of New York City for her *West Side Studies* (1915). Earlier, she had written *The Truth About Wage-Earning Women and the State: A Reply to Miss Minnie Bronson* (1912). But also her love of wilderness inspired her to collect whimsical Adirondackesque pieces for *The Gypsy Trail: An Anthology for Campers* (1915). William hit the mark when he observed that Pauline enjoyed a good hike in the mountains. But that didn't mean she was the innocent child of nature William liked to imagine.

In the coming years, William fostered occasional but intense contacts with Pauline. As he put it in one of his many flirtatious letters to her, "A cousin of mine"—was it William's old crush Minny?—"said years ago that life was made up of painful partings and confused meetings." And he had cultivated both with Pauline. In September 1897, two years after they'd met, William tried to give Pauline a puppy. At a mutual friend's, Pauline had fallen in love with a young dog that William had already spoken for. But William saw an opportunity to show his generosity or his fervor. "I also fell in love with it and bought it," he wrote Pauline, "but no sooner had I done so than I said to myself, 'What a jolly present that would make to Miss P.G.'"

For her own reasons—perhaps because the word *love* occurred so readily in William's letter—Pauline declined this gift. To provide Pauline with a replacement, William presented her with a pencil sharpener that Christmas—hardly a romantic gift or a satisfying substitute for the beloved setter Pauline had recently lost. But, especially with its intricate accompanying instructions from William, the sharpener qualified as a strangely burdened Freudian offering.

Back in the Adirondacks again in June 1898, William worked hard on a lecture series he'd soon give in Scotland, which would eventually grow into his marvelous book *The Varieties of Religious Experience* (1902). In a quietly revolutionary way, this collection of lectures looked at religion from an academic and specifically a scientific point of view, understanding spiritual experience as a matter of psychological needs. This work, one of William's finest, would also be one of his most personal; the spiritual journey he described, by means of a compendium of world religions, was in many ways his own. It led from what he called the "Sick Soul"—his own experience as a depressed young man—toward a positive and life-affirming philosophy. Highly American in its optimism, *Varieties* would become one of William James's most enduringly popular books. As an example of its wide appeal, it would even be an inspiration for the founding of Alcoholics Anonymous in the 1930s. William didn't discuss alcoholism in his book, per se. But as the son of an alcoholic, he had reason to know how addictions could rule people's lives, and how religion, broadly and open-mindedly construed, could help in overcoming such personal and psychological problems.

In *The Varieties of Religious Experience*, William would laud what he called *healthy-mindedness*. This ideal of mental health premised a basic and natural human desire for happiness: healthy-mindedness was "the tendency which looks on all things and sees that they are good." In a particular way, William's love for the Adirondacks had helped him shape this philosophy, which he would go on to develop further in his future philosophy of pragmatism. For him, the mountains had played an important role in his own rediscovery of happiness, their stimulation of natural appetites and urges that his overcivilized life had squelched. It was no accident that William worked on these ideas in the surroundings of Putnam Camp, or that one of his unstated inspirations to happiness was Pauline Goldmark.

In that summer of 1898, as a break from his writing, he arranged an overnight trek up Mount Marcy with Pauline, her sister Josephine, and a party of young mountaineers. As the moon rose before midnight, the mountaintop swam with biting-cold air, "either inside or outside the cabin." Stimulated, William swelled with "spiritual alertness of the most vital description." He wrote his again-absent wife, Alice, "[The] influences of Nature, the wholesomeness of the people round me, especially the good Pauline, the thought of you and the children, dear Harry on the wave [William's nineteen-year-old son, now crossing the Atlantic in the great James tradition], the problem of the Edinburgh lectures, all fermented within me till it became a regular Walpurgis night." Here William framed Pauline as a wholesome distraction; he insisted on "wholesomeness" just as his brother Harry had long craved "innocence." But William clearly had a lot of idealized, pent-up erotic energy, even if his "Walpurgis night" took place only in his own mind.

Veiled eroticism often charged William's letters to Pauline, such as when he tried to claim her as a houseguest in the spring of 1899. "Pray find it possible to come!" he coaxed. "If I don't see you now I shall never see you again, for I spend this summer in Cambridge, and the next summer in Europe." When Pauline hesitated (and in a letter forwarded to William by Mrs. Alice), William wittily complained:

> What a winter of estrangement it has been! With no lectures given or heard, no pups offered and ignored and contemptuously rejected by telegraph, no snatches of conversation in the midst of crowds, no basking on the lawn at Bryn Mawr, no nothing at all in short; and yet all sorts of real things to talk about accumulating on my side of the fence. You may say, "Why, since you have a week of holiday, don't you run down here [to New York], and come and see me and talk them over." Well, it sounds natural; but, apart from the lack of dignity it would argue for a man at my time of life to spend the *whole* of his time in running after the girls.

Though ardent in his pursuit—and perhaps, in a sense, "running after the girls"—William persisted in viewing Pauline as an innocent manifestation of nature, all "magnanimity, generosity and freedom." He feared getting to know the "hidden selfishness and sinister recesses of [her] character indoors"—a tellingly Freudian anxiety. "Ah Pauline," William pleaded, "don't ever let me be disappointed!"

Little is recorded of what Mrs. Alice thought about Pauline or William's other embroilments. But as the 1890s went on, William indulged in crushes on a number of young women, also including his cousin Elly Temple's young daughter, Rosina Emmet—who had a waist, William noticed, "about twice round a human thumb." "I, as you know, love her (although not blind to her defects!)," William wrote his cousin in 1895, "and Alice likes her thoroughly, though I sometimes think she wishes she were young and rapid enough to 'keep up' with her." Alice evidently felt the need to "keep up" with such young women and to compete with them for the admiration of her husband. (William had also maintained an intense friendship with Sarah Whitman, the woman who had helped him prepare his *Psychology* for the printers.)

The claim that Mrs. Alice didn't mind, that William remained "completely loyal to his wife though he could not resist the temptation of harmless flirting with every pretty woman," has been repeatedly made. But, though William's attractions remained "wholesome" in most senses, "harmless flirting" implies that he never hurt or worried Alice, a claim that Alice's 1895 depression would seem to disprove. As a late-Victorian wife, of course, Alice had been schooled to put up with more than William's small indiscretions; the notorious "double standard" still flourished. And though he sometimes felt some compunction about Alice, William took his masculine privileges as freely as his father, Henry Senior, had done before him: he flirted widely while proclaiming his own wholesomeness as well as his undiminished love for his wife.

But William's peccadilloes really do appear mild in comparison to one of William's own siblings. Bob James, though still married to Mary, hardly ever saw her; in 1892, with the death of her father, Edward Holton, she achieved financial independence, and Bob was left to drift as he pleased, moored nominally to the Boston area and to his brother William. More than any other James, Bob had a tendency to act on his sexual impulses, and his experience more fully illustrates the seamier fringes of Victorian philandering.

Ten years before, back in 1884, when he was still living in Milwaukee, Bob had pursued an extramarital affair. Afterward, he had come to Cambridge corpulent and bogged down by his "drinking habits." He confided his confusion to William. Bob felt surprised that his affair had "crushed" Mary. He was equally unprepared for the emotional damage it had done to him and to the unnamed young woman in question, though she had idealistically and naively hoped to "raise him [Bob] from the gutter." Before her death Aunt Kate had expressed herself "pained, shocked, disgusted" by the "reprobate" Bob's behavior. She thought Mary Holton should divorce him (as she had unofficially done with her own husband), but she also blamed the other woman, who in her eyes was "so devoid of morality, decency and common sense, as to accept the overtures of a married man."

William secretly believed Bob to be a "mere hollow shell of a man, covering up mental disease." In spite of his own flirtations, William felt that full-fledged adultery counted as dysfunctional; it certainly wasn't "wholesome." Still, William had pledged to be "tender" with Bob, because, as he admitted, "I seem now to be his only friend here, and it is good to have one refuge." William had long looked after the maladjusted Bob, on his side of the Atlantic, as Harry had looked after Alice on the other side.

Bob most often boarded in Concord, Massachusetts—near enough to William to remain a cautionary tale about excesses of many kinds. (Harry hated it when Bob visited him in England and spent the whole time resentfully grumbling about wanting to divorce his long-estranged wife.) By 1898, when William's cheerful pursuit of Pauline Goldmark had become an established ritual, Bob's lifelong alcohol addiction had grown so severe that he checked himself into an establishment called the Dansville Asylum in the Genesee Valley of New York State. There he would spend five years trying to cure himself by drinking "All-Healing Spring Water" and taking "Moliere-Thermo Electric Baths."

In many senses, William's own marriage, like his career, stood in stark contrast to Bob's rank failure. In spite of his crushes on young women, William maintained a deep and authentic connection to Alice. "I can hardly live away from your sweetness, surrounded as I am with so much that reminds me of it in its pristine bloom, both in doors and in the face of nature," William wrote his wife from Putnam Camp in 1897. "Though your hair is paler, your heart is as ruddy and your will far more trenchant and your intellect more active than you were then, and altogether your personality more significant and important, and I tremble with hope that things with us may continue indefinitely thus." Yet even in this tribute, William asserted his sense of masculine superiority. He implied that, if Alice had steadied him, he had trained her to be a more "significant" personality than she'd have become on her own.

Surprisingly, Harry also claimed the privilege of admiring and annexing admirers—though few enough of his contacts had seemed very sexual so far. In the late 1890s, Harry seemed more concerned about styling himself as a literary "Master"—in spite of his recent failures in the theater. Still, Harry also increasingly wanted more of a household than his inveterate bachelor lodgings. At the beginning of December 1897, Harry wrote his sister-in-law Alice to announce a "peculiar little complication" that he'd been keeping from the family. "Don't be scared," he added, coyly, repeating a worn joke, "I haven't accepted an 'offer.'"

No, Harry didn't plan to get married. But he now contemplated a stroke almost as bold.

❧

LAMB HOUSE, IN the small Sussex town of Rye, didn't take its name from the credulous wooly ruminant that for poets like William Blake had embodied pure innocence. Yet the association with purity might have fit the chaste Harry, fifty-five years old when he signed his first lease on the property. All of a sudden, after decades of city living, Harry found himself eager to live in the countryside, to simplify his life. A few years after moving into Lamb House, in fact, Harry would scrap the urbane beard he had worn since his dashing young manhood. He would present the world with the joweled but surprisingly babylike face that would be iconically identified with "the Master."

Lamb House actually derived its name, appropriately, from an entrenched family with proud traditions, not altogether different from the Jameses. The Lambs had been a minor Sussex dynasty, beribboned with local mayors. In 1723, when they had erected their handsome little Georgian estate, they hadn't built in a country park, but chose the place that had been their chief glory in life—the tightly packed, ancient hill-town of Rye.

After his disappointments in London, Harry hoped to make himself happy in Rye, a "little old, cobble-stoned, grass-grown, red-roofed town," as he described it for William. On a round hill that had once been an island, the town proudly staked its claim as one of the royal Cinque Ports from the Middle Ages. But, like the social-climbing Jameses themselves, Rye rated as an add-on to the list, an afterthought when that mercantile league had expanded to seven (and hence became the

Sept Ports in all but name). Over the years the sea had receded along with the town's wool-bale prosperity. By the 1890s, Rye traded primarily on its tea-shop picturesqueness, its robust gossip, and its convenient golf links. A tiny steam train provided a regular service out for the gaily clad players, their expensive clubs, and their caddies with local accents. Though Harry didn't golf much himself, a sturdily built Georgian mansion in this realm of genteel leisure just might suit him "perfectly," he thought.

When Harry first prowled through Lamb House in September 1897, the old place definitely had the look of a fixer-upper. The price of the house hovered just above the range of a hypersubtle novelist whose increasingly thorny fictions—*The Spoils of Poynton* and *What Maisie Knew* in 1897—hardly netted him a wide audience or a fat income. A high old eighteenth-century doorway led Harry into two cramped parlors—one on each side of the entry, each of them plastered with ghastly Victorian wallpaper. But Harry saw hints of paneling underneath, and he also approved of the solid oak staircase with its twisting helix-shaped balusters.

Having lived in lodgings for most of his adult life, Harry knew that living in his own house would burden him in new ways. For one thing, he'd have to " 'pick up' a sufficient quantity of ancient mahogany-and-brass odds and ends" to furnish the old place, as well as to renovate it from the ground up. And he'd have to find a different constellation of servants to replace the trusty if difficult Smiths, who disliked the transition from Kensington to a backwater like Rye. On top of it all, he would have to hire a new local amanuensis to help him handle his correspondence, now almost as voluminous as that of a government ministry.

At Rye, Harry would set up his own bachelor version of a James household—his answer to William and Alice's Irving Street house in Cambridge and their farm at Chocorua. Harry, depressed after his theatrical failures and the loss of his friends, craved a warm and comfortable home. For the time being, he would people it with guests and of course servants. Eventually, his establishment would include a faithful typist named Mary Weld and a manservant, Burgess Noakes, who'd start out as a "knife boy" at the age of fourteen and later mature into Harry's loyal valet.

Harry's inspection of the upper windows of Lamb House showed him views across a jostle of town roofs and chimneys, over a sweeping estuary and the salt marshes beyond. In bad weather, the marshes provided a surprisingly bleak vista for the Home Counties of England. But atmosphere—even the glum, sea-foggy Victorian variety—suited his desire for a refuge from London's increasingly exhausting world of cabs, receptions, clubs, and theaters. For the present, he hung on to his pied-à-terre in De Vere Gardens in Kensington; it wouldn't do to rusticate too much. But the pleasures of the metropolis had now mostly worn thin.

Out back, Harry found, his house rapturously opened up into a wide garden. Overlooked by only a few rear windows and the tower of the church, the garden was shielded by high walls of ruddy brick. Smothered in roses and jasmine in the summertime, these walls satisfyingly shut in almost an acre of luxurious privacy. A vegetable garden lurked among the greenhouses; the larger plot nearby teemed with "flourishing old espaliers, apricots, pears, plums and figs"—a miniature private Eden, conveniently stocked with fig leaves.

Harry's secret garden, what's more, contained one more sanctuary-within-a-sanctuary. Harry could climb the steps to a "most delightful little old architectural garden-house," which begged to be turned into a novelist's lair. A wisteria branch arched across the porch—a promise for the first month of Harry's initial occupation in May. This detached room, or "garden room," in a more ocherous brick than the main house, had originally been conceived as a "banqueting room" for the mayoral *fêtes champêtres* of the eighteenth century. Though the little annex came with a fireplace, robust drafts would render it largely uninhabitable except during the brief warm episodes of an English summer. Such a place wouldn't really lend itself to dalliances or trysts. Harry's respectable bachelor life didn't and wouldn't rival Oscar Wilde's. And yet Harry would find his own uses for such a refuge.

The room—later obliterated by a German bomb during World War II—was conveniently equipped with a broad bow window that overlooked a steep cobbled street running down toward the main market thoroughfare of Rye. If properly curtained with lace, the outlook gave opportunities for old-maidish spying on what Harry recognized as a "gossiping little town."

In fact, this secret vantage point would later intrigue the subsequent owner of Lamb House, the comic novelist Edward Frederick Benson (1867–1940). After Harry's death, Benson created the immortal character of Miss Elizabeth Mapp, a relentless gossip and social climber, to inhabit Harry's quirky little house and his intriguing garden room. In Benson's highly popular 1922 novel, *Miss Mapp*, the redoubtable title character sits "like a large bird of prey at the very convenient window of her garden-room, the ample bow of which formed a strategical point of high value." For Harry as well as for Miss Mapp, most of the doings of Rye could be "proved, or at least reasonable conjectured, from Miss Mapp's eyrie." Harry was above such petty gossip, but that would in fact render Rye a more boring place than he had anticipated.

The coincidence of E. F. Benson's later residence in Lamb House—in the same provincial milieu, incidentally—underlines Harry's earnest construction of himself as a high-art novelist, in contrast to Benson's more accessible and popular fare. But though Harry's fictions undeniably labored in deeper and darker psychological realms, though they were undeniably weightier and more beautiful than Benson's, his altitude above the gossipy, middle-aged world of Miss Mapp may not be as stratospheric as his biographers, buying into his myth of high-art genius, have claimed. No doubt Harry would have recoiled from Benson's undignified spoof of Rye life. But his own spinsterish retirement in the town wasn't all that dissimilar. Still, as a piece of feminine overrefinement, Harry more resembled Benson's high-toned, Italophilic, excruciatingly pretentious Lucia Lucas than the conniving, locally grown Elizabeth Mapp.

Strikingly, though, it was actually popular culture that enabled Harry's eventual purchase of Lamb House. Though he'd fallen flat on the stage, Harry would succeed wildly at a different art form. In 1898 the novelist sold a ten-part ghost story to *Collier's*, a fashionable illustrated New York weekly, for a proverbial bundle. *The Turn of the Screw* would endure as Harry's best-known and most-read work besides *Daisy Miller*, his sensation from the late 1870s, and *The Portrait of a Lady*, his exquisite novel of manners from the 1880s. Evidently, Harry could manage about one popular success per decade.

Harry's new novella, a self-consciously light work for him—though one that plumbed unexpectedly deep recesses—follows the narrative of an unnamed governess who, trying to protect her young orphaned charges Miles and Flora, glimpses a series of menacing ghosts. She claims to have seen specters of the children's old servants, including the sinister Peter Quint, a former valet, and Miss Jessel, her own now-dead predecessor in the nursery. *The Turn of the Screw* would later be understood as a protomodernist text, an epistemological puzzle with an unreliable narrator: the several layers of the story created fictions swirling inside fictions. But in its preoccupation with weirdly sexualized ghosts that appeared to a heavily repressed shut-in, the story made good use of Harry's own gothic and involuted sexual desires. And in the wake of the failure of his play and the loss of his intimate friends, these desires were about to find new and complicated objects.

IN ROME, IN the late spring of 1899, through mutual friends, Harry met a young artist named Hendrik Andersen. Now fifty-six, Harry immediately took an interest in the lanky, twenty-six-year-old sculptor, with his big frame, his strong hands, and his cap of wheat-colored hair. Hendrik had been born in the smoky fjord town of Bergen; he had emigrated from Norway to New England while still a child. Along with thousands of other Scandinavian immigrants, he had joined the "huddled masses" at Ellis Island and elsewhere. But in his adolescence, Hendrik had been adopted into Harry's more comfortable class; he had been enrolled as an art student in Newport and then in Boston by well-heeled acquaintances of the Jameses—in a strange recapitulation of William's and Harry's own art-student adolescence.

Hendrik Christian Andersen—such was the young man's complete Norwegian name—wasn't to be confused with Hans Christian Andersen, the well-known Danish writer of fanciful stories, including "The Ugly Duckling," who'd died back in 1875. But in a deliberate joking conflation, Harry nicknamed Hendrik "Hans" during their early correspondence, as if trying to render his "dearest boy," as he called him, even more childlike and filial, by means of this reference to a writer of fairy tales.

This craggy young marble worker with his "magnificent stature" had many strange points of commonality with Harry. Whether or not the young man's name sounded like "Roderick Hudson," as one biographer spookily noticed, Hendrik (Norwegian for "Henry," after all) bore an uncanny resemblance to the handsome young sculptor from Harry's formative 1875 novel. And in another instance of life imitating art, Harry himself would soon reprise the role of Rowland Mallett, his fictional aesthete and patron, in this strangely gripping if lopsided friendship.

That Hendrik worked in a studio in the Via Margutta stirred Harry's envy and admiration. This narrow shadowy street, tucked underneath the Pincian Hill between the Piazza del Popolo and the Spanish Steps, had famously attracted penniless and aspiring bohemian artists, many of them foreign, since the seventeenth century. Hendrik's studio stirred up passionate yearnings from Harry's youthful first impressions of Rome thirty years before, when he himself had just turned twenty-six. Hendrik chiseled out oversized nude figures, obvious and almost crude in their male anatomy. This acutely recalled Harry's primordial gawk at his naked cousin at Newport, his appalled brush with the flamboyance of Paul Zhukovsky's friends at Posillippo, and his subsequent bottled-up visits to galleries of unclothed statues with Constance Fenimore Woolson in Florence.

Hendrik would seemingly wrap much of Harry's long history into one bundle—as the future would unfold. His appearance in Henry's life, now, "must have seemed like something in a ghost story," as one critic suggested. In fact, Hendrik might have walked straight out of one of Harry's most gothic tales. But in fact he'd emerged—as truth sometimes really does prove stranger than fiction—from that equally murky Freudian region, so familiar already to the Jameses and their century: the realm of repression.

⁓

HARRY HAD COME to Rye to be happy, but he didn't immediately shake the deep depression that had dogged him since his theatrical fiasco. At Lamb House, he often experienced raw loneliness, worsened by the loss of friends and his distance from London. The winter of 1899 brought heavy gales. His old roof wouldn't, miraculously, lose any tiles;

his sturdy old walls wouldn't even shudder. But his chimneys would "cavernously regurgitate," and the house would deeply absorb the cold. Worse, his shut-in solitude would stir up other presences: "all ghosts and memories," as he put it to William. But, he confided to his brother, "I live with them anyhow. It's midnight, now—farewell." At the stroke of midnight, in his storm-battered manse, Harry himself could scarcely tell, any more than his mad governess in *Turn of the Screw* had been able to do, what these visitations of ghosts might mean.

By his later fifties, Harry had accumulated plenty of ghosts: his rough-shorn cousin Minny, his limping father, his sock-darning mother, his diary-keeping sister, Alice, his old friend Fenimore with her rusty black gowns. All of them came to Lamb House, now, to make curtain calls.

Yet one of the most troubling, stirring presences in Harry's life wasn't dead but instead liable at any moment to catch one of the turn-of-the-century's ever-more-leviathan Atlantic steamships. In the coming late hours of the family's life, the one who would preoccupy Harry the most would be his distant but loomingly monumental brother William.

THE IMPERIAL TWILIGHT

When Harry arrived in New York Harbor on August 30, 1904, he knew his brother William wouldn't be at the dock to meet him. Harry hadn't touched the soil of the United States for almost two decades, and he hadn't seen William for two whole years. Still, his brother had been heavily involved in Harry's fretful decision to cross the Atlantic, but the two men had disagreed about the particulars. Harry, at sixty-one, had taken William's high-handed interference with less wifely patience than he'd done in previous years—but not, probably, because he loved his brother less. If anything, with the loss of most of the rest of their family, the two brothers had grown closer, more embroiled, than they had ever been before.

For the moment, though, Harry had other matters on his mind. His ship had passed the lighthouse at Fire Island. Even from a distance, he could come to grips with the unfolding spectacle of a radically altered New York—the "vast bristling promontory," as he later described it, of Manhattan. The surrounding waters streamed with tugs and freighters. The long wharves and smoke-smudged skyline was alive with circling and plunging seabirds, "white-winged images of the spirit, of the restless freedom of the Bay."

Harry himself felt lifted up by his return; New York Harbor stirred up memories of his family's long history of comings and goings. For several years now he had been hankering to see his native country again.

Throughout the spring of 1903, as his sixtieth birthday approached, he had longed to go "home" (he put the word in quote marks) for an extended period, before he was too old to make the trip. More and more, he told William, his "native land" had begun to appear as "romantic" and remote as Europe had once seemed to him. He remembered kicking fallen leaves on Fifth Avenue, and he wondered if the city still had such leaves or if it was "nothing but patriotic arches, Astor Hotels and Vanderbilt Palaces." Yet as he strained to make out the skyline, he stood on the upper promenade deck of a sumptuous ship, the floating equivalent of the Waldorf-Astoria. In true James style, he had crossed the Atlantic on the massive German-built twin-screw steamship *Kaiser Wilhelm II*—a suitably imperial vessel for the Master's return to the country of his birth.

As it steamed toward the Hoboken docks, the *Kaiser Wilhelm II*, a towering and baroque steamer launched in 1903, displaced some twenty thousand tons of seawater. With its sleek black hull, its four gold-colored steam funnels and two masts, it prefigured the great liners, outfitted with deck chairs and chandeliered dining rooms, that would cruise in and out of New York Harbor during the coming twentieth century. This behemoth had whisked Harry across the summer Atlantic in just six days. With engines capable of 23.5 knots, the ship claimed the Atlantic Blue Ribbon speed record. It could vanquish the Jameses' ocean in less than half the time that the *Atlantic*, the family's steamship from 1855, had churned out that same crossing with its now-quaint paddle wheels.

Harry was no longer the bearded forty-year-old who had departed these shores in 1883. Clean-shaven, bald, and heavyset, he had transformed into a magisterial novelist, a recognizable figure on both sides of the Atlantic. He had just published, in fact, an extraordinary novel about Americans in Paris, *The Ambassadors* (1903). Perhaps the best of his ponderous, brooding "late" novels, the book was a psychological tour de force, following the point of view of an elderly American editor encountering Paris for the first time. This fictional editor, Lambert Strether—modeled to some extent on William Dean Howells—had Harry's tendency to live secondhand: he observed, almost voyeuristically, an affair between a young American, Chad Newsome, and his

French mistress, Marie de Vionnet. (This twosome echoed the trans-atlantic romance in *The American* between Christopher Newman and Claire de Cintré, but now these youthful figures were more removed in comparison to Harry's lonely protagonist.) Against the charming mirages of Paris, Harry's central character found himself in what the novel called a "false position"—a shaky moral position, in which he had defended the rights of a young couple who, it turned out, were apparently living in sin. (The novel left the real content of their relation in question.) With its exquisitely realized, almost impressionistic portrait of the French capital and its complex portrayal of an older man's half-understood desires for love, the book would be considered an important precursor of literary "modernism" by future critics. Harry himself would come to deem *The Ambassadors* his masterwork, and many of his admiring readers would agree. Yet his insights into Lambert Strether had come at a cost. Down deep, Harry was not essentially the accomplished "Master" he liked to bill himself as, but someone more insecure and worried—someone who felt as lost and shut out, as beguiled by the false appearances of things, as his protagonist.

Harry had long fretted about the expense and trouble of his crossing: for over a year, his letters to William had been full of prevarications and fears. Friends, among them Constance Fenimore Woolson's relatives, the Benedicts, had enthusiastically vouched for the safety and comfort of the new liners. On them, the Benedicts said, one might even forget one was at sea.

The ultimate new liner, in fact, would launch just eight years later in 1912. The White Star Line's crown steamship would boast a displacement of some forty-six thousand tons, more than double the mass of the *Kaiser Wilhelm II*—although its top speed of 21 to 23 knots wouldn't in this case quite match German ingenuity. The iron hull of the RMS *Titanic* would soon rise in its Belfast shipyard, and that behemoth's maiden voyage would give the lie to the Benedicts' blithe confidence in the bravado of "unsinkable" ships. Harry, with his "imagination of disaster," would acquire rich vindication for his neurosis. Yet if the Jameses sometimes feared the great ships of their time, they also embodied a parallel grandiosity and pride. The family and their chosen sea gods had in fact proved weirdly symbiotic and coextensive—both complex products of a gigantic cultural hubris now on its last legs or perhaps rushing on into cataclysmic change.

Queen Victoria, corpulent and confined to a bath chair, had died a few years before, in 1901, at the age of eighty-one. The queen had been buried—in a strangely telling detail about herself and her era—in a white dress and with the veil from her wedding to Prince Albert in 1840. (Harry might well have remembered that Victoria had been married in the same year as his parents.) With the burial, the Victorian age had come to an end. Its Edwardian and Georgian successors would soon founder with the *Titanic* and sink into the mires and trenches of the First World War—along with much that the Jameses had variably embodied, amended, or resisted—the Victorian conventions of love, marriage, and family, for example. The Jameses' darker complications had already suggested the preoccupations of the new century. Yet Harry, for his part, dreaded the brash and galvanized new century now taking hold all around him. And he was about to confront it as never before.

The rapid technological advancement of steamships only hinted at the kinds of change Harry would soon find in his native city. This new Manhattan had in fact embraced change on an even more gigantic and incomprehensible scale, and its feats of architecture and engineering alone—its skyscrapers and vast new suspension bridges—would both attract and appall Harry during his visit. Yet the grandiose rebuilding of New York was only one facet of the many changes in American society. The United States had now surpassed Britain as the premier economic and industrial nation on the planet. It had also declared itself an imperial power, in competition with Europe. In its recent war with Spain (1898), the United States had added Puerto Rico, Cuba, Guam, and the Philippines to its overseas possessions. (William had had mixed feelings about this war. Though he wasn't as anti-imperialist as many of his intellectual friends, he decried what he saw as the misguided attempt after the war to Americanize the Philippines.)

Harry would also have mixed feelings about the new, more aggressive America. As he would later mythologize New York in his monumental travelogue and cultural critique, *The American Scene* (1907), the city embodied "dauntless power." "The aspect the power wears then is indescribable," he wrote, in the swelling convoluted style that he had cultivated in his recent novels,

> it is the power of the most extravagant of cities, rejoicing, as with the voice of morning, in its might, its fortune, its unsurpassable conditions, and imparting to every object and element, to the motion and expression of every floating, hurrying, panting thing, to the throb of ferries and tugs, to the plash of waves and the play of winds and the glint of lights and the shrill whistles and the quality and authority of breeze-born cries—all, practically, a diffused, wasted clamour of *detonations*—something of its sharp free accent and, above all, of its sovereign sense of being "backed" and able to back.

For Harry, the matter of power was personal as well as industrial and political. In this passage, he left it hanging in the air, just mentioning who was being "backed" and who "able to back." As a function of his "late style," Harry's grammatical antecedents dodged easy definition; they came up mysterious or missing.

Yet the question of being "backed" mattered to Harry, personally. Faced with this modern dynamo, as his friend Henry Adams might have called it, Harry hinted at a more intimate quandary about love and support. Did he himself want to be "backed" by New York, to be authenticated and nurtured, as his family had often vainly hoped, from his mother's ancestral city? Or was Harry now, as a well-known novelist, able to back himself, as the city so powerfully seemed to do? The sight of Manhattan both raised and troubled Harry's spirits. In *The American Scene*, the city would stimulate his style to a grandiosity similar to itself. But in both cases, this grandiosity covered for some gnawing anxieties.

❧

IT HAD BEEN a strain for Harry to cross to William's side of the Atlantic, and partly because, in spite of William's brotherly kindness or interference, Harry didn't feel always "backed" by his elder brother. For his part, William found it equally taxing to brave Harry's side of the water. For seven years during the 1890s, William had stayed away from Europe. He had only boarded a steamer in July 1899 thanks to a worrying development.

While climbing the peaks of the Adirondacks in June of that year, he had found himself gasping for breath. In confusion, he had wandered the labyrinthine mountain paths, unsure of where he was; he had barely made it back to Putnam Camp. After this scare, William and his physicians determined that his heartbeat struggled along, arrhythmically. Out of the blue, William had discovered he had a heart problem.

Bad Nauheim, near Frankfurt, a cure resort on the edge of the steep Taunus Mountains, exactly fit William's needs. Its salt springs were conveniently reputed to cure both heart and nerve diseases, and William's new troubles, typically, were both physical and psychological. At the age of fifty-seven, William was perennially stressed and overworked as a lecturer, and he was once again, as he'd so often been in his life, depressed. Once more, he had been thrown back onto the sanatoriums of his youth. But this time, at least, he traveled in the company of his capable and loving wife, Alice.

From Nauheim, William got into trouble with Harry—though the cure resort seemed a safe Teutonic distance from Harry's undersized parlors at Lamb House. Buried tensions between the two brothers were waiting to erupt. At the end of July 1899, Harry wrote to his brother in painful anxiety. He wished himself nearer so that he could "consult" with William about a "material matter touching [him]," which had suddenly cropped up. "I don't mean—don't be alarmed—that I've received a proposal of marriage," Harry wrote, recapping an old joke. No, Harry was fretting now about a sudden opportunity to purchase Lamb House outright, after his first lease on the property expired. The prospect made Harry feel as flustered and vulnerable as if some intrepid woman *had* proposed to him.

William wrote back with big-brotherly advice: he thought two thousand pounds was a "very extravagant price" to pay for Lamb House. He couldn't imagine how anybody could ask so much for a drafty and out-of-repair period piece: "Don't be in a hurry—no one will gobble it—till you have consulted some business friend."

Reviewing her husband's draft, Alice felt "trepidation"; she sensed William's brotherly *no* wouldn't play well on the other side of the Channel. But William blithely misunderstood both Harry's acute need to settle down and his pride in his own financial prowess. He sent the letter.

As soon as he got it, Harry shot back: "I do, strange as it may appear to you, know more or less what I'm about." He protested that, thanks to Rye's prettiness and its golf links, property there would swell in value more than the uninformed William could possibly know. Wounded, Harry poured out pages and pages. "My joy has shriveled under your lucid warnings," he lamented, "but it will re-bloom."

But hadn't Harry, after all, asked for advice? Harry's paroxysms betrayed how much he craved William's approval and how helpless he felt in the face of his brother's criticisms. "It has filled this home with grief," William wrote back, unconsciously implicating the innocent Mrs. Alice, "to find that our letters about the purchase 'rubbed you the wrong way.'"

But such fraternal friction not infrequently kicked up sparks between William and Harry. Through the 1890s and into the new century, William's public stature increased: he taught at Harvard, wrote copiously, and lectured all over the United States. It wasn't that Harry's reputation as a novelist had decreased; he continued to attract a dogged band of readers and to win extravagant critical praise. But Harry's books still sold poorly, and not since *The Turn of the Screw* (1898) had he enjoyed the kind of public success that William had experienced with his recent popular books on psychology. *The Varieties of Religious Experience* (1902) had already gone through a dozen editions by the time Harry crossed the Atlantic in 1904.

Even at this stage of their lives, the two James brothers jostled for the celebrity, approval, and validation that had always been an acute family need. If anything, their rivalry deepened with time. In 1898 when the National Institute of Arts and Letters was founded, both siblings were tapped as members—an unusual example, then as now, of two brothers who'd both risen to conspicuous fame. But in 1905, when the same institute assembled an American imitation of the Académie Française (both groups would eventually merge into what is now called the American Academy of Arts and Letters), Harry was elected on the second ballot and William on the fourth—a slight, as William saw it. When he got his offer, he refused the chair. Quite as much as Harry, William could show himself prickly and fragile. Even when both brothers entered their sixties, their childhood rivalry remained keen, fraught, and painful to themselves and to each other. The loss of the rest of the family left the field to them, rendering Harry's and William's long-running conflicts stark, isolated, and titanic. And their very closeness, their very need for each other, exacerbated their disagreements.

Still, the deaths of their parents and other family members had also brought the two brothers closer together. All their siblings were gone now except the perpetually ailing Bob, currently trying to cure his chronic alcoholism in western New York State. William and Harry were the last bastions of the family and its signature wit. Each had a lively interest in all the other's doings. They wrote tremendous letters to each other—hundreds of pages of them—long, loving, and warm.

At tender moments, William could address his brother as "Dearest Henry" or (more jocularly) "Beloved H'ry." Usually, though, William just wrote "Dear H.," as if Harry were the only *H* in the world. Harry, courtlier but perhaps not more extravagant, insisted on his devotion to both William and to Mrs. Alice: "Dearest William & dearest Alice: never more dear!" This tender language—the language of romance conflated with that of family love—strangely echoed William's mock romance with his sister, Alice, of four decades before. But now the deep and complicated family affection didn't costume itself as a joke. Its protestations, if anything, fell short of the brothers' real and profound attachment.

William's Bad Nauheim cure in 1899 brought out tenderness as well as conflict. When Harry first heard about "William's revealed deli-cacy," his emerging heart problem, he found himself "interested & even agitated to the depths." In turn, William was moved by Harry's "heartbreakingly beautiful and loving letter"—"And I, who through all these years have 'claimed' that the Jameses were deficient in simple family affection, and that [C]eltic doubleness of nature and XIXth cen-tury 'critical spirit' had warped us far away from those anchorages." But, William movingly concluded, "We live and learn; and even if I live as if a slave to family affections!" Looking back over the history of the family, William could see that he and Harry, at least, had grown into a deeper connection.

Still, Harry's plan to revisit America had freshly strained the ties between them. William recognized that his overrefined and excitable brother hadn't traveled to the United States since the early 1880s. The country had since pressed through two decades of dizzying technological, industrial, and economic progress—arguably as great as any two decades in U.S. history. In this, the twilight of the so-called Gilded Age, railroads branched out all over the continent, knitting the agricultural hinterlands with a widening industrial belt through the Northeast and Midwest. Cities had exploded in size; Chicago, for example, had grown from half a million people in 1880 to more than a million and a half by 1900. Wealth, at least for industrialists like the Vanderbilts and Rockefellers, had burgeoned as never before. In consequence the United States was more confident, more aggressive, and sometimes more contemptuous of Harry's beloved Europe than ever before.

William worried how Harry would react to the new national assurance. In the spring of 1903, he predicted that his brother would feel "physical loathing" at what he would see as the prosperous vulgarity of Americans. William cited a pet peeve of his own: "the sight of my fellow beings at hotels and dining-cars having their boiled eggs bro't to them, broken by a negro, two in a cup, and eaten with butter." He dreaded that the more fastidious Harry would find even the American "*vocalization*," or accent, "simply *incredibly* loathsome."

In response, Harry misunderstood William's caution. He complained that William didn't want him to come over; he found William "dissuasive—even more than [he] expected." "What you say of the Eggs(!!!) of the Vocalisation, of the Shocks in general, and of everything else, is utterly beside the mark," Harry wrote back. "I want to see them, I want to see everything."

∽≈∾

WHEN THE *KAISER WILHELM II* docked, Harry knew he was walking into a "trap (very kindly) set on the wharf." One of his American publishers, the patron of *The American Scene*, Colonel George Harvey of Harper Brothers, would soon—after Harry paid a courtly initiatory visit to friends in Gramercy Park—whisk the author off to Deal Beach, New Jersey. There Harry would sit on a "deep piazza" open to the summer light and air. There he'd hold a conversation with the snowy-headed and recently widowed Mark Twain—a fellow critic, although in a widely different style, of the so-called Gilded Age. Twain would die a few years later, in 1910, and the two prodigious novelists, who had met only once before in London, would never again have a similar private moment together. If anything looked monumentally American, it might have been these two scarred titans hunkering together in summer chairs on Harvey's terrace, gazing out over the summer Atlantic Ocean with their senatorial eyes. In their sweeping vista, a chain of smart villas marched along the sea spray of the Jersey Shore. "There was gold-dust in the air," Harry remembered.

Earlier, in the "waterside squalor" of Hoboken, Harry hadn't felt like a grandee. There, on that bright and breezy last-of-August day, a more tender and fragile New York past had confronted Harry. The long-forgotten smells and noises of a New York dockside conjured up Harry's "extremest youth." Also, Harry's handsome twenty-six-year-old nephew, William's eldest son, waited to take charge of Harry's brand-new steamer trunk and to brace his uncle up. Characteristically, Harry would later write his nephew out of the lyrical, agonized opening of *The American Scene*. But during Harry's actual arrival, the young man stood out as a "rare benediction" in the dockside crowds.

Back at Lamb House, Harry had gotten tears in his eyes when his nephew had offered to meet him in Hoboken. "I can't tell you how I thank you," he wrote, "for offering me your manly breast to hurl myself upon in the event of my alighting on the New York dock . . . in abject and craven terror." He half-jokingly warned this young lawyer, his nephew, that he might possibly prove "the most awful burden, nuisance, parasite, pestilence and plaster that you have ever known." As it turned out, Uncle Harry disembarked with his inveterate calmness and composure. No messy scene ensued. As for a burden, the game young man mostly got to wrestle with Harry's morass of luggage, to haul it back to the family nest that was waiting for Harry in Massachusetts and New Hampshire.

This nephew, Henry James III—who'd in fact now fully inherited Harry's old nickname—filled a profound role. He qualified as one of the missing antecedents, grammatically and historically, in Harry's elusive *American Scene*. He embodied a third generation of Henry Jameses. As such, he uncannily resurrected Henry Senior, now dead for more than two decades. He provocatively embodied Harry's own lost youth. And he also represented a new generation of Jameses, confident and apparently unflappable—as powerful in their way as the great city across the water.

What's more, this nephew also met Harry as an emissary of his always formidable, always beloved brother William.

AFTER A STAY in the Chocorua woods, at William's farm, Harry returned to Cambridge. He wrote his letters and his impressions of America upstairs in the shingled house at 95 Irving Street that William had built for his family a decade before. William's plain professorial abode, William's practical wife, and William's four complicated children anchored Harry, more deeply than he knew, to his now-lost history at Quincy Street. "The Dead that we cannot have," Harry wrote to Bob, inviting him to join them, "but I feel as if they would be, will be, a little less dead if we three living can only for a week or two close in together here."

This reunion took place a few tree-shaded streets away from the old James house. Harvard was almost as near—Harry's onetime alma mater and William's established milieu. Once, Harry scorned this former theological school. But in the last twenty-odd years Harvard had grown "into a mass so much larger" that Harry was impressed by the "swarm of distinguished specialists" who had gathered there. Also, the once-detested Cambridge presented Harry with fewer irritations now— though the "very ancient and mellow" Charles Eliot Norton still hung on there, teaching Dante at Harvard College, living with his three plain daughters whom the undergraduates had wittily dubbed "Paradiso, Purgatorio, and Inferno."

Mostly, though, Harry spent time with William and his family. He had already come to know William's children, but he now witnessed them in their own milieu, confronting young adulthood and facing conflicts derived, in part, from James history.

William's eldest son, Harry, sometimes appeared a confident throwback to his savvy entrepreneurial ancestors. As a young lawyer, he had become a "regularly booked" man of affairs, "cool in his affections and judgments," his father thought, "sans haine & sans amour [without hatred and without love], but absolutely fair & benignant." Billy, who'd entered medical school in his father's footsteps, more resembled his father in a long childhood history of hypochondria. He continued to perplex his father with his moods. The athletic Aleck, the baby of the family, "tall and taciturn," would eventually yearn to be an artist, as his father and uncle Harry had longed to do in the 1860s.

Peggy, like her aunt, Alice, the only James daughter, sometimes despaired at dealing with her sharp-elbowed brothers. She wasn't sure how she fit into a world that, for all the educational and professional advances of women during the Jameses' collective lifetimes, still insisted on male superiority. But her father understood her, in spite of her tendency toward "morbidness," as a "big souled and large minded pattern of humanity."

Harry warmed to his nephews and niece as he stayed at Irving Street, but he'd already encountered them frequently on his own side of the water. Both before and after the dramas of 1899, William's family, as apt to climb aboard steamships as their older relatives, had graced England regularly. Harry had often put up a nephew or niece as a guest at Lamb House.

In 1900, William and Mrs. Alice had come to England trying to arrange European schooling—as the elder James had done half a century earlier—for their daughter. Peggy gradually became a favorite niece to Harry, just as Billy, William's second son, became a favorite nephew. Though Henry III had wondered while staying with his uncle in 1898 if his uncle really cared for him, Billy had reported in 1902 that his uncle's treatment of him was "kinder to him than that of a mother." (Harry had always taken after his mother, Mary, and here he even achieved a maternal role.) Harry appreciated that Billy and his younger brother, Aleck, both wanted to be painters. And William, far from opposing their inclination as his father had done, encouraged his two sons, when he could, in their chosen vocations. His child rearing had improved on his father's on many points—and Harry, as an interested, generous uncle, achieved a similar distinction.

Both William and Harry, having passed through their own struggles, worked hard to help the next generation escape from the lingering damage of Henry Senior's mental illness—visible in their physical ailments and outsized ambitions. But this very family madness, if that's what it was, had also given birth to the agonized genius of William and Harry and Alice's generation. For complicated reasons, William's children, further from the turmoil of the old James household, wouldn't discover the same electric inspiration that even their aunt, with her "bottled lightning," had experienced. But they would grow up with more security and self-confidence than their father, their aunt, and their uncles had done.

AS THE NEW England autumn deepened, with its improbable paintbox colors in the woods, Harry traveled out to the Berkshire Hills of Massachusetts. He was delighted to stay with his fairly new friend Edith Wharton, at her lavish Georgian-style manor, "the Mount," built in 1902. Harry called the place a "chateau mirrored in a Massachusetts pond," and a credit to the taste of the woman who had created it. An amateur architect, Wharton had designed the house and gardens herself, and as a well-to-do New Yorker and the wife of the rich Edward ("Teddy") Wharton, she had the wherewithal to do so. The brilliant, elegant, chestnut-haired Mrs. Wharton—who would publish her stirring critique of American aristocracy, *The House of Mirth* (1905), during Harry's American visit—figured as Harry's latest cherished friend and literary protégée, a breezier and more confident Constance Fenimore Woolson.

Harry had first met Edith in the late 1880s, but they had only recently become friends. For years, Wharton had idolized the work of Henry James; in 1900 she had sent him a copy of her story "The Line of Least Resistance." Harry had returned it with a mixture of praise and criticism that had at first overwhelmed the sensitive thirty-eight-year-old fiction writer. As with Fenimore, Harry insisted on being regarded as a *"cher Maître"* to an admiring woman artist; at the same time, his warmth and charm endeared him to Edith as the two got to know each other better during the first years of the new century. Their easygoing literary friendship was made safer, perhaps, by Edith's status as a married woman as well as by Harry's increasingly venerable age. Nobody expected him, now, to get married—not even William.

"The Whartons are kindness and hospitality incarnate," Harry wrote a friend in England that October, "the weather is glorious-golden, and the scenery is high class." From the Mount, Teddy, Edith, and Edith's Pekinese whisked Harry off to the Hudson Valley and the New England hills in her up-to-date automobile. Harry could relax and enjoy himself. As a loyal friend, tireless cosmopolitan, and adept literary artist, the talented, well-dressed Edith gave Harry another good proof of the superiority of aesthetic American females, as he saw it, to their business-oriented menfolk. But even with Edith's sumptuous house always open to him, Harry had more to see and more business to conduct—not only with his publishers but with his past.

In the late autumn of 1904, Harry traveled to New York, a city both he and Wharton knew well and had in common. In Manhattan, he stayed with his friend Mrs. Cadwalader Jones at her house on East Eleventh Street, then after New Year's 1905, with Edith Wharton in her apartment on Park Avenue. Dinners and engagements filled some of his time, but he had plenty of leisure, that winter, to walk around the city and witness the progress, as some saw it, of twenty years of fast-paced American life. The new Manhattan as well as the old would become monumental characters in Harry's *American Scene*.

As he wrote about the changed city for *Harper's* and the *North American Review*, Harry could only understand it by means of metaphors. Harry's friend H. G. Wells likened the Manhattan skyline to a crown, a "clustering group of tall irregular crenellations." In contrast, Harry used images of common domestic objects gone weirdly awry. He saw the new skyscrapers spinning up "like extravagant pins in a cushion already overplanted"—although he admitted these tall buildings at least had the charm of "taking the sun and the shade in the manner of towers of marble." For him, the newborn skyline resembled "some colossal hair-comb turned upward and deprived of half its teeth."

Harry's analogies could grow even darker. Sometimes, he compared the city to a python or an entangling monster, with its "bold lacing-together, across the waters, of the scattered members of the monstrous organism." Other times, he saw New York as a colossal machine. Its "immeasurable" bridges served as "the horizontal sheaths of pistons working at high pressure, day and night." One of these bridges was the towering Gothic-arched Brooklyn Bridge, which Harry had probably glimpsed under construction before its completion in 1883; in his New York childhood there had been a public ferry that had stirred the passions of Walt Whitman. It was one example of the huge technological and architectural changes that caused Harry to see New York as unimaginably, chaotically, and freakishly modern.

If Harry had previously styled himself as a passionate pilgrim, he now took on the role of a "restless analyst" or "brooding analyst." In the lyrical, curmudgeonly, and portentous jeremiad of *The American Scene*, Harry would object to many of the innovations he would witness in Manhattan and the United States. For example, Harry lodged a protest against the mobility and transience of "hotel culture." He deplored the empty grandiosity of the Waldorf-Astoria on Fifth Avenue (on the present site of the Empire State Building), its lobby crowded with "huge-hatted" ladies who found "in the gilded and storied labyrinth the very firesides and pathways of home." He himself, though, had been a "hotel child"; and even before his birth, his own parents had lived at the Astor House, the Waldorf of their day.

As he floated around a wintery New York, Harry would likewise lament the "cult of candy"—the "great glittering temples, the bristling pagodas," where New Yorkers—women especially—worshipped pyramids of "chocolate creams." Chocolates were an innovation; Milton S. Hershey, the Pennsylvania factory mogul and fanciful town planner, would introduce a small dollop of chocolate called a "kiss" in 1907. But sweets had a long history in New York and in Harry's own life—his dental problems in his sixties were traceable to this past. The James children had enthusiastically patronized the cheerful New York pastry shops and confectioners of the middle century, Harry himself recollecting a fragrant bakery on the corner of Eighth Street, a "repository of doughnuts, cookies, cream-cakes and pies."

To some degree, Harry's hatred of the increasingly frenetic consumer culture of the "great commercial democracy" made sense. It fit the fussy, decorous temperament of an exiled novelist. But Harry tended to blame this "culture" largely on women (women being the avid shoppers he saw on the street in New York) and to critique it all from a sometimes hypocritical altitude. More troublingly, Harry objected to the "aliens" of New York, especially to the Italian and Jewish immigrants who thronged many of the city's now-dilapidated downtown neighborhoods. At Ellis Island, Harry uneasily dreaded the "affirmed claim of the alien, however immeasurably alien," to share in his "supreme relation" to his ancestral city. He rued "*their* monstrous, presumptuous interest, the aliens, in New York." Harry would devote many fascinated but agonized pages to the Jewish ghetto of the Lower East Side, to the "social question" that the mass immigration of the late nineteenth century had raised and which Harry only poorly understood.

As he tried to get used to the new Manhattan, Harry took refuge in a nativist fantasy of the past. He recollected a purely white, genteel, Anglo-Saxon New York that had never really existed, even in Ward McAllister's social register. Contrary to this myth, "aliens" had built New York; through the centuries the city had been a roiling entrepôt of class, ethnicity, and race. New York's jostling heterogeneity had in fact stood out even in Harry's parents' days. Its class conflicts had shown in the Panic of 1837 and exploded in that theatrical dispute turned uprising, the Astor Place Riots of 1849. In fact, both frictional and harmonious racial and ethnic diversity had dominated the city since the days of the first dirty wooden taverns and assertive step gables of New Amsterdam, with its tropic-burned Dutch traders, its ubiquitous black servants and freedmen, and its astonishing parade of polyglot sailors. Of course, Harry's own ancestors hadn't qualified as Dutch or English "founders"; they were immigrants themselves. The Jameses had come from boggy Ulster, the Walshes from wind-scoured Scotland.

Harry soon uncovered more personal objections to New York. The city's tendency to rebuild and reinvent itself bothered Harry more than almost anything, and for crucial reasons. Manhattan no longer sheltered bay-windowed row houses and Grecian churches and trim brick warehouses stocked with cotton as it had at the time of Harry's birth in 1843. Nor did it resemble any longer the porticoed, pig-ridden Manhattan of his mother's young womanhood in the 1830s. Over the years, the city had massively built up like a giant brick-and-stone reef—increasingly sprouting with exotic and fantastic marble-built corals. The old Trinity Church opposite Wall Street, Harry noted, now found itself overshadowed and "cruelly overtopped" by new stone high-rises.

Harry stared at the new tall buildings. Other writers would admire or decry the age of the new steel-cage "skyscrapers," which soared ten or twenty or forty floors from the streets. The Flatiron Building, completed in 1902, thrilled the visiting English writer H. G. Wells. Wells gaped approvingly at the Flatiron's lavishly lit limestone wedge "ploughing up through the traffic of Broadway and Fifth Avenue." (Harry, who later read Wells's book on America, scoffed at his "cheek" in writing about the "Future!" as embodied by New York, after a visit of only five weeks.) In contrast, Philip Burne-Jones—the globetrotting son of the noted Pre-Raphaelite painter—dismissed this same New World prodigy as nothing but a "vast horror." Keeping him company, Harry pronounced these towers as "grossly tall and grossly ugly." To him, such upstarts amounted to a personal as well as an architectural affront. They'd replaced and usurped his cherished childhood universe.

Harry made a pilgrimage to the family's old neighborhood on West Fourteenth Street. He hoped these quieter streets would help him keep the "boa-constrictor" of the busy modern city at bay. In front of the family's old steps and bay window, he basked in the delicacy of old memories. Farther downtown at Washington Place, however, Harry received a great shock. The house where he'd been born—in addition to an adjacent "castellated and gabled" university hall—had "vanished from the earth." In an odd reference to his father's disfigurement, Harry felt he had been "amputated of half my history."

In Washington Square, near his mother's old home, Harry recoiled from Stanford White's triumphal arch commemorating George Washington, finished in 1895. Through this arch and around the once-quiet square, horse-drawn traffic noisily coursed along the cobbles—joined by the "loud-puffing motor-cars" that had already begun to jostle with the "sharp-ribbed horses" of New York's thoroughfares. Harry lamented the new arch's "poor and lonely and unsupported and unaffiliated state." Here Harry projected onto this monument his own losses; he was the one who felt "unsupported and unaffiliated." In many of Harry's exquisitely spun analyses of the "scene," a simple, personal anxiety lurked, terrified to bare itself.

Over and over again in *The American Scene*, Harry lamented New York's obsession to reinvent itself as bigger and more monumental. He couldn't understand why Manhattan loved to tear down an old brick townhouse in favor of a fifty-floor office building. To Harry, it made no sense to exchange "an old staircase, consecrated by the tread of generations," for a brand-new Otis elevator—that modern contraption first conceived by Elisha Graves Otis as far back as the 1850s, though in 1903 the Otis Elevator Company introduced the gearless traction electric elevator, which would briskly serve the heavily trafficked skyscrapers of the future. But Harry didn't hold with such improvements. He resented what he saw as repeated desecrations of his family past.

Ironically, though, Harry had come to New York partly for his own self-aggrandizing reasons. He would soon seal a deal with the distinguished literary publisher Charles Scribner for the so-called New York Edition of his collected works. Over the next few years, he would make sure that each text would be rebuilt and remodeled; each would be painstakingly rewritten and mediated by a ponderous preface as though by an elegant new classical-revival portico. If New York was reinventing itself, so was Harry—and likewise on an enlarged and impressive scale. In his own way, Harry remained a true son of the ambitious and overweening city whose pretensions he so readily criticized.

THE WHITE HOUSE was brightly lit on the evening of January 12, 1905, with carriages unloading distinguished guests at its semicircular portico of classical columns. Harry, arriving as a fussily dressed dinner guest, was welcomed or at least ushered by crisply uniformed aides-de-camp, as he passed along red silk ropes into the inner sanctum of the president's residence. It was a "big and quite pompous function," in keeping with the grander and more powerful America to which Harry had returned. The mansion, first occupied in 1800, had been officially called "the President's House" or the "Executive Mansion" for a hundred years. Theodore Roosevelt, who had taken over the presidency after the assassination of William McKinley in 1901, had been the first to stamp THE WHITE HOUSE (an informal nickname dating from 1811) on his official stationery. He had also masterminded other improvements to his increasingly royal or at least imperial residence—among them, to handle the overflow of the new bureaucracy, the West Wing. Roosevelt was a youthful improver, just forty-two when he took office. Harry nick-named this young firebrand as "Theodore Rex" or "Theodore I"—and worried that he just might start a war.

Harry took his seat at the president's table, one chair and one cabinet member's wife away from him. He found Roosevelt full of "native intensity, veracity and *bonhomie*." The chief executive was interested in practically everything, with the gusto of a six-year-old, people said; at the moment his head was full of the Panama Canal, the construction of which the United States had taken over from the French in 1904. Harry found the president's colorful talk "indescribable" and "overwhelming." But all in all, Harry could only regard the Roosevelt as a "wonderful little machine," overdone and artificial, "*like* something behind a great plate-glass window 'on' Broadway."

For his part, Roosevelt had only invited Harry at the urging of John Hay, the secretary of state, one of Henry James's many influential friends. Also, Harry was (once again, as he'd been during his last visit to Washington in 1882) a guest of Henry Adams, now an eminent historian of the period from 1801 to 1817 in America (he had published nine volumes between 1889 and 1891). Like Harry, he was now beardless, with carefully parted hair; he was more embroiled than ever in political Washington circles, even if he had never become president like his Adams ancestors. In 1904, though, he would publish privately, for his nieces, a version of his *Mont Saint Michel and Chartres*, a musing on the nature of medieval Europe that also reflected on his somewhat skeptical view of the new "dynamo" of American civilization.

Definitely a "dynamo" himself, Roosevelt, like Harry, had grown up as a New Yorker, in the Gramercy section of Manhattan. He had passed through a sickly childhood not unlike the Jameses'—and had since made a career out of overcompensation. His efforts to define himself as masculine, by way of San Juan Hill and big game hunts, dwarfed William's program of wood chopping in the Adirondacks. Roosevelt in his forties had become a vigorous philistine who took his cabinet members for brisk walks and staged boxing matches in the state rooms of the White House. Not surprisingly, he thought Harry was "effete" and a "miserable little snob." The two men bowed and smiled and politely listened to each other's remarks, but there was no love gained or lost between them.

❧

AFTER HIS WASHINGTON engagements, Harry traveled to the South and West in the spring of 1905, but he maintained his brother's family and their Cambridge household as his center of gravity. It was natural for him to stay in William's orbit. But proximity sometimes generated conflict between them. Harry disagreed with William quite as much as with Theodore Roosevelt.

Some of Harry and William's disagreements would surface in Harry's book about the United States, *The American Scene* (1907). In his writings as he traveled around America, Harry adopted a sometimes dark and skeptical vision of the country that contrasted strongly with William's more upbeat and down-to-earth hopes. William, it's true, would pronounce Harry's book "*köstlich* [delicious] stuff" and find himself "fairly melting with delight" as he read it. But in spite of this genuine "tribute," Harry's book would only underline the brothers' temperamental and philosophical differences.

Even in their sixties, the two could still play the roles of man and wife, in an echo of their parents' marriage. Harry was still mostly supportive and encouraging. When critics misunderstood and attacked William after his introduction of an optimistic and accessible philosophy in his *Pragmatism* (1907), Harry soothed and reinforced his brother: "You are immensely and universally *right*," Harry reassured him.

William had built his *Pragmatism: A New Name for Some Old Ways of Thinking*, ultimately one of his most influential works, on a series of popular Lowell lectures—the venue at which he had courted Alice three decades before and which in the next century would spawn the public television station WGBH in Boston. Beginning with his 1904 lecture "What Pragmatism Means," William had set up a method that cut through the thorny tangle of traditional philosophy and focused on facts, practicality, and concrete action. It was such action, William felt, that had delivered him from the mire of depression and confusion in his younger days. "Pragmatism," the product of his life experience, was offered as a positive, commonsense philosophy that anyone could adopt.

William's populist pragmatism countered Harry's increasing tendency toward obscure, elitist, protomodernist, high-art fiction. And yet Harry heartily endorsed his brother's work, still playing the all-approving, all-supporting role his mother had lavished on Henry Senior. "It may sustain & inspire you to know that I'm *with* you, all along the line," Harry wrote William about pragmatism in 1909: Harry could "conceive of no sense in any philosophy" that wasn't his brother's.

Contrastingly, when reviewers attacked Harry's complex and arcane novel *The Golden Bowl* (1904), published during Harry's American tour, William joined Harry's detractors. This novel, like *The Ambassadors* before it, created a mesh of deep psychology in its story of marriage, adultery, and vexed family interactions. But William didn't like this book, so rich in its portrayal of the complexities of consciousness. He asked Harry to "sit down and write a new book, with no twilight or mustiness in the plot, with great vigor and decisiveness in the action, no fencing in the dialogue, no psychological commentaries, and absolute straightness in the style." "Publish it in my name," William added, in a flippant joke that underscored their rivalry, "and I will acknowledge it, and give you half the proceeds." Understandably, Harry was devastated, but he declared he would rather "descend to a dishonoured grave" than conform to William's idea of literature. "I'm always sorry when I hear of your reading anything of mine," Harry went on wearily, "and always hope you won't—you seem to me so constitutionally unable to 'enjoy' it."

Yet despite their rivalries, William confided to Harry his deepest aspirations. William remained dissatisfied with *Pragmatism*, which many had misunderstood as a "philosophy got up for the use of engineers, electricians, and doctors." With characteristic James ambition, William longed, he would tell Harry in 1907, to "write and publish, if I can do it, another immortal work, less popular but [with] more originality than 'pragmatism.'" Harry, as usual, sympathized both with William's distress and with his high ambitions; the two were deeply enmeshed, no matter what side of the Atlantic they were on.

A set of striking images from the early twentieth century illuminates the brothers' relationship. This series of photographs reveals the two of them as they must have appeared during the year of Harry's visit to the United States. Against a dark background, Harry surprisingly stands out as the more assertive of the two figures. He is sharply dressed in a discreet bow tie and high collar, his clean-shaven face anxious but authoritative. Beside him, William appears more comfortable with himself, in his element; he settles back in a tweedy professorial suit brightened with a fob and watch chain. Patriarchically masked in the beard he has worn for decades, William is now mostly grizzled to gray. But both brothers share a penetrating gaze—each version abstracted, complicated, elaborately riddled with running thoughts. Between the two, as the foundation of the photograph, lies a region of darkness as pitch-black as the Atlantic Ocean at night.

❧

AFTER A YEAR in the United States, Harry crossed the Atlantic again in July 1905 to dispossess his bothersome tenants at Lamb House. He returned to Britain like the fabled King Arthur, in order to right the realm and rescue his able cook-housekeeper and his other beleaguered servants. Not everyone at Rye flooded with joy on Harry's return. Harry's cook-housekeeper, improbably named Mrs. Paddington, showed more offense than gratitude. Joan Paddington—though in the household she retained no discernible first name—tended to stand on her dignity. She amounted to a "big authoritative" presence, Harry thought, even if she'd proved, culinarily, a "pearl of great price." She'd replicated Harry's mother's abilities as an "absolutely brilliant economist" and a "person of the greatest order, method, and respectability"—in spite of her tendency toward huffs. She'd almost quit, during the evil reign of the tenants, thanks to a dispute over a bosomy parlor maid, one Alice Skinner.

Harry also returned to his trusty young houseboy, Burgess Noakes. Burgess wasn't at all "pretty" like the controversial parlor maid. Standing in the room waiting for orders, he was slight, dark, and stubby, with a pug nose and a granitelike void of expression. "The eternally babyish Burgess," Harry called him. But the young man was good-natured and loyal, and he worked like a small demon cleaning shoes, knives, doorsteps, and windows. For these efforts he'd soon catapult to the enviable post of Harry's valet—choosing suits and turning socks inside out in the morning so that Harry could slip his feet easily into ready-to-wear booties. Harry hadn't grown rich from his books, but he could afford to live like a gentleman—quietly, an aging bachelor, alone.

The "help" were all Harry had at Lamb House. Not all of his employees, though, planned to stay. Mary Weld—the typist-assistant who'd taken Harry's dictation of *The Ambassadors*, *The Wings of the Dove*, *The Golden Bowl*, and reams of correspondence—had nefarious plans to get married and leave Harry's service. But by way of consolation, Harry also came home to the warm wet kisses of his dachshund, Max, "the best and gentlest and most reasonable and well-mannered as well as the most beautiful, small animal."

Inevitably, Harry also came home to a mountain of notices, packages, and letters. One of these letters, postmarked from the steamer port-of-call at Gibraltar, contained some rather crushing news. Hendrik Andersen, the friend whom Harry had eagerly expected, wasn't coming to stay at Lamb House; the young sculptor wouldn't join Harry in savoring the summer glories of Rye, the walks along the salt marshes, and the rounds of golf.

Harry had half expected his own disappointment. "That I *should* have you here at this lovely moment . . . was somehow too good to be true," he wrote; "and as your silence lengthened out I felt, more and more, that I was losing you." In his loneliness Harry dreaded losing any houseguest. But "losing you" amounted to passionate, loaded language even in 1905.

Harry's language hit an even higher and more revealing pitch: "Hold on tight, at any rate, till I can get you somehow and somewhere and have you *back* me," he wrote to his friend. There was that outcry again, "*back* me"—the curious expression that he would apply to New York City in *The American Scene*. This repeated word opened a window into Harry's deep need to be "backed"—supported, understood, embraced. Harry closed his letter by reaching out to his friend with both force and "benediction." *Benediction* was a religious word, but Harry used it (as the Jameses tended to do) in a brooding, romantic way. He addressed these resonant phrases—laced with still more yearning, tender words—to "My dear, dear Hendrik": "But good-night, dearest boy," Harry wrote; "how I yearn after you to Montefiascone!"

Montefiascone lay hundreds of miles from Rye; it was a tiny town just north of Rome, crammed with churches and perched on a volcanic ridge above the azure Lake Bolsena. Harry had previously walked the streets of this Italian hill town with Hendrik Andersen, his "dearest boy." The young Norwegian-American sculptor whom Harry had met in 1899 mostly lived in Rome on the Via Margutta, that ghetto of foreign artists, but he sometimes escaped from his studio for the cleaner air of the hills.

When he had met Hendrik Andersen, Harry had immediately tried to demonstrate his respectable intentions by seizing on the role of patron. He had promptly bought a piece of Hendrik's art—and not one of the artist's muscular, graphically naked male figures. Instead, Harry paid fifty pounds—$250, the fee for one of his magazine stories—for a small terra-cotta bust of a child noble, Alberto Bevilacqua Lazise. "Brave little Bevilacqua," a bust sculpted by the "braver still big Maestro," was packed in shavings and shipped to Rye. And this delicate adolescent had since gazed out from the mantelpiece in Harry's dining room, while he chewed Mrs. Paddington's heavy, stewed dinners alone.

Contrary to any unconscious wishes Harry might have had, the "Maestro" himself didn't come in the crate with his statue. Though over the seventeen-year course of this friendship Harry would write the young sculptor more than seventy letters—many of them longing and affectionate—Hendrik would visit Lamb House only four times.

Such starvation rations were reminiscent of Harry's long liaison with Fenimore. Like his friendship with Fenimore, his connection with Hendrik also required silence and secrecy—though Harry's close friends and his brother knew a little about it. As a "queer," or unorthodox, relation, this friendship struggled to find any space, time, or venue in which it could exist.

The age difference between the two men also added to its fragile poignancy. Although Hendrik wasn't indifferent to Harry, he had the advantages of being young and free. The aging Harry frequently felt mortal in the face of his friend's youth. He felt the urgency, in this friendship, more than he had with Fenimore. In fact, an earlier dynamic had now been reversed. If Harry had sometimes disappointed Constance's expectations, he now found himself on the receiving end of such unconscious snubs. Hendrik, that is, apologetically specialized in crushing Harry's hopes, in being too busy, too taken up, too embroiled, to visit or meet up.

Harry often had to send his love by mail, but also his hugs. These days, he was extravagantly embracing many of his friends in a startling Latin manner. To Hendrik, he had to translate these physical impulses into verbal ones: "Every word of you is as soothing as a caress of your hand . . . I pat you on the back lovingly, tenderly, tenderly" (1904); "I've tenderly loved you and yearningly embraced you" (1906). With Hendrik so often at a distance, these hugs had sometimes stretched wide in Harry's imagination, in a huge geographic arc: "I pat you affectionately on the back, across Alps and Apennines," Harry had written in 1903; "I draw you close, I hold you long." As late as 1910 he would still invoke this same unbridgeable, yearning distance: "I put out my arms & hold you fast, across Channel & Alps & Apennines." In spite of this long-distance courtship, disguised as avuncular affection, little evidence of physical contact between the two men has survived. It is unclear if the inexperienced Harry consciously thought of Hendrik sexually, for all his tender phrases and Latin hugs.

In one telltale displacement, Harry's erotically charged worries about Hendrik often focused on the young man's stock of poorly selling nude statues. Tossing feverishly on his bed at Rye, Harry fretted about Hendrik's "horribly expensive family of naked sons & daughters." He lost himself in a "troubled vision" of Hendrik's having to "feed and clothe" his naked marble children, imagining the artist as a bankrupt prodigal with a rakish sex life that had resulted in offspring: "And then I reflect that you are always (terrible fellow!) begetting new ones as fast as possible—& I do lie awake at night asking myself what will become either of them or of you." Pointedly, Harry imagined Hendrik creating his statues by means of illicit (heterosexual) sex. But, Harry added, quoting Shakespeare's *King Lear*—where the issues were paternal rather than erotic—"But 'that way madness lies.'" Clearly, Harry's psyche couldn't handle even this imagined erotic misconduct.

For similar reasons, Harry wanted Hendrik to concentrate his sculpture on busts, not full-figure nudes: "It is fatal for you to go on . . . neglecting the *Face*, never doing one, only adding Belly to Belly—however beautiful—& Bottom to Bottom, however sublime." Even in the Edwardian era, *bottom* (not even *buttocks*!) struck a jarringly nursery-ish or auntish note. And the addition of *sublime* rang strangely in this combination. Could a "Bottom" be "sublime"? Harry visibly struggled with the issue of graphic nakedness, and the sexuality it suggested.

Yet Hendrik's own sexual desires, in spite of his riots of stripped statues, remained almost as obscure as Harry's. True, his artist brother Andreas painted a canvas of a youthful Hendrik "waking up in bed, the covers slipping off his naked body, while another young man, also naked, sits beside him, pulling up his socks"—possibly Hendrik's fellow art student from Newport, John Briggs Potter. But otherwise Hendrik didn't leave any more evidence of affairs than Harry did. As a sexual puzzle, he rivaled his older friend, so that this secretive young artist made for a "safe match," as one critic phrased it, for Harry's own evasions.

Before the end, Harry would incinerate all of Hendrik's correspondence. One of Hendrik's three surviving letters to Henry James, accidentally preserved by his sister-in-law Olivia, hints at Harry's possible motives. The letter opens up a strange glimpse of how Hendrik may have consciously or unconsciously collaborated in the highly colored father-son fantasies that had developed over the course of this relationship. Worried about Harry's disapproval of an exhibition he was plotting in 1912, the sculptor, then almost forty years old, wrote, "[I am] afraid that you will take your son Hendrik and lay him across your stout knee and spank him on both cheeks of his fat backsides."

In this Scandinavian-flavored English, Hendrik created a weird and vivid picture. The stipulation of "both cheeks" rendered this fantasy oddly specific—almost as graphic as Andersen's strapping statues. Did Harry blush with disapproval, as he'd done more than thirty years before at Posillipo? Or did he find the image compelling? In "A Child Is Being Beaten" (1919), Sigmund Freud would explore the relation between some children's perverse fantasies about being beaten to the development of a range of adult sexual "abnormalities," including sadism and masochism.

Whatever his own sexual tastes, Hendrik clearly saw Harry as a father figure in a broader sense. He regarded Harry as a patron and as a paternal established artist who could help boost his career. As late as 1912, Hendrik could wonder "what right has this tall pale, yellow headed Norwegian, Andersen, a poor beggar of a sculptor living in the slums and shadows of Rome, a right to approach the King of writers and impose any obligation on him." In 1913, Hendrik could propose a visit to Harry and the "Emperor of Germany" in the same breath.

Hendrik could also write intimately, as when he declared, "I wish you could be here, I would love to embrace you and talk with you and assure you ever again of my deep sympathy and affection." At the same time, Harry urged some of his young friends, like Hendrik, to address him as *"très-cher Maître"* (very dear Master). He played the role of a distant, almost imperial figure; he wasn't at all displeased to have Hendrik conflate him with the Kaiser. On an unconscious level, as time would prove, Harry in fact yearned to identify himself with grand authority figures like emperors.

Despite such grandiosity, Harry's long liaison with Hendrik had its more intimate moments. In 1902, Harry comforted Hendrik on the loss of his elder brother Andreas: "How can I express the tenderness with wh[ich] it makes me think of you," Harry wrote. He himself qualified as a second son; he had his own beloved elder brother, the thought of whom fueled Harry's "aching wish" to be near Hendrik and "put [his] arms around [him]." For this important occasion, Harry even crossed out the otherwise snobworthy name of the Athenaeum Club that was embossed on his stationery. Sincerity in 1902 couldn't ask for more.

In 1903, Harry enjoyed a photograph of his young friend dressed up as a "Bearded Bandit; very charming for all its savagery." Harry, like many overserious people before him, longed to love a rogue, even one in costume.

In May 1907—two years after his homecoming letdown at Rye— Harry made a rare rendezvous with Hendrik in Rome. Hendrik offered to put Harry up in his digs, but Harry insisted on a hotel. Tellingly, Harry didn't want to "encumber [Hendrik's] apartment with [his] large and heavy presence." Self-conscious, Harry felt the weight of his sixty-four-year-old body, increasingly plumped by age and good living; he had always liked to drink, even if there is no real evidence of his father's kind of alcoholism. Like his father, though, he sank under his "personal habits & traditions & eccentricities," his accumulated emotional burdens. A photograph taken in Hendrik's studio during this visit shows a stern-looking Harry, in formal dress, sprawling imposingly. Beside him the young, whimsical-looking Hendrick, in a rippling artist's smock, leans in toward his patron, pleasantly. The photograph captures a moment of this odd, hard-to-imagine relationship. Nevertheless, the two enjoyed many "happy studio hours," Harry claimed. In his old Roman haunts, the two men spent what Harry called "romantic" days together.

The evidence for Harry's attraction to men, sparse prior to 1890, grows much stronger afterward, as illustrated by his many letters to Hendrik. The change seems sudden, but it was probably less so than it appears. Harry's impulses had presumably been eroding his deep reserve for a long time. With the deaths of his parents, with the losses of his sister, Alice, and his friend Fenimore in the 1890s, with the failure of his plays on the London stage, he had experienced tremendous stress. With his depressions in the mid-1890s, he had bent and buckled. As one critic, Hugh Stevens, described this development, Harry grew "increasingly daring in the way he constituted himself as a sexual and desiring subject, and acknowledged freely—indeed with pleasure—that his desires were for (young and attractive) men." And though he hadn't abandoned his reserve and discretion—his Victorian conventionality—such restraints couldn't any longer contain all of Harry's desires.

A particular deluge of epistolary passion burst forth around 1899, the year Harry bought Lamb House. In 1904 and 1905, Harry's emotionally fraught return to the United States also unleashed floods of feeling—and precipitated a poignant rendezvous with Hendrik on their common ground of Newport. The sheer force and variety of these new confessions of feeling are astonishing—and partly because Hendrik Anderson wasn't the only young man Harry would secretly find fascinating after the turn of the century.

❧

THE CHUNKY, MUSTACHED American novelist Howard Sturgis didn't want to be kept secret: back in 1900, he and Harry had even contemplated living together. If circumstances had allowed, he and Harry might have changed history—and history's view of Henry James—and set up a male version of a "Boston marriage" at Lamb House, complete with bow ties, urns, and fine china. Harry had finally shied away from the plan. Still, the two men had continued to spend time together in Rye and Windsor and other locations.

Of Harry's late love interests, the dapper Howard Sturgis most broke the novelist's now-established May-December pattern. Sturgis, a heavily Anglicized and nattily tailored American expatriate novelist and socialite, trailed Harry only by twelve years in age—not by the three decades of Hendrik Andersen. Harry had known Howard for some years when their friendship suddenly warmed up at the turn of the century. And their off-and-on companionship remained warm as well as erotically charged well into Harry's sixties.

In the late summer of 1907, the sixty-four-year-old Harry ran into his friend Howard at Cernitoio, a villa owned by artist friends near Vallambrosia in Tuscany. Howard Sturgis had holed up in this bucolic "eyrie," with its rich pastoral views, to recover from London stresses. There his companion, William Haynes Smith, "excellently" took care of him, as Harry observed. Surprisingly, gay couples circulated freely in Edwardian England, even in the wake of the humiliation of the Oscar Wilde trials of the 1890s, at least among the open-minded and unconventional cosmopolitans who formed Harry's circle. Such couples often gravitated to France and Italy, countries where the Code Napoléon, the revolutionary set of laws that Napoléon Bonaparte had bequeathed to much of continental Europe, had decriminalized homosexuality.

Harry, though, traveled to Cernitoio alone. A mysterious, solitary figure at train stations, he continued to keep his amatory interests away from family and public notice. What's more, he kept his amorous friendships separate from one another, compartmentalized and private. The chameleonic Harry would become a different man for each of these new friends—and each of these complicated fin-de-siècle figures would prove as hard to pigeonhole as Harry himself.

Whether in England or Tuscany, Harry found Sturgis a colorful, flamboyant figure. Unlike the more cagey and ambiguous Andersen, Sturgis flouted conventions as boldly as John Addington Symonds, another of Harry's English friends, had always done. He had even talked about homosexuality, as Harry had nervously noted, in print. In 1891, Sturgis had published a frank novel about same-sex love at English public schools, based on his own experiences at Eton, called *Tim: A Story of*

School Life. But since English schoolboys were often thought to pass through a homosexual phase, the book excited less of a stir than it might otherwise have done.

More provocatively, Sturgis swanned around West London with a domestic companion, a distant cousin of his named William "the Babe" Haynes Smith—an almost exact stocky, mustached replica of himself. The two lived at an exquisite potted estate called, appropriately, Queen's Acre (or "Quacre") at Windsor.

"The Babe" shot billiards while Howard, wrapped in a shawl, happily worked bold colors of yarn into a fancy needlework frame. Such an outright parody of Victorian gender roles qualified these two men as openly homosexual by the standards of Edwardian England. They insisted on a good deal of openness even in a country where sodomy was a criminal offense. Surprisingly, Harry wasn't appalled, as he'd so often been with Oscar Wilde; he actually found his "dear dear Howard" obscurely comforting.

Back in 1900, after a particularly commodious cohabitation with Howard at Lamb House, Harry committed an "indiscretion." Harry declared to Howard, "I could live with you." The idea proved more of a longing than a practical plan. Because of "the Babe" or because of social convention, Harry felt he could ultimately "only try to live without" his friend. Still, the two often stayed at each other's exquisite Lilliputian estates; Harry was moved to find Howard's Windsor house his "natural asylum." The two gossiped, confabulated, and exchanged sympathetic letters. After all these years, Harry discovered a Posillipo-like side of himself. He campily referred to one meeting as a "tryst" and joked about being "ravished" when Howard stayed over. ("I mean as to my inner being," he added somewhat coyly.) The friendship, what's more, remained reciprocal: "Keep a-wanting of me all you can," Harry wrote in the fall of 1907, after their time together in Tuscany, "you won't exceed the responsive desire of yours [truly], dearest Howard."

❧

BY CONTRAST, HARRY enthusiastically embraced a different side of himself—a manly and Irish one—when he met the young Jocelyn Persse at a society wedding in 1903. The fair-haired, good-looking, strong-chinned

Persse was thirty years old—half of Harry's age. Harry would subsequently help him become a member of various London clubs, yet Persse wasn't a helpless young man in search of a patron. The young Irishman had considerable savoir faire and carried the distinction of being the nephew of Lady Augusta Gregory, friend of the poet William Butler Yeats and cofounder of the Irish National Theatre. As his first overture of friendship, Harry sent Persse a copy of his exquisite just-published novel, *The Ambassadors* (1903).

Coincidentally, Persse long carried on an intrigue with a married woman, Lorna Hutton Black, whom he finally married decades later in 1938. This real-life heterosexual affair, however, didn't apparently faze Harry—or prevent him from writing to Jocelyn suggestively and passionately, enjoying secondhand the young man's taste for guns and grouse shooting. In one instance of this infatuation, Harry imagined that Jocelyn had brought Mediterranean swear words from a trip to Greece in 1904. Harry hoped to hear them "rip" from his friend's "moustachioed lips," as well as see a traveler's sunburn on Persse's "manly cheeks." Thus Harry echoed his father's and his brother William's decades-old obsession with the "manly." Yet he added to this family preoccupation an erotic twist that grew plainer as he grew older. As for Persse, the young man was grateful to have Henry James sponsor him for the Athenaeum. But he claimed never to understand quite what the distinguished, balding novelist saw in him.

❧

THE LAST OF Harry's flames knew just what he saw. Harry first corresponded with the youthful Hugh Walpole—who was just launching a career as a novelist—in December 1908. The gung-ho, shortsighted Hugh would later befriend Virginia Woolf and other urbane high-modernist literary figures. At twenty-four, though, the future "dearest little Hugh" had set his sights on Henry James. In one of their first encounters, the two enjoyed a coruscating supper together at the Reform Club, Harry's pied-à-terre in London. Afterward, Hugh, with youthful gusto, declared Harry to be "by far the greatest man [he] had ever met—and yet amazingly humble and affectionate—absolutely delightful."

The two men differed vastly in age. In 1908, Harry had turned sixty-five and increasingly suffered from failing health. Four decades younger, Hugh gyrated with childlike energy—"as filled with vitality," as he himself later phrased it, "as a merry-go-round at a fair." With such an age difference, no wonder Harry admired Hugh for his lithe, sweaty "lawn tennis greatness." Harry marveled at the magnificence, splendor, and prowess of Hugh's youth, exotically imagining this spectacled young screwball as a "peerless pearl-diver," with his enviable rounds of "contacts & conquests."

Painful contrasts of youth and age both fueled and checked Harry's crush. In comparison to the youthful Hugh, who tended to "bleat & jump like a white lambkin" in the green new vastness of letter writing, Harry felt he'd been "writing letters for a hundred years." More than ten thousand of Harry's letters, many of them charming and feeling, would in fact survive after his death. By contrast to all this dewy-eyed youth, the sexagenarian Harry felt ponderous and unwieldy, like an elephant: "*this* elephant," he signed himself in 1909, "—who accordingly winds around you, in a stricture of gratitude & affection all *but* fatal, his well-meaning old trunk."

Such a pachyderm of age and restraint could only "paw" at his young friend—not even paternally hug and pat, as Harry had done in earlier years with Hendrik. "The Elephant paws you oh so benevolently," Harry touchingly, painfully wrote. With such a view of himself—and with so many decades of restraint behind him—Harry felt a deep physical and sexual divide. Hugh, though, felt it less.

According to one famous story, Hugh even offered to sleep with Harry. And the novelist, according to this legend, protested in horror, "I can't, I can't." This story was maliciously circulated by Hugh's sworn enemy, the English novelist Somerset Maugham, and may or may not represent what actually took place between the two men.

In any case, Harry took his own revenge against marauding youth and its advantages. Early in their relation, in 1909, Harry told Hugh to address him as "'*Très*-cher Maitre [sic]', or 'my very dear Master' (for the present)." From this posture, Harry freely and trenchantly criticized Hugh's novels, just as he'd earlier railed against Hendrik's colossal nudes. Harry's reactions to Hugh's novels remained "tepid"—although

Hugh's review of Harry's *The Outcry* in 1911 hyperbolically exalted the elderly novelist, causing Harry to "swim in a blaze of glory." In this case, Hugh had his own motivations for praise. The novel's young protagonist, Hugh Crimble, physically resembled him. "You will sell the edition for me," Harry playfully but hopefully remarked, envisioning both Hugh's fictional charm and his real-life flattering review; "and no edition of mine has ever sold yet!"

Such criticism, though, helped Harry confirm his literary and artistic superiority to his younger friends, both male and female. Most of these untried aspirants cowered in the face of Harry's now-colossal reputation. Harry's sharp criticisms reenacted, weirdly, William's old habit of insulting his own work. Harry seemed to take out a lifetime of frustrations on these little brothers—on these metaphorical sons and nephews and grandchildren, cherished as they were. Harry lashed back against his father's early disapproval of his career in fiction as well as against William's "manly" and philosophical disapproval of his complicated prose. Decades before, Harry had likewise blitzed Fenimore's work. But Constance Fenimore Woolson, to judge at least from her few surviving letters, had actually criticized back—a source of equality and intimacy not accorded these later friends, who seldom dared to controvert "the Master," even when his own interfering and condescending reviews irritated or wounded them.

Harry may have meddled, but his letters to these late friends also lavished them with warmth, tenderness, care, and even erotic engagement. Yet these letters ultimately testified as much to Harry's isolation as to his newfound powers of connection. In one of his most lyrical addresses to Hugh Walpole, Harry dreamed of a Freudian "floppy sail" that filled with wind on a voyage to the "golden islands" of a tropical literary fantasy—with "you there, along with me, for my man Friday." In conjuring up a paradise, Harry alluded to Daniel Defoe's *Robinson Crusoe* (1719). He imposed on Hugh the part of his "man Friday"—a bosom companion, yes, but also a servant, an assistant, and a racial other, with Harry himself playing the marooned and isolated Crusoe.

The evidence suggests that Harry wanted complicated things from Hugh. In part, he craved a family—both the one he'd had and the one he'd never had. "Cultivate with me, darlingest Hugh," Harry wrote in

1913, "the natural affections." Harry left hanging just what these might be—family connections or the deep, mysterious passions natural to human beings, including sex? In either case, it paid not to "wait till you are 80 to do so," Harry cautioned. Yet in the same letter, he hastened to retract, claiming that he himself had "made the most of them"—passions? family connections?—"from far back." True, the dutiful Harry had long cultivated family pieties and connections—in his own skittish way. But he had evidently only begun to cultivate "natural affections" motivated by erotic desire.

Harry evidently knew he had shunted sexual matters to very late in his life, perhaps too late. The theme of "too late" abounds in his fiction, as critics have noticed—in a myriad of characters who have missed crucial life opportunities. Lambert Strether in the Ambassadors was one of them. John Marcher in Harry's masterpiece of a novella, *The Beast in the Jungle* (1903), was another. In it, Marcher waits all his life for a momentous event that never comes, a "beast in the jungle" that is lying in wait for him. But a faithful woman, who waits with him, *is* the important thing that he never recognizes, and the "beast" is the tragedy of his not recognizing her importance to him before her death. The story has often been interpreted as referring to Constance Fenimore Woolson. But it also applies equally well to other "natural affections" that Harry had squelched or deferred for most of his life.

In his sixties, as an erotic late bloomer, what did Harry want? What was he looking for? A host of recent studies, exposés, and critiques have debated how to label Harry and his late-breaking Roman spring: "homosocial male, homoerotic male, homosexual, repressed homosexual, gay-inflected author, exemplar of 'male homosexual panic,' nonheterosexual." The recent term and theoretical innovation of *queer*—sexually complicated, idiosyncratic, and unconventional—might fit Harry's tangled contradictions better. The term *queer* can apply to anyone whose sexuality doesn't conform to the social norms of his or her time; Harry, for all his buttoned-up gentlemanliness, had long harbored hard-to-categorize, unconventional desires, whether for the company of Paul Zhukovsky or Constance Fenimore Woolson. Yet by that same token, the other members of his family—erotically unconventional for most of their lives—also qualified, by this definition, as *queer*.

After all, Harry's late-in-life flames were matched in number, intensity, and naïveté by his brother William's. The two brothers psychologically had much in common, in spite of William's hardy masculine objections to Harry (and perhaps because of them; William criticized in Harry what he was afraid existed in himself). Both James sons shared many traits and many experiences—for example, their "unmasculine" escape from the Civil War, their sexual backwardness and inexperience, and their obsession (inherited partly from their disabled, alcoholic father) with things "manly." Although one brother could certainly be described as *heterosexual* and one *homosexual*—these terms, brand-new to English as of 1892, were themselves a construction of the late nineteenth century, an oversimplified dichotomy set up by German sexologists and adopted by Anglo-American bourgeois culture. This opposition didn't always fully or meaningfully describe the "queer" complications of these brothers' sex lives. In many fundamental ways, as their later infatuations showed, William and Harry resembled peas in a pod.

William's continuing flirtations and romantic friendships with young women in the first decade of the twentieth century—with Rosina Emmet and Pauline Goldmark—largely paralleled Harry's pattern. Strikingly like Harry's entanglements, William's liaisons stayed flirtatious, epistolary, paternal, evasive, clandestine, and doggedly "innocent." Although both brothers bore a palpable family resemblance to the addictive, moody Bob—the bad seed and infant id of the family—both William and Harry favored chaste infatuations. (Bob evidently knew how to seduce a woman, and he didn't adopt protégés as his brothers did.) In their tendency toward flirtation, William and Harry remained temperamentally indebted to their father, who had perhaps cadged kisses but had otherwise stayed faithful to their mother, to the Victorian "angel of the house." Like their moralistic, iconoclastic, mentally ill father, too, they'd both evolved into strange and florid paradoxes of passionate unconventionality and Victorian restraint. No doubt the "sensual education" their father had designed for them had, in unexpected ways, shaped these contradictions. In a sense, both brothers qualified as *queer*. In a narrower and more useful term, they remained *Jameses;* they were both idiosyncratic according to the dynamics of their long, itinerant, incestuous, ambitious family history.

In one important contrast between the brothers, Harry hadn't centered his life on one person, as William had done with Mrs. Alice. True, Harry often attached himself to a primary woman friend, as he had earlier with Constance and as he often did, now, with Edith Wharton. Yet these relations did not impinge on his interest in young men. And for William, even the capable and long-suffering Mrs. Alice hadn't really curbed his impish proclivities or entirely filled his needs. His impulses, like his brother's, proved gaping, labyrinthine, and imperial, requiring the admiration and approval of a kingdom, a whole public, and not just a single well-meaning person.

These late affairs no doubt manifested other long-buried motives. For his part, William apparently suffered off and on from impotence. Both brothers remained insecure in spite of their successes—in need of praise, support, and love. Both of them also seem to have plunged into affairs partly to stave off the deep depression that hit them with renewed ferocity in their old age. If that was their motivation, these liaisons didn't always help; Harry told Hugh Walpole in 1910 that his "black devils" had made him unfit to accept a visit from his young friend.

All in all, Harry and William carried on their affairs with a funny hybrid of openness and secrecy. (Mrs. Alice continued to put up with William's flirtations.) Though the two aging men didn't exactly confide in each other, each knew at least a little about the other's young friends. Their loves created still more competition between them. But their affairs, in the end, would anchor them less to these winged, fleeting youths than to each other.

This was especially true when, by 1909, the brothers, both in their late sixties, fell victim to another old James legacy, ill health.

AT LAMB HOUSE, Christmas 1909 eerily pantomimed other gloomy James holidays of the past. It marked, though, the last of an era, the last one when the scattered remnants of Henry Senior and Mary's offspring might have reassembled. But no earnest James crossed the stormy Atlantic. And none of Harry's young men, either, managed to join him at Rye. Instead, Harry welcomed only one houseguest, a journalist by the name of T. Bailey Saunders. Harry described him as a "rather dreary lone and lorn and stranded friend"; he'd been having marital problems with his wife.

Harry, now sixty-six, found comfort where he could. He spent Christmas Eve at the nearby ancient, shrunken Cinque Ports town of Winchelsea, at a "child's afternoon party." The day after, he invited his faithful typist, Theodora Bosanquet, and her friend to Christmas dinner. Harry received his guests cheerfully, dressed to the nines, and the two young women discovered boxes containing gloves laid out on their plates. "Miss Bosanquet," as Harry respectfully addressed her, while courteously spelling out difficult words for her during his long dictations, had received exactly the same elegant present the year before. "This seems to be his one idea of gifts for ladies!" Theodora recorded in her diary.

Harry had unwittingly chosen an extremely old-fashioned present. To Theodora Bosanquet, the gloves already appeared antediluvianly Victorian. Likewise to her friend Nelly—Miss Bradley, as Harry addressed her—the gloves no doubt rated as a touching, fussy gift, such as one's aunt might give. For his part, Harry thought of Miss Bosanquet's friend as a "pal or second self of hers (a lady-pal)"—shades of his departed sister, Alice, and her "lady-pal," Katharine Loring.

For Theodora qualified as yet another self-confident, ambitious "New Woman," a female determined to succeed in the world through education and professionalism. Other such women had threaded through Harry's long life, although Theodora belonged to a bold generation distinct from Alice James's and Katharine Peabody Loring's. Though she'd received a finishing-school education at Cheltenham Ladies' College, Theodora had gone on to earn an eggheaded university degree, formerly the exclusive province of males, at University College, London. Then she'd taught herself to type and had joined a London secretarial agency, with the firm intention of landing the post of Henry James's assistant. She'd triumphed at last in the autumn of 1907, after the inconvenient marriage of Harry's ex-assistant Mary Weld had opened up the position. Trim, erect, efficient, and intelligent, Theodora was actually seldom in need of having Harry's references explained to her—in his slow, steady voice that she found so hard to interrupt. She had quickly proved herself an "excellent amanuensis." "The young, boyish Miss Bosanquet," he called her; he evidently admired in her something like the pluck of Daisy Miller and the intelligence of Isabel Archer. But Theodora hadn't mired herself in these characters' Victorian limitations.

After dinner, Harry and his guests pulled open "crackers," those customary English Yuletide party favors and noisemakers, containing prizes and paper Christmas crowns. But these particular crackers contained masks, the "pleasant, benevolent sort of masks only down to the mouth with a hole for the nose," Theodora observed. Harry's mask caused an immediate sensation. In it, he hilariously transformed into a "fat old lady with side curls." The young women laughed uncontrollably. Harry rang for a shaving mirror in order to see himself. "Why . . . don't we all wear masks," he said, "and change them as we do our clothes." He spoke charmingly, banteringly, but with a perhaps unintended reference to his own masked life.

A few days after this high-spirited celebration, Harry fell ill—and with a battery of characteristic James ailments that would pummel him over the coming "dismal and dreary" months. Harry had at least partly inherited his mother's iron constitution, but he now fell victim to digestive crises, attacks of gout, and bouts of depression. At first he protested that his illness had "no more to do with a 'nervous breakdown' than with Halley's comet"—that astronomical feature known since antiquity that had reappeared, fiercely bright, in the night skies of 1910. But soon Harry had to admit that an omen was indeed streaking across his psychological heavens. By April 1910, Harry described to Jocelyn Persse a "*nervous* condition—trepidation, agitation, general dreadfulness." To Hugh Walpole in May, he reported himself entirely unfit to be visited. In a whiff of his father's old language of mental illness, he explained, "[I am down] with the black devils of Nervousness, direst, damnedest demons, that ride me so cruelly and that I have perpetually to reckon with."

It was Miss Bosanquet who informed William and Alice, back in Cambridge, Massachusetts, that Dr. Ernest Skinner had visited Lamb House. The doctor apprehended "no cause for anxiety"—in itself an anxiety-producing diagnosis, in 1910. William wrote back with physicianly and big-brotherly advice: "Walk a minimum (using cars and hacks [cabs] when required) take no morning bath . . . and a *bain de propreté* [a real bath] only once a week, lie down for a quarter of an hour 3 or four times a day, avoid cerebral and social fatigue, and take a 1/250 of a grain of nitro-glycerine . . . 3 or 4 times a day." Mrs. Alice, by contrast, proposed a different cure: she had the immediate impulse to board a steamer for England, to come and take care of her brother-in-law. Now a sturdy woman of sixty-two, with a rich head of snow-white hair, Alice embodied all of the sensible practicality, and at least as much of the tenderness, of William and Harry's long-dead mother.

For now, Alice had to dispatch her thirty-year-old son, Henry III, across the Atlantic as a proxy; his uncle Harry received him as a "blessed support." Alice herself couldn't get away from Irving Street as immediately as she'd hoped; there, as William gratefully put it, she was taking care "of all my duties to other people as she takes care, as far as she can, of those of all the family. Its [sic] a wonder how she keeps up!" It turned out that William's prescription to Harry in fact amounted to his present regimen for himself. His angina had only worsened. Since his retirement from Harvard in 1907, William had kept up his active lecturing and writing. But by the winter of 1910, when the news of Harry's illness reached Cambridge, William's own health was crumbling. "I *dream* of the companionship of Alice," Harry wrote movingly in March, "—but all that is infinitely difficult for you, & I am your poor clinging old Brother always."

All that spring, a rapid and touching international exchange of family care passed across the Atlantic. On April 1, nephew Harry left Liverpool on the Canadian Pacific Line's tall, double-funneled *Empress of Britain*. Harry had to pine for only a week before William and Alice themselves alighted from the White Star Line's brand-new, red-hulled *Megantic*. The couple stayed with Harry at Lamb House for a month before William—restless even when seriously ill—plunged on to Paris, to revise the proofs for the French edition of *Pragmatism*.

Afterward, Alice took William on to Bad Nauheim in Germany, the sanatorium where he had sought a coronary cure back in 1899. Diagnosing his brother's apprehensive and agitated condition as "neurasthenic melancholia," William persuaded Harry to join him there in June. Harry seemed willing: "I want to be *with* you more than anything & am your loving struggling brother," he wrote.

In a spectral reprise of their itinerant childhood, when they'd had nothing in strange European towns so much as each other, William and Harry boarded together that June at the overpriced but commodious Hotel Hohenzollern—an establishment appropriately named after the centuries-old but soon-to-be-dethroned Prussian-German imperial family. After his arrival, Harry described this spa town as a "place of thick woods, groves, springs, and general *Kurort* [spa town] soothing-ness." Once they'd drunk the obligatory waters and consulted the oblig-atory physicians, the brothers launched on what would be a last tour together—a strange reprise of their first independent, youthful travels together in the Swiss mountains in 1860.

But now the country to which their father had moved his family in the 1850s had transformed into a "nightmare of Switzerland." The fail-ing William fumbled at a "Nach-Kurs" [after cure] at low breezy alti-tudes in the Alps. And Harry himself needed a cure and an after cure, as well as all of the attention his sister-in-law could spare, both because of his ailments and William's. He couldn't bear any more illness or bad news. As he wrote his faithful friend Edith Wharton, "I simply *fear* to challenge you on your own complications. I can *bear* tragedies so little."

But in July, unexpected tragic tidings arrived for both William and Harry. Though the family had previously noticed some improvements, their youngest brother, Bob, had fallen into renewed drinking binges af-ter he'd left the Dansville Asylum in the Genesee Valley in 1901. Also, marital and financial problems had continued to dog him; he and his long-estranged wife, Mary Holton, had mostly lived apart, each of them not even knowing most of the time where the other one was. Bob had contemplated suicide, as his sister, Alice, had done in the 1870s. But he'd appealed to his father's single-minded vision of a rationalist Swe-denborgian God in order to survive: "I don't believe God likes a cow-ard," Bob had written. Meanwhile, Bob's heart condition had worsened, and on July 3, 1910, he had a heart attack alone in his house in Concord. The neighbors didn't find his body for two days.

William, his own health crumbling, admired Bob for "go[ing] as quickly." Having had a lifetime of invalidism, William had been trying cures for his manifold physical and psychological ailments now for over four decades. But William and Alice had weathered the now-difficult voyage to Europe for an additional reason. Especially after Harry's recent health crisis, they were worried about him living alone as he did; they'd schemed to bundle him back to America with them.

As it turned out, however, it was Harry and Alice who took William back to America. By the summer of 1910, when the news of Bob's death reached England, William's health was failing fast. Harry and Alice hurried him on board the *Empress of Britain* to Quebec City in early August. The voyage was "beautiful, quick, in itself auspicious" on a calm Atlantic—as Harry wrote his now-ancient New England spinster friend Grace Norton—as if the iron-hulled *Empress* really did, like the fabled but already-fading imperial Britannia, rule the waves. But even at sea William could scarcely breathe, which Harry found "terrible" to witness. Like his father and his sister, Alice, before him, William lay under the hazy spell of morphine. And Alice and Harry had scarcely brought William home to the family summer house at Chocorua, to the thick air of an American summer and the attentions of a "local" doctor nine miles off, when, on August 24, 1910, at the age of sixty-eight, William died.

"I sit heavily stricken and in darkness," Harry wrote one of his oldest friends, Thomas Sergeant Perry, from New Hampshire, "—for from far back in dimmest childhood he had been my ideal Elder Brother, and I still, through all the years, saw in him, even as a small timorous boy yet, my protector, my backer, my authority and my pride. His extinction changes the face of life for me." For Alice Howe Gibbens James, William's death had as profound an impact. Grieving for her husband, Mrs. Alice would wear black until her own death twelve years later in 1922.

William's "extinction" devastated Harry—as not even his own parents' deaths in the early 1880s had done. Significantly, though, Harry phrased his new, nearly fatal loss in the family's long-running terminology of damage and disability, recalling Henry Senior's amputations of many decades before: "My beloved brother's death has cut into me," he wrote Edith Wharton, "deep down, even as an absolute mutilation." Crushed with this loss, Harry spent almost a year with his sister-in-law and her family on Irving Street. "We cleave intensely together," Harry confided to his friend Howard. But after he returned to England in July 1911, Harry began to recover his health, as if his brother's death—in another instance of that old, peculiar, paradoxical James symbiosis—had given Harry a new rush of life. After all, Harry had previously always gained health in William's absence. "My life, thank God, is impregnated with him," as Harry had curiously written to H. G. Wells.

Harry's gains, in the final dusk of his lonely life, would feature an astonishing literary energy. With William's burial at the humble, now thickly planted plot at the Cambridge Cemetery, the flesh-and-blood life of the Jameses as interacting siblings had ended. But the afterlife of the family had only begun.

THE EMPEROR IN THE ROOM

I n the dark, early days of the year 1913, the final scene of
Harry's life opened in Cheyne Walk, at Carlyle Mansions—a
solid, newly built redbrick block of flats in Chelsea. Boxes of
books and papers had just arrived from Lamb House, and this whole
midwinter move had been "like a rather blackish nightmare," Harry
wrote to Mrs. Alice. The sixty-nine-year-old novelist was suffering from
gastric troubles as well as from shingles, a tenacious neurological disease
that had raised pink blisters on his skin. Yet it was all in a good cause.
He often needed to be in London, and a place of his own was better
than staying in temporary quarters at the Reform Club in Pall Mall.

Here in Chelsea Harry had a view. From his high, L-shaped, up-to-
date flat, he overlooked the stodgy bulwark of the Thames embankment, with its still-young trees, heavy balustrades, and cast-iron gas
lamps. Fifty-four acres had been reclaimed from the river by Queen
Victoria's engineers in 1874; in earlier years, as Harry remembered his
visits to Chelsea when he was a child, the neighborhood had been
rough, run-down, susceptible to cholera contagions from the mud.
Chelsea had definitely come up since the 1850s. But the old associations, far from being forgotten, filled Harry with memories.

Beyond Victoria's embankment, the dirty river ebbed and flowed
with its relentless tides. To some, the Thames brought to mind not only
the long history of the city on its banks but also the promise of a future.

Lately the river had suggested London's complicated status as an imperial capital; for Joseph Conrad in his *Heart of Darkness* (1902), the river, like the Congo in Africa, had hinted at the darker aspects of European imperialism. For T. S. Eliot in *The Waste Land* (1922), the Thames would embody some of the darker qualities of both history and modernity. In a strange parallel to Harry's vantage point over the river, Eliot's poem would envision "the brown fog of a winter dawn" downriver at London Bridge. It would imagine the river as sweating "Oil and tar" and "The barges wash / Drifting logs / Down Greenwich reach / Past the Isle of Dogs."

Harry's view of the Thames took in a higher, more genteel stretch to the west of Westminster. But he also felt the massive darkness of the river, noticing the heavy barges and the tarry water: to Hugh Walpole, the old man described the Thames as a "black-barged yellow river." Harry was at least as haunted by the past as Eliot would be; he was frequently depressed or retrospective these days. At the same time, his eye remained Victorian and painterly, from his years of prizing art. Harry often wrote like an artist, suggestively, impressionistically; that was one way that he clung to an aesthetic vocation that had both enticed him and eluded him since the days in William Morris Hunt's studio in Newport.

Even now, in Chelsea, Harry hovered close to where the groundbreaking painters J. M. W. Turner (1775–1851) and James McNeill Whistler (1834–1903) had lived and where they had concocted their own polychromatic visions of the moody river that Harry saw every day from the windows of his well-appointed flat. He was also only a stone's throw from the house of his father's long-dead friend Thomas Carlyle, on Cheyne Row. Yet he had come to Chelsea for the convenience, not for the ghosts. He wanted light, space, and air, even in the heart of the great metropolis, and he boasted that he'd been able to put up his three faithful house servants from Rye, "separately," in their own quarters—an unusual circumstance in London. Supervised by the formidable Mrs. Paddington, Minnie or Joan brought him his tea, now—as in his earlier bachelor days—in relative metropolitan splendor.

Harry still hoped to summer in his tiny Georgian manse with its rose-covered secret garden. But, weary of the quiet life of Rye—of "melancholy, dreary, diluvian" autumns and winters, with the wind howling in the chimneys—Harry had moved back to London. His retirement in Sussex had almost proved "fatal" to him. Whenever a "crisis" struck, a bout of depression, Harry had "fled to London at once," as he confided in James Jackson Putnam, a Boston psychiatrist friend of William's. Putnam, incidentally, was one of the first American practitioners of Freudian theory: the "Freud method," as he called it. Not that he had ever seen Harry as a patient. Harry had other methods for coping with his psychological stresses. He had faddishly tried "Fletcherism," the chewing of all food to liquidity—an invention of the American health crackpot, the "Great Masticator," Horace Fletcher. Chewing might not have cured Harry's now-entrenched depression, but possibly it soothed his stomach.

London, on the other hand, promised Harry a real panacea. The "big Babylon, with its great spaces for circulation, for movement, and for variety," always provided him with distraction. In fact, London alone matched both Harry's aspirations and his agitations, in scale; it had become his cure-all, as travel had been for his father and brothers. For years now, the moment Harry sensed the presence of his family's resilient demons, he had hastily applied what he called "the remedy of London—of the blessed miles of pavement, lamplight, shopfront, apothecary's beautiful and blue jars and numerous friends' teacups and tales!" Or so he told Putnam. But the city wasn't just a diversion; it was also a connection to his now-dead family. He could still remember, vividly and tenderly, where his parents had lived in St. John's Wood; where his sister had received visitors in Mayfair; and where his brother William, a fourteen-year-old in a top hat, had led him through the crowded, rainy streets of the city during the winters of the mid-1850s.

Such memories had been comforting Harry lately; in fact, he'd been fondling them, spinning them into words, while writing an account of his childhood, *A Small Boy and Others* (1913). He had been basking in these beautiful recollections for many reasons. He'd been mourning his brother William, coping with his aging body, and battling his own loneliness. His problem wasn't only the "isolation of Rye" but his own profound, essential solitude, with all its deep and tangled roots.

In the past few years at Rye, Harry had mostly cultivated connections, so to speak, with ghosts. To summon the past, he hadn't used Leonora Piper's spiritualist methods; Harry was outraged, in fact, when one of his brother's old psychical acquaintances claimed to have raised William in a séance. Instead, Harry had bent himself on the haunted project of sorting through William's old letters and turning them into an account of his own life, in a second volume of memoirs, *Notes of a Son and Brother* (1914). Curiously, Harry had not previously written autobiography but rather had disguised his experiences, with characteristic James obliqueness, in a magnificent wordy web of fiction. Now that his parents and all his siblings were dead, he embarked on reviving them through prose. In *Notes of a Son and Brother*, he would audaciously revise his father's and brother's old letters in order to tell his own version of the family story. When his nephew Henry III objected to Harry's editing of Henry Senior's and William's voices, Harry admitted, "[I] did instinctively regard it at last as all my truth, to do with what I would wish."

Henry *intended* to transform this material. A grander, more monumental account of his family history was foremost in his mind, and this project was parallel to what he had already been doing with his own writings. Beginning in 1907, he had enlarged and rewritten his earlier novels for the monolithic "New York Edition" of his work. He had transformed his magazine fictions from the 1870s and 1880s into grander, more ponderous versions of the original texts. Now he wanted to recast his own family's history. From his solitary house on a hill above the Sussex marshlands, he had been rebuilding the James family history in the elaborate and erudite style of his late novels.

In earlier years, in his young manhood of Roman horseback riding, Harry had learned from his "sensual education" to live out each day as it came—even if he had only admired the shepherds of the Campagna from afar, while spending much of his time with women. Now he was increasingly concerned with how his life would look after his death; he worried about his control over what later literary critics would describe as his "construction of authorship"—his literary reputation as a genius. Such an image as Harry had in mind would have to be heavily edited. To begin with, that meant expurgating or burning old letters. As Kate had done a generation earlier, Harry worked to make sure a dignified and respectable version of the James family history would survive.

Aunt Kate had perhaps covered up a religious indiscretion in her youth—her association with her brother-in-law's radical Presbyterians—though maybe she had something more to hide. What Harry was covering up appeared to be much more complicated. With his aloof, polite, and careful life, it's true, he hardly had a wealth of scandal to wipe out, although he may well have cropped a few incidents out of his notes or correspondence. But his secrecy wasn't simply a matter of his emotional or erotic impulses; these were becoming bolder and more obvious in his old age, anyway, than ever before. His impulse to correct, to heighten, to expunge, had an even more complicated impetus. Down deep, his old insecurities still hounded him, no matter how substantial his reputation had became. After all these years, did he feel that he didn't measure up—that he had to transform himself, with his literary gift, into someone else? To do that, he had to transform his family, too. He still saw himself as a small boy among others, as a son and brother of difficult men. Significantly, he never managed to push his autobiography beyond his young manhood, beyond those days saturated with his father and William. He began a volume he titled *The Middle Years*, but he would never finish it.

Harry's literary impulses were increasingly grand—even grandiose, like those of his father—but he maintained a certain Jamesian critical perspective. After William's death, in 1911, Harry had observed how strange it was that "with Death and recession a man of genius becomes a *figure*—a representative of two or three stateable things that have to be *made* stateable—to the public at large, save for the few who knew him best and saw the whole complexity." At the same time, Harry consciously and unconsciously worked to hide his own complexity. By rewriting his novels as well as his life, he insisted on portraying himself as "the Master," as a mythical, monumental high-art novelist—and not the vulnerable, struggling Harry James.

To his friends, Harry could make fun of this hyped-up magnificence. In 1913, he described *A Small Boy and Others* to Hugh Walpole as a "lump of twaddle." In the same letter, he complained about the potential for posturing in other writers' "cheap and humbugging autobiographic form." Again to his young friend Hugh, Harry dismissed the "fatuous & presumptuous Small Boy; an extraordinarily impudent attempt surely, that of regaling the world with the picture of my rare consciousness from the age of 6 months to that of my earlier teens." Harry was still vulnerable and self-denigrating, beneath his sumptuous costume of words.

His words, though, came from an extraordinary and pure depth; he savored what he called the "crystal stream" of memories that had welled up in him as he wrote. He confessed to having "*liked* the way of its coming"—to have enjoyed the process of summoning up his boyhood. "It's full at any rate of an ancient piety & a brave intention," he told Hugh. He was disconcerted that his young friend felt "defeated" by many of the passages of the book, having found them "difficult, obscure or *entortillés* [twisted]." Hugh Walpole, in fact, shared this point of view with many readers of the time, including old friends, who wrote Harry in various states of mystification, craving clarifications and explanations. Many people found themselves "defeated." To the end, it seemed, Harry would doggedly remain an "uncommunicating communicator." Such indirection might prove an asset for a protomodernist novelist writing about the elusiveness of language, consciousness, and human connection. But this unwillingness to communicate was also personal, symptomatic, a leftover shard of Victorian self-hatred.

ALMOST EVERYONE, NOW, knew the author Henry James. The "Junior" had dropped away years ago, and after having written more than twenty novels and dozens of short stories and articles, he was well known on both sides of the Atlantic. His name regularly appeared in the newspapers, and his bald head and jowly face were almost as well known, having been caricatured by Max Beerbohm and others. He couldn't walk the streets without being recognized, and his heavy, besuited, magisterial figure was about to become even more of an archetype of the literary genius.

Harry had been painted before, but now that he was back in London, a more magisterial portrait was in the offing. Early in 1913, Harry's favorite nephew, Billy, tipped him off about a plot that was afoot to commission a majestic portrait of him. The scheme had been launched by Edith Wharton, who had conceived of a piece for the National Portrait

Gallery in London, to be painted in honor of his seventieth birthday. "How can I sufficiently thank you," Harry wrote his nephew in a panic, "for the blessed notifying Cable about the dreadful project you had got wind of?" In a flurry of letters and telegrams, Harry tried to halt this "fond conspiracy to raise a sum of money" in order to create what he thought of as an "expensive effigy," something funereal and grandiose, akin to effigies, those marble sculptures of recumbent knights in English churches.

Nevertheless, Harry acquiesced to his friends. By late that spring, after he'd turned seventy on April 15, he sat for his brother's onetime companion from Venice in the 1880s, the now-famous expatriate painter John Singer Sargent. A long list of British and American notables had subscribed money to pay for Harry's portrait: Rupert Brooke, John Galsworthy, Rudyard Kipling, Lord Rosebery, H. G. Wells, Edith Wharton, and Virginia Woolf—not to mention Harry's "beloved boys" Jocelyn Persse, Howard Sturgis, and Hugh Walpole. (Hendrik Andersen, perennially broke and chronically distant, didn't pitch in.) Over the course of several sittings—for which Harry urged his friend Jocelyn, in vain, to drop by and keep him company—the magnificent Sargent portrait of "the Master" emerged. A ponderous image of Harry surfaced from a dark background, with his hand hooked in the armpit of his vest, his gaze skeptical and authoritative, as though he were on the verge of oracular utterance.

Harry posed for this portrait at Tite Street in Chelsea, not far from his London flat. Sargent's studio was on the same street as the "house beautiful" residence of Harry's old rival, dead since 1900, Oscar Wilde.

A year later, the finished portrait was exhibited at the Royal Academy in Mayfair. But it would not simply rest there; a strange twist would highlight Harry's lifelong issues with women and women's rights. On the day the exhibition opened, in May 1914, a white-haired woman, wrapped in a purple cloak, paused in front of the painting. Without warning, she struck out at it with a meat cleaver, smashing the glass and slashing three rents in the canvas before being restrained. The attacker was Mary Wood, a suffragist who knew nothing about either James or Sargent. By vandalizing the portrait, she wanted to protest the fact that no woman would be paid seven hundred pounds for a painting, as Sargent had been.

Though he wasn't present at the scene, the incident shook Harry. It enacted a strange revenge on the last surviving member of a family that had habitually treated women—his mother, Mary, and his sister, Alice, included—as second-rate. But the painting could be patched by experts, and it would soon be mended. And as for mending Harry, he would receive "390 notes of condolence," by his own count—many of them from his lifelong women friends and faithful female readers.

Still, even with the support of friends like Edith Wharton, Harry's life was growing harder. He was suffering now from a wide range of old-age as well as Jamesish afflictions, including angina, nerves, depression, tooth extraction, and gastric trouble. And his life grew sharply more difficult during the summer of 1914. In late June, a Serbian nationalist named Gavrilo Princip shot Archduke Franz Ferdinand, heir to the Austro-Hungarian Empire, in Sarajevo. In August, the armies of imperial Germany, with resounding cannonades, overran the small kingdom of Belgium. The old dynastic order of Europe—the deep-seated traditions that Harry had spent his life cultivating, which he had embraced instead of American plainness—would soon dissolve in thunder.

THE WAR, EVERYONE said, would be won by Christmas. During the First Battle of the Marne in September 1914, the British and French armies had halted the German advance toward Paris, and it seemed only a matter of time before the invaders would be pushed back out of France. But Harry's own darker instincts contradicted such optimism, and the deadly trench warfare that was unfolding on the Western Front in the autumn of 1914 would soon justify his fears.

Harry watched his world crumble from his garden at Lamb House. In spite of the richness of his fruit trees and the comforts of his small Georgian mansion, he felt his whole life had been blighted: "We eat and drink . . . we sleep and wake and live and breathe only the War," he wrote an American friend, "and it is a bitter enough regimen . . . I hoped I shouldn't live on, disillusioned and horror-ridden, to see the like of it." It comforted him a little to have two of William's children to keep him company. His youngest nephew, Aleck, who aspired to be a painter, had recently daubed his own portrait of his distinguished uncle. Harry's twenty-seven-year-old niece, Peggy, also sat with him in his garden, reading to him the war bulletins. Although high-strung like her aunt, Alice, Margaret Mary James also had her mother's and grand-mother's ability to listen, to soothe, and to comment intelligently.

Even so, William's children belonged to a generation of young Americans who, with their noisy and uneducated friends, struck Harry as wholly uncouth. Civilization seemed under attack everywhere. Writing to a seasoned friend in August 1914, Harry rued that the "ornaments" of his own generation, himself and his sophisticated friends, had lived to witness "this wreck of our belief that through the long years we had seen civilization grow and the worst become impossible." He averted his face from "such a monstrous scene," hoping only that "we shall again be gathered into a blessed little Chelsea drawing-room—it will be like the reopening of the salons, so irrepressibly, after the French revolution." Mostly he felt his own helplessness to do anything about it. "I go to sleep, as if I were dog-tired with action," he wrote Edith Wharton from Lamb House, "yet feel like the chilled vieillards [old men] of old epics, infirm and helpless at home with women, while the plains are ringing with battle."

In Chelsea that winter, as the fighting bogged down in the mud of France, Harry was "infinitely" troubled by the radical wartime changes he saw in London. The scintillating life of a golden age had quickly faded, he thought, into "grey mists of insignificance." Certainly, the rigors of the war had further exacerbated Harry's isolation and social alienation. He spent the long afternoons and evenings at his lonely perch above the yellow, barge-laden river. As Harry reported to Hugh Walpole, "People 'meet' a little, but very little, every social habit and convention has broken down." Harry, at seventy-one and feeling his age, only wanted to see a few people, old friends who knew and understood him.

As the servants laid his lonely tea during the dark winter of 1914–15, Harry repeatedly faced both a frightening future as well as a lacerated past. He had stark reasons for feeling abandoned. Again, as during the

Civil War, young men were signing up, boarding transports, and dying on distant battlefields: not Antietam and Gettysburg, now, but Mons, Ypres, and the Marne. And, at least as much as in the earlier war, these were young men whom Harry loved.

Harry's handsome young friend Rupert Brooke had already fought in Belgium, in the ill-fated expedition to Antwerp. This young Cambridge poet, with his sweeping forelocks, would grow famous for his wartime sonnets and his premature death from septicemia off of the Greek island of Skyros in 1915. Jocelyn Persse had joined the Royal Fusiliers. Only Hugh Walpole tried to make himself an exception to this rule. Excused from war service because of poor eyesight, Hugh found himself accused of shirking by society women who sent him white feathers betokening cowardice. Whenever he had the chance, Harry roundly defended his young protégé. But all too soon Hugh, too, went off to Russia, to serve as a war journalist and later to join the Red Cross.

Even Harry's faithful valet, Burgess Noakes, would sign up for service with the British army in France. Wounded later by an exploding shell, little Burgess would suffer multiple injuries including the permanent loss of most of his hearing. Harry, stripped of his longtime assistant, had resorted to borrowing Edith Wharton's man, Frederick, to turn out his socks and arrange his vested suits. Yet such creature comforts or discomforts paled in comparison to what Harry clear-sightedly understood as the "huge enormity" of the war, "the younger lives, the fine seed of the future, that are offered and taken."

Harry visited hospitals, as he'd done during the Civil War. He haunted St. Bartholomew's Hospital, near St. Paul's Cathedral, as casualties from Belgium poured in. There, in the relative shelter furnished by James Gibbs's graceful Georgian quadrangle, Harry "almost discovered [his] vocation in life to be the beguiling and drawing-out of the suffering soldier." Though Harry was genuinely moved to compassion, his *almost* was telling. It rang with the echoes of that earlier war in which he'd also been both deeply embroiled but strangely aloof. Although he could speak fluently and beautifully to the Francophone wounded—as few others could—Harry still kept his distance, as he'd done as a dapper young man during the 1860s. It still wasn't his nature to abandon himself to Walt Whitman's kind of instinctive, physical, compassionate devotion to dying young soldiers. His personal reserve still ruled him, holding him at arm's length from such raw suffering. Yet something broke through his reserve, one night at Victoria Station. As he was buying an evening newspaper, he encountered the "bad lameness of a poor hobbling khaki convalescent," which flooded him with impulsive generosity. Perhaps on an unconscious level this maimed soldier had reminded Harry of his amputated father or wounded brother Wilkie.

Harry did what he could for the war effort. In the cause of Belgian refugees, he found himself less suited to nursing than to philanthropic fund-raising. In March 1915, in the first dark spring of the war, Harry told Edith Wharton that he had assisted at a charitable voice recital by a Belgian baritone, presided over the mesmerizing Réjane—Gabrielle-Charlotte Réjane, the legendary French comedienne, then in her late fifties.

At this afternoon event, Harry helped host two exiled Belgian Napoleonic aristocrats, Prince Victor Napoléon and Princess Clémentine. The fortyish Clémentine of Saxe-Coburg-Gotha, princess of Belgium, lively and dark-haired, had recently married her longtime forbidden sweetheart and then duly provided him with two small dynastic offspring. Through various family machinations, Prince Victor had been designated imperial heir of the ambitious Napoléon Bonaparte and the vainglorious Louis-Napoléon; he was the embodiment, with his handlebar mustache, of the now-deposed French imperial house. From exile, he was still hammering away at the lost cause of a once-brilliant upstart dynasty, now cobwebbed and anachronistic. In his role as prince imperial, Victor Napoléon would leave Harry with a profound conscious and unconscious imprint. He and his wife, briefly Harry's collaborators, would furnish the novelist with one of his most bizarre and telling late-in-life obsessions, as would soon unfold.

Meanwhile, Harry was mostly focused on the tragedy of the war. With his beloved France being reduced to rubble—Rheims Cathedral, literally so, during 1914—he was increasingly furious with the United States for not supporting the Entente Powers, and he now mulled a symbolic gesture of protest. During the summer of 1915—with the trench war turning into a bloodbath, with the United States hanging back even after the dramatic sinking of the steamship *Lusitania* and the loss of a hundred American civilian lives—Harry contemplated acquiring British citizenship. In one sense, his naturalization seemed perfectly natural to him; he dated his becoming British from long before this crisis. He was ripe for the transfiguration, and he welcomed the intervention of his influential friends H. H. Asquith, the prime minister of Great Britain, and the young Winston Churchill, then the first lord of the Admiralty. After all, he'd lived in England for almost forty years and had long possessed something "so remarkably like" citizenship that, he said, "I wonder anyone can tell them apart—I myself being all but unable to."

At the same time, Harry's transmutation—which would prove unpopular in the United States—marked a bold move for a sensitive and battered old man. Harry wished to protest what he saw as pro-German American neutrality when, at home in Chelsea, he could see and hear the ominous drone of the night-flying German Zeppelins, "with their peculiarly unerring instinct for poor old women and young children," as he put it. Zeppelins actually made poor bombers, being vulnerable to fire and almost as combustible as Henry Senior's small balloons had been at the Albany Academy back in 1824. Still, more than a hundred civilians would be killed in raids on East Anglia in 1915, and the newspaper accounts filled Harry with indignation. "I daresay many Americans *will* be shocked at my 'step,'" Harry wrote John Singer Sargent, "so many of them appear in these days to be shocked at everything that is not a reiterated blandishment and slobberation of Germany."

He'd waited "long months, watch in hand," Harry said, for help from the country of his birth. "But it seemed never to come," he said, his war concerns tapping into a deeper and more complex resentment. Harry felt fury with the American government, to be sure, but he was also still wrestling with his own lifelong, deeply felt Jamesian need for approval and acknowledgment. "It would really have been so easy for the U.S. to have 'kept' (if they had cared to!) yours all faithfully."

For decades, Harry's political and cultural allegiance to the United States had always been fraught. And the nation shared this distinction with Harry's own family. During some of his medical sufferings in the spring of 1913, Mrs. Alice—ever solicitous about a beloved brother-in-law she'd promised her late husband to look after—invited Harry to come stay with her and her family in Cambridge.

"You can see, can't you?" Harry wrote back in alarm,

> how strange and desperate it would be to "chuck" everything up, Lamb House, servants, Miss Bosanquet, *this* newly acquired and prized resource [Carlyle Mansions], to come over, by a formidable and expensive journey, to spend a summer in the . . . utterly arid and vacuous Cambridge. Dearest Alice, I could come back to America (could be carried back on a stretcher) to *die*—but never, never to live . . . but when I think how little Boston and Cambridge were of old ever *my* affair, or anything but an accident, for me, of the parental life there to which I occasionally and painfully and losingly sacrificed, I have a superstitious terror of seeing them at the end of time again stretch out strange inevitable tentacles to draw me back and destroy me.

Harry's "superstitious terror" of Cambridge proved alive and on guard even after decades of exile. It especially seemed so, now that he was increasingly weak, lonely, and troubled by illness. Even two years later, at the age of seventy-two, a British citizen being considered for knighthood in 1915, Harry could still dread the "strange inevitable tentacles," as he saw them, of the old family life that had so thoroughly defined and deformed him.

As the winter of 1915 deepened, it seemed the trench war had frozen into a horrifying permanent fact of life—though the German general Erich von Falkenhayn was plotting to break out of the trenches later that winter with his assault on the French garrison town of Verdun.

On December 1, Harry tore himself away from the newspapers to write his niece Peggy, to thank her for some photographs of San Francisco that she had sent him. He tried to cover other topics of family interest, as he had done for so many years, but soon he had to give up in exhaustion. He had dictated the letter to Theodora Bosanquet, his assistant, but at the close of it he said, "The pen drops from my hand!"

The next day, on December 2, Harry suffered what one of his live-in maids at Carlyle Mansions described as "a kind of stroke." In alarm, the capable Theodora Bosanquet immediately cabled the United States.

Mrs. Alice, though nearly seventy years old, immediately booked passage on a steamer and packed her trunk.

In Chelsea, meanwhile, Harry's stroke had made him even more vulnerable than ever before. He told one friend who visited him, Fanny Prothero, that he had heard a voice in the room, not his own, speaking distinctly. "So here it is at last," the voice had said, "the distinguished thing." But what was this "distinguished thing," and how was it now going to manifest itself? And how could Harry face it, as alone as he was?

With his mind starting to unravel, Harry clung to his longtime habit of formulating narratives out loud. For years now, since long before the days of Miss Bosanquet, Harry had dictated his massive correspondence, his intricate short stories, and his magisterial novels. Harry's sister, Alice, too, had dictated through her last hours, and Harry was now following her into that twilight realm. From habit, now—from James family tradition, almost—Harry summoned Miss Bosanquet and her notepad. And, patiently attending her failing employer and personal hero, Harry's assistant would soon take down some of the most curious correspondence in literary history.

In his disorientation after his stroke, Harry mixed up the history of the James family with that of the Bonapartes. Perhaps remembering his recent charity appearance with the uprooted royals, he hit on a weird but strangely apt parallel between these two clans that had risen from obscurity (wealthy Scots-Irish obscurity, in the case of the Jameses) to surprising prominence.

"Dear and most esteemed brother and sister," Harry intoned, taking on the voice of a Bonaparte, "I call your attention to the precious enclosed transcripts of plans and designs for the decoration of certain apartments of the palaces, here, of the Louvre and the Tuileries." He saw, inside his head, the grand facade of the Tuileries Palace, which had been burned down in 1871, and of the Second Empire Louvre as it had risen up, clean and new, near the Jameses' modest hotel during the family's visit to Paris in 1855.

In another "letter," which Theodora carefully took down, Harry conjured up the long-dead sister of Napoléon Bonaparte, Princess Caroline Murat, the queen of Naples: "There have been great families of tricksters and conjurers, so why not this one, so pleasant withal? Our admirable father keeps up the pitch," Harry confided to the princess. "Great families of tricksters and conjurers" weirdly described the Jameses as well as the Bonapartes. In this "letter," Harry signed himself "Napoléone," using the Corsican version of the late emperor's name. He even spelled it out, meticulously and considerately, for Miss Bosanquet.

In a later dictation on December 12, Harry veered back toward his own family, without, however, abandoning his imperial illusion. He had conquered, Harry said, and he wanted William and Mrs. Alice to share in the spoils. "My dear brother and sister," Harry dictated—forgetting that his brother had been dead now for six years and that his sister-in-law was at sea and unreachable, "I offer you great opportunities in the exchange for the exercise of a great zeal . . . I have displayed you as persons of great taste and judgment. Don't leave me a sorry figure in consequence but present me rather as your very fond but not infatuation able [sic] and ready to back you up." Significantly, that odd phrase had cropped up again—about wanting to "back" his family and be backed. It was a strange, grandiose way of asking for love or of offering it. And it was a need that had dominated Harry's life long before his first and second strokes began to break down the great Roman walls of his reserve.

On the evening of December 13, Mrs. Alice arrived in Chelsea after a stormy Atlantic crossing. The old lady had passed through submarine-ridden wartime waters, at the very real risk of becoming a shipwreck casualty, like the passengers on the *Lusitania*. But her love for William, and for Harry himself, had steeled her to danger.

In the last half of December, as Christmas approached, Harry sometimes left his bed, moving vaguely and restlessly from one chair to another in the drawing room. He murmured about going back to Rye. Disoriented, he even imagined he'd gone there while having a conversation with Burgess Noakes, who had now returned from the front. All the while, Harry had a nervous, twitching impulse to write, but his hands wouldn't form letters, and he resorted to dictations once again. With his mind sinking, the messages were briefer, amounting to mere muttered fragments. Peggy, too, was now on hand, and Harry's niece obligingly took down what she could in longhand, in the occasional absences of the capable Miss Bosanquet.

"Across the border," Harry said. "All the pieces," Harry said.

"Problems are very sordid," he said. Then: "I never dreamed of such duties as laid upon me."

The old man was increasingly slipping out of lucidity. No one in the family now knew if anything they told him really reached him—there in that infinitely distant place where he'd withdrawn. "Beloved Alice," Harry said, recognizing his sister-in-law briefly. He told her to tell William he was leaving in two days—again forgetting his brother was dead. "Stay with me Alice," Harry muttered, "stay with me." And Alice did stay. But before the end of February 1916, Harry would be dead—willing his house at Rye to his square-jawed eldest nephew and name-sake, leaving his whole estate to William's family. To avoid the complications of wartime, Mrs. Alice would smuggle Harry's ashes back into the United States, and they would be buried beside his parents, William and Alice, in Cambridge Cemetery.

Two months before he died, Harry was awarded one of his greatest honors, although, for his family, it was a bittersweet moment. Alice, Peggy, and Henry III (still called "Harry" in the family, as his uncle had been) gathered around the half-paralyzed man who lay in a lounge chair by his big windows overlooking the river, sometimes gripping Burgess Noakes's small rough hand, and told him that in the New Year's Honours List on January 1, 1916, he had received the Order of Merit. Harry's friends had persuaded the prime minister, Herbert Asquith, to have King George V grant him this high distinction, previously bestowed on only two other British novelists.

The family tried to convey what Harry had earned—the kind of validation the exiled Jameses had pursued all their lives and that he himself had long craved. But in his last days, Harry was elsewhere. He'd entirely glided away. Mrs. Alice observed a ravaged old man, once again child-like, who appeared to think he was "voyaging and visiting foreign cities." Had he become again the twelve-year-old Harry, pinkened with the fever of malaria, bumping along in a nest of family luggage, bound for a distant garden of orange blossoms? Or had he reverted to another Chelsea, one not torn by war, one not bleared by sickness, where he drank tea at Carlyle's house with his father, more than half a century before? His father's bright-eyed limp, the rustle of his mother's dress, were finally more real to him than the empires he had won.

Notes

Abbreviations Used in Notes

PEOPLE

AHGJ	Alice Howe Gibbens James ("Mrs. Alice")
AJ	Alice James
CFW	Constance Fenimore Woolson ("Fenimore")
CW	Catharine Walsh ("Aunt Kate")
GWJ	Garth Wilkinson James ("Wilkie")
HJ	Henry James Jr. ("Harry")
HJSr	Henry James Sr.
JJGW	Dr. James John Garth Wilkinson
MJ	Mary Walsh James
MT	Mary Temple ("Minny")
RJ	Robertson James ("Bob")
WJ	William James

LIBRARIES AND ARCHIVES

H	Houghton Library, Harvard
MHS	Massachusetts Historical Society, Boston
S	Swedenborg Society Library, London
W	Rare Books Collection, Wellesley College

PRINTED SOURCES

(For full publication information, see Bibliography.)

A	Henry James Jr., *The American*
AJB	Jean Strouse, *Alice James: A Biography*

AJD	Alice James, *Diary*
AM	*Atlantic Monthly*
AS	Henry James Jr., *The American Scene*
BB	Rosella Mamoli Zorzi, *Beloved Boy*
BBF	Jane Maher, *Biography of Broken Fortunes*
CCL	Thomas Carlyle and Jane Welsh Carlyle, *Collected Letters*
CLHJ	Henry James Jr., *Complete Letters of Henry James*
CWE	Henry James III, *Charles William Eliot*
DBF	Susan E. Gunter and Steven H. Jobe, *Dearly Beloved Friends*
DLAJ	Ruth Bernard Yeazell, *The Death and Letters of Alice James*
EEL	Ellen Tucker Emerson, *Letters*
EJ	Ralph Waldo Emerson, *Journals and Miscellaneous Notebooks*
EL	Ralph Waldo Emerson, *Letters*
F	Alfred Habegger, *The Father*
HJAL	Leon Edel, *Henry James: A Life* (1 vol.)
HJL	Henry James Jr., *Letters*
HJWB	Alfred Habegger, *Henry James and the Woman Business*
JHM	Julian Hawthorne, *Memoirs*
LHJ	Leon Edel, *The Life of Henry James* (5 vols.)
LM	Henry James Sr., *Lectures and Miscellanies*
LR	Henry James Sr., *Literary Remains*
NHJ	Henry James Jr., *The Complete Notebooks*
NSB	Henry James Jr., *Notes of a Son and Brother*
NYTimes	*New York Times*
NYTrib	*New York Tribune*
PL	Henry James Jr., *The Portrait of a Lady*
PP	Henry James Jr., *Portraits of Places*
RH	Henry James Jr., *Roderick Hudson*
RS	William Walsh, *A Record and Sketch of Hugh Walsh's Family*
SBO	Henry James Jr., *A Small Boy and Others*
SC	Edward Emerson, *The Early Years of the Saturday Club*
SRFM	Henry James Sr., *Society the Redeemed Form of Man*
TS	Henry James Jr., *Transatlantic Sketches*
VRE	William James, *The Varieties of Religious Experience*
WJL	William James, *Correspondence*
WS	Henry James Jr., *Washington Square*
WWS	Henry James Jr., *William Wetmore Story and His Friends*

Introduction: A Contemporary Portrait of the Jameses

PAGE

1 "Success has always been the biggest liar": Friedrich Nietzsche, *Beyond Good and Evil*, trans. R. J. Hollingdale (New York: Penguin, 2003), 207.

1 "In everything they undertake they do well": Alice Miller, *The Drama of the Gifted Child [Drama des begabten Kindes]*, trans. Ruth Ward (New York: Basic Books, 1981), 6.

1 "When you travel, your first discovery is that you do not exist": Elizabeth Hardwick, *Sleepless Nights* (New York: Random House, 1979), 5.

1 "We were, to my sense, the blest group of us": Henry James Jr., *A Small Boy and Others* (New York: Charles Scribner's Sons, 1913), 2. Hereafter *SBO*.

2 "geniuses": see, for example, Maxwell Geismar, *Henry James and His Cult* (London: Chatto, 1964).

6 Henry Senior lived for nearly three decades as an alcoholic: Alfred Habegger is the one biographer who substantially acknowledges Henry's alcoholism, but even his discussion is limited to several scattered references: See Alfred Habegger, *The Father: A Life of Henry James, Sr.* (New York: Farrar, Straus and Giroux, 1994), 57, 90–92, 118–20, 151. Hereafter *F*. In the historical source material, many references to Henry Senior's alcoholism are indirect, though they are persistent in his life at least until the 1850s.

6 a lively debate about the novelist's sexuality: This debate is extensive, ongoing, and sometimes hotly contested. Eve Kosofsky Sedgwick provided early landmarks in this dispute, with her sophisticated analysis of HJ as reflected in his fiction. See Sedgwick, *The Epistemology of the Closet* (Berkeley: University of California Press, 1990), 182–212; see also Sedgwick's influential definition of *homosocial desire* in *Between Men: English Literature and Male Homosocial Desire* (New York: Columbia University Press, 1985), 1–20. Other critics have argued against Sedgwick's readings of HJ's sexuality: see Philip Horne, "Henry James: The Master and the 'Queer Affair' of 'The Pupil,'" *Critical Quarterly* (Autumn 1995), 75–92. Biographers have also differed in their depictions. Leon Edel, HJ's main twentieth-century biographer, systematically downplayed the evidence of homoerotic desire in HJ's life, though late in his career acknowledged "psychosexual problems" in his final version of HJ's biography: see Leon Edel, *Henry James: A Life* (New York: Harper and Row, 1985), 723–75 (hereafter *HJAL*). Fred Kaplan creates an effective portrait of HJ's repression and his enmeshment with his family in *Henry James: The Imagination of Genius: A Biography* (New York, William Morrow, 1992); and Sheldon M. Novick argues for actually gay sexual experience in *Henry James: The Young Master* (New York: Random House, 1996), xi–xvii. For general discussions of the sexuality of Henry James Jr., see Hugh Stevens, *Henry James and Sexuality* (Cambridge, England: Cambridge University Press, 1998), who views HJ as increasingly daring in his late life, although still constrained by his Victorian upbringing; John R. Bradley, ed., *Henry James and Homo-Erotic Desire* (London: Macmillan, 1999), and Peggy McCormack, ed., *Questioning the Master: Gender and Sexuality in Henry James's Writings* (Newark, DE: University of Delaware Press, 2000), two collections of scholarly essays on this subject; and Susan E. Gunter and Steven H. Jobe's introduction to *Dearly Beloved Friends: Henry James's Letters to Younger Men* (Ann Arbor: University of Michigan Press, 2001), 1–12 (hereafter *DBF*), which gives an excellent overview of the issue.

Chapter 1: The Voyage of the *Atlantic*

11 "thoroughly hot": *NYTrib*, 28 June 1855.

12 "acquisition of the languages"; "New York fetish": *SBO*, 195.

12 "fool's paradise"; "Society everywhere is a conspiracy"; "Whoso would be a man": Ralph Waldo Emerson, "Self Reliance" in *The Complete Works of Ralph Waldo Emerson*, with a biographical introduction by Edward Waldo Emerson, 10 vols. (Boston: Houghton Mifflin, 1903), 2:81, 49, 50.

13 a public declaration . . . that he had given up drinking: JJGW to HJSr, 13 July 1849; 3 August 1849, Swedenborg Society Library (hereafter S); "Intemperance," *NYTrib*, 26 August 1851.

14 "sensuous education": Henry James Jr., *Notes of a Son and Brother* (New York: Charles Scribner's Sons, 1914), 195–96, hereafter *NSB*; Ralph Barton Perry, *The Thought and Character of William James*, 2 vols. (Boston: Little, Brown, 1935), 1:59.

14 "social consciousness"; "race": Henry later declared that "the family is literally the seminary of the race, or constitutes the sole Divine seed out of which the social consciousness of man ultimately flowers": Henry James Sr., *The Literary Remains of the Late Henry James*, ed. with an introduction by William James (Boston: Houghton Mifflin, 1884), 175. Hereafter *LR*.

14 "chickens": HJSr to Samuel Ward, 9 March 1854, James Papers, Houghton Library (hereafter H): bMS Am 1093.1 (15).

15 "hotel children": *SBO*, 30.

15 "lolling and bumping": Ibid., 236.

16 an enormous trunk: This trunk, and Henry James Sr.'s traveling volumes, with their annotations, have been preserved at the Swedenborgian Library in Berkeley, California.

16 "vast, even though incomplete"; "strain"; "Father's Ideas": *NSB* 156, 158.

16 *Mansions of England in the Olden Time*: *SBO*, 19.

17 "not to be drowned"; laughing assurances": HJ to Catharine Barber James, 28[?] August 1860, Henry James Jr., *Henry James Letters*, ed. Leon Edel, 4 vols. (Cambridge, MA: Belknap Press of Harvard University, 1974–84), 1:34. Hereafter *HJL*.

18 "Byzantine": George Templeton Strong, *The Diary of George Templeton Strong*, ed. Allan Nevins and Milton Halsey Thomas (New York: Macmillan, 1952), 1:357.

18 "telegraph line on the premises"; "wearily trailed through it": Isabella Bird, quoted in Kenneth T. Jackson and David S. Dunbar, eds., *Empire City: New York Through the Centuries* (New York: Columbia University Press, 2002), 235.

18 "covered with gaudy paintings": William Chambers, *Things as They Are in America* (Philadelphia: Lippincott, Grambo, 1854), 175.

18 "National Baby Show": *NYTrib*, 4 May 1855.

18 "bottled mermaids": *SBO*, 155.

19 "missed fire": Alice James, *The Diary of Alice James*, ed. Leon Edel, with a new intro. by Linda Simon (Boston: Northeastern University Press, 1999), 63. Hereafter *AJD*.

19 "iridescent and gilded card": *SBO*, 21.

19 "covetable things" and "appetizing nuggets": Strong, 2:132.

20 "Mr. James"; "Legitimacy and Significance of the Institution of Property"; "no news"; "no tidings"; "no trace": *NYTrib*, 4 February 1851.

20 "I am surprised": Ibid., 13 February 1851.

20 THE ATLANTIC SAFE AT CORK!: Ibid., 17 February 1851.

20 "Ladies and gentlemen": *SBO*, 278.

20 "*abords* [outskirts] of the hot town"; "rank and rubbishy"; "where big loose cobbles": Ibid., 69–70.

21 "supported right and left by a gilded mermaid": "The Collins Line of Steamships," *NYTrib*, 22 April 1850.

21 English travelers: Quoted in John Malcolm Brinnin, *The Sway of the Grand Saloon: A Social History of the North Atlantic* (New York: Delacorte Press, 1971), 173.

21 "floating palace"; "the most beautiful specimen of marine architecture afloat": "The Collins Line of Steamships."

21 "exclusive use of extra-size state-rooms"; "experienced surgeon": Advertisement, *NYTrib*, 7 May 1855.

21 "lemonade (frozen)": Quoted in Brinnin, 180.

22 escutcheons of the states: "The Collins Line of Steamships."

22   brocatelle marble, etc.: Quoted in Brinnin, 171.
22   "white holly, satin-wood, and rosewood"; "their numbers quadrupled": "The
     Collins Line of Steamships."
22   "Demon of the Sea": HJ to Thomas Sergeant Perry, 18 November [1859],
     HJL, 1:7.
22   "very nasty weather nearly the whole of the passage": HJSr, "An American in
     Europe I," *NYTrib*, 3 September 1855.
23   "rich carpeting": "The Collins Line of Steamships."
23   But only two members of the family felt well enough: See Jean Strouse, *Alice
     James: A Biography* (Boston: Houghton Mifflin, 1980), 35. Hereafter *AJB*.
23   green turtle soup, etc.: Quoted in Brinnin, 180.
24   "to 'the lower classes' ": Quoted in *F*, 364.
24   "manly and good-hearted"; "the menace plucked out of every storm": "An
     American in Europe I."
25   "What account of us all": *NSB*, 177.
25   "mother's heart paints a future for [her] boys": MJ to Emma Wilkinson, 29
     November 1846, James Papers, H: bMS Am 1093.1 (65).

Chapter 2: Panic

28   "balloon-flying"; "motive power"; "heated air supplied from a tow ball satu-
     rated with spirits of turpentine"; "roll of fire"; "thinking only of the confla-
     gration": William James, *The Letters of William James*, ed. Henry James III, 2
     vols. (Boston: Atlantic Monthly Press, 1920), 1:7–8.
29   "a glowing fire of animal spirits"; "under the magical light of the morning":
     LR, 186.
29   working-class rebellion: *F*, 56. My account owes much to Habegger's excellent
     and painstaking reconstruction of the details of Henry's teenage accident as well
     as other earlier points in the history of the James family. Habegger conceives of
     the shoemakers' group as a sort of "revolutionary salon for young boys."
29   $1.2 million: Ibid., 112. This figure is Habegger's estimation, correcting the
     long-assumed figure of $3 million.
30   "exhibition of authority towards us": *LR*, 188.
30   emotional distance: See Habegger's discussion in *F*, 48–50.
30   "awash in spirits": Ibid., 57.
31   gallon of corn whiskey cost only about twenty-five cents: See Thomas R. Pe-
     gram, *Battling Demon Rum: The Struggle for a Dry America, 1800–1933*
     (Chicago: Ivan R. Dee, 1998), 9.
31   "the habit of taking a drink of raw gin or brandy": HJSr to RJ, [c. 1875–77],
     quoted in *F*, 57.
31   "protect them from becoming drunkards": W. J. Rorabaugh, *The Alcoholic Re-
     public: An American Tradition* (New York: Oxford University Press, 1979), 14.
31   the highest per capita consumption of alcohol in American history: Ibid., 10;
     Pegram, 7.
31   "strangely self-contradictory": *F*, 44. For an in-depth discussion of the com-
     plexities of Henry's early family, see *F*, 44–57.
32   "anxiety": *LR*, 188.
32   "certainly a very easy parent": Ibid., 147.
32   "never so happy at home as away from it"; "horse talk"; "rheumatism,
     [M]ethodism, and miracle": Ibid., 188–89.

32 the Erie Canal: For a description of the cutting-edge technology used to create the Erie Canal, see Ruth Schwartz Cowan, *A Social History of American Technology* (New York: Oxford University Press, 1997), 102–5.

33 "burned-over district": Michael Barkun, *Crucible of the Millennium: The Burned-Over District of New York in the 1840s* (Syracuse, NY: Syracuse University Press, 1986), 2. Barkun notes, about the origin of this phrase, that the "incendiary metaphor evoked the emotional conflagrations of religious excitement that later led the greatest nineteenth-century revivalist, Charles Grandison Finney, to observe, 'I found that region of the country what, in the western phrase, would be called, "a burnt district."'"

33 more than thirteen hundred revivals: Ibid., 23.

33 Rochester rappings: See Janet Oppenheim, *The Other World: Spiritualism and Psychical Research in England, 1850–1914* (Cambridge, England: Cambridge University Press, 1985), 11.

34 "had to be amputated"; "ill-done": Caroline Dall, Journals, 25 June 1866, Caroline Wells Healy Dall Papers, Massachusetts Historical Society (hereafter MHS).

34 "gun-shot wound"; "an exalted sense of his affection"; "My wound had been very severe": *LR*, 147.

35 "revulsion": *NSB*, 113.

36 "an excellent whip": Ibid., 192.

36 abused and gifted children: See Alice Miller's discussion of grandiosity and "depression as the reverse of grandiosity" in Miller, 33–39.

37 "The militia are under arms, as riots are expected"; IOUs for . . . oysters: Frederick Marryat, *A Diary in America, with Remarks on Its Institutions* (New York: D. Appleton, 1839), 17.

38 an estate valued at $25,000: *F*, 172.

39 "quiet and genteel retirement": Henry James Jr., *Washington Square* (New York: Modern Library, 1950), 21. Hereafter *WS*.

39 "great shock"; "overwhelmed . . . with grief"; "she secluded herself"; "allowed to display their finery"; "best, second best, and calico"; "warm-hearted, kind, [and] hospitable": William Walsh, *A Record and Sketch of Hugh Walsh's Family* (Newburgh, NY: Newburgh Journal, 1908), 9-10, H: bMS Am 1092.9 (4600), folder 9. Hereafter *RS*.

41 "strong"; "properly made"; "Her appearance of health": *WS*, 18.

41 she appreciated the novel: "I am very pleased that you have liked *Washington Square* and hope you will to the end," Henry wrote to his mother. HJ to MJ, 31 October 1880, *HJL*, 2:312.

42 "love-story": *NSB*, 282.

42 "oratorio concerts": *RS*, 9.

42 breakfasts of fried ham and salt fish: For typical details of an American lady's life in the 1830s, see Frances Trollope, *Domestic Manners of the Americans*, ed. Donald Smalley (New York: Knopf, 1949), 281–82.

42 Mary and Kate plied at their needlework: As they did also in later years; see WJ to HJSr, [1860], William James, *The Correspondence of William James*, ed. Ignas K. Skrupskelis and Elizabeth M. Berkeley, with the assistance of Wilma Bradbear and Bernice Grohskopf, 12 vols. (Charlottesville: University Press of Virginia, 1992–2004), 4:27. Hereafter *WJL*.

43 favorite cousin, Helen Wyckoff: *SBO*, 122–23.

43 "a large roll of all those indescribable matters": Trollope, 281.

43 "prudent dispenser of charities": *RS*, 10.

43 "long, shrill city": *WS*, 22.

43 pigs often trotted: Charles Dickens, *American Notes* (New York: St. Martin's Press, 1985), 78.

44 "a moving bed of tulips": Henry Tudor, *Narrative of a Tour in North America* (London: J. Duncan, 1834), 1:32.

44 "flaunting air," etc.: Thomas Colley Grattan, *Civilized America*, 2 vols. (London: Bradbury and Evans, 1859), 1:102.

44 "high flyer at Fashion": The phrase comically describes the overdressed Mrs. Boffin in Charles Dickens's *Our Mutual Friend* (1864–65).

44 "in spite of her taste in fine clothes": *WS*, 20.

45 "old Scotch Presbyterian divine"; "Darkly must her prospect"; "divine"; "fulminate": HJ to Thomas Sergeant Perry, [1 November 1863], *HJL*, 1:44.

45 "public worship, and private tea-drinkings": Trollope, 75.

46 "good Cork leg": Joseph Henry, *Papers*, ed. Nathan Reingold et al., 10 vols. to date (Washington, DC: Smithsonian Institution Press, 1972–), 3:380, 429.

46 tried to deal with his alcohol addiction: In 1835, Habegger theorizes, Henry stayed in a temperance hotel in Canandaigua, New York, and was hence "off the bottle"; see *F*, 120. But Henry's drinking habits are usually much more difficult to read, from historical evidence. Alcoholics then as now were good at keeping their problems a secret, even from the people nearest to them.

47 "so intoxicated with the roads and lanes": *NSB*, 270.

47 "the power to dazzle": Ibid., 266.

47 "morbid doctrinal conscience": *LR*, 178.

47 "colour and savour": *NSB*, 156.

48 "talk and temper"; "original charm": Ibid., 211.

48 "superior intellect, easy and affable manners"; "new element"; "generous hospitality": *RS*, 9–10.

49 "strong attraction": Ibid., 10.

49 The word *attraction* in the nineteenth century: See *F*, 174, where Habegger argues that this word is ambiguous at best and doesn't necessarily offer proof that Kate Walsh, too, had erotic feelings for Henry James Sr. Caution is definitely warranted, but the power of the bonds between these people was still strong in William Walsh's memory in 1903, six decades after these events occurred: "There is such a thing in human life as a strong attraction taking place between parties on a short acquaintance," he wrote. "Such seems to have been the case with Mr. James and Mary and Catharine Walsh": *RS*, 10.

49 "reduced to driving"; "could circulate": *NSB*, 192.

50 "grief": *RS*, 10.

51 "loveliest of women": Quoted in *F*, 141.

51 "listen with the whole of her usefulness": *NSB*, 177–78.

51 "complete availability": Ibid.

52 "caught the reverberations of the inward mystic choir": Ibid., 160.

52 "romantic youth"; "Bohemia": Ibid., 275.

53 "a firm rein": Quoted in Leon Edel, *The Life of Henry James* (Philadelphia: Lippincott, 1953–72), 1:43. Hereafter *LHJ*.

53 "essentially a *civil* contract": John Walker, *Essays and Correspondence*, 2 vols. (London: Longman, 1838), 2:309.

54 "wondrous gold headband": *SBO*, 233.

55 "ancient Astor House": Ibid., 7.

55 Astor House Hotel: See Eric Homberger, *Mrs. Astor's New York: Money and Social Power in a Gilded Age* (New Haven, CT: Yale University Press, 2002), 71n.

55 "better than anywhere else": William Chambers, quoted in Jackson and Dunbar, 226.

Chapter 3: Shadow Passions

58 "brilliantly lighted": *New Yorker*, 28 November 1840, quoted in Austin Baxter Keep, *History of the New York Society Library* (New York: De Vinne Press, 1908), 400–401.

59 "in my own house": HJ to Joseph Henry, Henry, *Papers*, 5:17.

59 "I love the fireside rather than the forum"; "passive"; "manly": "Intemperance," in Henry James Sr., *Lectures and Miscellanies* (New York: Redfield, 1852), 427–28. Hereafter *LM*.

59 In the temperance tracts of the time: For a discussion of nineteenth-century temperance tracts and their portrayal of "fallen drunkards and redeeming women," see Elaine Frantz Parsons, *Manhood Lost: Fallen Drunkards and Redeeming Women in the Nineteenth-Century United States* (Baltimore: Johns Hopkins University Press, 2003), 1–17.

60 "an unbusinesslike character"; "value of money"; "Wall Street people": Dr. James John Garth Wilkinson to HJSr, 20 February 1847, S.
Cult of True Womanhood: See Barbara Welter, *Dimity Convictions: The American Woman in the Nineteenth Century* (Athens, OH: Ohio University Press, 1976), 21–41.

60 A minor mystery surrounds this birth: Biographers disagree on this point; see *F*, 188; Linda Simon, *Genuine Reality: A Life of William James* (New York: Harcourt Brace, 1998), 18.

60 Grand hotels: I am indebted to Alfred Habegger for this historical insight.

61 "a certain lack of oxygen": *LR*, 152.

61 THE TIMES: Ralph Waldo Emerson, *The Letters of Ralph Waldo Emerson*, ed. Ralph L. Rusk, 6 vols. (New York: Columbia University Press, 1939), 3:14 (hereafter *EL*); John McAleer, *Ralph Waldo Emerson: Days of Encounter* (Boston: Little, Brown, 1984), 385.

62 "humorous scenes"; "mermaid"; "exhibition of learned canary birds": *EL*, 3:129–30n.

62 "low prices": Ibid., 3:14.

63 "commodious": *New Yorker*, 28 November 1840, quoted in Keep, 400–401.

63 "punctual as a clock"; "time-worn black body-coat and trousers"; "scarcely acknowledge the applause"; "not at us"; "grave music"; "His gestures were few and restrained"; "the Eagle of Olympian Jove": Julian Hawthorne, *The Memoirs of Julian Hawthorne*, ed. Edith Garrigues Hawthorne (New York: Macmillan, 1938), 103. Hereafter *JHM*.

63 "cold and embarrassed"; "warm[ed] into genuine eloquence"; "deep and clear": Emerson's reviews from Philadelphia, January 1843, cited in *EL*, 3:128n.

63 "The Times are the masquerade of the Eternities": From the version of this speech Emerson delivered a few months earlier: "Lecture on the Times, Read at the Masonic Temple, Boston, December 2, 1841," in Emerson, *Complete Works*, 1:259.

64 "one of the richest and most beautiful compositions": Walt Whitman, *Walt Whitman of the New York Aurora, Editor at Twenty-Two: A Collection of Recently Discovered Writings*, ed. Joseph J. Rubin and Charles H. Brown (State College, PA: Bald Eagle Press, 1950), 105.

64 "This *Ennui*, for which we Saxons had no name"; "Is there less oxygen": "Lecture on the Times," in Emerson, *Complete Works*, 1:284.

64 "glowed with many a true word," etc.: HJSr to Ralph Waldo Emerson, 3 [March 1842], quoted in Perry, 1:39–40.

65 "love letters": *EL*, 3:144.

66 "city of magnificence and steam"; "an imperial prosperity"; "Me my cabin fits better": Ibid., 3:20.
66 transcendentalism: For an accessible discussion of the transcendental movement, see Joel Myerson, *Transcendentalism: A Reader* (Oxford: Oxford University Press, 2000), xxv–xxxvii.
66 "I become a transparent eyeball": Emerson, *Nature*, in *Complete Works*, 1:10.
66 "wholly guiltless": *EL*, 3:18.
67 Martin Gay: For a discussion of this passage of Emerson's life, see Evelyn Barish, *Emerson: The Roots of Prophecy* (Princeton, NJ: Princeton University Press, 1989), 90–95.
67 "cold blue eyes": Ralph Waldo Emerson, *Journals and Miscellaneous Notebooks*, ed. William H. Gilman et al., 16 vols. (Cambridge, MA: Harvard University Press, 1960–82), 1:39. Hereafter *EJ*.
67 "a very manlike thorough seeing person": *EL*, 3:23.
67 "an independent right minded man"; "ten or twelve"; "expressed a strong sympathy": Ibid., 3:30.
67 "true comfort,—wise, gentle, polished, with heroic manners, and a serenity like the sun": *EJ*, 11:248.
68 on Henry's table: *EL*, 3:33.
68 "castellated and gabled"; "hallowed": Henry James Jr., *The American Scene*, ed. with an introduction by Leon Edel (Bloomington: Indiana University Press, 1968), 91. Hereafter *AS*.
68 wealthy Bond Street coterie: See Homberger, 87.
69 "When I take a few glasses of wine": "Temperance," in *LM*, 428.
69 as much as forty dollars per lecture: *EL*, 3:5.
69 "an accomplished scholar": *New York Evening Post*, 23 January 1843.
69 "outgoing to the world"; "I came to night": Perry, 1:41; *NSB*, 181–82.
70 "the most tranquil and wise of all the Round Table": *EL*, 3:147.
70 "young Washington phoenix": Ibid., 3:137.
70 "a good deal": Ibid., 3:144.
70 "another fine little boy"; "Tell Mrs. James": Quoted in *LHJ*, 1:42; Thomas Carlyle and Ralph Waldo Emerson, *Correspondence of Thomas Carlyle and Ralph Waldo Emerson*, 2 vols. (Boston: J. R. Osgood, 1883), 1:308; 2:38, 83, 252.
70 "But I must stop": HJSr to Ralph Waldo Emerson, 5 November [1843], quoted in *F*, 205.
71 Emerson maddeningly half invited: My account owes to Alfred Habegger's anatomy of this friendship. For a full treatment of Henry's early relation with Emerson, see *F*, 191–202.
71 "Invisible Emerson"; "Whenever I am with you": Perry, 1:42.
71 "man without a handle": *NSB*, 185; Perry, 1:51, 352.
72 "the best people flow off," etc.: *EL*, 3:203–104.
72 "good for his health": As quoted or paraphrased by Emerson in ibid., 3:212.
73 "love": Ibid., 3:213.
73 "winter in some mild English climate, Devonshire perhaps": *NSB*, 185.
73 "appalling and horrible to the last degree": Dickens, 14.
74 "Where the bowsprits of ships": Ibid., 74.
74 "escorted down the bay by seventeen steamboats": Strong, 1:86.
74 Isambard Kingdom Brunel: For a lively account of Brunel's contributions to steamship technology, see Peter Petroski, *Remaking the World: Adventures in Engineering* (New York: Knopf, 1997), 126–45.
74 "club-houses of London": Quoted in Brinnin, 56–57.
74 "a horsehair slab," etc.: Dickens, 1–2.
75 system of bells: See Brinnin, 57.

76   "really these Yankees"; "take the poker"; "If Mr Carlyle's *'increasing reputa-tion'* ": Thomas Carlyle and Jane Welsh Carlyle, *The Collected Letters of Thomas and Jane Welsh Carlyle*, ed. Charles Richard Sanders et al., 34 vols. (Durham, NC: Duke University Press, 1970–2006), 17:190. Hereafter *CCL*.

76   "drawling and *Sir*-ring": Ibid., 17:235.

77   "James is a very good fellow": Ibid., 17:180–81.

77   "Not a *bad* man"; "wife and wifes-sister"; "Of his two women": Ibid., 17:263.

78   "make up for her diffidence of speech"; a "witty person": *WS*, 19.

78   "the many hours of unalloyed entertainment": *LR*, 422.

78   "old Covenanting stock": Ibid., 428.

78   "gnashed his teeth": Ibid., 440.

78   "great critic"; "man of genius"; "man of ideas": Ibid., 422.

79   these judgments decades later: In the *Atlantic Monthly*, May 1881; *LR*, 470.

79   "almost sure finally to disappoint one's admiration": *LR*, 423.

79   "bibliomanical propensity," etc.: Dr. Wilkinson's memory, JJGW to HJSr, 2 March 1846, S.

79   "screamed incessantly": HJSr to Catherine Barber James, 5 January 1844, quoted in *F*, 218.

79   "as a baby in long clothes," etc.: *SBO*, 53–54.

80   "long walks and drives": *LR*, 59.

80   "looking down from her castle": HJSr to Catherine Barber James, 5 January 1844, H; quoted in *F*, 219.

80   "Divine seed": *LR*, 175.

81   "embers in the grate," etc.: Ibid., 59.

81   "insane career"; "infernal": Henry James Sr., *Substance and Shadow* (New York: AMS Press, 1983), 126.

82   "eminent physicians"; "overworked [his] brain"; "a life in the open air"; "cheerful company": *LR*, 60.

82   hydropathy: See *F*, 225–26.

82   "interference with [his] personal liberty"; "at this dismal water-cure": *LR*, 60, 62.

82   "the rich light and shade": Ibid., 61.

83   "one early spring morning through Hampstead": MJ to Emma Wilkinson, 29 November 1846, James Papers, H: bMS Am 1093.1 (65).

83   "happy time spent in and about London": *SBO*, 82.

83   "a lady of rare qualities": *LR*, 63–64.

83   "charmed": *NSB*, 174.

83   "It is very much as I had ventured to suspect": *LR*, 64.

83   "one of the stages of a regenerative process": Ibid., 65.

83   "possessed himself of certain volumes": *NSB*, 173.

83   "frantic"; "instead of standing any longer shivering on the brink"; "boldly plunge into the stream": *LR*, 66.

84   "independent and disturbingly irregular": *NSB*, 175.

84   "ghastly condition of mind": *LR*, 60.

Chapter 4: The Nursery of Geniuses

86   "It was here": *WS*, 22–23.

87   "buoyant": WJ to AJ, 25 December 1866, *WJL*, 4:149.

87   "delightfully amiable & genial": WJ to RJ, 23 May 1870, ibid., 4:407.
88   "treasure"; "imbibed": *SBO*, 83.
89   "bawl a good bit": MJ to RJ, 16 December [1874], quoted in *AJB*, 24.
89   "ought to husband all her strength": MJ to RJ, 27 September [1874], quoted in ibid.
89   "extreme": MJ to Emma Wilkinson, 28 May [1846], S.
89   "primitive steamboat": *AS*, 52.
89   Robert Fulton: See Cowan, 106–7.
89   "night of huge strange paddling," etc.: *SBO*, 178.
89   "softly-sighing widowed grandmother," etc.: Ibid., 4.
90   "pinkish red picked out with white," etc.: Ibid., 11.
90   "confined to [her] mother's sickroom"; "faithful nurse"; "little pets": MJ to Emma Wilkinson, 28 May [1846], S.
90   "stout brave presence": *SBO*, 122.
90   "Our admirable aunt": Ibid., 152.
91   "Henry's philoprogenitiveness"; "any increase of beauty in the family"; "shoved off"; "into his own hand the redress of his grievances"; "the ruling spirit of the nursery": MJ to Emma Wilkinson, 29 November 1846, James Papers, H: bMS Am 1093.1 (65).
91   "nurse": MJ to Emma Wilkinson, 28 May [1846], S.
92   "wet nursing often involved trading the life of a poor baby": Janet Lynne Golden, *A Social History of Wet Nursing in America: From Breast to Bottle* (Cambridge, England: Cambridge University Press, 1996), 97.
92   a rosy and mostly recovered Henry: As early as 1844, Thoreau's friend Ellery Channing described Henry "as a little fat, rosy Swedenborgian amateur, with the look of a broker & the brains and heart of a Pascal": Henry David Thoreau, *Correspondence*, ed. Walter Harding and Carl Bode (New York: New York University Press, 1958), 161.
92   "a region where the extension of the city": *WS*, 23.
92   "the poplars, the pigs, the poultry"; "world of quieter harmonies"; "dragons and sphinxes"; "anchorage of the spirit": *SBO*, 97–100.
93   "rural picturesqueness": *WS*, 23.
93   "mandatory ways": RJ to AHGJ, 24 February 1898, quoted in *AJB*, 24.
94   "How feeble and diluted": *AJD*, 32.
94   "torture chamber," etc.: *SBO*, 64–66.
94   "lying with folded hands": AJ to WJ, 29–30 January 1889, in Alice James, *The Death and Letters of Alice James*, ed. Ruth Bernard Yeazell (Berkeley: University of California Press, 1981), 158. Hereafter *DLAJ*.
95   "hanging on [her] skirts"; "the familiar Stewart headache": *SBO*, 66.
95   "overwhelmingly and irresistibly English": Ibid., 81.
95   "a small periodical in quarto form, covered in yellow": Ibid., 83.
95   "broad-bosomed, broad based old lady"; "blue cup": *WS*, 23.
95   " 'at home' among the theatres": *SBO*, 101.
96   "lived and moved at that time"; "flight across the ice-blocks": Ibid., 158–59.
97   "shocking bad manners": *NSB*, 196.
97   "Father used to spank me with a paper cutter": WJ to AJ, 31 August [1865], *WJL*, 4:116.
97   "*I* play with boys who curse and swear!": *SBO*, 259.
97   "All boys": Ibid., 260.
97   "at seated play with his pencil under the lamp": Ibid., 259.
97   "No stroke of it that I have recovered": *NSB*, 17.
97   "plied the pencil"; "critically, rapidly, or summarily": *SBO*, 260.

98   "standing five feet six or eight inches in [his] shoes": "The Laws of Creation," in *LM*, 317.

98   "frankly independent and disturbingly irregular . . . connection": *NSB*, 175.

98   "Mr. Emerson's room": Ibid., 205.

98   met the now-legendary Washington Irving on a Hudson steamboat: *SBO*, 61.

98   "I 'visualise' . . . the winter firelight": *NSB*, 204.

101   "You will like it better than anything he has ever written"; "It fills too with new meaning and beauty": MJ to Catharine Barber James, 14 January [1849 or 1855?], James Papers, H: MS Am 1093.1 (63).

101   "with an appreciation of that modest grasp": *NSB*, 176.

101   "the full music of the 'papers'": Ibid., 178.

101   "somehow too philosophic for life": Ibid., 180.

101   "might be 'wrong'": Ibid., 228.

101   "singularly unvaried and few"; "bundle of truths": *LR*, 9.

102   "Your father's *ideas*, you know—!": *NSB*, 161–62.

102   "delightedly derisive": Ibid., 179.

102   "vague grand things within"; "sat on the steps"; "caught reverberations of the inward mystic choir": Ibid., 159–60.

102   "the lovely Mother and Aunt": *NSB*, 43.

102   "sort of sub-antagonism": WJ to RJ, 23 May 1870, *WJL*, 4:407.

103   "cheery strenuousness": HJSr to ET, fragment [1853?], H, quoted in *F*, 302.

103   Lajos Kossuth, the dashingly bearded Hungarian nationalist: See *AJB*, 32.

103   "So Miss Walsh is in hot water!"; "We do not wonder at it"; "doctrinal": JJGW to HJSr, 18 September 1847, S.

103   "more in the intellect than the affections": WJ to the James family, 15 December [1861], *WJL*, 4:58.

103   "at about the hour of our upward procession to bed," etc.: *NSB*, 199.

104   "gusty street-lamp"; "ideal comfort": Ibid., 199–200.

104   "loud-mouthed imbecility": Ibid., 200.

105   "poltroonery"; "the old rules": JJGW to HJSr, 27 June 1850, S.

105   "hemorrhage": JJGW to HJSr, 3 October 1849, S.

106   "inferior to man . . . in passion": See Henry James Sr., "Woman and the 'Woman's Movement,'" *Putnam's Monthly* 1 (March 1853), 279–88.

106   "man has shown no reluctance": "The Proper Sphere of Men," *Putnam's Monthly* 4 (July 1854), 305–10.

106   "Who will then ever be caught in that foolish snare again?"; "I did nothing but tumble": *NSB*, 240.

106   many female correspondents: See ibid., 248.

107   editorial in the *New York Tribune*: "Intemperance," *NYTrib*, 26 August 1851. Henry was proud enough of this piece to have it reprinted in his collection of lectures printed in 1852: *LM*, 425–32.

107   urged him to give up alcohol: JJGW to HJSr, 13 July 1849; 3 August 1849, S.

107   "quite as curable under proper care"; "How stupid to preach to the drunkard"; "infinitely keener sense"; "The drunkard never lived": "Intemperance," in *LM*, 430.

108   "*Like all habits, its strength lies in a diseased will*": Ibid., 426–27.

108   "sympathy and help": Ibid., 429–30.

109   lonely without her: see *AJB*, 32.

109   procession of uncles: See *SBO*, 131.

110   "sixteen days and a pirouette": Quoted in Brinnin, 14.

110   "rises at five winter and summer"; "Captain Marshall's assiduities"; "steady stream of skirt and chemisette"; "speak to the Captain"; "has always been a

most loving and provident husband": HJSr to Edmund Tweedy [fragment, 1853?], James Papers, H: MS AM 1092.9 (4288).

110 claimed to remember the romance: See *AJB*, 33.

112 "so numerous has waxed our family"; "Looking upon our four stout boys": *NSB*, 195–96; Perry, 1:59.

112 "headlong impatience": *SBO*, 86.

113 "little sheath-like jacket"; "not so adequately dressed": Ibid., 87.

113 "Buttons": Ibid., 88.

113 "common conspiracies against her"; "explosive": Ibid., 86.

114 with a marble bust of a Bacchante: Ibid., 270.

114 as Harry's biographer Leon Edel observed: See *HJAL*, 35–38.

114 "Say I am a philosopher": *NSB*, 69.

114 "What church do you go to?"; "pewless state"; "could plead nothing less than the whole privilege": *SBO*, 233–34.

115 "small vague spasms of school": Ibid., 172.

115 "dispensaries of learning"; "We couldn't have changed oftener": Ibid., 16.

115 "supposedly supreme benefits of Swiss schooling": *NSB*, 1.

115 "solutional 'Europe'": Ibid., 195.

116 "frightful mistake," etc.: HJSr to Ralph Waldo Emerson, 18 June 1855, James Papers, H: MS Am 1092.9 (4110).

116 "productive of happiness to either party"; "retired from his house": *RS*, 11.

Chapter 5: Hotel Children

119 "two throbbing and heaving cabs": *SBO*, 317.

119 "coign of vantage"; "for the first time since [their] babyhood": Ibid., 276.

119 "but vaguely 'formed'": Ibid., 312.

119 "much too big to be agreeable"; "a great huge unwieldy metropolis with a little brown river crawling through it": WJ to Edgar Beach Van Winkle, 1 July 1856, *WJL*, 4:1.

120 "hotel children": *SBO*, 30.

120 "the same old sausage, fizzing and sputtering in his own grease": *NSB*, 201.

120 "the great bleak parlours of the hotels": Ibid., 425.

120 "the great fusty curtained bed"; "dull seed": *SBO*, 278.

120 "black-whiskered"; "fresh-coloured, broad-faced and fair-braided": Ibid., 283.

121 "much frequented by English travellers": Karl Baedeker, ed., *Paris and Northern France: A Handbook for Travellers* (Coblenz: Baedeker, 1867), 4–5.

121 "such a galaxy as never was or should ever be again"; "shining second Empire": *NSB*, 59.

122 "in the splendid coach"; "*cent-gardes* [imperial guard troopers], all light-blue and silver": *SBO*, 332.

122 "whole perfect Parisianism": Ibid., 280.

122 "appalled but uplifted, on brave Nadali's arm": Ibid., 350.

122 "People talk about Paris being such a beautiful city!"; "Harry sentimentalises, as usual": WJ to Edgar Beach Van Winkle, 1 July 1856, *WJL*, 4:2, 4.

123 "ancient inn"; "bobbed up and down"; "the romance of travel"; "of abated illness and of cold chicken": *SBO*, 282–83.

124 "a stone's throw"; "the most exquisite *morceaux*"; "as if our tie was one of friendship instead of francs": "An American in Europe, I," *NYTrib*, 3 September 1855.

124 "superior talent for life": *SBO*, 287.

124 "extrusive but on the whole exhilarating": Ibid., 306.

125 $350 a year: *F*, 371.

125 "nine-pin alley"; "amply fostered and directed"; "They go down every fair day to the Rhone": "An American in Europe, I."

126 "greatly overrated": HJSr to Catharine Barber James, 29 September 1855, quoted in Robert LeClair, *Young Henry James* (New York: Bookman, 1955), 171–72.

126 "glamour of the Swiss school"; "stale": *SBO*, 294.

126 "delicious infant": *AJD*, 57.

126 "settle": *NSB*, 231.

126 "entire inability or indifference 'to stick to a thing for the sake of sticking'": *AJD*, 57.

126 "queer old city": WJ to Edgar Beach Van Winkle, 1 July 1856, *WJL*, 4:1.

126 "Swiss schools are all humbug": WJ to Edgar Beach Van Winkle, 4 January 1858, Ibid., 4:10.

127 "a fatigued and famished American family"; early Victorian London; "thick gloom of the inn rooms": *SBO*, 297–98.

128 boiled beef, snipe kidneys, steaks and chops, etc.; "colossal proportions": Peter Cunningham, *London in 1856* (London: John Murray, 1856), x.

128 "gin-shops": "Nationalities—Vice in London," *NYTrib*, 15 Nov 1855.

128 "There's nothing like it after all!": *SBO*, 298.

128 "lumpish 'mansions'": Ibid., 299.

128 "a considerable garden and wistful view": Ibid., 303.

128 "draped in December densities": *AJD*, 46.

129 "bobbery"; "St. Nicholas, the merry old elf": "Christmas at London," *NYTrib*, 16 January 1856.

129 "used to spoil our Christmases so faithfully for us": *AJD*, 72.

129 "a poor and arid and lamentable time"; "but walk about together"; "walked and dawdled and dodged": *SBO*, 301–2.

130 "queer old obsequiosities and appeals": Ibid., 310.

130 "the postmen in their frock-coats": Ibid., 309.

130 "knew no other boys at all": Ibid., 308.

131 "Come now, be getting on!": Ibid., 300.

131 "sport[ing] a beaver": WJ to Edgar Beach Van Winkle, 4 September 1857, *WJL*, 4:6.

131 "buns and ginger-beer": *SBO*, 313.

131 "little boys in the streets who stared at us": Ibid., 265.

131 "Few English boys know that the English language is spoken in the United States!!": WJ to Edgar Beach Van Winkle, 4 January 1858, *WJL*, 4:10.

131 "came from New York by the Cape of Good Hope"; "thought Americans had no beards"; "if it was not very muddy"; "such ignorance is rare": WJ to Edgar Beach Van Winkle, 1 March 1858, ibid., 4:15.

132 "breathed inconsistency and ate and drank contradictions"; "The presence of paradox": *SBO*, 216.

132 "grey dusk"; "the millinery point of view of Neufchâtel"; "came forth green shirred silk and pink roses": *AJD*, 46.

133 "little coloured oil-lamps": *SBO*, 331.

133 "odd relic of a house"; "redundancy of mirror": Ibid., 326–27.

133 "Our house is furnished"; "about ten times as much French": WJ to Edgar Beach Van Winkle, 1 July 1856, *WJL*, 4:2.

134 "gigantic improvements": Baedeker, *Paris*, xx.

134 "Many unwholesome purlieus": Ibid., Preface.

134   "that all the houses should be whitewashed," etc.: WJ to Edgar Beach Van Winkle, 1 July 1856, *WJL*, 4:2–3.

135   "wide-faced apartment": *SBO*, 334.

135   "queer way of living": WJ to Edgar Beach Van Winkle, 1 July 1856, *WJL*, 4:3.

135   "softly-crusty crescent-rolls": *SBO*, 335.

135   chateaubriand, etc.: Baedeker, *Paris*, 9.

135   "parvenus": *NSB*, 221.

136   "the blinding glare of the new Empire": *SBO*, 333.

136   "My mother anxiously urg[ed] me": Ibid., 378.

136   "heels grinding into [her] shins": *AJD*, 128.

136   "little flounced person"; "Crinoline?—I was suspecting it!": *SBO*, 89.

136   Crinoline, linen stiffened with horsehair: See Daniel Pool, *What Jane Austen Ate and Charles Dickens Knew: From Fox Hunting to Whist—The Facts of Daily Life in 19th-Century England* (New York: Simon and Schuster, 1993), 214–15.

137   "constant comic star": *SBO*, 253.

137   William's teasing: See Strouse's brilliant, in-depth discussion of this dynamic in *AJB*, 51–55. My understanding of Alice in the context of the James family also owes much to Strouse's thorough and insightful analysis of William James's mock courtship of Alice.

137   "a cave of emotional borborygmus": *AJD*, 176.

137   "an object of fraternal curiosity": *AJB*, 55.

137   "beautiful poetry": WJ to HJSr, [1860], *WJL*, 4:27.

138   "I was asked w'ether I wanted to belong": HJ to Edgar Beach Van Winkle, [1856], *HJL*, 1:5.

138   "a certain amount of English comfort with French taste": Baedeker, *Paris*, 203.

138   "This might certainly be called pleasure under difficulties!": *AJD*, 128.

139   "the malignant typhus"; "scant possibilities": *SBO*, 398.

139   "raw-boned": WJ to Edgar Beach Van Winkle, 4 January 1858, *WJL*, 4:9.

139   "imperilled or curtailed": *SBO*, 397.

139   "bluer and darker"; "blue with collapse"; "dangerous classes": Strong, 2:357, 363, 369.

140   "high reputation": Baedeker, *Paris*, 203.

140   "An Engineer in the present state of society"; "go out into the country"; "as many discoveries as possible"; "I'll be kicked": WJ to Edgar Beach Van Winkle, 1 March 1858, *WJL*, 4:14–15.

140   "as a general thing, Americans had better keep their children at home"; "gained in some things": WJ to Edgar Beach Van Winkle, 26 May 1858, Ibid., 4:16–17.

141   "cauda virilis": WJ to Edgar Beach Van Winkle, 1 July 1856, ibid., 4:6.

142   "scientific pursuits," etc.: HJSr to Catharine Barber James, 15 October [1857], James Papers, H: MS Am 1092.9 (4188).

142   "*l'ingénieux petit* Robertson": *NSB*, 375.

142   "destined for commerce": WJ to Edgar Beach Van Winkle, 18 December 1859, *WJL*, 4:25.

143   "reducing decimal fractions"; "high destiny": Quoted in Leon Edel, "Portrait of Alice James," in *AJD*, 4.

143   "none of them cut out for intellectual labors": HJSr to Edmund Tweedy, 18 July [1860], James Papers, H: MS Am 1092.9 (4285).

143   "The question of 'what to be' has been tormenting me": WJ to Edgar Beach Van Winkle, 4 January 1858, *WJL*, 4:8.

144   "In the first place, what ought to be everyone's object in life?": WJ to Edgar Beach Van Winkle, 1 March 1858, ibid., 4:11.

144 "marked prejudices," etc.: *NSB*, 112.
145 "rather disorderly": WJ to Edgar Beach Van Winkle, 1 July 1858, *WJL*, 4:18.
145 "very comfortable cottage with four acres of land": WJ to Edgar Beach Van Winkle, 12 August 1858, ibid., 4:20.
145 "hot beds of corruption"; "very unjust": WJ to Edgar Beach Van Winkle, 1 July 1858, ibid, 4:19.
145 "Willy, that wretched dog is on the bed again"; "Willy, the dog is tearing the buttons off the sofa"; "Never, never before did I so clearly"; "dreary": WJ to Edgar Beach Van Winkle, 12 November 1858, ibid., 4:23.
146 "not the place to bring up such 'ingenuous youth' ": WJ to Edgar Beach Van Winkle, 18 September [1858], ibid., 4:21.
146 "New Englander of genius": *SBO*, 341.
146 "a little too much attraction to painting"; "break that up"; "philosophical": HJSr to Edmund Tweedy, 24–30 July [1860], James Papers, H: MS Am 1092.9 (4286).
147 "enlarge[d his] experience and mind"; "nothing could be more advantageous": WJ to Edgar Beach Van Winkle, 18 December 1859, *WJL*, 4:25.
148 "I swore to ask thy hand, my love"; "very cooly"; "almost desert": WJ to HJSr., [1860], ibid., 4:27–29.
148 "sudden returns"; "at the end of 36 hours"; "with Mother beside him holding his hand": *AJD*, 57–58.
149 "guided us to country walks": *NSB*, 31.
149 "plums are now 50 for a groschen": WJ to HJSr and MJ, 12 August [1860], *WJL*, 4:36.
150 "I never value my parents": WJ to HJSr, [19 August 1860], ibid., 4:37.
150 "Alice [at] the [window]": WJ to HJSr and MJ, 12 August [1860], ibid., 4:34–35.
151 "I confess": Perry, 1:191.
151 "ought to be weighed down": WJ to HJSr, [24 August 1860], *WJL*, 4:40.
151 "isolation had been utter": *NSB*, 62.
152 "our national defeat and humiliation": Quoted in Brinnin, 198.

Chapter 6: Implosion

153 "artificial daylight of more than ten-thousand torches"; "patriotic war dance round and round the astonished statue of Washington"; "fair Republican Floras": "The Presidential Campaign; Grand Wide-Awake Demonstration": *NYTimes*, 4 October 1860.
154 "strangers from all parts of the country": "The Wide-Awake Demonstration; Influx of Strangers," ibid., 3 October 1860.
154 "the busy, the tipsy, and Daniel Webster": *SBO*, 49.
155 "services as an able-bodied and willing young man": HJ to Thomas Sergeant Perry, 26 September 1860, *HJL*, 1:38.
155 "in tears over the news": *SBO*, 50.
156 two Newports: For a history of Newport as a resort, see Jon Sterngrass, *First Resorts: Pursuing Pleasure at Saratoga Springs, Newport and Coney Island* (Baltimore: Johns Hopkins University Press, 2001), chap. 2.
157 William S. Wetmore: Antoinette F. Downing and Vincent J. Scully Jr., *The Architectural Heritage of Newport, Rhode Island, 1640–1915* (Cambridge, MA: Harvard University Press, 1952), 125.
157 ladies were required to change outfits nine times a day: Homberger, 169.
158 "the barren isle of our return from Europe": *NSB*, 415.
158 "its opera-glass turned for ever across the sea": Ibid., 304.

158 "sharp reverberation": *SBO*, 56.
159 "to learn to paint": *NSB*, 62–63.
159 "hovered and flitted"; "vivid and whimsical": Ibid., 79–80.
160 "all muscular spareness and brownness and absence of waste": Ibid., 83.
161 "I also plied the pencil"; "critically, rapidly or summarily": *SBO*, 260.
161 "hummed with promise": *NSB*, 81.
161 "sublime uplifted face": Ibid., 80.
161 "serious"; "divested of every garment"; "niggle for months"; "perfect gymnastic figure": Ibid., 95.
161 "the most beautifully made athletic little person"; "rare radiance," etc.: *SBO*, 172–73.
163 "parvenus and comical"; "up to [their] knees"; "a cordial Pan"; "magnificent experiments": *NSB*, 221–23.
163 Bush, with its nine famous chestnut trees: McAleer, 208–10.
163 "surrounded by the great, fresh outdoors"; "a week's encampment": *JHM*, 85.
164 Frank Sanborn: Jane Maher, *Biography of Broken Fortunes: Wilkie and Bob, Brothers of William, Henry, and Alice* (Hamden, CT: Archon Books, 1986), 14–16. Hereafter *BBF*.
164 "a tall, wiry, long-limbed young scholar"; "passion and self-control": *JHM*, 77.
164 "tall, erect, long-haired and freckled"; "between the eyes": *NSB*, 221–22.
165 "urchins under her roof": Ibid., 221.
165 "perfectly delightful characters": *JHM*, 121.
165 "good-looking, open-hearted fellows": Ibid., 120.
166 "the glass of fashion and the mould of form"; "best dressed boy in the school"; "[Wilkie] was of middle height": Ibid., 121.
166 "robust and hilarious, tough, tireless as hickory": Ibid., 120–21.
166 "full of fun and pranks and audacities"; "a perfect gentleman": Ibid., 121.
167 "carte blanche to go at any expense of health"; "reduce [Alice] to the ordinary domestic routine"; "foretaste": HJSr to Ralph Waldo Emerson, 22 December [1861], James Papers, H: MS Am 1092.9 (4115).
168 *Godey's Lady's Book*: See the discussion in *AJB*, 63–64.
168 "enforced uselessness": Ibid., 82.
168 "artificial and sophisticated": *AJD*, 93.
169 "very handsome": *NSB*, 96.
169 "boisteroso triumphissimo," etc.: WJ to Katharine Temple Emmet, [November 1861], *WJL*, 4:48.
170 "slim and fair and quick": *NSB*, 78.
170 "the most affected creature"; "bullied": Quoted in Alfred Habegger, *Henry James and the "Woman Business"* (Cambridge, England: Cambridge University Press, 1989), 130. Hereafter *HJWB*.
170 "delightful": AJ to WJ, 28 May 1867, *WJL*, 4:168.
170 comic sketches: See HJ to Thomas Sergeant Perry, 18 April 1864, *HJL*, 1:53.
170 "highly disgusted"; "very very weak"; "I don't at all like the way he looks at Slavery": Quoted in *HJWB*, 131.
170 "dazzled": *NSB*, 118.
170 "young and shining apparition," etc.: Ibid., 76–78.
171 "catastrophe"; "Was she all alone," etc.: *WJL*, 4:49.
171 "insanity": Quoted in *HJWB*, 129.
171 "as *lovely* as ever"; "the same strange youth as ever, stranger if possible": Quoted in ibid., 421.
171 "brilliant, original, and affectionate": Edward Waldo Emerson, *The Early Years of the Saturday Club, 1855–1870* (Boston: Houghton Mifflin, 1918), 327. Hereafter *SC*.

171 "instantly corrected or disputed by the little cock-sparrow Bob"; "bright as well as motherly"; "Don't be disturbed"; "smiling, close to the combatants": Ibid., 328.

172 "absorbing into the bone"; "the better part is to clothe oneself in neutral tints": *AJD*, 95.

172 "anathematized"; "Oh, Alice, how hard you are!"; "I can remember how penetrated I was"; "hard core": Ibid., 192.

173 "muscular circumstances"; "How I recall the low grey Newport sky": Ibid., 95.

173 "lone and perverse even in [his] own sight"; "Nobody in those days walked, nobody but the three or four of us": *NSB*, 108.

174 "the honest Jack Tar of the family": *WJL*, 4:72.

174 "the happiest, queerest boy in the world"; "equally queer"; "dancing eyes"; "contemplated the vivacious row"; "Look at the five potatoes!"; "it did look very funny": Ellen Tucker Emerson, *The Letters of Ellen Tucker Emerson*, ed. Edith E. W. Glegg, 2 vols. (Kent, OH: Kent State University Press, 1982), 1:295–97. Hereafter *EEL*.

174 "entertaining treat," etc.: E[dwin] L[awrence] Godkin, *Life and Letters of Edwin Lawrence Godkin*, ed. Rollo Ogden, 2 vols. (London: Macmillan, 1907), 2:218.

176 "coat tails of my Willy & Harry"; "found some charming conjugal Elizabeth or other"; "vituperate": HJSr to [Cranch?], [March–April 1861], quoted in *F*, 430.

176 William's enlistment: See *F*, 429.

177 "Science, physical Science, strenuous Science in all its exactitude": *NSB*, 122.

177 "a queer fusion or confusion": Ibid., 296.

177 "the smoke of Charleston Bay still so acrid in the air", etc.: Ibid., 297–98.

177 Historical sources, however, confirm only a back problem: This point of view, now generally accepted, was first argued by Leon Edel, who cited two letters by William James, from 1867 and 1869, and a memory of Edmund Gosse, that confirmed this idea. See *LHJ*, 1:181.

178 "idleness": HJSr to RJ, 29 August 1864, quoted in *BBF*, 71.

179 "[Cabot and I] lay beside each other on our bellies"; "not inclined to make friends with bullets": GWJ to parents, December 29, 1862, quoted in ibid., 34.

179 "vulgar contempt of color": Luis Emilio, *A Brave Black Regiment: History of the Fifty-Fourth Regiment, 1863–1865* (New York: Johnson Reprint, 1968), 3.

180 "vastly attached to the negro-soldier cause": *NSB*, 242.

180 "bright breezy air and high shanty-covered [fields]," etc.: Ibid., 372–73.

180 Henry Senior . . . also felt proud of Wilkie: *BBF*, 39–40; Peter Burchard, *One Gallant Rush: Robert Gould Shaw and His Brave Black Regiment* (New York: St. Martin's Press, 1965), 93–94.

180 the departure of the Fifty-fourth Massachusetts: See Yacovone in George E. Stephens, *A Voice of Thunder: The Civil War Letters of George E. Stephens*, ed. Donald Yacovone (Urbana: University of Illinois Press, 1977), 36–38; Duncan in Robert Gould Shaw, *Blue-Eyed Child of Fortune: The Civil War Letters of Colonel Robert Gould Shaw*, ed. Russell Duncan (Athens, GA: University of Georgia Press, 1992), 1–2; *Boston Evening Transcript*, 28 May 1863.

182 "heebin' "; "right well": Shaw, 335–36.

182 "Our artillery peppered it a little, as we came up": Ibid., 342.

183 "the post of honor": Emilio, 74.

183 One bullet ripped Wilkie's side: Wilkie's 1883 account, quoted in *BBF*, 44–47.

184 "with his jaw shot away"; "deluged [him] with blood": HJSr to Elizabeth Peabody, 11 August 1863, Horace Mann Papers III, reel 38, MHS.

184 As it was, Wilkie had to have the inch-and-a-half canister ball: *NSB*, 241–42.

184 "for his friends gone and missing": Ibid., 242.

185 "*l'ingénieux petit* Robertson": Ibid., 375.

186 "irreproachable"; "Cheer up then"; "Keep yourself from vices": HJSr to RJ, 29 August 1864, quoted in *BBF*, 72. For Maher's excellent discussion of Bob's probable struggles with liquor and women, see *BBF*, 71–74.

186 "so much manhood suddenly achieved": HJSr to Samuel Gray Ward, 1 August [1863], quoted in *F*, 442.

187 July 1861: Harry remembered it as the summer of 1862; see *LHJ*, 1:169.

187 "hadn't come armed like him with oranges and peppermints"; "the pitch of the last tenderness of friendship": *NSB*, 314.

187 "attaching and affecting"; "amusing figure[s] of romance": Ibid., 313.

187 Gus would fight his way: Rufus W. Clark, *The Heroes of Albany: A Memorial of the Patriot-Martyrs of the City* [. . .] (Albany, NY: S. R. Gray, 1866), 410–19.

Chapter 7: Athenian Eros

191 a new and different Boston in the making: See Alex Krieger and David Cobb, eds., *Mapping Boston* (Cambridge, MA: Massachusetts Institute of Technology Press, 1999), 122–32; Jane Holtz Kay, *Lost Boston* (Boston: Houghton Mifflin, 1999), 178–79.

192 Faneuil Hall Market: Krieger and Cobb, 121.

192 Massachusetts Society for the Suppression of Intemperance: Pegram, 15.

192 "before the fall"; "[I am] apt (as often before I have said in regard to some other married ladies of my acquaintance)": Quoted in Codman Hislop, *Eliphalet Nott* (Middletown, CT: Wesleyan University Press, 1971), 177, 300.

193 "honest florid and ornate ministers": WJ to HJJr, 26 September 1867, *WJL*, 1:20.

195 "worth all the men in the Club put together": *AJD*, 68–69.

195 "loved each other like David and Jonathan"; "I cannot help thinking": *SC*, 33.

196 "rogue who suddenly finds himself in the company of detectives": Ibid., 331.

196 "Henry James of New York": Ibid., 8.

196 "Celtic"; "Northern Erin"; "best": *SC*, 322.

196 Irish as not "white": See Noel Ignatiev, *How the Irish Became White* (New York: Routledge, 1995), 1–3.

197 "vague golden November": *NSB*, 331.

198 "product of New England at its sparest and dryest": Ibid., 329.

198 "young types, or rather with the members of a single type": Ibid., 317.

198 "moot-court": Ibid., 340.

198 "went to the same lectures and recitations"; "became attached to each other by all manner of ties": Henry James III, *Charles W. Eliot, President of Harvard University, 1869–1909*, 2 vols. (Boston: Houghton Mifflin, 1930), 1:186. Hereafter *CWE*.

199 "*his* people": *NSB*, 327.

199 "singularly alien": Ibid., 120.

199 red silk handkerchiefs: see *CWE*, 1:79.

200 "I don't believe he is a *very* accomplished Chemist": WJ to the James family, 16 September 1861, *WJL*, 4:43.

200 "Mathematics, Chemistry, Physics": *CWE*, 1:95.

200 "as much in advance of us in all that pertains to higher education": Ibid., 1:117.

202 But Beacon Hill had another identity: See Stephen Kendrick and Paul Kendrick, *Sarah's Long Walk: The Free Blacks of Boston and How Their Struggle for Equality Changed America* (Boston: Beacon Press, 2004), 21–28.

202 "Nigger Hill"; "Mount Whoredom": Ibid., 21, 26.

202 "the very taste of the War ending and ended": *NSB*, 426.

203 "bronzed, matured faces and even more in bronzed, matured characters"; "worn toggery put off": Ibid., 427.

203 "one's own . . . pulses matched"; "huge general gasp": Ibid., 430.

204 "certain door of importances": Ibid., 414.

205 Alfred Habegger has discovered an incident: See *F*, 456–57.

205 "an electric shock"; "prolonged, steadfast, and compelling"; "a divine pity— seemed to stream from his eyes"; "I write this down"; "tender kiss"; "Phenomenally it must mean something": Caroline Dall, Journals, 25 April 1866, Caroline Wells Healy Dall Papers, MHS.

206 "dilate on the vanity of riches": AJ to WJ, 13 October 1867, *DLAJ*, 54.

206 "Shakespeare, Goethe and Charles Lamb"; "I cannot again stand the pressure of avowed authorship": HJ to Thomas Sergeant Perry, 25 March 1864, *HJL*, 1:49–50.

207 "lump": HJ to Charles Eliot Norton, 1 December 1864, ibid., 1:57.

207 "I am frequently in the way of reading French books": HJ to Charles Eliot Norton, 9 August 1864, ibid., 1:54.

207 "What an awful thing this war is! I mean for wives": HJ to Thomas Sergeant Perry, 28 October 1864, ibid., 1:56.

207 "the very greenbacks"; "first earned wage"; "the golden light of promise": *NSB*, 404–5.

210 "[Father is] going to break your head for spending so much!": WJ to the James family, 15 December [1861], *WJL*, 4:55.

210 "prodigal philosopher," etc.: WJ to the James family, 16 September 1861, ibid., 4:44.

210 "old character of a beggar"; "I am [in] very great want of stockings," etc.: WJ to HJSr, [1863], ibid., 4:80.

211 "higher nature"; "I want you to become familiar": WJ to MJ, [2 November 1863], ibid., 4:86.

211 "Don't let *more* than a fortnight pass": MJ to WJ, 27 May [1867], ibid., 4:166.

211 "My darling Hubby": MJ to HJSr, [n.d., 1869?], James Papers, H: MS Am 1093.

212 "Cherie, charmante"; "That you should not have written to me for so long": WJ to AJ, 13 September [1863], *WJL*, 4:83.

212 "private"; "interesting": HJ to WJ, 21 May [1867], ibid., 1:15.

213 "a deep Prussian blue over a sea of the same color": WJ to HJSr and MJ, 21 April [1865], ibid., 4:103, 100.

213 "his charlatanerie is almost as great as his solid worth": WJ to HJ, 3 May 1865, ibid., 1:6.

213 "sinful"; "in a marble sarcophagus": WJ to HJSr and MJ, 21 April [1865], ibid., 4:103.

214 "an immense ripe raspberry": WJ to HJSr, 3 June 1865, ibid., 4:105.

214 "neuralgic pain": WJ to MJ, 6 July [1865], ibid., 4:109.

214 "speculative"; "exploring expeditions": WJ to HJSr, 3 June 1865, ibid., 4:107.

214 "totally uneducated": WJ to MJ, 23 August 186[5], ibid., 4:111.

214 "Genius, in truth, means little more than the faculty of perceiving in an unhabitual way": *AJD*, 165; see William James, *The Principles of Psychology*, 2 vols. (New York: Henry Holt, 1890), chap. 19.

214 "What would the blessed mother say"; "hacked up": WJ to AJ, 31 August [1865], *WJL*, 4:115.

214 "sensuality": WJ to HJSr, 3 June 1865, ibid., 4:109.

215 "ball"; "lovely Indian maidens"; "Ah Jesuina"; "with her long hair floating free": WJ to AJ, 31 August [1865], ibid., 4:120.

215 "eating & drinking & dancing with the Indian maidens"; "studying them-selves into fevers"; "even churches"; "almost too good for this world": WJ to MJ, 9 December 1865, ibid., 4:132.

216 "Bob has some artistic taste": MJ to GWJ, 14 March [1866], quoted in *BBF*, 80.

219 "temperament"; "groan[ed] for hours": GWJ to HJSr, 21 July 1867, quoted in ibid., 95.

219 "the most deplorable looking place you ever saw": AJ to WJ, 28 May 1867, *WJL*, 4:167.

219 "intermittent fever"; "thin and sallow"; "The crops have been an almost en-tire failure this year": MJ to WJ, 21 November [1867], ibid., 4:230.

220 "frowned at him": WJ to GWJ, 21 March [1866], ibid., 4:135.

221 "eloquent dome of the State House": HJ to Thomas Sergeant Perry, 1 De-cember 1866, *HJL*, 1:68.

221 "Vandal hand": WJ to AJ, 14 September 1861, *WJL*, 4:46.

221 "heave a beautiful sigh": WJ to HJSr and MJ, 21 October [1865], ibid., 4:128.

221 "social intercourse": WJ to Thomas Wren Ward, 27 March 1866, ibid., 4:137.

222 "so much influenced"; "very pretty"; "fascinating": AJ to WJ, 6 August [1867], ibid., 4:191.

222 "*A*1, if any one ever was": WJ to GWJ, 21 March [1866], ibid., 4:135.

222 "not impossible she": William quoted the seventeenth-century English poet William Crashaw; WJ to MJ, [2 November 1863], ibid., 4:86, 87n.

223 "aged parents": WJ to Katharine Temple Emmet, 3 August [1864], ibid., 4:92.

223 "exciting"; "fishballs lying heavy on [his] stomach": HJ to AJ, 3 February [1867], *HJL*, 1:69.

223 "The undergraduates of course are too young": HJ to Thomas Sergeant Perry, 15 August [1867], ibid., 1:71–72.

223 "rigid, frigid": HJ to Thomas Sergeant Perry, 27 March 1868, ibid., 1:83.

223 "relaxation"; "only a ghostly simulacrum of it"; "about as lively as the inner sepulchre": HJ to WJ, 22 November [1867], ibid., 1:80–81.

224 "Can Cambridge answer Seville?": HJ to Thomas Sergeant Perry, 1 Decem-ber 1866, ibid., 1:66.

224 "provincial, common, and inelegant": HJ to Thomas Sergeant Perry, 15 Au-gust [1867], ibid., 1:72.

224 "woman hater": WJ to AJ, 23 June 1868, *WJL*, 4:326.

224 "an epic self-contained"; "undazzled eye": WJ to MJ, [31 March 1865], ibid., 4:98.

224 "standing remedy": *NSB*, 444.

224 "very cheerful": William James, *The Varieties of Religious Experience* (New York: Longmans, Green, 1902), 128. Hereafter *VRE*.

225 sucking on oranges: WJ to AJ, 27 April [1867], *WJL*, 4:157–59.

226 "Triton among minnows"; "great swollen hunk of a premature Leviathan": Quoted in Brinnin, 216–17.

226 "couronner l'édifice": WJ to AJ, 5 April 1867, *WJL*, 4:156.

226 "alterations of our old haunts": WJ to HJSr and MJ, 27 May 1867, ibid., 4:160.

226 "noble"; "grand old language": WJ to Catherine Elizabeth Havens, 23 March 1874, ibid., 4:486.

227 "heyday of youth is o'er": WJ to HJSr and MJ, 27 May 1867, ibid., 4:160.

227 "mere physical nervousness"; "come of age"; "Boys will make mistakes"; "The tho't of what *might* have happened": WJ to Thomas Wren Ward, 14 March 1870, ibid., 4:403–4. Simon theorizes that this experience may also

have been either a visit to a prostitute or masturbation, a practice highly condemned in nineteenth-century America; see Simon, 103.

227 "akin": WJ to HJSr and MJ, 27 May 1867, *WJL*, 4:160.

228 "feminine system of espionage"; "exceedingly pretty": WJ to AJ, 27 May 1867, ibid., 4:164.

228 "attentive"; "a gift of the gab": WJ to HJ, 4 March 1868, ibid., 1:35.

228 "comic"; "listening fair"; "The cold water cure at Divonne": *NSB*, 445.

229 "blisters"; "over the diseased muscles": WJ to HJ, [22 September 1868], *WJL*, 1:58.

229 "having his back nicely tuned up": WJ to AJ, 25 December 1866, ibid., 4:149.

229 "family peculiarity": WJ to Thomas Wren Ward, ibid., 4:197.

230 "*thin*": WJ to HJ, 4 March 1868, ibid., 1:36.

230 "anything to write about": WJ to HJSr, 5 October 1868, ibid., 4:343.

230 "neat alpaca coat": WJ to AJ, 23 June 1868, ibid., 4:325.

230 "Substance and Shadder": WJ to AJ, 19 November 1867, ibid., 4:228.

231 "mental isolation": WJ to HJSr, 26 September [1867], ibid., 4:203.

231 "*mainly* from the purely *scientific* cast"; "puerile stage of progress": HJSr to WJ, 27 September [1867], ibid., 4:204–5.

231 "a lone outcast among the unfeeling foreigners": WJ to HJ, 12 February 1868, ibid., 1:31.

231 "one of the emptiest years of [his] life": WJ to AJ, 16 March 1868, ibid., 4:265.

231 "library of books in the house"; "clean"; "dealing his snubs around": WJ to AJ, 19 November 1867, ibid., 4:227.

231 "bump like a moth": WJ to AJ, 9 January 1868, ibid., 4:253.

Chapter 8: Bottled Lightning

233 "splendor, picturesqueness, and oceanic amplitude"; "heavy, low, musical roar": Walt Whitman, *Democratic Vistas*, in *Whitman: Poetry and Prose* (New York: Library of America, 1996), 962.

234 "sheds and marble palaces are huddled together": Jules Verne, *A Floating City [Une Ville Flottante]*, ed. and trans. I. O. Evans (Westport, CT: Associated Booksellers, 1958), 164.

234 George Herbert Taylor: Taylor's name is sometimes given as George Henry Taylor, but Herbert is his correct middle name.

235 "neurasthenia": See *AJB*, 103; George Miller Beard, *American Nervousness: Its Causes and Consequences* (New York: Putnam, 1881); Marijke Gijswijt-Hofstra and Roy Porter, eds., *Cultures of Neurasthenia from Beard to the First World War* (Amsterdam: Rodopi, 2001).

236 "pretty little boy"; "I hope that the Doctor has not pushed matters too hard": AJ to WJ, 28 May 1867, *WJL*, 4:168.

237 "You've no idea how *delightful* your letters are": WJ to AJ, 12 December [1866], ibid., 4:148.

237 "fine accounts of [her] blooming appearance": MJ to AJ, [January 1867], James Papers, H: MS Am 1093.1 (22).

237 "fat as butter": MJ to AJ, [December 1866], ibid., MS Am 1093.1 (20).

237 "We are delighted to hear such fine accounts": HJ to AJ, 7 November [1869], *HJL*, 1:69.

237 "weary & empty place": WJ to AJ, [30 January 1867], *WJL*, 4:151.

237 "Alice seems bright and is an immense joy to us": MJ to WJ, 27 May [1867], ibid., 4:166.

237 "head troubles": Ibid., 4:167n.
238 New England Women's Club: See *F*, 466–67.
238 "impatient for the moment": *AJD*, 26.
238 "the admirable mother": AJ to WJ, 8 June 1867, *WJL*, 4:172.
238 "one of her attacks"; "little overexertion": MJ to WJ, 10 June 1867, ibid., 4:174n.
239 "in the most improper way"; "How much I wish"; "I feel myself to be a more respectable human being": AJ to Frances Rollins Morse [undated], quoted in *AJB*, 92.
240 "By the time you get back": AJ toWJ, 8 June 1867, *WJL*, 4:174.
240 "like an angel"; "putting up cornices and raking out the garret room like a little buffalo": WJ to AJ, 14 November 1866, ibid., 4:145.
240 "the perfection of health as of everything else": HJ to WJ, 10 May [1867], ibid., 1:14.
240 "stiff stupid house in Cambridge," etc.: Quoted in Van Wyck Brooks, *From the Shadow of the Mountain* (New York: Dutton, 1961), 45.
240 "solid proportions": AJ to Sara Sedgwick, 1 February 1874, *DLAJ*, 63.
240 "ringing the changes upon the Mother's perfections," etc.: *AJD*, 79.
241 "May I have some of those brown-rolls," etc.: AJ to WJ, 13 October 1867, *DLAJ*, 52–53.
241 "your Father's immortal work": HJ to AJ, 7 November [1869], *HJL*, 1:170.
241 "He is about my size"; "all doubled up in a deep arm-chair," etc.: AJ to WJ, 6 August [1867], *WJL*, 4:192.
241 "energetic expletives"; "cool remarks": WJ to AJ, 31 August [1865], ibid., 4:114.
242 "well-digested"; "Why, that's very true"; "meant for one eye"; "delightful remarks"; "Bee"; "Cambridge misses"; "There is the longest list of engagements and weddings": AJ to WJ, 13 October 1867, *DLAJ*, 51–53.
243 "the peerless child of Quincy Street": WJ to AJ, 16 March 1868, *WJL*, 4:264.
243 "that idle & useless young female": WJ to MJ, [2 November 1863], ibid., 4:86.
243 "too serious for much letter writing to one's childlike sisters": ibid., 4:223.
243 "Your loving *idiotoid* sister": AJ to WJ, 6 August [1867], ibid., 4:192.
244 "You lovely babe": WJ to AJ, 14 September 1861, ibid., 4:46.
244 "Cherie de Balle!": WJ to AJ, 5 March [1865], ibid., 4:97.
244 "go *mad*, mad, MAD!": WJ to the James family, 16 September 1861, ibid., 4:45.
244 "at home sitting on the sofa, with my arm around your waste": WJ to AJ, [30 January 1867], ibid., 4:151.
244 "sass": WJ to AJ, 9 January 1868, ibid., 4:253.
244 "clinging yet self sustained, reserved yet confidential," etc.: WJ to HJ, 22 January 1868, ibid., 4:256.
244 "bold-faced jay": AJ to WJ, 8 June 1867, ibid., 4:174.
245 "being 'good' "; "burst out and make every one wretched for 24 hours"; "embody selfishness": *AJD*, 64.
245 *hysteria:* For Freud's analysis of hysteria, see Sigmund Freud and Josef Breuer, *Studies in Hysteria [Studien über Hysteria]*, trans. Nicola Luckhurst, with an introduction by Rachel Bowlby (New York: Penguin, 2004); for further varieties of hysteria, as culturally understood, see Sander L. Gilman et al., *Hysteria Beyond Freud* (Berkeley: University of California Press, 1993).
245 "violent revolt in [her] head": *AJD*, 149.
246 "never-ending fight"; "constabulary"; "violent inclination"; "abandon it all, let the dykes break and the flood sweep in": Ibid.
246 "The only difference between me and the insane"; "luminous and active

and susceptible to the clearest, strongest impressions"; "abandon": Ibid., 148–50.

247 "degrading"; "amiable": Ibid., 64.

247 "bottled lightning": Ibid., 60.

248 "Beloved Sisterkin"; "I earnestly hope you get better": WJ to AJ, 4 June 1868, *WJL*, 4:311, 315.

248 "What I have always maintained": *AJD*, 61.

248 "waves of violent inclination"; "benignant pater," etc.: Ibid., 149.

250 "free disclosure of the handsome largish teeth"; "becoming": *NSB*, 468.

250 "raid," "thirteen Emmets," etc.: Ibid., 455–56.

250 "sound": Ibid., 467.

251 "a desire to know something about her life": Quoted in *HJWB*, 132.

251 "wholly detestable"; "the right thing for her": *NSB*, 469.

251 "I don't expect to see him again": Ibid., 467.

252 "in a queer condish": WJ to Henry Pickering Bowditch, 24 January 1868, *WJL*, 4:362.

252 "horribly damp and bleak"; "invaluable"; "much *en rapport* with Charles": HJ to MJ, 20 March [1869], *HJL*, 1:103, 105.

253 "a marvelous phenomenon": HJ to AJ, 10 March [1869], ibid., 1:91.

253 "*grand homme*": HJ to WJ, 19 March [1869], ibid., 1:99.

253 "rich virginal brogue", etc.: HJ to MJ, 20 March [1869], ibid., 1:103.

253 "short, burly, and corpulent"; "stained glass windows, tiles, ecclesiastical and mediaeval tapestry altar-cloths"; "cut out of a missal": HJ to AJ, 10 March [1869], ibid., 1:93–94.

254 "delicious melancholy old house"; "almost": HJ to John La Farge, 20 June [1869], ibid., 1:120.

254 "loneliness and gloom": HJ to AJ, 10 March [1869], ibid., 1:95.

254 "letter of darksome blue"; "bathe and walk and feed and read the newspapers": HJ to Grace Norton, 6 April [1869], ibid., 1:106, 107.

255 "douche rectale": WJ to HJ, 23 April 1869, *WJL*, 1:66.

255 "the mighty lads of England"; "lounging down the stream"; "at the right of the Carver": HJ to WJ, 26 April [1869], *HJL*, 1:110–12.

256 "a movement every day": HJ to WJ, 13 May [1869], *WJL*, 1:73.

256 "*Never resist a motion to stool*": WJ to HJ, 1 June 1869, ibid., 1:78.

256 "I blush to say": WJ to HJ, 12 June 1869, ibid., 1:84.

256 "I am much obliged to you all for your good advice"; "magnificently ugly—deliciously hideous," etc.: HJ to HJSr, 10 May [1869], *HJL*, 1:115–17.

257 "fairytale of privilege": *NSB*, 470.

258 "I am watching for Aunt Kate's arrival": HJ to HJSr, 10 May [1869], *HJL*, 1:118–19.

258 "Down, down—on, on into Italy we went": HJ to AJ, 31 August [1869], ibid., 1:128–29.

259 "a species of investment": HJ to John La Farge, 21 September [1869], ibid., 1:133.

259 "recreation"; "serious culture"; "The only economy": HJ to MJ, 28 June [1869], ibid., 1:124–25.

259 "Your letters from Italy are beyond praise": WJ to HJ, 5 December 1869, *WJL*, 1:128.

260 "extremely like it in atmosphere and color": HJ to John La Farge, 21 September [1869], *HJL*, 1:134.

260 "love a bath-tub and they hate a lie": HJ to HJSr, [26 October 1869], ibid., 1:153.

260 "bare-chested, bare-legged, magnificently tanned and muscular"; "picturesque"; "rotting and crumbling": HJ to WJ, 25 September [1869], ibid., 1:142.

261 half-understood homoerotic inclinations: The word *homosexuality* was not used in English until 1892; see David M. Halperin, *One Hundred Years of Homosexuality* (New York: Routledge, 1990), 15. More oblique and complex references to homoerotic behavior, of course, occurred much earlier in human history.

261 John Addington Symonds: See Phyllis Grosskurth, *John Addington Symonds: A Biography* (New York: Arno Press, 1964); Paul Robinson, *Gay Lives: Homosexual Autobiography from John Addington Symonds to Paul Monette* (Chicago: University of Chicago Press, 1999).

261 "vulgar, vulgar, vulgar": HJ to MJ, 13 October [1869], *HJL*, 1:152.

261 "bitterness of exile": HJ to HJSr, 26 October 1869, ibid., 1:153.

262 "getting better and locating some of their diseases in me": HJ to WJ, 26 October [1869], ibid., 1:158.

262 "little cities of pasteboard"; "reeling and moaning thro' the streets"; "dusky Hindoo idol": HJ to WJ, 30 October [1869], ibid., 1:160.

262 "grassy arena"; "flaccid old woman waving his ridiculous fingers"; "As you revert to that poor sexless old Pope": HJ to AJ, 7 November [1869], ibid., 1:163–65, 171n.

263 *"Manly!"* HJ to WJ, 8 November [1869], *WJL*, 1:122 and n.

263 "a useful distraction from the unbroken scrutiny of each other's characters": HJ to WJ, 27 [December 1869], *HJL*, 1:185.

264 "bald-headed": Quoted in *HJWB*, 133.

264 "if all other women felt the eternal significance of matrimony"; "queer"; "they wouldn't be [her] for anything": Quoted in ibid., 129.

264 "neither reasonable nor consoling"; "not only highly unpractical, but ignoble & shirking"; *"pride & conceit"*: Quoted in ibid., 135.

264 " 'pride' and aristocracy and 'spirited nature' "; " 'Noblesse oblige' ": *AJD*, 155.

265 "snub": Quoted in *HJWB*, 137.

265 "first rate": WJ to HJ, 1 November 1869, *WJL*, 1:121.

265 "elegant invalidity"; "propriety": HJ to HJSr, 10 May [1869], *HJL*, 1:118.

265 "delightful in all respects," etc.: WJ to HJ, 5 December 1869, *WJL*, 1:129.

265 "azure demon": HJ to WJ, 26 April [1869], *HJL*, 1:109.

265 "sick of life": WJ to HJ, 22 March 1869, *WJL*, 1:61.

266 "steadily deteriorating"; "galvanic disk"; "stomach, bowels, brain": WJ to HJ, 27 December 1869, ibid., 1:132.

266 "It fills me with wonder and sadness that [Bob] should be off in that Western desolation": HJ to WJ, 8 March 1870, *HJL*, 1:210.

266 Kitty Van Buren: See *BBF*, 110–11.

267 "hardly exchanged ten words with a human creature": HJ to MJ, 5 February [1870], *HJL*, 1:194.

267 "unlimited tomatoes and beans and peas and squash and turnips and carrots and corn": HJ to WJ, 8 March 1870, ibid., 1:207.

267 "amber-tinted surface of the scalloped oysters": HJ to HJSr, 19 March 1870, ibid., 1:216–17.

268 "as if I were pressing all England to my soul": Ibid., 1:215.

268 "dear, bright, little Minny": HJ to MJ, 26 March 1870, ibid., 1:219.

268 "My dear young lady," etc.: *NSB*, 513.

268 "immense little spirit": HJ to HJSr, 19 March 1870, *HJL*, 1:214.

269 "It comes home to me": HJ to MJ, 26 March 1870, ibid., 1:219.

269 "Minny has lost very little by her change of state"; "sleeping less and less": HJ to WJ, 29 March 1870, ibid., 1:227.

269 "Such a burden has been taken off my heart"; "not wishing to add to my anxiety": MJ to AJ, [14 January 1870], James Papers, H: MS Am 1093.1 (25).

269 "It's a good deal like dying"; "Farewell, beloved survivors": HJ to Grace Norton, 28 April [1870], *HJL*, 1:233.

270 "*palazzo*"; "soaring *campanile*"; "*piazza*": HJ to Grace Norton, 20 May 1870, ibid., 1:238.

270 "the end of [their] youth": *NSB*, 515.

271 "asylum"; "a sort of sculptured Egyptian cat or Peruvian mummy"; "*That shape am I*"; "Nothing that I possess can defend me against that fate"; "a horrible dread in the pit of his stomach"; "The eternal God is my refuge," etc.: *VRE*, 128–29.

271 "first act of free will shall be to believe in free will": Quoted in *WJL*, 4:431n; Gay Wilson Allen, *William James: A Biography* (New York: Viking, 1967), 168.

271 his own agonies: See *VRE*, 118–19.

271 "Florence is within and not without": HJ to Grace Norton, 20 May 1870, *HJL*, 1:239.

Chapter 9: Heiresses Abroad

272 Vanderbilts or Belmonts, General Philip Sheridan or General William Tecumseh Sherman: See Sternglass, 152.

272 "pools"; "frowsy betting men"; "blew a loud summons on a horn": Henry James Jr., "Saratoga, 1870," in *Portraits of Places* (Boston: James R. Osgood, 1884), 332–33, Rare Books Collection, Wellesley College (hereafter W). *Portraits of Places* hereafter *PP*.

273 "blue Mediterranean": Ibid., 326.

273 "duster"; "satin-shod feet": Ibid., 332–33.

274 "San Francisco, from New Orleans, from Alaska"; "diamonds and laces": Ibid., 327.

274 "at any hour of the morning or evening"; "dusty clapboards"; "with her beautiful hands": Ibid., 330–31.

274 "vacuous grandeur": Ibid., 327.

274 "money and finery and possessions": Ibid., 331.

275 "European gains": HJ to Grace Norton, 26 September [1870], *HJL*, 1:245.

275 "*might* be lodged in one of the innermost circles of the Inferno—in Wisconsin"; "quiet, stay-at-home life": Ibid., 1:268–69.

276 "When one sits down to sum up Cambridge life": HJ to Charles Eliot Norton, 4 February 1872, ibid., 1:271.

276 the respectable sum of $150: WJ to RJ, 25 July 1870, *WJL*, 4:410.

276 "shut up face to face with [his] impotence to do anything": WJ to HJ, 25 May 1873, ibid., 1:209.

276 "glanced": *AJD*, 127.

277 insisted that . . . he would be able to serve his guests: see McAleer, 598.

277 Wilkie would cross the Missouri at Council Bluffs, etc.: See *BBF*, 112–13; McAleer, 598–99; James Bradley Thayer, *A Western Journey with Mr. Emerson* (Boston: Little, Brown, 1884).

278 "burly, bull-necked man of hard sense": Quoted in McAleer, 599.

278 "acute and constant"; "barely remunerative": HJ Sr. to GWJ, 4 June [1871], quoted in *BBF*, 114.

278 incoming editor: Howells, an assistant editor, would take over the editor's chair in July 1871.

279 "marvelous creatures"; "not lightly to be thrown aside"; "*atelier* and *salon*": HJ to Elizabeth Boott, [April 1871], *HJL*, 1:255.

281 "one of the greatest works of 'this or any age' ": HJ to James Thomas Fields, 15 November [1870], ibid., 1:249.

281 "slight": HJ to Charles Eliot Norton, 9 August 1871, ibid., 1:262.

281 "under-valued man": Henry James Jr., *Watch and Ward*, *Atlantic Monthly* 28 (August 1871), 232. Hereafter *AM*.

282 "every whorehouse in Boston"; "I admire the old fellow": WJ to Henry Pickering Bowditch, 8 April 1871, *WJL*, 4:417.

282 "long-headed"; "wrangle grimly"; "not great choice of company": HJ to Charles Eliot Norton, 4 February 1872, *HJL*, 1:273.

283 "just the thing to work my salvation": WJ to AJ, 27 July 1872, *WJL*, 4:426.

283 "smallness of College pay"; "up to the very limit of physical endurance": *CWE*, 87.

283 "decidedly a roller": HJ to HJSr and MJ, 20 May [1872], *HJL*, 1:283.

283 "scribbl[ing] on the tumbling washstand in the malodorous stateroom": HJ to HJSr and MJ, 4 June [1872], ibid., 1:290.

284 the foibles of the other Jameses: See *AJD*, 57.

284 "cry for two hours, after he goes": Ibid., 74.

285 "introductions, photographs, travellers' tales": Henry James Jr., *William Wetmore Story and His Friends: From Letters, Diaries, and Recollections*, 2 vols. (Boston: Houghton Mifflin, 1903), 1:10–11. Hereafter *WWS*.

285 "the poor bewildered and superannuated genius": Henry James Jr., "Swiss Notes," in *Transatlantic Sketches* (Boston: J. R. Osgood, 1875), 63, W. Hereafter *TS*.

285 "introduction to English verdure"; "a quiet stroll through the town"; "*valet de place*": HJ to MJ, 23 May [1872], *HJL*, 1:286.

286 "The country has no disappointments"; "We of course interpose"; "[d]ear house-cleaning mother": HJ to HJSr, 29 May [1872], ibid., 1:287–88.

286 "show region," etc.: HJ to Charles Eliot Norton, 1 June [1872], ibid., 1:289.

286 "I have been playing at first impressions for a second time": "Chester," in *TS*, 7.

287 "unsophisticated young person": "Florentine Notes," in *TS*, 282–83.

287 "companion"; "Elizabethan": "Lichfield and Warwick," *TS*, 28.

287 "embedded in his pages [are] many pearls": *AJD*, 212.

287 "capital traveler"; "rhosy-dendrons": HJ to HJSr and MJ, 4 June [1872], *HJL*, 1:292.

288 "genius of the house": HJSr to AJ, 27 June [1872], James Papers, H: MS Am 1092.9 (4157).

288 "the epithet of Mme de Sevigné"; "undreamt by any of us"; "lioness": WJ to HJ, 24 August 1872, *WJL*, 1:165.

288 "thoroughly launched in journalism"; "radical"; "obvious"; "what the public was going to want": Henry James Jr., *The Portrait of a Lady* (Boston: Houghton Mifflin, 1882), 43–44.

290 "My daughter a child of France!"; "mere delights of eating and drinking and seeing and dressing"; "What has become of that high moral nature": MJ to AJ, 18 July [1872], James Papers, H. MS Am 1093.1 (26).

290 the Irish patriot Charles Stewart Parnell: See *AJD*, 158–59.

291 "Montreux dress": HJ to AJ, 10 February 1873, *HJL*, 1:340.

291 "amiability & sweetness"; "various thin-flanked Englishmen with par-boiled faces": HJ to WJ, 24 July [1872], *WJL*, 1:161–62.

293 "over excitement"; "Her verdict": Quoted in *AJB*, 154–55.

293 "the center of the stage": Ibid., 156. For Strouse's analysis of Alice's break-down in Switzerland, see ibid., 152–56.

293 "bath of light and air—color and general luxury"; "enough to support [him]self in affluence": HJ to HJSr and MJ, 9 September [1872], *HJL*, 1:296, 298.

294 "delightful pictures and memories": HJ to WJ, 22 September [1872], ibid., 1:299.

294 "'*Ah Monsieur*'"; "older and wiser"; "innumerable delightful days and hours and sensations": HJ to HJSr and MJ, 29 September [1872], ibid., 1:302–3.

295 "The dresses are unpacked": HJ to HJSr, [November 1872], ibid., 1:307.

295 "glittering bauble": HJ to HJSr and MJ, ibid., 1:305.

295 "walking, strolling, *flânant*": HJ to WJ, 30 November [–1 December] 1872, ibid., 1:312.

295 "serene": HJ to Grace Norton, 5 March 1873, ibid., 1:350.

295 "struck up a furious intimacy"; "queer places": HJ to HJSr, [November 1872], ibid., 1:308.

296 "guilty of a stroke of business": *SBO*, 190.

296 "realization of [his] investments": HJ to HJSr, 22 December 1873, *HJL*, 1:422.

296 "modernized air in the streets": HJ to HJSr, 25 December [1872], ibid., 1:315.

297 "nail": Ibid., 1:314.

297 "age of Mrs. Jack": See ibid., 2:266n.

297 "one upholstered in cobalt and the other in yellow": HJ to MJ, 24 March 1873, ibid., 1:360.

298 "pathetic old-world situation"; "*moeurs Italiennes*": HJ to WJ, 9 April 1873, ibid., 1:368.

298 "interesting or 'cultivated' native society": HJ to HJSr, 4 March [1873], ibid., 1:348.

298 "sight-seeing barbarians": HJ to AJ, 10 February 1873, ibid., 1:338.

298 "Cambridge tea fights": HJ to MJ, 29 December [1872], ibid., 1:318.

298 "dark side to a brilliant picture": HJ to Grace Norton, 5 March 1873, ibid., 1:350.

298 "*caro sposo*": HJ to WJ, 8 January [1873], ibid., 1:321.

298 "all her sweetness": HJ to HJSr, 19 January 1873, ibid., 1:328.

298 "a very poor affair indeed"; "sonorously announced"; "*roof*, not a ceiling"; "friendly, humorous and clever"; "fair, fat, and fifty": HJ to MJ, 26 January 1873, ibid., 1:331–32.

299 "*prosperous* pretention"; "His cleverness"; "brazen hussy": HJ to Charles Eliot Norton, 31 March [1873], ibid., 1:362.

300 "criticism would be graceless": HJ to MJ, 29 December [1872], ibid., 1:318.

300 "lavender satin lavishly *décolleté*": HJ to WJ, 8 January [1873], ibid., 1:322.

301 "tolerable seat"; "an excellent fellow": HJ to HJSr, 1 February [1873], ibid., 1:335.

302 "the Marchese somebody"; "remarkably ugly little grey-haired boy": HJ to AJ, 10 February 1873, ibid., 1:339.

302 "a Yankee girl can do anything she pleases": *WWS*, 1:255.

302 "too independent by half": Ibid., 1:256.

302 "that strange sisterhood of American 'lady sculptors'": Ibid., 1:257.

303 "hard as flint": HJ to HJSr, 4 March [1873], *HJL*, 1:347.

303 "mouselike": HJ to HJSr, 30 March [1880], ibid., 2:277.

303 "if she would only paint a little less *helplessly*": HJ to WJ, 9 April 1873, ibid., 1:368.

303 "fierce energy": HJ to HJSr, 19 January 1873, ibid., 1:328.

303 "beautiful Bore"; "Tell it not in Philadelphia"; "brutal phrase": HJ to MJ, 26 January 1873, ibid., 1:331.

304 "exclusive diet of women": WJ to HJ, 11 May 1873, *WJL*, 1:203.

304 "high sounding": WJ to HJ, 13 February 1873, ibid., 1:189.
304 "ran a little more to *curliness*"; "directness of style": WJ to HJ, [10] October 1872, ibid., 1:172.
304 "cold, thin blooded & priggish": WJ to HJ, 24 November 1872, ibid., 1:176.
305 "*fratello mio*": HJ to WJ, 9 April 1873, ibid., 1:200.
305 "spouse": WJ to GWJ, 16 November 1873, ibid., 4:454.
305 "oysters and cold beef, tomatoes and apple-pie"; "carte": MJ to HJ, 27 April [1873], James Papers, H: MS Am 1093.1 (46).
305 "parasitic life": WJ to HJ, 14 July [1873], *WJL*, 1:215.
305 "A compliment to me!": HJ to HJSr, 2 November [1873], *HJL*, 1:408.
305 "wedded to Europe": WJ to MJ, 6 November [1873], *WJL*, 4:451–52.
306 "the angel"; "He is wholly unchanged": WJ to the James family, ibid., 4:453.
306 "utter slave": WJ to AJ, 17 December 1873, ibid., 4:472.
306 "look out for a wife"; "positively refuse[d] to think of such a thing": WJ to RJ, 8 December [1873], ibid., 4:465.
306 "sinister"; "damned blood soaked soil"; "fled howling from the place": WJ to HJSr, 30 November 1873, ibid., 4:462.
307 "I greatly value *his* impressions"; "sun-bathed": HJ to HJSr, 3 December [1873], *HJL*, 1:412–13.
307 "in "wedding costume"; "with the flush of successful literary effort": WJ to AJ, 17 December 1873, *WJL*, 4:471.
307 "dip into": WJ to AJ, [22 December 1873], ibid., 4:473.
308 "ministering angel": HJ to HJSr and MJ, 5 February [1874], *HJL*, 1:430.
308 "angelic patient": WJ to MJ, 23 January [1874], *WJL*, 4:479.
308 "The strongest forces are not the most visible forces": WJ to RJ, 8 December [1873], ibid., 4:465–66.
308 "I expected to find Germany hideous after Italy": WJ to Catherine Elizabeth Havens, 23 March 1874, ibid., 4:486.

Chapter 10: Matches

310 "pendant from her ears"; "obstinate will"; "firm & energetic will"; "I cant [sic] for the life of me": HJSr to WJ and HJ, 21 November [1873], *WJL*, 4:456.
311 "hard nonentity": WJ to AJ, 13 February 1874, ibid., 4:484.
312 "This is a crisis in Wilky's life": MJ to HJ, 21 January [1873], James Papers, H: MS Am 1093.1 (42).
312 "Wilky's fortunes seem to be brightening": MJ to to HJ, 3 April [1873], ibid., MS Am 1093.1 (54).
312 "Such flowers!"; "Such meats and drinks!": HJSr to WJ, 21 November [1873], *WJL*, 4:457.
313 "sexual intercourse begins regularly"; "mental troubles": WJ to RJ, 22 June 1872, ibid., 4:424.
314 "economical talents": HJ to HJSr and MJ, 29 September [1872], *HJL*, 1:303.
314 "a few natural flowers": From the Holtons' family journal, quoted in *BBF*, 119.
314 "won all hearts"; "prettiness, amiability, vivacity, & modesty"; "dash and pluckiness": WJ to HJ, 24 November 1872, *WJL*, 1:175.
315 "panacea for all his woes": WJ to AJ, 13 February 1874, ibid., 4:483.
315 "queer, so sandwiched between infancy and maturity": HJ to HJSr, 22 December 1873, *HJL*, 1:421.
315 "become a magazinist": WJ to AJ, 17 December 1873, *WJL*, 4:467.

315 "conjugal sentiment": MJ to HJ, 8 December 1873, James Papers, H: MS Am 1093.1 (52).
316 "arctic cold and torrid heat": *AJD*, 36.
316 "wintry levels": RJ to HJSr, 28 January 1873, James Papers, H: MS Am 1095.2 (18).
316 "Wilky sends good news of his housekeeping": WJ to MJ, 23 January [1874], *WJL*, 4:479.
318 "none but failures & invalids": WJ to Catherine Elizabeth Havens, 22 February 1876, ibid., 4:534.
318 "the 'last hair' ": WJ to RJ, 7 May [1876], ibid., 4:536.
319 "strong longings"; "the normal state both for men and women"; health; "resolution": WJ to RJ, 20 April 1873, ibid., 4:434.
319 "Were she mine": WJ to RJ, 11 June [1876], ibid., 4:538.
320 "a high congress of souls": See Laura E. Richards and Maud Howe Eliot, *Julia Ward Howe, 1819–1910*, 2 vols. (Boston: Houghton Mifflin, 1916), chap. 13.
320 a third of what men earned: See Barbara Miller Solomon, *In the Company of Educated Women: A History of Women and Higher Education in America* (New Haven, CT: Yale University Press, 1985), 33.
321 "young person with a patent costume": WJ to AGHJ, [14 March 1876], *WJL*, 4:535.
322 "docile passivity": WJ to HJ, 3 June 1876, ibid., 1:261.
323 the St. Regis House, etc.: For an architectural history of Adirondack resorts, see Bryant Franklin Tolles, *Resort Hotels of the Adirondacks, 1850–1950* (Hanover, NH: University Press of New England, 2003).
323 "unpainted farmhouse"; "poor dislicensed Boston": "Saratoga, 1870," in *PP*, 334–35.
325 "leading a natural animal life": WJ to Catherine Elizabeth Havens, 25 December 1876, *WJL*, 4:550.
325 "break through [his] bonds"; "I *depend* on Mrs. Ward"; "pretty scenery": WJ to Thomas Wren Ward, [4 August 1876], ibid., 4:542.
326 "seven weeks of insomnia"; "To state abruptly the whole matter"; "My duty in my own mind is clear"; "It seems": WJ to AGHJ, [September 1876], ibid., 4:543.
327 "tragic"; "normal"; "scholastic and pedantic"; "general mania for theorizing at unseemly hours": WJ to AGHJ, [September 1876], ibid., 4:545–46.
327 "self contained and self supported at a distance, not needing [him]": WJ to AHGJ, 12 November 1876, ibid., 4:548.
327 "marriage of unhealthy persons"; "crime": WJ to AHGJ, [September 1876], ibid., 4:546.
328 "My friend": WJ to AHGJ, 12 November 1876, ibid., 4:548.
328 "Christmas token": WJ to Catherine Elizabeth Havens, ibid., 4:549.
328 "delirious affair"; "She cares no more for me"; "bury": WJ to Thomas Wren Ward, 30 December 1876, ibid., 4:552.
329 "the nicest face & the sweetest smile"; "I hope I shan't see him again": AJ to Annie Ashburner, 2 November 1873, *DLAJ*, 60.
330 "I can't get reconciled"; "features": AJ to Sara Sedgwick, 1 February 1874, ibid., 61.
330 "all Canadians . . . are by nature several degrees lower"; "dirty desolate hole"; "Earthly Paradise": AJ to Annie Ashburner, 26 September 1873, ibid., 56–57.
330 " 'company manners' ": *AJD*, 49.
330 "tender and apparently undesired": AJ to Annie Ashburner, 26 December 1875, *DLAJ*, 69.

330 "elope with the handsome butcher-boy": AJ to Sara Sedgwick, 16 February 1874, ibid., 63.
330 "cruel and unnatural fate for a woman": *AJD*, 57.
331 "They seem to be such an impossible couple": AJ to Sara Sedgwick, 16 February 1875, *DLAJ*, 63.
331 "stay at home in a constant state of matrimonial expectation"; "attracted by depressed & gloomy females": AJ to Annie Ashburner, 12 April 1876, ibid., 73.
331 "rarely"; "beautiful & seductive"; "My passion grows"; "not bad-looking": AJ to Annie Ashburner, 26 December 1875, *DLAJ*, 69.
331 intimacy of equals: See *AJB*, 90–96; see also Lillian Faderman's excellent discussion of women's romantic friendships in the nineteenth century in *Surpassing the Love of Men: Romantic Friendship and Love Between Women from the Renaissance to the Present* (New York: William Morrow, 1981), 145–230.
332 "(1) a high age at marriage": The demographic historian John Hajnal, quoted in Mary S. Hartman, *The Household and the Making of History: A Subversive View of the Western Past* (Cambridge, England: Cambridge University Press, 2004), 21.
333 Mount Holyoke Seminary: The new academy, interestingly, led to its own late-marriage pattern for its graduates. See Solomon, 31.
333 "started making teaching a women's field": Ibid., 32.
334 "violently declining"; "meekly succumbed"; "You can laugh": AJ to Annie Ashburner, 26 December 1875, *DLAJ*, 70.
334 "[I am] deeply hurt at yr. ridicule"; "I assure you it is not a thing to be laughed at"; "only too happy to sit at [her] feet": AJ to Annie Ashburner, 12 April 1876, ibid., 74.
334 "historical professorship"; "immense thing": WJ to HJ, 12 December 1875, *WJL*, 1:247–48.
335 "kept unknown to any": Quoted in *DLAJ*, 70n.
335 "great fancy bazaar": HJ to HJSr, 18 November [1875], *HJL*, 2:6.
335 "Mr. James is always fascinating": MJ to HJ, 3 April [1874], James Papers, H: MS Am 1093.1 (54).
336 "very charming notice": HJ to William Dean Howells, 3 February [1876], *HJL*, 2:23.
336 "emancipation": HJ to Grace Norton, 8 June [1879], ibid., 2:241.
336 "bosom of the Orleans family": HJ to MJ, 24 January [1876], ibid., 2:20.
337 "the skim of the milk of the old noblesse": Henry James Jr., *The American* (Boston: Houghton Mifflin, 1907), 54. Hereafter *A*.
337 "ugly"; "old, corpulent, and deaf"; "what princesses are trained to [be]": HJ to MJ, 24 January [1876], *HJL*, 2:20.
337 "prehistoric monster[s]"; "specimens": *A*, 54.
337 "*Je suis lancé en plein Olympe*": HJ to Thomas Sergeant Perry, 3 February [1876], *HJL*, 2:24.
338 "a magnificent creature"; "manlier": HJ to CW, 3 December [1875], ibid., 2:10.
338 "touches that are too *raffiné*": HJ to WJ, 8 February [1876], ibid., 2:26.
338 "meat for men"; "too many flowers and knots of ribbon": "Ivan Turgenev" (1903), quoted in *HJAL*, 184.
338 "in a way that he had rarely spoken": HJ to WJ, 25 April [1876], *HJL*, 2:42.
338 "*amour d'homme*": HJ to WJ, 8 February [1876], ibid., 2:26.
338 Paul Zhukovsky: The relationship between Harry and Zhukovsky was mostly neglected or deemphasized by Harry's twentieth-century biographers. The exceptions to this neglect are Fred Kaplan and Sheldon M. Novick. Leon Edel,

who reviewed this second book before his death in 1997, was characteristically skeptical of the degree to which Novick turned Paul Zhukovsky into an affair, an active, emotional romance for the young Henry James. He was mistaken, however, that the evidence for an emotional entanglement is flimsy; on the contrary, it is all too plentiful. But my treatment of this loaded romantic friendship takes a middle ground, which seems to me more in keeping with the repressed and unconscious sexual habits of the 1870s, of which Henry James Jr. was an exemplar.

339 "about [his] own age"; "great friend": HJ to WJ, 25 April [1859], *HJL*, 2:42.

339 "intimate friend"; "dandled by Empresses": HJ to MJ, 8 May [1876], ibid., 2:46.

339 "valuable background in Germanism"; "delicate and interesting mind"; "*l'épicurien le plus naif* "; "one of the pure flowers of civilization": HJ to AJ, 24 May [1876], ibid., 2:50.

340 "pretty girl"; "I can at least show you a pretty boy": Henry James Jr., *Roderick Hudson* (Boston: Houghton Mifflin, 1910), 16. Hereafter *RH*.

340 "remarkably handsome"; "admirably chiselled and finished": Ibid., 20.

340 "Northampton is not so gay as Rome": Ibid., 141.

341 "great deal of *mollesse*"; "amateurish": HJ to WJ, 25 April [1876], *HJL*, 2:42.

341 "He lacks vigor": HJ to MJ, 8 May [1876], ibid., 2:46.

341 "young Russian": HJ to WJ, 25 April [1876], ibid., 2:42.

341 "dear young friend Joukowsky": HJ to AJ, 24 May [1876], ibid., 2:49.

341 "*extremement sympathique*": HJ to WJ, 22 June [1876], ibid., 1:55.

342 "relics"; "awful": HJ to AJ, 24 May [1876], ibid., 1:50.

342 "Parisian Babylon": HJ to WJ, 25 April [1876], ibid., 2:42.

342 "jovial, prattlesome, and entertaining": HJ to MJ, 8 May [1876], ibid., 2:45.

342 "all sorts of interesting Russians": HJ to AJ, 24 May [1876], ibid., 2:50.

342 "as easy as an old glove": HJ to MJ, 8 May [1876], ibid., 2:46.

342 "us": HJ to HJSr, 11 November [1876], ibid., 2:74.

343 "picturesque": HJ to AJ, 24 May [1876], ibid., 2:50.

343 "sworn an eternal friendship": See ibid., 2:42, 50.

343 "most tender affection": HJ to AJ, 24 May [1876], ibid., 2:49.

343 "So you see I don't love beneath my station": HJ to WJ, 25 April [1876], ibid., 2:42.

343 "I envy you the possession": WJ to HJ, 3 June 1876, *WJL*, 1:262.

343 "send Joukowsky's Portrait": WJ to HJ, 5 July [1876], ibid., 1:269. Harry evidently did send William a portrait, as one survives in the William James papers, dated from this era of his life.

343 "extreme purity of life": HJ to AJ, 24 May [1876], *HJL*, 2:50.

343 Harry's most authoritative biographer: See *HJAL*, 253.

343 "effeminacy, celibacy, and sublimation of eros": Wendy Graham, *Henry James's Thwarted Love* (Palo Alto, CA: Stanford University Press, 1999), 4.

Chapter 11: Boston Marriage

346 "soft strong air"; "stiffen his backbone"; "It was impossible": WJ to AHGJ, 30 May [1877], *WJL*, 4:565–66.

346 "Oh thank you, thank you": WJ to AHGJ, [27 February 1877], ibid., 4:554.

347 "Ah Friend!": WJ to AHGJ, 15 March 1877, ibid., 4:554.

347 "Some day, God willing": WJ to AHGJ, 15 April 1877, ibid., 4:557.

347 "bowed down with solemn happiness"; "I will try to be a mate": WJ to AHGJ, 23 April [1877], ibid., 4:558.

347 "friend & lover": WJ to AHGJ, [3 May 1877], ibid., 4:562.

347 "standard of wholesomeness"; "crime": WJ to AHGJ, [September 1876], ibid., 4:545–46.

347 "old stone cottage": WJ to AJ, HJ, and CW, 30 May [1872], ibid., 4:422.

348 "restless striving after new architectural effects"; "no look of domesticity"; "a prevailing commonness": WJ to RJ, 11 June [1876], ibid., 4:537.

348 "little salary": WJ to RJ, 2 September 1873, ibid., 4:443.

349 "rushing, slapping, and tinkling music of the boat"; "wicked"; "Don't think either": WJ to AHGJ, 30 May [1877], ibid., 4:568–69.

349 "embarrassed"; "a certain aridity & bleakness of mind": WJ to AHGJ, 7 June 1877, ibid., 4:572.

349 *"doctrines"*; "I renounce you!": WJ to AHGJ, [15 June 1877], ibid., 4:574.

350 "We cannot separate so lightly"; "You and I can never mean nothing each for the other"; "lonesome, dreary Canada": WJ to AHGJ, [20 July 1877], ibid., 4:577–78.

350 "physical renovation and invigoration": WJ to AHGJ, 24 August [1877], ibid., 4:584.

350 "I charge you to breathe no word of it": WJ to RJ, 15 September 1877, ibid., 4:586.

350 "musical séance": HJ to HJSr, 11 November [1876], *HJL*, 2:73.

350 "enchanting studio and apartment": HJ to MJ, 8 May [1876], ibid., 2:46.

350 "ravishing young widow"; "I was bored"; "They are quite the most (to me) fascinating people"; "all round the horizon": HJ to HJSr, 11 November [1876], ibid., 2:73–74.

351 "an insatiable collector"; "walls were covered with rusty arms": *A*, 140.

352 "potent moralist"; "the tale and the moral hanging well together": Henry James Jr., "Gustave Flaubert," in *French Poets and Novelists* (London: Macmillan, 1893), 201.

352 "You're the great Western Barbarian": *A*, 45.

353 "certain admirable wash-tubs": Ibid., 158.

353 "I made up my mind tolerably early in life": Ibid., 50.

353 "sitting, bareheaded"; "a rapid inspection of Newman's person": Ibid., 60.

353 "a friend already made": Ibid., 114.

353 "free and adventurous nature"; "destined to understand one another": Ibid., 126.

353 "Well, here I am for you as large as life"; "interested": Ibid., 128.

354 "a long 'pull' dangling in the young man's conscious soul": Ibid., 129.

354 "so fabulously!"; "the flower of [his] magnificent manhood": Ibid., 132.

354 *"mollesse"*: HJ to WJ, 25 April [1876], *HJL*, 2:42.

354 "dead failure": *A*, 132.

354 "fell into step together"; "formally swearing an eternal friendship": Ibid., 139.

354 "eternal friendship": HJ to AJ, 24 May [1876], *HJL*, 2:50.

354 Leon Edel: Edel remarks that Harry's "warm friendship with Paul Zhukovsky is reflected in the friendship between Newman and Valentine: it has the same quality of camaraderie." *LJH*, 2:261. Late in his life, Edel ridiculed the idea, floated in Sheldon M. Novick's *Henry James: The Young Master* (1996), that Zhukovsky had ever been Harry's lover. Zhukovsky may not have been in the physical sense, but the significance of this intimate friend in Harry's emotional development has been systematically overlooked or underestimated, and partly thanks to Edel's uneasiness.

355 "It's a pity you don't fully understand me"; "Old races have strange secrets!": *A*, 163.

355 "You're charming, innocent, beautiful creatures"; "Valentin holds that women should marry"; "I adore some one I *can't* marry!": Ibid., 280.

355 "really quite a bad bore": Ibid., 355.

355 "the exposure, the possible sacrifice"; "only knew that he did yearn now as a brother": Ibid., 358.

355 "See here . . . if anyone hurts you again!": Ibid., 360.

356 "psychosexual"; "homoerotic": See *HJAL*, 82–83, 244–46, 722.

356 "a most *attachant* creature"; "My few Russian friends here are what I most regret": HJ to HJSr, 11 November [1876], *HJL*, 2:73–74.

356 "Russian snow scene"; "as smooth as . . . paper": HJ to AJ, 13 December [1876], ibid., 2:82–83.

356 "curious temper": See Novick, 412.

357 "I must be a born Londoner": HJ to MJ, 24 December [1876], *HJL*, 2:86.

357 "*fires*": Ibid., 2:90.

357 "detached"; "absolutely *glutinous*"; "mammy": HJ to MJ, 24 December [1876], ibid., 2:85–86.

358 "excellent lodgings in this excellent quarter"; "dusky"; "the exquisite English loaf": HJ to AJ, 13 December [1876], ibid., 2:82.

358 "bachelor": For a thoroughgoing study of the relation of bachelorhood to other forms of middle-class manhood in the nineteenth century, see Katherine V. Snyder, *Bachelors, Manhood, and the Novel, 1850–1925* (Cambridge, England: Cambridge University Press, 1999).

358 The Albany: During the nineteenth century, this famous residence was known primarily as "the Albany." At some point in the twentieth century, however, the fashionable use became simply "Albany." I have used the historical version, as favored by Oscar Wilde, in this book.

359 "civilizing part played . . . by the occasional unmarried man": HJ to Elizabeth Boott, 11 December [1883], *HJL*, 3:17.

359 "I'm too good a bachelor to spoil": HJ to Grace Norton, 28 December 1880, ibid., 2:323.

359 "*Non mi sposero mai—mai!*": HJ to Elizabeth Boott, 11 December [1883], ibid., 3:17–18.

360 "I dined one day at Lady Rose's"; "I lead a very quiet life": HJ to HJSr and AJ, 20 March [1877], ibid., 2:113.

361 "all the great chairs and lounges and sofas filled": HJ to AJ, 2 March [1877], ibid., 4:103.

361 "seem like a festering sore on the bosom of Justice": HJ to WJ, 12 January [1877], ibid., 2:91.

362 "a good many hypochondriac feelings": WJ to RJ, 9 July 1878, *WJL*, 5:18.

362 "Was ever woman in such humor wooed?": WJ to AHGJ, 8 May 1878, ibid., 5:5.

363 "Engaged!": WJ to Oliver Wendell Holmes Jr., 13 May [1878], ibid., 5:6.

363 "dear delightful good for nothing nephew"; "bombshell"; "Imagine us all": Mary Tweedy to WJ, 14 May [1878], ibid., 5:10.

363 "contentment and happiness"; "the greatest piece of news": GWJ to WJ, 16 May 1878, ibid., 5:10.

363 "We are delighted beyond our power to express in the good news": MJ to AHGJ, [May 1878?], James Papers, H: MS Am 1093.1 (32).

364 "for her moral more than her intellectual qualities": WJ to RJ, 9 July 1878, *WJL*, 5:18.

364 "blessings"; "as she will need it most"; "of Miss Gibbens"; "from another hand than your's": HJ to WJ, 29 May [1878], *HJL*, 2:174.

365 "I am greatly disappointed in not being able to go in to see you this morning": MJ to AHGJ, [May 1878?], H: MS Am 1093.1 (32).

365 "the pink of perfection": WJ to Mary Holton James, 12 May [1878], *WJL*, 5:5.

365 "heavy lassitude": WJ to AHGJ, [1 July 1878], ibid., 5:15–16.

366 "very quietly": AHGJ to John Greenleaf Whittier, [n.d.], quoted in Simon, 163.

366 "unwholesome excitement of an engagement"; "all right again": WJ to RJ, 9 July 1878, *WJL*, 5:18.

366 "well"; "a fine red on [his] cheek": WJ to AHGJ, [1 July 1878], ibid., 5:15–16.

366 "hymeneal felicity"; "romantic and irresponsible isolation": WJ to James Jackson Putnam, 21 July 1878, ibid., 5:19.

367 "abruptness"; "As I was divorced from you": HJ to WJ, 15 July [1878], *HJL*, 2:177.

368 "homoeroticism": See *HJAL*, 82–83, 244–46, 722.

368 "with no other country": WJ to AJ, 29 July 1889, *WJL*, 6:517.

369 "clumsy pen": HJ to WJ, 15 July [1878], *HJL*, 2:177; *HJAL*, 244.

369 "painfully silent as to details": HJ to WJ, 23 July [1878], *HJL*, 2:178.

369 "big tranquil library"; "strangely and profoundly at home": HJ to HJSr, 29 May [1878], ibid., 2:175–76.

370 "great hit"; " 'Everyone is talking about it' "; "comprehended"; "sufficiently subtle": HJ to WJ, 23 July [1878], ibid., 2:179.

371 "thin"; "I don't however think you are always right"; "queer and narrow": HJ to WJ, 14 November [1878], ibid., 2:193.

372 "the most contradictory accounts"; "a very clever foreign lady": Henry James Jr., *Daisy Miller* (New York: Harper and Brothers, 1906), 133.

372 "too much as if an artistic experiment": HJ to WJ, 14 November [1878], *HJL*, 2:193.

372 "passive part"; "bare, crude blankness": AJ to Frances Rollins Morse, 25 November 1878, *DLAJ*, 78.

373 "dark waters": *AJD*, 230.

373 "My friend, my sister": WJ to AHGJ, 23 April [1877], *WJL*, 4:558

373 "peerless specimen of 'New England womanhood' ": HJ to AJ, 5 June [1878], James Papers, H: MS Am 1094 (1584).

373 "sunshine transforms Mount Blanc": *VRE*, 126–27.

373 "inconsiderate of William": HJ to AJ, 5 June [1878], James Papers, H: MS Am 1094 (1584).

374 "hideous summer of '78"; "[I] went down to the deep sea": *AJD*, 230.

374 "patience, courage & self control"; "moral prostration": *DLAJ*, 78.

374 "empty pea pod": *AJD*, 230.

375 "a little staggered by the length of time": *WJL*, 5:14.

375 "great joy"; "She is a truly lovely being"; "poor family an immense amount of trouble"; "learning to behave [her]self better": AJ to Frances Rollins Morse, 25 November 1878, *DLAJ*, 78.

376 "strength of wind and limb"; "all about": HJ to WJ, 1 May [1878], *HJL*, 2:172.

376 "panacea for all earthly ills"; "nothing in the way of discomfort"; "all the mere brute superiority"; "most wonderful being": AJ to Sara Sedgwick, 9 August 1879, *DLAJ*, 80–82.

377 "most sustaining optimist": *AJD*, 164.

377 confided in her husband what no other James . . . dared conjecture: See *AJB*, 201; Allen, 227.

Chapter 12: Abandonment

378 "I must try and seek a larger success than I have yet obtained": HJ to William Dean Howells, [14 or 15 July 1879], *HJL*, 2:252.

378 "not brilliant": HJ to Frederick Macmillan, 28 September [1879], ibid., 2:257.

378 "Look out for my next big novel": HJ to Isabella Stewart Gardner, 29 January [1880], ibid., 2:265.

378 "always to keep the pot a-boiling": HJ to William Dean Howells, 17 June [1879], ibid., 2:243.

380 "marched up"; "a rather awkward thing": HJ to MJ, 6 July [1879], ibid., 2:248. 107 times; "folly": HJ to Grace Norton, 8 June [1879], ibid., 2:240.

381 "witty or clever person"; "kind, honest and genial"; "doing sums on the table cloth"; "looked exactly the same"; "drop out of existence so suddenly": HJ to MJ, 6 July [1879], ibid., 2:249.

382 "the portrait of the character and recital of the adventures of a woman": HJ to William Dean Howells, 2 February [1877], ibid., 2:97.

382 "aching fragment": HJ to William Dean Howells, 17 June [1879], ibid., 2:244.

383 "bestride the [B]ritish lion"; "paying visits": WJ to HJSr, MJ, and AJ, 13 July [1880], *WJL*, 5:120–21.

383 "much interesting talk"; "descant on his observations": HJ to HJSr, 20 June [1880], *HJL*, 2:290.

383 "knocking about London": HJ to MJ, 4 July [1880], ibid., 2:292.

383 "swellish looking people"; "buyer"; "Papa gone!": WJ to AHGJ, [5 June 1880], *WJL*, 5:99.

384 "repent"; "the date of that strange performance"; "I want to tell you": WJ to AHGJ, 7 July [1880], ibid., 5:117–19.

385 "queerest repetition of [his] old bachelor outward circumstances": WJ to AHGJ, 13 June [1880], ibid., 5:101.

385 "unfeasible"; "make psychological feathers fly"; "My wife": WJ to Granville Stanley Hall, 16 January 1880, ibid., 5:81.

386 "an easy & natural state": WJ to Arthur George Sedgwick, 20 September 1878, ibid., 5:22.

386 "an enduring haven of refuge from the rocks of life": WJ to AGHJ, 4 [September 1882], ibid., 5:239.

386 "the little animal"; "domestic catastrophe": WJ to RJ, 26 May 1879, ibid., 5:52.

386 "strong, intelligent, and rosy"; "bratling"; "the fatness of his own body": WJ to RJ, 21 November 1879, ibid., 5:67.

386 "baby hobgoblin"; "bewitching": WJ to RJ, 28 April [1880], ibid., 5:92.

386 "speciously"; "non-parlor"; "It would be as awkward for him": HJ to MJ, 31 October [1880], *HJL*, 2:312.

386 "concocting the design": WJ to RJ, 21 March 1880, *WJL*, 5:89.

387 "cares of a nursing father"; "Farewell to the tranquil mind!": WJ to RJ, 18 August [1879], ibid., 5:55–56.

387 "fussing about nurses": WJ to Granville Stanley Hall, 3 September 1879, ibid., 5:61.

388 "noble trustful helpful heart": WJ to AHGJ, 22 June [1880], ibid., 5:105.

389 "coming to live there as a blushing bridal pair"; "a new kind of sympathy"; "the great roaring foreign tide"; "Better late than never!"; "afflictions"; "more of a comfort": WJ to HJSr, MJ, and AJ, 13 July [1880], ibid., 5:120.

389 "unmanliness"; "rolling down hill"; "*honest*": WJ to AHGJ, 31 July [1880], ibid., 5:127–28.

390 "terrible algebra": HJ to Grace Norton, 28 July [1883], *HJL*, 2:424.

391 "slender and blond"; "like a German youth out of Schiller": Quoted in Curt von Westernhagen, *Wagner: A Biography*, trans. Mary Whittall (Cambridge, England: Cambridge University Press, 1978), 556.

391 "Ah, this old robber!": Friedrich Nietzsche, *The Case of Wagner*, in *The Birth of Tragedy and the Case of Wagner*, trans. Walter Kaufmann (New York: Random House, 1967), 185.

391 "long-promised": HJ to HJSr, 30 March [1880], *HJL*, 2:278.

391 *"bonne cuisine, excellent vin, vue paradisique, air excellent"*; *"présent"*: Paul Zhukovsky to HJ, 25 September 1879, James Papers, H: bMS Am 1094 (277).

391 "peculiar": HJ to HJSr, 30 March [1880], *HJL*, 2:278.

391 "the musician of the future"; "intelligible"; "manners and customs"; "carry [him] too far"; "lovely"; "the mutilated Psyche" : HJ to Grace Norton, 9 April 1880, ibid., 2:282–83.

392 "aesthetics"; "immoralities": HJ to AJ, 25 April [1880], ibid., 2:288. Edel emphasizes Harry's sexual discomfort; see *HJAL*, 253. Novick underlines Harry's objections to nihilism; see Novick, 410–12.

393 "ridiculous mixture of Nihilism and bric à brac"; "always under someone's influence"; "H.J.Jr. (!!)": HJ to AJ, 25 April [1880], *HJL*, 2:287.

393 "epistemology of the closet"; "'Closetedness' itself": Sedgwick, *The Epistemology of the Closet*, 3.

394 *"Non ragioniam di lui—ma guarda e passa"*: Henry James Jr., *The Complete Notebooks of Henry James*, ed. Leon Edel and Lyall H. Powers (New York: Oxford University Press, 1987), 216. Hereafter *NHJ*.

394 "vast pale-blue floor"; "wonderfully distinct in the clear still light": HJ to Grace Norton, 9 April 1880, *HJL*, 2:282.

394 *"adorable"*; *"Et votre bonne et chère figure"*: Paul Zhukovsky to HJ, 25 September 1879, H: bMS Am 1094 (277).

395 "admirable, honest, reasonable, wholesome"; "fantastic immoralities and aesthetics": HJ to AJ, 25 April [1880], *HJL*, 2:288.

395 *"Mon bien cher ami"*: Paul Zhukovsky to HJ, 19 March 1898, James Papers, H: bMS Am 1094 (278).

395 "She was looking at everything": From the opening of this novel as it first appeared in the serial. Henry James Jr., *The Portrait of a Lady*, in *AM* (November 1880), 592.

396 based to some degree on Paul Zhukovsky: For a developed comparison of Gilbert Osmond and Paul Zhukovsky, see Novick, 419.

396 "pure-minded"; "tea-parties"; "pursuing [Harry] through Europe": HJ to AJ, 25 April [1880], *HJL*, 2:288.

398 "amiable"; "deaf, and asks me questions": HJ to AJ, 25 April [1880], ibid., 2:288.

398 "code names"; "The Costanza"; "The Littératrice": See Lyndall Gordon, *A Private Life of Henry James: Two Women and His Art* (New York: Norton, 1998), 92.

399 "Of course you admired"; "No, I did not"; "Ah yes"; "not sufficiently acquainted with torsos": Constance Fenimore Woolson's diary, quoted in *LHJ*, 2:417.

400 "Father's": WJ to AHGJ, [9 July 1882], *WJL*, 5:221.

400 "Miss Loring has been a real savior to her": WJ to Frances Rollins Morse, 25 December 1879, ibid., 5:71.

401 "the wisdom of the serpent with the gentleness of the dove": HJ to MJ, 20 July [1880], *HJL*, 2:296.

401 "who could be everything to her": *AJB*, 197.

401 "built a monument somewhere": HJ to MJ, 20 July [1880], *HJL*, 2:296.
401 "wonderful being": AJ to Sara Sedgwick Darwin, 9 August 1879, *DLAJ*, 82.
401 "conspicuous object": WJ to AHGJ, [29 June 1882], *WJL*, 5:221.
401 "delicious": WJ to AHGJ, 12 July [1882], ibid., 5:222.
401 "the sea close to the piazzas": *NHJ*, 230.
402 "great bristling Valhalla"; "laurels to the dead and dinners to the living": *AS*, 61.
402 "very graceful"; "great credit to her intellectual audacity"; "Alice's Whim": HJ to MJ, [31 May 1879], *HJL*, 2:236.
402 Alice and Katharine as lovers: *AJB*, 201; Allen, 227.
403 Mark DeWolfe Howe and "unions"; "Whether these unions": See Faderman, 190; Helen Huntington Howe, *The Gentle Americans: Biography of a Breed* (New York: Harper and Row, 1965), 83.
404 "one of the happy ingredients of her life": WJ to Frances Rollins Morse, 26 December [1878], *WJL*, 5:30.
405 "rude career"; "sorry account": HJ to WJ, 28 January [1878], *HJL*, 2:151.
405 "cross"; "bad day with liquor": Mary Holton James's notebook, quoted in *BBF*, 132–33.
406 "selfish tyrannical turbulent spirit": MJ to GWJ, 1 April [1881], quoted in ibid., 134.
406 "asylum treatment": WJ to AHGJ, [1 February 1881], *WJL*, 5:150.
406 "no duty to these other folks at all"; "orderly"; "less expensive": WJ to AHGJ, [3 February 1881], ibid., 5:151.
407 "upper middle class manners": RJ to HJSr, 23 September [n.y.], James Papers, H: MS Am 1095.2 (18).
407 "bachelor house"; "patron of the Turf"; "disappointingly"; "a very delightful creature": HJ to MJ, 10 January [1881], *HJL*, 2:330–31.
408 "gorgeous residence"; "manner of life"; "golden thrones, belonging to ancient Doges of Venice"; "living like Longfellow": HJ to MJ, 28 November [1880], ibid., 2:317–19.
409 "made up his mind not to marry": Quoted in *HJAL*, 236.
409 "shooting accident": Richard Ellmann, *Oscar Wilde* (New York: Knopf, 1988), 426.
409 "successful and glorified": HJ to MJ, 10 January [1881], *HJL*, 2:331.
409 "princely"; "It is so long since I have had any money": GWJ to HJ, [1882], quoted in *BBF*, 139.
410 "*maquillage* [makeup] on one's grandmother"; "I adore it": HJ to Grace Norton, 12 June 1881, *HJL*, 2:355.
410 "a queer, but almost delightful, creature": Quoted in *HJAL*, 265.
411 "passion"; "the sun, of the south, of colour"; "queer little wineshop"; "A great deal might be done with Herbert Pratt": *NHJ*, 221.
411 "After a year or two of marriage"; "psychological": Ibid., 13.
412 "by the back-door": HJ to Clover Adams, 6 November 1881, *HJL*, 2:361.
412 "*les miens*"; "entering into their lives": *NHJ*, 214.
412 "worn and shrunken": Ibid., 229.
413 "a fifth wheel to their coach": HJ to HJSr and MJ, 9 September [1881], James Papers, H: MS Am 1094 (1920).
413 "poor"; "wonderfully unchanged": *NHJ*, 224.
413 "sympathetic, expressive and effusive": HJ to Grace Norton, 10 January [1882], *HJL*, 2:369.
414 "cultivated Americans": HJ to Grace Norton, 20 September 1880, ibid., 2:307.
414 "commodious and genial": HJ to Grace Norton, 10 January [1882], ibid., 2:369.
414 "a perfect Voltaire in petticoats": HJ to Grace Norton, 20 September 1880, ibid., 2:307.

414   "cockatrice": WJ to HJSr, MJ, and AJ, 13 July [1880], *WJL*, 5:122.

415   "cyanide of potassium": Edward Chalfant, *Better in Darkness: A Biography of Henry Adams: His Second Life, 1862–1891* (Hamden, CT: Archon Books, 1994), 502.

415   "The sky is blue"; "business"; "air of leisure": HJ to Sir John Clark, 8 January [1882], *HJL*, 2:367.

415   "provisional"; "an immensely painted but unfinished cloth"; "rank outsider": *AS*, 339.

416   "big and gorgeous banquet"; "personable": HJ to MJ, 22 January [1882], *HJL*, 2:370.

417   "repulsive and fatuous": HJ to Isabella Stewart Gardner, 23 January [1882], ibid., 2:372.

417   "unclean beast": Quoted in Ellmann, 26.

417   "It has too many bronze generals": Quoted in *LHJ*, 2:459.

417   "Really? You care for *places*?": Oscar Wilde, *The Letters of Oscar Wilde*, ed. Rupert Hart-Davis (London: Rupert Harte-Davis, 1962), 509.

418   "devotion of the family": HJ to MJ, [29 January 1882], *HJL*, 2:375.

418   YOUR MOTHER EXCEEDINGLY ILL; "closing dusk"; "saw her lying in her shroud": *NHJ*, 228.

418   "the two who presumably might suffer most": WJ to Thomas Davidson, 16 April 882, *WJL*, 5:204.

419   "Without her"; "splendid winter's day"; "She was patience": *NHJ*, 229.

420   "She was sweet"; "I thank heaven": HJ to Isabella Stewart Gardner, [13 February 1882], *HJL*, 2:377.

420   "exquisite maternity": *NHJ*, 229.

420   "divine maternity": *AJD*, 221.

420   "country, the sea, the change of air and scene"; "dry, flat, hot, stale and odious Cambridge": *NHJ*, 230.

420   "house": Ibid., 229.

421   "The blessed memory": *DLAJ*, 86.

421   "severe loss to all of us": WJ to Thomas Davidson, 16 April 1882, *WJL*, 5:204.

422   "keystone": *NHJ*, 229.

Chapter 13: Steamer News

424   whose features reminded her all too much of her own mother: *AJD*, 27. This portrait later crossed the Atlantic "without a scratch"; when it arrived, it "seem[ed] somehow to include mother," Alice remarked.

424   "stifled sense": Ibid., 31.

424   "Poor human nature can stand but a slight strain": Ibid., 53.

424   "haunted by the terror that [she] should fail him": Ibid., 79.

424   "look after [their] father"; "person of great ability"; "exert"; "tranquil"; "his own way of taking the sorrows of life": HJ to Florence Wilkinson Mathews, 13 February [1882], *HJL*, 2:379.

425   "her Mother's death seem[ed] to have brought new life to Alice": CW to Mary Holton James, 26 February 1882, quoted in *AJB*, 202.

426   "scragginess"; "charming drives": *NHJ*, 230.

427   "For the sake of pleasing Willy"; "nothing but horror"; "It seems like a dark thing": RJ to HJ, 26 March 1882, quoted in *BBF*, 143.

428   "pretty": *NHJ*, 230.

428   "equal"; "vague terrors"; "I used to think I loved my dear Mother": AJ to Frances Rollins Morse, 11 September 1882, *DLAJ*, 86.

429   "desperately homesick for London": HJ to Lord Rosebery, 27 February 1882, *HJL*, 2:380.

429   "sacrifices": HJ to Frances Anne Kemble, ibid., 2:381.

429   "My darling boy": HJSr to HJ, 9 May [1882], James Papers, H: MS Am 1092.9 (4205).

431   "some very green fields and dirty cabins"; "whirlpool of the Season": HJ to Grace Norton, 3 September [1882], *HJL*, 2:382.

431   "battered and depressed": NHJ, 231.

432   "old salve to a perturbed spirit"; "poor": Ibid., 230.

432   "I have a certain fear that you miss me": HJ to Grace Norton, 25 May [1882], *HJL*, 2:383.

432   "wild"; "night falling and gathering about a lonely ship"; "*terra firma* conditions of solidity"; "kiss"; "Cover Harry": WJ to AHGJ, [2 September 1882], *WJL*, 5:238–39.

433   "Kiss for Harry": WJ to AHGJ, 27 September [1882], ibid., 5:257.

434   "Instead of horse cars"; "Your poor Dad": WJ to Henry James III, [1 October 1882], ibid., 5:261.

434   "peppered over": WJ to AHGJ, 27 September [1882], ibid., 5:258.

435   "stay the winter": WJ to HJ, 23 January [1883], ibid., 1:354.

436   "mystery of womanhood"; "the Mothers!"; "own dear Mother": WJ to AHGJ, 24 September 1882, ibid., 5:255–56.

436   "exquisite little"; "as good as they can be"; "colossal dimensions"; "grand style": WJ to AHGJ, 11 October 1882, ibid., 5:268.

437   "fall back upon": WJ to AHGJ, 3 October 1882, ibid., 5:264.

437   "I feel sorely tempted"; "You & she are a regular pair of twins"; "rapidly falling in love"; "grammar-school"; "no right to resent"; "once"; "I would give millions of dollars"; "everlasting bride"; "shoot to an unexampled height"; "Alice, I ought never to have come abroad alone": WJ to AHGJ, 11 October 1882, ibid., 5:269–70.

438   "*such* eyes"; "ravishingly beautiful": WJ to AHGJ, 6 October [1882], ibid., 5:267.

439   "nevermore to be separated"; "piazzas"; "six years"; "the same fresh boy as then"; "violently in love": "brandished the [J]ewish flag"; "converted her from pessimism to optimism": WJ to AHGJ, [25 July 1882], *WJL*, 5:227.

441   "Miss Lazarus"; "I think the power of *playing* with thought and language"; "dear wife": WJ to Emma Lazarus, 26 August 1882, ibid., 5:233.

441   "one race hating another"; "*Emma*"; "Dearest": WJ to AHGJ, 11 October 1882, ibid., 5:271.

442   "must feel rather bewildered and abandoned"; "Abandoned by your husband"; "William's own doctrines": HJ to AHGJ, 16 October [1882], *HJL*, 2:385.

442   "furies at temporary lodgings"; "Never, never again": WJ to AHGJ, 25 November [1882], *WJL*, 5:307.

443   "soft chuckling": WJ to AHGJ, 29 November [1882], ibid., 5:311.

444   "attack of nausea and faintness"; "gentle vigilance": AHGJ to WJ, 30 November [1882], ibid., 5:312, 314.

445   "Brain softening"; "great perplexity & anxiety"; "Harry & I were both ready to start": WJ to AHGJ, 11 December [1882], ibid., 5:321–22.

446   "very rapid and prosperous, but painful passage": HJ to WJ, 26 December [1882], *HJL*, 2:393.

446   "inside of [an] old church"; "poor dear old father"; "no clear light": WJ to AHGJ, 11 December [1882], *WJL*, 5:321–22.

447 "The dear, dear old man lies there": AHGJ to WJ, 6 December [1882], ibid., 5:320.

447 "hurried": AHGJ to WJ, 3 December 1882, ibid., 5:316.

449 "very quiet"; "tranquil"; "painless"; "series of swoons"; "little of the sick-room"; "softening of the brain"; "simply a gradual refusal of food": HJ to WJ, 26 December [1882], *HJL*, 2:394–95.

449 "spiritual life"; "perfectly cheerful"; "the most picturesque and humorous things": HJ to WJ, 26 December [1882], ibid., 2:395.

449 "fade day by day": *AJD*, 79.

450 "Mary—my Mary"; "Oh, I have such good boys—*such* good boys!": HJ to WJ, 28 December [1882], *HJL*, 2:397.

450 "going with great joy": AHGJ to WJ, 18 December 1882, *WJL*, 5:336.

450 "terribly emaciated": HJ to WJ, 26 December [1882], *HJL*, 2:395.

450 "tied [up] his manuscripts": AHGJ to WJ, 18 December 1882, *WJL*, 5:337.

451 no more urgent personal reasons: See *F* 500.

452 "extraordinarily close to Mother": HJ to WJ, 1 January 1883, *HJL*, 2:398.

452 "Darling old Father"; "peculiarities"; "creature"; "Good night my sacred old Father": WJ to HJSr, 14 December [1882], *WJL*, 5:327–28.

453 "houses": HJ to WJ, 28 December [1882], *HJL*, 2:397.

454 "Grecian portico": HJ to WJ, 23 January [1883], ibid., 2:402.

454 "placed a limitation upon [Bob's] share of the estate": HJ to RJ, 30 December [1882], quoted in *BBF*, 147.

454 "The more I think of this discrimination"; "base cowardly act"; "death stab": GWJ to RJ, 26 December [1883], quoted in ibid., 150.

455 "to absolutely ignore": WJ to HJ, 22 January [1883], *WJL*, 1:353.

455 "sadly broken and changed"; "pretty well finished"; "imbecility"; "lectured and preached": HJ to WJ, 23 January [1883], *HJL*, 2:402.

455 "loving, tender, moderate and wise counsels": GWJ to HJ, 6 February 1883, James Papers, H: bMS Am 1095 (18).

456 "gain strength"; "peg out": GWJ to WJ, 25 September [1883], *WJL*, 5:465.

457 "ghastly"; "Alone, Alone!"; "echoed thro' the house": *AJD*, 45.

457 "medicalization of womanhood": see Jane Wood, *Passion and Pathology in Victorian Fiction* (New York: Oxford University Press, 2001), 8–58.

457 "a Russian electrician"; "quackish quality": AJ to Sara Sedgwick Darwin, 5 May 1884, *DLAJ*, 91.

458 "flimsy houses"; "Jews": AJ to Frances Rollins Morse, [spring 1884?], ibid., 89.

459 "banged"; "soft mass of formless virtue"; "tomb-like closet": AJ to CW and WJ, 22 November 1884, ibid., 93.

459 "only anchorages": AJ to CW, 31 January 1885, ibid., 101.

460 "pincushion of a woman": See ibid., 93n.

460 "a little round ball": AJ to CW and WJ, 22 November 1884, ibid., 94.

460 "not the least shame"; "sense of leisure": *AJD*, 36.

460 "excellent servant": AJ to CW and WJ, 22 November 1884, *DLAJ*, 93.

460 "brought the science of dawdle to perfection": AJ to AHGJ, 8 December 1884, ibid., 96.

460 "You are indeed very delicate": AJ to CW and WJ, 22 November 1884, ibid., 94.

460 "Your illness is a very pleasant one"; "elaborate coiffée"; "mildewed"; "varied & dressy locks"; "round, genial ball of seventy": AJ to AHGJ, 8 December 1884, ibid., 96–97.

461 "percussing & stethoscoping": AJ to WJ, 23 December 1884, ibid., 100.

461 "small pamphlet": AJ to AHGJ, 8 December 1884, ibid., 97.
461 "excessive nervous sensibility"; "Oh! dear me yes"; "I have seen people"; "organic trouble": AJ to CW, 31 January [1885], ibid., 102.
461 "gentlemanly-Punchinello type": HJ to WJ, 2 January 1885, *HJL*, 3:63.
463 "joy and despair"; "stifled sense": *AJD*, 31.
463 "discrete intervals"; "She is a very intelligent woman": HJ to William Dean Howells, 21 February 1884, *HJL*, 3:28.
464 "haunted by fears and anxieties": HJ to Grace Norton, 29 October 1883, ibid., 3:12.
464 "conjugal Mrs. H.": HJ to Elizabeth Boott, 11 December [1883], ibid., 3:17.
464 "un-dependent and independent"; "*cling* no more than a bowsprit"; "her own plans"; "wreck and blight": HJ to Grace Norton, 3 November 1884, ibid., 3:53.
465 "winter of infinite domestic worry": HJ to Violet Paget [Vernon Lee], 10 May [1885], ibid., 3:85.
465 "lady-nurse, or companion": HJ to Grace Norton, 9 May [1885], ibid., 3:82.
465 "No one understands what she has been & done for me": *AJD*, 84.
466 "female Jacobin": Henry James Jr., *The Bostonians* (New York: Penguin, 1984), 37.
466 "far from brilliant": Ibid., 433.
467 "tremble": HJ to Elizabeth Boott, 11 December [1883], ibid., 3:17.
467 "drama of [Alice's] separation"; "bereavement[s]": HJ to AJ, 29 February [1884], ibid., 3:34.
467 "as soon as they get together Alice takes to her bed": HJ to WJ, 29 January [1885], *WJL*, 2:5.
467 "As of her giving her legs to be sawed off": HJ to CW, 12 May [1885], James Papers, H: MS Am 1094 (1336).
469 "with the 'naughty' pages gummed together"; "deliciously droll": *AJD*, 67.
469 "unmentionable"; "magnificent, superb"; "feminine point of view"; "*Do* like the *Bostonians*, dear Grace": HJ to Grace Norton, 4 March [1885], *HJL*, 3:75–76.

Chapter 14: Spirits

471 "the poor little Humster"; "hooked nose": WJ to AHGJ, 26 June [1885], *WJL*, 6:40.
472 "little Israelite": HJ to WJ, 20 February [1884], ibid., 1:374.
472 "human turtle": AJ to WJ, 23 December 1884, *DLAJ*, 98.
472 "moribund": WJ to AHGJ, 26 June [1885], *WJL*, 6:40.
472 "a labor fit to break the back of Hercules": WJ to CW, 28 June 1885, ibid., 6:41.
472 "like an elephant"; "play he was papa and I William"; "I want the whip, I want the whip": WJ to AHGJ, 22 June 1885, ibid., 6:35.
473 "practically separated": WJ to Katharine James Prince, 23 June [1885], ibid., 6:37.
473 "like an antique leperess"; "babies, callers, witnesses, notes to write, or duties to perform": WJ to Katharine James Prince, 21 March [1885], ibid., 6:23.
473 "ladylike": WJ to AJ, 20 March 1885, ibid., 6:21.
473 "constitution proved so tenacious": WJ to Katharine James Prince, 12 July 1885, ibid., 6:44.
473 "Dear little Hummer! Dear little soul!"; "flower of the flock"; "aggrandized and illuminated"; WJ to CW, 11 July 1885, ibid. 6:43–44.

473 "soft memories"; "Alice will always throb": HJ to WJ, 24 July [1885], *HJL*, 3:94.

474 "taste of the intolerable mysteriousness": WJ to CW, 11 July 1885, *WJL*, 6:44.

474 "*esprit fort*": Alta L. Piper, *The Life and Work of Mrs. Piper* (London: Kegan Paul, 1929), 22.

474 "Grecian": Ibid., 11.

475 "great muscular unrest": Quoted in Allen, 284.

475 "a flood of light": Piper, 17.

475 "a sharp blow on her right ear"; "Aunt Sara, not dead, but with you still": Ibid., 12.

476 "actual historical person": See *WJL*, 6:614n.

476 "probably a mere name": Oppenheim, 374.

477 "No spirit form came directly to any one of us": Quoted in Allen, 283.

478 "Rochester rappings": Oppenheim, 11.

478 "simple, genuine, unassuming Yankee girl": WJ to Leonora Evelina Piper, [November 1889], *WJL*, 6:617; Piper, 50.

478 "Light should be the demand of every spiritualist": Quoted in Oppenheim, 14.

479 "preoccupied with spirit rappings": WJ to HJ, 2 April 1890, *WJL*, 2:134.

479 "I wish to determine a fact": WJ to Elizabeth Wild Blodgett, 21 June [1888], ibid., 6:419.

479 "social side": WJ to HJ, 23 November 1890, ibid., 2:157.

480 "fraud or simulation of fraud": Edmund Gurney to WJ, 31 July [1885], ibid., 6:48. Such fraud destroyed Edmund Gurney's career and also his life. The English psychologist was found dead in his hotel room in Brighton, England, in June 1888. The cause of death was an overdose of chloroform. Officially, Gurney had taken this dangerous chemical to relieve his facial neuralgia and help him sleep. But Trevor Hall argued that Gurney administered a deliberate overdose, spurred by his discovery of "egregious deceit" in two men who had earlier starred in his highly publicized experiments in thought transference. Alice James, for one, felt "little doubt" that Edmund Gurney had committed suicide. This horrible scandal, clearly, gave him the motivation. See Oppenhim, 144; *AJD*, 52; Trevor H. Hall, *The Strange Case of Edmund Gurney* (London: G. Duckworth, 1964).

480 "base trick"; "I thought it a much better test": AJ to WJ, 3 and 4 January [1886?], *DLAJ*, 105–6.

480 "frivolous treatment of so serious a science": Ibid., 106.

480 "vast sea of mews"; "larger repertory"; "keeper"; "debased": AJ to CW, 21, 23, and 24 November [1885?], ibid., 103.

480 "little modest day"; "greenish": AJ to CW, 23 April [1886?], ibid., 113.

481 "London salon": *AJB*, 253.

481 "the greatest capacity for diminishing itself": *AJD*, 49.

481 "smug and comfortable": Ibid., 55.

481 "heiress": AJ to WJ, 31 March 1889, *DLAJ*, 166.

481 "bloated capitalist": *AJD*, 113.

482 "very considerable, social winter"; "the provinces": HJ to Francis Boott, 25 May [1886], *HJL*, 3:120.

482 "company manners": Ibid., 49.

482 "trans-Atlantic neurasthenia": AJ to WJ, 10 September 1886, *DLAJ*, 118.

483 "awfully tired of reading"; "round, bustling, cheery-in-the-morning": *AJD*, 35.

483 "no excitements"; "occasionally a new old-maid": AJ to WJ, 10 September 1886, *DLAJ*, 118.

483 "Barnum monstrosity which had missed fire": *AJD*, 63.

483 "human good outweighs human evil": Ibid., 201.

483 "a sheet of note paper"; "diseased jelly-fish"; "abrupt and arbitrary streaks": AJ to CW, 15 November [1887?], *DLAJ*, 133.

483 "reduced to Nurse and Miss C.": *AJD*, 45.

483 "potency of Bismarck"; "Oh! Nurse"; "Inside of you, Miss": Ibid., 48.

484 "*only* women, so far as she now sees anyone": HJ to WJ, 29 October 1888, *HJL*, 3:243.

484 "friendless wisp of femininity": *AJD*, 130.

484 "*wüttend*"; "robust health": HJ to WJ, 29 October 1888, *HJL*, 3:245.

485 "insanitary Florentine hotel": HJ to Francis Boott, 26 November [1886], ibid., 3:138.

485 "The word villa"; "young lady's room": *CWE*, 150.

485 "landlady"; "*sans bornes*": HJ to Francis Boott, 26 November [1886], *HJL*, 3:138.

486 "roomy and rambling": HJ to John Hay, 24 December [1886], ibid., 3:153.

486 "big wood fires": HJ to WJ and AHGJ, 23 December [1886], ibid., 3:151.

487 "a lonely spinster who carries a torch for the icy James all over Europe": Cheryl B. Torsney, *Constance Fenimore Woolson: The Grief of Artistry* (Athens, GA: University of Georgia Press, 1989), 11.

487 Woolson and the Mediterranean climate: Cheryl B. Torsney theorized that the warmth-loving Fenimore suffered from seasonal affective disorder—that she unknowingly needed light in order to battle the deep depression that ran in her family. In this respect she resembled Harry's Washington friend Clover Adams, who had tragically committed suicide in 1885. See ibid., 17.

487 "male culture": Ibid., 36.

488 "on the continent flirting with Constance": AJ to WJ, 4 November 1888, *DLAJ*, 149.

488 "an impassioned Gondolier": AJ to AHGJ, 3 April 1887, ibid., 124.

488 "amiable friend"; "She is a deaf and *méticuleuse* old maid"; "an excellent and sympathetic being": HJ to Francis Boott, 25 May [1886], *HJL*, 3:119.

488 "good"; "worked in"; "an immense power of devotion (to H.J.!)": HJ to Elizabeth Boott, 18 October [1886], ibid., 3:135.

489 "H.J.Jr. (!!)": HJ to AJ, 25 April [1880], ibid., 2:287.

489 "You know I have found fault with you": CFW to HJ, 30 August [1882], ibid., 3:546.

490 "a calculated betrayal; it carried an armory of stings in its velvet glove": Gordon, 213.

490 "competing with, even feeding off of, women's fiction": Anne E. Boyd, "Anticipating James, Anticipating Grief: Constance Fenimore Woolson's 'Miss Grief,'" in *Constance Fenimore Woolson's Nineteenth Century: Essays*, ed. Victoria Brehm (Detroit: Wayne State University Press, 2001), 196.

490 "lesbian impossibility": Kristin M. Comment, "Lesbian 'Impossibilities' of Miss Grief's 'Armor,'" in ibid., 207.

491 "humble pilgrims"; "fall"; "rise"; "that glorious object"; "wondrous things": *AJD*, 46.

492 "Renunciation remains sorrow"; "The frightful separateness of human experiences": Alice's notebook, quoted in *AJB*, 269.

493 "I think that if I get into the habit of writing," etc.: *AJD*, 25.

493 "vigorous"; "signs of a loss of memory": AJ to WJ, 29–30 January 1889, *DLAJ*, 157–58.

493 "I am devoutly grateful": AJ to WJ, 22 March 1889, ibid., 162.

493 "contemplation"; "Poor human nature": *AJD*, 53.

494 "A dozen times a day"; "farbackedness": Ibid., 29.

494 "poor Aunt Kate": Ibid., 53.

494 "failure"; "independence & a 'position'"; "absorb herself in a few individuals"; "how much the individuals resisted her"; "a great & ungrateful betrayal": AJ to WJ, 22 March 1889, *DLAJ*, 162.

495 "with whom her life had been passed"; "with whom we had always considered her so united": HJ to WJ, 25 May [1889], *WJL*, 2:110.

495 "usurpation by 'Kate Walsh'"; "strikingly personal thing"; "old crank"; "much impressiveness of manner"; "great similarity of temperament": WJ to Richard Hodgson, 7 November 1889 and 9 November 1889, ibid., 6:618–19.

495 "ghost microbes": *AJD*, 78.

495 "highest attainable abode"; "my fancy plays about the soup-plates & gravey boats": AJ to WJ, 31 March 1889, *DLAJ*, 166.

495 "life-interest"; "theft, fire, or flood"; "A life-interest in a shawl": AJ to WJ, 7 April [1889], ibid., 167.

496 "publicly humiliated"; "limited little helpless life": HJ to WJ, 13 June 1889, *WJL*, 2:112.

496 "some small personal possession to Harry": AJ to WJ, 7 April [1889], *DLAJ*, 168.

496 "[My own] wifeless, childless, houseless": HJ to WJ, 31 July [1891], *HJL*, 3:350.

496 "chaste and secluded"; "like a photographer's studio"; "commune with unobstructed sky": HJ to WJ, 9 March [1886], ibid., 3:114.

497 "wooden-faced"; "orders of the day": HJ to WJ, 1 October 1887, ibid., 3:199.

497 "convenience": HJ to Grace Norton, 25 January [1887], ibid., 3:158.

497 "furtive manners & scuttling motion"; "But never lisp a word": AJ to AHGJ, 9 January 1890, *DLAJ*, 178.

497 "Alice has kindly taken my rooms and servants off my hands": HJ to Grace Norton, 27 February [1887], *HJL*, 3:165.

497 "splendid spring of water": WJ to Carl Stumpf, 6 February 1887, *WJL*, 6:205.

497 "My live-stock is increased": WJ to Henry Pickering Bowditch, 26 March 1887, ibid., 6:213.

498 "more than a clown": WJ to AJ, [February 1885], ibid., 6:2.

498 "he is a girl"; "elevate the tone of the house": AJ to AGHJ, 3 April 1887, *DLAJ*, 123.

498 "protect the innocent darling": AJ to WJ, 24 April 1887, ibid., 126.

498 "queer look"; "I must tell you something"; "You're not going to be married!"; "shrieked"; "No, but William is here"; "looked white as a ghost"; "large repertory": *AJD*, 50–51.

499 "somewhat dreaded": WJ to HJ, 8 July 1889, *WJL*, 2:117.

499 "brought Alice pretty low"; "slap in the face": HJ to WJ, 25 May [1889], ibid., 2:110.

499 "distress her": HJ to WJ, 13 June 1889, ibid., 2:111.

499 "Enter Wm. *not à la* Romeo via the balcony"; "simply himself"; "a creature who speaks in another language"; "exquisite *family* perfume of days gone by": *AJD*, 51.

500 "*biggest* book on Psychology in any language": WJ to AHGJ, 24 May 1890, *WJL*, 7:38.

501 "the best woman in Boston": WJ to AJ, 23 July 1890, ibid., 7:68.

501 "idiotic review"; "disgust and indignation": HJ to WJ, 31 July [1891], *HJL*, 3:351.

501 "For several years past"; "My little girl"; "Invalid": AJ to Edwin Lawrence Godkin, 4 July 1890, *DLAJ*, 183.

502 "of a coral insect building up [her] various reefs of theory": *AJD*, 109.

502 "How dreary to be somebody": As quoted in ibid., 227.

502 "feeble ejaculations over the scenery": Ibid., 37.

502 "The paralytic on his couch"; "Let us not waste then the sacred fire"; "admitting defeat isn't the way to conquer"; "from every failure imperishable experience survives": Ibid., 146.

503 "I do pray to Heaven": Ibid., 231.

Chapter 15: Curtain Calls

505 "calm as a clock": *AJD*, 161.

505 "mighty and magnificent book": HJ to WJ, 6 February [1891], ibid., 3:331.

505 "Don't be hard on me": HJ to Robert Louis Stevenson, ibid., 3:326.

505 "pale little art of fiction"; "limited and restricted substitute": HJ to WJ, 6 February [1891], ibid., 3:329.

506 "grey mediocrity": HJ to Edmund Gosse, 28 April [1891], ibid., 3:340.

506 "state of abject, lonely fear": HJ to WJ, 3 January [1891], ibid., 3:318.

507 "all Liberty"; "good Liberty": HJ to AJ and Katharine Peabody Loring, [4 January 1891], ibid., 3:321.

507 "queerest": HJ to Robert Louis Stevenson, 18 February 1891, ibid., 3:338.

508 "flushed with the triumph of his first ovation": *AJD*, 161.

508 "author, *author*, AUTHOR!": HJ to AJ and Katharine Peabody Loring, [4 January 1891], *HJL*, 3:320.

508 "One (after a decent and discreet delay) simpered": HJ to Hugh Bell and Florence Bell, 8 January [1891], ibid., 3:323.

509 "UNQUALIFIED TRIUMPHANT MAGNIFICENT SUCCESS"; "wondrous"; "fifty vivid words"; "laid on every breakfast table": HJ to AJ and Katharine Peabody Loring, [4 January 1891], ibid., 3:320–21.

509 "I think it's a play that would be much more likely"; "divine mission"; "roast prig, done to a turn": *AJD*, 162.

510 "gaiety": *HJL*, 3:470.

510 "honourable death": *AJD*, 224.

510 "only appeal to that limited public": Ibid., 198.

510 "3000 miles of sea-sickness"; "tangle of shawls": Ibid., 176.

511 "a decidedly silly little house": Ibid., 200.

511 "had only to wave her magic wand"; "excellent Louisa"; "Jack the Ripper part"; "Slavey"; "House-and-parlour-maid"; "beautiful dream"; "strenuous": Ibid., 181–82.

511 "rich beyond compare"; "broadened and strengthened"; "human comedy": Ibid., 183.

512 "going downhill at a steady trot"; "cardiac complications"; "To him who waits, all things come!"; "monstrous mass of subjective sensations"; "pathological vanity": Ibid., 206–7.

513 "uncompromising verdict"; "picturesque"; "cameo"; "*see* it all, whilst I shall only *feel* it": Ibid., 207–8.

513 "*force d'âme*": HJ to WJ, 31 July [1891], *HJL*, 3:349.

513 "archangels"; "infinite tenderness and patience": *AJD*, 208.

513 "philosophy of transition": AJ to WJ, 30 July 1891, *DLAJ*, 186.

513 "mortuary attractions"; "feed almost exclusively on poisons"; "Poor strange and wonderful little being that she is": WJ to AHGJ, 23 September 1891, *WJL*, 7:203.

513 "one-eyed monster"; "woman's inhumanity to woman"; "refulgent beauty": AJD, 218–19.

514 "so excessive in the normal": Ibid., 193.

514 "certain male virtues": Ibid., 184.
514 "unexampled genius for friendship and devotion": Ibid., 225.
515 "the New England Professor of doing things"; "making sentences"; "get her head quiet"; "Physical pain however great": Ibid., 232.
515 "One sank down on one's knees": *NHJ*, 240.
515 "footlights of [her] last obscure little scene": *AJD*, 222.
515 "perfectly gentle sleep"; "constant sort of whistle in the lung"; "Her face then seemed in a strange, dim, touching way": HJ to WJ, 8 March 1892, *HJL*, 3:376–78.
516 "more attentive": quoted in *HJAL*, 377.
517 "free, independent, and successful": HJ to Katherine De Kay Bronson, [20 March 1894], *HJL*, 3:467.
517 "exquisitely morbid and tragically sensitive"; "chronic melancholia": HJ to William Wilberforce Baldwin, 2 February 1894, ibid., 3:464.
518 "some word which they thought was an Italian one for cold": Quoted in Gordon, 276.
518 "fatal form": HJ to William Wilberforce Baldwin, 2 February 1894, ibid., 3:463.
518 "ghastly amazement and distress": HJ to William Wilberforce Baldwin, 26 January [1894], ibid., 3:457.
518 "Constance Fenimore Woolson committed suicide": Quoted in Gordon, 277.
518 "some misery of insomnia": HJ to John Hay, 28 January 1894, *HJL*, 3:460.
518 "some sudden explosion of latent brain-disease": HJ to Rhoda Broughton, ibid., 3:462.
518 "sudden *dementia*"; "hypothesis"; "too sickened with the news": HJ to Francis Boott, 31 January [1894], ibid., 3:462–63.
519 "suggest why she may well have committed suicide": Torsney, 15.
519 "had no dread of death": HJ to William Wilberforce Baldwin, 26 January [1894], *HJL*, 3:457.
519 "topple out of with ease in a dizzy spell": Gordon, 276.
519 "poor helpless clinging": HJ to William Wilberforce Baldwin, [17 April 1894], *HJL*, 3:475–76.
519 "dolorous"; "sad death-house"; "stare[d] down at one": HJ to Francis Boott, ibid., 3:494.
519 "horrid predicament": HJ to WJ and AHGJ, 25 May [1894], ibid., 3:477.
520 "that might have been interpreted as incriminating": Torsney, 15; see *HJAL*, 394–95.
520 "convenient": Gordon, 286.
520 "one's eternal exposures, accidents, disasters": *NHJ*, 89.
520 "The truth about Mr. James' bachelorhood": From the *New York Herald*, quoted in Gordon, 282.
520 "strange story": See Gordon, 288–89.
521 "never left us until all her precious things were packed and boxed and sent to America": Quoted in *LHJ*, 3:367.
521 "*Non ragionam di lor!*": HJ to Francis Boott, 15 December 1894, *HJL*, 3:494.
521 "*Non ragionam di lui—ma guarda e passa*": *NHJ*, 216.
522 "Alice's magnificent diary"; "rare—wondrous"; "immense impressedness"; "[I have been] terribly scared and disconcerted"; "sunk a few names, put initials": HJ to WJ and AHGJ, 25 May [1894], *HJL*, 3:476–77.
522 "unique and tragic impression of personal power"; "*deep* humor"; "strange compunctions and solemnity"; "ought to be published"; "I am proud of it": WJ to HJ, 24 March 1894, *WJL*, 2:302.
522 "one of the neglected masterpieces of American literature: Gay Wilson Allen in the *Saturday Review* (5 September 1964); *AJB*, 326.

524 "swept away like a cobweb": *AJD*, 223.

524 "too preoccupied, too terrified, too fundamentally distracted"; "a death's head at the feast": HJ to Elizabeth Lewis, [15? December 1894], *HJL*, 3:496.

525 "florid 'poster' "; "Psychical intervention": HJ to WJ and AHGJ, [5 January 1895], ibid., 3:507.

525 "extremely human and extremely artistic little play"; "gallant, prolonged and sustained applause"; "hoots and jeers and catcalls"; "weary, bruised, sickened, disgusted"; "forces of civilization"; "roughs"; "episode in the history of an old English Catholic family": HJ to WJ, 9 January 1895, ibid., 3:507–9.

526 "I'm the last, my lord, of the Domvilles!"; "It's a bloody good thing y'are": quoted in *HJAL*, 420.

526 "so helpless, so crude, so bad, so clumsy, feeble and vulgar": HJ to WJ and AHGJ, 2 February 1895, *HJL*, 3:514.

526 "deliberate trap"; " 'cheeky' and paradoxical wit"; " '*décadent*' and *raffiné*": HJ to Florence Bell, [23 February 1892], ibid., 3:372.

527 "with a metallic blue carnation": Ellmann, 367.

527 "alive": WJ to AHGJ, 2 September 1895, *WJL*, 8:80.

528 "groundless melancholy"; "normality"; "efficiency"; "I cannot *imagine* anything different"; "That's why I haven't answered"; "I bless you day and night": WJ to AHGJ, 29 August [1895], ibid., 8:79.

529 "falling in love, passing honeymoons and the like": WJ to AHGJ, 5 September 1895, ibid., 8:82.

529 "flooded"; "simmering with a happiness"; "holy girlhood": WJ to AHGJ, 3 September 1895, ibid., 8:81.

529 "up at sunrise, out of door, and mountain-top kind of girl": WJ to Pauline Goldmark, 18 April 1899, ibid., 8:517.

529 "very sweet"; "little serious rosebud of a [M]iss Goldmark"; "She climbs cliffs like a monkey"; "happy, *happy*, HAPPY": WJ to AHGJ, 5 September 1895, ibid., 8:82.

530 "first person in literature"; "delighted"; "Dear Professor James"; "Dear Miss Stein": Gertrude Stein, *The Autobiography of Alice B. Toklas* (New York: Vintage, 1990), 78–79.

530 "ultra simple in mind": WJ to HJ, 21 June 1899, *WJL*, 3:65.

531 "A cousin of mine": WJ to Pauline Goldmark, 26 December [1897], ibid., 8:329.

531 "I also fell in love with it and bought it": WJ to Pauline Goldmark, 26 September 1897, ibid., 8:313.

532 "the tendency which looks on all things and sees that they are good": *VRE*, 73.

532 "either inside or outside the cabin"; "spiritual alertness of the most vital description"; "[The] influences of Nature": WJ to AHGJ, 9 July 1898, *WJL*, 8:390.

533 "Pray find it possible to come!": WJ to Pauline Goldmark, 14 April 1899, ibid., 8:515.

533 "What a winter of estrangement it has been!"; "magnanimity, generosity and freedom"; "hidden selfishness and sinister recesses of [her] character indoors"; "Ah Pauline": WJ to Pauline Goldmark, 18 April 1899, ibid., 8:515–17.

533 "about twice round a human thumb": WJ to Rosina Hubley Emmet, 3 August 1896, ibid., 8:178.

533 "I, as you know, love her": WJ to Ellen James Temple Emmet Hunter, 22 February [1895], ibid., 8:19.

534 "completely loyal to his wife": Edward H. Madden in *WJL*, 8:xxx. Gay Wilson Allen (1967) makes the same point by describing Pauline Goldmark as a

young friend William had met on camping trips: Allen, 390. But Linda Simon (1998) rightly notes both William's enthusiasm for Pauline and his hope that she would serve as a "model of feminine" character for his daughter, Peggy: Simon, 261.

534 "drinking habits"; "crushed"; "raise him [Bob] from the gutter": *WJL*, 5:527.

534 "pained, shocked, disgusted"; "reprobate"; "so devoid of morality, decency and common sense": CW to Mary Holton James, 25 October 1884, quoted in *BBF*, 171.

535 "mere hollow shell of a man"; "tender"; "I seem now to be his only friend here": WJ to Mary Holton James, 4 October 1884, *WJL*, 5:527.

535 "All-Healing Spring Water"; "Moliere-Thermo Electric Baths": See *BBF*, 187.

535 "I can hardly live away from your sweetness": WJ to AHGJ, 13 September 1897, *WJL*, 8:303.

536 "peculiar little complication"; "Don't be scared"; "I haven't accepted an 'offer'"; "little old, cobble-stoned, grass-grown, red-roofed town"; "perfectly"; "'pick up' a sufficient quantity": HJ to AHGJ, 1 December 1897, *HJL*, 4:61–65.

538 "flourishing old espaliers, apricots, pears, plums and figs"; "most delightful little old architectural garden-house": Ibid.

538 "gossiping little town": HJ to WJ and AHGJ, 9 August [1899], ibid., 4:114.

539 "like a large bird of prey"; "proved, or at least reasonable conjectured": E. F. Benson, *Miss Mapp* in *Lucia Rising* (London: Penguin, 1991), 237–38.

540 "magnificent stature": HJ to Hendrik C. Andersen, 7 September 1899, in Henry James Jr., *Beloved Boy: Letters to Hendrik C. Andersen, 1899–1915 [Amato Ragazzo: Lettere a Hendrik C. Andersen, 1899–1915]*, ed. Rosella Mamoli Zorzi, with an introduction by Millicent Bell (Charlottesville: University of Virginia Press, 2004), 5. Hereafter *BB*.

541 "Roderick Hudson": See *HJAL*, 489.

541 "might have seemed like something in a ghost story": Millicent Bell, in *BB*, xv.

542 "cavernously regurgitate"; "all ghosts and memories"; "I live with them anyhow": HJ to WJ, 26 January 1899, *WJL*, 3:48.

Chapter 16: The Imperial Twilight

543 "vast bristling promontory"; "white-winged images of the spirit": *AS*, 73.

544 "home": HJ to WJ, 10 April 1903, *WJL*, 3:231.

544 "native land"; "romantic": HJ to WJ, 24 May 1903, ibid., 3:238.

544 "nothing but patriotic arches, Astor Hotels and Vanderbilt Palaces": HJ to Mary Cadwalader Jones, 23 October 1902, *HJL*, 4:246.

545 "false position": This was a key phrase for Henry James, and he also used it in *The Wings of the Dove* (1902), another novel about deception and self-deception.

546 William had had mixed feelings about this war: See Simon's excellent discussion in Simon, 276–79.

546 "dauntless power"; "The aspect the power": *AS*, 74–75.

548 "consult"; "material matter touching [him]"; "I don't mean—don't be alarmed—that I've received a proposal of marriage": HJ to WJ, 31 July 1899, *WJL*, 3:66.

548 "very extravagant price"; "Don't be in a hurry": WJ to HJ, 2 August 1899, ibid., 3:68–69.

548 "trepidation": WJ to HJ, 3 August 1899, ibid., 3:71.
549 "I do, strange as it may appear to you"; "My joy has shriveled": HJ to WJ, 4 August 1899, ibid., 3:71–75.
549 "It has filled this home with grief": WJ to HJ, 8 August 1899, ibid., 3:76.
550 "Dearest Henry"; "Beloved H'ry": See ibid., 3:63, 76.
550 "Dearest William & dearest Alice: never more dear!": HJ to WJ and AHGJ, 3 June [1889], Ibid., 3:61.
550 "William's revealed delicacy"; "interested & even agitated to the depths": HJ to WJ and AHGJ, 3 June [1899], ibid., 3:61.
550 "heartbreakingly beautiful and loving letter"; "And I, who through all these years"; "We live and learn": WJ to HJ, 21 June 1899, ibid., 3:63.
551 "physical loathing"; "the sight of my fellow beings at hotels"; "*vocalization*"; "simply *incredibly* loathsome": WJ to HJ, 3 May 1903, ibid., 3:232–33.
551 "dissuasive—even more than [he] expected"; "What you say of the Eggs": HJ to WJ, 24 May 1903, ibid., 3:237, 239.
551 "trap (very kindly) set on the wharf"; "deep piazza": HJ to WJ and AHGJ, [31 August 1904], *HJL*, 4:319.
552 "There was gold-dust in the air": *AS*, 8.
552 "waterside squalor"; "extremest youth": Ibid., 1.
552 "rare benediction": HJ to WJ and AHGJ, [31 August 1904], *HJL*, 4:319.
552 "I can't tell you how I thank you"; "the most awful burden": HJ to Henry James III, 26 July 1904, ibid., 4:308.
553 "The Dead that we cannot have": HJ to RJ, 4 September 1904, ibid., 4:320.
553 "into a mass so much larger"; "swarm of distinguished specialists"; "very ancient and mellow"; "Paradiso, Purgatorio, and Inferno": HJ to Edmund Gosse, 27 October 1894, ibid., 4:332–33.
554 "regularly booked"; "cool in his affections and judgments": WJ to HJ, 9 September 1903, *WJL*, 3:244.
554 "tall and taciturn": HJ to WJ, 17 November 1906, *HJL*, 4:424.
554 "morbidness"; "big souled and large minded pattern of humanity": WJ to HJ, 1 January 1904, *WJL*, 3:254–55.
554 "kinder to him than that of a mother": Quoted in *HJAL*, 553.
555 "chateau mirrored in a Massachusetts pond"; "The Whartons are kindness and hospitality incarnate": HJ to Howard Sturgis, 17 October 1904, *HJL*, 4:325.
556 "clustering group of tall irregular crenellations": H. G. Wells, *The Future in America: A Search After Realities* (New York: Harper and Brothers, 1906), 35–36.
556 "like extravagant pins in a cushion already overplanted"; "taking the sun and the shade in the manner of towers of marble": *AS*, 76.
556 "some colossal hair-comb": Ibid., 138.
556 "bold lacing-together"; "immeasurable"; "the horizontal sheaths of pistons": Ibid., 75.
557 "huge-hatted"; "in the gilded and storied labyrinth": Ibid., 105.
557 "cult of candy"; "great glittering temples, the bristling pagodas"; "chocolate creams": Ibid., 196–97.
557 "repository of doughnuts, cookies, cream-cakes and pies": Ibid., 91.
557 "great commercial democracy": Ibid., 92.
558 "aliens"; "affirmed claim of the alien"; "supreme relation"; "*their* monstrous, presumptuous interest": Ibid., 85–86.
558 "social question": Ibid., 114.
558 "cruelly overtopped": Ibid., 78.
559 "ploughing up through the traffic": Wells, 42–43.

559 "cheek"; "Future!": HJ to WJ, 17 November 1906, *WJL*, 3:329.
559 "vast horror": Philip Burne-Jones, *Dollars and Democracy* (New York: D. Appleton, 1904), 58, 60.
559 "grossly tall and grossly ugly": *AS*, 86.
559 "boa-constrictor": Ibid., 89.
559 "castellated and gabled"; "vanished from the earth"; "amputated of half my history": Ibid., 91.
559 "loud-puffing motor-cars": HJ to Edmund Gosse, 27 October 1904, *HJL*, 4:331.
559 "sharp-ribbed horses": *AS*, 2.
559 "poor and lonely and unsupported and unaffiliated state": Ibid., 90.
560 "an old staircase, consecrated by the tread of generations": Ibid., 112.
560 "big and quite pompous function"; "Theodore Rex": HJ to Mary Cadwalader Jones, 13 January 1905, *HJL*, 4:337.
561 "Theodore I": HJ to Edith Wharton, 16 January 1905, ibid., 4:341.
561 "native intensity, veracity and *bonhomie*": HJ to Mary Cadwalader Jones, 13 January 1905, ibid., 4:337.
561 "indescribable"; "overwhelming": HJ to Jessie Allen, 16 January 1905, ibid., 4:339.
561 "wonderful little machine"; "*like* something behind a great plate-glass window 'on' Broadway": HJ to Edith Wharton, 16 January 1905, ibid., 4:341.
561 "effete" ; "miserable little snob": Quoted in *HJAL*, 604.
562 "*köstlich* stuff"; "fairly melting with delight": WJ to HJ, 6 October 1907, *WJL*, 3:346.
562 "tribute"; "You are immensely and universally *right*": HJ to WJ, 17 October 1907, *HJL*, 4:466.
563 "It may sustain & inspire you to know"; "conceive of no sense in any philosophy": HJ to WJ, 18 July 1909, *WJL*, 3:393.
563 "sit down and write a new book"; "Publish it in my name": WJ to HJ, 22 October 1905, ibid., 3:301.
563 "descend to a dishonoured grave"; "I'm always sorry when I hear of your reading anything of mine": HJ to WJ, 23 November 1905, *HJL*, 4:382. For a full survey of the complexity of William's and Harry's reactions to each other's works, see F. O. Matthiessen, *The James Family, Including Selections from the Writings of Henry James, Senior, William, Henry, & Alice James* (New York: Knopf, 1947), 315–45.
563 "philosophy got up for the use of engineers, electricians, and doctors"; "write and publish, if I can do it": WJ to HJ, 8 September 1907, *WJL*, 3:344.
563 Photographs of William and Harry from the early twentieth century: Leon Edel dates these photographs from Cambridge, Massachusetts in 1905 (see *HJAL*, x), but penciled notes in the James Papers at Houghton Library, Harvard, suggest the images were taken in England between 1899 and 1901.
564 "big authoritative": HJ to Jocelyn Persse, 27 October 1910, in *DBF*, 106.
564 "pearl of great price"; "absolutely brilliant economist"; "person of the greatest order, method, and respectability"; "pretty": HJ to Louise Horstmann, 12 August 1904, *HJL*, 4:312–13.
564 "The eternally babyish Burgess": HJ to AHGJ, 1 [and 16] April 1913, ibid., 4:658.
565 "the best and gentlest": HJ to Louise Horstmann, 12 August 1904, ibid., 4:313.
565 "That I *should* have you here"; "Hold on tight, at any rate, till I can get you somehow and somewhere and have you *back* me"; "benediction"; "My dear, dear Hendrik"; "But good-night, dearest boy"; "how I yearn after you to Montefiascone!": HJ to Hendrik C. Andersen, 6 August 1905, ibid., 4:369–70.

566 "Brave little Bevilacqua"; "braver still big Maestro": HJ to Hendrik C. Andersen, 19 July 1899, *BB*, 1.

567 "Every word of you is as soothing as a caress of your hand": HJ to Hendrik C. Andersen, 10 August 1904, ibid., 55.

567 "I've tenderly loved you": HJ to Hendrik C. Andersen, 31 May 1906, ibid., 68.

567 "I pat you affectionately on the back, across Alps and Apennines": HJ to Hendrik C. Andersen, 3 December 1903, ibid., 49.

567 "I put out my arms": HJ to Hendrik C. Andersen, [1 January 1910], ibid., 91.

567 "horribly expensive family"; "troubled vision"; "feed and clothe"; "And then I reflect"; "But 'that way madness lies'": HJ to Hendrik C. Andersen, 5 November 1905, ibid., 64.

567 "It is fatal for you to go on...neglecting the *Face*": HJ to Hendrik C. Andersen, 25 November 1906, ibid., 75.

568 "waking up in bed, the covers slipping off his naked body": As described by Millicent Bell, *BB*, xviii.

568 "safe match": See Fred Kaplan, 463.

568 "[I am] afraid that you will take your son Hendrik": Hendrik C. Andersen to HJ, 31 March 1912, *BB*, 128.

568 "what right has this tall pale, yellow headed Norwegian": Hendrik C. Andersen to HJ, 14 April 1912, ibid., 131.

569 "Emperor of Germany": Hendrik C. Andersen to HJ, 31 August 1913, ibid., 132.

569 "I wish you could be here": Hendrik C. Andersen to HJ, 31 March 1912, ibid., 130.

569 "*très-cher Maître*": See *DBF*, 9.

569 "How can I express the tenderness," etc.: HJ to Hendrik C. Andersen, 9 February 1902, *BB*, 26.

569 "Bearded Bandit; very charming for all its savagery": HJ to Hendrik C. Andersen, 22 September 1903, ibid., 48.

569 "encumber [Hendrik's] apartment with [his] large and heavy presence"; "personal habits & traditions & eccentricities": HJ to Hendrik C. Andersen, 3 April 1907, ibid., 77.

570 "happy studio hours"; "romantic": HJ to Hendrik C. Andersen, 18 July 1907, ibid., 80.

570 "increasingly daring in the way he constituted himself": Stevens, 167.

571 "eyrie"; "excellently": HJ to Edith and Edward Wharton, 11–12 August 1907, *HJL*, 4:458.

572 "dear dear Howard": HJ to Howard Sturgis, 24 August 1905, *DBF*, 142.

572 "indiscretion"; "I could live with you"; "only try to live without": HJ to Howard Sturgis, 25 February 1900, ibid., 124.

572 "natural asylum": HJ to Howard Sturgis, 18 September 1902, ibid., 127.

572 "tryst": HJ to Howard Sturgis, [5 May 1909], ibid., 151.

572 "ravished"; "I mean as to my inner being": HJ to Howard Sturgis, 22 January 1904, ibid., 137.

572 "Keep a-wanting of me all you can": HJ to Howard Sturgis, 23 April 1908, ibid., 149.

573 "rip"; "moustachioed lips"; "manly cheeks": HJ to Jocelyn Persse, 3 March 1904, ibid., 90.

573 "dearest little Hugh": HJ to Hugh Walpole, 14 October 1913, ibid., 221.

573 "by far the greatest man [he] ha[d] ever met": Walpole diaries, quoted in ibid., 176.

574 "as filled with vitality as a merry-go-round at a fair": Walpole diaries, quoted in ibid., 179.

574 "lawn tennis greatness": HJ to Hugh Walpole, [16 August 1909], ibid., 188.

574   "peerless pearl-diver"; "contacts & conquests": HJ to Hugh Walpole, 24 August 1909, ibid., 189.

574   "bleat & jump like a white lambkin"; "writing letters for a hundred years": HJ to Hugh Walpole, 8 January 1909, ibid., 183.

574   "*this* elephant"; "The Elephant paws you oh so benevolently": HJ to Hugh Walpole, [23 October 1909], ibid., 193.

574   "I can't, I can't": See *HJAL*, 652.

574   " '*Très*-cher Maitre": HJ to Hugh Walpole, 27 April 1909, *DBF*, 186.

574   "tepid"; "swim in a blaze of glory"; "You will sell the edition for me": HJ to Hugh Walpole, 13 October 1911, *HJL*, 4:585.

575   "floppy sail"; "golden islands": HJ to Hugh Walpole, [23 October 1909], *DBF*, 193.

575   "Cultivate with me, darlingest Hugh, the natural affections"; "wait till you are 80 to do so"; "made the most of them from far back": HJ to Hugh Walpole, 21 August 1913, ibid., 219.

576   "homosocial male, homoerotic male": As phrased by Susan E. Gunter and Steven H. Jobe in *DBF*, 3.

578   "black devils": HJ to Hugh Walpole, 13 May 1910, ibid., 199.

579   "rather dreary lone and lorn and stranded friend"; "child's afternoon party"; "This seems to be his one idea of gifts for ladies!": *NHJ*, 311.

579   "pal or second self of hers (a lady-pal)": HJ to Edith Wharton, 13 December 1909, *HJL*, 4:539.

580   "excellent amanuensis"; "The young, boyish Miss Bosanquet": HJ to WJ, 17 October 1907, ibid., 4:467.

580   "pleasant, benevolent sort of masks"; "fat old lady with side curls"; "Why . . . don't we all wear masks": *NHJ*, 311.

580   "dismal and dreary": HJ to WJ, 8 February 1910, *HJL*, 4:547.

580   "no more to do with a 'nervous breakdown' than with Halley's comet": *NHJ*, 312.

580   "*nervous* condition—trepidation, agitation, general dreadfulness": HJ to Jocelyn Persse, 28 April 1910, *HJL*, 4:551.

580   "[I am down] with the black devils of Nervousness": HJ to Hugh Walpole, 13 May 1910, ibid., 4:551.

580   "no cause for anxiety"; "Walk a minimum (using cars and hacks [cabs] when required): WJ to HJ, 4 February 1910, *WJL*, 3:407–8.

581   "blessed support": HJ to Theodora Bosanquet, 2 March 1910, *HJL*, 4:548.

581   "of all of my duties to other people": WJ to HJ, 7 January 1910, *WJL*, 3:406.

581   "I *dream* of the companionship of Alice": HJ to WJ and AHGJ, 15 March [1910], Ibid., *WJL*, 3:418.

581   "neurasthenic melancholia": WJ to HJ, 28 May [1910], ibid., 3:421.

582   "I want to be *with* you more than anything": HJ to WJ, 5 June [1910], ibid., 3:426.

582   "place of thick woods, groves, springs": HJ to Edith Wharton, 10 June 1910, *HJL*, 4:554.

582   "nightmare of Switzerland"; "Nach-Kurs": HJ to Edith Wharton, 29 July 1910, ibid., 4:557.

582   "I simply *fear* to challenge you on your own complications": HJ to Edith Wharton, 10 June 1910, ibid., 4:555.

582   "I don't believe God likes a coward": RJ to AHGJ, 28 October 1898, quoted in *BBF*, 189.

582   "go[ing] as quickly": AHGJ to Mary Holton James, 6 September 1910, quoted in ibid., 193.

583 "beautiful, quick, in itself auspicious"; "terrible"; "local": HJ to Grace Norton, 26 August 1910, *HJL*, 4:559.

583 "I sit heavily stricken and in darkness": HJ to Thomas Sergeant Perry, ibid., 4:561.

583 "My beloved brother's death has cut into me": Quoted in R. W. B. Lewis, *The Jameses: A Family Narrative* (New York: Farrar, Straus and Giroux, 1991), 584.

584 "We cleave intensely together": HJ to Howard Sturgis, 18 October 1910, *HJL*, 4:564.

584 "My life, thank God, is impregnated with him": HJ to H. G. Wells, 11 September 1910, ibid., 4:562.

Chapter 17: The Emperor in the Room

585 "like a rather blackish nightmare": HJ to AHGJ, 5 January 1913, *HJL*, 4:647.

586 "the brown fog of a winter dawn"; "Oil and tar"; "The barges wash": T. S. Eliot, *The Waste Land* (New York: Boni and Liveright, 1922), lines 61, 264, 273–75, W.

586 "black-barged yellow river": HJ to Hugh Walpole, 21 August 1913, *DBF*, 220.

586 "separately": HJ to AHGJ, 5 January 1913, *HJL*, 4:647.

586 "melancholy, dreary, diluvian"; "fatal": HJ to WJ, 17 October 1907, ibid., 4:467.

587 James Jackson Putnam: For a contrast between Putnam's and William James's therapeutic methods, see Simon, 362–63.

587 "crisis"; "fled to London at once"; "big Babylon, with its great spaces for circulation"; "the remedy of London—of the blessed miles of pavement": HJ to James Jackson Putnam, 4 January 1912, *HJL*, 4:595–97.

587 "isolation of Rye": See Edel's note in *HJL*, 4:598n. I would disagree that Harry's real isolation happened only in this provincial town, though he felt his disconnection there more than elsewhere.

588 "[I] did instinctively regard it at last as all my truth": Quoted in *HJAL*, 672–73.

588 "construction of authorship": See, for example, David McWhirter, ed., *Henry James's New York Edition: The Construction of Authorship* (Stanford, CA: Stanford University Press, 1995).

589 "with Death and recession a man of genius becomes a *figure*": HJ to Josiah Royce, 30 June 1911, *HJL*, 4:578.

589 "lump of twaddle"; "cheap and humbugging autobiographic form": HJ to Hugh Walpole, 18 March 1913, *DBF*, 215–16.

589 "fatuous & presumptuous Small Boy"; "crystal stream"; "*liked* the way of its coming"; "It's full at any rate"; "defeated"; "difficult, obscure or *entortillés* [twisted]"; "uncommunicating communicator": HJ to Hugh Walpole, [29 April 1913], ibid., 217.

591 "How can I sufficiently thank you": HJ to Henry James III, 29 March 1913, *HJL*, 4:653.

591 "fond conspiracy to raise a sum of money"; "expensive effigy": HJ to Percy Lubbock, 30 March 1913, ibid., 4:654.

592 "390 notes of condolence": HJ to Jessie Allen, 6 May 1914, ibid., 4:712.

592 "We eat and drink": HJ to Lilla Perry, 22 September 1914, ibid., 4:718.

593 "ornaments"; "this wreck of our belief"; "such a monstrous scene"; "we shall

again be gathered into a blessed little Chelsea drawing-room": HJ to Rhoda Broughton, 10 August 1914, ibid., 4:713–14.

593 "I go to sleep, as if I were dog-tired with action": HJ to Edith Wharton, 19 August 1914, ibid., 4:715.

593 "infinitely"; "grey mists of insignificance"; "People 'meet' a little": HJ to Hugh Walpole, 21 November 1914, ibid., 4:729.

594 "huge enormity": HJ to Mary Margaret James, 1 December 1915, ibid., 4:784.

594 "the younger lives, the fine seed of the future, that are offered and taken"; "almost discovered [his] vocation in life": HJ to Hugh Walpole, 21 November 1914, ibid., 4:729.

595 "bad lameness of a poor hobbling khaki convalescent": HJ to Edith Wharton, 23 March 1915, ibid., 4:743.

596 "so remarkably like"; "I wonder anyone can tell them apart": HJ to Edmund Gosse, 25 August 1915, ibid., 4:776.

596 "with their peculiarly unerring instinct for poor old women and young children": HJ to Lilla Cabot Perry, 17 June 1915, ibid., 4:758.

596 "I daresay many Americans *will* be shocked at my 'step'"; "long months, watch in hand"; "It would really have been so easy for the U.S. to have 'kept'": HJ to John Singer Sargent, 30 July 1915, ibid., 4:774.

597 "You can see, can't you?": HJ to AHGJ, 1 [and 16] April 1913, ibid., 4:657–58.

597 "The pen drops from my hand!": HJ to Mary Margaret James, 1 December 1915, ibid., 4:784.

597 "a kind of stroke": Theodora Bosanquet's diary, quoted in *HJAL*, 706.

598 "So here it is at last": Fanny Prothero, as told to Edith Wharton and recorded in Edith Wharton, *A Backward Glance* (New York: Charles Scribner's Sons, 1934), 366–67.

598 "Dear and most esteemed brother and sister"; "There have been great families of tricksters and conjurers"; "Napoléone": *NHJ*, 583–84.

599 "My dear brother and sister," etc.: Ibid., 584.

599 "Across the border," etc.: Ibid., 584.

600 "Beloved Alice"; "Stay with me Alice"; "voyaging and visiting foreign cities": Quoted in *HJAL*, 714.

Selected Bibliography

Adams, Henry. *Democracy: An American Novel.* 1880. New York: Henry Holt, 1908.

Agassiz, Louis, and Elizabeth Agassiz. *A Journey to Brazil.* Boston: Fields, Osgood, 1869.

Allen, Gay Wilson. *William James: A Biography.* New York: Viking, 1967.

Anbinder, Tyler. *Five Points: The 19th-Century New York City Neighborhood That Invented Tap Dance, Stole Elections, and Became the World's Most Notorious Slum.* New York: Free Press, 2001.

Anderson, James William. "In Search of Mary James." *Psychohistory Review* 8 (1979): 63–70.

Auchincloss, Louis. *Reading Henry James.* Minneapolis: University of Minnesota Press, 1975.

Baedeker, Karl, ed. *Italy: A Handbook for Travellers.* Leipzig: Baedeker, 1877.

———. *Paris and Northern France: A Handbook for Travellers.* Coblenz: Baedeker, 1867.

———. *Switzerland, Together with Chamonix and the Italian Lakes: Handbook for Travellers.* Leipzig: Baedeker, 1922.

Banks, J. A. *Prosperity and Parenthood: A Study of Family Planning Among the Victorian Middle Classes.* London: Routledge and Paul, 1954.

Barish, Evelyn. *Emerson, The Roots of Prophecy.* Princeton, NJ: Princeton University Press, 1989.

Barkun, Michael. *Crucible of the Millennium: The Burned-Over District of New York in the 1840s.* Syracuse, NY: Syracuse University Press, 1986.

Battersby, Christine. *Gender and Genius: Toward a Feminist Aesthetics.* Bloomington: Indiana University Press, 1989.

Beard, George Miller. *American Nervousness: Its Causes and Consequences.* New York: Putnam, 1881.

Bell, Millicent. *Edith Wharton and Henry James: The Story of Their Friendship.* London: Peter Owen, 1966.

———. "James and the Sculptor." *Yale Review* 9 (October 2002): 18–47.

Benedict, Clare. *Constance Fenimore Woolson.* London: Ellis, 1945.

———, ed. *Five Generations (1785–1923), Being Scattered Chapters from the History of the Cooper, Pomeroy, Woolson and Benedict Families.* 3 vols. London: Ellis, 1930.

Benson, E. F. *Final Edition: Informal Autobiography.* London: Longman's Green, 1940.

———. *Memories and Friends.* London: John Murray, 1924.

———. *Miss Mapp,* in *Lucia Rising.* 1922. London: Penguin, 1991.

658 · *Selected Bibliography*

Boott, Francis. *Recollections of Francis Boott: For His Grandson F.B.D.* Boston: Southgate Press–T. W. Ripley, 1912.

Bosanquet, Theodora. *Henry James at Work.* London: Hogarth Press, 1927.

Bradley, John R., ed. *Henry James and Homo-Erotic Desire.* London: Macmillan, 1999.

———. "Henry James's Permanent Adolescence." *Essays in Criticism* 157 (October 1997): 287–314.

Brehm, Victoria, ed. *Constance Fenimore Woolson's Nineteenth Century: Essays.* Detroit: Wayne State University Press, 2001.

Brinnin, John Malcolm. *The Sway of the Grand Saloon: A Social History of the North Atlantic.* New York: Delacorte Press, 1971.

Brodhead, Richard F. *The School of Hawthorne.* New York: Oxford University Press, 1986.

Brooks, Peter. *Henry James Goes to Paris.* Princeton, NJ: Princeton University Press, 2007.

Brooks, Van Wyck. *The Dream of Arcadia: American Writers and Artists in Italy, 1760–1915.* New York: Dutton, 1958.

———. *From the Shadow of the Mountain.* New York: Dutton, 1961.

———. *The Pilgrimage of Henry James.* New York: Dutton, 1925.

Burchard, Peter. *One Gallant Rush: Robert Gould Shaw and His Brave Black Regiment.* New York: St. Martin's Press, 1965.

Burne-Jones, Philip. *Dollars and Democracy.* New York: D. Appleton, 1904.

Burr, Anna Robeson, ed. *Alice James, Her Brothers—Her Journal.* New York: Dodd, Mead, 1934.

Burton, Elizabeth. *The Early Victorians at Home, 1837–1861.* London: Longman, 1972.

Carlyle, Thomas, and Jane Welsh Carlyle. *The Collected Letters of Thomas and Jane Welsh Carlyle.* Edited by Charles Richard Sanders et al. 34 vols. Durham, NC: Duke University Press, 1970–2006.

Carlyle, Thomas, and Ralph Waldo Emerson. *Correspondence of Thomas Carlyle and Ralph Waldo Emerson.* 2 vols. Boston: J. R. Osgood, 1883.

Chalfant, Edward. *Better in Darkness: A Biography of Henry Adams: His Second Life, 1862–1891.* Hamden, CT: Archon Books, 1994.

Chambers, William. *Things as They Are in America.* Philadelphia: Lippincott, Grambo, 1854.

Chauncey, George. *Gay New York: Gender, Urban Culture, and the Making of the Gay Male World, 1890–1940.* New York: Basic Books, 1994.

Clark, Rufus W. *The Heroes of Albany: A Memorial of the Patriot-Martyrs of the City [. . .].* Albany, NY: S. R. Gray, 1866.

Clark, T. J. *The Painting of Modern Life: Paris in the Art of Manet and His Followers.* Princeton, NJ: Princeton University Press, 1986.

Clinton, Catherine. *The Other Civil War: American Women in the Nineteenth Century.* Consulting editor Eric Foner. New York: Hill and Wang, 1984.

Cott, Nancy F. *The Bonds of Womanhood.* New Haven, CT: Yale University Press, 1977.

———. *Public Vows: A History of Marriage and the Nation.* Cambridge, MA: Harvard University Press, 2000.

Cowan, Ruth Schwartz. *A Social History of American Technology.* New York: Oxford University Press, 1997.

Cross, Whitney R. *The Burned-Over District: The Social and Intellectual History of Enthusiastic Religion in Western New York, 1800–1850.* Ithaca, NY: Cornell University Press, 1950.

Crewe-Milnes, Robert Offley Ashburton. *Lord Rosebery.* New York: Harper and Brothers, 1931.

Cunningham, Peter. *London in 1856.* London: John Murray, 1856.

Davidoff, Leonore. *The Best Circles: Society, Etiquette and the Season.* London: Croom Helm, 1973.

Davidson, Caroline. *A Woman's Work Is Never Done: A History of Housework in the British Isles, 1650–1950*. London: Chatto and Windus, 1986.

Dean, Sharon L. *Constance Fenimore Woolson: Homeward Bound*. Knoxville, TN: University of Tennessee Press, 1995.

Dickens, Charles. *American Notes*. 1842. New York: St. Martin's Press, 1985.

DiMaggio, Paul. "Cultural Entrepreneurship in Nineteenth-Century Boston: The Creation of an Organizational Base for High Culture in America." *Media, Culture, and Society* 4 (1982): 33–50.

———. "Cultural Entrepreneurship in Nineteenth-Century Boston, Part II: The Classification and Framing of American Art." *Media, Culture, and Society* 4 (1982): 303–22.

Downing, Antoinette F., and Vincent J. Scully Jr. *The Architectural Heritage of Newport, Rhode Island, 1640–1915*. Cambridge, MA: Harvard University Press, 1952.

Dugan, James. *The Great Iron Ship*. New York: Harper and Brothers, 1953.

Edel, Leon. *Henry James: A Life*. New York: Harper and Row, 1985.

———. *The Life of Henry James*. 5 vols. Philadelphia: Lippincott, 1953–72.

Egan, Michael. *Henry James: The Ibsen Years*. London: Vision Press, 1972.

Eliot, T. S. *The Waste Land*. New York: Boni and Liveright, 1922.

Elliott, Maud Howe. *This Was My Newport*. Cambridge, MA: Mythology Company, A. Marshall Jones, 1944.

Ellmann, Richard. *Oscar Wilde*. New York: Knopf, 1988.

Emerson, Edward Waldo. *The Early Years of the Saturday Club, 1855–1870*. Boston: Houghton Mifflin, 1918.

Emerson, Ellen Tucker. *The Letters of Ellen Tucker Emerson*. Edited by Edith E. W. Gregg. 2 vols. Kent, OH: Kent State University Press, 1982.

Emerson, Ralph Waldo. *The Complete Works of Ralph Waldo Emerson*. With a biographical introduction by Edward Waldo Emerson. 10 vols. Boston: Houghton Mifflin, 1903.

———. *Journals and Miscellaneous Notebooks*. Edited by William H. Gilman et al. 16 vols. Cambridge, MA: Harvard University Press, 1960–82.

———. *The Letters of Ralph Waldo Emerson*. Edited by Ralph L. Rusk. 6 vols. New York: Columbia University Press, 1939.

Emilio, Luis. *A Brave Black Regiment: History of the Fifty-fourth Regiment, 1863–1865*. 1894. New York: Johnson Reprint, 1968.

Faderman, Lillian. *Surpassing the Love of Men: Romantic Friendship and Love Between Women from the Renaissance to the Present*. New York: William Morrow, 1981.

Fields, Mrs. James T. [Annie Adams]. *A Shelf of Old Books*. New York: Charles Scribner's Sons, 1894.

Feinstein, Howard M. *Becoming William James*. Ithaca, NY: Cornell University Press, 1984.

Foucault, Michel. *The History of Sexuality: An Introduction*. 1979. New York: Vintage, 1990.

———. *Language, Counter-Memory, Practice: Selected Essays and Interviews by Michel Foucault*. Translated by Donald F. Bouchard and Sheery Simon. Edited by Donald F. Bouchard. Ithaca, NY: Cornell University Press, 1977.

Freedman, Jonathan. *Professions of Taste: Henry James, British Aestheticism, and Commodity Culture*. Stanford, CA: Stanford University Press, 1990.

Freud, Sigmund, and Josef Breuer. *Studies in Hysteria [Studien über Hysteria]*. Translated by Nicola Luckhurst, with an introduction by Rachel Bowlby. 1895. New York: Penguin, 2004.

Geismar, Maxwell. *Henry James and His Cult*. London: Chatto, 1964.

Gijswijt-Hofstra, Marijke, and Roy Porter, eds. *Cultures of Neurasthenia from Beard to the First World War*. Amsterdam: Rodopi, 2001.

Gilbert, Sandra M., and Susan Gubar. *The Madwoman in the Attic: The Woman Writer in* the Nineteenth Century Literary Imagination. New Haven, CT: Yale University Press, 1979.

Gilman, Charlotte Perkins. "The Yellow Wallpaper" and Other Stories. Edited by Robert Schulman. Oxford: Oxford University Press, 1995.

Gilman, Sander L., et al. Hysteria Beyond Freud. Berkeley: University of California Press, 1993.

Godkin, E[dwin] L[awrence]. Life and Letters of Edwin Lawrence Godkin. Edited by Rollo Ogden. 2 vols. London: Macmillan, 1907.

Golden, Janet Lynne. A Social History of Wet Nursing in America: From Breast to Bottle. Cambridge, England: Cambridge University Press, 1996.

Gordon, Lyndall. A Private Life of Henry James: Two Women and His Art. New York: Norton, 1998.

Graham, Wendy. Henry James's Thwarted Love. Stanford, CA: Stanford University Press, 1999.

Grattan, Clinton Harley. The Three Jameses: A Family of Minds, Henry James, Sr., William James, Henry James. New York: Longmans, Green, 1932.

Grattan, Thomas Colley. Civilized America. 2 vols. London: Bradbury and Evans, 1859.

Green, Martin. The Problem of Boston: Some Readings in Cultural History. New York: W. W. Norton, 1966.

Greenberg, Amy S. Manifest Manhood and the Antebellum American Empire. Cambridge, England: Cambridge University Press, 2005.

Grosskurth, Phyllis. John Addington Symonds: A Biography. New York: Arno Press, 1964.

Habegger, Alfred. The Father: A Life of Henry James, Sr. New York: Farrar, Straus and Giroux, 1994.

———. Gender, Fantasy and Realism in American Literature. New York: Columbia University Press, 1982.

———. Henry James and the "Woman Business." Cambridge, England: Cambridge University Press, 1989.

Hall, Trevor H. The Strange Case of Edmund Gurney. London: G. Duckworth, 1964.

Halperin, David M. One Hundred Years of Homosexuality: And Other Essays on Greek Love. New York: Routledge, 1990.

Hart-Davis, Rupert. Hugh Walpole: A Biography. New York: Macmillan, 1952.

Hartman, Mary S. The Household and the Making of History: A Subversive View of the Western Past. Cambridge, England: Cambridge University Press, 2004.

Hawthorne, Julian. The Memoirs of Julian Hawthorne. Edited by Edith Garrigues Hawthorne. New York: Macmillan, 1938.

Haynes, Renee. The Society for Psychical Research, 1882–1982: A History. London: Macdonald, 1982.

Henry, Joseph. Papers. Edited by Nathan Reingold et al. 10 vols. to date. Washington, DC: Smithsonian Institution Press, 1972–.

Herbert, Robert L. Impressionism: Art, Leisure, and Parisian Society. New Haven, CT: Yale University Press, 1988.

Hislop, Codman. Eliphalet Nott. Middletown, CT: Wesleyan University Press, 1971.

Holmes, Oliver Wendell. The Autocrat of the Breakfast-Table. 1858. Boston: Houghton Mifflin, 1891.

Homberger, Eric. Mrs. Astor's New York: Money and Social Power in a Gilded Age. New Haven, CT: Yale University Press, 2002.

Horne, Philip. Henry James: A Life in Letters. New York: Penguin, 1999.

———. Henry James and Revision. Oxford: Clarendon Press, 1990.

———. "Henry James: The Master and the 'Queer Affair' of 'The Pupil.'" Critical Quarterly (Autumn 1995): 75–92.

Horowitz, Helen Lefkowitz. Rereading Sex: Battles over Sexual Knowledge and Suppression in Nineteenth-Century America. New York: Knopf, 2002.

Howe, Helen Huntington. *The Gentle Americans: Biography of a Breed*. New York: Harper and Row, 1965.

Howe, Julia Ward. *Reminiscences, 1819–1899*. Boston: Houghton Mifflin, 1899.

Howells, William Dean. *Life in Letters of William Dean Howells*. 2 vols. Edited by Mildred Howells. 1928. New York: Russell and Russell, 1968.

———. *Literary Friends and Acquaintance: A Personal Retrospect of American Authorship*. New York: Harper, 1900.

Hyde, H. Montgomery. *Henry James at Home*. New York: Farrar, Straus and Giroux, 1969.

Ignatiev, Noel. *How the Irish Became White*. New York: Routledge, 1995.

Jackson, Kenneth T., and David S. Dunbar, eds. *Empire City: New York Through the Centuries*. New York: Columbia University Press, 2002.

James, Alice. *The Death and Letters of Alice James*. Edited by Ruth Bernard Yeazell. Berkeley: University of California Press, 1981.

———. *The Diary of Alice James*. Edited by Leon Edel, with a new introduction by Linda Simon. 1939 and 1964. Boston: Northeastern University Press, 1999.

———. "The Letters of Alice James to Anne Ashburner, 1873–78 (Part 1)." Edited by Rayburn S. Moore. *Resources for American Literary Study* 27.1 (2001): 17–64.

———. "The Letters of Alice James to Anne Ashburner, 1873–78 (Part 2)." Edited by Rayburn S. Moore. *Resources for American Literary Study* 27.2 (2001): 196–236.

———. *Substance and Shadow*. 1863. New York: AMS Press, 1983.

James, Henry, Jr. *The Ambassadors*. 1903. New York: Harper, 1948.

– ———. *The American*. 1877. Boston: Houghton Mifflin, 1907.

———. *The American Scene*. Edited with an introduction by Leon Edel. 1907. Bloomington: Indiana University Press, 1968.

———. *Beloved Boy: Letters to Hendrik C. Andersen, 1899–1915 [Amato Ragazzo: Lettere a Hendrik C. Andersen, 1899–1915]*. Edited by Rosella Mamoli Zorzi, with an introduction by Millicent Bell. 2001. Charlottesville: University of Virginia Press, 2004.

———. *The Bostonians*. 1886. New York: Penguin, 1984.

———. *The Complete Letters of Henry James, 1855–1872*. Edited by Pierre A. Walker and Greg W. Zacharias. Introduction by Alfred Habegger. 2 vols to date. Lincoln: University of Nebraska Press, 2006–.

———. *The Complete Notebooks of Henry James*. Edited by Leon Edel and Lyall H. Powers. New York: Oxford University Press, 1987.

———. *Daisy Miller*. 1878. New York: Harper and Brothers, 1906.

———. *Dearly Beloved Friends: Henry James's Letters to Younger Men*. Edited by Susan E. Gunter and Steven H. Jobe. Ann Arbor: University of Michigan Press, 2001.

———. *English Hours*. Edited by Alma Louise Lowe. 1905. New York: Orion Press, 1960.

———. *French Poets and Novelists*. 1878. London: Macmillan, 1893.

———. *Henry James Letters*. Edited by Leon Edel. 4 vols. Cambridge, MA: Belknap Press of Harvard University, 1974–84.

———. *Italian Hours*. Boston: Houghton Mifflin, 1909.

———. *Letters of Henry James*. Edited by Percy Lubbock. 2 vols. New York: Charles Scribner's Sons, 1920.

———. *Letters to A. C. Benson and Auguste Monod*. Edited by E. F. Benson. London: Elkin Mathews and Marrot, 1930.

———. *Notes of a Son and Brother*. New York: Charles Scribner's Sons, 1914.

———. *The Portrait of a Lady*. Boston: Houghton Mifflin, 1882.

———. *Portraits of Places*. Boston: James R. Osgood, 1884. Copy in W.

———. *Roderick Hudson*. 1875. Boston: Houghton Mifflin, 1910.

———. *A Small Boy and Others*. New York: Charles Scribner's Sons, 1913.

———. *The Tragic Muse*. 1890. Boston: Houghton Mifflin, 1892.

————. *Transatlantic Sketches*. Boston: J. R. Osgood, 1875. Copy in W.

————. *Washington Square*. 1880. New York: Modern Library, 1950.

————. *William Wetmore Story and His Friends: From Letters, Diaries, and Recollections*. 2 vols. Boston: Houghton Mifflin, 1903.

James, Henry, Sr. *Lectures and Miscellanies*. New York: Redfield, 1852.

————. *The Literary Remains of the Late Henry James*. Edited with an introduction by William James. Boston: Houghton Mifflin, 1884.

————. *Society the Redeemed Form of Man, and the Earnest of God's Omnipotence in Human Nature: Affirmed in Letters to a Friend*. Boston: Houghton, Osgood, 1879.

James, Henry, III. *Charles W. Eliot, President of Harvard University, 1869–1909*. 2 vols. Boston: Houghton Mifflin, 1930.

James, William. *The Correspondence of William James*. Edited by Ignas K. Skrupskelis and Elizabeth M. Berkeley, with the assistance of Wilma Bradbear and Bernice Grohskopf. 12 vols. Charlottesville: University of Virginia Press, 1992–2004.

————. *The Letters of William James*. Edited by Henry James III. 2 vols. Boston: Atlantic Monthly Press, 1920.

————. *The Principles of Psychology*. 2 vols. New York: Henry Holt, 1890.

————. *The Varieties of Religious Experience*. New York: Longmans, Green, 1902.

Johnson, Alexandra. *The Hidden Writer: Diaries and the Creative Life*. New York: Random House, 1997.

Kaledin, Eugenia. *The Education of Mrs. Henry Adams*. Philadelphia: Temple University Press, 1981.

Kaplan, Fred. *Henry James: The Imagination of Genius: A Biography*. New York: William Morrow, 1992.

Kaplan, Justin. *When the Astors Owned New York: Blue Bloods and Grand Hotels in a Gilded Age*. New York: Viking, 2006.

Katz, Jonathan Ned. *The Invention of Heterosexuality*. New York: Dutton, 1995.

Kay, Jane Holtz. *Lost Boston*. Boston: Houghton Mifflin, 1999.

Keep, Austin Baxter. *History of the New York Society Library*. New York: De Vinne Press, 1908.

Kendrick, Stephen, and Paul Kendrick. *Sarah's Long Walk: The Free Blacks of Boston and How Their Struggle for Equality Changed America*. Boston: Beacon Press, 2004.

Kern, John Dwight. *Constance Fenimore Woolson: Literary Pioneer*. Philadelphia: University of Pennsylvania Press, 1988.

Klein, Carole. *Gramercy Park: An American Bloomsbury*. Baltimore: Johns Hopkins University Press, 1987.

Köhler, Joaquim. *Richard Wagner, the Last of the Titans*. Translated by Stewart Spencer. New Haven, CT: Yale University Press, 2004.

Krieger, Alex, and David Cobb, eds. *Mapping Boston*. Cambridge, MA: Massachusetts Institute of Technology Press, 1999.

Lambert, Angela. *Unquiet Souls: The Indian Summer of the British Aristocracy, 1880–1918*. London: Macmillan, 1984.

LeClair, Robert. *Young Henry James*. New York: Bookman, 1955.

Levine, Lawrence W. *Highbrow/Lowbrow: The Emergence of Cultural Hierarchy in America*. Cambridge, MA: Harvard University Press, 1988.

Lewis, R. W. B. *Edith Wharton: A Biography*. New York: Harper and Row, 1975.

————. *The Jameses: A Family Narrative*. New York: Farrar, Straus and Giroux, 1991.

Loving, Jerome. *Walt Whitman: The Song of Himself*. Berkeley: University of California Press, 1999.

Maher, Jane. *Biography of Broken Fortunes: Wilkie and Bob, Brothers of William, Henry, and Alice*. Hamden, CT: Archon Books, 1986.

Marryat, Frederick. *A Diary in America, with Remarks on Its Institutions*. New York: D. Appleton, 1839.

Matthiessen, F. O. *The James Family, Including Selections from the Writings of Henry James, Senior, William, Henry, & Alice James*. New York: Knopf, 1947.

McAleer, John. *Ralph Waldo Emerson: Days of Encounter*. Boston: Little, Brown, 1984.

McCall, Dan. *Citizens of Somewhere Else: Nathaniel Hawthorne and Henry James*. Ithaca, NY: Cornell University Press, 1999.

McCormack, Peggy, ed. *Questioning the Master: Gender and Sexuality in Henry James's Writings*. Newark, DE: University of Delaware Press, 2000.

McWhirter, David, ed. *Henry James's New York Edition: The Construction of Authorship*. Palo Alto, CA: Stanford University Press, 1995.

Menand, Louis. *The Metaphysical Club: A Story of Ideas in America*. New York: Farrar, Straus and Giroux, 2001.

Miller, Alice. *The Drama of the Gifted Child [Drama des begabten Kindes]*. Translated by Ruth Ward. New York: Basic Books, 1981.

Montgomery Hyde, H. *Henry James at Home*. London: Methuen, 1969.

Myers, Gerald E. *William James: His Life and Thought*. New Haven, CT: Yale University Press, 1986.

Myerson, Joel. *The New England Transcendentalists and the Dial: A History of the Magazine and Its Contributors*. Rutherford, NJ: Farleigh Dickinson University Press, 1980.

———. *Transcendentalism: A Reader*. Oxford: Oxford University Press, 2000.

Neuhaus, Robert. *Unsuspected Genius: The Art and Life of Frank Duveneck*. San Francisco: Bedford Press, 1987.

Nietzsche, Friedrich. *Beyond Good and Evil*. Translated by R. J. Hollingdale. 1886. New York: Penguin, 2003.

———. *The Case of Wagner*. In *The Birth of Tragedy and the Case of Wagner*. Translated by Walter Kaufmann. 1872 and 1888. New York: Random House, 1967.

Norton, Charles Eliot. *Notes on Travel and Study in Italy*. Boston: Ticknor and Fields, 1860.

Novick, Sheldon M. *Henry James: The Young Master*. New York: Random House, 1996.

Oppenheim, Janet. *The Other World: Spiritualism and Psychical Research in England, 1850–1914*. Cambridge, England: Cambridge University Press, 1985.

Owen, Alex. *The Darkened Room: Women, Power and Spiritualism in Late Victorian England*. Philadelphia: University of Pennsylvania Press, 1990.

Owen, Michael, and Carole M. Osborne. *Duveneck: Frank Duveneck and Elizabeth Boott Duveneck*. Exhibition: 12 February–23 March 1996. New York: Owen Gallery, 1996.

Ozick, Cynthia. *What the Jameses Knew and Other Essays on Writers*. London: Cape, 1993.

Parsons, Elaine Franz. *Manhood Lost: Fallen Drunkards and Redeeming Women in the Nineteenth-Century United States*. Baltimore: Johns Hopkins University Press, 2003.

Pegram, Thomas R. *Battling Demon Rum: The Struggle for a Dry America, 1800–1933*. Chicago: Ivan R. Dee, 1998.

Perry, Ralph Barton. *The Thought and Character of William James*. 2 vols. Boston: Little, Brown, 1935.

Petroski, Henry. *Remaking the World: Adventures in Engineering*. New York: Viking, 1999.

Piper, Alta L. *The Life and Work of Mrs. Piper*. London: Kegan Paul, 1929.

Pool, Daniel. *What Jane Austen Ate and Charles Dickens Knew: From Fox Hunting to Whist—The Facts of Daily Life in 19th-Century England*. New York: Simon and Schuster, 1993.

Pursell, Carroll. *The Machine in America: A Social History of Technology*. Baltimore: Johns Hopkins University Press, 1995.

Richards, Laura E., and Maud Howe Eliot. *Julia Ward Howe, 1819–1910*. 2 vols. Boston: Houghton Mifflin, 1916.

Richardson, Robert D. *Emerson: The Mind on Fire*. Berkeley: University of California Press, 1995.

————. *William James: In the Maelstrom of American Modernism: A Biography*. Boston: Houghton Mifflin, 2006.

Robinson, Paul. *Gay Lives: Homosexual Autobiography from John Addington Symonds to Paul Monette*. Chicago: University of Chicago Press, 1999.

Rolt, L. T. C. *Victorian Engineering*. London: A. Lane, 1970.

Rorabaugh, W. J. *The Alcoholic Republic: An American Tradition*. New York: Oxford University Press, 1979.

Rotundo, E. Anthony. *American Manhood: Transformations of Masculinity from the Revolution to the Modern Era*. New York: Basic Books, 1993.

Sargent, Mrs. John T. *Sketches and Reminiscences of the Radical Club of Chestnut Street, Boston*. Boston: James R. Osgood, 1880.

Sarotte, Georges-Michel. *Like a Brother, Like a Lover: Male Homosexuality in the American Novel and Theater from Herman Melville to James Baldwin*. [*Comme un frère, Comme un amant*.] Translated by Richard Miller. 1976. New York: Anchor Press, 1978.

Sedgwick, Eve Kosofsky. *Between Men: English Literature and Male Homosocial Desire*. New York: Columbia University Press, 1985.

————. *The Epistemology of the Closet*. Berkeley: University of California Press, 1990.

Semenko, Irina M. *Vasily Zhukovsky*. Boston: Twayne, 1976.

Seymour, Miranda. *A Ring of Conspirators: Henry James and His Literary Circle, 1895–1915*. Boston: Houghton Mifflin, 1988.

Shand-Tucci, Douglas. *The Art of Scandal: The Life and Times of Isabella Stewart Gardner*. New York: HarperCollins, 1997.

————. *Built in Boston: City and Suburb, 1800–1950*. Boston: New York Graphic Society, 1978.

————. *The Crimson Letter: Harvard, Homosexuality, and the Shaping of American Culture*. New York: St. Martin's Press, 2003.

Shannon, Martha A. S. *Boston Days of William Morris Hunt*. Boston: Marshall Jones, 1923.

Shaw, Robert Gould. *Blue-Eyed Child of Fortune: The Civil War Letters of Colonel Robert Gould Shaw*. Edited by Russell Duncan. Athens, GA: University of Georgia Press, 1992.

Simon, Linda. *Genuine Reality: A Life of William James*. New York: Harcourt Brace, 1998.

Smith-Rosenberg, Caroll. *Disorderly Conduct: Visions of Gender in Victorian America*. New York: Oxford University Press, 1986.

Snyder, Katherine V. *Bachelors, Manhood, and the Novel, 1850–1925*. Cambridge, England: Cambridge University Press, 1999.

Sofer, Naomi. "Why 'Different Vibrations . . . Work Hand in Hand': Homosocial Bonds in *Roderick Hudson*." *Henry James Review* 20 (Spring 1999): 185–205.

Solomon, Barbara Miller. *In the Company of Educated Women: A History of Women and Higher Education in America*. New Haven, CT: Yale University Press, 1985.

Spurlock, John C. *Free Love: Marriage and Middle-Class Radicalism in America, 1825–1860*. New York: New York University Press, 1988.

Stein, Gertrude. *The Autobiography of Alice B. Toklas*. 1933. New York: Vintage, 1990.

Stephens, George E. *A Voice of Thunder: The Civil War Letters of George E. Stephens*. Edited by Donald Yacovone. Urbana: University of Illinois Press, 1977.

Sterngrass, Jon. *First Resorts: Pursuing Pleasure at Saratoga Springs, Newport and Coney Island*. Baltimore: Johns Hopkins University Press, 2001.

Stevens, Hugh. *Henry James and Sexuality*. Cambridge, England: Cambridge University Press, 1998.

Still, Bayrd. *Mirror for Gotham: New York as Seen by Contemporaries from Dutch Days to the Present*. New York: New York University Press, 1956.

Stoddard, Henry L. *Horace Greely: Printer, Editor, Crusader*. New York: Putnam's, 1946.

Strong, George Templeton. *The Diary of George Templeton Strong*. Edited by Allan Nevins and Milton Halsey Thomas. 4 vols. New York: Macmillan, 1952.

Strouse, Jean. *Alice James: A Biography*. Boston: Houghton Mifflin, 1980.

Stowe, William W. *Going Abroad: European Travel in Nineteenth-Century American Culture*. Princeton, NJ: Princeton University Press, 1994.

Sturgis, Howard Overling. *Belchamber*. 1909. Oxford: Oxford University Press, 1935.

Sutton, Robert P. *Communal Utopias and the American Experience: Religious Communities, 1732–2000*. Westport, CT: Praeger, 2003.

———. *Communal Utopias and the American Experience: Secular Communities, 1824–2000*. Westport, CT: Praeger, 2004.

Taylor, Andrew. *Henry James and the Father Question*. Cambridge, England: Cambridge University Press, 2002.

Thayer, James Bradley. *A Western Journey with Mr. Emerson*. Boston: Little, Brown, 1884.

Thompson, F. M. L. *The Rise of Respectable Society: A Social History of Victorian Britain, 1830–1900*. Cambridge, MA: Harvard University Press, 1988.

Thoreau, Henry David. *Correspondence*. Edited by Walter Harding and Carl Bode. New York: New York University Press, 1958.

Tintner, Adeline. *Henry James and the Lust of the Eyes*. Baton Rouge: Louisiana State University Press, 1993.

Tóibín, Colm. *The Master*. New York: Scribner, 2004.

Tolles, Bryant Franklin. *Resort Hotels of the Adirondacks, 1850–1950*. Hanover, NH: University Press of New England, 2003.

Torsney, Cheryl B. *Constance Fenimore Woolson: The Grief of Artistry*. Athens, GA: University of Georgia Press, 1989.

Townsend, Kim. *Manhood at Harvard: William James and Others*. New York: Norton, 1996.

Trollope, Frances. *Domestic Manners of the Americans*. Edited by Donald Smalley. 1832. New York: Knopf, 1949.

Tudor, Henry. *Narrative of a Tour in North America: Comprising Mexico, the Mines of Real del Monte, the United States, and the British Colonies, with an Excursion to the Island of Cuba*. 2 vols. London: J. Duncan, 1834.

Turner, James. *The Liberal Education of Charles Eliot Norton*. Baltimore: Johns Hopkins University Press, 1999.

Vanderbilt, Kermit. *Charles Eliot Norton, Apostle of Culture in a Democracy*. Cambridge, MA: Harvard University Press, 1959.

Veblen, Thorstein. *The Theory of the Leisure Class*. 1899. Boston: Houghton Mifflin, 1973.

Verne, Jules. *A Floating City [Une Ville Flottante]*. 1871. Edited and translated by I. O. Evans. Westport, CT: Associated Booksellers, 1958.

Vrettos, Athena. *Somatic Fictions: Imagining Illness in Victorian Culture*. Stanford, CA: Stanford University Press, 1995.

Walker, John. *Essays and Correspondence*. 2 vols. London: Longman, 1838.

Walsh, William. *A Record and Sketch of Hugh Walsh's Family*. Newburgh, NY: Newburgh Journal, 1903. Copy at H: bMS Am 1092.9 (4600).

Ward, J. A. *The Imagination of Disaster: Evil in the Fiction of Henry James*. Lincoln: University of Nebraska Press, 1961.

Warren, Austin. *The Elder Henry James*. New York: Macmillan, 1934.

Weber, Hermann, and F. Parkes Weber. *The Spas and Mineral Waters of Europe: With Notes on Baines-Therapeutic Management in Various Diseases and Morbid Conditions*. London: Smith, Elder, 1896.

Webster, Sally. *William Morris Hunt, 1824–1879*. Cambridge, England: Cambridge University Press, 1991.

Weissbourd, Katherine. *Growing Up in the James Family: Henry James, Sr., as Son and Father*. Ann Arbor, MI: UMI Research Press, 1985.

Wells, H[erbert] G[eorge]. *The Future in America: A Search After Realities*. New York: Harper and Brothers, 1906.

Welter, Barbara. *Dimity Convictions: The American Woman in the Nineteenth Century*. Athens, OH: Ohio University Press, 1976.

Westernhagen, Curt von. *Wagner: A Biography*. Translated by Mary Whittal. Cambridge, England: Cambridge University Press, 1978.

Wharton, Edith. *A Backward Glance*. New York: Charles Scribner's Sons, 1934.

Whicher, Stephen. *Freedom and Fate: An Inner Life of Ralph Waldo Emerson*. Philadelphia: University of Pennsylvania Press, 1953.

Whitman, Walt. *Walt Whitman of the New York Aurora, Editor at Twenty-Two: A Collection of Recently Discovered Writings*. Edited by Joseph J. Rubin and Charles H. Brown. State College, PA: Bald Eagle Press, 1950.

———. *Whitman: Poetry and Prose*. New York: Library of America, 1996.

Wilde, Oscar. *The Letters of Oscar Wilde*. Edited by Rupert Hart-Davis. London: Rupert Hart-Davis, 1962.

Winner, Viola Hopkins. *Henry James and the Visual Arts*. Charlottesville: University of Virginia Press, 1970.

Wood, Jane. *Passion and Pathology in Victorian Fiction*. New York: Oxford University Press, 2001.

Woolf, Judith. *Henry James: The Major Novels*. Cambridge, England: Cambridge University Press, 1991.

Yalom, Marilyn. *A History of the Wife*. New York: HarperCollins, 2001.

Yeazell, Ruth Bernard. *Language and Knowledge in the Late Novels of Henry James*. Chicago: University of Chicago Press, 1976.

Acknowledgments

I have been working on the Jameses for many years and am indebted to the mentors, teachers, friends, and colleagues who have inspired and enlightened me. At Harvard, William Alfred (1922–1999) first epitomized for me what a deep and passionate understanding of literature could be. At Yale, R. W. B. Lewis, Brian Wolfe, Jon Butler, Nancy Cott, and Richard Brodhead nurtured my fascination for the Jameses as expatriates and enabled me to see them in a broader and deeper historical context. I'm grateful to Bill Stowe at Wesleyan for stimulating conversations about transatlantic culture; and to Steven Biel, Jeanne Quinn, and Ann Holder from Harvard History and Literature for encouragement on this project while I was teaching there, only a few yards from the site of the Jameses' Quincy Street house. I would also like to thank my colleagues at Wellesley, who over many years have offered encouragement and support; thanks to Bill Cain, Larry Rosenwald, and Alex Johnson for specific insights on this book. None of these people is responsible for my errors, and all of them have helped me shape deeper and more meaningful perspectives on history and literature.

Any study of all the Jameses is a vast undertaking and a humbling one. I owe a debt to many previous able and painstaking biographers, and I feel particular gratitude to Jean Strouse and Jane Maher, who have done groundbreaking work on the less-known James children; and to Alfred Habegger, Linda Simon, and the late Leon Edel, superlative biographers who have dedicated distinguished careers to the study of the James family. Al Habegger and Linda Simon kindly read chapters, corrected errors, and gave valuable suggestions. Colm Tóibín illuminatingly discussed the James family with me one memorable day at the University of Massachusetts. For help in my research, I'm grateful to Joan Campbell at the Wellesley Library; Richard Lines at the Swedenborg Society Library; Peter Drummey and Elaine Grublin at the Massachusetts Historical Society; and Susan Halpert and Jennie Rathbun, who worked especially hard on my behalf, at the Houghton Library at Harvard. For financial support for this research, I would like to acknowledge the Roberta L. Keydel Fund and the Wellesley College Dean's Office.

The writing of this book took some five years, and I am enormously indebted to my agent, Brettne Bloom; I can hardly express adequate thanks for her acumen, her kindness, and her tireless support. I would also like to thank Jill Kneerim and Ike Williams, whose good advice helped me through this complicated process. I'm also grateful to George Hodgman, my editor, who believed in this book and spent many evenings and weekends putting his soul into it; and Helen Atsma, for her good sense in shepherding this project through its final stages.

For their support and friendship during the years of writing this book, I would also like to offer my warmest thanks to Marjorie Agosin, James Burns, Larry Civale, Kevin Connor, Kim Crawford-Harvie, Scott Fisher, Jeffrey Friedman, Patricia Gibbons, Julie Gordon, Nick Gordon, Esther Iwanaga, Sibyl Johnston, Paul Larson, Susan Lyddon, Heidi Macfarlane, Tim and Sibella Makower, Joy Renjilian-Burgy, Lori Roses, John Sedgwick, Camille Serchuk, Karen Sontag, Ryan Warner, and Sarah Wykes. I am especially grateful to Charlotte Gordon, my dear friend of more than a quarter century, without whom this book could never have been written.

Grateful acknowledgement is made to the following for permission to use both unpublished and published materials:

Harvard University Press: Excerpts from Henry James letters throughout are reprinted by permission of the publisher from *The Letters of Henry James: Volumes I–IV*, edited by Leon Edel, Cambridge, Mass.: Harvard University Press, Copyright © 1974, 1975, 1980, 1984, by the President and Fellows of Harvard College.

Houghton Library, Harvard University: Excerpts from the William James papers, the Henry James Papers, and the James Family papers all used by permission. Call numbers for each quoted excerpt may be found in the end notes of this book.

Bay James: Permission to quote portions of *The Death and Letters of Alice James* (© 1981 by Alice James; Ruth Bernard Yeazell, ed.) has been generously granted by Bay James.

Massachusetts Historical Society: Caroline Dall, journal, 25 April 1866, Caroline Wells Healey Dall papers (microfilm reel 36); Caroline Dall, journal, 25 June 1866, Caroline Wells Healey Dall papers (microfilm reel 36); Henry James Sr. to Elizabeth Peabody, 11 August 1863, Horace Mann papers III (microfilm reel 38), all used by permission.

The Swedenborg Society: Unpublished portions of letters from Dr. J.J.G.W. Wilkinson to Henry James Sr., and unpublished portions of a letter from Mary James to Emma Wilkinson, used by permission.

University of Virginia Press: Excerpts from William James's letters throughout are reprinted by permission of the publisher (William James, *The Correspondence of William James*, 12 vols. © 1992–2004).

William Morris Agency: Permission to quote portions of *The Diary of Alice James*, edited by Leon Edel (Northeastern University Press, 1999) has been generously granted by the William Morris Agency.

Index

Individuals are referred to by surname with the exception of the following abbreviations:

AHGJ - Alice Howe Gibbens James
AJ - Alice James
GWJ - Garth Wilkinson James ("Wilkie")
HJ - Henry James, Jr. ("Harry")
HJSr - Henry James, Senior
"Kate" or "Aunt Kate" - Catherine Walsh
"Minny" - Minny Temple
MJ - Mary Walsh James
RJ - Robertson James "Bob"
WJ - William James

About the Author

PAUL FISHER grew up in Wyoming, was educated at Harvard and Trinity College, Cambridge, and received his Ph.D. from Yale. The author of *Artful Itineraries: European Art and American Careers in High Culture, 1865–1920*, he has had a long professional fascination with the James family and teaches American literature at Wellesley. He lives in Boston, Massachusetts.